THE CHILD
A Book of Readings
SECOND EDITION

Jerome M. Seidman
MONTCLAIR STATE COLLEGE

Holt, Rinehart and Winston, Inc.

New York   Chicago   San Francisco   Atlanta   Dallas
Montreal   Toronto   London   Sydney

Copyright © 1969 by Holt, Rinehart and Winston, Inc.
Copyright © 1958 by Jerome M. Seidman
All Rights Reserved
SBN: 03–080798–0
Library of Congress Catalog Card Number: 69–17662
Printed in the United States of America
1 2 3 4 5 6 7 8 9

Preface

This second edition has been revised completely. The 64 selections represent current scholarship. All but four have been published since 1962, more than half have been published since 1965.

Since 1958 when the first edition of this book appeared, important work in child psychology has moved forward at an ever accelerating pace. Change and growth have marked the investigations in several areas, while new theories and improved methods of research have opened up entirely new areas. The selections in this revision provide authoritative, interesting, and useful examples of these new perspectives, emphases, and developments.

The focus of this edition is on recent advances in child development and behavior. The selections include new findings in such areas as: the crucial role of heredity; the significance of early sensory and motor experiences; the selectivity of perception; the influence of sociocultural factors on intellectual growth, language acquisition, achievement motivation, and moral development; current interest in the multidimensional nature of the human intellect; the relationship between childhood experience and adult behavior; new intervention techniques to develop problem-solving skills and to change child behavior.

Three criteria have guided the choice of the materials contained in this volume: 1) adequacy of treatment of the important problems, 2) exemplary research and experimentation in the areas most fruitful for understanding and helping children, and 3) appeal to students through form, content, and style.

As an aid to students who may wish to pursue the many problems raised by these readings, the bibliographical references that accompanied the original selections have been retained in a single compilation in the back of the book. Materials that did not appear when the selections were originally published have been appended to five selections (20, 21, 42, 53, and 63). To encourage critical and creative probing, concise introductory headnotes introduce each selection.

This new edition, like the first, is designed for instructors who prefer to make the reading of original publications a basic ingredient of their course. As a supplementary text, this book simplifies the instructor's task of compiling lists of assignments and the student's difficulties in obtaining scattered readings. However used, this collection of readings is invaluable in giving students the flavor of primary sources, firsthand experience with the contributions of leading psychologists, sociologists, and biologists, and an awareness of how hypotheses are made, research conducted, and learning achieved.

It is a pleasure to acknowledge the cooperation of colleagues and students who evaluated the selections of the first edition and suggested articles for this volume. Special thanks are extended to Sister Mary T. Amatora, Donald M. Baer, Katherine M. Banham, Roger W. Brown, Dorothy H. Eichorn, Susan Ervin-Tripp, Robert L. Fantz, C. B. Ferster, John H. Flavell, Harry Fowler, John L. Fuller, Eleanor J. Gibson, Eugene S. Gollin, S. B. Gusberg, Jerry Hirsch, Marjorie P. Honzik, Rollin D. Hotchkiss, Elizabeth B. Hurlock, Lewis P. Lipsitt, Carson McGuire, Merle N. Ohlsen, Seymour B. Sarason, Irving E. Sigel, Lois Meek Stolz, Ruth Strang, Hilda Taba, Leona E. Tyler, Steven G. Vandenberg, Joachim F. Wohlwill, and Joseph Zubin.

I am especially grateful to the authors and publishers for permission to reprint their material; acknowledgment accompanies each selection. And finally, for her invaluable suggestions and criticisms, I dedicate this book to my wife, Cindy.

Upper Montclair, New Jersey   *J. M. S.*

Contents: An Overview

(For complete Table of Contents see pages vii-xi.)

Part Five   Understanding and Helping the Child   543

Contents

Part Three *Personal-Social Development and Behavior: I*   265

Part Four *Personal-Social Development and Behavior: II*   405

PART ONE

Infancy and Childhood: Two Periods of Growth and Development

Principles of Development

1 Theories in Child Psychology

GEORGE G. THOMPSON

One of the chief objectives of science is to create theories. A theory is a set of principles or assumptions advanced to explain existing data. It serves as a guide for further research and predicts new and future events. A fruitful theory is a powerful tool for the extension of scientific knowledge. In child psychology a number of theories have been influential in research activity and clinical practice. The following reading describes several of these theories, including the psychoanalytic model, "critical periods" conceptions, cognitive-field theories, and neobehavioristic approaches to learning.

PSYCHOANALYTIC THEORY

Freud constructed the first psychological theory that emphasized the developmental dimensions of childhood experiences. Although his clinical data were largely drawn from the verbal reports and free associations of adults, his inferences about psychological structures and dynamics were principally related to the events of early childhood, experiences during the first four or five years of life. Freud conceived of these early experiences as highly dramatic and significant events that laid the foundations and sketched the blueprints for adult character, personality, and style of living.[1]

Reprinted from *Child Psychology: Growth Trends in Psychological Adjustment,* Second Edition (Boston: Houghton Mifflin, 1962), pp. 14–22. By permission of the author and the Houghton Mifflin Company.

According to Freud's conceptions, the human infant is a striving organism with but limited capacities for satisfying his needs. The first of these capacities to be utilized is the sucking response. This activity brings nutrition and libidinal pleasure. If the infant is thwarted in his search for pleasure via sucking by too early or too abrupt weaning practices—a substantial portion of his libidinal strivings is forever cathected (fixated, or reserved for use) at this level of activity. In later childhood and in adult life he will devote a disproportionate amount of his time and energy to the pursuit of oral-erotic activities — thumb sucking, eating, smoking, talking, and sundry other oral stimulations along with certain social regards of dependency.

Toward the middle of the first year of life the human infant acquires teeth and is thereby provided another pleasurable outlet—biting and chewing. Frustration and ambivalence over this activity may again result in a disproportionate cathexis of libidinal energy at this level of personality formation—the oral-sadistic with associated behav-

---

[1]The basic concepts of Freud's psychoanalytic theory are presented succinctly in Freud (1949) and Hall's primer (1954). The genetic, or developmental, aspects of the theory are summarized in Blum (1953). The annual volumes (since 1945) of *The psychoanalytic study of the child* (Freud, A., *et al.*, 1945) include modern interpretations of psychoanalytic theory and much of the more interesting research related to the developmental features of the conceptualization. Also see DeMonchaux (1957), Escalona (1958), and Freud (1951) for appraisals of the influence of psychoanalytic theory on child psychology.

iors in later childhood and adult life of biting, teeth grinding, sarcasm, gossip, and other forms of oral hostility and aggressiveness.

During the latter part of the first year and the beginning of the second year of life the infant develops primary pleasurable outlets via the elimination of the body's waste materials—urination and defecation. If frustrated unduly during this period by too early or too severe toilet-training procedures, he cathects (fixates) disproportionate amounts of libidinal energy at this level of personality formation. The resulting character formation may be of either the anal retentive or anal expulsive type. The personality characteristics associated with the anal (retentive) character were inferred by Freud as involving abnormally high standards of cleanliness, punctuality, pedantry, stinginess, frugality, parsimony, acquisitiveness, and stubbornness. The anal expulsive character—not as fully delineated by Freud—retains into later childhood and adult life a heightened interest in the elimination of all body waste materials and an associated concern for the manipulation of plastic materials: the artist, painter, baker, or all who displace, arrange, and mold semi-solid materials.

A little later in infancy the genitalia develop an erotic sensitivity that permits new pleasurable outlets via stroking, rocking, and brushing behaviors. Parental attitudes of indulgence or punishment for these autoerotic activities again determine the relative amounts of libidinal energy cathected at this developmental level of personality and character formation. Extreme narcissism (self love) is the usual consequence of severe parental punishment for the autoerotic pleasures of masturbatory behaviors.

Freud postulated the availability of a limited quantity of libidinal energy[2] for each individual. Energy cathected (reserved for use) at one stage of personality development restricted the amount of energy available for later personality-world transactions. Therefore extreme frustrations (too early or too abrupt weaning, too early or too severe toilet training, too punitive a regard toward phallic pleasures) impoverish the personality with respect to the resolution of subsequent frustrating circumstances. And the most severe conflict was inferred to arise later during the preschool years. This most stressful of adjustments, the Oedipus and Electra complexes in boys and girls respectively, demands the child giving up the possibility of an anaclitic (or dependent) "love" relationship with the parent of the opposite sex.[3] Freud believed this was forced upon the male child by castration anxiety, but remained puzzled and unclear in his conception of the antecedent conditions leading to the resolution of the Electra complex for the little girl; he often referred to this conceptual enigma as the "riddle of femininity." In any event, the child with sufficient libidinal energy at his, or her, disposal gives up the parent of opposite sex as a love object and identifies with the behavior, attitudes and interests of the parent of the same sex. Failure to resolve this most difficult of adjustments, or only partial success, eventuates in "feminization" for the boy and "masculinization" for the girl—conditions that set the stage for later social conflicts. Freud conceived of the years of middle childhood as a period of relatively inactive "latency" as far as basic personality structure is concerned. The sexual maturing of pubescence instigated the arousal of previously latent, and partially unresolved, Oedipal (or Electra for the female) conflicts which were finally resolved in the "normal" growth pattern by sex-social heterosexual experiences of dating, courtship and eventual marriage.

This loosely defined and interrelated set of constructs has been instrumental in initiating more research activities in child psychology than any other theoretical proposal. Freud's developmental concepts plus his dynamic principles of personality integration and adjustment (sublimation, repression, identification, projection, introjection, etc.) have stimulated more research in child psychology during the last twenty years than all of the other theories combined. These research efforts have yielded only ambiguous support for the psychoanalytic theories (classic Freudian and numerous variations of neo-psychoanalytic conceptions). This ambiguity of findings is an understandable outcome because of the lack of precision in conceptual and coordinating definitions. Numerous critics have attacked psychoanalytic theory as an inadequate

---

[2]Libidinal energy as employed by Freud is a hypothetical construct without reference to the conceptual properties of energies in the physical sciences.

[3]See Mullahy (1952) for an extended discussion of the postulated significance of the Oedipus complex, including the full text of Sophocles' *Oedipus Rex,* the literary analogy upon which Freud based this conception.

conceptual model. However, it continues to survive and gain stanch supporters because it has no serious competitor with the same comprehensive scope of behavior and personality coverage. As Sir Isaac Newton once wisely noted, "poor" theory is never destroyed by its critics; it is dismissed only after the availability of a demonstrated better theory.

PSYCHOANALYTIC-BEHAVIORISTIC THEORIES

A number of American behaviorists have tried to blend the perceptiveness of psychoanalytic theory with the relatively greater deductive and operational rigor of behaviorism in an effort to maximize the fruitful aspects of both theories. The most detailed of these combinations is skillfully presented by Dollard and Miller (1950). Their approach has emphasized Freud's dynamic principles rather than his ontogenetic stages. For example, Miller (1948) has proposed a behavioristic description of the antecedent-consequent conditions of displacement and has produced experimentally in rats phenomena with similar attributes to displacement as defined by Freud on the basis of clinical observations.[4]

Sears and associates (1957) have leaned heavily on psychoanalytic theory, liberally tempered by behavioristic

---

[4]A figure, omitted here, illustrates "an experimental production of behavior that is similar to psychoanalytic 'displacement.' Rats given electric shock through the grid at the bottom of the apparatus learn to strike at each other, and ignore the doll. In the absence of the other animal the doll becomes the recipient of the 'generalized' or 'displaced' aggression."

learning concepts, in their classic investigation of child-rearing practices and inferred consequences for child behavior and personality development. Their approach borrows from both the dynamic principles and the ontogenetic stages of Freud's conceptualization. Whiting and Child (1953) have ingeniously adopted a combination of psychoanalytic-behavioristic theory in their study of the effects of child-rearing practices on the belief systems of individuals growing up in very different cultures. For example, they have obtained tentative but promising support for the notion that weaning, toilet training, and similar experiences influence the later adult belief system related to the onset and cure of human illness.

All of the foregoing research studies demonstrate the feasibility of blending different theories into a more powerful and rigorous conceptual tool for integrating presently available empirical knowledge. However, the blending also almost necessarily leaves out some of the contradictory or unreconcilable features of both theories, and these omissions bring unhappiness to many psychologists. There is also the question whether a blending of these theories can do more than further the integration of *present* knowledge. Will this combination of conceptual models point the way toward an extension of empirical relationships, or is it restricted to the potential of the more fruitful of the two theories that are combined?

THEORIES INVOLVING "CRITICAL PERIODS"

Scientists have an almost irresistible tendency to view an evolving events-system as being comprised of more-or-less nonoverlapping periods; e.g., Darwinian theory about the evolution of organisms, various theories about the evolution of the universe, the earth's structure, and so on. Description based on a "periods" approach permits communication, low level prediction for "repeatable" sequences, and a primitive sense of understanding. The development of the human organism in its ontogenetic history is an obvious evolving events-structure system. It is also repeatedly open to observation and description across different individuals. These circumstances have favored the proposal of numerous theories involving discrete stages or critical periods during childhood, adolescence, and adult life.

The developmental aspects of Freud's psychoanalytic theory constitute a critical periods approach. Gesell's (1942, 1946) behavioral descriptive system with age as the independent variable has discrete stages as one of its most salient properties. Piaget's[5] theories of conceptual, intellectual, linguistic, social, and moral development utilize discrete stages in psychological growth as primary descriptive and explanatory vehicles. In Piaget's proposals chronological age is recognized as only a very crude indicator of progression in developmental stages.[6]

_____

[5](1929, 1930, 1948, 1952, 1953[a], 1960.)

[6]See Anthony (1957) and Berlyne (1957) for recent trends in Piaget's theorizing. Also see the three volumes of proceedings of the World Health Organization Study Group on child development (Tanner and Inhelder, 1957, 1958) for multiple references to Piaget's theories by internationally recognized specialists in developmental psychology.

In recent years Hebb's (1949, 1958) theory, differentiating primary and secondary learning experiences, has been highly influential on research activities among comparative psychologists. These "critical periods" hypotheses[7] have been instrumental in extending our knowledge of the consequences of sensory deprivation and selective stimulation as differential functions of the developmental maturity of rats, dogs, monkeys, and various other infrahuman organisms. They extend substantial promise to the child psychologist for guiding much needed research but have stimulated very little research activity to date with human subjects.

The "discrete" stages and "critical" periods in human development have yet to be defined in child psychology. It is obvious to all that the psychological processes of the two-year-old are considerably different than those of the six-year-old. However, the dimensions of difference are largely unidentified in modern psychology. We know more about the periods of primary socialization in the puppy (Scott and Marston, 1950) than we do about the stages of socialization in the young *homo sapiens*. At our present state of ignorance it is the sheerest of nonsense to partition the developmental sequence with respect to psychological principles. All such subdivisions—psychology of infancy, psychology of the preschool child, psychology of the preadolescent, etc.—are based on social and anthropometric rather than psychological criteria.

_____

[7]Much of the recent research on critical periods has been summarized by the contributors to the volume on *The concept of development*, edited by Harris (1957).

COGNITIVE-FIELD THEORIES

These theories are principally derived from Gestalt psychology which emphasizes a continuity of psychological growth (perceptual, intellectual, social) from an *initially* organized structure toward an ever increasing differentiation of this original structure. Psychological growth takes place by a differentiated elaboration of mental processes already present rather than by the addition of new functions —by differentiation rather than by accretion and integration. Koffka (1925) related the principles of Gestalt psychology to child development in his *organismic* approach.[8]

The most influential of the Gestalt psychologists on research in child psychology was Lewin[9] who used topology (a nonmetric branch of mathematics dealing with spatial relationships rather than with quantities) and vector analysis (forces and resultants of field forces) to represent the cognitive field, the need-valence system, and psychological locomotion. Lewin postulated a gradual differentiation of the cognitive field as a primary function of psychological development. He also postulated rigidity of boundaries (between need systems and between differentiated areas of the cognitive field) as an increasing function of the aging process. These postulates have been employed ingeniously and effectively to guide a number of highly interesting investigations of child behavior and development. The difficulties in using Lewin's hypothetico-deductive model fall into two general classes: (a) identifying and measuring the structure of the cognitive field and the intrapersonal need system for a given individual at a particular moment of time, and (b) coordinating conceptual conditions to observable behaviors. Tolman (1952), the American psychologist who pointed the way toward the use of intervening variables in modern learning theory, was much impressed with Lewin's conceptual model and borrowed liberally from it to implement the belief-values and need-systems properties of his own approach in his last hypothetico-deductive system. Despite Lewin's profound influence on group dynamics and social action programs (Cartwright and Zander, 1953; Lewin, 1948), on the only sustained investigation of psychological ecology (Barker and Wright, 1955), and on the dynamics of interpersonal perception and response (Heider, 1958), his provocative postulates related specifically to child *development* have been given only a minimum of research attention in the last fifteen years. The problems of constructing fruitful coordinating and operational definitions remain largely neglected and unsolved.

NEO-BEHAVIORISTIC THEORIES

The theoretical constructions of Hull (1943, 1951, 1952) have had an almost definitive effect on experimental studies of learning in this country during the last twenty years. His students have been most zealous in their efforts to extend his miniature theory of learning to cover the entire domain of psy-

---

[8]The organismic theory has been given variant expression in the writings of Goldstein (1939, 1940) and Maslow (1954[a]).

[9](1935, 1936, 1938, 1951, 1954.)

chology (see the introductory textbook based on Hullian principles by Kimble, 1956). Although Hull (1943, p. 399) did not live to see his theory extended to the conceptual problems of *developmental* psychology, it was a part of his long-range program to extend his theory in this direction. Sears' investigations of the socialization process (Sears, Maccoby, and Levin, 1957) are related to a part of Hull's original blueprint for elaborating his miniature conceptual model. In recent years a large number of psychologists have conducted research studies, based either explicitly or implicitly upon Hull's hypothetico-deductive system, in which children have been the principal subjects rather than the white rats on which Hull's constructions were originally based. These investigators have been highly productive in extending our knowledge of the empirical relationships existing between various types of stimulus displays and young children's abilities to discriminate and generalize their response tendencies. One of their most promising contributions has been an experimental attack on the postulated mediating processes of response-produced stimuli ($r_g{\rightarrow}s_g$) and a search for conceptual and empirical links between these mediating processes and conceptual-linguistic facilities of the developing human organism (Osgood, 1953). Because of his limited language functions the preschool-aged child makes an ideal subject for these important investigations.

The philosophical orientation on which these neo-behavioristic approaches to child psychology appear to be based has been presented in a lucid manner by McCandless and Spiker (1956). The hope is that a large number of carefully conducted studies with children will yield empirical relationships on which a fruitful theory of developmental and socialization dimensions can be constructed (e.g., see the reasoning by Terrell, 1958). The majority of these neo-behaviorists obviously favor a learning approach which identifies the limits of the developing organism's ability to discriminate, generalize, and alter his response patterns in a direction that maximizes the acquisition of positive reinforcement.

This virile movement in child psychology has already made substantial contributions to empirical knowledge in this area. It draws on a rich empirical and conceptual background of research with infrahuman organisms, therefore has a clear focus for emphasizing the theoretically relevant variables and ignoring the adjudged trivial. It embodies a clear recognition of the tedious accumulation of empirical relationships that has always been the precursor of fruitful theories in the physical sciences. Although this viewpoint cannot but augur favorably for the long-term future of child psychology, it offers little comfort to the applied social services faced with immediate problems related to child guidance and welfare. Professional educators, child guidance workers, and clinical psychologists working principally with children are naturally impatient with this theoretical position. Their problems are pressing, so they turn understandably to psychoanalytic theory and naïve phenomenology in the hope that these "leaps into the future" of a relatively undeveloped science will support remedial and therapeutic practices that will prove more helpful than guesses based on common intelligence. These differences in purpose between the scientist and the artful applier of scientific knowledge have ever marked interrelationships between the biological sciences and the physician, between physics and engineering, and now between psychology and its applied branches. The history of the older sciences fails to record any easy theoretical victories. Every major theoretical contribution has been solidly based on a wealth of empirical knowledge, "ripe" for integration by an inspired conceptual model. The neobehavioristic approach deserves encouragement—even though its contributions may not be immediately relevant to the solution of socially important problems—because it emphasizes the collection of a coherent body of empirical relationships. There appears to be no other known route to the construction of valid and fruitful conceptual models.

OTHER THEORIES INFLUENCING RESEARCH IN CHILD PSYCHOLOGY

Almost every theory in general psychology and personality has had some influence on the investigations that make up the research literature of child psychology. Murray's (1938) conceptions of need and press have stimulated a variety of psychological instruments for measuring dimensions of child personality. The factor analytic theories of Cattell (1950) and Eysenck (1953) have promoted a large number of investigations with children directed toward a developmental description of the growing child's personality structure. Skinner's (1938, 1953) techniques and schedules of reinforcement for conditioning operant responses have initiated a substantial number of similar investigations with children—even though Skinner (1950) professes to eschew all theoretical conceptions, preferring to restrict himself to empirical inquiries.

All these theories—and many more—have directed, and will continue to direct, experimental studies in child psychology. In view of the widely differing concepts and syntactic procedures among these different psychological theories, it is fortunate that the resulting empirical relationships provide common sustenance for all theories and applied efforts.

2   *Behavioral Genetics: An Overview*[1]

GERALD E. McCLEARN

This selection provides a perspective from which to view the relationship between genetics and behavior. Starting with the heredity-environment issue, evidence concerning the influence of heredity on behavior is presented, implying that with increased genetic knowledge, greater specification of the hereditary basis for greater arrays of behavior can be expected. Different genetic models illustrate how genetics contributes to development. Especially pertinent is the model that discusses genes having different effects at different times in the life of the organism.

The inheritance of "mental" traits was discussed by Darwin and was the central focus of Galton's inquiries. In the early years of this century, the work of Pearson and others seemed to demonstrate that behavioral properties were inherited in the same manner as were physical traits, and prospects for advances in understanding of behavioral inheritance appeared to be very good indeed. Then came Behaviorism and the futile nature-nurture controversy. The old natural and easy relationship between psychology and biology was sundered, and the dogma was established that, however much heredity might determine physical and physiological characteristics, behavioral characteristics were immune and subject only to environmental influence.

This attitude came to be emotionally charged, and, as a consequence, behavioral scientists in the past several decades not only did not encounter genetics during their training, they typically acquired a feeling of estrangement toward that subject matter. The enormous recent advances in genetics have therefore had but a limited impact upon psychology in general.

There has been, however, increasing activity in the interdisciplinary field of behavioral genetics, and there is now compelling evidence concerning the

[1]Presented at The Merrill-Palmer Institute Conference on Research and Teaching of Infant Development, February 9–11, 1967, directed by Irving E. Sigel, chairman of research. The conference was financially supported in part by the National Institute of Child Health and Human Development.

From *Merrill-Palmer Quarterly*, 1968, **14**, 10–24. Reprinted with the permission of the author and The Merrill-Palmer Institute.

influence of heredity on a wide variety of traits in a wide variety of organisms. These findings are of relevance to all psychologists, and one of the purposes of this paper is to provide examples of the types of evidence that have been adduced. An equally important purpose is to describe the general theoretical perspectives which genetical ro search can bring upon a problem, behavioral or otherwise.

In the space available, it has been necessary to simplify and condense, but never, I hope, to the jeopardy of the general argument. Readers interested in more extensive literature reviews might consult the papers listed in "review references" in the bibliography. More detailed accounts of genetic theory may be found in any number of recent texts. Specific applications of various genetic models, techniques and procedures to behavioral genetics are discussed in Hirsch (1967).

SIMPLE GENETIC SYSTEMS

The conceptually simplest genetic system is one in which a single gene has a large effect upon the trait under consideration. A formal description of such a system of inheritance is quite simple. A given gene can exist in two or more alternative forms called *alleles*. Each individual has two of a given gene, one having been contributed by each parent. Different combinations of the alleles give different outcomes. For example, consider the letter *A* to represent one allele of a gene, and *A'* to represent another allele. Three combinations are possible: *AA*, *A'A*, and *A'A'*. If the *phenotype*, which is the observed or measured characteristic, for *AA* is the

same as for *AA'*, it is said that *A* is dominant, and that *A'* is recessive. Various degrees of dominance and recessiveness are possible, with *AA'* yielding a phenotypic value somewhere between or even outside the range of *AA* and of *A'A'*. If *AA'* is exactly intermediate between *AA* and *A'A'*, the situation is described as additive.

A number of examples could be cited in which single genes have an important influence upon a behavioral characteristic. One of the best known is that of phenylketonuria in man. The dominant allele of this gene may be symbolized by *P* and the recessive allele by *p*. Both *PP* and *Pp* individuals are within the normal range of intelligence, but *pp* individuals suffer from mental retardation. Several other conditions of mental defect have been ascribed to single genes. Certain circumscribed conditions of sensory deficit have also been demonstrated to have a single gene basis. Ability to taste phenylthiocarbamide is an example of such a condition. Individuals who have two of the recessive alleles (these individuals being described as *homozygous* for the recessive allele) cannot taste the substance. People who are *homozygous* for the dominant allele find the substance to be bitter, as do those who are *heterozygous* (having one of each allele).

Several studies have demonstrated an effect of single genes in the behavior of laboratory mice. Winston and Lindzey (1964), for example, showed that homozygosity for the *c* allele of a particular gene, which results in albinism, also leads to inferior performance in a water-escape learning task by mice. DeFries, et al. (1966) further showed that *cc* mice had reduced activity and heightened emotional (defecation) scores as compared to their *Cc* or *CC* siblings.

Still another example may be drawn from the literature on mating behavior of Drosophila fruit flies. In this particular instance, a modification of the basic Mendelian rules is involved. In female Drosophila, animals who are homozygous *yy* have a yellow pigmented body, with *Yy* and *YY* animals having the normal darker color. In male Drosophila, on the other hand, there are only two possible states, *Y*— and *y*—, since the gene is located on the X chromosome, as described below. *Y* males are normal, and *y* males are yellow bodied. In addition to the effect on body color, it has been found that yellow males are less successful in mating competition studies than are the normal males. An analysis of their behavior during courtship has revealed that their wing vibration, which appears to be a crucial part of the courtship procedure, is significantly less frequent and less intense than that of normal males (Bastock, 1956).

CYTOGENETICS

Physically, the genes are located on small thread-like bodies called chromosomes, which are found within the nucleus of all body cells. For present purposes, the chromosomes may be regarded as linear arrays of many genes each. The chromosomes occur as paired structures, with one chromosome of each pair having come from the mother, and the other from the father. The number of chromosomes is quite constant from cell to cell within an organism, and from individual to individ-

ual within a species, although the number varies substantially from species to species. In human beings, there are 23 pairs of chromosomes; in mice there are 20 pairs; in the crayfish there are 100 pairs; and in Drosophila only four, for example. A large part of the original research work relating genes to chromosomes was performed with fruit flies, where in certain tissues the chromosomes are unusually large and easy to see. Research on chromosomes in mammals has been much more difficult, but the development of new techniques has recently made possible much more refined research on mammalian tissues in general and on human tissues specifically. There has been an exciting burst of activity in this area, and a number of findings relating chromosomal anomalies to behavioral characteristics have been described.

Ordinarily, in the process of development of sperm and eggs, a very precise mechanism guarantees that each egg or sperm will contain one of each of the pairs of chromosomes characteristic of the species. Thus, when fertilization occurs, the joining of the nuclei of the two germ cells gives rise to a single cell with the normal chromosomal complement. However, it occasionally happens that a mistake occurs, which results in a sperm or an egg containing either both members of a pair instead of only one, or containing no representative at all of a given pair. When such a germ cell is involved in fertilization, the resulting organism will possess three instead of two of one pair (which condition is called *trisomy*) or only one instead of two chromosomes (which condition is called *monosomy*). Trisomy of many of the chromosomes appears to be lethal. In some cases, the organism survives, but is affected by a number of abnormalities. One of these latter conditions is mongolism, more frequently known today as Down's syndrome. The chromosomes of man are classifiable according to size and certain other characteristics and a standard nomenclature has been established. The chromosome identified as number 21 has been found to be present in triplicate in many cases of Down's syndrome, and the condition is therefore also widely known as trisomy 21. It has become apparent that it is not necessary for all of chromosome number 21 to be present in triplicate for the multiple defects including mental retardation to occur; in certain cases only part of the third chromosome number 21 is present. (See Polani, et al., 1960).

In most cases, the individual members of the chromosome pairs appear to be equal, in the sense that each contains genetic information comparable to that contained on the other. In the case of sex chromosomes, however, this is not so. In man, as well as in many other organisms, females have two equivalent chromosomes, called the X chromosomes, while males have one X and a small Y chromosome. It seems that much of the genetic material carried on the X chromosome is not represented by corresponding material on the Y. The Y chromosome in mammals, however, does contain male-determining genetic information of some kind. As is true of the other, non-sex, chromosomes (called the *autosomes*) the distribution of sex chromosomes is usually quite precise, giving rise to XX daughters and XY sons through the generations.

However, mistakes also occur occasionally with respect to the sex chromosomes. A clinical condition involving incomplete sexual development in ostensible males, called Klinefelter's syndrome, has been shown in many cases to involve the presence of two X chromosomes in addition to a Y chromosome. In addition to the symptoms of retarded sexual development, there are behavioral concomitants in a generally reduced intelligence level. Another condition of retarded sexual development, in this case of ostensible females, is Turner's syndrome. In many Turner's patients, it has been found that there are only 45 instead of the normal number of 46 (23 pairs) of chromosomes. Detailed analysis has revealed that only one sex chromosome, an X, is present. A very specific type of cognitive defect appears to occur in these XO females. Money (1966) has discussed a number of observations which suggest that Turner's syndrome patients are grossly defective with respect to spatial abilities, although verbal I.Q. measures may fall within the normal range. A more recently reported condition is the XYY male. Jacobs, et al. (1965) found seven out of a population of 203 male inmates of a maximum security hospital to have an XYY constitution. This incidence is greatly in excess of that in the non-institutionalized population. They seemed to be characterizable as tall, aggressive, and mentally subnormal. Price and Whatmore (1967) have since compared the behavior of XYY individuals with XY ("normal") males in the same hospital. The aggression of the XYY individuals appears to be more directed to property than persons, and disturbed behavior was manifested earlier in the *XYY* than in the *XY* patients.

QUANTITATIVE GENETICS

The basic rules governing the transmission of genetic elements were worked out with reference to dichotomous, qualitative traits. After the generality of these rules had been demonstrated for many traits and in many organisms, efforts were made to apply them to continuously varying, quantitatively distributed characteristics. The analytical models that have been developed in this context assume that there are a number of different genes that exert influence upon the trait, with the individual effect of any particular gene being relatively small. The effect of the individual gene cannot therefore be followed by examination of progeny of various mating types, as in "Mendelian" traits. Instead, the effect of all of the genes, working in concert, must be assessed by statistical measures. There are several important ideas and terms that pertain to the analysis and interpretation of quantitative inheritance. The total system is sometimes described as a multiple-factor system, but a more frequently employed term is *polygenic*. As mentioned above, the basic notion of a polygenic system is that a number of genes each have an effect on the same character. A related term is *pleiotropy*, which is used to describe situations in which a given single gene has an effect upon several phenotypic characters. An example of this has already been presented, in that the albino gene in the mouse has behavioral effects in addition to the obvious effect upon coat color.

Perhaps the central concept of quantitative genetics is that of *heritability*. In a very general sense, heritability is the extent to which the phenotype is a reliable guide to the genotype. Phenotype has been defined as that which is measured. Genotype is the genetic makeup respecting all of the genes relevant to the particular character in question. One reason for a lack of one-to-one correspondence between genotype and phenotype is the phenomenon of dominance, where different genotypes (one homozygous for the dominant allele, the other heterozygous) give rise to the same phenotypic result. Another major source of discrepancy between genotype and phenotype is the effect of environment. Figure 1 is a pictorial representation of some of these ideas. This figure shows two normal distributions with representative individuals within each. An individual is represented by two connected symbols; one, a circle, represents the phenotypic value; the other, a triangle, represents the genotypic value. The latter is not directly measurable, of course, although estimates can be attempted by various procedures. One way of conceptualizing the genotypic value is to consider it to be the mean of the phenotypic values that would result if the given individual could be indefinitely replicated and reared under all of the environmental conditions to which the population is exposed. It may be seen that in the top distribution, phenotypic and genotypic values are quite close together. In the bottom distribution, however, the average discrepan-

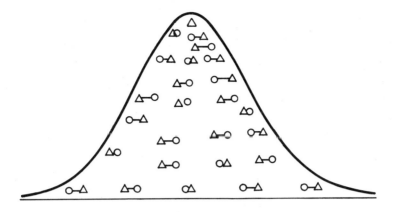

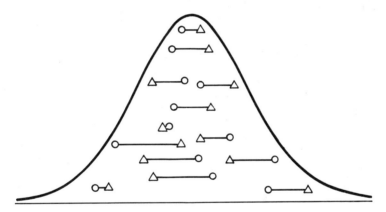

Fig. 1.   Two normal distributions with representative individuals
within each one. Each set of connected symbols represents an
individual—the circle standing for a *phenotypic* value (a characteristic as observed or measured), the triangle for a *genotypic*
value (the individual's actual genetic makeup relevant to that
characteristic). As can be seen, the two values are quite close
together for all of the individuals in the top distribution, in contrast to those in the bottom one. In the top distribution, therefore, the heritability of the particular characteristic is higher,
and the phenotypic value of an individual a more reliable index
of his genotypic value.

cy between phenotypic and genotypic
values is relatively high. In the top
distribution, therefore, the heritability

of the character in question is higher
and the phenotypic value of an individual is a far more reliable index of

the individual's genotypic value than in the bottom distribution.

It is worth repeated emphasis that consideration of environmental sources of variance forms an integral part of any discussion of quantitative genetics. During the old nature-nurture controversy, the question was frequently asked: Is a given trait due to heredity or environment? This dichotomous implication is easily seen to be faulty. With our modern perspective, we may inquire as to the relative proportions of phenotypic variance attributable to genetic differences among the individuals in the population and the proportion due to differences in their environments. In a somewhat simplified form, we may state that the phenotypic variance is equal to the genotypic variance plus the environmental variance:

$$V_P = V_G + V_E$$

However, as we have already seen, certain types of genetic interactions (e.g., dominance) contribute to a lack of one-to-one correspondence between genotype and phenotype. Without rigorous derivations (for which the interested reader should consult Falconer, 1960), it can be appreciated that the covariance among relatives of different degrees could be converted to statistical form which permits the estimation of heritability. The examination of such resemblances among relatives has indeed been widely used in human behavioral genetics. They were, in fact, an important source of data in the nature-nurture controversy and a brief review of some of the difficulties of interpretation is therefore in order.

It is a common finding that the parent-offspring correlation for intelligence tests is around 0.5, which is of the same general magnitude as the correlation found for traits of bodily dimension and so on. Rather smaller correlations have been typically found for measures of personality. These values are rather complicated to interpret (see McClearn, 1962a) and one of the principal difficulties is in the confounding of genotype and environment. It should be intuitively reasonable, from the above discussion, that it is necessary to have unambiguous assessments of environmental and genetic variance sources. If these are confounded, interpretation becomes very difficult indeed. Just such confounding appears to be rather the rule in the case of socially valued human traits. Those individuals who, on the average, are contributing the greater number of alleles for superior intelligence to their children, are most likely contributing also the environmental supports for intellectual attainment.

Another widely used technique in human behavioral genetics is that of studying twins. Problems similar to those encountered in correlational research present themselves in twin-study methodology. The basic logic of the twin technique is quite simple. Identical (monozygotic or MZ) twins are identical genetically. Any differences that may appear between MZ twin pairs must be some function of environmental variance sources. Fraternal (dizygotic or DZ) twins differ genetically as much as do ordinary siblings. Thus the differences that exist between DZ twin pairs are attributable both to genetic sources and environmental ones. If we assume that the environmental variance component in MZ twins is the same as that for DZ twins, then by a simple subtraction of the former from the latter we should obtain an index of the genetic variance source. One of the principal difficulties in interpreting such data is the likelihood that fraternal twins are exposed to a wider array of environmental forces than are identical twins, and that the two environmental variances cannot be regarded as equal.

In spite of all this and other difficulties of interpretation, the twin-study approach has been quite useful in behavioral genetics research. As in the case of data from correlations among relatives, the twin-study data suggest that the heritability of intellectual traits, as a class, is higher than that of personality traits, as a class. Recent research has emphasized finer grained analyses of the intellectual domain, with the interesting result that different varieties of intellectual function appear to have different proportions of genetic determination (Vandenberg, 1965). Various considerations of quantitative inheritance have suggested differential evolutionary significance of some of these intellectual sub-units in man's evolutionary history (Roberts, 1967).

The preceding comments concerning difficulties in the interpretation of human data should not be construed as a criticism of current research or a discouragement to further research. The implication rather is that conclusions from such human data must be interpreted with circumspection. Many traits are capable of study only in man. If man's conditions of social existence are such as to confound the available techniques, then the techniques must be used as best they can, with the interpretation always being made in the total context of information about heredity in general, and specifically including the data obtained on behavioral genetics in animals, where control procedures can circumvent many of the difficulties of human research.

Studies of the resemblance of relatives in animals is, of course, possible, and indeed is much less subject to the confounding of environmental and genetic variables that occurs in research on man. Likewise, the basic twin-study paradigm could be applied to animal species in which twinning occurs. In point of fact, however, the techniques most frequently used in the study of quantitative aspects of animal behavioral genetics have been two which are not possible in human research. The first of these techniques is the use of highly inbred strains. The mating of relatives in consecutive heterozygosity. In some cases, for in- generations leads to a reduction in stance sib mating, there is an asymp- tomatic approach to a condition of homozygosity for all genes in a strain thus derived (with certain complications not necessary for the current discussion). That is to say, every animal of a single strain in which each generation is derived from a single sibling mating pair will be homozygous in like allelic state for practically all genes. There is, therefore, no (or very little) genetic variability within such a strain, and the exhibited phenotypic variance must be attributable to environmental sources. If different inbred strains, reared in the same environment, exhibit different behavioral characteristics, these differences must be attributable to genetic differences between the strains. A comparison of various inbred strains on a particular behavioral characteristic is therefore a good indicator of the existence of genetic influence on a behavioral trait.

Many such strain differences have been described with respect to such behavioral characters as learning ability, activity level, sexual behavior, alcohol preference, and aggressiveness (see McClearn, 1962a). A particularly interesting type of strain difference, and one that has important implications for methodology in animal research generally, is that in which strains respond differentially to the application of an independent variable. An example of this type of outcome is that of the effects of administration of alcohol fumes upon activity level of mice (McClearn, 1962b). Some strains of animals have activity increased as a consequence of forced inhalation of alcohol vapor; some strains are unaffected; and some strains have their activity level decreased by the identical treatment.

The establishment of strain differences is only an indicator of genetic determination, and more detailed analysis of the inheritance requires the comparison of means and variances of the inbred strains and of generations derived from them. The F_1 generation, that is to say the offspring of the mating of animals of two inbred strains, is also uniform genetically, although these F_1 animals will be heterozygous for all genes which were homozygous in different allelic states in the parent strains. Phenotypic vari-

ance in the F_1 populations, therefore, like phenotypic variation of the inbred strains, must be attributable to environmental sources. The F_2 generation is obtained by mating F_1 animals with other F_1 animals. This generation is genetically heterogenous, and this fact permits the comparison of the variance in F_1's to the variance of the F_2 and other generations in which both environmental and genetic variance exist. This comparison can yield a type of heritability estimate. Fuller and Thompson (1960), for example, studied activity in descendant populations from two strains of mice and found that 60% of the variance of the F_2, under the existing environmental conditions, was due to genetic variability within the group.

The other principally used mating technique in animal behavioral genetics has been selective breeding. In selective breeding, subjects with extreme manifestation of the trait in question are mated together with the objective of shifting the population mean. In practical efforts—such as those directed toward increase in milk production in cattle, or egg size in chickens, for example—this selective breeding is usually carried out only in the more desirable direction of the trait. In laboratory research, however, it is customary (indeed for proper analysis, essential) to breed in both directions. The rate of differentiation of the high and low selected lines is dependent upon the heritability of the trait. This can be appreciated by referring again to Figure 1. In the upper distribution, selection of an animal with an extreme score will provide an animal with an extreme genotype. In the lower distribution, an animal with an extreme phenotype may be genotypically quite ordinary or average. Since none of the effects of environment can be transmitted to the next generation, only the genotypic value is of importance in determining the changes in population mean as a consequence of selective breeding. Thus traits of high heritability provide a more rapid divergence of strains selected bidirectionally and traits of low heritability show slower progress.

Successful selective breeding has been accomplished for a variety of behavioral traits. The classic example, of course, is that of Tryon (1940) who selectively bred rats for maze "brightness" and maze "dullness" in a 17-unit multiple T-maze. Other workers (see McClearn, 1962a) have selectively bred for learning in rats, activity in rats, aggressiveness in mice, geotaxis in fruit flies, mating speed in fruit flies, and other characteristics. Not only do these successful breeding programs reveal retrospectively that there was genetic contribution to the variability of the trait in the foundation population from which selection was begun, they also provide research animals with different values of the behavioral trait of interest. These animals therefore make excellent subjects for research on correlated characters and especially on physiological mechanisms. An excellent example of such procedures is the history of research on Tryon's bright and dull rats which have been investigated for the association of their performance differentials with motivational factors (Searle, 1949), specific "hypotheses"

preferences (Krechevsky, 1933), brain size (Silverman, et al., 1940), and enzyme differences (Rosenzweig, et al., 1960).

PHYSIOLOGICAL AND BIOCHEMICAL GENETICS

The past fifteen years has witnessed an explosion of knowledge concerning the mechanisms through which the genes express themselves, and the whole new field of molecular biology has emerged. The chemical nature of the gene is now quite clearly understood. The fundamental component of the hereditary material is deoxyribonucleic acid (DNA). The molecule of DNA has a double helical structure. This may be visualized as two strands of phosphate and deoxyribose sugar groups wrapped around each other, but held a fixed distance apart by pairs of bases on the interior of the helix. The space limitations of the molecular structure are such that the four bases involved are always paired in a certain way: adenine pairs with thymine; guanine pairs with cytosine. The doubled nature of this molecule and the pairing restrictions on the bases give it the capacity of self-duplication. This property is of course a requisite of the hereditary material, since the basic genetic information available in the fertilized egg must be duplicated many times over in the development of a multicellular organism. Essentially, what appears to happen is that the two helices unwind, and each carries with it one base of each base pair. The composition of the cell nucleus, in which this takes place, is rich in unattached bases. These attach themselves to the single bases that are in turn attached to the helix. Because of the strict rules governing which base may pair with which other base, the newly formed pairs are exact duplicates of the original. The process also involves duplication of the phosphate and deoxyribose sugar strands.

The DNA is, of course, located in the nucleus of cells. However, it is known that much of the vital work of the cells takes place in the cytoplasm. In some fashion, therefore, the information that is contained in the DNA molecule must be transmitted to the cytoplasm. This is accomplished by another nucleic acid, in this case single-stranded, called ribonucleic acid (RNA). By a process similar to that involved in DNA replication, an RNA molecule is transcribed on the DNA molecule, so that the sequence of bases in the DNA determines the sequence of bases in RNA. (In RNA, uracil substitutes for thymine.) The RNA molecule then goes into the cytoplasm, where it is involved in protein synthesis. The genetic "information" is coded by the sequence of bases and the code has been shown to consist of three letter "words." Each succeeding triplet of bases specifies an amino acid. For example, three uracils in a row (UUU) specifies phenylalanine; AUG (adenine, uracil, guanine) specifies glutamic acid. These amino acids join and ultimately form proteins. Of particular interest are the proteins that act as enzymes. These act as catalysts and are vital to the operation of the organism. The reactions that are the very basis of behavior and indeed, of life itself, could not take place in their absence.

A particularly cogent example relating gene to enzyme to behavioral consequence is that of phenylketonuria. As we have seen earlier, the evidence is clear that phenylketonuria arises from the homozygous recessive state of a particular gene. Phenylketonurics are deficient with respect to the enzyme, phenylalanine hydroxylase. With this deficiency, the metabolism of phenylalanine is stopped or greatly reduced, and there is an accumulation of phenylalanine and a number of related metabolic products. Some of these are evidently toxic to the developing nervous system, and lead to mental retardation if the individual is untreated. Fortunately, knowledge of the metabolic difficulty has given rise to a rational therapy. With special diets lacking phenylalanine, it is possible to keep the biochemical status of phenylketonuric patients within normal bounds, and there appears to be substantial improvement in mental status if the treatment is begun early enough. To the latter end, many states now require the testing of all newborn infants.

A number of other defects of amino acid metabolism with mental retardation have now been identified, and research is proceeding rapidly on problems of identification and therapy. A review of these and other conditions of mental retardation is given by Anderson (1964).

In research on animals, one of the most thorough attempts to trace the biochemical route from gene to behavior has been the work of Rosenzweig and co-workers (1964). Descendants of the selectively bred Tryon "bright" and "dull" rats have been found to differ in brain levels of acetylcholinesterase and acetylcholine. These results, combined with data from other strains selectively bred for the level of enzyme activity, suggest that the ratio of these two substances is correlated with learning ability.

Other research implicating physiological differences as mediators of strain differences in behavior include the finding by Feuer and Broadhurst (1962) that rats bred for high reactivity (emotional defecation) were hypothyroid relative to the strain selected for low reactivity.

Another sort of evidence suggesting basic biochemical differences underlying behavioral ones is that reported by Kakihana, et al., (1966), who found that mice of two inbred strains which differ in duration of narcosis after injection of alcohol evidently metabolize the alcohol at the same rate. Thus, the more quickly recovering animals are regaining consciousness with blood alcohol levels that maintain unconsciousness in the other strain. Evidently the tissue of the latter is more sensitive to alcohol than is that of the former genetic strain.

DEVELOPMENTAL GENETICS

An area of genetical research especially pertinent to the interest of the 1967 Merrill-Palmer Conference is that which deals with the role of genes in developmental processes.

Occasionally, confusion arises between the concepts of "hereditary" and "congenital." Consideration of the inheritance of adult traits that do not appear in the newborn should make clear, however, that not all genes are "turned on" at birth or at conception. A specific example is provided by the condition, Huntington's Chorea, which is due to the presence of a dominant allele of the particular gene involved. The average age of onset of the condition is about 35 years. Other characters, such as blood groups, do seem fixed at birth. Still others, for example, hemoglobin type, change systematically with age. Presumably, genes that are part of polygenic systems have differing times of onset, as well.

In addition to these temporal considerations, there are many interesting aspects of spatial differences in gene functioning. A key biological problem, in fact, concerns the way in which a single cell, the fertilized egg, can differentiate into a complex multicellular organism, each cell of which presumably carries the same set of genetic information. Part of this differentiation can probably be accounted for in terms of initial lack of homogeneity of the egg cytoplasm, with resulting nonequivalence of the cytoplasm in various descendant cell lines.

The operon model of gene action (Jacob and Monod, 1961) has provided suggestions as to how genes themselves may be "turned on" or "turned off" in developmental sequences. Although the basic data have been obtained from microorganisms, it seems a reasonable working hypothesis that similar mechanisms occur in higher organisms (Ursprung, 1965). The model postulates different types of gene: regulator genes and structural genes. The latter type is what we have previously been discussing simply as "genes," the function of which is to produce a type of RNA that will in turn produce enzymes. A structural gene has an "operator" adjacent to it.

The operator is apparently the critical starting point for the molecular copying involved in transcribing RNA from DNA. A regulator gene, which need not be physically adjacent to operator or the structural gene, produces a repressor substance which attaches to operator and thus prevents RNA transcription.

An "inducer" introduced into the cell, for example, by diffusion from adjacent cells, or from the external environment, combines with repressor, which then cannot occupy the strategic site on operator. RNA transcription and enzyme production can begin. The gene has been "turned on." If one of the metabolic products of the reactions initiated by the enzyme happens to be the inducer, or a similar molecule, it effectively keeps the system locked on. A similar mechanism can turn off or lock off a gene that is initially on.

The complexity of interactions between different genes, where the product of one might intervene in the controlling system of another, is easy to imagine. For such situations, the type of model described by Waddington (1957) might be required. It is possible to imagine, for example, that a given genotype fixes the developmental "trajectory"; that environmental forces act to move development from this path, and that the lability of the system depends upon the extent to which feedback information causes compensatory readjustment in trajectory.

It is probably correct to say that behavioral geneticists have only begun to apply developmental genetic considerations to analyses of the de-velopment of behavioral patterns. Yet sufficient has been accomplished to indicate the high promise of this approach. Descriptively, there are several examples of timed action such as that provided by Huntington's Chorea. An example taken from the mouse research literature is that of audiogenic seizure susceptibility. Many strains of animals are resistant to audiogenic seizures. In one of the most thoroughly investigated susceptible strains, there is a very sharply peaked distribution of sensitivity, with the peak occurring at 21 days (Schlesinger, et al., 1966). A rather different example is provided by another strain of mice, which shows a moderate preference for alcohol until about 9 weeks of age, at which time there is an abrupt decline in alcohol preference (Kakihana and McClearn, 1963). Other strains that are non-preferring as adults do not show this developmental function.

Another type of research that is relevant involves experimental intervention of some sort in early life, with an examination of the differential responsiveness to the treatment by different genotypes of animals. Lindzey and his co-workers (1963), for example, have investigated strain differences in the effect of handling and of auditory stimuli presented during infancy on learning performance and tests of temperament in the adults. Weir and DeFries (1964), and De-Fries (1964), investigated strain differences in the effect of prenatal stress on behavior of the offspring. In all of these studies significant strain differences have been identified, indicating that the effect of environmental variables in influencing a developmental sequence is strongly dependent upon the genotype of the organism to which the environmental treatment is offered.

SUMMARY

To summarize, the evidence implicating heredity in the determination of behavior is compelling. Some behavioral traits are affected by single genes. In other cases, abnormalities are attributable to the presence of many extra genes in the form of a surplus chromosome. Many, perhaps most, traits are determined by a number of genes acting in concert with environmental forces. The routes by which the genes affect behavior are under investigation, and gene-enzyme-behavior relationships are beginning to emerge. The potential for genetic control of behavioral development is suggested by yet other research.

In brief, the rules of behavioral inheritance appear to be no different from the rules of inheritance of other traits. We might reasonably expect no less a return, therefore, from the application of a genetic perspective in studying behavior than that which has rewarded similar efforts elsewhere in the biological sciences.

3 *Infant Malnutrition and Adult Learning*

NEVIN S. SCRIMSHAW, M.D.

There is growing evidence that the quality and quantity of the food we consume affects not only our health and physical growth but also mental ability and social development. The following selection stresses that since malnutrition may result in permanent impairment of learning and behavior, such knowledge impels public concern and action. Further evidence of the influences of nutrition on health and physical development, mental performance, and social behavior, and suggestions for meeting the nutritional needs of children, are found in Breckenridge and Vincent (1965, pp. 102–133).

Two-thirds of the world's children live in the developing countries of the world, and for most of them malnutrition during their early years is a fact of existence. The consequent retardation in physical growth and development is reflected in the almost universally smaller body size of members of low - income populations in these countries. Genetic differences are a minor factor. Many underprivileged children among poor families in the industrialized countries are also malnourished at an early age.

Attention was focused until recently mainly on the high mortality of malnourished infants and preschool children of developing countries, with no particular concern for the smaller body size of the survivors. In the 1920s, experiments with rats began to show that nutritional deficiencies not only retarded physical growth and development but affected the central nervous system as well. In recent decades, early malnutrition sufficient to impair growth in experimental animals has repeatedly and conclusively demonstrated its effect on their subsequent learning, memory, and adaptive behavior. This has led to the stunning implication that infants and young children whose physical growth is stunted by malnutrition may also be prevented from attaining their full mental capacity and social development.

At an International Conference on Malnutrition, Learning, and Behavior at MIT last March, more than 500 medical, biological, and social scientists from thirty-seven countries reviewed the evidence and emphasized the urgent need for better understanding of consequences of early malnutrition in man. Investigations are now required in a variety of cultural situations, taking into account not only malnutrition, but also infectious disease and the social, psychological, and educational influences in the young child's life.

Although the conditions under which malnutrition exerts a permanent influence on learning and behavior need to be defined further and the effects measured with greater precision, present knowledge impels public concern and action. Aid programs for industrialization and for the development of material resources are of limited value if essential human resources are neglected and inadequate. Even in advanced countries, remedial programs for underprivileged school children come too late when children have already suffered permanent physical and psychological damage.

In the rat, 80 per cent of brain growth occurs by four weeks of age; in the pig, by eight to ten weeks. The total body weight of both at these ages is less than 20 per cent of their usual weight at maturity. Rats which are underfed in the first few weeks after weaning and then placed on an adequate diet have smaller brains at maturity than control animals. Since the brain is growing so much faster than the rest of the body during these early weeks, the result of early undernutrition is a brain which is abnormally large for the body weight but small for the age of the animal. Recently, Dr. John Dobbing, Dr. R. A. McCance, and Dr. Elsie Widdowson, in the department of experimental medicine, University of Cambridge, England, have demonstrated more marked postnatal retardation in brain

IMPAIRED LEARNING AND BEHAVIOR
AMONG UNDERPRIVILEGED POPULATIONS

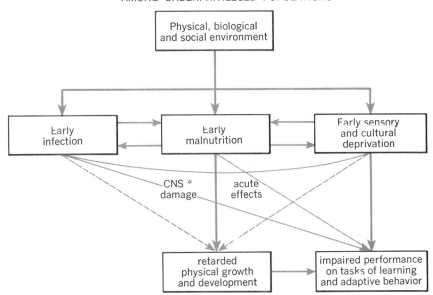

Fig. 1.   Schematic indication of interrelations among environmental factors which may cause physical and mental retardation. (*CNS: Central Nervous System).

growth of infant rats by having a single mother suckle fifteen to twenty young. In this way undernutrition was made to coincide with the period when the brain was growing most rapidly.

Beyond about three weeks of age for the rat and five weeks of age for the pig, the effect on brain size of short periods of undernutrition becomes progressively less pronounced. The adult brain is remarkably resistant to changes in weight, even during severe starvation, provided it is able to grow normally to a mature size before the starvation begins. Prisoners of war and concentration camp internees in World War II who survived long periods of severe food restriction showed no loss of intelligence after rehabilitation.

Food restriction in animals simulates the form of undernutrition in young children known as marasmus. Marasmus is particularly common in children less than one year of age, when the rate of postnatal brain growth is at its peak. It occurs because, under conditions of poverty and ignorance, children who are weaned early in the first year of life are likely to be given substitutes for breast milk which are inadequate in both calories and protein. Marasmus is found with growing frequency in the mushrooming cities of the developing countries because recent arrivals imitate the early weaning practices of the middle-and upper-income groups without either the knowledge or the resources to provide a proper substitute for mother's milk.

Children who are not weaned until the second or third year of life—until recently, the common practice in nearly all unsophisticated societies—are likely to receive sufficient calories but inadequate dietary protein. The type of malnutrition which then results is called kwashiorkor, a dramatically acute and often fatal disease which is due primarily to protein deficiency.

In experimental animals, central-nervous-system damage is still more pronounced on a diet deficient in protein but adequate in calories. When Dr. R. J. C. Stewart, Dr. B. F. Platt, and collaborators at the Human Nutrition Research Unit of the National Institute for Medical Research, Mill Hill, in London, fed diets severely deficient in protein though adequate in calories to weanling rats, piglets, and puppies born of well nourished mothers, the animals exhibited signs of central-nervous-system damage. Electroencephalograms showed diminution of rhythmic activity, and degenerative changes were found postmortem in the nerve cells and neuroglial cells of the spinal cord and brain medulla.

Similarly depleted animals were subsequently fed a high-protein diet for one to three months, and their clinical condition improved promptly; but again, when these animals were examined postmortem, cells in the central nervous system were still obviously damaged. The severity of such changes was increased by lowering the age at which the deficiency was established, by further reducing the protein value of the diet, or by increasing the duration of the deficient diet.

Dr. Richard Barnes and his colleagues at Cornell University have observed rats deprived of adequate food from the second to the twenty-first day of life. The animals were foster-nursed in large litters of fourteen to sixteen and further deprived on a low-protein diet for eight weeks after weaning. Five to nine months after rehabilitation on an adequate diet the rats still showed significantly poorer learning performance in a Y-shaped water maze. The Cornell observers concluded from these and other studies that, in rats and swine, simple undernutrition induced by general food restriction during the nursing period produces behavioral changes but has little effect upon the animals' ability to learn to solve complex problems. Severe protein deficiency in early life, however, causes not only the behavioral changes seen in food-restricted groups but also impairs the capacity to perform well in tests requiring the animals to learn from multiple trials.

In the studies of the Mill Hill group, in which the diets of the animals during pregnancy were deficient in protein and the animals' offspring were fed deficient diets after weaning, the effects were similar but even more pronounced. Dr. Bacon Chow at Johns Hopkins University and Dr. Sanford Miller at MIT have observed that young rats born of malnourished mothers show behavioral changes when they continue to be fed by their mothers. Dr. Miller has demonstrated that these effects can be avoided if the young are transferred at birth and suckled by a well nourished mother.

At the University of Aberdeen in Scotland, Dr. John Cowley found that a low-protein diet fed in unrestricted amounts to rats after weaning had no effect on their problem-solving ability in a maze. But the progeny of these rats, also maintained on such a diet, showed markedly reduced intelligence by the same test, as did second- and third-generation rats continued on this protein-deficient diet.

In the child, the brain achieves 80 per cent of its adult weight by age three, while the body reaches little more than 20 per cent of adult weight. The child's first three years of development are thus comparable to the first four weeks in the life of a rat or eight to ten weeks for the pig. At birth the human brain is gaining weight at a rate of one to two milligrams per minute. It could be expected, therefore, that protein deficiency serious enough to limit gain in height and weight during the first two to three years of life can also limit brain growth. While head circumference is of no value in predicting normal variations in intellectual capacity, it is a useful—if not absolute—indicator of brain size. When children are undernourished at an early age, their brain growth, as judged by head circumference, is significantly poorer than that of matched children who are well fed.

Dr. Mavis B. Stoch and Dr. P. M. Smythe in Capetown, South Africa, have followed twenty grossly undernourished infants, first examined in 1955–1960, and compared their gain in weight and head circumference with a matched control group of the same racial background which was considered adequately nourished. When the measurements were last made in 1967, the head circumferences of the control group were within normal limits for United States children of the same age, while those undernourished as infants averaged a full inch smaller. Similar differences in the head circumference of individuals of comparable genetic background but different nutritional histories have been reported by other observers.

To the extent that brain growth is impaired concurrently with early retardation in linear growth, more than 300 million children are in jeopardy today. Dr. Moisés Béhar, director of the Institute of Nutrition of Central America and Panama (INCAP), bases this calculation on the almost universal finding that the great majority of young children in the lower socioeconomic groups of developing countries show a decreasing growth rate after the first few months of life. This is true whether they are compared with children of the same ages in North America and Europe or with those of middle- and upper-income groups in their own countries.

Speakers at last year's MIT conference and at an international meeting held in Washington, D.C., in 1964 on Preschool Child Malnutrition presented data from more than forty developing countries, illustrating widespread growth failure among young children. Characteristically, growth retardation begins after the first four to six months of life and becomes progressively worse until the child passes the critical weaning period or succumbs to kwashiorkor or an infectious disease. Poor growth is associated with the inadequacy of breast milk as the sole source of protein after a child is six months old.

This inadequacy is serious because the supplementary foods offered during the generally prolonged period of breast feeding also are often insufficient. One result is a mortality rate for children one to four years of age in developing countries which is twenty to forty times higher than that in North America and Europe. Too, average height and weight for children of developing countries are well below the fifteenth percentile of children in the industrialized countries.

Genetic differences appear to be of minor importance in accounting for these findings, for children of middle- and upper-income families who are well fed in the developing countries generally share the growth patterns of children in Europe and North America. Whether the racial composition of the more privileged groups within a country differs from that of lower-income groups or is identical, the less privileged children fail to grow as well. Countries in which retardation in growth and maturation due to malnutrition is common among preschool children include nearly all of those considered to be technically underdeveloped. Some particularly underprivileged groups in industrially advanced countries would be included as well.

The most serious complication in designing field studies of these problems is the fact that social and psychological factors may independently have the same adverse effects as malnutrition on learning and behavior and on the anatomical and biochemical development of the brain. Studies with rats, kittens, and monkeys have clearly indicated that animals which are protected from stimulation and prevented from exploring their environments have not only smaller brains with fewer nerve cells but also develop functional impairment of the central nervous system.

Similarly, institutionalized children, well fed and genetically normal, but deprived of affection and stimulation at an early age, may show marked mental impairment. The many kinds of psychological and social deprivation common among malnourished children can exert a direct effect on intellectual performance. Unstimulating home environment, poor educational facilities, isolation resulting from illness, limited recreational opportunities, and lack of incentive due to repeated discouragement are examples of such deprivations.

In industrialized countries, inadequate intellectual or social performance in a child is more likely to be the result of a complex interaction over a period of time between genetic variables and primarily non-nutritional factors in the social or cultural environment than a consequence of malnutrition. In the rural areas of many developing countries, however, and often in city slums and ghettos, variations from family to family in education, economic status, and cultural practices may be relatively slight. In such populations, deficiencies in intellectual performance due to malnutrition and its synergism with infection may be detectable. While genetic factors are important determinants of individual potential, they do not account for most differences between privileged and underprivileged populations.

Very few long-term field studies in human learning and behavior have been completed, and most have failed to separate adequately the effects of malnutrition from those of other environmental factors. In the Capetown study, a series of intelligence tests revealed consistently lower scores in malnourished children when compared with the control group's scores over a period of approximately ten years. The disparity in living conditions between the two groups, however, was equally marked. Wretched housing with no sanitary facilities, alcoholism, unemployment, illegitimacy, and broken homes were the rule for the initially malnourished group. By contrast, the families of the control group lived in clean brick houses with running water and flush toilets; the children were legitimate and their parents employed.

The Capetown observers believe that the smaller body size and brain size in the malnourished group, as well as an increased frequency of abnormal brain waves and impaired visual perception, indicate organic brain damage. Despite this there is no way to separate the nutritional from other environmental influences in evaluating performance on various intelligence tests. Unfortunately, this was also the case in a number of studies of Serbian, American, and Indian children.

Dr. Fernando Mönckeberg of the University of Chile has reported a more critical study of the same type. Fourteen children with severe marasmus diagnosed at ages one month to five months were treated for long periods, discharged, and observed during visits to the out-patient department. As each child was discharged from the hospital, the mother was given 20 liters of free milk per month for each preschool child in her family. Three to six years later the children were clinically normal and some had weight-to-height ratios above normal. Their height, head circumference, and intelligence quotients, however, were significantly lower than in Chilean children of the same age without a history of clinical malnutrition. Significantly, language skill was the most retarded.

The information gathered in the town of Tlaltizapán, Mexico, by Dr. Joaquin Cravioto, Dr. Rafael Ramos-Galván, and their collaborators, is the outstanding pioneering effort in this field. Their studies have played the major role in attracting attention to the association of nutritional retardation of growth and development with performance on tests of learning and behavior. Because the economic, educational, and social status of families in Tlaltizapán was very uniform, these factors were judged to influence the variation within the study population to a lesser degree than the differences in nutritional status.

Retardation in physical growth and development was found to depend upon family dietary practices and on the occurrence of infectious disease. It was not related to differences in housing facilities, personal hygiene, proportion of total income spent on food, or other indicators of social and economic status. Under these circumstances, the investigators found test performance of preschool and school children to be positively correlated with body weight and height.

In order to extend these studies to another population and also to make more prolonged observations, Dr.

Cravioto and several members of his team joined forces with INCAP in Guatemala. They selected school-age children living in Magdalena Milpas Altas, Guatemala—a predominantly Mayan Indian village of 1,600. More than 10 per cent of the children born in this village died in their first year, and mortality in the one-to-four-year age group was more than forty-five times higher than in North America and Western Europe.

Variations in height and weight among the children of this community were not related to height of the parents or to the minor differences in economic and social status among families. The major reason for short stature was malnutrition at an early age. Two years of intensive work in this village showed once again that retardation in height for age relative to other children in the village was accompanied by poorer performance on psychological tests.

A growing body of evidence indicates that primary learning and the development of adaptive capacity is based on the development of interrelation among the separate senses. During ages six to twelve years, intersensory relationships follow a well defined growth pattern in normal children. Dr. Cravioto gave principal emphasis, therefore, to tests of intersensory integration. The tests involved manipulating eight differently shaped wooden blocks. The examiner determined visual integration by asking the child to put the blocks into their corresponding holes as rapidly as possible. The integration of visual stimuli with the complex sensory input required by active manual manipulation of a test object was judged by asking the child whether a block

placed in his hand behind a screen was the same or different from one in front. Kinesthetic-visual integration was measured by moving the child's hand behind the screen to trace a shape which he had to judge to be the same or different from that of a block in front of him.

Each of these types of intersensory relationship improved with the age of the child. This was true for both children of the study village and those from middle- and upper-income families in Guatemala City. The rural children clearly lagged in the development of intersensory competence when compared with the privileged urban children. Of even more significance, the relationship between poorer test performance and shorter physical stature in the rural village did not apply to the well nourished urban children. Among the urban children there was no correlation between the height of the child for age and test performance.

Dr. Cravioto returned to Mexico and obtained similar information on intersensory integration among school children in Tlaltizapán. He found that here, as in Guatemala, the smallest children in the village show poorer intersensory integration for their age than those who are tallest. Among children of upper-income families in Mexico City, no such correlation exists. Clearly, where the child is more nearly able to realize his genetic potential for growth, differences in height lose their nutritional and social significance.

The most comprehensive and well controlled study to date is now under way in Guatemala under the direction of Dr. Cipriano Canosa of INCAP. Children in three villages are being given adequate supplementary food from an early age. An extensive battery of psychological tests is being used to compare their performance over the next seven years with that of children in three control villages.

There are circumstances in which the effects of early malnutrition on mental development are firmly established. A number of hereditary diseases induce a nutritional deficiency through an inborn error of metabolism. The resulting impairment of brain development is so disastrous that it illustrates dramatically the way in which nutritional factors can influence development and function of the central nervous system if operative at an early postnatal age. These inherited nutritional defects should dispel any doubt that nutritional deficiency, if sufficiently early and severe, can have profound and permanently detrimental consequences for the learning and behavior of children.

It is clear that under circumstances common to developing countries, malnutrition can interact with infection, heredity, and social factors to bring about physical and mental impairment. The social factors responsible are multiple and difficult to correct, but the elimination of malnutrition and infection among underprivileged populations is a feasible goal. For each child in the world, of any race or heritage, of any social or economic background, the events of early childhood determine whether he will suffer some degree of permanent physical and mental impairment. Every child should have the opportunity to attain his full potential. Measures to ensure the maximum mental development and optimum learning and behavior of children deserve a high priority. Among these the prevention of malnutrition is of fundamental importance.

4   The Developmental Viewpoint

ERNEST R. HILGARD

RICHARD C. ATKINSON

Each child has his own pattern of growth and development. His readiness to learn changes day by day as a result of his biological maturing and his daily experiences. This selection helps us to understand the extent to which a child's development and behavior is a product of maturation and learning. Data are also presented on the continuity between early and later development, on the way in which early experiences of stress and unusual stimulation affect one in later years.

Reprinted from *Introduction to Psychology*, Fourth Edition, by Ernest R. Hilgard and Richard C. Atkinson, copyright 1953, © 1957, 1962, 1967 by Harcourt, Brace & World, Inc. and reprinted with their permission.

. . . The main assumption of the developmental point of view is that there is continuity from the past to the present, so that the present can be understood in terms of its history; this is so obvious that it would not lend much theoretical interest in development except for some more puzzling and controversial aspects of this continuity. One possibility is that there may be *critical periods* in development, where both favorable and unfavorable outcomes may have lasting and well-nigh irreversible consequences. For example, it has been hypothesized that a person's basic trust in other people is a characteristic developed in the first year of life through the warmth and affection of those who care for him (Erikson, 1963). If this hypothesis is true, and the child who lacks such early affectionate care grows up to be inadequate and mistrustful in social relationships, then the first few months of life would represent a critical period with respect to the development of basic trust.

Another possibility is that growth proceeds in definable *stages,* so that behavior and personality become somewhat restructured (in definable ways) as growth proceeds. The shifts in interest with the onset of adolescence would be one of the familiar aspects of such restructuring, but there are others of less obvious kind. The concepts of critical periods and of stages suggest that there are aspects of the developmental process inherent in growth, and not the result solely of learning. Hence the issue between inherent growth aspects, or *maturation,* and the result of experi-

ence, or *learning,* is one that has to be faced.

EMBRYOLOGICAL DEVELOPMENT AS MATURATION

In all the higher forms of life a good deal of development takes place before birth, so that much hereditary potential has already manifested itself by the time the infant is born. At the same time, the infant is so relatively helpless at birth that we may think of development in the early months after birth as being an extension of the same sort of process that went on in the fetus, that is, an orderly development whose timing is determined more by the nature of the organism than by how it is handled. This is the assumption that *maturation* is important, which means that the timing and patterning of changes, beyond birth, are relatively independent of exercise and experience, and they go on despite wide variations in the environment, assuming, of course, that these variations occur within limits favorable to survival and growth. If birds whose wings have been restrained from birth learn to fly as quickly as birds that have fluttered their wings many days before they fly, we may reasonably say that flying is controlled more largely by maturation than by learning.

In its earliest stages the human embryo resembles that of other animals, but by the eighth week of existence it has acquired rudimentary human characteristics; from then until birth it is known as a *fetus.* Fetal development goes on in the uniform environment of the mother's body according to a relatively fixed time schedule. Fetal behavior, such as turning and kicking, also follows an orderly sequence, depending on the growth stages of the fetus. Studies have been made of the responsiveness to outside stimulation of the human fetus born prematurely, and more systematic studies have been made of fetal behavior in animals such as the guinea pig and cat. When the fetus is surgically removed from the mother in animal studies, the circulation of the blood in the fetus is maintained through the umbilical cord, which is not severed. Then the fetus is placed in a salt solution at body temperature. Now the response of the fetus to stimulation can be studied at successive stages, with the physiological condition of the fetus essentially normal. Such studies show the appearance of behavior patterns in a developmental sequence depending upon growth (i.e., fetal age) rather than upon prior external stimulation (Carmichael, 1954).

Transplantation experiments with simpler forms of life, such as sea urchins and salamanders, have helped biologists to understand the nature of the developmental processes in the embryo. At an early stage of the salamander's development a small group of cells known as "the organizer" becomes very important. The *organizer* determines which will be the head end and which the tail end of the growing embryo. Previously undifferentiated cells begin to differentiate appropriately to their location, so that the embryonic salamander develops properly.

As development proceeds, subregions, such as the mouth region or eye region, are also "organized" by the environment of cells around them. That is, tissue from the belly region, if transplanted to the eye region or the mouth region at the appropriate stages, will conform to the new environment of cells and form an eye or a mouth.

Because the transplantation experiments work only when the developing organism is young enough, they also provide an illustration of *critical periods*. We find in embryological development many of the problems that will have to be considered in the study of development generally: species characteristics, internal and external environmental influences, critical periods and stages.

ORDERLY BEHAVIOR PATTERNS IN INFANT DEVELOPMENT

As we have noted, the orderly development of the human organism begins long before birth. The regulation of fetal development lies within the organism's own tissues, although normal development requires the continuing protection and sustenance provided by the mother's body. Evidence that the timing of development is internally regulated can be found in prematurely born infants who, kept alive in an incubator that simulates the intra-uterine environment, develop at much the same rate as infants remaining in the uterus full term. The regularity of development before birth provides a clear picture of what is meant by maturation, for growth goes on in regular and predictable ways.

Postnatal maturation is regulated much like growth before birth. That is, many kinds of behavior follow orderly sequences little affected by environmental influences, provided only that the environment is sufficiently favorable to support the necessary growth. Such sequences are found in standing, walking, using hands and fingers, and talking. For example, every infant goes through such regular sequences of crawling and creeping before he walks upright that a uniform growth pattern is evidently responsible for the behavior.

Maturation of structure continues into adult life. Some of the growth changes at adolescence are internally regulated in a sequence not unlike the regulation of fetal development. To the extent that adolescent behavior corresponds to bodily changes, maturational principles apply. The changes associated with aging also go on at their own rates. While maturation is thus a lifelong process, its nature is most readily understood through observing infants and young children, in whom behavioral changes dependent upon growth are rapid and apparent.

Long before learning to walk, the infant goes through a number of movement stages related to this later and more complex behavior. An early form of "locomotion" is learning to roll over. Again this regularity of sequence suggests that a growth process determines the order of behavior. The alternative conclusion would be that all parents go through a training ritual which leads to this uniformity of performance from one child to another. We know, of course, that *all* parents do nothing of the sort. Not all children go through the sequence at the same rate; in general, the *order* in which they go from one stage to the next is more alike from infant to infant than the *age* at which they reach each stage. An idea of the range of variation from child to child is given if Figure 1, showing the age zones within which 95 percent of a group of infants reached a stated level of performance. Some of the zones spread over four or five months, indicating that some infants are four or five months ahead of others in reaching the stage of standing alone or walking alone.

The sequences of normal behavior lead to the conviction that growth lies beneath the development of behavior, and further evidence of the influence of maturation comes from experiments in which the environment is either restricted or enriched. If environmental variations produce little change in the rate of change of behavior, then it becomes clearer that the process is determined by growth *within* rather than by influence from *without*.

Observations of the effects of restricted movements have been made on human infants. Hopi Indians, for example, have traditionally kept their infants bound to a board carried on the mother's back. Some Hopi mothers continue to follow the custom, while others, because of contact with white American culture, do not. Although the cradleboard markedly restricts movements of the infant's arms and legs during the early months, children raised on it began (on the average) to walk at the same age as

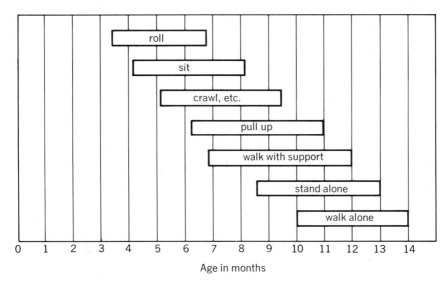

Fig. 1. Although development is orderly, some infants reach each stage
ahead of others. The bars show the zones of age within which 95 percent of
infants in a well-baby clinic achieved the stated performances. From C.
Anderson Aldrich and Mildred A. Norval, "A developmental graph for the
first year of life," *J. Pediat.* 29: 304–308, 1946.

those who were never bound on it
(Dennis and Dennis, 1940).

A similar study, made with a pair of
fraternal twins (twins developed
from separate eggs), provided similar
results. The twin girls were kept in
their cribs from the age of one month
until the age of nine months. They
were given no training of any kind
and only a minimum of handling.
They spent most of the time lying on
their backs, their hands and feet under the bedclothes. Despite this
marked restriction of activity, they
developed normally in such behavior
as putting their hands to their
mouths, grasping objects, playing
with their hands, and sitting up when
propped. They did, however, fall
slightly behind the norms for other
children in the age at which they
were able to walk holding onto furni-

ture and that at which they were able
to stand alone. There was no report of
any permanent effect upon the ability
to walk or upon other muscular skills
(Dennis, 1935). Maturation thus appears to be an important influence,
but too severe restrictions may cause
some delay in development.

MATURATION AND
READINESS TO LEARN

The practical (and theoretical) importance of recognizing the influence
of maturation lies in the relation of
maturation to the results of training at
different ages. The idea here is that
maturation may provide a *readiness
to learn.* Most behavior is developed
by *both* maturation and learning.
Language provides a useful illustration. The child learns to talk only

when he has *grown* old enough to learn (maturation), but the language he learns to talk is the one he *hears* (learning).

Imprinting

The manner in which inborn readiness affects what is later learned is well illustrated by the process of *imprinting,* a kind of learning that capitalizes upon an inherited tendency when the time is ripe. The clearest example is given by the tendency of a young duckling to start following its mother shortly after it is hatched, and then to follow only this particular female duck. Incubator-hatched ducklings can be imprinted upon artificial models, both inanimate and human. For example, mallard ducklings exposed to a moving model for 10 minutes between 12 and 17 hours after hatching will continue to treat that model as though it were the "mother" and will remain with it against the attraction of live mallard ducks. Once imprinting has occurred, the response of following will be elicited only by the imprinted object (Ramsay and Hess, 1954; Hess, 1959).

Critical Periods

The discussion of imprinting suggests that this is a learned bit of behavior, but that it can be learned only at the right age. Later experiments have shown that the results are not quite as simple as this. Part of the reason that imprinting is difficult when the ducks are older is that they have developed fear responses which interfere with the imprinting; when they are given tranquilizers to reduce the fear, then they can be imprinted later (Hess, 1957). Still, in the normal course of events, we find one period

much more favorable for this kind of learning than other periods in the life of the organism.

It has been noted in the training of seeing-eye dogs that the handling has to be adjusted very carefully to produce a faithful dog. In an experiment to test when human handling best produced a tame dog, Freedman, King, and Elliott (1961) raised puppies in a large field with tame mothers but without human handlers. They were then removed at various ages to spend 10 minutes a day with a human handler who was passive, that is, who waited for them to approach him. If this was delayed as long as 14 weeks the puppies had become wild dogs, frightened and timid with human beings. The best time for taming was shown to be between five to seven weeks of age; when tamed at these ages, the dogs remained tame, as was seen when they were tested again 14 weeks later. Thus we have evidence for another critical period. Whether or not such critical periods occur for human infants is a matter of some dispute, but we need to be prepared to find evidence for them.

SOME GENERALIZATIONS ABOUT MATURATION AND LEARNING IN INFANCY AND CHILDHOOD

Studies of efforts to train young infants at different ages permit us to make a few generalizations about learning and maturation. Although most of these apply to muscular skills rather than to more subtle aspects of personal and social behavior, it may be that in the long run we will discover that critical periods have more to do with such matters as anxiety and self-confidence than with skills such as typing or bicycle riding.

1. *Skills that build upon developing behavior patterns are most easily learned.* In almost all languages there are words for mother and father with sound patterns similar to *pa-pa* and *ma-ma.* The words which the infant usually acquires first are words like these which fit in most readily with his natural babbling. He can be taught words like *ma-ma, pa-pa, da-da, ba-ba, bye-bye,* because these words are like the sounds that he makes spontaneously.

2. *The rate of development remains uniform within wide ranges of stimulation.* The maturation of performance often requires environmental support, since growth alone is not enough to account for the resulting behavior. But maturation may still be fundamental in accounting for the *rate* of development. A study of stair-climbing by a pair of twins bears this out.

Twins T and C were identical twins, that is, twins developed from a single egg and with identical heredity. Because of their common heredity and similarity in development, they made an ideal pair for purposes of study. At the age of 46 weeks, the two twins showed no discernible difference in their behavior when placed at the bottom of a small staircase consisting of four treads and a platform that formed the fifth tread. As an initial test, the experimenter placed each twin before the staircase, while holding both hands. Each twin stepped forward and lifted one foot, but neither was able to place a foot or knee on the first tread.

Twin T was then given a daily 10-minute practice period in stair-climbing, while twin C (the "control" twin) was given no practice on stairs. At the end of six weeks, T could climb the steps in a little over 25 seconds, while C had not progressed further than putting the left knee on the first tread. Now T's training was discontinued, and a week later C began a two-week period of training. In these two weeks she caught up with and surpassed T's performance at the end of six weeks of training. Twin C had the advantage because she was older when she began her practice. One week later, when both T and C were 56 weeks old, their performances on the experimental stairs were essentially alike. It did not matter at the end that one twin had had three times the specific training of the other (Gesell and Thompson, 1941).

Within very wide limits of encouragement and exercise (i.e., environment), the child learns to walk and talk only when old enough and continues to improve at his own rate (i.e., maturation).

3. *The more mature the organism, the less training is needed to reach a given level of proficiency.* Many experiments point to the faster gains of older children over younger, with the same amount of directed practice. Maturation thus produces a certain *readiness* for specific kinds of learning. The generalization applies only within the period of growth; after adult status is achieved, a decline in learning rate may set in.

An experiment on typing was conducted in the first five grades of a school. After one year of practice, children in the second grade were typing at an average rate of less than five words per minute, while those in the fifth grade were typing at an average rate of 10 words per minute. In each grade the average gain with one year's practice was greater than in any lower grade.

The experiment went on for two years. It was then found that children who had had two years of typing experience were typing no faster than children in the same grade who had only one year of experience (Wood and Freeman, 1932).

The results of this experiment show that the final rate of typing depends more upon the level of maturation than upon the amount of typing experience, thus conforming to the stated principle that the more mature organism learns more readily. This principle would be limited were "critical periods" the rule for most kinds of learning.

4. *Training given before maturational readiness may bring either no improvement or only temporary improvement.* In an experiment in training in bladder control, conducted with two pairs of twins, an effort to train *one* member of each pair was begun shortly after birth, while no effort was made to train the other member of each pair. Training was ineffective until the infants were old enough; at that time the other two babies, previously untrained, learned very promptly. Although the two pairs of twins differed by some months in the time at which control was achieved, the trained and untrained member of each pair acquired control at the same time (McGraw, 1940). The necessary understanding awaited maturational readiness, and premature training was wasted. Any gains made under premature training are short-lived.

The temporary nature of improvements made beyond the natural maturational level is shown in some additional experiments done with the pair of identical twins who participated in the stair-climbing experiment.

When twins T and C were four years old, they participated in a number of experiments in which one was trained while the other received no training. The experiments included learning to cut with scissors, reciting digits, learning a ring-toss game, and maintaining balance while walking on boards of various widths. The experiments were so arranged that after a pretest of both twins only one was trained. Then there was a retest of both twins, followed by a period in which the second twin was trained. When training was stopped, both twins were retested three additional times at approximately 10-week intervals.

The typical result was that both twins profited by training, but that the one trained second gained more than the one trained first. After training was discontinued, there was loss in skill in both twins, as the performance dropped back to the level typical for children of their maturational development. . . . (J. R. Hilgard, 1933).

There was thus no evidence of permanent gain from training that had taken place too near the ceiling of ability for these twins.

5. *Premature training, if frustrating, may do more harm than good.* Although lack of training delays development, the lack appears to do no harm, for the retardation is overcome when practice begins. What

is the effect of overstimulation, that is, premature training, before maturational readiness? May it also retard development?

The child who has been exposed too early to an activity for which he is not ready may lose his natural enthusiasm for the activity when he reaches the stage of development appropriate for it. This loss was noted in an experiment in which there was a daily effort to teach a one-year-old to ride a tricycle. The experimenter observed, after the experiment was over, that the child's seven months of futile effort to ride the tricycle curtailed the interest that he would have shown later had the training been delayed (McGraw, 1943).

Experiments concerned with methods of drilling in arithmetic suggest that pressure for speed before the child is ready may actually interfere with learning. When tested after two years of speed drill, children who had been able to master arithmetic in the first grade when taught without pressure for speed did not do as well as they had in the first grade (Myers, 1928). . . .

EVIDENCE FOR REMOTE CONSEQUENCES OF EARLY DEVELOPMENTAL EXPERIENCES

The developmental point of view stresses the continuity between early and later development. To the extent that this is a matter of maturation it is characteristic of the species, and (unless there has been severe deficit with stunting of development) we merely wait for the interactions with the environment to produce their expected

effects. But this is by no means the whole story, and we wish to know how individual experience, of either deprivation or unusual stimulation, is reflected in later years.

Infant chimpanzees were reared in the dark for seven months. When removed from the dark, they failed to show the normal blinking response to an object moving toward their eyes. Even when a large yellow- and black-striped disk was connected repeatedly with electric shock, they showed no signs of recognizing (and avoiding) it, although normal animals develop avoidance responses after one or two mild shocks. Three such animals were used in this part of the experiment; a fourth, of the same age, had been in the light for one and a half hours each day. His reactions to light after seven months were entirely normal. Being raised in the dark may cause some injury to the eyes, but in addition there are behavioral defects that are gradually removed by practice, such as the inability to, converge the eyes upon an object. These results led to more careful study of normal chimpanzee infants, and it was found that their visual development was rather slow, with blinking in response to moving objects in the visual field not appearing until the age of two months. The animals raised in the dark took about two weeks to acquire the response after they had been brought into the light. Thus fully adequate use of vision in the chimpanzee depends both upon internal growth factors continuing after birth and upon practice in the use of vision (Riesen, 1950).

In another experiment, dogs reared in confined quarters so that they did not have the opportunity to explore the environment were perfectly healthy, but in some respects appeared stupid (Melzack and Scott, 1957). For one thing, they seemed quite insensitive to pain. They did not respond to a pin prick or to having their tails stepped on. They would investigate a lighted match by putting a nose into the flame; this would be repeated time after time, without any of the avoidance reaction expected from a normal dog. Whatever the felt experience may have been to the dog, certainly the pain stimulus did not evoke the compelling responses found in the normal dog.

A curious effect of early experience upon emotional responsiveness, and development generally, has been reported, based on experiments with white rats. The experimenter subjected one group of young rats to mild electric shocks, expecting to produce some abnormalities in behavior later on. As controls he had two other groups of young rats, one handled as the shocked rats were, but without shocks, the other merely left in the nest and not handled at all. The result of the experiment was unexpected: the shocked rats after they grew up were not distinguishable from those handled but not shocked; it was the non-handled rats that showed the abnormalities! They were particularly timid when placed in a new environment, crouching in the corner rather than exploring the open cage as normal rats do. Other lines of evidence showed that the handled (or shocked) rats developed more rapidly in many respects, opening their eyes

sooner, gaining weight more rapidly, growing larger. Later, under stress, the handled animals were found to have a more rapid response from the adrenal glands than the nonhandled ones. Thus the handling produced profound changes in development, reflected in changes of the regulatory systems within the body as well as in overt behavior (Levine, 1962).

We may well ask whether or not we can find comparable evidence in human growth for the effects of stressful experiences in early infancy. One place to look might be for effects on adult height, for the experiments on animals showed pronounced changes in size as a result of infantile stress. Two investigators set out to find what evidence they could for stress in infancy and adult height in men (Landauer and Whiting, 1964).

For many years anthropologists have been gathering information on nonliterate cultures all over the world. A cooperative enterprise has resulted in the depositing of relevant information on all available cultures in collection known as the Human Relations Area Files, originating at Yale University but with copies now deposited in many libraries. Evidence on both infant care and adult size exists for many cultures in these records. Landauer and Whiting (1964) found 80 cultures for which the evidence seemed adequate, and then they proceeded to classify these cultures separately for (a) stressful treatment of infant boys, and (b) adult male size. The stressful events that were selected for study were *piercing* (piercing the nose, lips, or ear to receive an ornament; circumcision, inoculation, scarification, or cauterization) and *molding* (stretching the arms or legs or shaping the head, usually for the sake of some preferred appearance). The study was repeated on two separate samples of cultures for whom the evidence was clear, with the usual care to avoid bias through having the classification into stressed and nonstressed child-care practices done by persons not familiar with the hypothesis being tested. The results for the two samples are given in Table 1.

TABLE 1.—Adult Male Height in Inches as Related to Infant Stress

| | PIERCING OR MOLDING DURING FIRST 24 MONTHS OF LIFE | |
	Present	Absent
First sample	65.2 ($N=17$)	62.7 ($N=18$)
Second sample	66.1 ($N=19$)	63.4 ($N=11$)
Combined sample	65.7 ($N=36$)	63.0 ($N=29$)

Significance of difference between combined means, by *t*-test, $P < .001$.*

SOURCE: After Landauer and Whiting (1964, pp. 1101–1112).

*Significant statements of this kind will appear in tables from time to time. The statement ("$P < .001$") can be interpreted as follows: "The probability that a difference of the magnitude found would arise through chance is less than 1 in 1,000." The letter N refers to the number of cases in a sample.

The somewhat surprising result for both samples was that the males stressed in infancy averaged 2.7 inches taller than those not so stressed.

This finding is in accordance with the animal studies, but it is, of course, subject to some reservations. The authors themselves looked for any confounding factors that they could find, such as different racial stock, different amounts of available food, or different climates, but they were not able to find any alternate explanation. The Spartan explanation that those cultures which treated their infants more harshly had only the fittest and strongest survive cannot be completely ruled out, for these practices may have gone on for many generations. A supplementary finding, which is of some interest in relation to the animal work, is that the adult stature appears to be affected when the stress occurs within the first two years rather than later in childhood. This has to do with the problem of "critical periods" in human development. It may be that the first two years are critical for the stresses affecting physical size.

These investigations, taken together, suggest that early experiences are very important in both higher animals and man in providing the background for coping with the environment when they are older. The implications for child-rearing practices are not firm, but they suggest that a certain amount of fondling and stimulation are important for development, and that neglect may be more harmful than some degree of stress. The parents who are so proud of the "good" baby who lies quietly in the crib may not in fact be giving to that baby what is best for him. . . .

5 *The Socialization Process*

BOYD R. MCCANDLESS

A child's behavior is always influenced by his interactions with his parents and family, relatives, playmates, teachers, and other adults. He depends upon other human beings, and his life is spent largely in interaction with others. The child stimulates people and they stimulate him; their responses to him determine many of the things he says and does and how he feels. The following excerpt describes some cultural differences in pressures toward socialization,[1] several theories of socialization, and the developmental learning of a personality characteristic, dependent-independent behavior.

PRESSURES TOWARD SOCIALIZATION

Every society has developed sanctions concerning the behavior of its members. The most nearly universal one is directed toward control of sexual behavior: all known contemporary societies include rigid incest taboos. Every organized society must have prohibitions concerning aggression. Such prohibitions range from forbidding physical combat among preschoolers to prohibiting murder. Rules, formal and informal, exist in all societies for the protection of proper-

ty. Certain minimal standards of parental conduct toward children are ordinarily prescribed. Some nations have state religions; others, such as the United States, have informal sanctions that encourage but do not require the individual to profess and practice religious belief.

In other words, through implicit and explicit codes, most of which have a moral, or right-wrong overtone, societies set up standards of behavior for their members. Great latitude may be granted the individual in some societies, relatively little in others; and a specific society may vary widely in permissiveness from one time to another. Freedom of political thought and action in a democracy is, for example, usually curtailed during a time of war and the period of read-

---

[1]The continuous process of learning—the shaping of individual characteristics and behavior through the training provided by the social environment. (Ed.)

From Chapter Ten from *Children: Behavior and Development*, Second Edition, by Boyd R. McCandless. Copyright © 1967 by Holt, Rinehart and Winston, Inc. Reprinted by permission of the author and Holt, Rinehart and Winston, Inc.

justment following war. The penalties for deviation from acceptable conduct vary widely: the death sentence for murder is common in Western European civilizations; but the middle-class mother who breast-feeds her baby beyond 18 months is only gossiped about. Random heterosexual activity by young males, although against formal canons of law and Judeo-Christian religious teaching, is winked at and even envied; the same sexual activity on the part of a girl may result in her being firmly, albeit informally, ostracized.

In short, the political-religious organization of any organized society blends with, influences, and is influenced by the informal sanctions of that society in defining correct conduct for its members and in setting up the methods by which parents and the community guide and direct children's conformity to social norms. For example, our society has quite clear expectations about dependency, sex, and aggressive behavior on the part of children and adults of different ages and sexes. It also says that parents should not use brutal punishment on their children or neglect them in obvious ways. It is assumed that parents should love and protect their children, and set good examples for them. Yet our culture is in many ways contradictory: the obedient, conforming, sexless *ideal* 9-year-old boy is expected to become the independent, enterprising, adequately masculine *ideal* 21-year-old who welcomes his chance to serve in the armed forces. Many things that are taught children must be unlearned by them before they become successful adults.

SOCIALIZATION THEORIES

The development of any individual depends upon how he sees and reacts to the socializing forces of the culture of which he is a member. How does the whole process look to the child? Society prescribes the sort of a man or woman he is to grow into, and lays down certain rules to guide his parents and teachers. But what are the forces and perceptions *within him,* as an individual, that cause him to respond in one way or another to these forces *on the outside?*

There are two broad theoretical orientations to the socialization process. The first is represented by both psychoanalytic and social-learning theory. Each of these subscribes to the idea that the adult end-product is a direct function of the teaching forces of the family and the environment as the child perceives them and as they affect him. If these forces are benign, the resulting human product is a happy one; if malign, the net result is unfortunate. The organism is thought of as shaped by its experiences. It becomes good or bad as these experiences are good or bad. Psychoanalytic or Freudian theory places more emphasis than social-learning theory on certain critical developmental stages, during which certain prescribed types of experience have a maximum effect, and somewhat discounts the influence on emotional or personality development of learning experiences after the ages of 5 to 7. Social-learning theory tends more to regard the human being as modifiable at any age. However, the influence attributed by each theory to *learning* is enormous.

The second broad strand of socialization theory holds that the forces of growth and development within the organism are essentially creative. If the child is *accepted*, if his developmental needs are not blocked by society, he will grow into a happy, creative, socialized individual. Such a theory does not discount the effect of learning, particularly when it is imposed in a negative, restrictive, and frustrating fashion. It simply argues that, given moderately constructive circumstances, the organism is self-directing, and that its self-direction is intrinsically constructive. Active teaching is assigned a lesser role in such theory than in Freudian or social-learning theory. The essential condition in the child's environment is acceptance. If that condition is met, everything will work out well. This theory was perhaps first enunciated in modern times by Jean Jacques Rousseau in *Emile*. Such contemporary theorists as Rogers (1951), Maslow (1954), and Gesell (1954) hold this viewpoint in common, although they differ in many of their derivations from it and their reasons for adopting it.

The difference between these two broad theories can perhaps be made clearer by an analogy from horticulture. The first theory would heartily endorse the principle, "As the twig is bent, so shall the tree grow." A good environment of proper soil, light, water, and fertilizer would be recommended. But active pruning, shaping, grafting, and cross-fertilizing would also be practiced. The second theory would also argue for an environment of proper soil, light, water, and perhaps fertilizer. But it would take the position that nature knows best how the tree is to grow. Pruning, shaping, grafting, and cross-fertilizing are to be left to the natural course of events plus the innate nature of the organism. There is a difference between the two theories (they are brutally simplified here) along the activity-passivity dimension, with *more* and *less* teaching activity, respectively, being regarded as "desirable" by the first and the second theory.

According to the first theory, the child will become social, altruistic, self-confident, or what have you, to the degree that he learns he must adapt himself to others in order to have his own needs gratified. The ease of this process, and the cost of it to the individual, will depend on the skill of the teacher and the appropriateness and effectiveness of the teaching process. According to the second theory, the germs of adequate adaptation or socialization are present in all people, and will come to soundest maturity in a benign and accepting but rather passive environment. It is probable that of the three theorists mentioned in connection with the second position, Gesell places more emphasis on inborn constitution and heredity than Rogers; that is, Gesell would not say that, given a suitable environment, everyone will turn out all right.

It is not known which of these two theories about socialization and development is correct—or whether, indeed, either of them is. Each places a heavy burden on those responsible for the environmental aspect of socialization—the first, or "learning," theory perhaps more than the second, or "developmental," theory. Both, with the possible exception of Freud as a representative of the first and of Gesell as a representative of the second, are optimistic. There are cross-overs between representatives of the two theories: Freudian theory seems almost to assume the "innate asociality of man," in the sense that the selfish, hedonistic, libidinous infant must be transformed into the altruistic and pleasure-postponing adult. Social-learning theory makes no assumptions about this issue, but postulates that altruism and pleasure-postponement are learned rather than innate. Freud, like Gesell, places heavy emphasis on universal, developmental-maturational sequences in growth, but does not put Gesell's emphasis on heredity as a determinant of individual differences.

LEARNING THAT OTHER PEOPLE ARE NECESSARY

Freud has spoken of the socialization process as a change from the *pleasure principle* of immediate need-gratification (characteristic of the very young child and infant) to the *reality principle,* which presumably governs the much older child an adult. This change seems to begin when the child realizes that his own gratification depends on the cooperation of other, older, stronger, and more proficient people, usually his parents. If he offends them by his own impulsiveness and "selfishness," then they in turn can keep gratification from him. At first it is likely that he conforms to their desires only to ensure that his own are met. Only later—often not until well into adolescence—does he begin genuinely to consider the needs of others because of an al-truistic, "highly socialized" pleasure that he takes in seeing them happy.

The foundation of socialization is simply this: A socialized individual attaches importance and pays attention to people and the rules that have been developed to mold them into and keep them functioning as a society. If he is successfully socialized, he also rather *likes* people and has a generally positive attitude toward the majority of the rules of his society. Both introverts and extroverts can be thought of as being successfully socialized, since there is more than one method of successful socialization. The scientist or artist working alone in his laboratory or studio, and the insurance salesman, politician, or reporter who deals with dozens of people every day, are both socialized, although in different ways, to the degree that they direct or inhibit personal behavior in deference to people and social rules.

How is this regard for people and social rules developed? In discussing this question, the author has drawn most heavily on the work of Dollard and Miller (1950), Whiting and Child (1953), Bandura and Walters (1963), and Sears and his co-workers (Sears, Maccoby, and Levin, 1957). They in turn have been influenced by such theorists as Freud (1933a) and Hull (1952), and have themselves been prolific in their research.

If a child is to learn to attach importance to people and rules, he must first attach *meaning* to them: to find out that they are useful, powerful, and associated with both rewards and punishments. The infant is helpless in satisfying his own needs. Without adults, he would die. Adults feed and warm and soothe and cleanse him. Soon, as a result of these ministrations, adults themselves come to have positive meaning for the baby; in the terminology of social-learning theory, they are perceived as "secondary rewards" or "reinforcements." The infant seeks them out not only to satisfy his *primary* needs, but also for themselves, to satisfy his newly developing *social* needs. As we have said, the smile that appears from 6 to 8 weeks of age is one of the first signs of socialization.

Evidence . . . indicates that babies who have had little opportunity to interact with adults are seriously retarded and perhaps permanently blunted in socialization. We might also speculate on the consequences for socialization of *complete and consistent reward* in infancy. It is reasonable to suppose that those who have never been cold fail to appreciate warmth, and that those who have never been insecure or afraid attach relatively little importance to security and freedom from fear. The child, in other words, to become socialized, must first have experienced many warm and loving relations with adults; but he must also have learned the importance and value of these relations by having experienced at least their temporary loss.

In real life, this question is largely academic. There is no way to rear a baby so that he does not experience temporary and rather frequent loss of attention and love. Not the most diligent of mothers can always feed her baby the instant he becomes hungry. In even the most child-centered family, there are times during the child's early life when his parents are not there at the moment he needs them. The child probably sees such experiences as "abandonment" or "deprivation of love." They presumably result in enhancing his appreciation of love and attention, and increase the reward value that adults have for him.

In addition to the deprivations that must of practical necessity occur for all children, parents impose deliberate deprivations or other penalties on their children in order to produce the behavior the parent considers desirable, or to eliminate undesirable behavior. These deprivations range from "love-oriented" manipulations ("Mommy thinks it would be nice if you went to the potty," or "It makes mommy feel bad when you are a naughty boy") to object- or thing-oriented techniques. These in turn range widely, from depriving or threatening to deprive the child of some of his television time, or outdoor play, or allowance, through depriving him of physical comfort by spanking or slapping him. Corporal discipline and "punitiveness" are commonly placed under this heading of "thing-oriented" discipline.

Love-oriented techniques, although they may be vicious in their extreme form (the mother who, when only slightly thwarted, retreats to her room in tears to place a damp cloth over her eyes), seem to result in more dependable social control through the exercise of the child's own conscience than thing-oriented techniques (see, for example, Sears, Maccoby, and Levin, 1957; and Miller and Swanson, 1960). But research in this important area is very incomplete.

To become socialized, in short, a child must have learned that his parents and (through generalization) other people are important, and that he is dependent on them. Dependency, as a *theoretical construct*, should be distinguished from dependent *behavior*. In the first sense, it refers to the *reward characteristics of the parents and others*, which have presumably been developed through a combination of good mothering and fathering, coupled with anxiety about the loss of this parental nurturance. In the second and more common sense, it refers to the clinging, lapsitting, affection- and assistance-seeking behavior usually referred to as dependent.

Those parents who have helped their child to acquire dependency (in the theoretical sense of the word) have provided a powerful tool for his later, more complicated socialization. If his parents, that is, are important and generally rewarding to him, then, through the process of generalization, other adults, children, and their rules also become important.

BASIC DRIVES AND PERSONALITY

As Freud and his followers, particularly Sullivan and Erikson, have recognized, the basic drives around which a child's dependency (and probably important aspects of his later personality) is organized are those that involve much interaction with adults. These are the drives he cannot satisfy himself, or whose expression he must alter to conform to adult standards.

The child can *breathe* on his own; no one tells him *how* to breathe; no one teaches him *to* breathe. Thus it is

not likely that air hunger and breathing are extensively involved in personality development. On the other hand, the baby interacts constantly with adults in such matters as eating and cleanliness and, as he grows older, he must *change* his ways of eating and eliminating to conform to adult expectations. In our culture, he must also learn to inhibit or hide sex behavior or interest. These changes, suppressions, and concealments are all based on interaction, some of it usually unpleasant, with adults, and the expression of dependency and aggressive needs must themselves be altered with increasing age. Curiosity is undoubtedly another drive that enters powerfully into socialization.

It is plausible, then, that the drives most significantly related to early personality development and socialization are the hunger, eliminative, sex, and curiosity drives. Because these drives require the mediation of adults for their satisfaction, the child learns dependency; through deliberate or spontaneous manipulation of his dependency need he is taught elimination, sex, and aggression control, and his expression of the dependency need itself is changed. The same is true for curiosity, or the activity drive.

ALTERATIONS IN DEPENDENCY

Although early learning of dependency, in the theoretical sense, logically appears to be the foundation of socialization, dependent *behavior* must be sharply modified during the developmental process. The sort of dependency typically shown by the child between 1 and 2 years of age is inappropriate in the later preschool years. It is typical for the child of 2 to cling to his mother, to be shy with strangers, and openly to seek affection; but the child of 4 is expected to have modified this "babyish" behavior.

It has been found that, by the preschool years, children who are most dependent on adults are least popular with their age-mates (Marshall and McCandless, 1957; McCandless, Balsbaugh, and Bennett, 1958; and Marshall, 1960[2]). Interestingly enough, being dependent interferes more with girls' than with boys' popularity (McCandless and Marshall, 1957), probably because of differences in the type of dependency shown by boys and girls (Heathers, 1955; McCandless, Balsbaugh, and Bennett, 1958). The latter seem more frequently to employ what might be called *emotional* dependency; they cling to adults, apparently seeking reassurance and affection, or openly ask for affection. Boys do not differ greatly from girls in amount of over-all dependency, but the type they show is different. They are more likely to be *instrumentally* dependent: that is, to seek help in accomplishing the aims of their work and play. "Help me put the wheel on the truck . . . Where is the big plane we had yesterday? . . . Will you move this ladder for me?" These are dependency requests of the type made more frequently by boys than by girls, and they seem not to interfere with popularity.

Boys also appear to be more task-oriented than girls (McCandless,

---

[2]Personal communication.

Balsbaugh, and Bennett, 1958). They will more often go to almost any length of compromise or combat to continue their activity, whereas preschool-age, girls, when blocked or engaged in conflict themselves, ask the adult in the situation to settle it for them.

There is some indication that these different modes of dependency and different ways of making use of adults in conflict situations result from learning: mothers of daughters more frequently than mothers of sons intervene in their conflicts and help them work out solutions.

For reasons probably similar to those implied above (society condones and perhaps even approves dependency in girls, but condemns it in boys), dependent behavior has been found to be more consistent from childhood to adulthood for girls than for boys. Kagan and Moss (1960) have found rather substantial relations between dependent behavior in girls, as rated from their case histories at the age of about 7 and as rated independently by a second investigator from interviews when they were in their early twenties. There was no indication in the behavior of young adult men whether they had been highly independent or dependent in their seventh year. The authors attribute this difference to the effect of the culture. It is all right for girls to be dependent; hence, they do not "disguise" their dependency as they move through later childhood and adolescence. The dependent boy, on the other hand, is "punished"; hence, whether he "feels" dependent or not, he assumes the cloak of independence.

Jakubczak and Walters (1959) have found that dependent 9-year-old boys are more suggestible than nondependent youngsters of the same age, and that they are swayed more by the opinions of adults than by the opinions of their peers. This finding suggests that the dependent youngsters were oriented more to adults than to their peers, and provides a possible clue about why dependent youngsters are less popular than nondependent ones.

Generally, in the preschool years, dependency and "seeking to do well at tasks," or achievement orientation, have been found to be negatively correlated. One study (Crandall, Preston, and Rabson, 1960) has found that the mothers of achievement-oriented 4- and 5-year-olds—presumably, nondependent children—reward their children when they seek *approval* and when they try to accomplish difficult tasks. The mothers' general affection and their pattern of reward when children sought emotional support or help, were unrelated to the children's achievement efforts, although it appears from the data in this study that those mothers who not only were affectionate but also rewarded their children's requests for help, emotional support, and approval may have been the mothers of children with the highest achievement orientation.

To some degree, a negative relation between dependent behavior and achievement orientation may be "built in." Achievement is usually defined as *independent* task-orientation, perseverance, and so on; hence, measures of dependency should be negatively correlated with it. But task-orienta-

tion which the child uses as a means of obtaining social reinforcers (approval, praise, affection) may well be positively related to dependency (Endsley[3]).

We have said that the behavioral manifestations of dependency must change with the age of the child—it is generally inappropriate for 8-year-olds to sit in the laps of their mothers in public. How does this change in behavior come about while the parent at the same time satisfies the child's "inner" need for dependency? There are five possible ways in which the change from immature dependent behavior to more mature independent behavior can occur. (1) The reward value of the parent is in some fashion reduced as the child grows older; or (2) the threat of the loss of love, which presumably intensifies theoretical (and behavioral) dependency, is reduced; or (3) the parents gradually transfer their rewards from dependent to independent behavior, yet continue to satisfy the drive for dependency; or (4) the reward value of peers increases; or (5) the child's increasing size, strength, and skill afford him increasingly frequent and wide-ranging opportunities to master his environment, thus reinforcing his independent and autonomous behaviors. Successful autonomous or independent behavior is probably strongly reinforcing, and is probably generalized widely, since it indicates to the child that he can now gain a given goal quite directly and *by himself*. In other words, he need no longer depend on a mediating agent

---

[3]Manuscript in preparation.

whose behavior he cannot always predict. If independence succeeds in one
area, the child will probably try to
extend it to other areas.

It is most likely that (2), (3), (4),
and (5) are the conditions that operate. With increasing ability to sym-
bolize, to incorporate past experience
by thinking about it, and to envision
future experience, the child of consistent and loving parents comes to see
that his parents have loved him in the
past, love him *now,* and will presumably continue to love him in the *future.* Thus the fear of loss of love is
reduced: the 8-year-old realizes, as
the 3-year-old does not, that a baby-
sitter for an evening does not signify
parental desertion. Parents (as indicated by the Crandall, Preston, and
Rabson, 1960 study) may combine affection with reward for achievement,
yet continue to accept and even reward immature requests for help and
emotional support,[4] thus helping their
children make the transition from the
more immature dependent to the more
mature achievement-oriented or independent behavior with a minimum of
sudden change and insecurity. It
seems certain (from the research
summarized above, and from observation) that peers become increasingly
important to children, and that peers
reinforce independent behavior, particularly that which does not obvious-

---

[4]This conclusion from the Crandall,
Preston, and Rabson (1960) study was
reached from an inspection of their pattern of correlation coefficients, but not
from a formal analysis of their data; nor
is it among the conclusions presented by
the authors.

ly seek to elicit adult affection and
support. Finally, with increasing age,
strength, vocabulary, and so on, the
child becomes more and more able to
master his environment.

This section, then, indicates that a
necessary condition for socialization—
in the sense of both social response
and social control—is learning that
other people are necessary, and that
one should therefore modify his behavior in accordance with their needs
and wishes as well as his own. The
fact that people are "important" can
be thought of as theoretical dependency, and it is the lever society uses
to mold the self-centered child into
the considerate adult. Good mothering
and fathering, plus anxiety about losing such a state of affairs, appear to
be responsible for the development
of dependency, so defined.

In the young child dependency is
expressed in dependent *behavior;* but
in our society the seeking of help, affection, and nurturance from adults
must be transformed into independent,
achievement-oriented behavior. This
change is apparently accomplished by
an increase in the importance of approval from peers; by a shift in parental approval from dependent to
independent behavior, while at the
same time the child is assured that he
continues to be loved; and by the
child's own ability to remember the
past, understand the present, and predict the future. The obvious fact that
increasing size, strength, and adapta-
bility help the normal child to master
more and more aspects of his environment also aids in acquiring independent behavior. . . .

Sensory and Motor Development

6 *Visual Experience in Infants: Decreased Attention to Familiar Patterns Relative to Novel Ones*[1]

ROBERT L. FANTZ

A visual stimulus presented to the infant repeatedly is paired with a comparable "novel" stimulus. Infants over two months of age show a consistent decrease in fixation of the repeated stimulus as it becomes more "familiar," whereas the "novel" stimulus brings out a corresponding increase in fixation. This finding suggests possible genetic determinants in the recognition and habituation of visual responsiveness to specific patterns.

The eyes of the human infant are open, active, and sensitive to light soon after birth, thus providing the means for visual exploration of the environment. For early visual exploration to be important in the develop-

[1]The study was made possible by support from grant M–5284 from the National Institute of Mental Health, USPHS, and by the cooperation of DePaul Infant and Maternity Home. The testing was carried out by Isabel Fredericson and Jean Dreifort.

ment of perception and behavior, it is further necessary that (i) the ocular movements and fixations be selective rather than random so that specific objects or areas of the environment can be looked at; (ii) what is looked at be seen with sufficient clarity that it may be distinguished from other objects or areas; (iii) what is seen be "remembered," as indicated by a change in later responsiveness to the same stimuli. Recent experiments have proved that requirements (i) and (ii) are met by the visual behavior of even the newborn infant: fixation times were found to be consistently different among stimulus targets differing in pattern, indicating both unlearned selective attention to patterning and the initial ability to resolve fine patterns (Fantz, 1961, 1963; Fantz, Ordy, and Udelf, 1962). In the study reported here, the aim was to obtain data on requirement (iii).

The visual preference test of early perceptual development (Fantz, 1961, 1963; Fantz, Ordy and Udelf, 1962) was adapted to reveal changes in preference during a test session. The infant was face up in a small hammock crib inside a test chamber which provided a uniform background for two stimulus cards. The cards were placed over holes (measuring 20 cm by 15 cm) in the chamber ceiling. The cards were 38 cm above the infant's head and were separated from each other by 15 cm. Illumination was provided by a 75-watt incandescent lamp underneath and between the cards and out of sight of the infant. Two window shades were drawn horizontally across the chamber to hide the patterns between exposures.

The patterns on the cards were 11 photographs or advertisements cut from magazines. They were chosen to give maximum variation among patterns in aspects such as size of detail, regularity, color, contrast, and predominant shape of contours, and yet so that each would be complex and have high attention value. Six were color photographs; five were black-and-white. Gross variations in overall brightness were avoided.

One of the photographs (varied among the subjects) served as a constant pattern. It was presented for 1 minute, ten times in succession. During each exposure period it was paired with one of the remaining ten photographs (variable pattern) in random order. Constant and variable patterns were reversed in right and left positions for the last 30 seconds of each exposure period; the initial positions were random. The entire test lasted about 15 minutes including between-exposure intervals.

The eyes of the subject were observed through a 0.6-cm hole in the ceiling of the chamber, midway between the patterns. Corneal reflections of the outline of the two patterns were clearly visible under the conditions of the experiment. The location of these reflections provided an objective criterion of fixation. Thus the superposition of the left reflection over the pupil of either eye indicated the left pattern was being fixated; this was recorded by pushing the left of two finger switches operating electric timers. A second person put the patterns in place so that the observer did

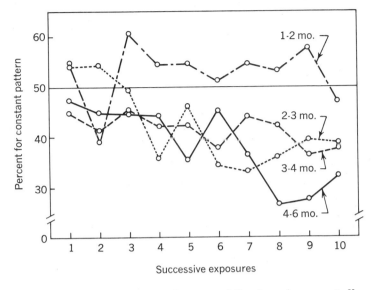

Fig. 1. Change in relative duration of fixation of a repeatedly exposed (constant) pattern relative to a novel (variable) pattern (the position of each being controlled) during a series of exposure periods. Each curve is the mean for six to eight infants.

not know which was the constant, except on those occasions when it was recognizable in the corneal reflection.

All the infants available at a foundling home who could be given the entire test without crying or falling asleep were used as subjects. They ranged from 6 to 25 weeks of age; six infants were under 2 months, seven were from 2 to 3 months, eight from 3 to 4 months, and seven over 4 months.

Figure 1 shows the percentage of the combined fixation time given to the constant pattern during successive exposure periods. While the variability in response during successive exposure periods and among individuals was high, the overall trend is clear. The curve for the youngest group showed no change in either direction; the suggested slight preference for the constant pattern was not consistent among infants. Each of the groups over 2 months of age gave decreasing attention to the constant pattern during the test. From the first five to the last five exposure periods the decrease was significant for the 2- to 3-month and for the 4- to 6-month groups separately ($p < .02$); and for the three older groups combined ($p < .01$), according to the Wilcoxon matched-pairs signed-ranks test. The decrease was significant for those infants over 2 months old exposed to an achromatic constant pattern as well as for those exposed to a chromatic one, indicating that color was not essential for recognition. During the last five exposure periods the novel pattern was fixated longer than the familiar one by all but four of the 22 infants over 2 months; these four were widely distributed in age.

Decreasing fixation of the familiar pattern was accompanied by increasing fixation of the novel pattern, resulting in a high response level throughout the test. Fixation of both patterns averaged 47 seconds out of 60 during the first five exposure periods and 46 during the second five. There is no evidence here of a response decrement due to fatigue, sensory adaptation, decreased arousal, or extinction of the orienting reflex. While infants under other conditions have shown some such nonspecific effects of being repeatedly exposed to stimuli, the present results indicate perception, recognition, and satiation of interest in a particular pattern. This effect of specific previous visual experiences is "learning" in the broad meaning of the term, even though it does not involve traditional experimental operations or explanations such as conditioning, practice, reinforcement, or association.

The initial attentiveness to all the patterns was a function both of novelty and of intrinsic stimulus characteristics such as complexity. The importance of novelty is evident from the differential fixation of novel and familiar patterns in the later exposure periods; the importance of intrinsic stimulus characteristics has been shown elsewhere by differential fixation of equally-novel targets, in which case the more complex are usually favored (Cantor, 1963; Fantz, 1961, 1963; Fantz, Ordy, and Udelf, 1962). The two factors probably function in a complementary way in the infants' visual explorations. Familiarization with potentially important parts of the environment is at first facilitated by selective attention and differential exposure to patterned surfaces and complex objects. Eventually, at least by 2 months of age, this information-gathering process is made more efficient by concentration of attention on the less-known objects and patterns. Response to novelty might thus be described as an unlearned visual interest in a complex stimulus which has not been habituated by experience.

Concurring results have been obtained by other investigators using different familiarization procedures (Saayman, Ames, and Moffett, 1964). Three-month-old infants were exposed for 4½ minutes to a cross or a circle, whichever form was preferred in initial exposure periods when both forms were presented simultaneously. During subsequent periods of exposure to both forms, the infants showed a decrease in fixation of the familiarized form. A greater effect of the familiarization period was shown when the two stimuli differed in color as well as form. No significant effect was shown as a result of exposure to the initially nonpreferred stimulus.

Evidently, incidental visual experiences can be retained by infants over 2 months of age, at least for a short period of time. This satisfies the third prerequisite given above for a possible developmental influence of early visual explorations. To what extent and under what conditions this influence actually occurs are questions for further study. The determination of changes in visual preferences following various types of experience will be useful in such studies, since the technique can be used at an age when other response measures are not available.

7 *Plasticity of Sensorimotor Development in the Human Infant*[1]

BURTON L. WHITE

RICHARD HELD

The plasticity of visual-motor development during the first months of life, particularly within the age range from one-and-a-half to five months, is demonstrated with institutionally reared infants. The onset of hand regard and visually directed reaching, and the growth of visual attentiveness are significantly affected by several kinds of environmental enrichment such as extra handling, suspending highly contrasting colors and forms over the infant, using multicolored sheets and crib bumpers, and making the ward activities visible by removing crib liners.

INTRODUCTION

The human infant engages in countless episodes of sensorimotor exploration during the first months of life (White, Castle, and Held, 1964). Prominent among these behaviors is visually directed reaching (prehension) which is, in turn, dependent upon orienting, accommodating, and pursuit responses of the eyes. Achievement of these sensorimotor abilities occurs during the first half year of life. This paper, and the research effort of which it is a report, focuses on the role of experience in these fundamental aspects of development.

Two considerations have guided

[1]At various stages, extending over the last six years, this research has received support from grant M–3657 from the National Institute of Mental Health, grant 61–234 from the Foundation's Fund for Research in Psychiatry, grant HD 00761 from the National Institute of Health, the Optometric Extension Program, grant NSG–496 from the National Aeronautics and Space Administration, grant AF–AFOSR 354–63 from the U.S. Air Force Office of Scientific Research, and the Rockefeller Foundation. The research was conducted at the Tewksbury Hospital, Tewksbury, Massachusetts. We are very grateful for the assistance of Mr. Peter Castle and Miss Kitty Riley and for the consideration and aid given by Drs. John Lu, Solomon J. Fleischman, Peter Wolff and Lois Crowell and head nurses Helen Efatathiou, Frances Craig and Virginia Donovan.

This paper has been complied in large part from an oral presentation to the American Association for the Advancement of Science, presented in Cleveland in December, 1963 by the senior author.

this research. On the one hand, we share with many other investigators an interest in the role of contact with the environment in the earliest development of infant behavior. On the other hand, we have been concerned with testing the implications of a specific theory of the development of sensorimotor coordination (Held and Freedman, 1963; Held and Hein, 1963). In testing for the contribution of early experience to development we are not prejudging the outcome of the complex issue of nature versus nurture. On the contrary, we are convinced that the endogenous mechanisms of development can best be delineated by increased understanding of the role of early contact with the environment.

The first steps in our research have been to trace the normal course of development of various fundamental sensorimotor behaviors such as reaching (White, Castle, and Held, 1964), exploratory activities (White and Castle, 1964), visual accommodation (Haynes, White, and Held, 1965), and blink to approaching objects. Subsequently, we have systematically modified the rearing conditions of several groups of infants. For humane reasons the modifications must necessarily be mild. Consequently, we have required normative scales of sufficient detail and precision to reveal small changes in rates of development. Our initial studies were designed to assess the modifiability of these rates by introducing relatively gross environmental alterations. Future research, now in the planning stage, will be more analytical, with the identification of specific experiential factors as their goal.

During the daylight hours, the new-born infant is visually alert less than 3% of the time, but at six months of age this percentage is approaching 50% (White, 1965). At birth, aside from a rudimentary ocular centralizing reflex, the infant does not exhibit any ability to orient himself to visible targets. Yet, at six months, he skillfully pursues visible targets viewed at various distances and moving with a wide range of speeds. In addition, he reaches swiftly and accurately for visible objects nearby (White, Castle, and Held, 1964). At birth the infant's accommodative mechanism is incapable of tracking a visible object in depth, but at six months he is at least as adept and accurate as the normal adult (Haynes, White, and Held, 1965). In these and other behaviors the six month old infant has attained a very high degree of competence. Does experience contribute to these developments? And, if so, in what ways?

Large individual differences in rates of infant development suggest that different rearing conditions have differential consequences. Hunt (1961) has made this thesis explicit in his analysis of the implications of Piaget's (1952) sensorimotor theory. However, it has not been experimentally tested prior to the present work.

One systematic approach to the problem of the development of sensorimotor coordination derives from consideration of modifiability of function in the adult. Some of the errors induced by rearrangement of sensory inputs are completely compensated for after the subjects of these experiments have undergone prolonged experience in their normal environments (Held, 1961; Held and Freedman, 1963). Activity, initiated by the subject performed in a dependably contoured surround, appears to be a necessary condition for full adaptation (Riesen, 1958; Denenberg and Karas, 1959; Levine, 1957). The fact that accurate visual-motor function can be fully re-established suggests that the mechanism underlying the adaptation may also be involved in the original acquisition of such perceptual-motor skills. Confirmation of this speculation has come from experimental studies with animals (Held and Hein, 1963). Kittens deprived solely of the opportunity for self-induced movements in the presence of a stable visual surround exhibited marked deficits in visual-motor development.

With infra-human species selective deprivation is a traditional tactic used for analyzing the role of experience. With human infants this procedure is inappropriate for obvious reasons. An alternative approach consists of selectively enriching the early experience of infants whose ordinary rearing conditions provide a comparatively bland psychological diet. The latter course is the one we have taken.

SUBJECTS

Our subjects were 63 infants born and reared in an institution because of inadequate family conditions. These infants were selected from a larger group after detailed evaluation of their medical histories[2] and those of their mothers along with relevant data

---

[2]Infants' daily records were screened under the supervision of Drs. P. Wolff and L. Crowell for signs of abnormality using standard medical criteria. Mothers' records were examined for possible genetic pathology and serious complications during pregnancy or delivery.

on other family members whenever available. All infants included in the study were judged physically normal. Reports based on studies of institutionally-reared infants generally include a statement acknowledging atypical conditions and, in addition, such infants may congenitally constitute a nonrepresentative sample. On the other hand, two factors make a group of such infants unusually suitable for experimental research. First, rearing conditions are virtually identical for each infant in marked contrast to the highly variable conditions for subjects reared in their own homes. Second, it is possible to systematically change rearing conditions in the institutional setting and to maintain continuous surveillance over their administration. . . .

BASELINE DATA

Using standard test and observational procedures we have acquired the following information concerning infants reared under the regular hospital routine.

A. *The Development of Visual Attention*

In order to determine the sheer amount of visual exploratory activities exhibited by infants, and also to gain a thorough knowledge of their spontaneous visual-motor behavior, we initiated weekly 3-hour observation periods for each of our subjects.

Briefly, visual attention is defined as the state in which the infant's eyes are more than half open, their direction of gaze shifting at least once within any 30-second period.

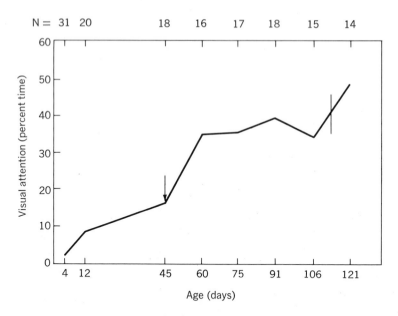

Fig. 1.   Visual attention data—control group.

Figure 1 illustrates the development of this activity from birth through 4 months (c. 120 days) of age. Each point represents the average of 2 scores taken during successive 2-week periods. It is interesting to note the correspondence between rather dramatic changes in the visible environment and the shape of this curve. For example, the sharp increase in slope at about 2 months (c. 50 days) of age occurs at about the same time as the onset of sustained hand regard (visual regard of the hands). (See arrow on Figure 1.) For the next 6 weeks or so, the child spends much of his waking time observing his fist and finger movements. The next major change in the visible environment occurred for these infants between 3½ and 4 months (c. 105–120 days, see vertical line on Figure 1). They were transferred to large open-sided cribs. The combina-

tion of greater trunk motility, enabling them to turn from side to side, and the more accessible visual surround gave them more visual experience. At about this time, the slope of the curve again shows a sharp increase.

B.   The Development of Visual Accommodation

Visual accommodation is the activity by which the image of a target is focused on the retina of the eye. This adjustment is largely accomplished by contraction or relaxation of the ciliary muscle which in turn changes the shape of the crystalline lens. Prior to the present research there has been no systematic study of the development of visual accommodation in human infants. We have used the technique of dynamic retinoscopy for this purpose. The test procedure is designed to measure the

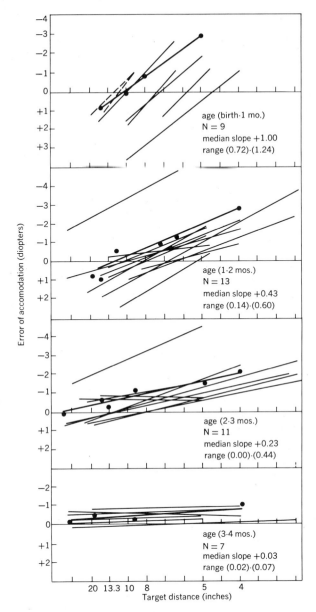

Fig. 2. Four stages in the development of accommodation in the first 4 months of life. The heavy lines fitted to the filled circles illustrate both the progress of a typical infant and also the closeness of fit of the lines to the plotted points. During the first month, the data that were estimated are represented by dashed lines. Plus values indicate myopic performance. Minus values indicate deviations in the hyperopic direction. Reprinted from Haynes, White, and Held (1965).

subject's accommodative ability under conditions more relevant to normal function than those used in traditional ophthalmological examinations. The subject's accommodation to targets placed at several distances is tested with eyes free of drugs. (Routine ophthalmological examinations employ cycloplegic drugs.) He is then tested for his capacity to track the target as it is moved toward and away from his eyes. Together with Dr. Harold Haynes of Pacific University, we performed 111 dynamic retinoscopy examinations on 25 of our infants.

With the use of lenses, objective measures of accommodative performance were obtained at target distances varying from 4 to 60 inches. The infant's capacity to track the target was also tested. The instrument used was a standard Copeland streak retinoscope with a white cardboard shield mounted so as to prevent the infant from seeing the examiner's head. The results of this study are shown in Figure 2.

Perfect adjustment to changing target distance would be presented by a slope of 0.00 on the graphs (Figure 2). Complete absence of accommodative change would be indicated by a slope of +1.00. Prior to one month of age (c. 30 days), the infant's accommodative response does not adjust to change in target distance. The system appears to be locked at one focal distance whose median value for the group is 7½ in. This is indicated by a slope value for the group of +1.00. Occasionally, infants of this age did not remain alert long enough to allow complete calibration of their responses. In these few instances, the magni-

tude of error was estimated (see caption of Figure 2). Flexibility of response begins at about the middle of the second month (c. 45 days). Performance comparable to that of the normal adult is attained by the fourth month (c. 120 days), as shown by a median slope value of +0.03.

In addition to the above measurements, eleven infants were retinoscoped while asleep in the nursery. In all eleven cases, the accommodative system was found totally relaxed. Infants less than one week of age occasionally exhibited slow changes in accommodation, but they were in no way related to distance of the target. Older infants, when drowsy, exhibited a gradual drift of accommodation towards optical infinity suggesting that drifting seen in the first week of life is a function of level of drowsiness.

C. Visually-Directed Reaching

To the best of our knowledge, no previous investigator, aside from Piaget (1952), has studied in detail the acquisition of visually-directed reaching. However, Piaget was not centrally concerned with prehension and he observed only three subjects. Consequently, his data, though very provocative, are primarily of suggestive value.

Figure 3 depicts the results of our normative study: a 10-step analysis culminating in visually-directed reaching (1) just prior to five months (c. 150 days) of age. Moreover, by the time swiping behavior occurs, at about 2 months (c. 60 days), the infant is prepared to focus his eyes on targets (Figure 2). Convergence of the eyes as checked by clinical pro-

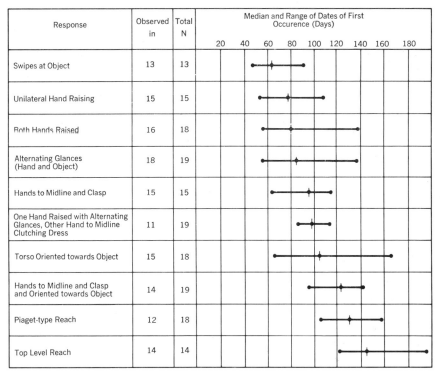

Response	Observed in	Total N	Median and Range of Dates of First Occurence (Days)								
			20	40	60	80	100	120	140	160	180
Swipes at Object	13	13									
Unilateral Hand Raising	15	15									
Both Hands Raised	16	18									
Alternating Glances (Hand and Object)	18	19									
Hands to Midline and Clasp	15	15									
One Hand Raised with Alternating Glances, Other Hand to Midline Clutching Dress	11	19									
Torso Oriented towards Object	15	18									
Hands to Midline and Clasp and Oriented towards Object	14	19									
Piaget-type Reach	12	18									
Top Level Reach	14	14									

Fig. 3. Normative data on the development of visually-directed reaching. These data were compiled by combining the scores of control and handled infants (which did not differ significantly). From White, Castle, and Held (1964). Reprinted by permission of the Society for Research in Child Development, Inc. and Burton L. White.

cedures was also found to be effective at this time. The range of accommodation increases rapidly during the period when hand regard makes its appearance.

Hands to the midline and clasp is characteristic of the bilateral behavior seen during the fourth month (c. 120 days) of life as the influence of the tonic neck reflex drops out. Torso-orienting reflects the child's growing capacities for gross motor action. What we have called a *"Piaget-type" reach* was described by Piaget as a raising of one hand to the vicinity of the object, followed by alternation of

glance between hand and object, a narrowing of the gap between them, and then contact. This response and the *"top level" reach* reflect a return to unilateral function in the fifth month (c. 150 days) of life.

We were particularly interested in the fact that swiping at objects appeared as early as the beginning of the third month (c. 70 days) whereas top level reaching did not appear until almost three months later (c. 160 days). Was this delay inevitable or a consequence of rearing conditions? Another point of interest was the question of the onset of sustained hand regard. Does this behavior presuppose a certain minimum level of acuity? What role did convergence of the eyes play here?

D. The Development of the Blink Response to an Approaching Visible Target

In Riesen's (1958) studies, young chimps deprived of experience with patterned light failed to develop the blink response to approaching visible targets. In Held and Hein's (1963) study of kittens deprived of self-induced motion in the presence of patterned light similar deficits developed with respect to this response. No such studies have been done with human infants. Even normative data on the development of this function are unavailable. The literature contains several references to the palpebral response but in each case the test circumstances combined the visual stimulus with touch or changes in air pressure as the target approached on the face.

We have performed a pilot study on 10 infants ranging in age from 1 month to 5 months of age. The apparatus we used consisted of a six inch bullseye target with ¼ in. red and white concentric rings. The object was mounted in a frame directly over the head of the supine infant. A plexiglass shield was placed 2 in. above the infant to preclude changes in air pressure as the target was dropped toward the subject. The range of target drop was from 2⅜ to 12½ in. Brightness changes were not totally prevented but the sources of light were arranged to minimize such effects. Recording procedures were also crude in this preliminary effort. One observer released the target and reported the magnitude and latency of response, the other recorded the data. The results were remarkably consistent.

The median age for the onset of blinking was 2 months (c. 60 days). The maximum target drop (12½ in.) had to be used to elicit the response and it was often slow and incomplete. By 3½ months (c. 105 days), the group exhibited very rapid and complete blinks and even occasional startles in at least 7 out of 10 trials. A target drop of but 2⅜ in. was sufficient to elicit these responses.

We have described baseline data for the development of four visual-motor functions, (A) visual attention, (B) visual accommodation, (C) visually-directed reaching, and (D) blinking to an approaching visible object. Are these developmental processes plastic? Is systematic contact with the environment instrumental in their development or does the infant simply grow into these skills?

EXPERIMENTAL RESULTS

A. First Modifications of Rearing Conditions—Handling Study

Many recent studies have reported the remarkable effects of postnatal handling on the subsequent development of laboratory-reared animals (Denenberg and Karas, 1959; Levine, 1957; Meier, 1961). Mice, kittens and dogs given small amounts of extra early handling grew up to be "better" animals as measured by a wide variety of tests. They were superior in

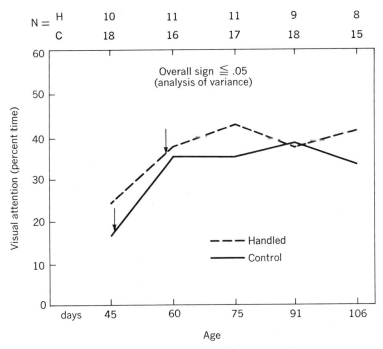

Fig. 4.   Comparative visual attention data.

many physical and adaptive respects. Recent surveys of maternal deprivation studies by Yarrow (1961) and Casler (1961) suggest that early handling appears necessary for adequate human development. Sylvia Brody (1951) in her book, *Patterns of Mothering,* noted that infants who received moderate handling were consistently more visually attentive than those receiving minimal handling. Would extra handling of our subjects, who normally receive minimal amounts, result in accelerated visual-motor development?

From day 6 through day 36, nurses administered 20 minutes of extra handling each day to each infant (N = 10). Measures of overall development, physical growth, general health, the development of reaching, and visual attention were taken regularly between days 37 and 152.

No changes were found in any developmental process except the growth of visual attention. The handled group was significantly more visually attentive than controls (Figure 4). Note that the shapes of the curves are quite similar. Sustained hand regard appeared about 1 week later in the handled group (day 58) than in controls (day 50). Upon relocation in large open-sided cribs the handled group, like the control group, exhibited a sharp increase in visual attentiveness.

Aside from the relationship between handling and visual attentiveness, the major finding of this study was that an environmental modification resulted in a significant alteration in the rate of growth of visual exploratory behavior. No evidence for comparable plasticity in other visual-motor developments was found following the extra handling. It is possible that further exploration of the effects of early handling would produce still greater increases in visual exploratory behavior.

B. Second Modification of Rearing Conditions— Massive Enrichment Study

Several recent studies seem to indicate that visual-motor performance depends to a significant extent on experience of some kind for its development. Riesen's (1958) work demonstrated that chimpanzees require exposure to patterned visual stimulation for normal visual-motor development. His later studies have suggested that movement within a patterned environment is also required for adequate development (Riesen, 1958). Held and his collaborators (Held, 1961; Held and Bossom, 1961; Mikaelian and Held, 1964) have repeatedly demonstrated the importance of self-induced movement in dependably structured environments for adaptation to rearranged sensory inputs in human adults. More recently, their study of neonatal kittens showed the applicability of these findings to developmental processes (Held and Hein, 1963). The results of this study indicated that movement *per se* in the presence of a dependable surround was insufficient for normal visual-motor development. Kittens whose movements were *externally-produced* rather than *self-induced* did not develop normally. Self-induced movement in a dependable surround

was found necessary for adequate development as well as maintenance of stable visual-motor behavior.

Our subjects are normally reared under conditions which are obviously less than optimal with respect to the types of experience discussed above. Motility is limited by soft mattresses with depressions in them as well as the supine posture in which these infants are kept. The visual surround is poorly figured. Consequently, according to our hypothesis, heightened motility in an enriched surround should produce accelerated visual-motor development.

As a first test we enriched environmental contact of a group of 19 infants in as many respects as feasible.

A. INCREASED TACTUAL-VESTIBULAR STIMULATION Each infant received 20 minutes of extra handling each day from day 6 through day 36.

B. INCREASED MOTILITY Infants were placed in the prone posture for 15 minutes after the 6AM, 10AM, and 2PM feeding each day from day 37 through day 124. At these times, the crib liners were removed, making the ward activities visible to the child. Movements of the head and trunk in the presence of a figured visual surround resulted from the normal tendency of infants to rear their heads under such circumstances. The crib mattresses were flattened, thereby facilitating head, arm, and trunk motility.

C. ENRICHED VISUAL SURROUND A special stabile featuring highly contrasting colors and numerous forms against a dull white background was suspended over these infants from day 37 through day 124. In addition, printed multi-colored sheets and bumpers were substituted for the standard flat white ones. These changes were designed to produce heightened visual interest and increased viewing of hand movements because of the normal tendency of infants to swipe at visible objects nearby.

Weekly measures of prehensory responses and visual attention were made. The rates of development of spontaneous behaviors related to visual-motor function such as hand regard, hands touching at the midline, mutual fingering, and torso turning were assessed from the records of the 3 hour observation periods. Performance on the Gesell tests was recorded at bi-weekly intervals to determine general developmental progress. Also, records of rate of weight gain and general health were kept.

RESULTS

1. *Hand regard and swiping* Hand regard as such was much less frequently shown by this group as compared with controls. Instead the hands were generally first observed as they contacted portions of the experimental stabile. We called this pattern monitored stabile play and considered it together with monitored bumper play as forms of hand regard. By these criteria the onset of hand regard was delayed for some two weeks in our experimental group (N.S. — Mann-Whitney U Test). The onset of swiping was also set back, but only by some 5 days (N.S.—Mann-Whitney U Test).

Response	Observed in	Total N	Median and Range of Dates of First Occurrence (Days)
Swipes at Object	11	14	40–70
Unilateral Hand Raising	12	13	40–80
Both Hands Raised	12	13	30–90
Alternating Glances (Hand and Object)	10	11	30–100
Hands to Midline and Clasp	7	10	80–180
One Hand Raised with Alternating Glances, Other Hand to Midline Clutching Dress	5	9	70–120
Torso Oriented towards Object	4	9	80–130
Hands to Midline and Clasp and Oriented towards Object	3	9	100–140
Piaget-type Reach	6	9	70–130
Top Level Reach	9	9	70–140

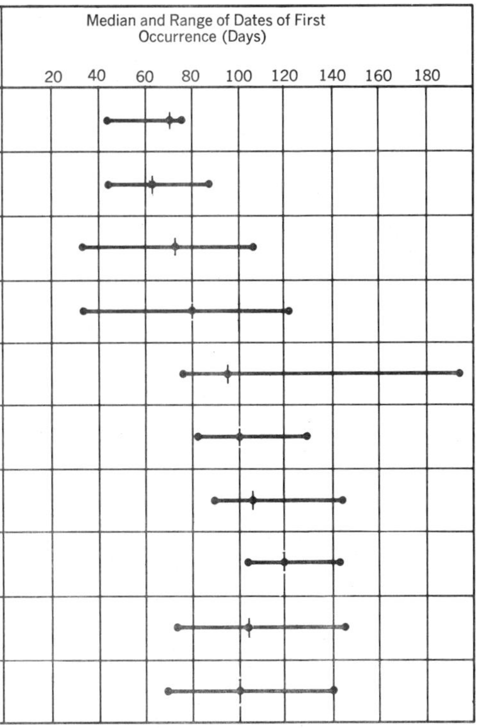

Fig. 5. The development of visually-directed reaching. Study B—massive enrichment.

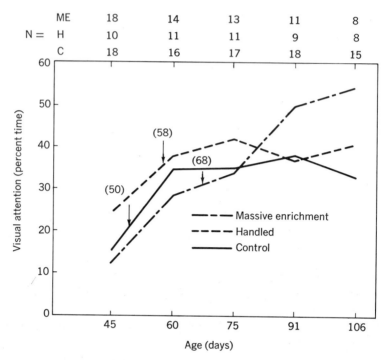

Fig. 6.   Comparative visual attention data.

Figure 5 illustrates the responses to the test object leading to reaching for this group.

2. *Prehension*   The median age for the first appearance of top-level reaching was 98 days for the experimental group, an advance of some 45 days (significant at .001—Mann-Whitney U Test). Some of the types of preliminary responses reported for our control group did not occur prior to the onset of top-level reaching.

3. *Visual attention*   The course of development of visual attention was also altered dramatically in our experimental group as illustrated by Figure 6. Concurrent with the unexpected delay in the onset of hand regard, was a marked decrease in visual exploratory behavior for the first portion of the test periods. On the other hand, once the group began to engage in prehensory contacts with the stabile and figured bumpers visual attention increased sharply.

Clearly the results of this study demonstrated the plasticity of several visual-motor developments. That the onset of hand regard is in part a function of environmental factors is not a novel notion. Hand regard is an 84th day behavior on the Gesell scale. Our control infants, with virtually nothing else to view, discovered their hands at less than 60 days of age. Piaget (1952) noted that the onset of this behavior varied by as much as three months among his own children as a function of differing environmental circumstances. Therefore, the fact that infants provided with enriched surrounds were late in discovering their hands as compared to controls was not totally unexpected.

We were surprised that the group exhibited less visual attention during the first five weeks in the enriched visible surround. In fact, not only did they tend to ignore the stabile and bumpers, but it is our impression that they engaged in much more crying than the control group during the same period. Starting at about 72 days of age the group as a whole began to engage in a great deal of stabile play. As we had suspected, the rattles were repeatedly swiped at, thereby producing far more monitored hand and arm movements than would normally have occurred. Subsequently, in less than one month, the integration of the grasp with approach movements had been completed. Control infants had required almost 3 months for this transition.

Earlier we had noted that the course of development of visual exploratory behavior seemed to reflect the availability of interesting things to look at. We had seen that in control and handled groups the slope of the curve of visual attention increased sharply when the hands were discovered and then decreased during the next six weeks. In this experimental group it appears that for about a month starting at day 37, the enrichment was actually ineffective and perhaps even unpleasant. However, once positive responses to the surround began to occur visual attention increased sharply in striking contrast to the previous groups. At 3½ months (c. 105 days) the enriched groups exhibited much more visual activity.

C.   Further Modification of the Environment

Until day 37 the procedures were the same as in study B, but instead of enrichment by prone placement and the stabile and printed sheets and bumpers, there was only one modification from day 37 until day 68. Two pacifiers were mounted on the crib rails. These devices were made to stand out visually by appending to them a red and white pattern against a flat white background. The objects were 6 to 7 inches away from the corneal surfaces of the infants' eyes. They were positioned so as to elicit maximum attention from a 6 to 10 week old infant (c. 42–70 days). The normal tendency of such infants is to accommodate at about 8 to 10 inches. It was assumed that the pacifiers might have the effect of orienting the infant toward the discovery of his own hands. It was further assumed that these objects might provide appropriate anchor points in space intermediate between the locus of spontaneous fixation and the ordinary path of motion of the hand extended in the tonic neck reflex posture.

At 68 days the infant was then placed in a crib with a stabile similar to that used in the previous study until he was 124 days of age. We hypothesized that these infants would be more consistently precocious in the attainment of visually-directed reaching. We also expected consistently higher visual attention from this group.

RESULTS

1. *Hand regard and swiping* In the control group the onset of sus-

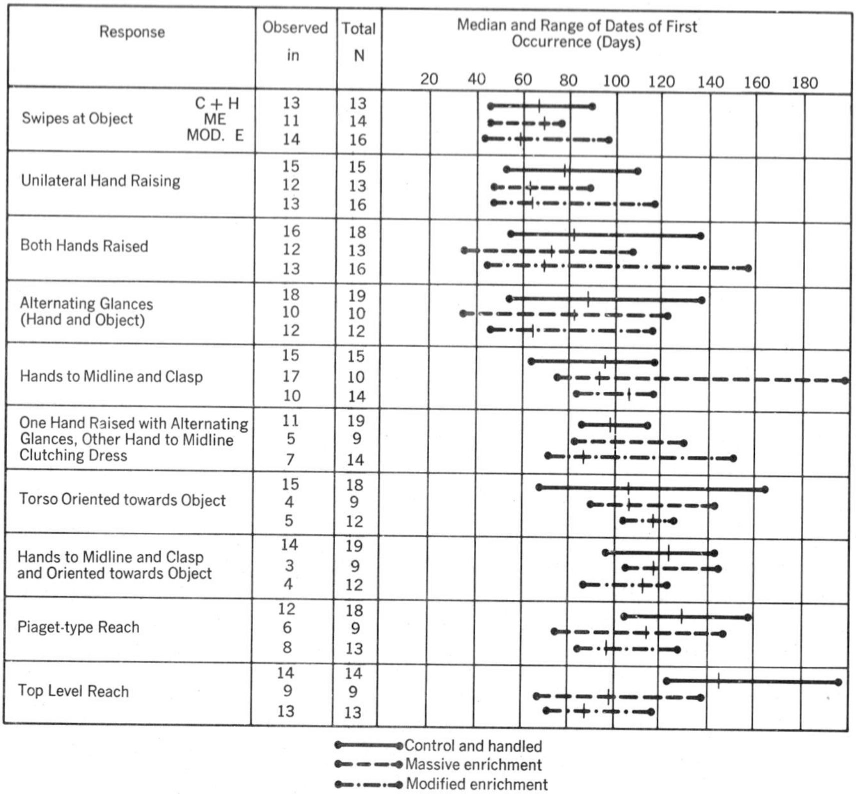

Response		Observed in	Total N	Median and Range of Dates of First Occurrence (Days)
Swipes at Object	C + H	13	13	
	ME	11	14	
	MOD. E	14	16	
Unilateral Hand Raising		15	15	
		12	13	
		13	16	
Both Hands Raised		16	18	
		12	13	
		13	16	
Alternating Glances (Hand and Object)		18	19	
		10	10	
		12	12	
Hands to Midline and Clasp		15	15	
		17	10	
		10	14	
One Hand Raised with Alternating Glances, Other Hand to Midline Clutching Dress		11	19	
		5	9	
		7	14	
Torso Oriented towards Object		15	18	
		4	9	
		5	12	
Hands to Midline and Clasp and Oriented towards Object		14	19	
		3	9	
		4	12	
Piaget-type Reach		12	18	
		6	9	
		8	13	
Top Level Reach		14	14	
		9	9	
		13	13	

Scale (Days): 20   40   60   80   100   120   140   160   180

●————● Control and handled
●— — —● Massive enrichment
●—·—·—● Modified enrichment

Fig. 7.   Comparison of prehensory responses among all groups.

tained hand regard occurred at day 46. Infants in the handling study were slightly behind (day 58). Infants in study B were even later in this respect (day 68) supporting the idea that the discovery of the hands is, in part, a function of the availability of interesting visible objects (White, Castle, and Held, 1964). The modified enrichment of this last study seemed more appropriate for the infant during the second month of life. Study C infants exhibited sustained hand regard at day 45. It should be noted that control infants reared in bland surroundings are about as advanced in this regard. The onset of swiping responses followed the same general pattern with study C infants exhibiting this behavior earlier than all other groups (day 58: Figure 7).

2. *Prehension* Apparently, the modified or paced enrichment of the last study was the most successful match of external circumstances to internally developing structures as indicated by the acquisition of top-level reaching at less than 3 months (day 89—significantly earlier than controls at <.001 —Mann-Whitney U Test).

3. *Visual Attention* Figure 8 shows visual attention data for the subjects of the several studies. The

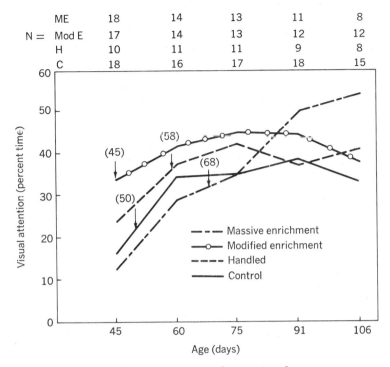

Fig. 8. Comparative visual attention data.

depression of visual interest shown by study B infants from day 37 to day 74 has been eliminated. Curiously, although the last group was more consistently attentive than the others, the reduction of such behavior at 3½ months (c. 105 days) appeared as it had in the first two groups. It would appear that some uncontrolled variable is interacting with our various attempts at modifying the function.

CONCLUSIONS

1. *The Significance of the Age Range from 1½–5 Months of Age*

The first major conclusion derivable from our research is that the age range from 1½ to 5 months (c. days 45–150) is a time of enormous importance for early perceptual-motor development. According to our findings and those of others, human infants reared under natural conditions show a dramatic surge in both visual activity and development at the middle of the second month of life (c. 45 days). During the next 3½ months the following events occur: (1) the development of flexible accommodative function culminating in virtually adult-like performance at 3½ months (c. 105 days), (2) discovery of the hands and gradual development of manual control by the visual system culminating in true visually-directed reaching, (3) the initiation and complete development of the blink reponse to an approaching visible target, (4) the initiation and complete development of visual convergence, (5) the onset of social smiling.

2. *Plasticity in Human Visual-Motor Development*

The studies reported above demonstrate that aspects of early visual-motor development are remarkably plastic. As yet we know neither the limits of this plasticity nor the range of visual-motor functions that fall within this classification. At the very least, the onset of hand regard and visually-directed reaching and the growth of visual attentiveness are significantly affected by environmental modification. Infants of both group B and C developed top-level reaching in approximately 60% of the time required by the control group, a result very much in line with the theory that self-initiated movement with its visual consequences is crucial for visual-motor development. Whether or not visual accommodation, convergence, pursuit, and blinking to an approaching target share this plasticity remains to be seen. Assessment of the extent to which various types of mobility and specific environmental factors contribute to these and other perceptual-motor developments is the goal of our continuing research.

8 *Olfactory Responses and Adaptation in the Human Neonate*[1]

TRYGG ENGEN

LEWIS P. LIPSITT

HERBERT KAYE

In this selection changes in infants' activity and breathing following different types and patterns of olfactory stimulation are reported. Babies from thirty-two to sixty-eight hours of age respond, and in different degrees, to odors such as asafoetida and anise oil. There is adaptation

[1]This research was made possible by the Institute for Health Sciences at Brown University under Research Grant B-2356 from the National Institute of Neurological Diseases and Blindness. The writers wish to thank Glidden L. Brooks, Director of the Institute for Health Sciences at Brown, and the staff of the Providence Lying In Hospital for facilitating this research.

Reprinted from the *Journal of Comparative and Physiological Psychology,* 1963, **56,** 73–77, by permission of Dr. Lipsitt and the American Psychological Association.

with repeated stimulations at least for these two substances, and recovery of response following a temporal delay. The order of presentation of odors affects the nature and amount of infants' reactions. They do not react differently to "pleasant" and "unpleasant" odors. In a follow-up study the authors (Engen and Lipsitt, 1965) present evidence that the adaptation effect is due to response habituation (learning) rather than sensory fatigue.

This paper reports the results of research in olfaction related to a general study program of sensory and learning processes of infants currently carried out at Brown University in co-operation with the Providence Lying In Hospital. The purpose of this study was to observe human neonates' responses to olfactory stimulation during the first few days of life and the change in such responses with repeated stimulation.

There is a lack of data concerning the newborn's capacity to smell, for virtually no research on this topic has been done in the past three decades. Until about 30 yr. ago, there had been a few such studies but with ambiguous findings (see Disher, 1934; Pratt, 1954 for reviews). Definite responses were obtained only to such stimuli as acetic acid and ammonia, but it was believed these responses were largely the result of pain or irritation (i.e., through stimulation of the trigeminal nerve) rather than smell. Some investigators believed they observed responses to so-called pure odor stimuli, e.g., valerian, mint, and essence of lavender, but others could not verify the observation. Some suggested that newborn infants are able to discriminate between pleasant and unpleasant odors, but others held that olfactory sensitivity is not present or is poorly developed at birth.

Perhaps the chief reason for the lack of clear-cut conclusions is that many of these studies relied on *E*'s rapid judgment rather than automatically recorded responses which could be viewed repeatedly, and most failed to establish interobserver reliability of the observations made. Recent developments in apparatus make possible a study of this sensory process under more objective experimental conditions, especially with respect to measures of the infant's responses (Lipsitt and DeLucia, 1960).

The present paper reports the results of two related experiments, the first designed to compare the responses made to acetic acid and phenylethyl alcohol, and the second to compare responses made to anise oil and asafoetida. On that basis of adults' reports, acetic acid would be classified as irritating or painful but phenylethyl alcohol would probably be described as a pure odor. Anise oil is typically called a "pleasant" and asafoetida an "unpleasant" odor. However, few describe asafoetida as "irritating" or "annoying" as in the case of acetic acid. Moreover, Allen (1937) obtained conditioned responses in the dog for asafoetida and anise only through the olfactory nerve and not through the trigeminal nerve. On the other hand, recent dual channel electro-physiological recordings from animal preparations have indicated that a so-called odor stimulus (e.g., phenylethyl alcohol) in relatively high concentration might elicit a response in

both the trigeminal and olfactory
nerves, while a lower concentration
of the same stimulus might produce a
response in only the olfactory nerve
(Tucker, 1961). There is reason,
therefore, to question the present
classification of chemical agents into
irritants vs. olfactory stimuli, for the
neural mechanisms mediating the response are not yet clearly understood.
The present concern is to determine
(*a*) to what extent the neonate responds to these stimuli and (*b*) how
the response changes with repetitive
stimulation.

METHOD

Subjects

Twenty apparently normal infants, 10
for each experiment, were Ss. There were
4 boys and 6 girls in each experiment.
The average age of the infants was 50 hr.
with a range from 32 to 68 hr.

Response Measures

Portions of the apparatus used to measure the infant's responses have been described earlier (Lipsitt and DeLucia,
1960), and only the essential details will
be discussed here. The major device sen-
sitively measures leg-withdrawal and
general bodily activity. Respiration was
recorded by attaching a Phipps and Bird
infant pneumograph around the abdo-
men. Heart rate was measured in the second experiment in connection with the
possibility of differential activity resulting
from anise oil and asafoetida, and was
recorded from the wrists with EEG elec-
trodes prepared with Bentonite paste. All
recordings were made on a four-channel
Grass polygraph, Model 5.

Stimuli

The experiments employed full-strength
acetic acid, phenylethyl alcohol, anise
oil (Anethol, U.S.P.), and tincture
asafoetida.[2] One cubic centimeter of each
odorant was kept in a 10 x 75 mm. pyrex
test tube stopped with a cork wrapped in
aluminum foil. The stimulus was presented to S on a commercial Q-Tip, one end
of which was attached to the cork, the
other end containing cotton saturated
with and positioned just above the liquid
odor.

Procedure

The experiments were performed in a
ventilated laboratory with the temperature at about 80°F. The Ss were tested
individually between 10 and 11 A.M., 15
to 90 min. after feeding. Noise and illumination were kept at a minimum. After
S had been placed in the apparatus, Es
waited until S appeared to be asleep (i.e.,
eyes were closed), respiration was steady
and regular, and activity was at a minimum. This state was required before the
presentation of all stimulus and control
trials.

Each S was presented two odors, either
acetic acid and phenylethyl alcohol (first
experiment), or anise oil and asafoetida
(second experiment). Half of the Ss received, for example, 10 trials with acetic
acid first and then 10 trials with phenylethyl alcohol, while for the other half this
order was reversed. A stimulus presentation consisted of E removing the cork
with the attached Q-Tip and placing it
between and about 5 mm. away from the
S's nostrils. The control trial involved the

---

[2]We are indebted to Fritzsche Brothers, Incorporated, of New York for supplying the odorants for the second experiment.

presentation of a clean (dry) Q-Tip in exactly the same manner. Presentation of stimulus and control trials was alternated. The duration of trials was recorded on the polygraph and was, with one exception, 10 sec. Responses to acetic acid were of such amplitude that the Q-Tip was maintained in the prescribed position for no more than 2.5 sec. The time between trials was approximately 1 min.; a longer period was required occasionally before S's behavior returned to pretrial standards.

With one minor exception, the procedure was the same in both experiments. In the second experiment, 4 posttest trials were added to obtain further data on order effects in the presentation of different odors. Two trials of the odor presented first in the session were reintroduced and again alternated with two control trials at the end of the session. There were thus a total of 40 trials per S in the first and 44 in the second experiment.

RESULTS

The raw data consist of simultaneous tracings of leg-withdrawal, general activity, respiration, and heart rate on the polygraph with paper speed at 5 mm./sec. A sample record is shown in Figure 1. For each odor two methods were used to evaluate individual records. Both methods yielded essentially the same results, and in both cases the frequency of response was evaluated with the Wilcoxon matched-pairs signed-ranks test. All p values reported are two-tailed. The three judges evaluating the records independently agreed on 86% of the total number of individual trials. Whether a response was ultimately judged to have occurred or not depended on the majority rule, i.e., the judgment of the two agreeing judges was taken as correct in the 14% of the trials where unanimity did not prevail.

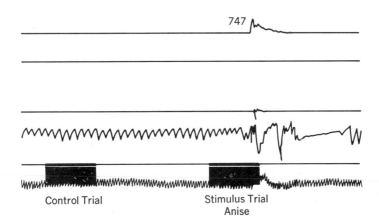

747

Control Trial

Stimulus Trial
Anise

Fig. 1. A sample record showing simultaneous records of stimulus and response events. (Reading from top to bottom, the lines shown are leg-withdrawal, an event marker not used in this study, stabilimeter movement, breathing, stimulus and control marker, and heart rate.)

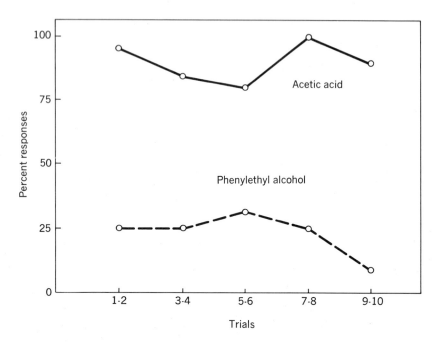

Fig. 2.   Percentage of responses as a function of trials.

The *E*s first judged whether or not any or all of the polygraph tracings during stimulus and control trials were larger than those observed for the 10-sec. interval immediately preceding the trial. The response measures tend to be correlated, although respiration appeared to be most sensitive with this particular stimulus material. The first analysis revealed a significantly higher frequency of differences for stimulus trials than for control trials ($p < .01$). However, the information of basic interest from this analysis was that about 15% of the controls gave a larger response than that obtained during the 10-sec. period immediately preceding it. This difference is not significant, nor are the differences among the control trials for the four odors. The responses observed on control trials appear to reflect the infants'

"baseline activity"; the fact that they sometimes do occur emphasizes the necessity for including such control trials in any study of olfactory responses in infants.

The control trial was used as baseline and a response on a stimulus trial was judged positive only when it was *greater* than that observed on the accompanying control trial. The average results of this analysis are presented below. Figure 2 presents the results obtained with the 10 Ss in the first experiment with acetic acid and phenylethyl alcohol. The points plotted indicate the percentage of Ss giving a larger response on a stimulus trial than on the control trial. Averages of two successive trials produce a smoothed but undistorted picture of the end of individual trials. It is evident that responses were obtained to both stimuli,

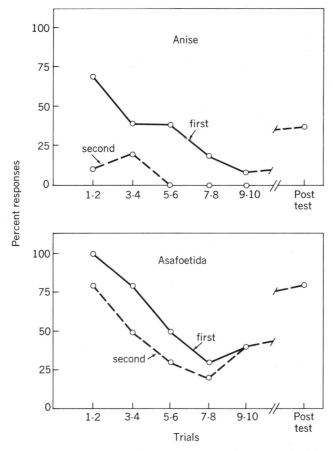

Fig. 3.   Percentage of responses as a function of trials.

but significantly more to acetic acid than to phenylethyl alcohol ($p<.001$). In the case of neither stimulus was there a reliable diminution of response from early to later trials, as determined by a t test for related proportions. Nor was there a reliable effect of presentation order of the two odors. In the second experiment heart rate was recorded along with leg-withdrawal, stabilimeter activity, and respiration, but the former measure seemed to show no differential effects of anise oil and asafoetida, nor did it prove feasible to count accurately

changes in heart rate resulting from the olfactory stimuli. (This difficulty was probably due to the relatively slow speed at which the polygraph had to be run to record the other three measures accurately. The heart rate record was often buffered by movement artifacts.)

Figure 3 presents the percentage of responses as a function of trials for anise oil and asafoetida when each of them is presented first and second in the session to subgroups of five Ss. A greater percentage of responses was obtained with asafoetida than anise oil ($p < .001$), and for both there is a decrement in response from the first to the last block of trials ($p < .001$ for asafoetida, and $p < .02$ for anise oil, all 10 Ss combined). The effect of order of presentation (i.e., first or second) on the frequency of response can also be observed. There is evidence of an interaction effect, for the order of presentation seems to affect response to anise oil significantly ($p < .001$), but not to asafoetida ($p > .05$). Finally, it can be seen in Figure 8.3 that in the posttest trials, the percentage of responses returns to nearly the level observed for the first several trials with each odor ($p < .08$ for anise, and $p < .05$ for asafoetida, based on five Ss, two-tailed t test for proportions between last block of trials and posttest trials). There occurred, then, both a decrement in response as a function of repeated stimulus presentations and recovery following stimulation with another odor.

DISCUSSION

The present experiments yielded clear-cut evidence that the neonate responds to olfactory stimulation. As might be expected on the basis of past findings, the largest number of responses was elicited by acetic acid, with asafoetida next and followed by phenylethyl alcohol and anise oil. The reason for this rank order is not clear. It could reflect differences in intensity of the odors, for intensity was not controlled in the present experiments. Another possibility is that magnitude of response is inversely related to pleasantness of the stimuli. However, an attempt to judge the obtained records as well as the behavior of the infant, e.g., facial expression and posture, provided no support for such speculation. In brief, infants can smell soon after birth, but the quantitative and reinforcing properties of various chemical agents are problems for future research.

The observed decrement in response as a function of trials (see also Bartoshuk, 1962; Bridger, 1961) presents an interesting problem of interpretation, because it is difficult to distinguish operationally between *sensory* adaptation (i.e., changes in receptor organs produced by repeated stimulation) and *response* habituation or adaptation (i.e., extinction of a response to an originally novel or effective stimulus) in the present experiment. The recovery from the adaptation observed in the posttrials and the cross-adaptation indicated by the effect of order of presentation of the stimuli seem consistent with a phenomenon of sensory adaptation, as does the relative absence of adaptation to a noxious stimulus, acetic acid. Only further study can illuminate the distinction between these two types of adaptation phenomena, and determine which of the two is occurring here.

A related experiment has been reported by Bronshtein, Antonova, Kamenetskaya, Luppova, and Sytova (1958) who used suppression of sucking as an indicator of smelling and hearing in newborns. The pacifier was placed in the infant's mouth and, during sucking, an odor or a tone was presented. If the infant stopped sucking, this was taken as a response to the stimulus. The suppression of sucking in response to the stimulus decreased over 10 trials, and eventually the stimulus failed to produce any change in sucking. Data showing suppression of sucking are presented, in order of

effectiveness, for iodoform, pepper-
mint, and anise oil. These investigators found that the weaker the stimulus, the more rapid and complete the
adaptation.

One final observation may be made
concerning qualitative aspects of the
infants' responses to the odor stimuli.
It was often observed that with successive presentations of some stimuli,
mostly acetic acid, but often asafoetida, S's response changed progressively from a diffuse, seemingly
disorganized response (similar to a
mild startle) to a smooth, efficient response in escaping the odor stimulus.

In early trials the baby's entire body
seemed to respond, while in later trials, a simple retraction or turn of the
head from the locus of the odorant
was executed. It is quite likely that
this *response differentiation,* similar to
that obtained by Marinesco and
Kreindler in older infants (Munn,
1955, pp 201–204), is a rudimentary
form of learning resulting from differential reinforcement of different response components. Further studies
should attempt to document either
photographically or mechanically these
changing characteristics of the infants'
head-movement responses.

9 *Conditioned Sucking in the Human Newborn*[1]

LEWIS P. LIPSITT

HERBERT KAYE

With increasing refinement of experimental techniques, analyses of
learning processes are now possible in young organisms whose immature neuromuscular status has been a barrier previously to extensive behavioral study. The following experimental study demonstrates
classical conditioning of the sucking response using a loud tone as the
conditioning stimulus. Sucking in response to a tone is greater in infants
who receive paired presentations of the tone and a sucking device than
in infants who receive unpaired presentations of the same stimuli.

[1]The writers thank Mrs. Dorothy West-
lake for her assistance. This study was
carried out as part of a project entitled
"Sensory Discrimination and Learning in
Human Infants" under a USPHS grant
(NB–04268) to Lewis P. Lipsitt. The
writers are indebted to the staff of the
Providence Lying in Hospital for their
co-operation.

Reprinted from *Psychonomic Science,* 1964, **1**, 29–30, by permission of the
senior author and Dr. Clifford T. Morgan, Editor.

PROBLEM

To determine whether classical conditioning is possible within the first days of human life, a tone was used as a conditioning stimulus (CS), and insertion of a nipple in the baby's mouth to elicit sucking movements constituted the unconditioned stimulus (UCS). If conditioning takes place, more sucking to the tone should occur following paired presentations of CS and UCS (experimental group, E) than following unpaired presentations (control group, C).

METHOD

Two groups of 10 hospital Ss in their third or fourth day were studied between 8 and 9:15 A.M., at least 3 hrs. after the previous feeding. For both groups, the CS was a low-frequency, loud (about 93 db) square-wave tone with a fundamental component of 23 cps and lasting 15 sec. For Group E, the nipple[2] was inserted in the infant's mouth 1 sec. after onset of the CS and remained to the end of the 15-sec. CS. For Group C, the CS and UCS were not paired; the nipple was inserted for 14 sec. approximately 30 sec. following offset of the CS.

----

[2]The non-nutritive nipple used was an automatic device for the recording of sucking responses developed by Grunzke (1961) for work with monkeys. For work with humans, Levin and Kaye (1964) adapted this stainless-steel mouthpiece, shaped like a nipple and containing a small lever attached to a microswitch, by covering it with a sterile rubber nipple. As the infant sucks, the lever is depressed and released, producing digital blips on a polygraph record.

All Ss first received 5 basal trials of CS alone. Presence and number of sucking movements to each 15-sec. tone were recorded independently by 2 Os. These trials were administered approximately 1 min. apart. Both groups then received 25 training trials, every 5th trial being a test in which sucking responses to the CS alone were recorded. For Group E, CS and UCS were paired for 14 sec. on the 20 conditioning trials. On these trials, Group C received the CS and UCS stimulations with a variable interval of 25–45 sec. (average, 30 sec.) between offset of CS and introduction of UCS. For Group E, intertrial interval was 1 min.; for Group C about 30 sec. Thus the conditioning session for Group E took approximately 31 min.; for Group C, about 38 min.

Following the conditioning period, all Ss received no less than 10 nor more than 30 extinction trials like the basal trials, these being discontinued when no responses occurred for 3 successive trials, the extinction criterion.

RESULTS

O agreement was high for both measures, the results being essentially identical when each O's results were considered independently. Averages for both Os are plotted in Figure 1 for the three phases of the study: 5 basal trials, 5 CS trials during conditioning, and 2 blocks of 5 extinction or test trials. The per cent measure, indicating proportions of trials in which sucking occurred during CS-alone presentations, showed an increase for Group E from beginning to end of the session, while this measure leveled off for Group C. A similar trend was present for the number-of-

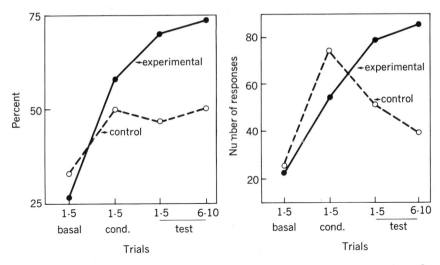

Fig. 1. Percentage and number of sucking responses to the CS (tone) in the Experimental and Control Groups.

sucks measure. Analyses of variance for both measures yielded highly significant interactions between groups and phases [F (3, 54) = 19.4 and 12.3, p < .001, respectively], indicating increasing differences between groups over time. Individual Ss in Group E showed a significantly greater amount of change from basal to extinction periods in both per cent of response and number of sucks [t(18) = 2.14 and t(18) = 2.41, p < .05, respectively]. Finally, the trials-to-criterion measure in extinction showed that Group E gave responses on the average of 24.1 of 30 trials compared with 11.1 for Group C [t(18) = 2.42, p < .05].

DISCUSSION

The study design attempted to control for sensitization or pseudoconditioning (Wickens and Wickens, 1940) by giving both groups identical stimulation but in different CS-UCS temporal relationships. There are two indications that this procedure did not completely eliminate such an effect: (1) Group C gave slightly (not significantly) more responses to CS than Group E during the conditioning period, and (2) Group C responded more during the extinction phase than during the basal phase. When the individual averages from the basal trials of Group C are compared with averages from the first 10 extinction trials, the t is 2.45 for the per cent measure (df = 9, p < .05) and for the number-of-sucks measure, the t is 2.59 (p < .05). Thus the Group C treatment was itself effective in increasing response, possibly due to (1) sensitization, (2) the unlikely possibility of trace conditioning having occurred in Group C, or (3) increase in hunger or other arousing condition, 35–40 min. having elapsed between the basal and extinction periods. Regardless, it has been established that the paired stimulation administered to Group E increased response more than did the control condition.

While 20 paired presentations of CS and UCS constitute a relatively small number of trials, the frequency of sucking during presentation of the UCS is such as to produce many "pairings" within each trial. Groups E and C responded with means of 13.1 and 13.0 sucks, respectively, per nipple presentation, and they did not differ over trials in numbers of sucks made to successive UCS presentations. If each sucking response is considered independently, then an average of 260 "pairings" of CS and UCS occurred in the conditioning session for the experimental Ss. Thus sucking is an efficient response for administering many paired CS-UCS presentations in a brief period.

These data agree with a much earlier experiment by Marquis (1931) and, more recently, with Papousek (1961) that conditioning of responses involving mouth-stimulation can occur in newborns, and contrast with reservations expressed by Kessen (1963) and Scott (1963). While age-determined changes in conditioning rate apparently occur (Kantrow, 1937; Morgan and Morgan, 1944; Papousek, 1961), failures to establish conditioning in neonates may be due as much to the use of ineffective experimental techniques as to chronological or neurophysiological deficiencies.

In His Society

10 A Cross-Cultural Study
of Correlates of Crime[1]

MARGARET K. BACON

IRVIN I. CHILD

HERBERT BARRY, III

Are there cultural factors that may be causal to criminal behavior, such as personal crime and theft? Among the findings in this study of a sample of 48 preliterate societies are: (1) a boy's inability or limitation to form an identification with his father is associated with both types of crime; (2) theft is associated with a high degree of anxiety in childhood, a low degree of indulgence in childhood, and a high degree of differentiation of status in adulthood; (3) personal crime is associated with a generalized attitude of suspicion and distrust. These relationships could be explored profitably in our own society.

[1]This research was supported by grants from the Social Science Research Council; the Ford Foundation; and the National Institute of Mental Health, United States Public Health Service (M–2681).

We wish to express appreciation to Selden D. Bacon for many helpful suggestions in the preparation of this manuscript, and to James Sakoda for generously providing us with a program permitting rapid calculation of our results on the IBM 709. We also wish to thank Pearl Davenport, Hatsumi Maretzki, and Abraham Rosman, who made many of the ratings employed in our calculations.

Reprinted from the *Journal of Abnormal and Social Psychology*, 1963, **66**: 4, 291–300, by permission of the authors and the American Psychological Association.

A number of researchers have analyzed the sociological and psychological background of delinquents and criminals and compared them with a noncriminal control population, in order to discover what conditions give rise to criminal behavior; for a recent review, see Robison (1960). The present paper reports on variations among a sample of preliterate societies in the frequency of crime, in order to determine what other known features of these societies are associated with the occurrence of crime. The cross-cultural technique (Whiting, 1954), in which each society is taken as a single case, is a unique method for studying crime and has certain advantages: The index of frequency of crime in a society represents the average among its many individuals and over a span of many years, so that the measure is likely to be more stable and reliable than a measure of criminal tendency in a single individual. Some of the cultural features which may be related to crime show wider variations among societies than within a single society, permitting a more comprehensive test of their significance. Results which are consistent in a number of diverse societies may be applied to a great variety of cultural conditions instead of being limited to a single cultural setting.

If certain cultural features foster the development of criminal behavior, they should be found preponderantly in societies with a high frequency of crime; factors which inhibit crime should be found largely in societies which are low in crime. Thus the cross-cultural method may help us discover psychological and sociological variables which have a causal relationship to the development of crime; the importance of these variables may then also be tested intraculturally. On the other hand, variables identified as possible causes of crime within our society may be tested for broader significance by the cross-cultural method.

The possible causal factors which we have explored are principally concerned with child training practices, economy, and social structure. Hypotheses concerning these factors, as they have been presented by other writers or as they have occurred to us, will be described in connection with the presentation of our results.

METHOD

Sample

The sample used in this study consists of 48 societies, mostly preliterate, scattered over the world. They were taken from a larger group of 110 societies which were selected on the basis of geographical diversity and adequacy of information on aboriginal child training practices. The present sample of 48 consists of those societies whose ethnographies were searched and found to provide sufficient information to permit comparative ratings on criminal behavior by three independent research workers.[2]

---

[2]The 48 societies included in the study are as follows: Africa—Ashanti, Azande, Bena, Chagga, Dahomeans, Lovedu, Mbundu, Thonga; Asia—Andamanese, Baiga, Chenchu, Chukchee, Lepcha, Muria, Tanala, Yakut; North America—Cheyenne, Comanche, Flatheads, Hopi, Jamaicans (Rocky Roaders), Kaska, Kwakiutl, Navaho, Papago, Tepoztlan, Western Apache; South America—Aymara, Cuna, Jivaro, Siriono, Yagua;

Ratings

We have included two types of crime in our study: *theft* and *personal crime.* These two were chosen because they are relatively easy to identify and almost universal in occurrence. Also, they represent two quite different types of behavior. Thus we are able to clarify antecedents common to both types of crime and those characteristic of only one. Judgments were always made in relation to the norms of the culture under consideration. Theft was defined as stealing the personal property of others. Property included anything on which the society placed value, whether it was a whale's tooth or a song. Personal crime was defined by intent to injure or kill a person; assault, rape, suicide, sorcery intended to make another ill, murder, making false accusations, etc., were all included.

The method of comparative ratings

Oceania—Arapesh, Balinese, Buka (Kurtachi), Ifaluk, Kwoma, Lau Fijians (Kambara), Lesu, Manus, Maori, Puka—pukans, Samoans, Tikopia, Trobrianders, Trukese, Ulithians, Vanua Levu (Nakoroka). All information was obtained from ethnographic studies available in the literature or in the Human Relations Area Files. Ratings were, so far as possible, of the aboriginal practices of the group in order to reduce the influence of acculturation. All ratings used in this study have been filed with the American Documentation Institute. Order Document No. 7450 from the ADI Auxiliary Publications Project, Photoduplication Service, Library of Congress; Washington 25, D. C., remitting in advance $1.75 for microfilm or $2.50 for photocopies. Make checks payable to: Chief, Photoduplication Service, Library of Congress. All intercorrelations among variables for our sample of societies appear in the same document.

was used to obtain measures of frequency. Three raters independently analyzed the ethnographic material on each society and made ratings on a seven-point scale as to the relative frequency of the type of crime under consideration. Thus a rating of 4 on theft would mean that the frequency of theft in a given society appeared to be about average for the sample of societies. Ratings of 5, 6, and 7 represented high frequencies and those of 3, 2, and 1 were low. Societies in which the behavior did not occur were rated as 0. Each rating was classified as confident or doubtful at the time that it was made. No rating was made if the analyst judged the information to be insufficient. We have included all societies on which all three analysts made a rating, whether it was confident or doubtful, and we have used the pooled ratings of all three analysts. The reliability of these pooled ratings is estimated as $+.67$ for Theft and $+.57$ for Personal Crime. These estimates were obtained by averaging (using a z transformation) the separate interrater reliabilities, and entering this average into the Spearman-Brown correction formula.

Most writers in this field make a distinction between delinquency and crime, largely on the basis of the age of the offender. The nature of our evidence does not permit us to make such a clear distinction. Ratings were made in terms of the relative frequency of specific types of criminal behavior in the adult population. Since the age at which adulthood is considered to have begun varies from one society to another, ratings may in some cases have included individuals young enough to be considered adolescent in our society and therefore delinquent rather than criminal. The distinction does not appear to be crucial in this study.

The measures of possible causal variables consist of ratings which have been derived from several sources. Each will be described in the following section. Except where noted (for certain variables in Tables 3 and 4), none of the three people who made the crime ratings participated in any of the other ratings.

HYPOTHESES, RESULTS, AND DISCUSSION

Our results will be presented under three main headings: Correlates of Crime in General, Correlates Specific to Theft, and Correlates Specific to Personal Crime. As this classification suggests, we have found it useful to consider the antecedents of crime as either general or specific, i.e., leading to a general increase in criminal behavior, or associated with only one major category of crime. A correlation of +.46 was found between frequency of Theft and frequency of Personal Crime. This indicates that the two variables show a significant degree of communality ($p < .01$) and also some independence.

Correlates of Crime in General

Our principal findings concerning common correlates of both Theft and Personal Crime are relevant to a hypothesis that crime arises partly as a defense against strong feminine identification. We will begin with an account of this hypothesis.

In our society crime occurs mostly in men, and we have no reason to doubt that this sex difference characterizes most societies. Several writers have called attention to the sex role identification of males as es-

pecially pertinent to the development of delinquency in our society. It is assumed that the very young boy tends to identify with his mother rather than his father because of his almost exclusive contact with his mother. Later in his development he becomes aware of expectations that he behave in a masculine way and as a result his behavior tends to be marked by a compulsive masculinity which is really a defense against feminine identification. Parsons (1954, pp. 304–305) notes further that the mother is the principal agent of socialization as well as an object of love and identification. Therefore, when the boy revolts he unconsciously identifies "goodness" with femininity and hence accepts the role of "bad boy" as a positive goal.

Miller (1958) has made a study of lower-class culture and delinquency which is also pertinent in this connection. He points out that some delinquent behavior may result from an attempt to live up to attitudes and values characteristic of lower-class culture. He also notes that many lower-class males are reared in predominantly female households lacking a consistently present male with whom to identify. He feels that what he calls an almost obsessive lower-class concern with masculinity results from the feminine identification in preadolescent years.

Whiting, Kluckhohn, and Anthony (1958), in a cross-cultural study of male initiation rites at puberty, found these rites tended to occur in societies with prolonged, exclusive mother-son sleeping arrangements. Their interpretation of this relationship is that the early mother-infant sleeping arrangement produces an initial feminine identification, and later control by men leads to a secondary masculine identification. The function of the initiation ceremony is to resolve this conflict of sexual identification in favor of the masculine identification. The authors further predict that insofar as there has been an increase in juvenile delinquency in our society, "it probably has been accompanied by an increase in the exclusiveness of mother-child relationships and/or a decrease in the authority of the father."

The hypothesis that crime is in part a defense against initial feminine identification would lead to the expectation that all factors which tend to produce strong identification with the mother and failure of early identification with the father would be positively correlated with the frequency of crime in the adult population. The factor that is easiest to study is the presence of the father. It seems reasonable to suppose that successful identification with the father is dependent on his presence. Therefore, societies which differ in the degree to which the father is present during the child's first few years should differ correspondingly in the degree to which the boy typically forms a masculine identification.[3]

Whiting (1959) has made use of Murdock's (1957) classification of household structure and family com-

position to distinguish among four types of households which provide a range from maximal to minimal degree of presence of the father. They are as follows:

Monogamous Nuclear. This household is the usual one in our society. The father, mother, and children eat, sleep, and entertain under one roof. Grandparents, siblings of the parents, and other relatives live elsewhere. The effective presence of the father in the child's environment is thus at a maximum.

Monogamous Extended. Here two or more nuclear families live together under one roof. A typical extended family consists of an aged couple together with their married sons and daughters and their respective families. In such a household, the child's interaction with his father is likely to be somewhat less than in the single nuclear household.

Polygynous Polygynous. The polygynous household consists of a man living with his wives and their various children. Here the child is likely to have even less opportunity to interact with his father.

Polygynous Mother-Child. This type of household occurs in those polygynous societies where each wife has a separate establishment and lives in it with her children. In these societies the father either sleeps in a men's club, has a hut of his own, or divides his time among the houses of his various wives. The husband usually does not sleep in the house of any wife during the 2 to 3 years when she is nursing each infant. Thus the mother may become the almost exclusive object of identification for the first few years of life.

---

[3]The whole problem of the mechanism whereby identification occurs has been omitted from this study. In all theories it would appear that identification with the father would be in some degree a function of the frequency of the presence of the father.

TABLE 1.—Frequency of Theft or Personal Crime in Relation to Family
Structure and Household

FAMILY STRUCTURE AND HOUSEHOLD[a]	FREQUENCY OF THEFT		FREQUENCY OF PERSONAL CRIME	
	Low	High	Low	High
Monogamous Nuclear	7	2	5	4
Monogamous Extended	7	3	6	3
Polygynous Polygynous	7	0	3	7
Polygynous Mother-Child	1	11	3	9

Note.—Each entry in the table gives the number of societies in our sample which have the particular combination of characteristics indicated for that row and column.

The total number of cases in the left-hand and right-hand parts of this table and in the various divisions of succeeding tables varies because lack of information prevented rating some societies on some variables. In testing each relationship we have of course been able to use only those societies for which the relevant ratings are available. The division into "low" and "high" was made as near the median as possible.

[a] See Murdock (1957).

Table 1 shows the number of societies with low and high frequency of Theft and Personal Crime within each of the four categories of household type. As the opportunity for contact with the father decreases, the frequency of both Theft and Personal Crime increases. This result agrees with our hypothesis. If the family structure and household is treated as a four-point scale, it yields a correlation of +.58 with frequency of Theft and of +.44 with frequency of Personal Crime; both correlations are statistically significant ($p < .01$). If we compare the extremes of the distribution—contrasting Monogamous Nuclear households (which provide the maximum opportunity for identification with the father) with Polygynous Mother-Child households (which provide the minimum opportunity for identification with the father)—this relationship is clearly demonstrated: 18 of the 21 societies fall in the predicted quadrants for Theft, and 14 out of 21 for Personal Crime.

Several results of empirical studies in our society appear consistent with this finding. One is the frequently reported relationship between broken homes and delinquency, since in the majority of cases broken homes are probably mother-child households. Robins and O'Neal (1958), for example, in a follow-up study of problem children after 30 years, refer to the high incidence of fatherless families. Glueck and Glueck (1950) report that 41.2% of their delinquent group were not living with their own fathers, as compared with 24.8% of a matched nondelinquent group. These data suggest that a relatively high proportion of the delinquents came from what were essentially "mother-child" households.

A recent book by Rohrer and Edmonson (1960) is also relevant. Their study is a follow-up after 20 years of the individuals described in *Children of Bondage* by Davis and Dollard (1941). The importance of the matriarchal household typical in a Southern Negro lower-class group, and its effect on the emotional development of the young boy and his eventual attitudes as an adult, are stressed throughout. The following passage summarizes, in its application to their (Rohrer and Edmonson, 1960, pp. 162–163) particular data, an interpretation consistent with those we have cited in introducing this hypothesis.

Gang life begins early, more or less contemporaneously with the first years of schooling, and for many men lasts until death. . . . Although each gang is a somewhat distinct group, all of them appear to have a common structure expressing and reinforcing the gang ideology. Thus an organizational form that springs from the little boy's search for a masculinity he cannot find at home becomes first a protest against femininity and then an assertion of hyper-virility. On the way it acquires a structuring in which the aspirations and goals of the matriarchy or the middle class are seen as soft, effeminate, and despicable. The gang ideology of masculine independence is formed from these perceptions, and the gang then sees its common enemy not as a class, nor even perhaps as a sex, but as the "feminine principle" in society. The gang member rejects this femininity in every form, and he sees it in women and in effeminate men, in laws and morals and religion, in schools and occupational striving.

Correlates of Theft

Although we shall consider correlates of Theft in this section and correlates of Personal Crime in the next section, each table will show in parallel columns the relation of a set of variables both to Theft and to Personal Crime. This will facilitate comparison and avoid repetition. How each of these variables was measured will be described in the section to which it is most pertinent.

The first variables to be considered are concerned with child training practices. Most of the child training variables have been developed in our research and described in an earlier paper (Barry, Bacon, and Child, 1957). These variables may be briefly described as follows:

Overall childhood indulgence. The period of childhood was defined roughly as covering the age period from 5 to 12 years, or to the beginning of any pubertal or prepubertal status change. In making ratings of childhood indulgence, factors relevant to indulgence in infancy—such as immediacy and degree of drive reduction, display of affection by parents, etc.—if operative at this later age, were taken into account. In addition, the raters also considered the degree of socialization expected in childhood and the severity of the methods used to obtain the expected behavior.

Anxiety associated with socialization during the same period of childhood. This was rated separately for each of five systems of behavior: Responsibility or dutifulness training; Nurturance training, i.e., training the child to be nurturant or helpful toward younger siblings and other dependent people; Obedience training; Self-reliance training; Achievement training, i.e., training the child to orient his behavior toward standards of excellence in performance and to seek to achieve as excellent a performance as possible.

In rating the training in these areas, an attempt was first made to estimate the Total Pressure exerted by the adults in each society toward making the children behave in each of these specified ways (Responsible, Nurturant, Obedient, Self-Reliant, and Achieving). The socialization anxiety measures were based on an estimate of the amount of anxiety aroused in the child by failing to behave in a responsible, self-reliant, etc. way, and they reflect primarily the extent of punishment for failure to show each particular form of behavior. The measures of Total Pressure reflect both this and the extent of reward and encouragement.

Wherever boys and girls were rated differently on any of the above variables of socialization, we used the ratings for boys.

The relation of the crime ratings to these and other variables of child training is presented in Table 2. It is clear that Theft is significantly related to several variables of child training.

First, Theft is negatively correlated with Childhood Indulgence, i.e., societies with a high rating of Childhood Indulgence tend to have a low frequency of Theft in the adult population; and, conversely, societies with a low rating of Childhood Indulgence show a high frequency of Theft.

TABLE 2.—Child Training Factors Associated with Theft or Personal Crime

FACTOR	THEFT		PERSONAL CRIME	
	N	r	N	r
1. Childhood Indulgence[a]	45	−.41**	42	−.10
2. Responsibility Socialization Anxiety[a]	43	+.48**	41	+.20
3. Self-Reliance Socialization Anxiety[a]	43	+.35*	41	+.24
4. Achievement Socialization Anxiety[a]	36	+.41*	35	+.20
5. Obedience Socialization Anxiety[a]	40	+.32*	39	+.06
6. Dependence Socialization Anxiety[b]	31	+.14	28	+.56**
7. Mother-Child Sleeping[c]	20	+.40	19	+.46*
8. Infant Indulgence[a]				
9. Age of Weaning[a]				
10. Oral Socialization Anxiety[b]				
11. Anal Socialization Anxiety[b]				
12. Sex Socialization Anxiety[b]				
13. Aggression Socialization Anxiety[b]				
14. Nurturance Socialization Anxiety[a]				
15. Total Pressures toward Responsibility, Nurturance, Self-Reliance, Achievement, and Obedience[a]				

Note.—In this and the following tables the correlations are Pearsonian coefficients, thus reflecting all available degrees of gradation in score rather than simply classifying societies as high and low.

Factors 8–15 showed no significant relationship with either Theft or Personal Crime.

[a]See Barry, Bacon, and Child (1957).

[b]See Whiting and Child (1953).

[c]See Whiting, Kluckhohn, and Anthony (1958).

*$p \leq .05$.

**$p \leq .01$.

TABLE 3.—Socioeconomic Factors Associated with Theft or Personal Crime

FACTOR	THEFT		PERSONAL CRIME	
	N	r	N	r
1. Social Stratification[a]	44	+.36*	40	+.16
2. Level of Political Integration[a]	43	+.34*	39	+.02
3. Degree of Elaboration of Social Control[b]	43	+.46**	40	+.04
4. Accumulation of Food[c]				
5. Settlement Pattern[a]				
6. Division of Labor by Sex[a]				
7. Rule of Residence (Patrilocal, Matrilocal, etc.)[a]				
8. Extent of Storing[b]				
9. Irrationality of Storing[b]				
10. Severity of Punishment for Property Crime[b]				
11. Severity of Punishment for Personal Crime[b]				

Note.—Ratings of Factors 3, 10, and 11 were made in connection with the analysis of crime by two of the three raters (H. Maretzki and A. Rosman). Ratings of Factors 8 and 9 were made by one of the raters (H. Maretzki) but in connection with an analysis of food and economy.

Factors 4–11 showed no significant relationship with either Theft or Personal Crime.

[a]See Murdock (1957).

[b]Bacon, Child, and Barry (unpublished).

[c]See Barry, Child, and Bacon (1959).

*$p \leq .05$.

**$p \leq .01$.

Frequency of Theft is also positively correlated with socialization anxiety during the period of childhood with respect to the following areas of training: Responsibility, Self-Reliance, Achievement, and Obedience. It should be emphasized that Total Pressures toward those four areas of socialization are not significantly correlated with Theft. Therefore it is apparently not the area or level of socialization required which is significant, but rather the punitive and anxiety provoking methods of socialization employed.

These findings on child training in relation to Theft may be summarized and interpreted by the hypothesis that theft is in part motivated by feelings of deprivation of love. Our data indicate that one source of such feelings is punitive and anxiety provoking treatment during childhood. Such treatment during infancy may tend to have a similar effect, as suggested by a correlation of −.25 between frequency of Theft and Infant Indulgence. This correlation falls slightly short of significance at the 5% level. It is of special interest that substantial correlations with socialization anxiety in childhood tended to occur in the areas of training in Responsibility, Achievement, and Self-Reliance. These all involve demands for behavior far removed from the dependent behavior of infancy and early childhood and close to the independent behavior expected of adults. If we assume that lack of adequate indulgence in childhood leads to a desire to return to earlier means of gratification and behavior symbolic of this need, then we would expect that pressures toward more adult behavior might intensify this need and the frequency of the symbolic behavior. Theft, from this point of view, would be seen as rewarded partly by its value as symbolic gratification of an infantile demand for unconditional indulgence irrespective of other people's rights or interests.

The results of the early study by Healy and Bronner (1936) seem directly pertinent to our findings and interpretation. They found that a group of delinquents differed from their nondelinquent siblings primarily in their relationships with their parents; the delinquent child was much more likely to give evidence of feeling thwarted and rejected. It seems reasonable to assume that such feelings would often, though not always, indicate a real deprivation of parental love. Glueck and Glueck (1950) also found that their delinquents, compared with matched nondelinquents, had received less affection from their parents and siblings and had a greater tendency to feel that their parents were not concerned with their welfare. It was also noted that fathers of the delinquents had a much greater tendency to resort to physical punishment as a means of discipline than fathers of the nondelinquents. This agrees with our observation that more punitive methods of socialization are associated with an increased frequency of theft.

Compulsive stealing (kleptomania)

has been interpreted by psychoanalysts (see Fenichel, 1945, pp. 370–371) as an attempt to seize symbols of security and affection. Thus this form of mental illness, in common with more rational forms of stealing, may be regarded as being motivated by feelings of deprivation of love.

Table 3 summarizes the relationship between our two measures of crime and a number of aspects of economy and social organization on which we were able to obtain ratings. Theft shows a significant relationship with only three of these measures: Social Stratification, Level of Political Integration, and Degree of Elaboration of Social Control. Social Stratification was treated as a five-point scale ranging from complex stratification, i.e., three or more definite social classes or castes exclusive of slaves, to egalitarian, i.e., absence of significant status differentiation other than recognition of political statuses and of individual skill, prowess, piety, etc. Level of Political Integration was also treated as a five-point scale ranging from complex state, e.g., confederation of tribes or conquest state with a king, differentiated officials, and a hierarchical administrative organization to no political integration, even at the community level.[4] Elaboration of Social Control is concerned with the degree to which a society has law making, law enforcing, and punishing agencies.

Our findings indicate that theft is positively correlated with each of

----

[4]Both variables are taken from Murdock (1957). Our manner of treating his data is described in Barry, Child, and Bacon (1959).

TABLE 4.—Adult Attitudes Associated with Theft or Personal Crime

ATTITUDE	THEFT		PERSONAL CRIME	
	N	r	N	r
1. Sense of Property	43	$+.45^{\circ\circ}$	40	$+.25$
2. Trust about Property	43	$-.31^{\circ}$	40	$-.27$
3. General Trustfulness	42	$-.28$	40	$-.40^{\circ\circ}$
4. Environmental Kindness in Folk Tales	23	$-.47^{\circ}$	21	$-.30$
5. Environmental Hostility in Folk Tales	23	$+.36$	21	$+.56^{\circ\circ}$
6. Communality of Property				
7. Competition in the Acquisition of Wealth				
8. Generosity				
9. n Achievement in Folk Tales[a]				

Note.—Attitude 3 was rated by one of the three raters (A. Rosman) in connection with the analysis of crime. Attitudes 1, 2, 6, 7, and 8 were rated by another of the three raters (H. Maretzki) in connection with the analysis of food and economy.

Attitudes 6–9 showed no significant relationship with either Theft or Personal Crime.

[a]See Child, Veroff, and Storm (1958).

$^{\circ}p \leq .05.$

$^{\circ\circ}p \leq .01.$

these three measures. In other words, with an increased Level of Political Integration, Social Stratification, and Elaboration of Social Control there is an increase in the frequency of Theft. These variables show no significant relationship with frequency of Personal Crime. Each of these institutional conditions seems capable of arousing feelings of insecurity and resentment, and hence may be similar in this respect to parental deprivation. Therefore the correlation of these institutional conditions with Theft might be tentatively interpreted as consistent with our hypothesis about motivational influences on Theft. It is obvious that other interpretations might be made from the same data. For example, a high frequency of crime may give rise to increased elaboration of social control.

Table 4 presents the relation of both Theft and Personal Crime to certain adult attitudes on which we were able to obtain ratings. Frequency of Theft is positively related to Sense of Property and negatively related to Trust about Property. This may indicate merely that the greater the importance of property, the greater the variety of acts which will be classified as Theft, or that a high frequency of Theft gives rise to an emphasis on property. But it may also mean that the greater the importance of property, the more effectively does Theft serve the personal needs to which it seems to be related.

Frequency of Theft is also negatively correlated with Environmental Kindness in Folk Tales. This folk tale measure requires some explanation. It was taken from an analysis of folk tales was taken. In making the anal-(MKB) without knowledge of the societies from which the sample of folk tales was taken. In making the analysis, each folk tale was divided into units of action or events as they related to the principal character or the character with whom the listener would be expected to identify. Each unit was then classified in one of a number of different categories including that of environmental kindness. Classification in this category means that the particular unit involved action or state of affairs definitely friendly or nurturant to the principal character. Thus our results show that societies high in frequency of Theft tend to have folk tales which do not represent the environment as kind. Thinking of the environment as lacking in friendly nurturance seems entirely consistent with the relative absence of parental nurturance which we have already found to be correlated with frequency of theft.

Correlates of Personal Crime

Inspection of Tables 2, 3, and 4 reveals that the significant correlates of Personal Crime are different from those for theft. In no instance does a variable in these tables show a significant correlation with both Theft and Personal Crime.

Frequency of Personal Crime shows a significant positive correlation with Dependence Socialization Anxiety, a rating taken from Whiting and Child (1953). In making this rating, an estimate was made of the amount of anxiety aroused in the children of a given society by the methods of independence training typically employed. This estimate was based on the following factors: abruptness of the transition required, severity and frequency of punishment, and evidence

of emotional disturbance in the child.

Ratings on mother-child sleeping are taken from Whiting, et al. (1958). In this study societies were placed into two categories: those in which the mother and baby shared the same bed for at least a year to the exclusion of the father, those in which the baby slept alone or with both the mother and father. According to our results there is a high positive relationship between prolonged, exclusive mother-child sleeping arrangements and frequency of Personal Crime.[5]

Inspection of the child training factors associated with frequency of Personal Crime suggests that the conditions in childhood leading to a high frequency of personal crime among adults are as follows: a mother-child household with inadequate opportunity in early life for identification with the father, mother-child sleeping arrangements which tend to foster a strong dependent relationship between the child and the mother, subsequent socialization with respect to independence training which tends to be abrupt, punitive, and productive of emotional disturbance in the child.

We would predict that this pattern of child training factors would tend to produce in the child persistent attitudes of rivalry, distrust, and hostility, which would probably continue into adult life. The results obtained with ratings of adult attitudes (Table 4)

---

[5]The variable of mother-child sleeping might be considered to favor feminine identification. In that event, the fact that it shows correlations in the positive direction with both types of crime tends toward confirmation of the findings in our earlier section on Correlates of Crime in General.

support this view. Frequency of Personal Crime is negatively correlated with General Trustfulness. Frequency of Personal Crime is also positively correlated with Environmental Hostility in Folk Tales. Classification of a folk tale unit in this category means that the particular unit involved definite deception, aggression, or rejection, in relation to the principal character. This variable was not highly related to that of environmental kindness, although the results obtained with the two are consistent with each other. The correlation between them was only −.34, most folk tale units not falling in either of these categories. Our results indicate that societies which are rated as relatively high in the frequency of Personal Crime have folk tales with a high proportion of events representing the environment as hostile. If we may infer that the content of folk tales reflects the underlying attitudes of the people who tell them, then this finding, as well as those with our other measures of adult attitudes, supports the view that personal crime is correlated with a suspicious or distrustful attitude toward the environment.

An analysis by Whiting (1959) of the socialization factors correlated with a belief in sorcery is relevant to this aspect of our results. He points out that a belief in sorcery is consistent with a paranoid attitude. According to Freudian interpretation, paranoia represents a defense against sexual anxiety. Whiting presents cross-cultural data in suppport of a hypothesis, based on Freud's theory

of paranoia, that a belief in sorcery is related to a prolonged and intense contact with the mother in infancy followed by a severe sex socialization. The same hypothesis might be applied to frequency of Personal Crime, since we have evidence that Personal Crime is correlated with a suspicious, paranoid attitude in adult life, and sorcery is after all one form of Personal Crime. Our results for Personal Crime, in common with Whiting's for sorcery, show a correlation with mother-child sleeping. However, we found no significant correlation with severe sex socialization but rather with severe dependence socialization. We do not feel that these findings negate the Freudian interpretation, because dependence socialization, bearing as it does on the child's intimate relation with his mother, necessarily is concerned with the child's sexual feelings in a broad sense.

GENERAL DISCUSSION

We would like to emphasize the value of the cross-cultural method for exploring the possible determinants of crime. When each society is used as a single case, and is classified according to crime and other variables for the entire society over a period of years, the measures are likely to be reliable; comparison among societies provides great diversity in frequency of crime and in the other variables to be related with it.

The cross-cultural method may help us to identify variables with a causal relationship to crime. For example, our cross-cultural data suggest that high differentiation of status within a society is a favorable condition for a high frequency of Theft, and that a high frequency of Personal Crime is associated with a generalized attitude of distrust. These relationships should be subjected to more systematic and intensive tests within our own society than has hitherto been done.

Variables which have been suggested, whether in empirical studies or theoretical discussions, as possible causes of crime within our society may be tested for broader significance by the cross-cultural method. It has been argued, for example, that within our society delinquent or criminal behavior is likely to develop if the boy has been raised without adequate opportunity to identify with the father. These suggestions have often been made in connection with family patterns that are said to characterize certain classes or groups within our society; the cross-cultural findings indicate that a high frequency of both Theft and Personal Crime tends to occur in societies where the typical family for the society as a whole creates lack or limitation of opportunity for the young boy to form an identification with his father. Therefore the cross-cultural method supports the theory that lack of opportunity for the

young boy to form a masculine identification is in itself an important antecedent of crime.

Another instance of such confirmation in a broader sense is the following: In our society delinquents have been reported to express feelings of alienation from their parents. It is unclear, however, whether this reflects their parents' actual treatment of them, or merely their own subjectively determined perceptions. Our cross-cultural data (in common with some of the findings within our own society) indicate that a high frequency of Theft is correlated with an actual low degree of indulgence during childhood.

Other theories about the antecedents of crime, when tested with the cross-cultural method, have not been confirmed in this broader framework. For example, pressures toward achievement were not significantly related to frequency of crime, although such a relationship is implied by theories of delinquency which emphasize the discrepancy between culturally induced aspirations and the possibility of achieving them. This negative result in our sample of societies does not deny the existence of such a relationship within our society, but it does indicate a limitation on its generality.

11 *Low-Income Outlook on Life*

LOLA M. IRELAN
ARTHUR BESNER

If we are to intervene successfully in the lives of children we must know that being poor is often a way of life into which people are locked from birth. There are many enemies of the poor: discrimination, inferior education, poor housing, unemployment, and so forth. Society restricts the poor from equal opportunity and from possible self-realization commensurate with their abilities. The following selection details characteristic behavior of the poor in certain important life areas. Such information is useful to those individuals and agencies trying to improve the quality of life of any group of people, especially the nonwhite and bilingual minority.

Currently, in our national concern for the alleviation of poverty and economic dependency, the need to know and understand what life looks like from the bottom of society is a crucial one. We can induce meaningful change only if we understand the situation where we intend it to occur. It is unlikely, for example, that we can change or reduce rates of dependency and poverty without knowing what the conditions of dependence and deprivation mean to people caught up in them. Nor can we bring any class of people into a different relationship to society without knowing the quality of the existing situation.

As yet, knowledge of this sort is fugitive and tenuous. Much needed research has yet to be designed. There are gaps and flaws in the exploratory research which has been done. The findings on hand are suggestive rather than definitive. There is enough known, however, to warrant inventory and judicious application. It behooves us to systematize and use such knowledge as we do have. In the long run, such a step will serve to refine and increase it.

This paper summarizes available findings, largely from studies in the United States, bearing on the approach to life of the poor, the people at the bottom of society's economic ladder. It will discuss the connection between the condition of poverty, the views of man and society which arise

Reprinted from L. M. Irelan, and A. Besner, *Low-Income Life Styles*, Welfare Administration Publication No. 14, U.S. Department of Health, Education, and Welfare, 1966, pp. 1–12, by permission of the authors.

there, and the apparent effect of those views on the lower class version of American goals and values.

LIFE CONDITIONS OF THE POOR

In our society, a continuously low income is directly associated with certain life situations. Poorer, more crowded living quarters, reduced access to education and recreation, occupational restriction to simpler, manual types of work—these and similar characteristics of the very poor are sufficiently obvious to need no underlining. The result of these circumstances is a set of life conditions which is not so obvious. They consist of four general limitations: (1) comparative simplification of the experience world, (2) powerlessness, (3) deprivation, and (4) insecurity. These limitations are, of course, relative. Indeed, they can be discerned only because of the different extent of their existence at the several levels of society.

1. Limited alternatives. The poor, of all the strata in society, have the slightest opportunity to experience varieties of social and cultural settings. Their own setting is one of the least intricacy and flexibility. Throughout life, they experience a very narrow range of situations and demands. Their repertoire of social roles is limited. They seldom participate in any activity which takes them out of the daily routine. They rarely play roles of leadership, or fill any position calling for specialized functioning. On their jobs they confront less complex situations and have fewer, less diverse standards to meet.

Socially, they seldom go beyond the borders of kinship and neighborhood groups—people very like themselves (Dotson, 1951).

2. Helplessness. The position of the poor vis-à-vis society and its institutions is one of impotence. They have practically no bargaining power in the working world. Unskilled and uneducated, they are the most easily replaced workers. The skills they do have are minimal, of little importance in productive processes. On the job itself, the very poor man can exercise little autonomy and has small opportunity to influence conditions of work. He is close to helpless even to acquire information and training which would change this situation. He has neither the knowledge nor the means to get it.

3. Deprivation. It is reasonable to suspect that this general condition, almost universally associated with poverty, is felt with particular intensity in American society. Deprivation is, after all, relative. When it is defined as lack of resources relative to felt wants and needs, it is evident that America has one of the greatest gaps between generally accepted goals and the extent to which the lower class can realistically expect to attain them. As a nation, we stress, perhaps inordinately, the value and virtue of high attainment. We expect and applaud efforts at self-improvement and upward social mobility. Commercial advertising attempts to stimulate and increase desire for status achievement. The richness of life in the rest of society is well displayed —on television, in newspapers, on billboards, in store windows, on the very streets themselves. All this, plus

awareness that some people have actually succeeded in the strenuous upward move, makes the condition of the unachieving poor one of unremitting deprivation. Their relative deprivation is, perhaps, the condition which more than anything else affects the life-view of the poor. Constant awareness of their own abject status and the "failure" which it rightly or wrongly implies understandably leads to embarrassed withdrawal and isolation.

4. Insecurity. People of low income are more at the mercy of life's unpredictability than are the more affluent. Sickness, injury, loss of work, legal problems—a range of hazardous possibilities—may overwhelm anyone. But to the poor man they are especially fearful. His resources are more sparse. His savings, if any, are quickly expended in any sizable emergency. Certain conditions of his life make emergencies more likely. His work skills are more expendable, sometimes more dependent on seasonal demands. He is more likely to lose his job on short notice. An emergency expenditure of funds may mean the postponing of rent payments and the fear of eviction. He is unable to secure for himself and his family the regular, preventive health measures which would fend off medical emergencies. He often finds that he cannot successfully navigate the channels involved in using public sources of emergency help, such as clinics and legal aid agencies (Cohen and Hodges, 1963).

LOW-INCOME VIEW OF MAN AND SOCIETY

Constant, fruitless struggle with these conditions is likely to produce estrangement—from society, from other individuals, even from oneself.

The wholeness of life which most of us experience—the conjunction of values, knowledge, and behavior which gives life unity and meaning—is less often felt by the poor. They see life rather as unpatterned and unpredictable, a congeries of events in which they have no part and over which they have no control.

Conceptualized as "alienation," this view of life is repeatedly found associated with lower social and economic status (Bell, 1957; Simpson and Miller, 1963; Dean, 1961). It is multifaceted—despair can be generated and felt in many ways. Generally, however, it seems to have four different forms of expression. The alienation of the poor is graphically seen in their feelings of: (1) powerlessness, (2) meaninglessness, (3) anomia, and (4) isolation.

1. Powerlessness. The objective condition of helplessness in relation to the larger social order leads naturally to the conviction that one cannot control it. The poor are widely convinced that individuals cannot influence the workings of society. Furthermore, they doubt the possibility of being able to influence their own lives. Correspondingly, they are likely to voice such pessimistic views as, "A body just can't take nothing for granted; you just have to live from day to day and hope the sun will shine tomorrow" (Cohen and Hodges, 1963, p. 322).

2. Meaninglessness. Powerlessness, the feeling of being used for purposes not one's own, usually is accompanied by conviction of meaninglessness. The alien conditions in which an individual may be caught up tend to be unintelligible. He does not grasp the structure of the world in which he lives, cannot understand his place in

it, and never knows what to expect from it. Oriented, by need, to the present, he is relatively insensitive to sequences in time. He often does not understand the continuity of past experience and current ones. And, not only does the poor man feel unable to control future events, he cannot even predict them.

3. Anomia. The term "anomie" was originally coined to describe situations in which social standards have been broken down, or have no influence upon behavior (Durkheim, 1951, p. 253). It has subsequently been pointed out that this normless condition is a probable result of the failure of prescribed behavior to lead one to expected goals (Merton, 1949, p. 128). The life view of individuals caught in such a discrepant situation is likely to be cynical, perhaps fatalistic. For example, the poor man who is taught in many ways that economic success is the most desirable thing in life—and then is barred from legitimate means of achieving it—may come to expect that illegal behavior is necessary to reach approved goals. The situation, moreover, induces people to believe in luck. The poor are in no position to comprehend the whole of society's structure and operation, or to understand its dysfunctions. Since they also have little control over it, its impact on them is frequently fortuitous. Understandably, they are quick to credit their difficulties to fortune and chance (Merton, 1949, pp. 138, 148–149).

4. Isolation. More than any other segment of society, the very lowest economic stratum is socially isolated. The poor man not only fails to comprehend society or his community, he is out of touch with it. He reads fewer newspapers, hears fewer news programs, joins fewer organizations, and knows less of the current life of either the community or the larger world than more prosperous, better educated people do. Nor do the poor associate among themselves more than minimally (Wright and Hyman, 1958; Leighton, et al., 1963; Myers and Roberts, 1959). Experiencing separation from society and each other, it is natural for them to feel alone and detached. And feeling no identity, even with each other, they view the world as indifferent and distant—"No one is going to care much what happens to you when you get right down to it" (Seeman, 1959; Simpson and Miller, 1961).

GOALS AND VALUES

What are the aims of life in such circumstances? In a situation of relative helplessness, knowing themselves worse off than the rest of society, living on the edge of chronic emergencies, and seeing their own circumstances as formless and unpredictable, how do the poor shape their lives? What values do they hold? What goals do they seek? Essentially, they seek and value the same things as other Americans. Naturally enough, since they are American poor, they absorb characteristic American values and preferences. And, just as naturally, the realities of low economic status are visible in the lower class version of American dreams and designs. The result is a constricted but recognizable variant of society-wide goals and standards.

Increased sophistication of research on lower income and deprived groups is correcting a long-held impression that the poor place no value on occupational and educational achievement. While the poor do have a more modest absolute standard of achievement than do those who are better off, they want relatively more improvement in their condition. They value the same material comforts and luxuries. Psychologically, they seek the securities that appeal to other Americans. They hold, with little qualification, to the same proprieties of social conduct.

Interest in improving one's status, however, seems to have different sources at different levels. To the middle-class youth, the idea of having a better job than his father is appealing, sometimes absorbing. Such achievement is attractive in itself. A lower-class youngster has more urgent, material reasons for wanting an improved future. His present is painfully unsatisfactory. His urge toward better, stabler occupations is not so much drive for achievement as flight from discomfort and deprivation. It is probably stronger for that difference. (Gould, 1941)

Reality—expenses of education and training, lack of resources—usually keeps less well-off high school students from aspiring to the highest level professions. But, more than their middle-class fellows, lower-class high school students want better jobs than their fathers'. They are more likely to value increased income. In significantly greater numbers, they are unwilling to enter the same occupations as their fathers. (Empey, 1956)

Although they may not expect to achieve it, most low-income people value advanced education. It has been found that up to 65 percent of parents will say they want a college education for their children. (Bell, 1965)

Materially, the lower classes are not satisfied with poor housing or living conditions. High on their list of desirable improvements are better hous-

ing and neighborhoods. Inside their homes, they value the same things as the general run of Americans—comfortable and durable furniture, a television set, an array of electrical appliances, and, to give life grace as well as comfort, a few ornaments and art objects. Tastes in style are definitely American—modern furniture, colored telephones, pole lamps, systematic color schemes (Lewis, 1963, pp. 26, 34). It sometimes happens, as in more affluent circumstances, that materialistic values win out over real human needs. Parents stint on children's clothing to save money for a car. Older children are pressed too early into adult responsibilities because both parents are working away from the home (Lewis, 1963, p. 37). A woman postpones an operation for herself because the family must have a car or a radio. (Koos, 1954, p. 35)

In common with other Americans, the lower class enjoys excitement and values the opportunity to escape routines and pressures of day-to-day existence. Spectator sports, television, visiting—all are valued leisure-time pursuits. (Riessman, 1962, p. 28)

Probably the most basic value held by the poor is that of security. Even more than "getting ahead," they value "getting by," avoiding the worsening of an already unstable situation (Kahl, 1959, pp. 205–210). They are unwilling to take risks, and seek security rather than advancement—also a frequent pattern in economically better-off segments of the population. (Centers, 1949, p. 62)

The moral code of the very lowest class is a moot subject. It has been said that they have an entirely separate set of moral and ethical values. They have also been described as subscribing so fully to the general

American code that they are frustrated by it (Rodman, 1963). The most realistic conception seems to be that which credits them with an adapted version of society's rules of behavior. They value stable marriages, perhaps even more highly than do middle-class Americans. They do not, however, reject out of hand other forms of sex partnership. A sliding scale seems to exist, whereon a good common-law marriage is valued less than legal union, but more than a transient arrangement. Illegitimacy is not devalued to the extent that it is elsewhere. Legitimate families are the ideal, but there is also some merit ascribed to the parent who acknowledges and supports children born out of wedlock. (Lewis, 1963, p. 29).[1]

LIFE THEMES

The anomaly of life at the poverty line is evident. When people live in conditions of such obvious helplessness, when they are themselves so aware of their condition as to feel alienated and apart from society, how can they retain, much less implement, the values of that society?

The apparent answer is reinterpretation. Paths to achievement, to security, to any goal—the very quality of the goal itself—are refracted by the lower-class view of life. They are interpreted in the light of what the poor man considers to be facts about life. The helplessness which he feels, the insecurity he experiences, the meaninglessness of life—all have their effect

[1]The problem of lower-class attitudes toward "deviant" behavior is currently being researched by Dr. Hyman Rodman of the Merrill Palmer Institute (Cooperative Research Project No. 243, Welfare Administration, U.S. Dept. of Health, Education, and Welfare).

upon the way he lives and behaves.

There are four distinctive themes peculiar to lower-class behavior, all apparently the result of a deprived, alienated condition: fatalism, orientation to the present, authoritarianism, and concreteness.

The genuine powerlessness experienced by the lower class is the source of persistent fatalistic beliefs. The natural counterpart of feeling helpless is belief in uncontrollable external forces. The attitude is reminiscent of belief in fate. People cannot avoid what is going to happen to them. Resignation is the most realistic approach to life (Miller, 1958). Even when optimism is expressed, it is likely to be in terms of the working of chance —"A poor person should never give up hope; there's always a chance that a lucky break will put him on top."[2]

[2]In research supported by the Welfare Administration (Cooperative Research Project No. 125, Leonard Goodman, principal investigator) it has been found that poor people are more likely, by 13 percent, to express "strong agreement" with this statement. At less than the .05 level of confidence, the difference is statistically significant:

Economic level and degree of agreement with the statement, "A poor person should never give up hope; there's always a chance that a lucky break will put him on top."

ECONOMIC LEVEL[a]	*PERCENT INDICATING—*	
	Strong Agreement	*Little or No Agreement*
Poor (N = 169)	31	69
Not poor (N = 166)	18	82
Percent difference	13	13

[a]According to the measure developed by Morgan, et al. (1962, pp. 188–196).

This attitude acts as a definite brake on occupational and educational aspirations, and retards health care. In various other ways fatalism minimizes efforts to cope with deprivation and its consequences.

Hand in hand with fatalism goes a persistent tendency to think in terms of the present rather than the future. It is, after all, fruitless to pay attention to the distant future or try to plan life when fortune and chance are considered its basic elements. Also, when so much of one's resources must be expended simply to survive the present, little is left over for the future (LeShan, 1952).[3] Results of this ad hoc orientation are pervasive. It handicaps people for the planning required in systematic economic improvement. It works against the frugality and rainy-day planning which could offset economic dependency. In the home, it results in child-training in terms of immediate reward

---

[3]An example of this trait is a recent finding by Leonard Goodman (Welfare Administration Cooperative Research Project No. 125): Economic level and agreement with the statement, "Nowadays a person has to live pretty much for today and let tomorrow take care of itself."

| | PERCENT INDICATING— | |
ECONOMIC LEVEL	Agreement	Disagreement
Poor (N = 169)	48	52
Not poor (N = 166)	34	66
Percent difference[a]	14	14

[a]Significant at less than the .05 confidence level.

and punishment. Children quickly evince their own present-time thinking. This low concern for future goals has been shown to be related to low academic achievement (Teehan, 1958) —and the cycle continues.

The authoritarian theme is a strong underlying factor in interpersonal relationships of the poor. Generally defined, it is the embodiment of belief, more prevalent in the lower classes than elsewhere, in the validity of strength as the source of authority, and in the rightness of existing systems. It seems to arise from simplification of life experiences, in which one learns to prefer simple solutions to problems, and from constant subordination of the poor. Authoritarianism is incarnate in the habit of classifying people as either "weak" or "strong," in belief that deviance or disobedience should be severely punished, and in reliance on authority, rather than reason, as the proper source of decisions. It has traceable effects on family relations, child-rearing patterns, and relation to community institutions—schools, clinics, the police, welfare agencies, even to churches (Lipset, 1960).

Concreteness, stress on material rather than intellectual things, is a believable but little-discussed theme of lower-class life. It is natural to people preoccupied by material problems. It shows itself in verbal patterns, in distrust of intellectualism, and in occupational values.

The concrete verbal style of the poor has been well-documented (Bernstein, 1960). It is characterized by less abstraction, fewer concepts, more frequent reference to concrete objects and situations, and a less discursive manner. It includes fewer generalizations, relies less on intellectual processes than on observation, and is more tied to the world of immediate happenings and sensations.

Consistent with its patterns of speech, the lower class inclines to withhold its admiration from "eggheads," reserving it instead for the practical, down-to-earth man of action. What counts is not abstract, intellectual pursuits, but the hard tangible products of action. Results are important (Miller and Riessman, 1961).

This pragmatic orientation has a vital effect upon the occupational values of the lower classes. They have been found, at as early an age as 10 years, to value occupations for more tangible rewards rather than for intellectual or emotional ones. That is, a boy will aspire to a certain profession because of what it offers in terms of money and prestige rather than the nature of the work itself (Galler, 1951; Morse and Weiss, 1955).

SUMMARY AND IMPLICATIONS

Our lower income population is insecure and comparatively powerless in relation to the rest of American society. Realizing their submerged position, they have come to feel apart from society rather than part of it. From their own helplessness, they have generalized to the belief that most of life is uncontrollable. They are convinced of their own impotence so that, while they accept typical American values they are frequently lethargic in trying to attain them.

It would be incautious, in view of the sparseness of our knowledge, to say just what program implications such knowledge has, or what techniques of improvement are most likely to succeed. But it would be irresponsible to close this discussion without underlining the precautions it suggests:

1. The entire life situation of the poor must be considered if any part of it is to be changed. Their attitudes arise in no vacuum but are logical results of real circumstances.
2. Lower-class citizens must be brought off the periphery into the structure of the community. Nothing which the community does for them can be durably effective until they are a functioning part of the community.
3. Energetic patience must prevail. The alienated adult cannot be completely reeducated. His children can be somewhat swayed. But it is with his grandchildren that one can really have hope.

12 *Children of Suburbia*

ALICE MIEL
with EDWIN KIESTER, JR.

"Affluent" suburban children and poor children[1] are both shortchanged, but in different ways. This selection is a small portion of the findings of a four-year study designed to learn about the ways of life of children in American suburbia.

INTRODUCTION

At first glance, the community of New Village, not far from New York City, seems an idyllic place for American children to grow up in. The homes are mostly ranged along quiet, winding streets. There are open spaces, greenery, woods to explore. The churches and community centers run dances, teen programs and other youth activities. The schools are new and modern, with well-kept lawns and the latest in playground facilities; they boast a curriculum tailored mostly to students headed for college. PTA meetings are among the best-attended events in town.

Yet children miss something in New Village. You do not recognize it at first, but as you drive along the streets, you suddenly realize that all the homes are pretty much of a stripe. None are very lavish, none are very poor. The people are of a stripe, too —almost all of them are white and young or fairly young. You will look long for a dark face or an old one. New Village has many things to offer young people, but diversity is not one of them.

The residents of New Village (which is not its real name) would resent hearing their town characterized as a look-alike suburb. And indeed the community, which began as a cluster of city people's summer cottages, does have a character, individuality and charm of its own that set it apart from other suburbs—even adjoining ones. Just the same, New Village is representative of America's postwar rush to "the country"—with all that is promising and all that is

[1]See preceding article in this volume.

Reprinted from Alice Miel and Edwin Kiester, Jr., *The Shortchanged Children of Suburbia: What Schools Don't Teach about Human Differences and What Can Be Done about It* (New York: Institute of Human Relations Press of the American Jewish Committee, 1967), pp. 10–14, 43–51. By permission of the authors and the publisher.

disquieting about that movement. Like hundreds of other new communities, it is made up largely of white middle-income families, clustering together and raising their children in an atmosphere where many of the basic differences among people are fenced out.

In another period of history, this sort of self-segregation might not have mattered. But today Americans cannot afford to shut themselves off from human differences, for these differences are precisely what the chief problems of our time are about. On the domestic scene, the crucial issues of the sixties include the Negroes' drive for equality, the Government's effort to bring a share of prosperity to the impoverished, the nation's concern with the welfare of the elderly, the ecumenical movement in organized religion. On the world stage we see the growing aspirations of the underdeveloped nations, the rise of nationalism and the ascendancy of the colored races. Moreover, hardly anyone believes these prickly questions can be solved during the present generation; our children and perhaps our children's children will have to face up to them as well.

How well is suburbia—the home of vast numbers of Americans, and increasingly the trend-setter for the entire population—preparing the young people of today for such a future? Lacking first-hand contact, how do suburban children learn about human difference, and what do they think about it? How can they acquire respect for persons whom their middle-class society brands less acceptable than themselves? And what can adults —parents, school administrators, class-room teachers, community organizations—do to groom the coming generation for a proper role in a multicultural society?

The Study: Why and How

Some time ago, a group of us— teachers, sociologists and researchers from Teachers College, Columbia University—set out to shed some light on these questions. We focused on New Village as a reasonably typical American suburb.

Of course, we knew that New Village was not a precise counterpart of every suburb. No single community could be, for each has developed according to its own pattern. Some were built on open land, others grew up around an existing community. Some belong almost wholly to one social class, others have at least a small range of socio-economic difference. In some, one faith predominates; in others, religious groups are more evenly represented. Some have stopped growing while others are still increasing in size. Yet, all seem to have a number of characteristics in common. They consist almost wholly of young adults and children. Fathers commute, and mothers dominate the children's upbringing. Adults have at least a high-school education and own their homes. Parents are greatly concerned with how their youngsters are raised. In all these respects, we found, New Village strongly resembles suburbs around the country.

Our study concentrated chiefly on the elementary schools as the chief training ground for American children today. We sought to discover how suburban youngsters are taught (or not taught) about human difference, and how their attitudes toward it are shaped and molded. We hoped to find out what opportunities for such "social learning" are available in the schools, and how teachers capitalize on them. We tried to delve into the values and predispositions of parents and teachers, and to gauge their awareness of problems connected with group differences. In short, we set out to learn what kind of background a suburb provides for educating children to live in a multicultural society. We also wanted to point up the need for social lessons in schools today, and to suggest how they might be included in the curriculum.

The actual study covered four years. In that time all the teachers in three elementary schools took part in group interviews, and over 200 teachers in seven schools filled out a lengthy questionnaire. Teachers were asked what their pupils seemed to know about human difference, and also how they taught about it. Numerous meetings were held with administrators. One researcher concentrated on the students themselves, using what are known as projective techniques—for example, asking the children to comment on or interpret photographs or imaginary situations. A sociologist on our research team talked to parents of children in three schools; and two other team members (one of them the study director) conducted a workshop for members of the faculty. In addition, some comparative research was done in urban, suburban and rural localities outside New Village.

The information obtained was then sorted out according to whether it had to do with racial, socio-economic, religious, ethnic or other differences between people. The next few chapters in this pamphlet set out our findings according to the same grouping. In later chapters we outline certain broader attitudes of suburban children (and, incidentally, their elders) that bear on our subject, and discuss the potential role of schools in helping the young get better prepared for life in the modern world. The concluding chapter suggests action programs which should prove useful to educators, parents and community groups in many places besides New Village.

Some General Impressions

The study points up certain troubling aspects of growing up in New Village—and, by extension, in any suburban community. To begin with, it was found that extraordinary effort was required to bring about any encounter between a child of the suburbs and persons different from himself. In big cities today—as in the small towns of the past—youngsters are virtually certain to encounter ethnic, economic or racial diversity, in the course of their school or social life. But the suburban child's life and social contacts are far more circumscribed; in fact they are almost totally controlled by his parents, whether or not the parents recognize this. He depends on his mother to chauffeur him wherever he goes. As a result, he knows little beyond his own home, the very similar homes of friends, the school, and the inside of the family car; he is largely insulated from any chance introduction to a life different from his own.

Second, we observed that children learn to be hypocritical about differences at a very early age. At first, many said things like "I wouldn't care if a person were white or black, I'd play with him if I liked him." But on further probing, it became evident that this supposed tolerance was only skin-deep: when the same children were given any test which involved just such a choice, they almost invariably shied from choosing the Negro. The prejudices of their society were still very much with them, but they had had it drilled into them that it was "not nice" to express such feelings.

Third, group prejudices, of whatever nature, evidently take root early and go deep. Many stereotypes about race and religion cropped up even among the youngest children. Six- and seven-year-olds, for instance, pictured Negroes as poor, threatening or inferior. With such early beginnings, any fight against prejudice is bound to be a difficult uphill struggle.

Fourth, and more hopefully, the study found a good many parents united in desiring more emphasis on certain kinds of human difference. For example, they were greatly in favor of children's learning about nationality differences; many also hoped the schools would help youngsters achieve respect for other faiths and even teach what the beliefs of these faiths were.

Finally, it appears that one area of human difference is almost completely ignored in the American suburb. Many parents and teachers were found eager to bridge religious differences; many recognized, however uneasily, the need for discussion of racial differences. But with a few notable exceptions, neither parents nor schools were facing up to economic inequality. Occasionally, a social-studies class would take up the poor of other na-

tions, or a fund drive would focus attention on the less fortunate in the United States; but the fact that there were impoverished families within a stone's throw of New Village was seldom noted, and how they got there or what kept them impoverished was seldom investigated.

The overall impression one carries away is that something is missing in New Village. People who have moved to the suburbs since the Second World War often say proudly that they did so "for the children." And, of course, the children of communities like New Village do have a host of advantages, by no means all of them material. But in one aspect of their education suburban children are underprivileged. Though other races, other nationalities, other generations have a great deal to teach them, there is little in their education, formal or otherwise, to familiarize them with the rich diversity of American life.

In this sense, despite the many enviable features of their environment, the children of suburbia are being shortchanged. . . .

PORTRAIT OF THE SUBURBAN CHILD

To understand the attitudes of suburban youngsters toward human difference, one needs to know something about their values and their family milieu. For it appears that this sort of influence has as much bearing on how they regard human diversity as do their more precisely measurable feelings about Negroes, Jews, poor people or foreigners.

To draw a general profile of the suburban child and his setting, we used not only our findings in New

Village, but also comparative data from other suburbs and from cities and rural areas. These comparisons indicate that while many of our conclusions apply solely to the suburban child, some may well be true of many or most children throughout the country.

As we have already seen, the child of suburbia is likely to be a materialist and somewhat of a hypocrite. In addition, he tends to be a striver in school, a conformist, and above all a believer in being "nice," polite, clean and tidy. Besides dividing humanity into the black and the white, the Jew and the Christian, the rich and the poor, he also is apt to classify people as "smart" or "dumb," "clean" or "dirty," "nice" or "not nice." What is more, he is often conspicuously self-centered.

In all these respects the suburban child patterns his attitudes and goals chiefly after those of his parents. But he can never be sure that he won't fall short of their hopes for him—that he is measuring up to the standards (especially of academic achievement, behavior and tidiness) that they have set for him. He is therefore likely to be an anxious child. Our study as well as other inquiries indicate clearly that to grow up in an American suburb today is not a wholly enviable lot.

There is a good deal of evidence to suggest that academic striving, conformism, self-centeredness, the urge for cleanliness and order, and related traits have a bearing on how children feel about persons different from themselves.

Academic Striving

One of the foremost yardsticks children use to measure difference is academic achievement. The suburban child is quite aware of who learns quickly and who does not, who gets good grades and who does not, who is articulate and who is not. And he judges the worth of his peers accordingly.

This observation should come as no surprise. Suburban parents, schools, and communities at large use the same yardstick; they fill the atmosphere with pressure for academic attainment. This came out clearly in interviews, though they were not intended to measure people's wishes for their children's education. When the sociologist on our team asked parents why they had moved to New Village, the largest single bloc said: "To have better schools"; and when he inquired what they liked best about the community, most mentioned the school system.

"Competition here is keen and strong; the push from the home is hard in some cases," one New Village teacher wrote. "We have kids here who are making 90 and 95, and still there is a terrific push and drive. If the child drops a few points, the mother is very much concerned and the child is made conscious of it."

Other teachers said that parents often became indignant when some child was put in a higher group on the grounds of ability and their own child was left out. The barest hint of partiality brought recrimination; individual pupils couldn't even be allowed to take a book home unless there were enough books for all. And not infrequently, the teachers continued, parents paid their children for academic effort, offering rewards for high marks on report cards.

Not all the pressure came from home, however. Teachers themselves, we observed, constantly urged the children into academic striving. They, in turn, were being prodded from above. At a fall orientation meeting, school administrators told the teachers that while they must take an interest in children's moral, spiritual and social values, acquiring academic concepts was more important than any other accomplishment.

Teachers' responses to our project sometimes echoed this thinking. "How will this study influence children's values?" one teacher asked us. "We have to prepare children for passing examinations, you know." Our tests were not always welcomed. At one point, for example, we asked teachers to distribute cards with words like *parents, neighbors, friendly, lonesome, not popular.* Children were to choose one of the cards and illustrate the concept with a drawing or a few sentences, so as to give a clue to their feelings. Some teachers allowed the children to write responses, but not to draw. One refused to participate at all, because "it would encourage the children to waste time."

As for the children of New Village, they readily joined in the quest for grades. "One thing I've run into this year that really amazes me is the importance attached to marks," a new teacher commented to us. "If one child gets an 'E,' other children want to know why they didn't get one. . . . They're very, very pushy." Children also discriminated sharply against classmates who could not keep up the pace. As noted earlier, a Puerto Rican boy and a Norwegian girl were slighted because of poor reading skills. A few youngsters even refused to play with children who did not read or otherwise do as well as they themselves did.

One of our tests showed graphically how children felt about grades and academic attainment. The children were given a brief unfinished story and asked to improvise an ending for it. The story went:

"Bill (Loretta) has always wanted to be chosen as chairman of one of the committees in his (her) classroom, but the children chose other boys and girls to be chairmen. Bill (Loretta) was not chosen because—"

Most frequently, the gist of the suggested endings was that Bill or Loretta had been passed over because of poor grades, not being smart enough, or poor performance in school subjects:

"Bill did not keep up with his classwork because he never did his homework. So he was not chosen for chairman."

"Loretta was not chosen because she couldn't spell and she could not do her arithmetic either, so the children didn't like her."

"Loretta was not a very intelligent girl. She had always gotten fair marks but her teacher always picked brighter children."

A second test asked students to complete the sentence, "Things would be better at school if—" Many of the responses stressed the need for obeying teachers and studying harder:

"Kids should do their homework and school work and not try to goof off."

"Things would be better if I could learn and do my work."

"It would be better if you would do your homework and bring it in when you are told and never get reported on."

These findings suggest that discrimination by suburban children does not necessarily fit the pattern we expect it to fit. The Negro or Puerto Rican, for instance, may be looked down on, not because of his race or ethnic origin, but because his background of deprivation has not allowed him to keep up with his school work. The academic record of one member of a minority group can of course be used to brand the whole group; the Puerto Rican boy with the reading problem may have led his classmates to label all Puerto Ricans backward or stupid.

The Blanket of Conformity

Passion for conformity seems to be a second trait which affects the suburban child's feelings toward "different" people. Our studies show clearly that he takes a dim view of anyone—adults, children, even himself—who deviates from the norm, and that he places a premium on being exactly what adults want him to be.

In New Village, at least, this is just what parents desire. We asked certain parents there whether they agreed with the statement: "Obedience and respect for authority are the most important virtues children can learn." The conformist response was extremely high, compared with findings of studies elsewhere. Of 47 fathers and 42 mothers questioned, 75 (or 84 per cent) agreed with the statement—31 strongly, 34 moderately, 10 slightly. Seventy-five per cent expressed strong or moderate agreement with a second statement: "Young people sometimes get rebellious ideas, but as they grow up they ought to get over them and settle down."

These parents would not have been disappointed by their children's responses to similar questions. When we asked children to complete the sentence, "Things would be better at school if—" we frequently got answers on the order of "All children should listen to their teachers," or "Everyone should pay attention and obey all the rules."

Of 258 fifth- and sixth-grade children who answered a questionnaire, more than half agreed with the statement that teachers should be more strict; more than a third agreed that teachers should tell children what to do, not try to find out what children want. Sixty per cent agreed that "if adults don't like what you're doing you know you are behaving badly."

In follow-up interviews, some children went even further. "What do you do when you're good?" we asked primary graders. "Do what they say I should do" or "Do things I'm asked to do" was the most common answer. Some children used the feminine pronoun, presumably referring to their mothers or teachers: "Do what she tells me to do" or "Listen to her and do what she wants."

While some of these answers could be construed as healthy respect for elders, that is not the whole story, as the children's overt attitudes toward other topics made clear. We observed, and teachers agreed, that the children thought it more important to get along with the system than to stand up for whatever they personally felt. They also judged other children by whether they conformed; anyone who did not was an outcast. "They tend to dislike another child when he can't get along with the group," one teacher explained. Sociability was the goal.

When we finally compared all of the children's responses, we found certain common threads running through them. Generally speaking, New Village children seemed to feel there was a single norm of behavior, considered conformity and academic achievement necessary for success, depended excessively on parents, blamed themselves when they failed to measure up to established standards, and believed there was always one right answer, dictated by authority. In short, they were confined to a narrow view of what people are and should be like.

Looking Out for Number One

The suburban child's self-centered and materialistic attitudes, besides bearing on his ideas about economic difference among people, have many other dimensions.

An earlier chapter describes a test in which New Village children were asked to name three wishes they would most like to have fulfilled. In one phase of our research, we concentrated on four sixth-grade groups and compared the results with similar replies by children in other communities: the core of a large Eastern city, some farm areas and some nearby suburbs. The responses were again classified as material or nonmaterial, and as being "for self" or "for others."

The tabulations showed New Village children clearly preoccupied with themselves. In one group, each child uttered at least two wishes on his own behalf. The majority of these wishes was nonmaterial. In the other three sixth grades, small percentages made wishes for others, all of them nonmaterial except in the case of one child. The responses were not unlike

those of groups outside New Village, although several of the latter, also in suburban areas, produced larger numbers of nonmaterial wishes for others.

Further sorting of the answers afforded some striking findings. The number of nonmaterial wishes rose with parental income and occupational status; the percentage was almost twice as high among children of professionals and managers as among those of the semi-skilled. The number of nonmaterial wishes also rose with children's vocabulary skills. (Those with the highest skills, of course, came from homes with the highest education and income levels.) Other findings confirmed that income and deprivation were controlling factors: more Negroes than whites expressed material wishes for themselves; and Jews, who in this instance came from high-income families, made more nonmaterial wishes—both for themselves and for others—than did Protestants and Catholics, whose responses were roughly identical.

Many of the nonmaterial responses reflected the suburban child's tensions and preoccupations. A great number of suburban children made wishes having to do with illness and death. "I wish I would never get sick," was a common response. So was "I hope my father and mother never die." Many other wishes dealt with academic achievement—"I wish I would get good grades and the teacher would like me" was typical.

All this would seem to indicate that sixth-grade children in New Village and similar suburban communities are almost totally wrapped up in themselves, whether they wish for material gain or nonmaterial benefits. They evidently have few thoughts of others, and even these few are mostly concentrated on persons close to them. Here and there, an answer betrays awareness of the outer world; a handful of responses had to do with social problems such as world health or racial prejudice, and there were some "material" wishes like "I wish I had money to stamp out illness." Generally, however, the children's wishes ended with themselves, highlighting one of the hurdles that must be cleared before suburban children can understand the nature of human difference.

"Nice and Tidy"

What was perhaps the most startling finding of all our studies related only indirectly to children's attitudes toward other people. It was the depth and breadth of their concern with neatness, cleanliness, tidiness, "being nice." Although we had been dimly aware of this passion when we began the study, we were not aware of its true dimensions, nor were the cooperating teachers.

The obsession with neatness was most notably brought to light by a test originally designed to delve into feelings about "different" people. We asked children to complete the following story:

"The Jones family like their home very much. They have worked hard to make it a nice, comfortable place to live. Then some new people moved next door to them. This disturbed the Joneses so much that they want to sell their home and move away from the neighborhood.

"1. The people who moved in probably were—

"2. The Joneses wanted to move away because—

"3. What do you think about the Joneses' reason for wanting to move?"

We had anticipated that children would speculate on the new neighbors' religion or, more likely, their race. Instead, 107 out of 270 said the new neighbors were "dirty." Some elaborated, adding that the newcomers "left garbage all over the lawn," or that "beer cans and lots of other trash" were strewn about. Others talked about how the value of the Joneses' property had been affected. A few went on at great length, stringing out adjectives to detail the new neighbors' offensive behavior.

Eleven per cent of the children said noise was the problem: the new neighbors had all-night parties, yelled at each other or made too much racket while moving in. Many mentioned a combination of noise and dirt; altogether, 55 per cent of the answers included one or both of these reasons, and in one group 90 per cent did. Others used more general words like "sloppy," "messy" and "disturbing," and 10 per cent said things like "The people were not nice," "disagreeable" or "unpleasant."

Interestingly, only seven children specifically mentioned race, religion or color as in any way related to the Joneses' moving away, and all of these went on to indicate they did not sanction such a reason. Yet the offenses listed closely resemble the common stereotype of the Negro as an "undesirable" neighbor. Quite possibly, New Village children, steeped in the notion that to express race prejudice is "not nice," used "dirt" and "noise" as cover-ups for their real feelings.

The same concern with dirt and noise turned up throughout the study in answer to other questions. "What do you like about and what would you like to see changed in your neighborhood, school and family?" we asked at one point. "I like my neighborhood because everyone keeps the outside nice and clean," one girl wrote. Others said:

"The kids I play with are clean-cut and nice."

"It's a quiet neighborhood."

"We are happy, neat and quiet."

Those who wanted changes mentioned things like, "Yard and cellar fixed up, house fixed up too," and "Mother cleans the house every day and we're not allowed past the basement."

The many responses stressing neatness and "being nice" indicate, we believe, that often, the really central values of the suburban child's life are cleanliness and order. It seems clear that the child's attitude toward "different" people is shaped, not only by their evident racial or religious differences, but also—perhaps even mainly—by their actual or supposed deviation from his strict and orderly norms.

For a Better Balance of Values

Amid the current "knowledge explosion," it is undeniably of value to our society that so many of the young appreciate the importance of education. A reasonable respect for authority and sense of self-interest are equally desirable traits. And at a time when the bulldozer and the wrecking ball are making rampageous headway across the nation, a generation with strong feelings about beauty can be a decided asset.

But these feelings, when exaggerated, can distort a child's judgment of people and do serious harm to the fabric of our varied society. It is therefore important for parents, schools and the general community to help balance such one-sided preoccupations with other important human values.

13 Effects of Social Class and Race on Responsiveness to Approval and Disapproval[1]

DAVID L. ROSENHAN

Rosenhan proposes a theory of social-class behavior in which lower-class children are presumed to be more alienated from and uncomfortable with middle-class people and institutions than middle-class children. As a consequence of alienation, it is deduced that relative to middle-class children, approval should facilitate the performance of lower-class children, whereas disapproval should retard it. Using 72 first-grade boys as subjects in this study, Rosenhan substantiates his hypothesis. There are no performance differences between lower-class Negro and white children, which indicates that for young children social-class differences are more potent determinants of behavior than racial differences. The implications of the data for longer term performance are noted.

Recent concern with the academic failure of the culturally deprived or the culturally different has yielded a number of hypotheses regarding the potential sources of this failure (cf. Passow, 1963; Riessman, 1962). Since the term culturally deprived implies primarily lower-class children, and particularly those who are nonwhite, these hypotheses have sought to explain the failures of these children in terms of characteristics that are presumed to be possessed primarily by the lower class. Thus, their relatively impoverished status is seen as relevant to their academic failure. So, too, their transient status in the community, their unstable parental iden-

[1]This research was supported in part by Grant HD–01762–01 from the National Institute of Child Health and Human Development, United States Public Health Service. Gratitude is expressed to Arthur Kender who collected the data, to Albert Beaton and Henrietta Gallagher who performed the analyses, and to Anthony Greenwald, Paul Jacobs, and Nathan Kogan who commented on the manuscript.

Reprinted from the *Journal of Personality and Social Psychology*, 1966, **4**, 253-259, by permission of the author and the American Psychological Association.

tifications, their negative self-images, the degree to which they are encouraged to achieve—all these and others are seen as potential sources for the academic performance discrepancies between young children from the lower and middle classes (cf. Passow, 1963, for a discussion of these issues).

Empirical research in this area has been meager and, to a large extent, inconclusive. Douvan (1956) has reported that lower-class children are less responsive to the idea of being correct than middle-class children. Zigler and Kanzer (1962) demonstrated further that middle-class children were more responsive to abstract reinforcers, that is, reinforcers directed at performance, while lower-class children responded more to concrete reinforcers, or those reinforcers that generally connoted praise. However, a replication of this study by Rosenhan and Greenwald (1965) did not bear out the findings. No differences were found between middle- and lower-class children in their tendency to respond to performance (i.e., abstract) or person (i.e., concrete) reinforcers.

The present study takes a social class interaction position (cf. Clark, 1963; Rosenhan, 1965) and examines the notion that the lower-class child may be more alienated than the middle-class child in a middle-class school system. Taking alienation to mean a lack of relationship with one's environment (English and English, 1958) and particularly an inability to comprehend environmental expectancies, the argument runs as follows: For the middle-class child, the middle-class school may be seen as an extension of his middle-class home.

Often, long before he has entered first grade, he anticipates going to school and has learned something about school from his parents. Commonly enough, he has been introduced to some of the materials that he will subsequently encounter in school. Moreover, he is reasonably familiar with middle-class institutions and is comfortable with middle-class people. Thus, for this child, the school is a comfortable situation with which he often has prior familiarity. For the lower-class child, however, the situation may be quite different. In his environment, attending school may not be an especially high-status activity. He has probably received little if any of the vicarious and anticipatory reinforcement that the middle-class child receives prior to going to school. Indeed, what with the larger family that he tends to come from and the greater need for both of his parents to be employed, the school may have subtly acquired negative reinforcing properties in the sense that it may be viewed as a repository in order to permit the parents greater freedom. From whatever source, then, it is conceivable that the lower-class child experiences greater alienation in middle-class institutions and with middle-class people than does the middle-class child.

In the present study we examine one hypothesis derivable from the above proposition: If lower-class children are more alienated in a middle-class institution, they should be more responsive to praise than middle-class children would be. By the same token, the performance of lower-class children should be more disrupted by disapproval than that of their middle-class peers. In general, the relationship of a lower-class child to middle-class institutions can be viewed in much the same way that a Westerner might experience, say, an Oriental wedding. Feeling quite unfamiliar with the rites and rituals, he would be more delighted than an Oriental would be by a remark that approved of his behavior. On the other hand, having done something that evoked disapproval, he would be more disturbed by the criticism than would one who was relatively more at home at such ceremonies.

In order to test the hypothesis, a middle-class male experimenter verbally reinforced the performance of first-grade lower- and middle-class subjects in a binary-choice game. Half of the subjects were given positive reinforcement when they made the correct response. No reinforcement was offered for incorrect responses. The remaining subjects were given negative reinforcement for incorrect responses, with no reinforcement given for correct responses.

It has been suggested (Riessman, 1962) that the Negro lower-class child suffers an especial handicap in that his color leads him to acquire a negative-identity image more rapidly and more deeply than the white child. We examine this hypothesis in this experiment by considering separately the effects of disapproval and approval on white and Negro lower-class children. (Negro middle-class children were not available for this study.) If both the alienation and the negative-identity hypotheses are correct, then Negro children should be more positively affected by approval than white children and more negatively affected by disapproval.

METHOD

Subjects

Subjects were 72 first-grade boys who were drawn from two public schools of mixed socioeconomic class.[2] Socioeconomic class was determined on the basis of parental occupation (Warner, Meeker, and Eells, 1949, p. 140). Subjects were randomly assigned to the approval and disapproval conditions. Twenty-four subjects were middle- and 48 were lower-class children. Of the lower-class children, half were Negro and half were white. A comparable Negro middle-class sample could not be obtained. Table 1 describes the composition of the groups.

A middle-class white male experimenter conducted the study. He was told that the experiment dealt with the effects of approval and disapproval on probability learning, but was not aware of the social class hypotheses. Nor did he realize that the subjects had been presorted on the basis of social class and race.

Apparatus

A black metal box, measuring $7 \times 12 \times 7$ inches, served as the binary-choice apparatus. Mounted on the lower right and left corners of the panel was a toggle-type automatic-return switch which the subject manipulated. The subject's responses activated either of two lights on the experimenter's clipboard indicating which lever the subject had depressed. The experimenter then responded accordingly. The apparatus is described fully in Rosenhan (in press).

[2]The assistance of the Trenton School System, and particularly of Olive Brown, director of instruction, Lester Blinn, and Merle Lloyd, principals, is gratefully acknowledged.

TABLE 1.—Composition of the Sample and Performance of the Subjects ($N = 12$ in Each Group)

SUBJECT GROUP	CA[a]		SOCIOECONOMIC CLASS		RESPONSES TO LEFT LEVER (PERCENTAGE OF 160 TRIALS)	
	M	Range	M	Range	M	Range
Middle-class white						
Approval	6:1	5:10–6:6	1.4	1–3	60	04
Disapproval	6:2	5:11–6:4	1.4	1–3	62	03
Lower-class white						
Approval	6:2	5:10–6:7	5.8	5–7	64	06
Disapproval	6:3	5: 9–6:8	6.0	5–7	55	04
Lower-class Negro						
Approval	6:3	5:11–6:10	6.4	6–7	63	09
Disapproval	6:1	5: 9–6:11	6.0	5–7	55	04

[a]At time of testing.

Procedure

The experimenter met the subject outside of his classroom and chatted with him on the way to the experimental room. Once inside, the subject was seated before a low table on which was the binary-choice game. The experimenter instructed the child in the use of the switches and, for the approval condition, told him that "each time you press the right button, I will say 'right.'" For the disapproval condition, the instructions were reversed, namely, "each time you press the wrong button, I will say 'wrong.'" The instructions were repeated several times.

Prior to the training trials, the subject was administered four practice trials, for which the first and last trials were correct (i.e., they were reinforced for the approval condition; for the disapproval condition the second and third practice trials were negatively reinforced).

When it was clear that the subject understood the instructions, he was administered 160 training trials. A reinforcement ratio of 70 : 30 to the left and right levers, respectively, was employed. That is, for the approval condition the left lever was positively reinforced 70% of the time, and the right lever 30% of the time. For the disapproval condition the reinforcement ratio was reversed— 70% of the right and 30% of the left lever presses were negatively reinforced.

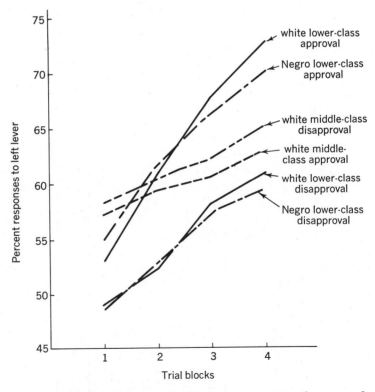

Fig. 1. Mean performance of subjects by experimental group and blocks of 40 trials.

Reinforcements were randomized in blocks of 20 trials. Thus, the response behavior demanded—pressing the left lever—was the same for both the approval and disapproval conditions and constituted the dependent variable for this study.

RESULTS

Three analyses of variance were applied to the mean performance data shown in Table 1. The first analysis considered the effects of approval and disapproval on lower-class children. It examined whether Negro and white boys responded differentially to these reinforcers. As will be seen in Table 2, no race differences emerged either as main effects or in interaction with other variables. The effects of reinforcers were such that lower-class children were much more responsive to approval than to disapproval.

The trials' main effect in this as in the subsequent analysis indicates that the tendency to respond to the left lever increased over the four blocks of trials. The subject's performance began at or near the 50% level and increased as he gained more experience with the reinforcement contingencies. The interaction between trials and the reinforcer valence demonstrated that the subject's tendency to respond to the left lever rose under approval conditions but remained relatively stable (and low) under conditions of disapproval. Figure 1 presents the data across trials for these lower-class subjects and for the middle-class subjects.

The second analysis of variance (Table 2) examined the responsiveness of lower- and middle-class white children to approval and disapproval. Again, the main effects of the reinforcement dimension were significant. However, they interacted with social class such that compared to middle-class boys, the performance of lower-class boys was facilitated by approval and retarded by disapproval.

Looking now to the between blocks-of-trials analysis, we find that the main effects of trials are marked: The subjects' performances improve over trials. The Trials × Social Class interaction is seen in Figure 1, where the early performance of lower-class subjects in the approval condition is below that of middle-class subjects in either condition. Terminal performance of lower-class subjects under approval is, however, higher than that of any other group.

Approximately similar results obtained from the third analysis which considered the effects of approval and disapproval on lower-class Negroes and middle-class whites (Table 2). While the overall effect of approval was greater than that of disapproval, lower-class Negroes performed better with approval and worse with disapproval than did middle-class whites. And while the performance of all groups improved over the four blocks of trials, the amount of improvement for Negroes in the approval condition (whose initial performance was below that of the middle-class boys in either condition) was substantially greater than it was for middle-class whites.

DISCUSSION

It is clear from these data that identical reinforcers—approval or disapproval—have differential effects ac-

TABLE 2.—Summary of the Analyses of Variance for the Color and Class Comparisons

SOURCE	DF	I LOWER CLASS: WHITE VERSUS NEGRO SUBJECTS		II WHITE SUBJECTS: LOWER VERSUS MIDDLE CLASS		III LOWER-CLASS NEGRO VERSUS MIDDLE-CLASS WHITE	
		MS	F	MS	F	MS	F
Between subjects							
Groups (A)	1	1.5052	.06	16.9216	1.27	28.5208	1.30
Reinforcers (B)	1	577.5469	22.05[a]	97.7552	7.32[a]	102.0833	4.65[b]
A × B	1	.0469	.00	194.0052	14.53[a]	200.0833	9.12[a]
Error (b)	44	26.1928		13.3509		21.9461	
Within subjects							
Trials (C)	3	313.4219	125.39	179.8108	158.26[a]	133.1875	71.94[a]
A × C	3	3.8108	1.52	38.6302	34.00[a]	19.4097	10.48[a]
B × C	3	13.3524	5.34[a]	4.5469	4.00[a]	1.3889	.75
A × B × C	3	1.0191	.41	6.4358	5.66[a]	2.3889	1.29
Error (w)	132	2.4995		1.1362		1.8513	

[a] $p < .05$.
[b] $p < .01$.

cording to the social class of the subject. Taking performance to mean the number of times the subjects pressed the left lever, the performance of lower-class subjects was substantially improved under conditions of approval relative to middle-class subjects. Under conditions of disapproval, however, lower-class boys performed more poorly than their middle-class peers.

The data are consistent with the view that lower-class children, at least on entry into middle-class institutions and with middle-class people, are unfamiliar with their surroundings and therefore experience a greater sense of alienation than do middle-class boys. This presumed sense of alienation leaves them especially sensitive to external social reinforcers that convey approval or disapproval of their behavior. Unable, as it were, to assure themselves that they are legitimate members of the environment in which they find themselves, they rely more heavily than middle-class children on external indexes of the quality of their performance.

At the same time we have an instance where alienation is not necessarily deleterious to performance. If learning is viewed as the tendency to respond to the more reinforced lever, then for lower-class children, approval facilitated learning. And while the paradigm is limited to a brief experimental event and to a small sample of performance, the data are sufficiently encouraging to speculate that the longer term effects of middle-class approval might produce a generally elevated performance in lower-class children. Long-term disapproval, on the other hand, might

have relatively enduring opposite effects, reducing the performance of lower-class children far below what it might be under other conditions.

It is also possible and consistent with the above interpretation that lower- and middle-class children differ in their approaches to a positively reinforced binary choice game. While children of both classes may recognize that the left lever is correct more often than the right one, middle-class children employ a problem-solving approach, attempting to get each item correct. Lower-class children, on the other hand, may tend to employ the more conservative strategy of maximizing their correct responses. Such differences in strategy are consistent with the relative incentive value of praise for lower- and middle-class children, since, in general, the greater the value of the reward the more the subject will tend to maximize (cf. Tune, 1964; Weir, 1964).

Under conditions of negative reinforcement, a problem-solving approach might similarly hold for middle-class children, the problem in this instance being the avoidance of wrong responses. Maximizing, on the other hand, makes little psychological sense where negative reinforcement is concerned, since locating rewards may be more important for the subject than avoiding punishment.

A problem-solving versus maximizing interpretation of these data, however, is limited by the fact that the children apparently did not achieve asymptotic performance (see Figure 1). Clearly, additional trials would have been necessary in order to reach asymptote, yet it is doubtful that such young children could have handled more trials. Moreover, an internal analysis of responses, such as the number of consecutive times the subject depressed the left lever (cf. Rosenhan, 1966) was not possible in this study because the responses to the levers were summarized on counters, rather than individually recorded. Nevertheless, a strategy interpretation remains a distinct possibility for these data.

Alternative Interpretations of These Findings

DIFFERENTIAL CHILD-REARING PRACTICES IN LOWER- AND MIDDLE-CLASS HOMES: THE EFFECT OF REINFORCER ADAPTATION AND VARIABILITY Sears, Maccoby, and Levin (1957) have shown that social classes differ in their methods of child rearing. Specifically, lower-class parents are more prone to employ physical punishment with their children while middle-class parents use verbal persuasions and penalties. It is conceivable that by the time the middle-class child is 6 years old, he has become relatively adapted to (satiated on?) verbal reinforcers such that neither approval nor disapproval affect him deeply or differentially. For lower-class children, however, who are relatively less adapted to verbal methods of behavior control, approval and disapproval have more potent effects.

There is in fact some experimental evidence that can be interpreted to support the notion that middle-class children are to some extent satiated on verbal reinforcers. Gewirtz and Baer (1958, 1958a) compared the responses to approval of children who had been experimentally satiated with or deprived of approval for a brief period of time. They found that compared to a matched untreated control group, deprived children were more responsive to approval. Subsequent evidence (Rosenhan, 1967) demonstrated that deprived subjects were more responsive to both approval and disapproval than were satiated subjects. The combined data would be consistent with the view that young middle-class children are relatively adapted to verbal reinforcement regardless of valence, that their responsiveness to such reinforcers increases only after periods of deprivation. While comparable data are not available for lower-class children, they might conceivably be more "deprived of sociality" than their middle-class peers and hence more responsive to it (cf. Zigler, 1961; Zigler and Williams, 1963).

If there is some difficulty with this interpretation, it rests with the strong effects of disapproval on lower-class children. For while lower-class parents tend to utilize physical means of punishment, they do not use such means exclusively. Presumably it is combined with verbal disapproval such that lower-class children ought to have become adapted to both kinds of disapproval, or perhaps to disapproval in general. Their performance in the disapproval condition, relative to middle-class children, indicates clearly that this is not the case, weakening thereby a child-rearing interpretation of these data or requiring a more complex model.

ANXIETY The data are clearly interpretable within an anxiety framework; namely, lower-class children are more anxious in a middle-class setting than are middle-class children. Thus, for lower-class children, approval reduces anxiety while disapproval heightens it. Since middle-class children, on the other hand, are presumed to be quite secure in this setting, neither approval nor disapproval affects them strongly.

Such an interpretation is not inconsistent with an alienation view of lower-class children's behavior in that these children may be anxious because they are alienated. Offered by itself, of course, an anxiety interpretation gives no clue as to why lower-class children should be more anxious. And since no independent measures of anxiety were obtained it was felt that the alienation interpretation offered was the more appropriate one at this time.

INTELLIGENCE Probability learning has been conceptualized as a problem-solving task in which the subject devises strategies to maximize his gain (i.e., to get the most correct answers). As such, one might expect intelligence to play something of a role. Numerous studies have shown that relative to the lower class, middle-class children possess superior IQs (cf. Deutsch and Brown, 1964), and one would therefore have expected such children to have performed better under all conditions. Since this did not in fact occur, an interpretation that rests on social class differences in intelligence is not appropriate to these data.

Class versus Color

While there is considerable evidence that young children are perceptive of and sensitive to racial differences, these differences do not appear to affect their responsiveness to verbal reinforcement. Ordinarily, one might have expected Negro lower-class children to experience most alienation with a middle-class white experimenter, by virtue of the combined effects of both class and color differences. Thus, their responsiveness to both approval and disapproval should have been heightened relative to lower-class white children. Since this did not occur it can be argued that, at least for very young boys, social class differences rather than color differences are the critical variables that determine responsiveness in reinforcement situations. It should be noted that a similar failure to obtain differences between Negro and white lower-class children, this time in a simple conditioning task, occurred previously (Rosenhan and Greenwald, 1965).

Clearly, the failure to obtain race differences in performance in two studies may simply reflect the restricted range of the experimental paradigms employed. Perhaps different experimental tasks or conditions might have elicited the presumed racial differences. At the same time, we note that this experiment *was* sufficiently sensitive to distinctions of social class which were presumably based on the same dynamics of alienation that should have affected Negro behavior more deeply than in fact they did. Thus, the argument that the experiment considers a restricted range of behavior is only partially compelling.

It is also possible that the tendency to be sensitive to racial differences reflects primarily the tendency to distinguish people and behaviors that are within one's social class from those that are outside of it. In other words, racial differences may be one aspect of social class differences, particularly insofar as relatively few Negroes are in the middle class. In any event, it seems clear that as far as the performance of young children is concerned (as distinguished from perceptions and attitudes), class is far more significant than color.

With His Family

4

14 The Accuracy of Parental Recall of Aspects of Child Development and of Child Rearing Practices[1]

LILLIAN CUKIER ROBBINS

On the basis of this and similar studies it is suggested that retrospective studies of child-rearing practices should no longer be acceptable. In the following three-year longitudinal study, begun with the birth of the child, despite the frequent rehearsal of child-rearing practices, retrospective parent accounts are quite inaccurate. Inaccuracies are greatest for items dealing with age of weaning and toilet training, occurrence of thumbsucking, and demand feeding. Inaccuracies tend to be in the direction of the recommendations of experts in child rearing, and of fathers recalling less correctly than mothers.

[1]This paper is based on a PhD dissertation submitted to the Graduate School of Arts and Science at New York University. The author wishes to thank Elsa E. Robinson and M. Brewster Smith for their valuable suggestions and helpful editorial criticism, Sidney Weinstein for his advice on statistical design, and Edwin S. Robbins for his invaluable assistance. The author is also grateful to Stella Chess and Alexander Thomas for making the data and sample of their longitudinal study of child development available. The research was supported in part by the Margaret E. Maltby Fellowship of the American Association of University Women.

Reprinted from the *Journal of Abnormal and Social Psychology*, 1963, **66**, 261–270, by permission of the author and the American Psychological Association.

The accuracy with which parents can recall and report, after a period of years, details of the early functioning of their children and of their own child care practices is a significant issue in view of the large number of investigations which have used retrospective parental reports as their primary data. Tests of theories of personality development, and discussions of similarities and differences in the child rearing patterns of various class and color groups (see, e.g., Davis and Havighurst, 1946; Miller and Swanson, 1958; Sears, Maccoby, and Levin, 1957), have been based on such data, often without sufficient regard for possible factual errors.

Only three studies have so far attempted to evaluate the extent to which retrospective reports of developmental data are accurate. The first two (McGraw and Molloy, 1941; Pyles, Stolz, and Macfarlane, 1935) demonstrated that inaccuracy is frequent, by comparing mothers' recollections with the observation of experts. Since there is no way of knowing which mothers, if any, had ever been aware of the highly specific material they were asked to remember, it is impossible to determine whether discrepancies were due to errors in the mothers' original perceptions, to differences in the frame of reference of experts and mothers, or to errors in recall. A more recent longitudinal study (Haggard, Brekstad, and Skard, 1960) has examined the reliability of maternal memory, as well as its validity. Maternal reports and independent observations were compared with the recollections of mothers as much as 8 years later. For

items dealing with such attitudinal questions as anxiety regarding childbirth and strength of wish for a given sex, reliability was lower than for the more factual questions, such as the birth weight. Where validity was ascertainable, R ranged from .71 to .89.

The present study endeavors to examine accuracy of recall by comparing retrospective accounts of child rearing obtained from parents of 3-year-olds with reports they previously gave in the course of a longitudinal study begun with the birth of the child (Thomas and Chess, 1957). It differs from other appraisals of parental accuracy by focusing on objective, nonattitudinal, yet long-term aspects of child development, such as the onset of toilet training and the duration of weaning—items which form the basis for most descriptive and comparative studies of child rearing patterns. Since it is not feasible to have an observer live with families for prolonged periods of time, there can only be assessment of the consistency of parental reports for material of this sort, and not of its validity.

The sample used is particularly favorable for maximizing the accuracy of recall since continued participation in the longitudinal study ensured parents' original awareness of the information sought. In addition, this is a middle-class group, whose practices are predominantly child centered, with the mothers accepting care of the baby as their prime responsibility, so that it can be presumed that maximum attention has been paid to details of the child's functioning.

This report will deal with two aspects of parental recall: the accuracy of retrospective parental reports,[2] and the relationship between errors in retrospective parental reports and recommendations made by authorities in the child rearing field.

METHOD

Subjects

The broader longitudinal study, in progress since March 1956, has been mainly directed at exploring the relationship between initial patterns of reactivity in infants, and subsequent personality development (Chess, Thomas, and Birch, 1959; Chess, Thomas, Birch, and Hertzig, 1960; Thomas, Birch, Chess, and Robbins, 1961; Thomas and Chess, 1957; Thomas, Chess, Birch, and Hertzig, 1960). Parents have been seen at frequent intervals and their participation in the study has been extensive. Interviews have been held, usually with both mother and father present, every 3 months during the child's first year, and at 6-month intervals thereafter. Questions were designed to elicit objective and specific description of the child's be-

---

[2]While it could be argued that only the consistency of retrospective reports is being measured when parental reports at two points in time are compared, it should be borne in mind that the original data were gathered close to the time of occurrence of events and are objective and noninterpretative in content. In addition, independent observations of children in this study showed that concurrent parental descriptions are valid (Thomas, Chess, Birch, and Hertzig, 1960). As a result, agreement between parental recall and original parental descriptions of the same events and behaviors can be held to represent accuracy rather than mere consistency of report.

havior during the normal routines of daily living, with items of a type which parents can usually answer easily and without defensiveness. Parents were used as the observers since their intimate contact with the child serves to make them the best reporters of consistent patterns and long-range activities. Other procedures have included independent observations of the children in order to check the validity of concurrent parental reports, the Stanford-Binet at 3 years, and direct observations in nursery school.

When the retrospective interviews were conducted, in the spring of 1959, 49 children of the families under study were approximately 3 years old. Recurrent illness and a recent divorce made scheduling impossible in two cases, so that only 47 families could be interviewed. Six fathers were not seen: four were no longer living with their wives, who had custody of the child; no appointment could be made with another because of the pressures of his business; and one family had moved to the midwest so that only the mother could be interviewed on one of her visits to New York.

In order to make this study more directly comparable to others, the data for three nonwhite families, among them one of the divorced couples, have not been included. As a result, the sample consists of 44 mothers and 39 fathers. All but five of the mothers have attended college, and many have advanced degrees in medicine, law, or psychology. The majority of the men work in a professional or executive capacity, and, with the exception of five, have gone to college. Most hold advanced degrees. The group is predominantly Jewish and is located in the Greater New York area. Its socioeconomic status is uniformly high, with the two men who have had no schooling beyond high school at the upper extreme. The median age of the children at the time of interview was 37.0 months, with a range of 29–45 months.

Procedure

Appointments were arranged through the project secretary, who had a long-standing acquaintance with the parents in the study. On the night of the interview, the author and her husband, a psychiatrist, arrived at the parents' home and introduced themselves. Arrangements

were made so that interviews could simultaneously be held in two different rooms. This technique made possible the assessment of individual attitudes and recall in a way that joint interviews with both parents could not achieve. At the same time, it eliminated the contamination which might ensue if parents were interviewed one after the other.

On the basis of a prearranged scheme, each interviewer spoke to a father on one visit and to a mother on the next. Tape recorders were used to ensure a complete record of the interviews and to eliminate

TABLE 1.—Description of the 19 Memory Items

AREA AND ITEM	QUANT.	QUAL.	RECOMMENDATION
Feeding			
C3. Schedule vs. demand?		X	demand
C4. Breast vs. bottle?		X	breast
C4b. If breast—how long?	X		7–10 months
C5. Cereal—when introduced?	X		
Weaning			
D1. Cup—when introduced?	X		5 months
D2a. Bottle—when stop?	X		by 24 months
D2b. If stop—type of transition?		X	
Sucking			
D3. Ever suck thumb?		X	opposes
D4. Ever suck pacifier?		X	favors
Toilet training			
Fla. Bowel training—when begun?	X		18–24 months
Fla. Bladder training—when begun?	X		18–24 months
Sleeping			
G5a. 2 A.M. feeding—when stopped?	X		
G5b. 10 P.M. feeding—when stopped?	X		
G5c. How well sleep at 6 months?		X	
Motor development			
I1. When first stood alone?	X		
I1a. When first walked alone?	X		
Medical history			
L2. First injection—when?	X		
L4. Birth weight?	X		
L4a. Birth length?	X		

Note.—Key: Quant. = Quantitative item: Qual. = Qualitative item. Recommendation = Advice of Spock (1957) regarding parental practices. Spock has been used as the authority, since all the parents in this sample were familiar with his writings. X signifies the presence of the category heading a given column.

the need for writing lengthy verbatim notes as well as the danger of selective recording. The interviewers possessed no information beyond the name and age of the child, and no previous attempt had been made to collect retrospective information.

The interviews, based on a specially designed interview guide, were primarily concerned with obtaining descriptions of parental behavior from which attitudes could be inferred.[3] The responses to the memory items, which took but a small fraction of the time spent in talking with the parents, were written in the course of the interview so as to expedite analysis of the present data. Table 1 cites the 19 memory questions that will be discussed in this report.

Immediately after the interview, which lasted anywhere from 1.5 to 3 hours, each parent was asked to fill out a modified version of the Schaefer and Bell (1957 unpublished, 1958) Parental Attitude Research Instrument. The scale was administered in order to obtain an objective and rapid measure of parental attitudes, which could be compared with the ratings based on the more extensive focused interviews.

While the parents were thus occupied, each interviewer had the opportunity to write a summary describing his impressions of the parent's personality and attitudes.

Scoring

After editing the retrospective records for ambiguities, the interview responses were tabulated in accordance with the

---

[3]The interview guide and all measures pertaining to recall are described and presented in Robbins (1961). An analysis of the attitudinal material is currently under way.

following conventions:

1. Ages were converted to weeks and weight to ounces, so as to obviate fractions.

2. Ranges were transformed into means. For example, if a parent said that something had happened between 3 and 4 months, his response was scored as "15 weeks."

3. Guesses were counted as actual responses but were set off by parentheses, so as to make possible, eventually, an analysis of the relationship between certainty and accuracy of recall.

For most of the items (e.g., birth weight, breast or bottle fed, age of onset of walking) coding proved relatively easy. The parents had been asked for specific information and by and large were able to give answers definite enough that no judgment was required in evaluating responses. Accordingly, these items were scored by the author alone.

There were only three questions where coding was more complex because the parental descriptions required interpretation. These were the items referring to feeding on schedule or demand, ease of weaning, and the sleeping pattern at 6 months. The responses to each of these items were entered on a worksheet and coded independently by the two interviewers.[4] The codings were then compared. Where disagreements occurred, the two coders re-evaluated the item independently, without reviewing the scores previously assigned. If the new scores were in agreement, this was the code entered. If not, both coders discussed the response until consensus was reached. Reliability of the first coding was computed by Cohen's (1960) K and

---

[4]Criteria are presented in Robbins (1961, Appendix B).

the degree of agreement was high, ranging from .78 to .96.

When coding of the retrospective data was finished, the original longitudinal records were consulted for the first time. The complete folder on each child was read. Precautions were taken to prevent contamination by masking the retrospective responses while the information from the longitudinal histories was entered.

In tabulating the longitudinal material, the following conventions were added to the previous set:

1. In the rare instances when the *exact* time at which a given behavior had begun or stopped was not specified, the midpoint between the date of the interview at which its presence or cessation was first noted, and that of the preceding interview, was tabulated. For example, if a child was described as not yet standing at 38 weeks, and as standing by the next interview, at 52 weeks, with no specific date of onset mentioned, the item was scored as "45 weeks."

2. When the longitudinal data for a specific item were vague or incomplete, the entry ODM (Original Data Missing) was made. This occurred typically when, as a result of error, some information was either not sought or not entered in the longitudinal histories.

Coding was done in the same manner as before, with K ranging from .84 to 1.00.

Once the data had been coded, two master charts, one for mothers and one for fathers, were set up to permit comparison of the retrospective and longitudinal material. Qualitative items, such as *whether* the child had been fed on schedule or demand, were scored as "correct" if the original and retrospective responses were identical, and "incorrect" if there was any difference between the two. Quantitative items, such as *when* the cup

had been introduced, were scored in terms of the discrepancy between the retrospective and original statements. A positive discrepancy score (+) indicates that the parent recalled the event as having occurred later than it really did; a negative discrepancy score (−), that the parent dated the event earlier than was actually the case.

Statistical Treatment

The question concerned with the accuracy of parental recall was evaluated by comparing retrospective responses with the original parental statements. For the quantitative items, t tests of the significance of differences between correlated means were computed. For the qualitative items, McNemar's (1949) test of the significance of changes was employed. Mothers and fathers were treated separately in order to compare their relative accuracy, and to facilitate comparison with other studies where mothers only have been questioned.

The effect of experts' recommendations on parental recall was evaluated by comparing the kinds of errors made with the advice of authorities. For example, if a mother who had originally described feeding on schedule stated in the retrospective interview that she had fed her baby on demand, this was scored as an error in the direction of the experts' recommendations. Spock (1957) was used as the basis of comparison since all the parents in the present group were more or less familiar with his work. However, his recommendations are so similar to those in other common sources of child rearing advice, such as *Infant Care* (United States Department of Health, Education, and Welfare, 1955), and women's magazines, that it was felt that parental agreement with experts in gen-

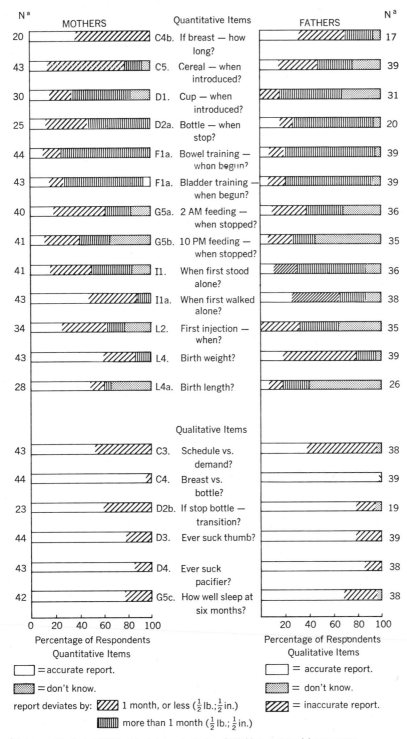

Fig. 1. Accuracy of parental recall.

eral, rather than with Spock alone, was being tested.

RESULTS

Question 1. How Accurate Are Retrospective Parental Reports of Child Rearing Practices?

In Figure 1, the percentage of parents whose reports were accurate, i.e., whose interview responses and original records were in exact agreement, is contrasted with the percentage whose retrospective reports were off by less, or more, than a month, and with the percentage who stated they were unable to recall. For the qualitative items, the percentage of parents who were correct is compared with the percentage giving incorrect or "don't know" responses. It may be seen that certain items, such as whether initial feeding was by breast or bottle, and the birth weight, were well-remembered by the great majority of the parents, both mothers and fathers. Other items, such as the cessation of bottle feeding and the onset of bowel and bladder training, were less accurately recalled by either parent, while two items—the introduction of the cup and the date of the first injection—were not recalled correctly by any of the fathers.

Table 2 further demonstrates that parental recall tends to be inaccurate. On 4 of the 13 quantitative items— those dealing with the age of weaning, beginning of bowel and bladder training, and the stopping of the 2 A.M. feeding—mean retrospective reports by both mothers and fathers differed significantly from the original records. Fathers' reports were also significantly inaccurate on the items

dealing with the introduction of cereal, the introduction of the cup, and the child's age when he first stood alone. For two of the six qualitative items—those dealing with feeding on schedule vs. demand, and thumbsucking—retrospective reports by both parents differed significantly from the original records.

For certain of the quantitative items, the main discrepancy scores showed extreme distortion in recall. For instance, with regard to the onset of bowel training, mothers erred by an average of +14.2 weeks and fathers by an average of + 22.7 weeks, both recalling the event as occurring *later* than was originally reported. As for bladder training, the average discrepancies were +22.3 and +25.5 weeks, respectively. These discrepancies of 3–6 months seem especially large when one considers that they are for behaviors that typically do not begin much before the end of the first year (Thomas, et al., 1961), so that they are relative to a maximum time span of approximately 2 years.

The age of first standing was recalled correctly by a far smaller percentage of parents than the onset of walking. Furthermore, the mean discrepancy scores were opposite in sign, with both mothers and fathers tending to recall standing as having occurred later than it did and walking as having started earlier. The parents considerably shortened the time required for the progression from one stage to the next, with the fathers believing that it took 14.8 weeks on the average and the mothers, 16.8 weeks. The average interval between standing and walking was actually 21.8 weeks.

TABLE 2.—Accuracy of Parental Recall

PARENTAL RECALL	N^a	MOTHERS' MEAN DISCREPANCY	T	N^a	FATHERS' MEAN DISCREPANCY	T
Quantitative items						
C4b. If breast—how long?	20	+.4[b]	<1	16	−.4[b]	<1
C5. Cereal—when introduced?	41	−.3	<1	29	+7.3	3.09**
D1. Cup—when introduced?	26	+1.1	<1	21	+12.7	2.48*
D2a. Bottle—when stop?	25	−13.6	3.52**	19	−18.2	4.74***
F1a. Bowel training—when begun?	44	+14.2	3.49**	38	+22.7	4.92***
F1a. Bladder training—when begun?	42	+22.3	5.23***	36	+25.5	4.86***
G5a. 2 A.M. feeding—when stopped?	34	+2.8	2.13*	25	+5.5	2.15*
G5b. 10 P.M. feeding—when stopped?	28	+2.3	<1	16	−5.9	1.23
I1. When first stood alone?	35	+1.9	1.31	31	+9.1	3.08**
I1a. When first walked alone?	43	−1.1	1.36	32	−1.1	1.08
L2. First injection—when?	27	−1.6	1.55	22	+4.0	<1
L4. Birth weight?	43	+.02 ounces	<1	37	−.1 ounces	<1
L4a. Birth length?	19	+.1 inch	1.56	10	+.2 inch	<1
		% Accurate	Significance[c]		% Accurate	Significance[c]
Qualitative items						
C3. Schedule vs. demand?	43	53	.05[d]	38	37	.05[d]
C4. Breast vs. bottle?	44	95	—	39	97	—
D2b. If stop bottle—transition?	23	61	—	19	74	—
D3. Ever suck thumb?	44	84	.01[e]	39	73	.05[e]
D4. Ever suck pacifier?	43	88	—	38	87	—
G5c. How well sleep at 6 months?	42	79	—	38	63	—

[a] Ns vary because of ODM (Original Data Missing), DK (Don't Know), or DNA (Does Not Apply) responses.

[b] In weeks except Items L4 and L4a.

[c] Significance depends upon the direction of errors, rather than the percentage of accurate responses. Thus, seven mothers denied thumb-sucking and none erroneously added it in the retrospective reports, so that the responses on original and retrospective interviews significantly differ from one another. For Item G5c, where the percentage accuracy is actually lower, change was not significant since four mothers said the child had slept well when he had slept poorly and three erred in the opposite direction.

[d] Significantly more modified demand and less schedule than had occurred were mentioned in the retrospective interview than in the original reports.

[e] Significantly less thumbsucking than had occurred was reported in the retrospective interview.

* $p \leq .05$.   ** $p \leq .01$.   *** $p \leq .001$.

133

In the case of weaning, the same tendency to shorten the learning process was found, with the age of introducing the cup recalled as having been later than was really the case, while the age of completion of weaning was placed significantly earlier. The former discrepancy was significant for the fathers only (at the .05 level); the latter for fathers and mothers alike (at the .001 and .01 levels, respectively).

With regard to bowel and bladder functions, the initiation of training was also recalled as significantly later by both sets of parents. Since a majority of the children had not yet been fully trained at the time of the retrospective interviews, information concerning the date of completion was not sought. However, in those families where training was complete, the parents tended to describe its accomplishment as taking place virtually overnight, and to gloss over the lengthy process of acquisition.

A larger percentage of both mothers and fathers were accurate in recalling the termination of the 2 A.M. feeding, which interrupts sleep, than of the 10 P.M. feeding. However, only the mean discrepancies for the 2 A.M. feeding were significant, because they were predominantly in the same direction, that of interfering longer with parental rest. In contrast, the discrepancies for the 10 P.M. feeding were random, with the fathers, who were less often involved, recalling its cessation as earlier, on the average. Finally, it should be noted that there was better recall of birth weight than birth length. The birth weight is considerably more important to the survival of the child, and is one of the most frequently mentioned items in descriptions or discussions of newborn babies, while the birth length is rarely brought up. However, the comparatively few parents who did recall the birth length were likely to be accurate, so that the mean discrepancy score was negligible.

As Bronfenbrenner (1958) anticipated, the recall of whether or not a particular practice was employed is somewhat more reliable than a parent's estimate of when the practice was begun or discontinued. However, even for the qualitative items, no fact was recalled accurately by *all* the parents, and there are two items with significant discrepancies. Both mothers and fathers reported a far greater incidence of demand feeding than had been described when their children were infants, and several stated that there had been no thumbsucking in instances where the evidence in the original records was undeniably to the contrary.

Table 3 presents the median ages for all quantitative items and the percentages for all qualitative items, as derived independently from the original records and retrospective interviews. These data should be utilized in comparing the present results with those obtained by other investigators.

Question 2. Is There any Relationship between the Recommendations of Experts in Child Rearing and Retrospective Parental Reports of Their Own Practices?

Although no cause and effect relationship can positively be established, the parallelism between experts' advice and prevailing direction of distortion is suggestive. As is shown in

TABLE 3.—Median Values and Percentages Given in the Original and Retrospective Interviews for the 19 Memory Items; Number of "Don't Know" Responses Given in the Retrospective Interviews

| | MOTHERS | | | | | FATHERS | | | | |
| | Original[a] | | Retrospective | | | Original | | Retrospective | | |
PARENTAL RECALL	N[b]	Median	N	Median	DK	N	Median	N	Median	DK
Quantitative items										
C4b. If breast—how long?	18	2.7[c]	20	2.7[c]	0	16	2.9[c]	16	2.8[c]	1
C5. Cereal—when introduced?	43	2.0	42	2.0	2	38	1.8	29	3.0	10
D1. Cup—when introduced?	30	8.0	39	6.0	4	26	8.0	29	10.6	10
D2a. Bottle—when stopped?[d]	25	23.8	25	17.4	0	20	24.0	19	17.4	1
F1a. Bowel training—when begun?	44	16.0	44	17.4	0	39	15.7	38	22.0	1
F1a. Bladder training—when begun?	44	16.4	42	19.4	1	39	15.9	36	21.4	3
G5a. 2 A.M. feeding—when stopped?	41	1.9	36	2.0	6	37	1.8	27	3.4	11
G5b. 10 P.M. feeding—when stopped?	41	2.9	29	3.0	13	37	3.0	18	4.0	19
I1. When first stood alone?	41	8.2	38	8.6	6	36	8.0	34	9.4	5
I1a. When first walked alone?	44	12.8	44	12.5	0	39	12.7	33	11.9	6
L2. First injection—when?	33	3.0	37	2.8	7	30	3.3	26	3.4	13
L4. Birth weight?	43	109.0 ounces	44	108.0 ounces	0	39	109.5 ounces	37	108.0 ounces	2
L4a. Birth length?	23	19.8 inches	33	20.2 inches	9	22	19.5 inches	22	19.4 inches	16
		% Accurate		% Accurate			% Accurate		% Accurate	
Qualitative items[e]										
C3. Schedule vs. demand?	43	56	44	77	0	38	53	38	76	1
C4. Breast vs. bottle?	44	41	44	46	0	39	41	39	44	0
D2b. Transition easy?	23	65	25	72	0	19	63	19	68	1
D3. Suck thumb? Yes.	44	57	44	41	0	39	59	39	44	0
D4. Suck pacifier? Yes.	43	42	44	50	0	38	42	39	41	0
G5c. How well sleep at 6 months?	42	74	40	78	2	38	71	36	72	2

[a] "Original" medians and percentages for fathers and mothers are not always identical because only the records of parents who participated in the retrospective interviews were used in these computations.

[b] N varies from item to item because of differences in the number of ODM (Original Data Missing), DK (Don't Know), or DNA (Does Not Apply) responses. The total number of respondents equals N plus DK.

[c] In months except Items L4 and L4a.

[d] For those already weaned.

[e] Percentages are given for the italicized categories, e.g., percentage fed on demand; percentage reported as sucking the thumb.

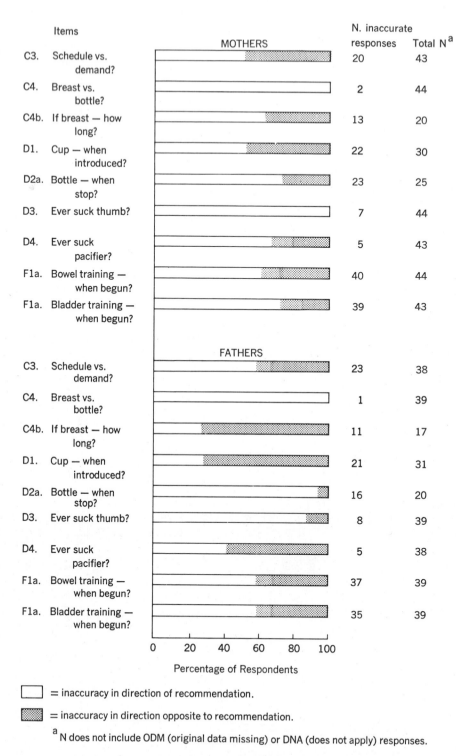

Fig. 2. Inaccuracies in parental recall as related to experts' recommendations.

Figure 2, mothers tended to be inaccurate in the direction of the recommendations on every one of the nine items for which suggestions were clearly made in the child rearing literature. For instance, of the 20 mothers who gave inaccurate responses regarding the mode of infant feeding they employed, 65% shifted in the direction of more demand feeding and only 35% toward less. This discrepancy suggests that mothers were desirous of appearing to have fed on demand even when they had not actually engaged in the practice. The age of weaning was markedly reduced in the retrospective reports, while the onset of toilet training was recalled as later than was really the case. In both instances, the shifts paralleled the recommendations of Spock (1957; see Table 1) regarding the ideal timing of these practices. Finally, with regard to thumbsucking, of which Spock disapproves, and the pacifier, whose use he favors, errors again reflected the recommendations. All seven of the mothers who were inaccurate in their reports of thumbsucking denied that their child had ever sucked his thumb. The original records showed not only that thumbsucking had occurred, in three cases for as long as a year, but also that several of these mothers had expressed concern about it at the time. In contrast, of five mothers who erred in their recall of the use of the pacifier, four stated that their child had used one when, according to the longitudinal records, he had not.

On items for which expert advice was relatively less specific or irrelevant, maternal errors were random in direction. Thus, with respect to the introduction of cereal, 17 mothers recalled the date of onset as later and 18 as earlier, while the birth weight was understated by 8 and overstated by 9.

As appears in Figure 2, the fathers tended to be less affected by expert advice than the mothers. While they all reported some acquaintance with Spock (1957), the fathers felt they were less thorough in their reading than their wives, and that he influenced them little.

DISCUSSION

In a widely quoted review of the literature, Bronfenbrenner (1958) inferred, on the basis of data which showed a rise in reports of demand feeding from 7% in 1932 to 71% in 1949–50, that self-demand feeding is becoming more common in the middle class. His conclusion must be assessed in light of the fact that 77% of the mothers in the current sample reported having fed their infants on demand 3 years previously. While this supports the trend noted by Bronfenbrenner, since the data were gathered subsequent to the last study he surveyed, an examination of the original records shows that only 56% of the mothers had *actually* fed on demand (see Table 3). The number of mothers whose reports were erroneous was sufficient to make this one of the items where inaccuracies were significant (see Table 2).

In the studies cited by Bronfenbrenner (1958), the age of weaning ranges from 10.3 to 14.4 months. This is considerably earlier than the recalled median age for completion of weaning found in the current sample

−17.4 months. The difference again appears to be consistent with the trend to permissiveness identified by Bronfenbrenner. Since the subjects of the other studies include a substantial number of children who were reared in the late thirties and early forties, when early weaning was commonly advocated (Wolfenstein, 1953), it is quite conceivable that a genuine change in practices has occurred. However, the actual median age of weaning of children in this study was 23.8 months. Parents were even more permissive in their practices than in their reports, perhaps because they had been influenced by such recommendations as Spock's (1957) to complete weaning before 24 months. In addition, the direction of error suggests that the tendency to report weaning as occurring earlier than was really the case may have been intensified for mothers in other studies, who were questioned about this event as much as 17 years after it took place.

The degree of inaccuracy found in the present study is only a minimal indication of the errors that may be present in other research. In part this is so because the children in this sample were considerably younger than those in other studies. In addition, the parents as a group were better educated and probably more intelligent than those interviewed by previous investigators. There is some indication that higher education is correlated with more accurate recall of details about child rearing (Pyles, Stolz, and MacFarlane, 1935). Because this sample has been participating in a longitudinal study in which extensive reports of the child's behavior

and development have been made at relatively frequent intervals, parents could be expected to observe, and therefore to retain, material relating to child rearing with greater precision than mothers whose first contact with an interviewer occurred some years after the events had taken place. Another factor that probably serves to enhance the relative accuracy of parents in this sample is that both parents were interviewed, rather than mothers alone. They might have shown greater care in their responses, knowing that their spouses were answering the same questions. Finally, the parents were aware that records were available against which their recollections could be checked—knowledge that might serve both as a deterrent to distortion and as an intellectual challenge for demonstrating their acuity to the personnel of the study.

The differences between original records and subsequent reports presented in Table 3 are in almost every instance as large as, or larger than, the differences between middle- and lower-class samples tabulated by Bronfenbrenner (1958, pp. 408–410). This is true even though the parents in the current study were talking about the same child at two points in time, while the class comparisons are based on different children. It is clear that a meaningful discussion of class differences in child rearing practices must await detailed longitudinal observations of representative samples of each group. Regardless of the accuracy of the reports reviewed by Bronfenbrenner, however, the way the mothers presented their child rearing practices at various points in time remains an important indicator of the values they have held.

As is apparent in Table 3, child rearing practices in the current sample by and large conformed to the recommendations of experts (see Table 1), in that demand feeding, relatively late weaning and toilet training, and a permissive attitude toward sucking are the mode. However, the experts also materially influenced parental recall, both in the sense of providing knowledge about child rearing around which memories could be organized, and in setting standards for appearing to be a good parent in the ways approved by "enlightened" judgment. This was especially evident for the mothers, who prefaced many of their responses with accurate statements of Spock's (1957) recommendations. In addition, many of the parents apologized for not always following the approved techniques, even when their modification seemed well-suited to the particular child.

It is possible that some of the inaccuracies in recall were due to more or less deliberate distortion. Yet the experts' recommendations are such a potent influence that in all likelihood many parents were not aware of the fact that they were incorrect in their reports. This factor should be kept in mind when evaluating the results of other studies, since it suggests that neither good rapport (Sears, Maccoby, and Levin, 1957), the asking of several questions in a given area (Miller and Swanson, 1960), nor internal consistency in maternal responses (Bronfenbrenner, 1958; Miller and Swanson, 1958, 1960; Sears, Maccoby, and Levin, 1957) is sufficient to insure accuracy.

The interplay between experts' opinions and parental practices is a complex one. The experts look to research for justification of their recommendations and for substantiation of their theories. Ironically, however, the responses of parents who furnish data for such research may already be colored by the advice that they have received and may not be accurate accounts of what they have actually done. As a result, there may be a self-perpetuating "validation," with experts' opinions influencing parental reports, which in turn influence the experts.

15 *Influence of Breast Feeding on Children's Behavior*

MARTIN I. HEINSTEIN

This summary of a longitudinal study (Heinstein, 1963) points to the danger of oversimplified recommendations for child-rearing practices —the hazards of a single approach to the relationship between early feeding experiences and later adjustment. The findings indicate that the relationship between breast-bottle feeding and child adjustment involves interaction of a complex of factors, such as warmth of the mother, marital adjustment of the parents and home atmosphere during the nursing period, length of nursing, and sex of child.

Breast feeding has at times been singled out as the royal road to successful mothering and mental health for the child. Freud, through his concept of orality, made the nursing experience of the infant a central issue in the study of personality. His clinical findings and speculations about oral gratification and deprivation have received a great deal of attention in the literature about child development.

Nevertheless, the effects of various nursing regimes on a child's physical and emotional development are still essentially unknown. Equally obscure are the influences which induce a mother to feed her child from the breast. Few facts have been established despite speculation dating back to Hippocrates and a considerable amount of recent research.

A decline in the proportion of mothers in this country who breast feed has been apparent over the past several decades, although significant geographic differences have been noted in the frequency of the practice (Bronfenbrenner, 1958; Meyer, 1958; Robertson, 1961). Research carried on in the 1930's and 1940's showed mothers from lower socioeconomic groups undertaking breast feeding more frequently and weaning their children later than mothers with higher socioeconomic status. Some recent studies indicate that these differences may now no longer exist or may even have been reversed (White, 1957; Bock, et al., 1957).

Much of the research about the influence of breast feeding on child development has suffered from some obvious defects. None of the studies have attempted to evaluate the personality of the mother doing the feeding as well as the type of feeding being done. Nor have the studies taken into account the possibility that a tense, breast-feeding mother may present a more disturbing environment for an infant than a relatively relaxed, bottle-feeding mother. Furthermore, few, if any, studies have looked for possible differences in reactions on the part of male and female children, or to possible variability of response with the age of the child. Behavior disturbances apparent at the time of weaning may not be present at subsequent stages of development.

Studies have usually relied too heavily on retrospective data. Reports from mothers several years later on how they fed their babies and their children's later reactions are likely to be unreliable. Moreover, investigators have usually studied only special groups, such as middle-class families or children being treated at a clinic. Few studies have used samples representative enough of the general population to permit broad deductions.

The study to be reported upon here made use of longitudinal data collected on a representative sample of children—a sub-sample of every third child born in Berkeley, Calif., from January 1, 1928, to June 30, 1929. The data covered a period from the birth of the child to 18 years of age. Be-

havior problems of the children during the preschool period, middle childhood, and adolescence were looked at in relation to whether or not the children were breast fed, the length of their nursing experience (whether from breast or bottle, or both), and the family atmosphere during the nursing period.

The term *nursing* will be used in this article, as it was in the study, to refer to the period of breast and bottle feeding, or both. *Length of nursing* was determined by fixing the time at which the child was weaned to the cup.

The 47 boys and 47 girls in the sample had been studied intensively for physical, mental, and personality development by the Institute of Human Development at the University of California, Berkeley. Data were also available on the general characteristics of the parents, the mother's relations to the child, and the socioeconomic status of the family. Testing and intensive, open-ended interviews had been conducted periodically over the 18-year period. The sample and program of data collection have been described in previous publications (MacFarlane, 1938).

STUDY VARIABLES

The main variables considered in this study were: (1) breast feeding without supplementary nursing; (2) length of nursing; (3) the warmth of the mother toward the child; (4) the nervous stability of the mother; (5) the marital adjustment of the parents; (6) and the behavior problems of the child. The warmth of the mother was determined by a combined average rating of the mother's closeness to the child, general friendliness, and expressiveness of affection toward her child.

The behavior of the child was evaluated both from reports of the mother, starting when the child was 21 months old, and interviews with the child starting when he was 6 years old. Ratings on behavior problems such as temper tantrums, thumbsucking, fears, and enuresis were used for the preschool period and middle childhood. The results of projective testing by the Thematic Apperception and Rorschach tests were the basis for behavior assessment in late childhood and adolescence. Ratings of the personalities of the parents, their relations to each other and to their children were based on the reports of the intensive interviews.

While no other studies to date have looked into the joint influence of the mother's personality and the nursing process on the child's behavior, a number have focused on the characteristics of mothers who did and of those who did not breast feed. Some of these studies have been based in part on the supposition that the mother's personality and her feelings toward the child are related to her decision to breast feed or not. For example, Levy at one time maintained that weaning was an index of maternal rejection (Levy, 1943).

On the other hand, two studies (Peterson and Spano, 1941; Sears, Maccoby, and Levin, 1957) reported 16 years apart found no evidence that breast feeding was related to whether the mother wanted the child or to the degree of warmth of the mother toward the child. One of them, however, indicated "that breast feeding probably does have some special implications for quite a good many mothers, and that those who have a strong sense of modesty or anxiety about sex, in general, may avoid breast feeding." (Sears, Maccoby, and Levin, 1957). Another study found that the "biologic type" of mother prefers to breast feed and to avoid a rigid schedule, while the "modern urban type" tends to bottle feed on a rigid schedule (Newton and Newton, 1950).

In the present study, none of the variables used to define the mother-child relations or the general family atmosphere was found to be significantly related to breast feeding. For example, factors such as the warmth of the mother toward the child or the marital adjustment of the parents were not associated with breast feeding or with the duration of breast feeding. Thus the data can hardly be interpreted as representing evidence that breast feeding is a reliable measure of maternal acceptance of the child.

The socioeconomic status of the family, however, was associated with the duration of breast feeding. For both boys and girls, the lower the socioeconomic status of the family, the older the age of the child at weaning from the breast.

The relationship of lower socioeconomic status with longer duration of breast feeding is consistent with the results of other studies using breast-feeding data from about the same period (1928–29). As already mentioned, more recent investigations tend to indicate no differences in this respect between social classes while some studies report longer or more breast feeding by middle-class mothers. Possibly the recent rise in the proportion of mothers from lower socioeconomic groups who are working outside the home has decreased the opportunity for breast feeding among them. At the same time, the emphasis in pediatric and child development publications on the psychological benefits of breast feeding for the child has probably been influential in fostering positive attitudes toward breast feeding among middle-class mothers. The relatively greater decline of breast feeding among mothers of the lower socioeconomic levels may also mean, at least in part, that these mothers have reached standards of child care followed by middle-class mothers several decades ago.

HEALTH AND BEHAVIOR PROBLEMS

The study gave no evidence of breast feeding being positively related to favorable growth or general health of the child. On the contrary, length of breast feeding for both boys and girls correlated negatively with the rate at which the children reached various heights—one index of maturation. Four of six overall health ratings also correlated negatively with breast feeding. The health ratings were based on periodic physical examinations and frequency of illness. The study was not designed, however, to answer specific questions about the relation of breast feeding to health.

The study also failed to reveal significant differences in incidence of problem behavior between breast-fed

or bottle-fed children—whether boys or girls. The findings of previous studies are noticeably inconsistent in this respect. In four studies, children who had been breast fed for 4 to 10 months were better adjusted than children who had been breast fed shorter or longer periods. Three studies reported that the later the weaning from the breast the fewer the behavior problems. Two other studies, in direct contrast to the first four mentioned, indicated that the best adjustment was among subjects breast fed for very short periods or not at all, or for a long period (11 or 12 months). Four other investigations found no significant differences in behavior according to the length of breast feeding (Heinstein, 1963).

PARENTAL FACTORS AND NURSING

Psychologists who are influenced by learning theory and psychiatrists who place more emphasis on interpersonal transactions than on libidinal drives have regarded the personal-social environment of the child as fundamentally more important than a particular nursing regime. They have maintained that positive, early relationships of the child with the parents, particularly the mother, are likely to carry over to other later interpersonal relations.

The results of this study revealed that in general the daughters of the more stable or of the warm mothers had fewer behavior problems. For boys, only the warmth of the mother was associated in any degree with positive behavior. The marital adjustment of the parents showed no noticeable association with the behavior of either boys or girls when this factor alone was considered in relation to behavior problems.

Findings based on such single factors in the child's environment as the warmth of the mother, her nervous stability, or the marital adjustment of the parents were not as pronounced as the associations apparent when both parental characteristics and the nursing situation were considered at the same time. In fact, the results of this study seem to indicate that the interaction of the nursing and parental factors are more important for the adjustment of the child than either the nursing situation or parental characteristics taken separately.

While the nursing situation by itself did not seem to relate significantly to later behavior, it became a variable of importance when considered in connection with parental attributes, the sex of the child, and differences between the experience of breast feeding and length of nursing as such.

The most pronounced maladjustment shown in any group in the study was among boys who were nursed (on breast or bottle) for a long period of time (15 months or longer) by a *cold* mother (distant, hostile, inexpressive of affection). Length of nursing, when considered apart from the personal characteristics of the mother doing the nursing, was not associated with any noticeable behavioral disturbances. Furthermore, boys who were nursed for a long period of time by a *warm* mother tended to be relatively free from behavioral difficulties. What became evident was the effects of experiencing *both* long nursing and a cold mother at the same time. (Table 1)

Extended nursing in our culture may be regarded as a sign of continuing dependency needs on the part of the child. The mother who accepts or fosters these dependency needs, but at the same time has feelings of rejection toward the child, is obviously ambivalent and providing an atmosphere of conflict for the child. Such a mother is perhaps not truly nurturant, but may use the dependence of the child as a basis for maintaining hostile control.

Dependence in the first years of life is not likely to be maladaptive if it is expressed and met within the context of genuine feelings of nurturance on the part of the mother. The boys in this sample, who were long-nursed by a cold mother were, in effect, experiencing oversolicitousness and hostility at the same time. Too much from a mother who in reality is able to give only too little is likely to result in confusion for the child.

Long nursing (weaned from the breast or bottle at 16 months or later) as such showed no significant overall association with behavior problems for girls, as it did for boys. However, when the results of the interaction between length of nursing and the maternal nervous stability were considered, girls who had a relatively unstable mother had fewer behavior problems when they were nursed for a long period of time. A shorter total nursing period was the most favorable duration when the mother was more stable.

Possibly mothers unable to provide a generally stable atmosphere for their daughters are able to compen-

TABLE 1.—Relation of Length of Nursing and Mother's Warmth to Incidence of Problem Behavior and Fantasy Expression in Boys

PRESCHOOL

	Diurnal Enuresis		Insufficient Appetite		Food Finickiness		Excess Attention Demanding		Specific Fears		Negativism	
	Present	Absent	Present	Absent	Present	Absent	Present	Absent	Present	Absent	Present	Absent
Long Nursing with Warm Mother	3	8	2	9	3	8	1	10	6	5	1	10
Long Nursing with Cold Mother	8	4	8	4	10	2	2	10	3	9	8	4
Short Nursing with Warm Mother	2	10	2	10	2	10	6	6	3	9	7	5
Short Nursing with Cold Mother	2	10	4	8	6	6	6	6	8	4	5	7
x^2	9.35		8.54		12.55		7.53		5.09		8.93	
p	.03		.04		<.01		.06		.10		.03	

LATER DEVELOPMENT

	Food Finickiness		Temper Tantrums		Rorschach Oral References		Independence Relinquished		Excessive Reserve	
	Present	Absent	Present	Absent	Present	Absent	Present	Absent	Present	Absent
Long Nursing with Warm Mother	7	4	3	8	2	9	3	8	3	8
Long Nursing with Cold Mother	8	4	10	2	8	4	10	2	4	8
Short Nursing with Warm Mother	4	8	6	6	6	6	5	7	9	3
Short Nursing with Cold Mother	1	11	7	5	3	9	5	7	6	6
x^2	11.02		7.49		7.33		8.75		6.44	
p	.01		.06		.07		.04		.09	

sate by added solicitousness in the nursing area. The capacity of the girl to benefit from a longer period of nurturance through nursing may reflect cultural differences in our demands for independence from boys and girls. Girls may be able to receive reinforcement of dependency needs longer than boys without being subjected to conflicting expectations that they become more independent and aggressive. This, of course, is clearly speculative. Apparently, however, boys and girls experience length of nursing in different ways depending, in part, on variations in personal-social environment.

BREAST FEEDING AND THE MOTHER

What about the effects of breast feeding generally when considered along with the feelings of the mother doing the feeding? For boys, breast feeding did not appear to be significantly related to problem behavior even when considered in the context of mother-child relations at the time of nursing. Whether the mother was warm or cold in her feelings toward her son was not associated with noticeably different kinds of behavior. In other words, the interaction of breast feeding and the warmth of the mother was not significant except when length of nursing was taken into account.

Girls, however, developed fewer behavioral difficulties if breast fed by a warm mother. However, those whose mothers were distant, unfriendly, and inexpressive of affection did better if bottle fed. (Table 2)

It is not unreasonable to suppose that the mother who breast feeds her daughter without real warmth provides an ambivalent and potentially more disturbing environment for her —a situation similar to the one experienced by boys fed by a long nursing, cold mother. The close, intense relationship between mother and daughter implied in breast feeding apparently should be part of a more generally warm mother-child relationship in order to effect lasting psychological benefits for the child. Where technical nurturance represents only a formal expression of love or when it occurs with feelings of rejection, the resulting confusion for the child again appears to be associated with behavior problems.

Why boys were unfavorably affected by the *long nursing* situation with a cold mother and girls by *breast feeding* with a cold mother is not readily apparent. The ambivalence present in both of these general conditions, however, is clear.

The fact that behavioral difficulties seem to be generated by the long nursing-cold mother experience of the boys in this study and the breast feeding-cold mother situation of the girls has some relevance for the "double bind" theory of Bateson et al. (1956). It also has implications for Harlow's (1958) findings on the importance of cuddling.

The main ingredients of the double bind, as described by Bateson, consist of two or more people in a repeated experience from which one, the victim, has no escape. The victim receives a primary negative (or positive) injunction which is in conflict with a more abstract secondary in-

TABLE 2.—Relation of Breast Feeding and Mother's Warmth to Incidence of Behavior Problems and Fantasy Expression in Girls

	Food Finickiness		Speech Problems		Excess Attention Demanding	
PRESCHOOL	Present	Absent	Present	Absent	Present	Absent
Breast Fed with Warm Mother	2	12	4	10	2	12
Breast Fed with Cold Mother	7	1	6	2	3	5
Formula Fed with Warm Mother	5	4	6	3	6	3
Formula Fed with Cold Mother	8	8	6	10	5	11
x^2	8.36		6.81		6.80	
p	.04		.08		.08	

	Nail Biting		Enunciation Defects		Excess Reserve		Controlled Aggression	
LATER DEVELOPMENT	Present	Absent	Present	Absent	Present	Absent	Present	Absent
Breast Fed with Warm Mother	8	6	4	10	3	11	9	5
Breast Fed with Cold Mother	5	3	5	3	5	3	5	3
Formula Fed with Warm Mother	7	2	3	6	5	4	4	5
Formula Fed with Cold Mother	4	12	12	4	11	5	3	13
x^2	7.54		8.05		7.41		7.56	
p	.06		.05		.06		.06	

junction. Thus the boys in this study who experienced a long nursing period with a cold mother were caught in a relationship in which the mother was expressing two orders of message, one of which denied the other. Technically, the long nursing or the breast feeding expressed a formal manifestation of nurturance or love, which was contradicted by a communication of the mother's feelings of hostility and lack of closeness.

Harlow's early work suggests the possibility that the amount and kind of cuddling the infant receives are more important psychologically than the nursing experience. While some of the evidence from the study described here indicated that the warmth and nervous stability of the mother as single factors in the child's early experience were more important than the nursing situation, the pattern of both factors together, nursing and the mother's personality, seemed to be the most decisive influence.

IMPLICATIONS
OF THE STUDY

The results of this study point to the dangers of making oversimplified recommendations in relation to specific child-rearing procedures without consideration of the family atmosphere in which these procedures are to take place. Breast feeding or long nursing are not efficatious *per se*. In each instance, we must ask who the nursing mother is and what the other relevant factors in the home environment are which impinge on the nursing experience of the child.

Further evidence supporting these observations may be gained from the study's findings in relation to thumb-sucking. Freud used thumb-sucking as a model for explaining the erogenous nature of the oral zone. As a result thumb-sucking has become a diagnostic sign for insufficient sucking satisfaction, disturbed emotional development, troubled mother-child relations, and a host of other ills. Levy (1937), for example, has stated that the main cause of finger sucking is insufficient sucking at the breast or bottle.

The greatest incidence of thumb-sucking in this study occurred among girls who were breast fed by mothers who had achieved a good marital adjustment and who were also judged better than average in regard to nervous stability. Not only are the results the reverse of what would be theoretically expected, but, again, the interaction of two factors, the breast feeding and the parental characteristics, was more significant than the effects of either variable considered separately.

Moreover, the results in this study and in two additional investigations based on large, representative samples of children, thumb-sucking was negatively correlated with other behavior problems in the preschool period. The thumb-sucking girl tended to come from a breast-feeding, stable environment, and girls and boys who as preschoolers sucked their thumbs were less likely than others to have other behavior problems.

Perhaps the most important conclusions of this study relate to the several methodological considerations raised in the early part of this article. Apparently sex differences *are* an important factor in evaluating the behavioral correlates of the nursing experience. Also, the pattern of the child's nursing experience within the context of varying personal-social conditions seems to provide a more decisive view of the child's emotional adjustment than do single factors, be they the nursing experience or particular characteristics of the parents.

The zeal of some people in trying to foster breast feeding or a particular child-rearing technique may derive from an oversimplified interpretation of psychoanalytic theory or a long held idyllic picture of mother-infant oneness. It is perhaps wiser without more definitive knowledge to view nursing as one aspect of the total life space of the infant or child. While the results of this study must also be viewed with caution, they do seem clear enough to raise serious doubts about some of the current *ex cathedra* pronouncements which appear on the topic of breast feeding or baby nursing in general.

16   *The Varieties of Children's Behavioral Problems and Family Dynamics*[1]

RICHARD L. JENKINS, M.D.

Three groups of children examined at child guidance clinics are described. The overanxious children are likely to have anxious, "infantalizing" mothers. The unsocialized aggressive child is likely to have a critical, depreciative, punitive, inconsistent mother or stepmother. Socialized delinquents are likely to come from large families characterized by parental neglect, delegation of parental responsibilities, parental pathology that is more parental than material, and an alcoholic father or stepfather.

A designation of three major symptomatic groupings of children referred to a child guidance clinic was presented by Lester Hewitt and myself in 1944 (Hewitt and Jenkins, 1946; Jenkins and Hewitt, 1944). At that time we recognized three large behavioral syndromes, which we called the overinhibited child, the unsocialized aggressive child, and the socialized

delinquent. We recognized a characteristic family background for each syndrome: family repression for the overinhibited child, parental rejection and particularly maternal rejection for the unsocialized aggressive child, and parental negligence and exposure to delinquent behavior for the socialized delinquents.

A paper presented at a research conference in child psychiatry in 1965 and subsequently published contrasted the family backgrounds of the overanxious (or overinhibited) children, the undomesticated (or unsocialized aggressive) children, and the socialized delinquents as these have been revealed in a number of studies (Jenkins, 1964).

In a study published in May of

---

[1] Read at the 123rd annual meeting of the American Psychiatric Association, Detroit, Mich., May 8–12, 1967.

This paper has been shortened by the omission of the supporting tables, which are scheduled for publication in the *Proceedings of the Conference on Adolescent Psychiatry*, held at Douglas Hospital, Montreal, June 7, 1967. Reprints of the tables are available from Dr. Jenkins upon request.

Reprinted from *American Journal of Psychiatry*, 1968, **124**, 1440–1445. Copyright 1968, the American Psychiatric Association. By permission of the author and the American Psychiatric Association.

1966, a computer analysis of 500 cases of children examined in a child guidance clinic and grouped on the basis of 94 symptoms revealed five more or less separate clusters. These included the three groups already mentioned and also a shy-seclusive and relatively withdrawn group and a hyperactive-distractible group. These five groups were found to come from characteristically different family backgrounds (Jenkins, 1966).

A further study based on the cases of 300 children examined in the child psychiatry service at the University of Iowa contrasted the responses of parents of six groups of children to an intake questionnaire. The groups were: an overanxious group, an undomesticated group, a socialized delinquent group, a withdrawn group, a brain-damaged group, and a mentally retarded group. There is some correspondence between the shy-seclusive group of the last study cited and the withdrawn group described here, and substantial overlap between the symptomatic group described as hyperactive-distractible and the etiological group described as brain-damaged. The retarded group is definable only in terms of developmental retardation, not in terms of characteristic behavior (Jenkins, Nur Eddin, and Shapiro, 1966).

METHOD

The present study is an effort to test, verify, and expand the description on a larger number of cases. The study is based upon data cards for 1,500 cases of children examined at the Institute for Juvenile Research, Chicago, Ill. IBM cards on these cases, with the results of examinations coded on them, were loaned to us through the courtesy of the Institute. These cards were subjected to a computerized clustering procedure on the basis of the symptoms, signs, and dynamic factors recorded from the examination. Five clinical clusters were determined. These are the overanxious-neurotic children, the undomesticated or unsocialized aggressive children, the socialized delinquents, the brain-damaged children, and the shy, seclusive, withdrawn, schizoid children. The first three clusters will be discussed here.

The procedure differed from the study reported in 1966 in requiring less exacting criteria for inclusion in a group and in having substantially larger numbers of cases available for comparison.

Children whose records showed at least two of the following entries were classified as overanxious: generally immature (402 cases), chronically anxious or fearful (188 cases), reluctance or fear of school (167 cases), shy (143 cases), overly conforming, submissive (85 cases), frequent nightmares (79 cases), sleep disturbance other than nightmares (70 cases), difficulty in separating from mother (66 cases). There were 287 children classified as overanxious.

Children whose records showed at least two of the following entries were classified as unsocialized aggressive: disobedience with hostile component (418 cases), temper (416 cases), bullying, domineering, aggressive (397 cases), lying (227 cases), destructiveness (159 cases), firesetting (70 cases). There were 445 cases classified as unsocialized aggressive.

Children whose records showed at least two of the following entries, including at least one of the first four, were classified as socialized delinquents: stealing (215 cases), truancy from school (116 cases), running away from home (67 cases), group stealing (45 cases), psychiatrist's judgment that primary problem area is socially unacceptable acts (276 cases), relationship made by child with psychiatrist is guarded, defensive, resistive (209 cases), relationship made by child with psychologist is guarded, defensive, suspicious (101 cases). There were 231 cases classified as socialized delinquents.

The selection of these groups is obviously very rough and approximate. However, the number of cases is large enough so that the approximation involved tends only to dilute the size of the phi value in such significant differences as we found.

Only about a third of our overanxious children and of our unsocialized aggressive children were over ten years of age, while about four-sevenths of our socialized delinquent group were over ten years of age. Thus, our socialized delinquent group is definitely older than our other two groups. Girls represented 35 percent of the overanxious group, 20 percent of the unsocialized aggressive, and 22 percent of the socialized delinquent groups.

The children in each group were compared on a long series of items with all children in our study *not* in that group. Chi-square values were calculated. If the degree of association, positive or negative, between one of the groups and an item were greater than would be expected once in 20

times purely on a chance basis the relationship was taken to be significant.

FINDINGS

Family Structure

The overanxious children tended to be the youngest in the family, a position unusual for the socialized delinquent or the unsocialized aggressive groups. The socialized delinquents tended to come from families with four or five children, not from families with one or two children. To a lesser degree, the unsocialized aggressive children also tended to come from larger rather than smaller families.

Both the socialized delinquents and the unsocialized aggressive children were unlikely to be living with both parents, for they tended to come from homes broken by separation or divorce. The socialized delinquent children were very frequently living with the mother and stepfather, the unsocialized aggressive children very frequently with either the mother and stepfather or with the father and stepmother.

Parental Characteristics

The mothers of overanxious children were more likely than the mothers of other clinic children to be characterized by the social worker as having an *infantilizing, overprotective* attitude toward the child—a description quite unlikely to be used for the mothers of the other two groups. Both of the aggressive groups were likely to have mothers whose attitude toward the child is described as *overt rejection* of the child, *punitive* toward the child, or as *acting out through the child.* A *critical, depreciative* attitude toward the child and a *lack of consistency* were characteristic of the mothers of unsocialized aggressive children. The attitude of the mother of the socialized delinquent toward the child is likely to be characterized as *cold, distant, and neglectful,* and it is recorded that she was prone to *delegate parental responsibility.* Her area of difficulty was likely to be *delinquency or promiscuity,* and she was likely not to be married to the father at the time the child was conceived.

From the social history, the father's attitude toward the unsocialized aggressive child was likely to be characterized by *lack of consistency.* The attitudes of the fathers of the socialized delinquents were characterized as *controlling, rigid,* as *acting out through the child,* as *punitive,* and as *cold, distant, neglectful.* In the case of the overanxious child, the father's area of difficulty was likely to be recorded as *mental health,* while in the case of the socialized delinquent it was likely to be *alcoholism.*

According to the social history, *withdrawal of privileges* and *physical punishment* tended to be used less with the overanxious child than with the average clinic child. The parents of the unsocialized aggressive children extensively reported *physical punishment* as a means of discipline; also, *withdrawal of privileges, physical restraint or confinement, physical or emotional isolation,* and that most inconsistent of methods of control, *bribery.* The parents of the socialized delinquents also reported substantial use of *withdrawal of privileges,* and,

less characteristically, *physical punishment* and *physical restraint or confinement.* Reports of *physical or emotional isolation* and of *bribery* as means of control were not associated with this kind of problem behavior. The parents of socialized delinquents did report the use of *extra chores* as a means of discipline.

The Child's Relationship with Environment, Parents, and Others

From the psychological examination the overanxious child's relationship with his environment was characterized as *withdrawn and passive,* a description negatively associated with the other two groups. *Acting out* was characteristic of the socialized delinquents and even more characteristic of the unsocialized aggressive child. The manifestation of hostility is *minimal, repressed* for the overanxious child and *excessive, easily elicited* for the socialized delinquent, and especially so for the unsocialized aggressive child. The relationship of the overanxious child with the examiner was *shy, withdrawn, inhibited* or *ill at ease, apprehensive* for the overanxious child and *provocative* for the unsocialized aggressive. The overanxious child was rated as *submissive* toward his parents, while the rating was *hostile, aggressive* for the socialized delinquent, and particularly so for the unsocialized aggressive child.

In the psychiatrist's judgments we find the mother's relationship to the overanxious child checked as *infantilizing, overprotective,* as *setting an example for the child's pathology,* and as sometimes involving a *marked preference for the patient.* The elements which were checked as most characteristic of the attitudes of mothers of the unsocialized aggressive children are *punitive, lack of consistency, acting out through child, overly permissive, critical, depreciative, conflicting with other authorities* (often the father), *delegates parental responsibility, and rivalous.* Such expressions certainly do not describe a maternal attitude which would make it easy for a child to learn to accept limits. The descriptive characterizations *cold, distant, neglectful,* and *overt rejection* were used for mothers of both the socialized delinquents and the unsocialized aggressive children. *Acting out through child* and *punitive* were used to describe the maternal attitudes toward the socialized delinquent as well as toward the unsocialized aggressive child. *Lack of consistency* was associated with the mothers of all three groups, but most conspicuously with those of the unsocialized aggressive children.

The mother's concept of her self-involvement in her child's problem was typically *ambivalent* in the case of the mothers of overanxious children. A *nonaccepting* attitude towards their self-involvement characterized the mothers of socialized delinquents. The attitude of the mother of the socialized delinquent toward therapy for herself is typically characterized as *reluctant, resistant, refusing.* The mothers of the unsocialized aggressive children were frequently checked as having a *character disorder or psychoneurosis.*

The psychiatrist's estimate of the relationship of fathers of the overanxious children to the child is one of *delegating parental responsibility*—a characteristic shared by the fathers of the socialized delinquents. In the case of the unsocialized aggressive children, the father's relationship is characterized by such elements as *acting out through child, punitive, lack of consistency, conflicting with other authorities, overly permissive,* and *rivalrous. Acting out through the child* and *conflicting with other authorities* were also checked as characteristic of the father's relationship with the socialized delinquent. *Overt rejection* of the child by the father was significantly related only to the socialized delinquent.

The fathers of the socialized delinquents were not accepting of their self-involvement in the patient's problem, nor were they accepting of therapy for themselves. The personality structure of the fathers of the overanxious children was likely to be characterized as involving a *character disturbance or psychoneurosis,* while in the case of the other two groups the problem is typically *alcoholism or delinquency.*

Thus both parents of socialized delinquent children showed a nonacceptance of their own involvement in the patient's problem and an unwillingness to be involved in therapy.

Stepmothers or *stepfathers* are often present in the family of the unsocialized aggressive children, *stepfathers* only with the socialized delinquents.

Paired Comparison of the Two Aggressive Groups

It should be clear that our overanxious children present a decided contrast with our other two groups and that the undomesticated children and the socialized delinquents resemble each other much more than either one resembles the overanxious children. Our next step was to confine ourselves to a comparison of these two aggressive groups.

Turning to our 445 unsocialized aggressive children and 231 socialized delinquents, we found that 129 cases fell into both groups. Eliminating these overlapping cases, we found that we had 316 cases remaining in the unsocialized aggressive group and 102 in the group of socialized delinquents. First we compared the total group of 316 unsocialized aggressive children with 102 socialized delinquents. As a second step we matched both age and sex for pairs of one unsocialized aggressive child and one socialized delinquent. This was done to eliminate the possible effect of differences between the two groups in age and sex on the comparison. This gave us 95 matched pairs, controlled on the variable of sex and reasonably well controlled on the variable of age. Our age groupings were: five-seven years, seven pairs; eight-ten years, 28 pairs; 11-14 years, 36 pairs; and over 14 years, 24 pairs. We had 76 pairs of boys and 19 pairs of girls.

In no case was the direction of the relationship reversed between the two comparisons, although, naturally, the comparison based on only 95 matched pairs showed fewer significant relationships.

The socialized delinquents were the more likely to have three or four siblings, while the unsocialized aggressive children were the more likely to be only children and were more likely to have a stepmother.

Both parents of socialized delin-quents were more likely to *delegate parental responsibility.* The mother was prone to be *cold, distant, and neglectful;* the father, *controlling and rigid.* The *punitive* mother, on the other hand, was more characteristic of the unsocialized aggressive child.

The relationship of each parent to the unsocialized aggressive child is characterized by *lack of consistency.* The father of the unsocialized aggressive child tended to prefer a sibling, while the mother of the socialized delinquent might prefer the patient to the other children.

The mothers of the socialized delinquents were more prone to *delinquency or promiscuity,* the fathers to *alcoholism.* The mothers of socialized delinquents often were characterized as *irresponsible, poor work record.* They were less likely than the mothers of the unsocialized aggressive children to be married to the child's father when the child was conceived. The mothers of unsocialized aggressive children are more likely to be considered as showing a *character disturbance or psychoneurosis.*

In the foregoing, the relationship, as measured by a phi coefficient, held up fairly well with the matched pairs although it often did not attain statistical significance with this smaller group. The use of extra chores as a method of discipline characterized the families of the socialized delinquents and the fathers did not accept their involvement in the patient's problem.

SUMMARY

In brief, the indications in this study are that the family background of the overanxious child frequently is one with an infantilizing, overanxious mother, overly concerned about the child, often preferring this child to her other children, and setting an example for the child's pathology with her own anxiety. The mother is ambivalent about her own involvement in the child's problem but is not nonaccepting of this involvement. The father delegates parental responsibility, and may have a problem of mental health, typically a character disorder or psychoneurosis.

Both parents of the unsocialized aggressive child are highly inconsistent in their relationship with the child. They are punitive, and yet they are often overly permissive. Parental immaturity is indicated by the fact that either parent may be rivalrous with the child; family instability is indicated by the frequency of a stepfather or a stepmother. The critical, depreciative, and rejecting mother or stepmother is typical. The mother is likely to have a character disturbance or psychoneurosis.

The home from which the socialized delinquent comes is more likely to involve delegation of parental responsibility and a cold, distant, neglectful parental attitude. These are in part the product of the large family in meager economic circumstances. The parental pathology is more paternal than maternal and frequently includes the alcoholic father or stepfather. Neither parent is likely to be accepting of his involvement in the patient's problem or accepting of therapy for himself.

If we contrast these two latter groups, we find that the unsocialized aggressive child is more likely than the socialized delinquent to be an only child, to have a stepmother or a punitive mother, and much parental inconsistency. The present findings support the formulation that, as compared with the unsocialized aggressive child, the socialized delinquent is more a product of parental neglect and delegated parental responsibility. The development of the unsocialized aggressive child appears to involve a large measure of direct response to parental rejection and inconsistency, while the parental contribution to the problem of the socialized delinquent appears to be more one of a failure of parental control, and particularly paternal control.

17 *Parent Discipline and the Child's Moral Development*[1]

MARTIN L. HOFFMAN

HERBERT D. SALTZSTEIN

In the development of moral standards and internalization of controls, parent discipline focusing on (1) consequences of the child's action for others is most effective, (2) power and authority over the child is least effective, and (3) love withdrawal—direct but nonphysical expression of anger and disapproval—stands midway between the other two techniques. This study of seventh-grade children further examines the roles of mothers and fathers in discipline, middle- and lower-class disciplinary practices, and evaluates several explanations of the effects of parent discipline on the child's moral development.

Recent years have seen the accumulation of a body of findings relating moral development, especially internalization of moral values and the capacity for guilt, to parental practices. In a recent review of this research (Hoffman, 1963a) the following propositions received support: (a) A moral orientation based on the fear of external detection and punishment is associated with the relatively frequent use of discipline techniques involving physical punishment and material deprivation, here called power assertive discipline; (b) a moral orientation characterized by independence of external sanctions and high guilt is associated with relatively frequent use of nonpower assertive discipline—sometimes called psychological, indirect, or love-oriented discipline.

Several explanations of these findings have been advanced, each focusing on a different aspect of the parent's discipline. Thus, Allinsmith and Greening (1955) suggest that the

[1]This study was supported by Public Health Service Research Grant M–02333 from the National Institute of Mental Health. It was carried out while both authors were at the Merrill-Palmer Institute. The authors wish to thank Lois W. Hoffman for her many helpful comments and suggestions.

Reprinted from the *Journal of Personality and Social Psychology*, 1967, **5**, 45–57, by permission of the authors and the American Psychological Association.

significant variable may be the difference in the model presented by the parent during the disciplinary encounter (i.e., parent openly expresses anger versus parent controls anger). The importance of this factor may lie in the model it provides the child for channeling his own aggression. Where the parent himself expresses his anger openly, he thereby encourages the child to express his anger openly; where the parent controls his anger, he discourages the child from openly expressing anger and therefore may promote a turning of the anger inward which according to psychoanalytic theory is the process by which the guilt capacity is developed.

Another explanation of the difference between power assertive and nonpower assertive techniques is in terms of the duration of the punishment; that is, whereas nonpower assertive discipline may last a long time, the application of force usually dissipates the parent's anger and thus may relieve the child of his anxiety or guilt rather quickly. A third possibility, suggested by Sears, Maccoby, and Levin (1957), is that punishing the child by withholding love, which is frequently involved in nonpower assertive discipline, has the effect of intensifying the child's efforts to identify with the parent in order to assure himself of the parent's love.

A still different formulation has recently been suggested by Hill (1960). According to this view, the crucial underlying factor is the timing of the punishment. Love-withdrawal punishment is believed more often to terminate when the child engages in a corrective act (e.g., confession, reparation, overt admission of guilt, etc.)

whereas physical punishment is more likely to occur and terminate at the time of the deviant act and prior to any corrective act.

Finally, the important variable may be the information often communicated by nonpower assertive techniques regarding the implications of the child's deviant behavior. For example, Aronfreed's (1961) view is that such information can provide the cognitive and behavioral resources necessary for the child to examine his actions independently and accept responsibility for them.

Though varied, all but the last of these explanations assume the key ingredient for nonpower assertive discipline to be its punitive—more specifically, its love-withdrawing—quality. This hypothesis stems from psychoanalytic and learning theories that emphasize anxiety over loss of love as the necessary motivational basis for moral development.

In examining instances of nonpower assertive discipline it became apparent that the amount of love withdrawal, real or threatened, varied considerably. In some cases, the love-withdrawal aspect of the discipline seemed to predominate. In others it seemed totally absent, and in still others it seemed to be a minor part of a technique primarily focused on the harmful consequences of the child's behavior for others. This suggested that the effectiveness of these techniques might lie in their empathy-arousing capacity rather than, or in addition to, their love-withdrawing property. In the present study we accordingly made the distinction between two kinds of nonpower assertive discipline. One, called *induction,* refers to techniques in which the parent points out the painful consequences of the child's act for the parent or for others. In the second, called *love withdrawal*, the parent simply gives direct but nonphysical expression to his anger or disapproval of the child for engaging in the behavior. In a sense by these latter techniques the parent points out the painful psychological consequences of the act for the child himself, that is, the withdrawal of love by the parent.

It is probable, of course, that the child experiences both these types of nonpower assertive techniques as involving a loss of love. However, as indicated above, the love-withdrawing component of the induction techniques is more subdued, and in addition they provide him with the knowledge that his actions have caused pain to others. By doing this the technique capitalizes on the child's capacity for empathy. In our view (see Hoffman, 1963b; Hoffman, in press; Hoffman and Saltzstein, 1960) it is this capacity for empathy which provides a powerful emotional and cognitive support for development of moral controls and which has been overlooked in other psychological theories of moral development. For this reason it was expected that *induction, and not love withdrawal, would relate most strongly to the various indexes of moral development.*

Affection has often been supposed to be a necessary condition for moral development. Measures of the parent's affection were therefore included for completeness. We expected, following the pattern of the previous research, that power assertion would relate negatively, and affection positively, to the moral indexes.

METHOD

Sample

The children studied were all seventh graders in the Detroit metropolitan area. The test battery was administered to groups of children in the schools during three sessions spaced about a week apart. Sometimes an individual class was tested in the homeroom, and sometimes several groups were tested together in the gymnasium or auditorium.

Data bearing on the various dimensions of moral development were obtained from over 800 children broadly representative of the population in the area. Because of the apprehension of some of the school officials, however, we were unable to obtain reports of parental discipline from about a fourth of these children, the loss being greater among the lower-class sample. In addition, children identified as behavior problems and those from nonintact families were screened from the sample. Further shrinkage due to absences, incomplete background information, and unintelligible or incomplete responses resulted in a final sample of 444 children. Included were 146 middle-class boys, 124 middle-class girls, 91 lower-class boys, and 82 lower-class girls.

Subsequently, interviews were conducted with a subsample consisting of 129 middle-class mothers (66 boys and 63 girls) and 75 middle-class fathers (37 boys and 38 girls). No interviews were conducted with parents of the children from the lower class.

Child Morality Indexes

Several different moral indexes were used—each tapping a different aspect of conscience.[2] The two major indexes pertain to the degree to which the child's moral orientation is internalized. These are (a) the intensity of guilt experienced following his own transgressions, and (b) the use of moral judgments about others which are based on internal rather than external considerations. The other indexes pertain to whether the child confesses and accepts responsibility for his misdeeds and the extent to which he shows consideration for others. Identification, though not a direct moral index, was also included because of its relationship to moral development, as hypothesized by psychoanalytic theory and by recent researchers (e.g., Sears, et al., 1957).

GUILT   Two semiprojective story-completion items were used to assess the intensity of the child's guilt reaction to transgression. The technique presents the child with a story beginning which focuses on a basically sympathetic child of the same sex and age who has committed a transgression. The subject's instructions

_____
[2]These dimensions were used because they clearly bear on morality and because they represent different levels (affective, cognitive, overt) and directions for behavior (proscriptions, prescriptions). Each dimension has its advantages and disadvantages, and since a strong case for including one and not the others could not be made we included them all. In doing this our intention was not to treat them as indexes of a single underlying "moral development." Doing this would seem premature, since, although the different aspects of morality presumably increase with age (empirical data on age progression are available only for moral judgment), they very likely begin to develop—and reach full development—at different ages and progress at different rates.

are to complete the story and tell what the protagonist thinks and feels and "what happens afterwards." The assumption made is that the child identifies with the protagonist and therefore reveals his own internal reactions (although not necessarily his overt reactions) through his completion of the story.

The first story used here was concerned with a child who through negligence contributed to the death of a younger child. The story beginning was constructed so as to provide several other characters on whom to transfer blame. The second story was about a child who cheats in a swimming race and wins. In both stories detection was made to appear unlikely. In rating the intensity of the guilt from the subject's completion of the story, care was taken to assess first that the subject identified with the central character. If such identification was dubious, the story was not coded for guilt, nor were stories involving only external detection or concern with detection coded for guilt. All other stories were coded for guilt. For a story to receive a guilt score higher than zero there had to be evidence of a conscious self-initiated and self-critical reaction. Given evidence for such a reaction, the intensity of guilt was rated on a scale ranging from 1 to 6. At the extreme high end of the scale were stories involving personality change in the hero, suicide, etc. In coding the stories the attempt was made to ignore differences in sheer style of writing and to infer the feeling of the subject as he completed the story.

A departure from the usual practice was to assign two guilt scores to each story—one for the maximum guilt experienced by the hero, usually occurring early in the story, and the other for terminal guilt. In relating discipline to this and other facets of morality extreme groups were chosen. In choosing the high- and low-guilt groups, attention was paid to both scores. That is, the high-guilt group included those who sustained a high level of guilt throughout the stories. The low-guilt group included children who manifested little or no guilt throughout the stories. Children who initially manifested intense guilt which was dissipated through confession, reparation, defenses, etc., were not included in the guilt analysis.

INTERNALIZED MORAL JUDGMENTS The moral judgment items consisted of several hypothetical transgressions which the children were asked to judge. These situations were of the general type used by Piaget, including moral judgments about persons committing various crimes, for example, stealing; choosing which of two crimes was worse, for example, one involving simple theft and the other a breach of trust; and judgments of crimes with extenuating circumstances, for example, a man who steals in order to procure a drug which he cannot afford and which is needed to save his wife's life.[3] In each case the child's response was coded as external (e.g., "you can get put in jail for that"), internal (e.g., "that's not right, the man trusted you"), or indeterminate. The individual internal scores were then summed for all items, and the sum constituted the child's internalization score on moral judgments.

OVERT REACTIONS TO TRANSGRESSION Two measures were used to assess the child's overt reactions to transgression. The first was the teacher's report of how the child typically reacts when "caught doing something wrong." The categories

included: "denies he did it"; "looks for someone else to blame"; "makes excuses"; "cries, looks sad, seems to feel bad"; "accepts responsibility for what he has done"; and "where possible tries on own initiative to rectify situation."

The second measure was a questionnaire item asked of the child's mother, similar to the item used by Sears, et al. (1957). The question was: "when . . . . has done something that (he) (she) knows you would not approve of, and you haven't found out about it yet, how often does (he) (she) come and tell you about it without your asking?" The mother was asked to check one of five alternatives, the extremes of which were "all the time" and "never."

Neither of these measures is ideal. The first has the disadvantage of asking for the child's reaction in the presence of an authority figure after detection. The second has the defect of being based on a report by the parent, who is the same person providing much of the discipline data and who is more likely to be influenced by "social desirability" than the teacher. Yet, the parent may well be the only person with enough background information and close contact with the child to make a knowledgeable estimate of how he acts before detection.

CONSIDERATION FOR OTHER CHILDREN This measure was obtained from sociometric ratings by the childen in the same classroom. Each child made three nominations for the child first, second, and third most "likely to care about the other children's feelings" and "to defend a child being made fun of by the group." The usual weights were used and the two scores summed.

IDENTIFICATION Our major measure of identification was based on the child's responses to several items bearing on his

---

[3]This item was an adaptation of one used by Kohlberg (1963).

orientation toward the parent: (a) admiration: "Which person do you admire or look up to the most?"; (b) desire to emulate: "Which person do you want to be like when you grow up?"; (c) perceived similarity: "Which person do you take after mostly?" Responses which mention the parent were coded as parent-identification responses and summed to obtain an overall identification score. It should be noted that this measure is designed to assess the child's conscious identification with the parents and not necessarily the unconscious identification of which Freud wrote.

CODING PROCEDURE The story completion and moral judgment coding were done by one of the authors (HDS). To avoid contamination, the procedure was to go through all 444 records and code one item at a time. Especially difficult responses were coded independently by both authors, and discrepancies were resolved in conference.

Before the final coding was begun, coding reliabilities of 82% for maximum guilt, 73% for terminal guilt, and 91% for internal moral judgment were attained by the authors. These figures represent the percentage of agreement in giving high (top quartile), low (bottom quartile), and middle ratings. There were no extreme disagreements, that is, no instances in which a child received a high rating of one judge and a low rating by the other.

Measures of Parent Practices

Two reports of each parent's typical disciplinary practices were available—one from the children who reported the disciplinary practices of both parents, another from the mothers and fathers who each reported their own typical disciplinary practices. The reports from the children were collected during the third testing session in the schools. The parents were interviewed separately by trained female interviewers. The interview typically lasted about an hour.

Assessment of parental discipline was made in the following way. Each respondent (the child or parent) was asked to imagine four concrete situations: one in which the child delayed complying with a parental request to do something, a second in which the child was careless and destroyed something of value, a third in which he talked back to the parent, a fourth situation in which he had not done well in school. Following each situation was a list of from 10 to 14 practices. The respondent was asked to look over the list, then rate the absolute frequency of each and finally to indicate the first, second, and third practice most frequently used.[4] These three choices were weighted, and the scores summed across the four situations. The practices listed represented our three main categories. The first category, *power assertion,* included physical punishment, deprivation of material objects or privileges, the direct application of force, or threat of any of these. The term "power assertion" is used to highlight the fact that in using these techniques the parent seeks to control the child by capitalizing on his physical power or control over material resources (Hoffman, 1960). The second category, *love withdrawal,* included techniques whereby the parent more or less openly withdraws love by ignoring the child, turning his back on the child, refusing to speak to him, ex-

---

[4] Ratings of the absolute frequency were included primarily to make sure the respondent thought about all the items in the list before ranking them.

plicitly stating that he dislikes the child, or isolating him. The third category, *induction regarding parents,* includes appeals to the child's guilt potential by referring to the consequences of the child's action for the parent. Included are such specifics as telling the child that his action has hurt the parent, that an object he damaged was valued by the parent, that the parent is disappointed, etc.

These lists were administered to each parent twice, once with instructions to select the techniques which he used at present, and next to select those he remembers using when the child was about 5 years old. Reports of past discipline were not asked of the children because it was unlikely that they could remember parent practices used several years before.

The above measure of induction is a limited one in that it only included instances where the parent made references to the consequences of a transgression for the parent himself. To supplement this, an additional measure of induction was constructed. This dealt with the parent's reaction to two situations in which the child's transgression had harmful consequences for another child. In the first situation the child, aged 5, aggresses against another child and destroys something the other child has built, causing the other child to cry. In the second situation the parent sees his child aged 6–10 making fun of another child. The parent was asked what he would have done or said in such a situation, and his reaction was coded along a 3-point scale for the degree to which he (the parent) makes reference to and shows concern for the *other* child's feelings. The scores were summed to arrive at a measure of the parent's use of *induction regarding peers.*

Assessment of the parent's affection for the child was also obtained from the child and from the parent. The child was given a list of 19 behaviors indicating affection, approval, criticism, advice giving, and participation in child-centered activities and asked to indicate along a 4-point scale how often the parent engaged in such behaviors. The affection score was a simple weighted sum for the affection and approval items.

A slightly different measure was used to obtain affection data from the parents. They were given a list of eight behaviors indicating affection, approval, qualified approval, and material reward and asked to indicate along a 4-point scale how often they engaged in such behaviors when the child "did something good." The affection score was a weighted sum for the affection items.

BACKGROUND INFORMATION   The family's social class was determined from the child's responses to questions about the father's occupation and education. The distinction was basically between white collar and blue collar. In a few cases, families initially classified as middle class were later recategorized as lower class as a result of more accurate and specific information from the parent about the father's actual occupation and education.

DATA ANALYSIS   The data were analyzed separately for middle-class boys, middle-class girls, lower-class boys, and lower-class girls. The procedure for each of these subsamples was to form two groups—one scoring high and one scoring low on each moral development index— and then to compare these groups on the child-rearing-practice scores obtained in the child reports and (in the case of the middle class only) the parent interviews. In forming the comparison groups, the cutoff points were made as close as pos-

TABLE 1.—Statistically Significant Relations between Child's Morality Indexes and Mother's Discipline Techniques: Middle Class

MORALITY INDEX	POWER ASSERTION			LOVE WITHDRAWAL			INDUCTION RE PARENT			INDUCTION RE PEERS[a]		
	Boys	Girls	Sum	Boys	Girls	Sum	Boys	Girls	Sum	Boys	Girls	Sum
Guilt (child's response)		−p*	−c*, −n*, −p*				+c*	+p*	+c*, +n*, +p*	+p*		+p**
Internal moral judgment (child's response)		−n*			−c*	−c*		+c*				
Confession (mother's report)	−p**		−p**				+n*		+c*			
Accepts responsibility (teacher's report)	−c*	−c*, −n*	−c*, −n**		+n*		+c*, +n*, +p*		+c**			
Consideration for other children (peers' ratings)	+n*	−p*	−p*	−p*				+n*, +p*	+c*		+p**	+p**
Identification (child's response)	−c*	−c*	−c**		−n*		+p*	+c*	+c*			

Note.—The data sources of the significant findings summarized in Tables 1, 2, and 4–6 are indicated as follows: c (child report), n (parent report of current practices), p (parent report of past practices).

[a] Data on induction regarding peers are incomplete since these data were obtained only from the parent reports of past practices.

* p < .05.

** p < .01.

sible to the upper and lower quartile points within each subsample.

The test of significance used throughout was the median test.

CONTROL ON IQ   An important feature of this study, which was not true in the previous moral development research, was the control on intellectual ability which was instituted. Scores on either the California Test of Mental Maturity or the Iowa Tests of Basic Skills were found —with social class controlled—to relate positively to internalized moral judgments and consideration for others, negatively to confession, and negatively to parent identification. This suggested that some of the findings previously reported in the literature might be the artifactual results of a lack of IQ control. In forming the high and low quartile groups for these variables we therefore controlled IQ—to the point of making the high-low differences in IQ negligible. Since IQ did not relate to guilt, there was no need to control IQ in the guilt analysis.

RESULTS AND DISCUSSION

To facilitate presentation of the results, the significant findings relating moral development indexes and parental discipline are summarized in Tables 1 and 2 for the middle-class sample and Tables 4 and 5 for the lower-class sample.[5] Included in each

_____
[5]Seven pages of tables giving medians for each of the high and low quartile groups have been deposited with the American Documentation Institute. Order Document No. 9079 from the ADI Auxiliary Publications Project, Library of Congress, Washington, D. C. 20540. Remit in advance $1.25 for microfilm or $1.25 for photocopies and make checks payable to: Chief, Photoduplication Service, Library of Congress.

table are relationships between each of the six indexes of moral development and each of the four measures of parental discipline: power assertion, love withdrawal, induction regarding parents, and induction regarding peers. Tables 1 and 2 are based on present discipline as reported by the child and present and past discipline as reported by the parent. Since the parent's report was not available for the lower-class sample, Tables 4 and 5 are based solely on the child's report of present parental discipline.

Middle-Class Discipline

The overall pattern of the findings in the middle class provides considerable support for our expectations, at least with respect to the mother's practices. Thus the frequent use of power assertion by the mother is consistently associated with weak moral development. The use of induction, on the other hand, is consistently associated with advanced moral development. This is true for both induction regarding parents and induction regarding peers. In all, there are a large number of significant findings especially for the major moral indexes —guilt and internalized moral judgments.

In contrast to the mothers, few significant findings were obtained for fathers—for boys as well as girls—and those that were obtained did not fit any apparent pattern.

A further step in the analysis of induction was to combine all indexes of this category into a composite index. The results, presented in Table 3, were quite striking in the case of mothers for all the moral indexes. Significant findings, all in the expected

TABLE 2.—Statistically Significant Relations between Child's Morality Indexes and Father's Discipline Techniques: Middle Class

MORALITY INDEX	POWER ASSERTION			LOVE WITHDRAWAL			INDUCTION RE PARENT			INDUCTION RE PEERS		
	Boys	Girls	Sum	Boys	Girls	Sum	Boys	Girls	Sum	Boys	Girls	Sum
Guilt (child's response)												
Internal moral judgment (child's response)		$-c^*$						$+c^*$				
Confession (mother's report)	$+p^*$		$+p^*$		$+c^*$		$-p^*$		$-p^*$			
Accepts responsibility (teacher's report)	$-c^{**}$		$-c^*$			$+c^*$						
Consideration for other children (peers' ratings)	$+n^*$		$+p^*$		$-c^*$			$+c^{**}$	$+c^{**}$			
Identification (child's response)												

$^*p < .05.$
$^{**}p < .01.$

TABLE 3.—Statistically Significant Relations between Child's Morality Indexes and
Parent's Composite Induction Score: Middle Class

MORALITY INDEX	MOTHER'S INDUCTION			FATHER'S INDUCTION		
	Boys	*Girls*	*Sum*	*Boys*	*Girls*	*Sum*
Guilt (child's response)	+*	+*	+*			
Internal moral judgment (child's response)	+*	+*	+**			
Confession (mother's report)	+**			+***		
Accepts responsibility (teacher's report)	+*			+*		
Consideration for other children (peers' ratings)			+**	+*		
Identification (child's response)	+*					

*$p < .05$.
**$p < .01$.
***$p < .005$.

direction, were obtained for boys on guilt, internal moral judgments, confession, and acceptance of responsibility; and for girls on guilt, internal moral judgments, and consideration for others. When both sexes are combined, the findings are significant for all the moral indexes. The findings on identification are significant only for boys, however.

In contrast to induction, love withdrawal relates infrequently to the moral indexes (see Table 1). Further, in most cases in which significant relations between love withdrawal and moral development do occur, they prove to be negative. Taken as a whole, the importance of the distinction between love withdrawal and induction has been clearly demonstrated by these findings.

In sum it is a pattern of infrequent use of power assertion and frequent use of induction by middle-class mothers which generally appears to facilitate the facets of morality included in this study.[6]

---

[6]The question might be raised here as to the extent to which these findings should be interpreted as independent. Do induction and power assertion exert independent influence on morality, or are they but two aspects of the same influence; for example, do the measures used require that someone high on induction is necessarily low on power assertion? The findings in Table 1 suggest the influences are largely independent. That is, there are only a few instances in which negative power assertion findings and positive induction findings for the same subsample were obtained with the same measure. In most cases the findings for the two types of discipline were obtained with different measures, and in some instances a finding was obtained for one but not the other (e.g., guilt in boys relates to induction, but not to power assertion).

There is, however, one major exception to this pattern. The peer's reports of the boy's consideration for other children is positively related to the mother's report of their present use of power assertion (Table 1). A possible explanation of this finding is that our measure of consideration is a poor one especially for the boys. In particular, there is no built-in provision to assure that the behavior is based on internal motivation. The motive behind such behavior in the case of boys might instead often be a need for approval by peers. Why this should be the case for boys and not girls remains unclear. It should be noted, however, that consideration is a more deviant value for boys than girls. Evidence for this is provided from a measure of values administered to the children. The largest sex difference found was on the consideration item ("goes out of his way to help others"). The girls valued this trait more than the boys ($p < .001$). Thus consideration does not appear to have a different meaning for the two sexes.

Lower-Class Discipline

In discussing the lower-class findings the lack of parent interview data must be kept in mind. Nevertheless, there are several very apparent contrasts with the middle-class sample. Foremost among these is the general paucity of significant relationships between the child's moral development and his report of parental discipline. This is especially striking in the case of the mother's discipline. Furthermore, of those significant relationships that emerge, two are inconsistent with

our expectations. First, as with the middle-class sample, the boy's consideration is related positively to the mother's use of power assertion. Second, in contrast with the findings for the middle-class boys, guilt is positively associated with the mother's use of love withdrawal, but unrelated to the mother's use of power assertion or induction. In summary, our expectations were not confirmed for the lower-class sample, and no general conclusion may be drawn.

The infrequent relationships between the child's moral development and the mother's discipline, compared to the middle-class sample, suggest that the lower-class mother's discipline may be less crucial and singular a variable. This in turn may be due to several factors. First, the mothers more often work full time in the lower than in the middle class. Second, the combination of large families and less space may result in the parent and child interacting with many other people besides each other. Third, according to the more traditional family structure usually found in the lower class (e.g., Bronfenbrenner, 1958), the father is more often the ultimate disciplining agent. In our sample, for example, boys more often reported that their mothers had the fathers do the disciplining ("says she'll tell your father") in the lower class than in the middle class ($p < .01$). Fourth, lower-class children are encouraged to spend more time outside the home than middle-class children. For all these reasons the socializing process may be more diffuse in the lower class; that is, it may be more equally shared by the mother with the father,

TABLE 4.—Statistically Significant Relations bewteen Child's Morality Indexes
and Mother's Discipline: Lower Class

MORALITY INDEX	POWER ASSERTION			LOVE WITHDRAWAL			INDUCTION RE PARENT		
	Boys	Girls	Sum	Boys	Girls	Sum	Boys	Girls	Sum
Guilt (child's response)				+c*				+c*	
Internal moral judgment (child's response)									
Accepts responsibility (teacher's report)									
Consideration for other children (peers' ratings)	+c*							+c*	
Identification (child's response)					−c*	−c*			

Note.—Interview data were not obtained from the lower-class parents. Thus all entries in Tables 3 and 4 are based on child reports. For the same reason lower-class data on confession and on induction regarding peers were unavailable.

*$p < .05$.

TABLE 5.—Statistically Significant Relations between Child's Morality Indexes
and Father's Discipline: Lower Class

MORALITY INDEX	POWER ASSERTION			LOVE WITHDRAWAL			INDUCTION RE PARENT		
	Boys	Girls	Sum	Boys	Girls	Sum	Boys	Girls	Sum
Guilt (child's response)	−c*				+c*				
Internal moral judgment (child's response)									
Accepts responsibility (teacher's report)									
Consideration for other children (peers' ratings)									
Identification (child's response)	−c*		−c*				+c*		+c*

*$p < .05$.

with siblings, members of the extended family, the child's peers, and others.[7]

Further research comparing the two classes needs to be performed. One might conjecture that because of the more diffuse socialization process in the lower class the basis of internalization may be quite different for children in the two classes, with consequent differences in the kind of morality that develops.

Affection

The relations between affection and the six moral indexes are presented in Table 6. The most notable features of this table are first, as expected, the relationships are positive; second, most of the findings, as with the discipline data, were obtained for middle-class mothers. It should also be noted that most of the findings are based on the child's report.

Role of the Father

Several studies of delinquency (e.g., Glueck and Glueck, 1950; McCord and McCord, 1958; Miller, 1958)

----

[7]Another possible explanation for the paucity of findings in the lower class is that the lower-class children are very low on morality. Thus if the upper quartile of the lower class on morality were like the lower quartile of the middle class, there would be no reason to expect similar associations for the two classes. This possibility can be discounted since there was no overlap between the lower-class upper quartile and the middle-class lower quartile. And although there was a general tendency for the lower class to be lower on morality than the middle class, the difference was significant only for internal moral judgment and consideration for others, and only for girls.

suggest that the father is important in the development of internal controls. Our findings, especially in the middle class, seem to suggest that this is not so. Relatively few significant relationships were obtained between paternal discipline and the child's morality, and several were in a direction opposite to that expected.

Of course, it is possible that the role of the father is more important than indicated in this study. For example, the father might provide the cognitive content of the standards by direct instruction rather than by his discipline techniques. Lacking data on direct instruction, we could not test this possibility. Another possibility is that the role of the father is a less direct one. That is, he may affect the moral development of the child by his relationship to the mother and his influence on the discipline techniques chosen by the mother. This is indicated in a study of preschool children where evidence was found suggesting that women who are treated power assertively by their husbands tend to react by using power assertive discipline on their children (Hoffman, 1963c). It may also be that the father's role is ordinarily latent in its effects and only becomes manifest under exceptional circumstances such as those often associated with delinquency. That is, under normal conditions with the father away working most of the time and the mother handling most of the disciplining, as in our middle-class sample, the father's importance may lie mainly in providing an adequate role model that operates in the background as a necessary supporting factor. Under these conditions, the specific lines along

TABLE 6.—Statistically Significant Relations between Child's Morality Indexes and Parent's Affection

MORALITY INDEX	MIDDLE CLASS						LOWER CLASS					
	Mothers			Fathers			Mothers			Fathers		
	Boys	Girls	Sum	Boys	Girls	Sum	Boys	Girls	Sum	Boys	Girls	Sum
Guilt (child's response)	+c*		+c*									
Internal moral judgment (child's response)		+c*	+n*			+n*						
Confession (mother's report)	+c*		+c*			+p*						
Accepts responsibility (teacher's report)		+n*			+n*							
Consideration for other children (peers' ratings)	+p*	+c*	+c* +n*				+c*			+c*		
Identification (child's response)	+c**	+c**	+c**				+c*					

* $p < .05$.
** $p < .01$.

which the child's moral development proceeds may be determined primarily by the mother's discipline. An adequate role model is lacking, however, in extreme cases as when there is no father, when the father is a criminal, or when the father is at home but unemployed, and this may account for the findings obtained in the delinquency research.

Methodological Issues

Any study of child rearing and moral development that relies on indexes of discipline and morality from the same source is open to the criticism that the relationships that emerge are due to the lack of independence of the sources. If that source is the child himself, the suspicion might be held that the child's report of parental discipline is simply another projective measure of the child's personality. It should be noted that in the present study the relationships between the child's morality and the parent's report of discipline were generally in the same direction as those involving the child's report of discipline. (We refer here to the middle-class-mother findings.) In addition, over half the significant findings for each sex involve relations between measures obtained from different respondents.

Further support for our findings comes from a recent review in which our threefold discipline classification was applied to the previous research (Hoffman, in press). Since most studies used a power assertive-nonpower assertive dichotomy, as indicated earlier, the raw data were examined (and recoded where necessary) to determine whether love withdrawal, induction, or some other form of nonpower assertion was responsible for

the findings. The results were clearly consistent with ours. Since a wide range of theoretical and methodological approaches were involved in the studies reviewed, our confidence in the findings reported here is considerably strengthened.

A common problem also relevant to the present design is that no definitive conclusion may be drawn about causal direction of the relationships obtained. Any solution to this will have to wait upon application of the experimental method or longitudinal studies. Nevertheless, some support for the proposition that discipline affects moral development, rather than the reverse, may be derived from the fact that several findings bear on the use of discipline in the past. If these reports are assumed to be reasonably valid, to argue that the child's moral development elicits different discipline patterns (rather than the reverse) necessitates the further assumption that the child's morality has not changed basically from early childhood. This is an unlikely assumption in view of common observations (e.g., about the child's changing acceptance of responsibility for transgression) and the findings about the developmental course of moral judgments obtained by Piaget (1948), Kohlberg (1963), and others.

Theoretical Discussion

In this section we will analyze the disciplinary encounter into what we believe to be some of its most basic cognitive and emotional factors.

First, any disciplinary encounter generates a certain amount of anger in the child by preventing him from completing or repeating a motivated act. Power assertion is probably most likely to arouse intense anger in the child because it frustrates not only the act but also the child's need for autonomy. It dramatically underscores the extent to which the child's freedom is circumscribed by the superior power and resources of the adult world. This is no doubt exacerbated by the fact that power assertion is likely to be applied abruptly with few explanations or compensations offered to the child. (The empirical evidence for a positive relation between power assertion and anger has been summarized by Becker, 1964.)

Second, a disciplinary technique also provides the child with (a) a model for discharging that anger, and may provide him with (b) an object against which to discharge his anger. The disciplinary act itself constitutes the model for discharging the anger which the child may imitate.

Third, as much animal and human learning research has now shown, what is learned will depend on the stimuli to which the organism is compelled to attend. Disciplinary techniques explicitly or implicitly provide such a focus. Both love withdrawal and power assertion direct the child to the consequences of his behavior for the actor, that is, for the child himself, and to the external agent producing these consequences. Induction, on the other hand, is more apt to focus the child's attention on the consequences of his actions for others, the parent, or some third party. This factor should be especially important in determining the content of the child's standards. That is, if transgressions are followed by induction, the child will learn that the important part of transgressions consists of the harm done to others.

Fourth, to be effective the technique must enlist already existing emotional and motivational tendencies within the child. One such resource is the child's need for love. This factor depends on the general affective state of the parent-child relationship, the importance of which may be seen in the consistent relationship obtained between affection and the moral indexes (Table 6). Given this affective relationship, some arousal of the need for love may be both necessary for and capable of motivating the child to give up his needs of the moment and attend to (and thus be influenced by) the parent's discipline technique. Too much arousal, however, may produce intense feelings of anxiety over loss of love which may disrupt the child's response especially to the cognitive elements of the technique. All three types of discipline communicate some parental disapproval and are thus capable of arousing the child's need for love. But it is possible that only inductions can arouse this need to an optimal degree because the threat of love withdrawal implicit in inductions is relatively mild. Also, it is embedded in the context of a technique which explicitly or implicitly suggests a means of reparation. Inductions are thus likely to disrupt the child's response—as well as his general affective relationship with the parent—than either love withdrawal which may arouse undue anxiety, or power assertion which arouses anger and other disruptive affects.

The second emotional resource, empathy, has long been overlooked by psychologists as a possibly important factor in socialization. Empathy has been observed in children to occur much before the child's moral controls are firmly established (e.g., Murphy, 1937). We believe that it is a potentially important emotional resource because it adds to the aroused need for love the pain which the child vicariously experiences from having harmed another, thus intensifying his motivation to learn moral rules and control his impulses. Of the three types of discipline under consideration, induction seems most capable of enlisting the child's natural proclivities for empathy in the struggle to control his impulses. As indicated in greater detail elsewhere (Hoffman, 1963b; Hoffman, in press; Hoffman and Saltzstein, 1960), we view induction as both directing the child's attention to the other person's pain, which should elicit an empathic response, and communicating to the child that he caused that pain. Without the latter, the child might respond empathically but dissociate himself from the causal act. The coalescence of empathy and the awareness of being the causal agent should produce a response having the necessary cognitive (self-critical) and affective properties of guilt.

It follows from this analysis that power assertion is least effective in promoting development of moral standards and internalization of controls because it elicits intense hostility in the child and simultaneously provides him with a model for expressing that hostility outwardly and a relatively legitimate object against which to express it. It furthermore makes the child's need for love less salient and functions as an obstacle to the arousal of empathy. Finally, it sensitizes the child to the punitive responses of adult authorities, thus contributing to an externally focused moral orientation.

Induction not only avoids these deleterious effects of power assertion, but also is the technique most likely to optimally motivate the child to focus his attention on the harm done others as the salient aspect of his transgressions, and thus to help integrate his capacity for empathy with the knowledge of the human consequences of his own behavior. Repeated experiences of this kind should help sensitize the child to the human consequences of his behavior which may then come to stand out among the welter of emotional and other stimuli in the situation. The child is thus gradually enabled to pick out on his own, without help from others, the effects of his behavior, and to react with an internally based sense of guilt. Induction in sum should be the most facilitative form of discipline for building long-term controls which are independent of external sanctions, and the findings would seem to support this view.

Love withdrawal stands midway between the other two techniques in promoting internalization. It provides a more controlled form of aggression by the parent than power assertion, but less than induction. It employs the affectionate relationship between child and parent perhaps to a greater degree than the other two techniques, but in a way more likely than they to produce a disruptive anxiety response in the child. However, it falls short of induction in effectiveness by not including the cognitive material needed to heighten the child's awareness of wrongdoing and facilitate his learning to generalize accurately to other relevant situations, and by failing to capitalize on his capacity for empathy.

The weak and inconsistent findings for love withdrawal suggest that anxiety over loss of love may be a less important factor in the child's internalization than formerly thought to be the case. Before drawing this conclusion, however, the possibility that love withdrawal is only effective when the parent also freely expresses affection, as suggested by Sears, et al. (1957), should be considered. We were able to test this hypothesis by examining the relation between love withdrawal and the moral indexes within the group of subjects who were above and below the median on affection, and also within the upper and lower quartile groups. The results do not corroborate the hypothesis: the relations between love withdrawal and the moral indexes do not differ for the high- and low-affection groups.

In an earlier study with preschool children, however, love withdrawal was found to relate negatively to the expression of overt hostility in the nursery school (Hoffman, 1963b). It was possible to make a similar test in the present study since teacher ratings of overt hostility were available. Here, too, love withdrawal related negatively to hostility outside the home ($p <$ .05).[8] We also found that love withdrawal is used more when the child expresses hostility toward the parent than in other types of discipline situations. These findings suggest that the contribution of love withdrawal to moral development may be to attach anxiety directly to the child's hostile impulses, thus motivating him to keep them under control. Psychoanalytic theory may thus be correct after all in the importance assigned love withdrawal in the socialization of the child's impulses. Our data, however, do not support the psychoanalytic view that identification is a necessary mediating process. That is, we found no relation between love withdrawal and identification (Tables 1–4). It remains possible, of course, that a form of unconscious identification which may not be tapped by our more consciously focused measure serves to mediate between the parent's love withdrawal and the child's inhibition of hostile impulses—as suggested in psychoanalytic theory.

In any case, our data do tend to show that love withdrawal alone is an insufficient basis for the development of those capacities—especially for guilt and moral judgment—which are critical characteristics of a fully developed conscience.[9]

---

[8]Power assertion related positively to hostility ($p <$ .05), and induction showed a slight nonsignificant negative relation.

Some relevant experimental evidence is also available. Gordon and Cohn (1963) found that doll-play aggression expressed by children in response to frustration decreased after exposure to a story in which the central figure, a dog, searches unsuccessfully for friends with whom to play. Assuming the story arouses feelings of loneliness and anxiety over separation in the child—feelings akin to the emotional response to love-withdrawal techniques—these findings may be taken as further support for the notion that love withdrawal may contribute to the inhibition of hostility.

[9]It should be noted that love withdrawal might relate positively to guilt as defined in psychoanalytic terms, that is, as an irrational response to one's own impulses. Clearly our concept of guilt is quite different from the psychoanalytic, pertaining as it does to the real human consequences of one's actions.

18 *Parents' Differential Reactions to Sons and Daughters*[1]

MARY K. ROTHBART

ELEANOR E. MACCOBY

This report explores parents' reactions to a child's voice as a function of sex of parent and sex of child. Fathers show greater permissiveness toward girls than boys for both dependency and aggression; mothers show greater permissiveness toward boys than girls. Parents' sex-role differentiation scores as measured by a questionnaire are found to relate to their responses to the child's voice, but the expectation that high differentiation parents would show a stronger tendency to promote stereotyped sex-role behavior in the child is not upheld. Several hypotheses for some unexpected findings are considered, and a suggestion is made for replication studies with different socioeconomic samples of parents.

The existence of sex differences in psychological functioning has been repeatedly documented in psychological literature. Often the differences have been unexpected and have taken complex forms (Oetzel, 1966). Any theory of sex typing that attempts to understand the sources of these differences must consider the possible effects of differential parent pressures occurring as a function of the sex of the child. Few studies have as yet explored the nature of differential parent behaviors toward boys and girls, and any complete study of this kind would have to consider sex of parents as another important source of variation. The present study therefore attempts to examine parent behavior toward a

[1] The authors would like to express their gratitude to Clarene Dong, Carol Spielman, and Paul Wick, who assisted in the development and administration of the initial pilot study, and to Aimée Leifer, who worked on all phases of the final study. This research was financed in part by Public Health Service Predoctoral Fellowship No. 5, F1 MH-20, 971-02, National Institute of Mental Health.

Reprinted from the *Journal of Personality and Social Psychology*, 1966, **4**, 237–243, by permission of the authors and the American Psychological Association.

child as a function of (*a*) sex of the parent, and (*b*) sex of the child.

Previous studies of mother-father differences in treatment of boys and girls have been of two major types. The first involves children's perceptions of their parents' behavior; the second involves parents' perceptions of their own behavior and attitudes toward their children. Numerous studies of children's perceptions of their parents have been carried out, and the literature is summarized and briefly criticized by Droppleman and Schaeffer (1963). Considering only studies with preadolescent children, a common finding has been that both boys and girls "prefer" the mother to the father and find her friendlier and easier to get along with (Hawkes, Burchinal, and Gardner, 1957; Kagan, 1956; Simpson, 1935).

Cross-sex findings suggesting an interaction between sex of parent and sex of child have also been reported. When Simpson (1935) questioned children ranging in ages from 5 to 9, the boys said they were punished (spanked) more by their fathers than their mothers. Girls said mothers spanked them more, but the inference from their projective responses was that the father punished more. Kagan and Lemkin (1960) interviewed children ages 3–8 and found few sex differences in reports of parent practices. Both boys and girls reported that the opposite-sex parent "kissed the most." Girls saw the father as more punitive and affectionate than the mother, while boys saw him only as more punitive. Kagan (1956) interviewed first-, second-, and third-grade children on four issues: Who (the mother or the father) would be on the child's

side in an argument; who punishes; who is the boss of the house; who is more feared. With children of all ages combined, there was little cross-sex difference in response. When the younger and the older children were treated separately, the older children showed a consistent tendency to see the same-sex parent as less benevolent and more frustrating.

In studies involving parents rather than children, Aberle and Naegele (1952) and Tasch (1952) used only fathers as subjects. Fathers reported different expectations for sons and daughters and said that they participated in different activities with their sons than with their daughters. Sears, Maccoby, and Levin (1957) used only mothers as subjects, interviewing at length mothers of nursery school children. Mothers reported that they permit more aggressiveness from boys when it is directed toward parents and children outside the family, no difference in permissiveness of aggression against siblings. No differences in severity of punishment for aggression nor in permissiveness for dependency were found. Mothers reported they did most of the disciplining of both sexes, but that the father took a larger role in disciplining his son when both parents were at home. In a study with both parents, Goodenough (1957) found that mothers were less concerned about their child's appropriate sex typing than were fathers. Fathers also reported they were actively involved in implementing sex typing of their children, while mothers reported they did not consciously attempt to influence sex typing.

Emmerich (1962) gave questionnaires for assessing nurturance and restrictiveness to parents of children ages 6–10, defining nurturance as reward for positive behavior and dependency, and restrictiveness as punishment for negative behavior. The two scales were combined as a measure of power. Mothers were found to be more nurturant and less restrictive toward children of both sexes. A marked trend was also found for fathers to exert more power toward their sons than their daughters, and a similar but less powerful trend for mothers to exert more power toward their daughters than toward their sons. Emmerich's data are suggestive of differences between mothers and fathers in their treatment of boys and girls, but only on a very general dimension. The questions asked of parents were also quite amorphous, for example, rating the extent to which he compliments his daughter "when she does what she knows she should do," or gives her "something at the time she wants it."

The present experiment is an attempt to study parents' reactions to specific child behaviors, including some regarded as sex typed, for example, dependency and aggression.

We are also interested in a test of a hypothesis proposed by social learning theorists to account for sex differences in behavior. Mischel (1966) suggests:

The greater incidence of dependent behaviors for girls than boys, and the reverse situation with respect to physically aggressive behavior, seems directly explicable in social learning terms. Dependent behaviors are less rewarded for males, physically aggressive behaviors are less rewarded for females in our cul-

ture, and, consequently there are mean differences between the sexes in the frequency of such behaviors after the first few years of life.

Assuming that the family constitutes the major "culture" to which the preschool child is exposed, we might predict from this learning-theory interpretation that both parents would consistently reinforce dependency more strongly in girls and aggression more strongly in boys. The present study is designed to test this prediction.

Parents were put in a hypothetical situation with a child and were asked to record their immediate reactions to what the child said and did. To avoid the additional variables that would compound an adult's reaction to an actual boy or girl, the recorded voice of a single child constituted the stimulus material. The voices of a number of 4-year-olds were recorded, and one was chosen which judges could not readily identify as to sex. Some of the parents were informed that it was a boy's voice, some that it was a girl's voice, and differences in their responses were examined. A questionnaire was also used to measure the extent to which a parent differentiates between the sexes by either (*a*) feeling boys and girls are different on selected characteristics, or (*b*) feeling boys and girls *should* differ on these characteristics. It was hypothesized that parents showing high differentiation between boys and girls would show greater differences in reaction to the boy's voice compared with the girl's voice than would parents who differentiated little between the sexes.

METHOD

This study was preceded by an initial individual testing of 58 mothers. A small pilot group of both mothers and fathers was then tested in a group-administered procedure, and the coding categories and questionnaire were revised. The final testing involved both fathers and mothers in a group administration.

Selection of the Stimulus Voice

The child speaker was chosen by recording nine nursery school children reciting a prepared script. Six adult judges rated the sex of each child after hearing the tape recordings. The voice selected (that of a boy) was judged to be a boy by half the judges and a girl by the other half. In the actual study, none of the parent subjects questioned the sex attributed to the voice they heard.

The statements comprising the script were adaptations of actual statements of 3- and 4-year-old children recorded in the same locality approximately a year before the final study. An attempt was made to make the script as realistic as possible, and a number of mothers in the individually administered pretest remarked that the recorded child sounded very much like their own nursery school child.

Subjects

Subjects were 98 mothers and 32 fathers of children enrolled in a parent-education nursery school. These parents came from a range of socioeconomic status levels, with a concentration of upper-middle-class families.

Of these parents, 60 mothers and 21 fathers were told that the voice was a girl's, 38 mothers and 11 fathers that it was a boy's. The reason for a larger number of parents hearing the girl's than the boy's voice was that only the number of parents expected to attend had been matched according to sex and age of the nursery school child and assigned to the two groups. More parents attended than had been anticipated, and the extra parents all heard the girl's voice.

The group hearing the boy's voice and the group hearing the girl's voice proved to be matched according to sex of nursery school age child, but it was later found that the two groups were not well matched with respect to whether the parent had children of only one or of both sexes. Our sample was divided according to this variable, and no differences in a direction that would influence our results were found.

Presentation of the Stimulus Voice

Parents were tested in four separate groups (fathers-girl's voice, fathers-boy's voice, mothers-girl's voice, mothers-boy's voice), with female experimenters. Each experimenter introduced the parents to the situation represented by the tape-recorded voice. The subject was asked to imagine that he (or she) was at home reading, with his 4-year-old boy, Johnny (or girl, Susan), playing with a puzzle in an adjacent room. With the child is the 1-year-old baby. Subjects were asked to give their immediate reactions to the 4-year-old's statements by writing down what they would say or do in response to each statement. The child's statements were as follows. (Due to some lack of clarity in the tape, each statement of the child was repeated by the experimenter to assure that it was understood by all subjects.)

1. Daddy (or Mommy), come look at my puzzle.
2. Daddy, help me.

3. Does this piece go here?
4. Baby, you can't play with me. You're too little.
5. Tell him he can't play with my puzzle—it's mine!
6. Leave my puzzle alone or I'll hit you in the head!
7. I don't like this game—I'm gonna break it!
8. I don't like this game. It's a stupid game. You're stupid, Daddy.
9. Ow! Baby stepped on my hand!
10. Daddy—it hurts.
11. Daddy, get me another puzzle.
12. It's not raining now—I'm going across the street and play.

After each statement, the experimenter stopped the tape while subjects recorded their reactions.

Parents' responses were coded for each item, and items were grouped according to 7 different scales: Help Seeking (Items 1, 2, 3, 11), Comfort Seeking (9, 10), Dependency (Help and Comfort Seeking scales combined), Aggression (6a, 7a, 8a), Allowing Child to Stop Game (7, 8), Siding with Child versus Baby (4, 5, 6), and Autonomy (12). Scores on all scales ranged generally from permissiveness for the child (low score) to nonpermissiveness for the child's actions (high score). For example, in response to the child's statement 9 ("Ow! Baby stepped on my hand!"), a rating of high comfort was given to the response, "Here, Mommy will kiss it," while a rating of low comfort was given to the response, "Keep your hand away from the baby's foot." In response to Statement 5 ("Tell him he can't play with my puzzle—it's mine!"), a

parent who said, "That's right. Let's find the baby something else," was rated as siding with the child. A response of "Johnny, let your brother help you" was rated as siding with the baby. All protocols were coded by one rater, and 25 were coded independently by a second rater. Reliabilities ranged from .83 to 1.00, with a mean scale correlation of .90.

Questionnaire

The parent questionnaire, administered immediately after the tape-recorded script, measured two aspects of parents' attitudes about sex differences. Part 1 asked parents' opinions about differences they felt actually existed between boys and girls. The items included were taken from statements given by mothers to open-ended interview questions about sex differences from the files of the Sears, et al. (1957) study. The format for the questionnaire was adapted from Sherriffs and Jarrett (1953). A sample from the 40-item list is as follows:

More likely to be obedient are: ___ ___ ___.
$$\text{G} \quad \text{B} \quad \text{X}$$

Here, G represents girls, B boys, and X no sex differences. The measure of sex-role differentiation for this part of the scale was the total number of X responses, with a large number of X responses indicating low sex-role differentiation.

Part 2 of the questionnaire measured what differences parents felt *should* exist between boys and girls. Boys and girls were rated separately on how important it was to the parent that his child be described by each characteristic. A sample item is:

Very important *not* to	Fairly important *not* to	Unimportant to	Fairly important to	Very important to	
					be obedient.

TABLE 1.—Mother's and Father's Reactions to Boy's versus Girl's Voice

VOICE	HELP SEEKING (High score-refuses help)		COMFORT SEEKING (High score-refuses)		DEPENDENCY (High score-refuses)		AGGRESSION (High score-does not permit)	
	Mothers	Fathers	Mothers	Fathers	Mothers	Fathers	Mothers	Fathers
Boy's								
M	8.71	8.45	4.24	5.82	12.95	14.18	4.95	5.64
SD	1.71	1.51	1.73	2.18	2.32	2.92	1.29	2.16
N	38	11	38	11	38	11	37	11
Girl's								
M	9.15	8.39	5.02	4.84	14.17	13.12	4.91	4.86
SD	1.93	1.61	1.86	1.56	3.05	2.55	1.32	1.62
N	59	18	59	19	59	17	56	21

VOICE	ALLOWING CHILD TO STOP GAME (High score-does not)		SIDING WITH CHILD VERSUS BABY (High score-sides with baby)		AUTONOMY (High score-does not permit)		AGGRESSION TOWARD PARENT (High score-does not permit)	
	Mothers	Fathers	Mothers	Fathers	Mothers	Fathers	Mothers	Fathers
Boy's								
M	3.62	4.18	6.13	7.64	1.97	2.27	1.59	2.27
SD	1.09	1.17	1.43	1.43	.64	.64	1.76	1.01
N	37	11	37	11	37	11	38	11
Girl's								
M	4.00	3.62	6.76	6.20	2.10	2.40	1.75	1.67
SD	1.09	1.16	1.47	1.61	.47	.60	1.16	1.11
N	57	21	59	19	60	20	60	21

Note.—Mean scores.

TABLE 2.—Summary of Analyses of Variance Interaction Tests between Sex
of Parent and Sex of Child's Voice

VARIABLE	INTERACTION (MS)	ERROR (MS)	F
Help Seeking	1.81	3.24	.56
Comfort Seeking	16.29	3.28	4.97**
Dependency	27.06	7.67	3.53*
Aggression	3.13	2.11	1.48
Allowing Child to Stop Game	5.54	1.31	3.70*
Siding with Child versus Baby	24.94	2.16	11.55***
Autonomy	.04	.32	.12
Aggression toward Parent	4.02	1.02	3.94**

*$p < .10$, $df = 1/121, 1/122$.
**$p < .05$, $df = 1/123, 1/125$.
***$p < .01$, $df = 1/123$.

As a measure of sex-role differentiation for Part 2 of the questionnaire, absolute differences between ratings of an item's importance for girls and importance for boys were summed. The higher this difference (D) score, the higher the sex-role differentiation that was indicated.

RESULTS

Parents' Response
to the Child's Voice

When the direction of differences for all scales are considered, a general trend emerges. Mothers tend to be more permissive for the boy's voice and fathers more permissive for the girl's voice (see Table 1). While only one main effect was significant (Scale 7—fathers allowed more autonomy than mothers, $p < .05$), interactions were significant for Scale 2 (Comfort Seeking, $p < .05$), Scale 3 (Dependency, $.05 < p < .10$), Scale 5 (Allowing Child to Stop Game, $.05 < p < .10$), and Scale 6 (Siding with Child versus Baby, $p < .01$) as shown

in Table 2. On all of these scales, the interaction was in the direction of mothers showing more permissiveness and positive attention to their sons than to their daughters, fathers showing more permissiveness and positive attention to their daughters than to their sons.

Our failure to find a significant interaction for the Aggression scale was somewhat surprising, since in the initial pilot study we had found a strong tendency for mothers to allow more aggression from their sons than from their daughters. In the pilot study, our measure of aggression had been composed chiefly of aggression directed against the parent. For this reason, Item 8a (Aggression toward Parent) was examined separately from the rest of the Aggression scale. Item 8a showed a significant interaction ($p < .05$), with fathers allowing more aggression from their daughters than from their sons and mothers allowing more aggression from their sons than from their daughters.

Questionnaire

Parents' X scores on the questionnaire (extent to which parents felt differences *do* exist between boys and girls) were correlated with parents' D scores (extent to which parent felt differences *should* exist between boys and girls). The correlation between X and D scores for mothers was $-.53$; the correlation for fathers was $-.40$. Since a high D score and a low X score both represent high sex-role differentiation, these findings indicate a positive correlation between the two measures.

There were no significant differences between mothers' and fathers' sex-role differentiation scores, but parents who had heard the girl's voice tended to have higher sex-role differentiation scores than parents who had heard the boy's voice. This trend appeared in mothers' X and D scores and in fathers' D scores, but was significant only for mothers' D scores ($p < .05$). This finding is difficult to explain, and it suggests that questionnaire scores may be influenced by situational variables.

Finally, parents with high sex-role differentiation scores were separated from parents with low sex-role differentiation scores. Both X and D scores for mothers and fathers were standardized, and divided approximately at the median for the high- and low-differentiation groups. Since not all parents received the questionnaire, Ns for the fathers' group were quite small. Parents' responses to the child's voice were then compared, with the expectation that high-differentiation parents would show larger differences between their treatment of boys and

girls than would low-differentiation parents. It was also expected that these differences would be in the direction of promoting sex-typed behavior. The first part of this prediction received some support in this study; the second part did not. When scores for all scales were standardized and summed for each subject, giving a general permissiveness score toward the child, high-differentiation parents tended to show greater permissiveness to the opposite-sex child (see Table 3). High sex-role differentiation parents showed larger differences between treatment of boys and girls than did low-differentiation parents for fathers separated on the basis of D scores ($p < .02$) and for mothers separated on the basis of X scores ($p < .05$). The differences were in the same direction but not significant for mothers separated according to D scores and fathers separated according to X scores.

In testing the hypothesis that differences would run in a sex-stereotyped direction, parents' responses on the Dependency and Aggression scales were more closely examined. On the basis of all parents' responses to the D questionnaire, it was expected that high-differentiation parents would act to promote dependency in girls and assertiveness in boys. When these scales are examined, however, the differences seem rather to be for high-differentiation parents to show greater relative permissiveness to the opposite-sex child than low-differentiation parents. These differences were significant only in Scales 1 and 3 for mothers separated according to D scores (high-differentiation mothers more permissive of dependency in boys, p

TABLE 3.—Mean Standard Scores Representing Degree of Overall Permissiveness for High- and Low-Differentiation Parents

VOICE	MOTHERS		FATHERS	
	High diff.	Low diff.	High diff.	Low diff.
	Groups assigned according to D scores			
Boy's				
M	48.71	47.72	50.75	50.92
SD	4.90	2.15	2.40	4.74
N	15	12	5	6
Girl's				
M	53.05	49.23	47.63	50.48
SD	5.45	4.09	4.49	4.57
N	10	11	8	9
	Groups assigned according to X scores			
Boy's				
M	48.62	48.52	55.15	53.05
SD	4.53	3.95	2.78	4.67
N	14	15	7	4
Girl's				
M	53.26	47.60	49.93	49.90
SD	4.81	5.12	3.85	4.52
N	11	9	9	10

Note.—High scores = nonpermissiveness.

$< .05$ for both scales), and Scale 3 for fathers separated according to X scores (high-differentiation fathers more permissive of dependency in girls, $p < .05$). The direction of these results suggests that high-differentiation parents do not necessarily promote sex-role stereotypes; they rather show an intensification of the kinds of differences found for parents as a whole. When the scores of all high-differentiation parents (regardless of which voice they heard) were compared with those of low-differentiation parents, there was an additional tendency for low-differentiation parents to show more general permissiveness than high-differentiation parents, but in no case was this difference significant.

DISCUSSION

Although previous studies have found clear differences between the behavior of mothers and fathers independent of the sex of the child, the present study found only one difference (permissiveness for autonomy) to be independent of the child's sex. A source of this discrepancy may be that earlier studies relied on verbal reports of children and parents; these reports might be expected to be influenced by the cultural stereotypes of the mother and father. The present study differed from the earlier ones in that a measure more closely approaching the behavior of a parent in an actual situation was used. Also, the fact that the fathers in this study were attending a meeting concerning their children indicates an involvement with the child that may not be found in the father population as a whole.

Another interesting discrepancy exists between some of the current findings and the predictions expected on the basis of commonsense notions of sex typing. For example, the mothers in this study were more likely to allow aggression toward themselves from their boys, as expected in sex-role stereotypes, but they were also more acceptant of comfort seeking in their sons than in their daughters, an entirely unexpected finding. Fathers, on the other hand, were more acceptant of their daughters' comfort seeking, but also allowed more aggression to be directed toward themselves from their daughters than from their sons. In short, the sex of parent seems to be a better predictor of his differential response to boys and girls than does a sex-role stereotype.

This finding presents some difficulties for the social learning theory interpretation of sex differences outlined at the beginning of this paper (Mischel, 1966). Rather than consistent reinforcement of sex-typed behavior by both parents, inconsistency between parents seems to be the rule, and while a parent may treat his child in a manner consistent with the cultural stereotype in one area of behavior, in another he may not.

It is, of course, possible that the only reinforcement counter to the cultural stereotype comes from the child's parents, and that reinforcement from other sources serves to counteract inconsistent parental pressures. It is also possible that parents shift their reinforcing behaviors as their children become older. These possibilities might apply to sex differences in dependency, which seem to emerge late enough to be affected by influences outside the home or later shifts in parental behavior. However, sex differences in aggression have been observed early, while the family is still the primary influence, and our findings fail to support the interpretation that differential reinforcement from both parents is of a kind to promote these differences at this early age level. Perhaps there is a biological component in these sex differences which is of importance either in its own right or in interaction with socialization practices.

There are several possible sources of the cross-sex interaction. In instances of permissiveness for the child's dependent behavior, the parent may be simply responding to the young child as a member of the opposite sex, reacting more favorably to the actions of the child who most resembles his marital partner. Or, reflecting the other side of the Oedipal coin, the parent may react less favorably to the same-sex child because of feelings of rivalry with this child. Another hypothesis, this one concerned with parents' differential responses to negative behavior in the child, suggests that parents may tend to punish the expression of impulses that they do not allow in themselves. As a child, the parent has been punished for certain actions and thoughts, and he may react negatively when he sees expression of these actions and thoughts in his child. When the child is of the same sex as himself, the parent may be more strongly reminded of the situation in which he had been punished, and more negative feelings are evoked. The parent is therefore more likely to punish the same-sex child for negative actions than the opposite-sex child.

The list of possibilities suggests that family interaction springs from multiple motivations, and that any tendency parents may have to reinforce culturally stereotypic behavior in their children may be outweighed by other determinants of their behavior. Parent behavior, then, may not always be consistent with preparing children for the social roles they will fill. Indeed, the child may acquire some aspects of his appropriate role behavior in spite of, rather than because

of, what at least one of his parents does as a reinforcing agent.

Although the questionnaire results are by no means conclusive, they suggest a pattern of differences for high-differentiation parents that is simply a stronger statement of the general findings of the study. Perhaps parents with high-differentiation scores are more aware of the differences that distinguish their sons and daughters, but tend to react in a sex-specific way to these sex differences rather than actively promoting sex-typed behavior in their children.

Parents taking the questionnaire for the most part had fairly low sex-role differentiation scores. If this study were replicated with a lower-class sample of parents, we would expect a wider range of sex-role differentiation scores and even stronger interaction effects than were found in this study.

In the School

5

19 *A Study of the Child's Concept of the Teacher*

GAYLE F. GREGERSEN

ROBERT M. W. TRAVERS

In this exploratory study of elementary school children's drawings of their classes and teachers, boys are more rejecting of their teachers than girls, but show no increase in rejection with advancing age-grade, whereas girls show increasing rejection. The degree to which girls show a negative attitude toward their teachers depends to some extent on the characteristics of the teacher.

Relatively few studies have explored the perceptions which elementary school pupils have of their classrooms and their teachers. One such study was conducted by Estvan and Estvan (1959) who presented first and sixth graders with a picture of a classroom and asked for interpretations. The younger children gave responses indicating greater positive effect than the older children. Estvan and Estvan interpreted the decline in enthusiasm for school shown by the older children as a result of increasing resistance to authority. Although more girls than boys produced positive responses to the classroom situation, the difference did not reach an acceptable level

Reprinted from the *Journal of Educational Research,* 1968, **61,** 324–27, by permission of Dr. Travers and Dembar Educational Research Services, Inc.

of significance. Powers (1962) found that girls were more accepting than boys of the teacher as an authority figure and that the brighter students tended to be more accepting than the less bright children. Meyer and Thompson (1956) found that three sixth-grade teachers showed more disapproval for the boys than for the girls, and they were also able to show that the children recognized this differential in teacher response.

This study investigates further the concepts that children of elementary school age have of their teachers. While the Estvan and Estvan study implies that pupils become more negative in their responses toward teachers as they progress through school, and the Meyer and Thompson study shows that teachers express stronger negative attitudes toward boys than toward girls, neither study provides any direct evidence concerning pupil responses to their particular classroom situation. This study attempts to provide some evidence concerning the latter. The study tests the following hypotheses: (a) girls show a more positive attachment to the teacher than do boys; (b) there are grade differences in students' perceptions of the teacher: boys show an increase in their rejection of the teacher with advancing grade, while girls continue to regard the teacher in a positive way as a person who interacts well with the class; (c) there are teacher differences which influence a pupil's concept of the teacher.

The use of drawings of children suggested itself as a technique for exploring the pupil's perception of the teacher, for there is considerable support for the position that the drawings of children reflect those features of the environment which have special significance for them.

The technical literature on drawing as a projective technique is too voluminous to review here. Of special significance is the early work of Goodenough (1926) who was the first to point out that the distortions shown in children's drawings are not just a result of technical inadequacy in the art of drawing but reflect also distortions related to what the child perceives as the important and essential features of the object displayed. Clinicians were quick to use the drawing technique as a means of exploring both the perceptual world and the personality structure of patients. The better known publications in this area include Machover's (1949) "Personality Projection in the Drawing of the Human Figure" and Buck's (1949) development of the house—tree—person drawing technique. These techniques were attempts to assess broad aspects of personality rather than a means of exploring a child's perception of particular aspects of his environment. One of the few studies in the latter category was undertaken by Hare and Hare (1956) who found that a child's drawing of the group in which he was participating was related to his social position in the group. In another study by Rabinowitz and Travers (1955) students of education in various stages of preparation were asked to "Draw a picture of a teacher with a class." The drawings reflected changes as the students passed through a program of teacher education designed to change their concept of the function of the teacher.

The plan of the present study was to explore the perceptions which children have of their teachers by asking them to draw a picture of their teacher and class.

METHOD

Drawings were obtained by a female research assistant preparing to be a school psychologist who contacted each classroom involved in the study and who, after an introduction by the teacher in charge, distributed mimeograph paper and gave the following instructions:

Write your name on the top left-hand corner of your paper. Put your room number under your name. Put your grade number under your room number. Now, turn your paper over. On this side draw a picture of your class and your teacher. Don't use stick figures. You may arrange your drawing any way you wish. This will be a quick drawing. We will take about twenty minutes.

In answer to questions asked by the pupils the administrator answered, "You may arrange your drawing in any way you wish."

Subjects

The subjects were 1,592 boys and girls in five metropolitan elementary schools covering a wide range of social and economic circumstances. The subjects were fairly evenly distributed over grades 1 through 4 and included 717 boys and 818 girls.

Scoring Procedure

Criteria were established for classifying the drawings into categories involving positive interaction, negative interaction, and unclassifiable. The following criteria were used:

1. Positive Interaction (+): (a) short distance between teacher and student(s); (b) pleasant, visible features of both teacher and student(s); (c) compatibility of activity between teacher and student(s); (d) pleased attention of student(s) when teacher is dominant figure; (e) size of teacher and student(s) in reasonable proportions.

2. Negative Interaction (−): (a) teacher well defined and student(s) not well defined; (b) aggressive motions of teacher toward student(s); (c) passive student(s) and active teacher; (d) forced attention of student(s) with dominant teacher; (e) heavy shadings of the student(s) figures(s); (f) extreme distance between teacher and student(s); (g) no relationship of activity between teacher and student(s); (h) presence of only teacher or only student(s); (i) no facial features or frowns on students while the teacher has (have) facial features.

3. Drawing cannot be classified: (a) room void of people; (b) human figures represented by circles with no discernible characteristics; (c) the drawings cannot be deciphered.

The drawings were classified into one of these three broad classes based on the judgment of the classifier. The above criteria were used as a general guide to judgment and no attempt was made to score each drawing on each criterion.

One of the judges was the graduate student who collected the data and the other was a practicing child psychologist who was uninformed about the purposes of the study. Precautions were taken to prevent contamination of the data. There were no identifying marks on the front of the drawings which were all shuffled by an independent person before any judgments were made by either judge. Each judge worked without a knowledge of the classifications assigned by the other judge. Neither judge received information about the child who had produced a drawing until all drawings had been judged. High agreement was found between the two judges on a sample of 417 drawings in which only 57 disagreements of over-all scoring were recorded. The only possible source of contamination would be the memory of the person who collected the 1,592 drawings, but who could hardly have been expected to remember whether particular drawings were undertaken by boys or girls.

RESULTS

The first hypothesis of the study, stating that boys are more rejecting of the teacher than are girls, was tested by comparing the frequency of positive and negative concepts presented by the boys and the girls. The data, presented in Table 1, show a clearly significant overall sex difference ($p < .001$). The hypothesis is accepted.

The second hypothesis stated that the boys would show an increased rejection of the teacher as they moved through the elementary school grades. This hypothesis was tested by examining the proportion of negative drawings for boys at each age level. The proportion in the negative category shows uniformity across grades.

The second hypothesis also stated that girls will continue through the four grades to represent the teacher as interacting positively with the class. This hypothesis was tested by comparing data for girls from grades 1 and 2 with grades 3 and 4. A comparison of the frequencies for the first two grades with the frequencies for the next two grades yields a value of chi square of 3.744 while a value of 3.841 would be significant at the .05 percent level of significance. The data are suggestive that the girls appear to show a decline in the relative frequency of positive responses. Estvan and Estvan found a similar differential.

TABLE 1.—Proportion of Drawings Falling in Positive and Negative Categories

		+	−	CHI SQUARE COMPARING THE PROPORTION BY SEX
First Grade	Boys	.33	.67	31.20 ($p < .01$)
	Girls	.64	.36	
Second Grade	Boys	.34	.66	44.34 ($p < .01$)
	Girls	.65	.35	
Third Grade	Boys	.32	.68	30.70 ($p < .01$)
	Girls	.61	.39	
Fourth Grade	Boys	.31	.69	14.03 ($p < .01$)
	Girls	.53	.47	

The third hypothesis was that there are teacher differences which influence a student's concept of a teacher. This hypothesis was tested by comparing the number of positive and negative concepts reflected in grade drawings produced in twelve third grade classes. A chi square test showed that there were significant departures from homogeneity for girls ($p < .05$) but not for boys.

CONCLUSIONS

Insofar as the drawings of children may be considered to represent projections of their concept of the classroom situations the following conclusions seem justified:

1. Boys have a more negative concept of the classroom than do the girls.
2. Boys show no change in the frequency of negative concepts over the grade range studied. The data for girls suggests an increase in negative concepts as the grade level rises.
3. The data suggest that there are differences in the frequency of negative drawings attributable to a teacher effect, but that girls may be more variable in their response to these differences than boys.

DISCUSSION

The findings that the negative responses are much more characteristic of boys than of girls suggests that the educational environment in the early grades is poorly planned to meet the needs of young males. This may be a consequence of the fact that the elementary school is largely run by women teachers and hence is likely to represent an environment planned in terms of the needs and characteristics of females. Elementary school functions are typically female-cen-

tered and the teacher is likely to show a preference for the well-groomed and docile girl to the untidy, dishevelled, and boisterous boy. The girl in the lower grades is verbally more advanced than the boy and also manifests greater social development which gives her an advantage in relation to the teacher. Boys show a higher incidence of aggressive behavior which does not fit well into a female planned environment. It is hardly surprising that with these disadvantages the boys' view of the teacher should be preponderantly negative. Our data fit well those of Meyer and Thompson and complement their findings that teacher disapproval is directed far more frequently against boys than against girls.

Our data also are consistent with Meyer and Thompson's hypothesis that the girls gain rewards from the teacher for activities in which they have been engaged for years. On the other hand, boys are likely to come into conflict with the teacher merely by practicing what they have long practiced. The vigorous physical activity of boys which is often accompanied by aggressive behavior leads the teacher to play an inhibiting role which may result in the boy's hostility being directed toward her.

Finally, a number of points may be made with respect to future research. First, although the technique involved overall judgments, it has shown itself to be relatively sensitive, but the sensitivity could, undoubtedly, be increased by scoring within each category. Second, the technique provides a basis for differentiating teachers who produce a higher frequency of positive responses from those who produce a higher frequency of negative responses. If teachers could be found who produced a high frequency of positive responses in boys, as well as in girls, then a study of the behavior of these teachers might reveal a pattern in which other teachers might be trained.

20 *Teacher Behavior toward Boys and Girls during First Grade Reading Instruction*[1]

O. L. DAVIS, JR.

JUNE JENKINSON SLOBODIAN

The study explores first-grade childrens' perceptions of teacher behavior and actual teacher-student interaction, in order to determine whether teachers discriminate against boys. Results indicate that children perceive that teachers discriminate against boys and favor girls; however, observations of actual teacher-pupil interaction reveal no differential treatment. Boys' and girls' reading achievement do not differ significantly.

The observation that girls demonstrate superior achievement in reading is generally acknowledged by teachers and substantiated in the research literature on school achievement. Girls seem to gain in reading achievement over boys during initial instruction (Gates, 1961; Stroud and Lindquist, 1942) and their superiority appears to persist through the secondary school (Loughlin, et al., 1965; Stroud and Lindquist, 1942). More boys attend reading clinics than do girls (Durrell, 1956; Newton, 1959). Even so, systematic research on sex differences is not as conclusive as expert opinion and some representative studies would suggest. Stroud and Lindquist (1942), in their review, noted "a conspicuous absence of significant differences," and some recent studies (Kowitz and Mahoney,

---

[1]An earlier version of this paper was presented at the American Education Research Association Convention, Chicago, Illinois, February 1966.

Reprinted from the *American Educational Research Journal*, May 1966, **3:**3, 261–269, by permission of the authors and the American Educational Research Association.

1964; Parsley, et al., 1963; Sinks and Powell, 1965) have reported generally nonsignificant sex differences.

In this ambiguous situation, belief in girls' superiority in reading, and efforts to both account for this difference and to act on it continue. Various factors such as growth and maturation have been advanced to explain girls' higher reading achievement (Chronister, 1964; Clark, 1959; Kowitz, 1964; and Nicholson, 1957). Elements of the general culture, expectations, and attitudes have been suggested (Dechant, 1964; Gates, 1961; Mazurkiewicz, 1960; and Preston, 1962). Also, for many years, the nature of the school and teacher behaviors have been asserted to contribute to boys' lower scholastic achievement in general, and reading achievement in particular. Ayres (1909) commented that "our schools as they now exist are better fitted to the needs and natures of the girl than of the boy pupils." The *feminized* school was attributed to the behaviors of women teachers by St. John (1932). He observed that boys' generally lower academic performance was "due chiefly to a maladjustment between the boys and their teachers which is the result of interests, attitudes, habits, and general behavior tendencies of boys to which the teachers fail to adjust themselves and their school procedures as well as they do to the personality traits of girls." While general observations such as these have appeared from time to time, McNeil (1964) has presented evidence which indicated that first grade (female) teachers do not treat boys and girls equally under reading instruction. Boys in his study

had achieved higher than girls under programmed instruction during kindergarten, but had been surpassed by the girls after a period of classroom instruction in first grade. The evidence employed by McNeil demonstrated teachers' apparent discrimination against boys by uses of pupil and teacher reports of their perceptions. Thus, McNeil (1964) suggested "an association between teacher behavior and performance in beginning reading."

Do female first grade teachers in fact discriminate against boys and favor girls in the situation of reading instruction? That is, do these teachers actually behave differently toward boys and girls during reading instruction? In the presence of meager, and, as yet only indirect evidence, the present study was designed as a portion of the continued inquiry that is obviously warranted.

PROCEDURE

This study was designed to incorporate a) collection and analysis of pupil perceptions of teacher behaviors in the setting of the reading instruction, b) collection and analysis of observed teacher-pupil interaction data gathered during regular reading instruction, and c) analysis of sex differences in reading achievement, if any, and the relation of these data to teacher-pupil interaction data.

Subjects

Ten first-grade teachers and their pupils provided data for this study. These classes were chosen from the first-grade sections in a large public school system in the Detroit, Michigan, suburban area. Eligible for selection were only those classes whose teachers had experience at the first-grade level, were on tenure in the system, and would agree to participate in the study. These teachers ranged in age from 23 to 38 years (median: 27.5). All teachers held baccalaureate degrees; one possessed a master's degree. Their teaching experience ranged from two to 9½ years (median: 4 years). Nine of the ten teachers were married; three had children of their own. All classes were heterogeneously grouped and used a system-wide-adopted basal reading series. In the ten classes, 276 pupils were enrolled. Since complete data were available on 238 (122 boys and 116 girls), this total served as the study population. Boys and girls in this study did not differ significantly with respect to age (boys: 82.3 months; girls: 82.4 months) and to reading achievement (Harrison-Stroud Readiness Test) (boys: $M = 95.30$, $SD = 23.25$; girls: $M = 97.71$; $SD = 22.14$). Data were collected during the Spring, 1965.

Data Collection

Pupil perceptions of pupil-teacher interactions during reading instruction were gathered in individual interviews employing a standard structured schedule. Questions asked pupils by McNeil (1964) were included in addition to four additional items. The pupils were told, "pretend you are in your reading group. To whom is the teacher talking when she says: a) Read that page out loud for us?, b)[2] Sit up and pay attention?, c) You did a fine job of reading?, d)[2] Who doesn't get to read very much in your group?, e) Who doesn't read

well?, and f) Who is the best reader in your group?" Pupils could name themselves if they so desired.

Following McNeil (1964), teachers were asked to rate each pupil in the classroom according to his motivation and readiness for reading, "considering the child's ability to pay close attention to explanations, stay with a task, and ask relevant questions." Instead of a five-point scale as used by McNeil, a graphic rating scale (Guilford, 1954) was employed.[3]

To guide the observation and systematic recording of teacher-pupil verbal interactions in the setting of reading instruction, a Reading Observation Record (ROR) was developed following procedures outlined by Medley and Mitzel (1963).[3] The ROR makes possible the sequential recording of verbal discourse segments, similar to the cycles of Bellack and Davitz (1963), and elements within these segments. Provided by the ROR, consequently, were data on the number of call-on response units, acceptance-response units, rejection-response units, interruption-response units, interruption-acceptance units, and interruption-rejection units. The sequence of interaction was also noted. The ROR also provided data regarding time spent by teachers on various standard reading instructional activities. Five experienced special reading teachers were trained as observers for this study. All reached a criterion of 95 percent agreement on all observations made during training. The reading instruction in each of the first grade classes participating in the

---

[2]Items used by McNeil (1964).
[3]Appended to the selection.

study was observed, employing the ROR, on four different days by different observers. Each reading group in a class was observed on the same day and data over all reading groups were pooled for analysis.

The Stanford Achievement Test, Primary Battery, Form X, provided data on pupils' general reading achievement. The raw score for reading was employed. This incorporated raw scores from the subtests of word meaning, paragraph meaning, word study skills, vocabulary, and spelling.

FINDINGS

To check on the possibility of interview-item overlap for each class, the difference was calculated between the percentage-of-boys-nominated to all-pupils-nominated and the percentage of boys in the class. These differences for each class were ranked for each question and intercorrelated (Spearman *rho* coefficients). The results, displayed in Table 1, indicate

that the percentage of boys nominated in each class was not consistent across questions and that the interview items evoked different percentages of boy nominations. Non-significant item overlap was revealed.

Analyzing the total number of nominations received by boys and girls, following McNeil (1964), boys were perceived as receiving more negative comments from the teacher ($X^2 = 43.94$, $p < .01$), as having little opportunity to read ($X^2 = 12.76$, $p < .01$), and as being poor readers ($X^2 = 9.98$, $p < .01$). Non-significant sex differences were obtained on analysis of nominations as receiving much opportunity to read, as receiving praise from the teacher, and as best reader. This number (three) of significant differences is itself significant ($p < .01$) (Sakoda, Cohen, and Beall, 1954).

These results, while consistent with those reported by McNeil, are suspect and conclusions based on them, as were McNeil's, seem unwarranted.

TABLE 1.—Intercorrelations (Spearman *rho*) of Interview Questions

ITEM[a]	1	2	3	4	5	6
1	—	.56	.15	.44	.50	.20
2		—	.35	.72*	.38	.13
3			—	.18	.16	.54
4				—	.22	.12
5					—	.00
6						—

* p .05

1—receiving more negative comments from the teacher.
2—little opportunity to read.
3—much opportunity to read.
4—receiving praise from the teacher.
5—being "best" reader.
6—being poor readers.

Based on the total number of nominations, they do not take into account the fact that multiple nominations received by an individual and credited to a sex group would exaggerate the real situation. For example, several nominations of the same boy as having little opportunity to read might exceed the number of single nomina tions of several girls. The assumption of independence underlying the chi-square tests employed is doubtful. While their use, therefore, may be questionable (Lewis and Burke, 1949), obtained results are particularly useful here in that they may be related to those obtained by McNeil. Consequently, nomination data were reexamined.

First, an analysis was performed on the number of individual boys and girls nominated on each interview item. As a result of this re-analysis, boys were still perceived as receiving more negative comments from the teacher ($X^2 = 7.50$, $p < .01$) and as being poor readers ($X^2 = 4.16$, $p < .05$). On each of the other four analyses, no significant sex difference was noted. This number of obtained significant differences (two of six) still being significant, the earlier conclusion of pupil's perceiving teachers' differentially treating boys and girls is supported.

Inasmuch as the results of these chi-square analyses were suspect because of the doubtful assumption of independence, a second and probably more appropriate set of analyses was performed. For each question, the percentage of boys nominated to all pupils nominated in each class was contrasted to the percentage of boys in that class. (Classes in which boys nominated/all pupils nominated $>$ boys/class members were assigned "1"; classes in which boys nominated/all pupils nominated $<$ boys/class were assigned "0.") These data were then subjected to sign tests. For none of the six interview items was a significant difference ($p = .05$) obtained. Thus, pupils in the classes did not nominate a significantly higher percentage of boys of those named than the percentage of boys in the classes.

Inspection of the nomination data further suggested that nominations on some of the items were sex-linked. Subsequent analysis revealed sex-linking in a significant number of contrasts. Boys were found to choose other boys and girls to select other girls when asked who received the most opportunity to read ($X^2 = 65.91$, $p < .01$), who was told he did a fine job after finishing reading ($X^2 = 7.18$, $p < .01$), and who read the best ($X^2 = 39.03$, $p < .01$). Boys were nominated significantly more by both boys and girls on the item relating to negative comments from the teacher ($X^2 = 5.52$, $p < .05$). On the items relating to who did not read well and who did not read much, nominations were not sex-linked.

Teachers' estimates of pupils' motivation and readiness for reading were treated by two analyses. Pupils rated at or above the mean were categorized as "motivated and ready for reading" while pupils rated below the mean were classified as being perceived by their teachers as having little motivation and readiness to read. Teachers were found to have assessed more boys as "less motivated and ready" than girls ($X^2 = 6.75$, $p < .01$).

Teachers did not so assess a higher proportion of boys than the percentage of boys in the class. Non-significant differences were also obtained between teachers' mean assessment of boys and girls ($t < 1.0$).

Tables 2 and 3 present summary results of the analyses of variance (Lindquist Type I) performed on the observation (ROR) data. A non-significant difference was noted between the number of times boys and girls were called on to respond by their teachers (see Table 2); too, teachers were not found to react differentially to boys' and girls' responses. A significant difference in the nature of teachers' reactions to pupils' responses was revealed; teachers employed more "acceptance" and "neutral" than "rejection" reactions. Boys were found to interrupt the reading group significantly more than girls (see Table 3), but teachers did not react differently to boys' interruptions than to girls'. Apparently, teachers were "accepting" or "rejective" of interruptions without regard to whether the interruptions originated with boys or girls. In addition, teachers did not react (acceptance, rejection, or neutral) in one way more frequently than another to interruptions.

General reading achievement of boys

TABLE 2.—Summary of Analysis of Variance (Lindquist Type I) of Observed Call-On Response/Treatments

SOURCE	D.F.	SUM OF SQUARES	MEAN SQUARE	F	F .05
Between (class and sex)	19	457.65			
Between sex	1	34.12	34.12	1.45	4.41
Error between	18	423.53	23.53		
Within (classroom and sex and response)	40	810.48			
Nature of response	2	712.12	356.06	134.36	3.28
Response × sex	2	3.35	1.68	.64	3.28
Error within	36	95.01	2.65		

TABLE 3.—Summary of Analysis of Variance (Lindquist Type I) of Observed Interruption/Treatment

SOURCE	D.F.	SUM OF SQUARES	MEAN SQUARE	F	F .05
Between (class and sex)	19	56.63			
Between sex	1	25.58	25.58	14.79	4.41
Error between	18	31.05	1.73		
Within (classroom and sex and response)	40	66.13			
Nature of response	2	4.41	2.21	1.38	3.28
Response × sex	2	4.02	2.01	.796	3.28
Error within	36	57.70	1.60		

($M = 92.74, SD = 30.48$) and of girls ($M = 93.86, SD = 26.99$) was not significantly different ($t < 1.0$). Subsequently, comparisons were made of the reading achievement of all pupils and of those nominated on the six interview items. Each of the comparisons revealed nonsignificant differences.

DISCUSSION

Results of this investigation do not support the hypothesis that female first grade teachers discriminate against boys and favor girls in reading instruction. In particular, these findings conflict sharply with those presented by McNeil (1964), provide empirical confirmation of several questions raised by Ingle and Gephart (1966), and suggest that explanations of boys' lower reading achievement under classroom teaching, if real, probably should be focused on the specific teacher-pupil interactions in the situation of classroom reading instruction.

Pupils' perceptions of teacher behavior toward pupils during reading instruction, at least in this study, must not be admitted as evidence of teachers' differential behavior toward boys and girls. Analysis of the interview data according to individuals nominated rather than the total number of nominations received by boys and girls yielded generally non-significant results. Had McNeil also analyzed the data in these ways, results quite different from those reported might well have been obtained. In addition, the finding of sex-linked nominations on a significant number of interview items, a possibility unexamined by McNeil, further points out the general unsuitability of these data on which to base conclusions about teachers' treatment of pupils during reading instruction.

More damaging to the notion of teachers' discrimination against boys, because it is more direct and relevant, is the observation evidence presented. Teachers were not found to call on girls more and boys less frequently or to direct more negative comments toward boys during reading instruction. Rather, teachers were observed as giving boys and girls essentially equal opportunity to read and/or respond during reading instruction. Teachers, further, did not treat (accept, reject, ignore) boys' responses differently than girls'. Even though boys interrupted the reading group more frequently than girls, teachers reacted to these interruptions essentially no differently than when the interruptions were originated by girls. Teachers' reactions to interruptions, in all likelihood, were framed primarily by the demands of the situation itself and not by noting if the interrupting pupil was a boy or a girl. These results obviously indicate that the female first grade teachers in this study did not act (at least in their verbal behavior) differently toward boys and girls. Apparently, the teachers worked at the task of teaching pupils to read, without considering the sex of the pupil relevant in this instructional setting.

These results underscore the importance of obtaining direct, behavioral evidence whenever possible in studies of teaching. Such data about the teaching behaviors of the teachers in McNeil's study might also have contributed to a different conclusion than that advanced. In such an event, an hypothesis other than teacher differential treatment would have been necessary to explain the achievement differences noted under the two situations (auto-instruction and classroom).

In light of these findings, continued inquiry is clearly dictated. A matter of basic concern is the reality or fiction of important sex differences in school achievement, reading in particular. The situation is ambiguous at present, to say the least. The value of auto-instructional procedures in reading instruction, demonstrated by Mc-Neil (1964), merits attention. If replications reveal a consistent finding of boys' higher achievement than girls' under auto-instruction, explanations should be sought that lie more directly within the context of these procedures. Obviously, additional studies of classroom teacher's behaviors, particularly during reading instruction and including attention to more than verbal behavior, and employing refined observational schedules, will be valuable.

DIRECTIONS FOR USE OF READING OBSERVATION RECORD (JUNE 1967)

I. *Materials Needed:*

Stop Watch
Reading Observation Record (ROR)
Pencil or Pen

II. *Procedures:*

a) Complete the information re. classroom, teacher, observer, time of beginning observation, and date.

b) Indicate the reading group being observed: high, middle, low.

c) Begin timing the moment children are seated for reading class or when the teacher makes the first comment re. the reading instruction.

d) Place in brackets under Act. (activity) the letter which corresponds to the activity in process.

e) Begin to check units of action, starting on a new line each time the unit changes. Begin numbering each unit in sequence 1–2–3–4–5, starting over again each time a new unit is started and

TEACHER FORM

                                    School _____
Date: _____   Teacher _____

Indicate on the scale below by placing an "X" on the line at approximately the point which best describes each child in your room in terms of readiness and motivation for reading. Base your decision on the child's ability to pay close attention to explanations, stay with a task, and ask relevant questions.

NAME: _____ Low _____ High

the observer moves down a line on the form.

A unit of action is completed when the originator of the action changes—when the action returns to the originator—or when a new activity or action is initiated. The exception to this is when an interruption occurs or multiple responses occur. Then the observer drops down one line on the form to record the interruption but does not return to the number 1, when the interruption is concluded and the action resumes, the observer either moves up to the preceding line to continue numbering, or if the return to the former unit is not made, he drops down a line and begins to number with the number 1, indicating a new unit of action was begun.

f) When an activity changes, return to a new line (vertically) and place the activity letter in brackets preceding the first number in the activity squares. Record time elapsed and clear stop watch in order to start timing the new activity.

g) Continue the observation until the reading class is dismissed (children rise and return to their seats—or teacher leaves group to move on to new group).

h) Total at the bottom of the schedule the number of checkmarks in each column. Total at the right side the number of actions which occur between one bracketed number and the next.

i) Record to the right of the bracketed numbers at the top of the sheet, the amount of time in minutes and seconds devoted to each activity.

III. Definitions of Terms and Recording of Information:

1. *Activities* (Act.) First Column— Post a letter in this column and check the stop watch to begin timing the activity in process. Definitions of the various activities are as follows:

a. *Developing Readiness/Establishing Background*—(R) Questions or statements with reference to the introduction of materials. This section may include board writing of children's statements and introduction of new words to be met in the lesson.

b. *Guided Reading*—(G) This section refers to silent reading done by students in order to answer questions or discover points mentioned by the teacher. It may directly follow establishment of background or may occur any time during the reading lesson. The crucial determining factor in this category is that the children read in response to either a question or direction from the teacher.

c. *Oral Reading*—(O) The category above refers to the "round-robin" type reading which goes on in a reading group. Children are called on and either stand to read or take turns to read orally. If a child reads only a portion of a page in response to a question or statement from the teacher this is considered guided reading, and not tabulated as fall-

ing in the oral reading category. The oral reading category is reserved only for rote
or routine reading activities
which enable the teacher to
evaluate reading skill. If the
children present a play or do
some kind of oral reading
from sequence in the book,
this is considered oral reading.

d. *Skill Development*—(S)
This category refers to direct
instruction in phonics, structural analysis, syllabication, or
techniques for improved comprehension. If the teacher
makes reference to these skills
in other sections, i.e. developing of readiness or guided
reading sections, the number
is not changed. It must be
clear to both teacher and students that word attack skills
are being taught in order to
record this number as a category.

e. *Extending Interests*—(I)
This category refers to teacher
making assignments, reviewing lessons or workbook pages
from the preceding day, or
teacher preparing students at
their seats prior to initiation of
group reading activities.

2. *Headings*—The major headings
are listed below with definitions
for each:

a. *Talk*—Presentation of information, structuring by use of
statements, possibly leading or
transferring to questioning.
Literally any statement which
is not in response to a question
or in response to teacher request for information falls in
the "talk" category. When a
teacher has not asked a question but merely calls on children by name who wish to
contribute information, tally
is recorded in boy talk or girl
talk columns.

b. *Calls on/Questions*—A teacher
or student asking a question or
requiring by command a response from a student is
marked in this column.

c. *Responds*—Answers given to
questions or replies made
when called on are indicated
by marking the appropriate
box under this column. Multiple responses are indicated
by checkmarks vertically on
the next lower line. Multiple
responses differ from confusion or yelling out of answers in that they can clearly
be heard and follow sequentially one another. However if
the teacher nods or the child
looks at the teacher to gain
approval before responding,
this is considered a call-on by
the teacher. When the teacher
calls for word recognition and
asks children to read a word
from the board, this is recorded as an "all" response
whether the action occurs simultaneously, or one at a time
in rapid succession. However,
if a question of another kind
intervenes individual re-
sponses, the tallies for board
word reading are recorded
individually by respondent
either b(boy) or g(girl).

d. *Interruption*—A sudden change
of topic which occurs before

the appropriate series of actions to close the unit of action is completed. Entrance of the reading group for information, etc. by a student outside the group. Teacher stopping the chain of discussion to speak to child either inside or outside the group for purposes of maintaining order or giving direction.

e. *Acts to*—In response to an interruption, the other party involved either accepts or rejects the interruption. Acceptance is indicated by a response such as "good," "fine," or a similar comment. Rejection also is indicated by such comments from the teacher as, "Take your seat, don't come to reading class until we are finished"; "I can't talk with you now"; etc. A motion of the hand or head indicating the interrupter is not being received should also be scored as a rejection. In similar manner, motions with hand or head indicating acceptance should be scored as accept-

ance. A child's correction of another child's response is scored as a multiple response. An answer of "no" even if followed by qualification is plotted as rejection. Example: "No, your answer is almost right." However, "the answer is pretty good but" is scored acceptance. If no comment is made, no recording is made. This is considered neutrality. Multiple acceptances are scored vertically—teacher who says, "fine," child continues and teacher's acceptance continues, "um huh," etc.

f. *Assistance given*—This column is to handle advice or words supplied during reading class by teacher or fellow student. This advice may be either accepted or rejected and thus following assistance number may appear in the Acts to column. Assistance differs from interruptions in that the unit is meaningful to on-going activities rather than disruptive of same.

3. *Abbreviations*—

T = Teacher   G = Girl   SR = Silent Reading
A = All   Ac = Accepts   BW = Board Writing
B = Boy   Rj = Rejects   O = Other

Classroom:_____ Observer:_____ Teacher:_____
Date:_____ Reading Group: _____

Reading Observation Record

Act	Talk			Calls on Questions			Responds			Acts to			Asst. Given by			SR	BW	O	Interruptions In				Out		
	T	B	G	A T	B	G	A T	B	G	A Ac	Rj T	B	G	A				T	B	G	A	B	G	A

21 *Scholastic Success and Attitude toward School in a Population of Sixth Graders*[1]

PHILIP W. JACKSON

HENRIETTE M. LAHADERNE

How accurate are teachers' judgments of their students' satisfaction with school? Are scholastic success and attitude toward school related? 292 sixth graders answer two questionnaires assessing attitudes toward their schools and their teachers. Each teacher estimates each of his students' overall satisfaction with school. The results show that the teachers' estimates are better than chance and relate more closely to the students' academic records than to their expressed attitudes. The correlations between students' satisfaction scores and scholastic scores are negligible.

Success and satisfaction are bound together by logic, if not by fact. Logically at least, successful people ought to appear satisfied, and unsuccessful people dissatisfied, when queried about the conditions surrounding their achievements. In educational terms, students who are doing well in school might be expected to express contentment when asked to describe their school experience, and those who are doing poorly might be expected to express discontentment. Surprisingly, however, educational research has not yet provided a confirmation of this logically compelling expectation. Indeed, over the past 25 years an impressive amount of evidence has accumulated showing that scholastic success and attitudes toward school are typically unrelated to each other (Diedrich, 1966; Jackson and Getzels, 1959; Malpass, 1953; Tenenbaum, 1944; Tschechtelin, Hipskind, and Remmers, 1940).[2]

[1]Expanded version of a paper presented at the American Educational Research Association meeting, Chicago, February 1966.

[2]One investigator (Brodie, 1964) does present evidence in support of the prediction, but his results, which seem to hold only for the girls in his sample, are difficult to evaluate because of the atypical performance of one of his experimental groups.

Reprinted from the *Journal of Educational Psychology*, 1967, **58**, 15–18, by permission of the authors and the American Psychological Association.

If confirmed by further investigation, the absence of a strong linkage between success and satisfaction in the classroom should provoke considerable thought among practitioners and researchers alike. Few of the questions to which it gives rise are more intriguing than those that concern the beliefs and behaviors of classroom teachers. How sensitive, for example, are teachers to differences in their students' views of school? When estimating the attitudes of their students do teachers act in accord with the popular expectation linking success and satisfaction or are their judgments in agreement with the results of empirical studies? The study reported here was designed to provide partial answers to these questions and to explore further the general relationship between scholastic success and attitudes toward school.

SUBJECTS AND PROCEDURES

The subjects (Ss) comprised the entire sixth grade of the public schools in a predominantly white, working class suburb (11 classes located in 6 schools; $N = 148$ boys, 144 girls). The pupils' mean IQ, as measured by the Kuhlmann-Anderson Intelligence Test, was 103.9, with a standard deviation of 19.2. The 11 sixth-grade teachers (7 women, 4 men) also participated in the study by estimating how satisfied each of the students was with his school experience.

Toward the end of the school term, one of the investigators administered two attitude inventories to Ss during regular class periods. To encourage honesty in replying, Ss were assured that their responses would not be seen by their teach-

ers nor by anyone else connected with the schools. The two inventories were:

1. The Student Opinion Poll II.[3] This was a revision of a questionnaire developed a few years ago (Jackson & Getzels, 1959) and designed to elicit responses concerning general satisfaction or dissatisfaction with four aspects of school life: the teachers, the curriculum, the student body, and classroom procedures. The version used in this study contained 47 multiple-choice items and was scored by giving one point each time S chose from within a set of multiple-choices the response indicating the highest degree of satisfaction with that aspect of school life. Thus, the possible range of scores was from 0 to 47. The mean scores for the sample of sixth graders were 25.3 for boys and 29.4 for girls. The standard deviation for both sexes was 8.2. Test reliability for the total sample, based on Kuder-Richardson formula 20, was .86. . . .

2. The Michigan Student Questionnaire (abbreviated version.)[3] This was a shortened form of a questionnaire developed by Flanders and his associates (Flanders, 1965) to assess students' attitudes toward their present teachers and schoolwork. The version used in this study contained 37 descriptive statements, each followed by four possible replies: strongly disagree, disagree, agree, and strongly agree. A student's response to each item was scored 4, 3, 2, or 1 depending on the degree to which his reply reflected a positive attitude toward his school and his teacher. Thus, the possible range of scores was from 37 to 148. The mean scores for the sample of sixth graders were 101.5 for boys and 109.3 for girls. Standard deviations were 19.2 and

[3]Appended to the selection.

16.9 for boys and girls respectively. Test reliability for the total sample, based on a variation of the Kuder-Richardson formula appropriate for weighted scores (Ferguson, 1951) was .94. . . .

The correlation between responses to the Student Opinion Poll II and the Michigan Student Questionnaire was .62 for the total sample. Thus, although the two questionnaires provide similar information, the relationship between them is low enough to justify the use of both in a study of students' attitudes.

At a special meeting held after school, the 11 sixth-grade teachers were shown sample items from the Student Opinion Poll II and were asked to predict how their students might respond to such a questionnaire. The exact procedure for obtaining the teachers' ratings was as follows. Each teacher was presented with an alphabetized list of his students. He was asked, first, to divide the group into thirds by classifying his students into three levels of satisfaction: "most," "average," and "least." He was then asked to identify from within the groups labeled "most" and "least" a smaller number of students (one-fourth of each group) who seemed to represent extreme positions

("*very* satisfied" and "*very* dissatisfied"). Thus, each student's attitudes were described by his teacher as falling into one of five categories. In each classroom the approximate fractions of students in the five categories were: 1/12, 1/4, 1/3, 1/4, 1/12. When the ratings were treated quantitatively the values 15, 12, 10, 8, and 5 were assigned to the five groupings, the highest number being used to represent the attitudes of students whom the teachers had described as "very satisfied."

Two measures of scholastic performance were used. The first consisted of four grades, given by the S's present teacher, in reading, language arts, arithmetic, and science. The second consisted of three scores, derived from the Stanford Achievement Test, in reading, language arts, and arithmetic.

RESULTS

The findings with respect to the relationship between the teachers' estimates of students' satisfaction and scores derived from the students' responses to the two questionnaires are presented in Table 1. That table also contains correlations between the

TABLE 1.—Correlations between Teachers' Estimates and Measures of Student Attitudes, Achievement, and IQ

	ATTITUDE MEASURES		*ACHIEVEMENT MEASURES*			
Students	*Student Opinion Poll II*	*Michigan Student Questionnaire*	*Reading*	*Language*	*Arithmetic*	*IQ*
Boys	.28**	.27**	.49**	.51**	.45**	.44**
Girls	.27**	.25**	.36**	.37**	.31**	.39**

Note.—$N = 148$ for boys; $N = 144$ for girls.
**$p < .01$.

teachers' estimates and measures of the students' academic performance. The findings reveal that students' satisfaction is at least partially visible to teachers and can be estimated with greater-than-chance accuracy. They also reveal, however, that teachers tend to expect achievement and satisfaction to be more closely related than they, in fact, are. Indeed, the correlations in Table 1 indicate that when teachers set out to estimate how a student will respond to an attitude questionnaire, they come closer to describing how well the student achieves in school than to how he feels about his school experience.

TABLE 2.—Correlations between Attitudes and Scholastic Performance

SCHOLASTIC PERFOR-MANCE	ATTITUDES			
	Student Opinion Poll II		Michigan Student Question-naire	
	Boys	Girls	Boys	Girls
Grades				
Reading	.15	.16	.01	.06
Language	.13	.16	.01	.01
Arithmetic	.08	.14	.00	.00
Science	.15	.19*	.06	.04
Achievement tests				
Reading	.14	.08	.08	−.07
Language	.11	.14	.02	−.06
Arithmetic	.13	.12	.06	−.05
IQ	.06	.14	−.08	.01

Note.—$N = 148$ for boys; $N = 144$ for girls.
*$p < .05$.

Table 2 contains correlations between attitudes toward school and measures of scholastic achievement.

Four features of that table deserve attention. First, and most important, all of the correlation coefficients are small. Second, they are of the same magnitude with teachers' grades as with achievement test scores. Third, although the coefficients are uniformly higher for the Student Opinion Poll II than for the Michigan Student Questionnaire, the difference between the two sets of statistics is trivial. Fourth, there are no significant sex differences. Thus, these data confirm the results of other investigators who have found no significant relationship between attitudes toward school and scholastic achievement. Furthermore, they extend our previous knowledge by demonstrating the absence of the success-satisfaction relationship with a wider variety of measuring instruments than has been used in earlier studies.

DISCUSSION

Several conditions might account for the unexpected lack of relationship between success and satisfaction. One possibility is that the range and intensity of student attitudes are not as great as responses to the questionnaire indicate and, thus, are not sufficiently powerful to affect behavior. Perhaps students typically do not either hate school or love it but, instead, feel rather neutral about their classroom experience. Another possibility is that teachers and parents behave in ways that effectively weaken whatever natural connection might exist between attitudes and achievement. In most classrooms students are required to master the minimal curricular objectives whether they want to or not. Assignments are clearly defined, deadlines are set, and frequent checks are made by teachers and parents alike to determine whether the work is being completed as expected.

Thus, in several ways teachers, parents, and general classroom conditions may counteract the natural consequences of differences in students' attitudes. The insignificant correlations between responses to questionnaires and achievement test scores could be interpreted as quantitative evidence of the effectiveness of that counteraction.

STUDENT OPINION POLL II

This is not a test. The answer to each question is a matter of opinion. Your true opinion, whatever it is, is the right answer. You will be asked a lot of questions about the school in which you are now studying. Wherever the words "school," "teacher," and "student" appear, they refer to *this* school, the teachers you have had while studying *here*, and your classmates in *this* school.

Here is an Example

Mark your answer in the box for PRACTICE QUESTIONS on your answer sheet.

O. In general I study
   a) too little
   b) too much
   c) about the right amount

If your answer is "a) too little," place an X in the box under a, like this:

	a	b	c	d
O	X			

If your answer is "b) too much," place an X in the box under b, like this:

	a	b	c	d
O		X		

Be sure the number on your answer sheet is the same as the question number.

If you have any questions, raise your hand and you will be helped.

Place your answer on the answer sheet.

Do not mark this booklet.

1. This school listens to parents' opinions
   a. too much
   b. just enough
   c. too little

2. The number of courses given in this school is
   a. too many
   b. just about right
   c. not enough

3. Although teachers differ in this school, most are,
   a. very good
   b. good
   c. fair
   d. poor

4. In some schools the principal sees and talks with the students often, while in other schools he rarely sees them. In this school the principal sees and talks with students
   a. too often
   b. just about the right amount
   c. too little

5. The chance to say or do something in class without being called upon by the teacher is
   a. too little
   b. too much
   c. about right

6. The things that I am asked to study are of
   a. great interest to me
   b. average interest to me
   c. of little interest to me
   d. of no interest to me
7. Getting to know other kids in this school is
   a. easier than usual
   b. about the same as in other schools
   c. more difficult than usual
8. As preparation for Junior High School, the program of this school is
   a. too tough
   b. about right
   c. too easy
9. The class material from year to year
   a. repeats itself too much; you learn the same material over and over
   b. repeats itself just enough to make you feel what was learned before helps you now
   c. is so new that the things learned in the last grade do not help much in this one
10. In this school the teachers' interest in the students' school work is
    a. too great
    b. just about right
    c. not great enough
11. When students in this school get bad grades, their classmates usually
    a. feel sorrier for them than they should
    b. admire them more than they should
    c. show the right amount of concern
12. Students in this school are
    a. too smart—it is difficult to keep up with them
    b. just smart enough—we are all about the same
    c. not smart enough—they are so slow I get bored

13. Most of the subjects taught in this school are
    a. very interesting
    b. above average in interest
    c. below average in interest
    d. dull and uninteresting
14. The teachers' interest in what the students do outside of school is
    a. too great
    b. about right
    c. too small
15. The student who shows a sense of humor in class is usually
    a. admired by the teacher more than he should be
    b. punished by the teacher more than he should be
    c. given about the right amount of attention
16. When teachers "go too fast," students do not know what is going on. In this school, most teachers teach
    a. too slowly
    b. about right
    c. too fast
17. Students who are good in sports are respected by classmates
    a. more than they should be
    b. less than they should be
    c. neither more or less than they should be
18. The practice of competing against each other or working together in this school
    a. leans too much toward competition
    b. leans too much toward working together
    c. is well balanced
19. On the whole, the things we study in this school
    a. are about right
    b. should be changed a little
    c. should be completely changed
20. The teachers I have had in this

school seem to know their subject matter
  a. very well
  b. quite well
  c. fairly well
  d. not as well as they should

21. Students may work either by themselves or in groups. In this school we work in groups
  a. too often
  b. just enough
  c. too little

22. Students get along together in this school
  a. very well
  b. about average
  c. not too well
  d. very badly

23. The amount of "school spirit" at this school is
  a. more than enough
  b. about right
  c. not enough

24. On the whole the school pays attention to the things you learn from books
  a. too much
  b. just enough
  c. not enough

25. Teachers in this school seem to be
  a. almost always fair
  b. generally fair
  c. occasionally unfair
  d. often unfair

26. The things we do in class are planned
  a. so badly that it is hard to get things done
  b. so well that we get things done
  c. so completely that we hardly ever get to do what we want

27. Our seats in class
  a. change too much; we can never be sure where we will sit and who will sit next to us

  b. change about the right number of times
  c. never change; we stay in the same place all year

28. The students who receive good grades are
  a. liked more than they should be by their classmates
  b. disliked more than they should by their classmates
  c. neither liked nor disliked more than they should be

29. In this school the teachers' interest in the students' school work is
  a. just about right
  b. not great enough
  c. too great

30. In my opinion, student interest in social affairs, such as clubs, scouts, and the "Y" is
  a. too great
  b. about right
  c. too little

31. In general the subjects taught are
  a. too easy
  b. about right in difficulty
  c. too difficult

32. When students need special attention, teachers in this school are
  a. always ready to help
  b. generally ready to help
  c. ready to help if given special notice
  d. ready to help only in extreme cases

33. The ability of the teachers in this school to present new material seems to be
  a. very good
  b. good
  c. average
  d. poor

34. In general, students in this school take their studies
  a. too seriously

b. not seriously enough

c. just about right

35. In this school teachers seem to teach
    a. too many things that are *not* useful to us now
    b. too many things that are useful to us now but not later
    c. both things that are useful now and can be useful later

36. When it comes to grading students, teachers in this school are generally
    a. too "tough"
    b. just "tough" enough
    c. not "tough" enough

37. The student who acts differently in this school is likely to find that most students
    a. dislike him for being different
    b. do not care whether or not he is different
    c. like him for being different

38. In my opinion, students in this school pay attention to their looks and clothes
    a. too much
    b. about right
    c. too little

39. In general, teachers in this school are
    a. very friendly
    b. somewhat friendly
    c. somewhat unfriendly
    d. very unfriendly

40. In general, I feel the grades I received in this school were
    a. always what I deserved
    b. generally what I deserved
    c. sometimes what I did *not* deserve
    d. frequently what I did *not* deserve

41. Teaching aids such as films, radio, and the like are used
    a. more than they should be
    b. as much as they should be
    c. less than they should be

42. Memory work and the learning of important facts are

a. stressed too much

b. used about right

c. not stressed enough

43. In some classes the teacher is completely in control and the students have little to say about the way things are run. In other classes the students seem to be boss and the teacher contributes little to the control of the class. In general, teachers in this school seem to take
    a. too much control
    b. about the right amount of control
    c. too little control

44. Some schools hire persons in addition to teachers to help students with special problems. In my opinion, this type of service in this school is
    a. more than enough—it is often forced upon us
    b. enough to help us with our problems
    c. not enough to help us with our problems

45. When a new-comer enters this school, chances are that other students will
    a. welcome him
    b. ignore him
    c. dislike him

46. Homework assignments in this school usually
    a. help us to understand
    b. have little to do with what we learn in class
    c. are just "busy work"

47. In general, teachers in this school pay
    a. too much attention to individual kids and not enough to the class as a whole
    b. not enough attention to individual kids and too much to the class as a whole
    c. about the right attention to individual kids and to the class as a whole

48. In general, my feelings toward school are
    a. very favorable—I like it as it is
    b. somewhat favorable—I would like a few changes
    c. somewhat unfavorable—I would like many changes
    d. very unfavorable—I frequently feel that school is pretty much a waste of time
49. In this school the teachers' interest in the students' school work is
    a. not great enough
    b. too great
    c. just about right

Key

1. b	26. b
2. b	27. b
3. a	28. c
4. b	29. a
5. c	30. b
6. a	31. b
7. a	32. a
8. b	33. a
9. b	34. c
10. b	35. c
11. c	36. b
12. b	37. b
13. a	38. b
14. b	39. a
15. c	40. a
16. b	41. b
17. c	42. b
18. c	43. b
19. a	44. b
20. a	45. a
21. b	46. a
22. a	47. c
23. b	48. a
24. b	49. c
25. a	

Note: Items 10, 29, and 49 check the subject's consistency of response.

One point is given when all three items indicate satisfaction.

MICHIGAN STUDENT QUESTIONNAIRE

This is not a test because there are no wrong answers. The answer to each question is *A MATTER OF OPINION,* and your true opinion, whatever it is, *IS THE RIGHT ANSWER.* You will be asked a lot of questions about how much you like this class, the teacher, and the work you are doing here. All the questions refer to *THIS ONE CLASS AND THIS PARTICULAR TEACHER.* No one in your school will see your answers. By giving frank, true answers to show exactly how you feel, you can help us understand the opinions of students.

Directions:

1. Do not skip any questions.
2. Make sure that the number on the answer sheet matches the question number when you mark your answer.
3. Work carefully, but quickly. Don't spend too much time deciding how to answer each question—mark the answer that comes to your mind first.

Here are Two Examples

Mark your answers to these in the box for PRACTICE QUESTIONS in the upper right hand corner of the answer sheet.

PRACTICE QUESTIONS:

O. I think we should have school on Saturday.

SD—STRONGLY DISAGREE
D—DISAGREE
A—AGREE
SA—STRONGLY AGREE

You have four alternatives to choose from. If you *STRONGLY DISAGREE* with the statement, put an "X" in the *SD* box on your answer sheet, like this:

O.   SD   D   A   SA

OO.   Girls talk more than boys do.

SD—STRONGLY DISAGREE
D—DISAGREE
A—AGREE
SA—STRONGLY AGREE

If you aren't really certain about this, but you are inclined to *AGREE*, you would put an "X" in the box marked *A*, like this:

OO.   SD   D   A   SA

However, if you *STRONGLY AGREE*, put an "X" in the box marked *SA*, like this:

OO.   SD   D   A   SA

DO NOT write on this questionnaire because other students will have to use it.

1. I get along well with this teacher.
2. This teacher has lots of fun with us.
3. This teacher helps to settle quarrels fairly.
4. This teacher lets some kids get by without working very hard.
5. This teacher praises us for good work.
6. This teacher lets us all have turns doing the jobs that are fun.
7. I think this teacher picks on some boys and girls unfairly.
8. This teacher will always listen to both sides of an argument.
9. This teacher is quick to see what mixes you up in your schoolwork.
10. This teacher is always fair with each boy and girl.
11. This teacher always asks the OTHER kids the EASY questions.
12. What we learn in this class makes me want to learn new things.
13. This teacher is one of the best I have ever had.
14. I get pretty bored in this class.
15. This teacher sometimes punishes the whole class for something one person did.
16. This teacher certainly knows how to teach.
17. This teacher really understands boys and girls my age.
18. This teacher knows a lot.
19. I find it easy to talk with this teacher.
20. Our teacher makes everything seem interesting and important.
21. This teacher makes sure not to hurt your feelings.
22. This teacher often "bawls you out" in front of the class.
23. I really like this class.
24. I like to be called on in this class.
25. This teacher makes it fun to study things.
26. This teacher doesn't listen to what SOME boys and girls have to say.
27. Our teacher helps us when we have problems with our work.
28. This teacher has some special favorites or "teacher's pets."
29. This teacher makes me nervous.
30. This teacher likes children.
31. I wish I could have this teacher next year.

32. This teacher likes to hear students' ideas.
33. This teacher makes sure no children get left out of things.
34. Our teacher is very good at explaining things clearly.
35. This teacher gives us a chance to show what we are good at.
36. When I'm in trouble I can count on this teacher to help.
37. This teacher punishes me for things I didn't do.

22 *Sequence of Speaking and Listening Training in Beginning French: A Replication Experiment*[1]

EVAN R. KEISLAR

CAROLYN STERN

LAWRENCE MACE

Among the findings of this study is the discovery that training in speaking a foreign language followed by training in listening produces better comprehension than either the reverse sequence or concurrent training. Some major tasks in learning a foreign language are noted and the effects of various sequences of these tasks are examined. Other results and their implications for teaching raise a number of research questions.

The relation of speaking and listening in second language acquisition has not been clarified. Some writers maintain that the child should first listen to a foreign language so as to be able to distinguish the sounds before beginning to speak utterances in the new language (e.g. Brooks, 1960). On the other hand, Lane (1965) has presented evidence to suggest that the child should begin by speaking the language in order to facilitate more careful discrimination among the sounds. Keislar and Mace (1965) have

[1]The research reported herein was performed under contract with U.S. Office of Education, DHEW, NDEA, Title VI, Contract No. OE 3–12–022.

Reprinted from the *American Educational Research Journal*, 1966, *3*, 169–178, by permission of the senior author and the American Educational Research Association.

indicated that, since many different definitions of listening and speaking are used, the problem should be defined in terms of tasks which clearly specify the instructions, the stimulus and the response required.

Mace (1966) conducted a study with primary children in which he attempted to throw some light on certain aspects of this problem. In his investigation he had four groups who were given fifteen minutes of French instruction each day for two weeks. One group was taught, during the first week, to speak French utterances appropriate to projected pictures and then, during the second week, to listen to and respond with understanding to the utterances they heard. A second group was given the same instruction in the reverse sequence: a week of training in listening comprehension followed by a week of speaking training. A third and fourth group received concurrent training combining both listening and speaking in fifteen-minute daily sessions over the two-week period. All four groups were given the same 600 frames of French instruction; the differences among the treatments lay entirely in the order in which the blocks of speaking and listening were presented.

On the test of listening comprehension, Mace found that the children who were first given the week of training in speaking were significantly better in listening comprehension than the group which had received the listening training first. On a test of speaking the difference between the two groups was not reliable. The unanswered question in Mace's study revolved around the effect of recency.

Did the speaking-first group surpass the listening-first group simply because the former had had a shorter forgetting period, one day instead of eight, between training and test?

The present investigation was conducted as a replication study primarily to assess the factor of recency as well as to improve on the precision of the experiment. The speaking-first and the listening-first groups, Groups 1 and 2, were treated in practically the same manner as in the earlier study. However, in place of the two concurrent treatments, two new groups, 3 and 4, were established to determine the effect of the unequal forgetting periods for Groups 1 and 2. The listening comprehension test served as the major criterion, since the test of speaking in the earlier experiment had revealed no reliable differences. Other modifications included the introduction of more rigorous controls during instruction, the use of voice relays to supply reinforcements for speaking, an automated method of presenting frames and scoring responses, and a complete record of the performance of subjects during listening training.

EXPERIMENTAL DESIGN

Group I was taught to speak the utterances during the first week and to listen during the second. Group 2 was given listening comprehension training for one week and then one week of speaking training. Groups 3 and 4 were given only listening training; Group 3 received this training during the first week, with no relevant instruction during the second, while Group 4 received no relevant training the first week and had the listening training during the second. All groups received the first posttest on the same day, at the conclusion of the two-week training program.

The factorial design of the experiment may be represented as follows:

Speaking Training	Listening Training	
	First week	Second week
present	Group 1	Group 2
absent	Group 3	Group 4

The hypothesis tested is whether the difference on the listening comprehension test between Groups 1 and 2 is reliable *after* adjustment for the difference between Groups 3 and 4. A 2×2 analysis of covariance, adjusting posttest scores for mental age, was used to test the significance of the interaction in this design.

A second method of attacking this problem was to reduce to a negligible amount the effect of the initial difference in forgetting periods by giving the posttest after one month and again after three months. Here, the hypothesis that Group 1 is superior to Group 2 on the test of listening comprehension can be tested directly.

SUBJECTS

A total of 109 third grade children from an elementary school in a middle class neighborhood were used as the subjects for the study. These children had a mean chronological age of seven years and seven months with a standard deviation of seven months. The mean mental age was eight years and eight months with a standard deviation of 13 months. At the conclusion of the two weeks of training, absenteeism had reduced the total number of subjects to 98, the numbers in each group ranging from 22 to 26.

APPARATUS

The experiment was carried out in an unused classroom to which children, in groups of ten, were brought for each day's training. Each child took his place in a separate booth which had been placed so that the child could see the screen at the front of the room but not the children on either side. A microphone and a headset were provided for each subject as well as an individual multiple-choice response panel.[2]

For the listening-comprehension program, each child saw a slide appear on the screen, and heard (over his earphones) the necessary instructions and a French utterance. A yellow light then appeared on his panel as a signal for him to respond. He registered his choice by pressing one of three buttons, the one with the same number as the picture selected. If the button pressed corresponded to the correct picture, it showed a green

---

[2] This instructional system, described originally by Keislar (1961), has been improved and developed for research purposes by many individuals at U.C.L.A. The contributions of John D. McNeil and M. C. Wittrock to the equipment in its present form are gratefully acknowledged. (See McNeil and Keislar, 1963, and Wittrock, Keislar, and Stern, 1964.)

light. If the choice was incorrect, a red light appeared; this light had to be turned out before another selection could be made.

For the speaking program, the experimenter was able to monitor the utterances spoken into the microphones by any individual child. The child's vocal responses activated a voice relay which turned on the yellow light in the response panel; the child was then able to produce a green light by pressing one of the buttons. This system for reinforcing vocal behavior proved to be highly effective. In the earlier study, Mace had encountered some difficulty in getting the children to speak when they were told to do so. With the new apparatus, even those children who were at first timid about talking soon began speaking regularly and clearly; unless they did so they could not get the reinforcing green light.

From the control panel at the rear of the room, 35 mm. black-and-white slides were projected on the screen from a modified *Kodak Carousel* slide projector called the Davis programmer. A hole punched in the appropriate spot on the mounting of each slide supplied information as to the correct answer for each frame. The display of lights on the control panel indicated to the experimenter the correct answer as well as the response made by each child. This information was stored in the master panel until the end of the response interval, at which time an impulse from the sound tape initiated a scanning operation; the data was automatically read and punched on paper tape by a *Clary Account-O-Punch Recorder*. Another impulse from the tape recorder then

cleared the panel, turned off the signal lights, and presented the next slide.

EXPERIMENTAL INSTRUCTION

With the exception of minor changes necessitated by the different equipment used, the instructions and commentary were identical to those used by Mace (1966). A new recording was made by a person who spoke French as a native speaker.

It is worthwhile to note the performance of the subjects in the four groups during speaking training. While the actual utterances were not recorded, the recording tape provided information as to whether or not the child had spoken. Since practically all subjects gave an overt vocal response on every frame, no reliable group differences on this variable of speaking were found.

In studying the performance of all four experimental groups during the listening comprehension training, important differences were noted. In Figure 1 are presented the mean performance scores of the four groups on each day's lesson, consisting of 60 multiple-choice frames. The performance of Group 1 during the week of listening training was far superior to any of the other groups. This was to be expected by virtue of the fact that they had received one week of speaking training prior to the listening instruction. Group 3, which received listening training during the first week only, demonstrated the poorest performance on each day's training. The performance of Group 2 on the comparable lessons is slightly superior. Group 4, which did not begin lis-

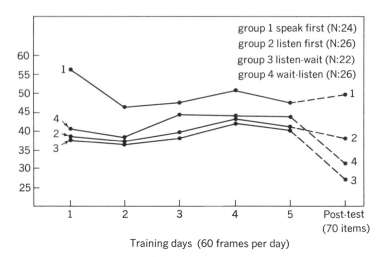

Fig. 1. Mean performance on listening comprehension during training and on post-test for four groups.

tening instruction until the second week, performed considerably better than either Group 2 or 3, even though this was also its first exposure to this material ($p < .01$).

A basic assumption of the experimental design was that Groups 2, 3, and 4, having been randomly selected from the same population, would show no systematic differences with respect to the level of comprehension attained during the week of listening training. According to this reasoning, differences on the posttest between Groups 3 and 4 would reflect only the difference in the length of the forgetting period: eight days for Group 3 versus one day for Group 4. Unfortunately, this assumption could not be maintained, as the results presented in Figure 1 clearly show. The initial difference in performance between Groups 3 and 4 was highly reliable. The major reason for the superiority of Group 4 appeared to be a motivational one. The experimenter and research assistant noted that the

children in this group, who were not called during the first week, became increasingly eager to take part in the experiment; when they were finally allowed to participate, they performed with great enthusiasm.

POSTTESTS

The listening comprehension posttest used by Mace was revised to provide two different forms, A and B. Each of these forms consisted of 70 items, representing a sample of all the tasks which had been taught during the program. Form A, used for the Immediate Listening Test, was administered to all subjects of the four experimental groups on the day following the second week of instruction. The testing conditions were the same as those during training, with two important modifications. First, the lights which had provided knowledge of results during the learning phase were turned off during testing. Second, while the children were brought for testing in groups of ten, these groups included subjects from all four treatments, randomly selected.

As a measure of retention for the One-Month Listening Test, Form B was administered one month later to Groups 1 and 2. Form A was administered to the same two groups after an interval of three months, the Three-Month Listening Test. On this occasion, the test of speaking which Mace had prepared, called the Three-Month Speaking Test, was also administered to these groups for the first time. This speaking test was given to six children at a time, with each child's spoken responses recorded on tape for later scoring. The subjects were seated in booths spaced so far apart in the room that the children, wearing earphones, heard only the taped voice and not each other's responses. The criterion, as in Mace's test, was comprehensibility, rather than fidelity of reproduction of the French utterance.

RESULTS

The results of the Immediate Listening Test, given in Table 1, show that while Group 1 was appreciably superior to Group 2 (49.8 versus 38.0), Group 4 was also superior to Group 3 (31.4 versus 27.6). An analysis of covariance, with posttest scores adjusted for mental age, failed to yield a significant interaction ($F = 3.53$, $df = 1, 93$). On the basis of these data, the possibility that Group 1 was superior to Group 2 on the listening test simply because it had one less week of forgetting could not be rejected.

As was previously noted, however, the training performance of Group 4 was significantly superior to that of Group 3. Thus the difference between these two groups on the posttest is confounded by the initial discrepancy and does not constitute an estimate of the effect of forgetting alone. Consequently, the posttest scores of the three groups who received listening training as the first exposure to French were adjusted by means of analysis of covariance for the initial differences in training performance. No significant difference between the adjusted mean posttest score for Group 3 of 29.6 and that for Group 4 of 28.7 was obtained, indicating that the differences between these two groups are entirely attributable to unequal performance during training rather than to the unequal retention inter-

TABLE 1.—Mental Age and Immediate Listening Test Scores Reported for Four Experimental Groups

	Group	N	*AVERAGE MENTAL AGE (in years and months)*		*IMMEDIATE LISTENING TEST (70 items)*	
			Mean	*S.D.*	*Mean*	*S.D.*
1.	Speaking-Listening	24	8–8	1–0	49.8	10.5
2.	Listening-Speaking	26	8–6	1–1	38.0	13.0
3.	Listening-Waiting	22	8–8	1–1	27.6	8.9
4.	Waiting-Listening	26	8–8	1–2	31.4	9.0

vals. When an analysis of covariance was carried out using adjusted scores for Groups 2, 3 and 4, the interaction was highly significant ($F = 10.9$, $df = 1, 94$). This finding clearly supports the hypothesis that the difference between Groups 1 and 2 is attributable neither to chance nor to the effects of forgetting, but rather to the sequence of speaking versus listening training.

This statistical method of compensating for unequal learning may be questioned, however, because these initial differences were not the results of chance but reflected a systematic bias. A more appropriate test of the hypothesis may be found in the results of the retention tests, shown in Table 2. The effect of the initial one-week difference in retention interval between the speaking-first and the listening-first groups is probably negligible after one month and certainly negligible after three months.

The results of the analysis of covariance, found in Table 3, clearly indicate that the speaking-first group was also superior on the listening comprehension test, Form B, given a month later. After adjustment for mental age, the difference is significant far beyond the .01 level. On the Three-Month Listening Test, the speaking-first group maintained its superiority in listening comprehension at the .05 level of confidence. The results of the Three-Month Speaking Test indicate that the speaking-first group was superior, also at the .05 level, in the ability to produce appropriate and comprehensible French utterances.

A comparison of the scores obtained by the two groups which received different sequences of instruction is presented graphically in Figure 2. It is of considerable interest that there appears to be so little for-

TABLE 2.—Results of Retention Tests

TEST	GROUP	N	M	S.D.
One-Month Listening Test (Form A—70 items)	1. Speaking-Listening	25	47.8	13.4
	2. Listening-Speaking	24	33.9	9.8
Three-Month Listening Test (Form A—70 items)	1. Speaking-Listening	24	45.9	13.2
	2. Listening-Speaking	26	35.8	14.0
Three-Month Speaking Test (320 items)	1. Speaking-Listening	20	202.8	77.9
	2. Listening-Speaking	19	144.8	59.3

TABLE 3.—Analysis of Covariance on Retention Tests with Mental Age as Covariable

	SOURCE	DF	MS	F	P
I. One-Month Listening Test	Treatment	1	2408.1	16.9	.01
	Error	46	142.1		
II. Three-Month Listening Test	Treatment	1	1201.3	6.4	.05
	Error	47	187.3		
III. Three-Month Speaking Test	Treatment	1	28150.7	6.9	.05
	Error	47	4065.3		

getting on the part of Group 1. Even after three months these young children appear to have retained a good deal of what they learned during a total of less than two-and-a-half hours of instruction.

describe a picture; the task for listening comprehension was that of selecting the appropriate picture when a French utterance was heard. As Keislar and Mace (1965) have indicated, speaking involved the task of saying

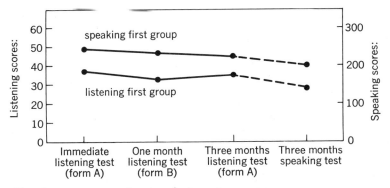

Fig. 2. Test scores for the speaking first and listening first groups.

CONCLUSIONS

This replication study has provided evidence that a two-week sequence of instruction in which speaking training is given during the first week and listening training during the second is better than the reverse. These experimental findings not only support the results obtained by Mace (1966), but also justify rejecting the alternative hypothesis that the obtained differences can be attributed to the unequal forgetting periods. The fact that the superiority of the speaking-first group held up one month and even three months later makes it clear that factors associated with the sequence variables were undoubtedly responsible.

For this replication experiment, as in the earlier study, speaking training and listening training were defined in terms of certain tasks. Training in the appropriate French utterance to

the findings of an experiment in which certain tasks are used for these terms cannot be generalized to situations where different tasks are involved.

The conclusions must be restricted even further to the type of materials, the instructional procedures, and the kind of subjects used. It is quite possible, for example, that the effects of sequence would not be found at the college level where students may already have acquired a varied repertoire of speaking skills. It is also possible that the obtained sequence effects were related to certain specific features of the instructional programs. Mace had made a careful effort to construct frames equivalent in all respects but the critical one, that of listening versus speaking, by matching the content of each frame of the listening comprehension program with the corresponding frame in the speaking program. Thus, if the child said *"C'est le garçon"* on the speaking program, this was the utterance he heard and had to identify on the corresponding frame in the listening program. However, it may very well be that this procedure did not produce programs equivalent in difficulty or effectiveness. A further test of the effect of sequence should be carried out in which speaking and listening programs, individually equated for effectiveness, are administered in a similarly designed experiment.

With His Peers

6

23 *Person Perception in Children*

JOHN D. CAMPBELL

How do children form impressions of others who are initially strangers? Do their perceptions correspond to adult observations? To what extent do momentary, situational, and personality factors account for children's perceptions of persons? These are some of the provocative questions explored by the authors.

How do people "perceive" one another? This question continues to invite research of many kinds. In many of these studies, behavioral responses are taken as perceptual indicators, but the meaning of the other person and the cognitive processes involved in achieving such meaning are left an inference. A needed extension of the work in this area is an inquiry into the ways in which other persons are experienced, as represented by the perceiver's description or conceptualization of the "other." In what dimensions is the other experienced; how uniquely and complexly is he comprehended? How do constant tendencies of the perceiver bring a screen into the situation? How do qualities of the particular other and the particular situation affect perception?

In research on person perception, investigators have proceeded along several different lines. One approach has emphasized *judgmental* aspects of person perception and has focused on

Reprinted from the *Merrill-Palmer Quarterly of Behavior and Development*, 1963, **9**, 57–72, by permission of the senior author and the Merrill-Palmer Institute.

factors correlated with an individual's empathic ability, insight, or accuracy in appraising the responses of others. Common to this research is a focus on a discrete judgment, an appraisal of the person perceived along specified dimensions preselected by the investigator, for example, prediction of a person's responses to a picture frustration test, a technique employed by Bieri (1953); prediction of the stimulus person's self description by an adjectival Q-sort, used by Baker and Block (1957); or prediction of another's sociometric choices, in work by Tagiuri, Kogan, and Bruner (1955).

Another approach less commonly employed was pointed to by MacLeod (1945) when he emphasized the need to ask the phenomenological question "What is there?" More recently Hastorf, Richardson, and Dornbusch (1958), among others, have echoed this view in the statement: "Researchers should make more of an attempt to study the perceptual categories that are actually employed by, and thus relevant to, the perceiver under consideration" (p. 55). Such an approach is basically taken in the work reported in this paper.

This study uses a meaningful real-life social situation as a setting for examining the characteristics of children's perceptions of one another as they occur in a behavioral context. The basic aims of the research are: (a) to examine the dimensions in terms of which children conceptualize and organize their impressions of others; (b) to explore ways in which characteristics of the perceiver and of the perceptual object contribute to interpersonal perceptions; and (c) to

assess effects of continued contact (the transition from stranger to acquaintance) on children's cognitive appraisals.

The setting and design of the research utilized the essentially natural laboratory of children's summer camps.[1] The 267 boys and girls, white and Negro, who served as subjects ranged in age from eight to 13. They came from low-income families in the greater Washington area. The children were placed in cabin groups of eight children per cabin. The cabins were homogeneous in age and sex. In half the cabins, groups were racially homogeneous; in half, biracial.[2] The groups were composed of children who were initially strangers to one another. The setting was isolated from familiar surroundings of family and friends. Children of the cabin were, therefore, the child's primary social group for two weeks of camp.

The data on children's perceptions derive from interviews with each child at the beginning and at the end of the two weeks of camp. In the interviews, individual snapshots of all the cabin members were spread out in front of the child, and he was asked to choose one child whom he felt he knew most about. He was encouraged to "tell all about him, as if you were telling a friend back home." The ques-

---

[1]We are indebted to Mr. John G. Theban, Executive Secretary of Family and Child Services of Washington, D.C., who made available the summer camp.

[2]The role of race in influencing interpersonal perception has not been reported in the present paper, since it has been examined elsewhere by the investigators (Yarrow, 1958).

tions were designed to learn what was most salient to the child (whom he selected, and what dimensions he used for description) and the quality of his interpretations. From sociometric questions, each child's ranking of his cabin mates on their desirability as friends was obtained.

For 20 of the 32 cabins studied, systematic behavior observations were made using a sampling of periods and locations in the camp day, on days at the beginning, middle, and end of camp. The observer made detailed running accounts of the behavior of each child in the cabin. This was done by observing for five minutes, followed by five minutes for additional writing-up of observations. In each five-minute record, the observer was required to account for each child present. There were 1,010 such observational records, representing slightly more than four hours in the life of each group studied.

CHARACTERISTICS OF CHILDREN'S PERCEPTIONS OF PERSONS

In order to present the data on children's perceptions of persons it will be necessary first to describe ways in which their "perceptual" reports have been analyzed. Descriptions were divided into psychological units, a unit being defined as a discrete action, or a single characteristic or evaluation. For example, the following response is broken up into twelve units:

He is nice — and plays all right, — but he likes to fight people. — Says he can

beat anybody in the cabin. — He likes to tell jokes a lot. He makes you laugh. — O.K.—but he likes to fight other kids. —Acts all right—except when gets mad, then he wants to punch on people. — Most of time he is on his bed telling jokes.—He says he don't like to play baseball but he likes to play horseshoes. — That's all I know.

A report was scored on: (a) number of psychological units present, (b) content of the units, and (c) nature of interpretation in the total description.

Content of Perceptual Report

The desire to examine content by using a framework that did not deviate too greatly from the children's phenomenal reports guided the development of a classification scheme. The one evolved has antecedents in the conceptualizations of interaction formulated by Coffey and his associates (Freedman, Leary, Ossorio and Coffey, 1951), but the categories (Table 1) were tailored to the content in the children's reports.

When asked to tell all they knew about another, children showed two very strong tendencies: (a) broad positive or negative judgments were given by 85 per cent, and (b) these judgments were elaborated primarily in terms of peer actions having direct interpersonal consequences. In contrast, noninteractive qualities appeared in only one-half of the reports, as relatively minor fractions of the descriptions. Physical appearance was the most frequently reported noninteractive aspect.

Behaviors described with greatest

frequency were "sociable" in nature (Table 1). They dealt with the "business" of camp—play and conversation of the children—described in personal and "feeling" terms—who was friendly, who shared with whom, how a child felt about another, the emotional consequences of play. One may ask whether these positive dimensions reflect strong affiliative needs in a new situation with new companions. Reports of direct aggression, domination, rebellion and nonconformity, which also appeared with considerable frequency, might have parallel immediate interpersonal relevance, though in the negative sense. The appearance of descriptions of fearfulness, dependence, indirect aggressive maneuvers, effective leadership behavior, documents the breadth of children's awareness of interpersonal relations, though the latter categories, which may not be so readily apprehended, occurred relatively infrequently.

Individual children contributed differently to the distribution of characteristics listed in Table 1. On the average, children reported 11 units of description, some reported as many as 27, others a single unit. When each child's description of another was summarized in terms of four major categories of interaction—aggressive, affiliative, assertive and submissive—forty-six per cent of the children concentrated their descriptions entirely in one of these broad dimensions. Thirty-one per cent were able to see opposite or contradictory features in the other child (i.e., both affectionate and hostile behavior, dominating and passive-dependent actions). Only two

per cent of the children described the other child in terms of all four categories. The remaining children, in using more than one dimension of content, did not present both ends of any given continuum.

Children's perceptions on the two interviews (in the first or second day at camp and at the end of camp) demonstrated noteworthy stability; content areas appeared in relatively the same frequency positions on the two interviews ($tau = +\ .76$; $p < .001$). Within this consistency, some shifts occurred; emphasis on interaction rather than noninteraction (proportion of interaction units in each description) became even more pronounced. Among children mentioning noninteractional factors in either interview, 56 per cent showed lessened emphasis and 35 per cent increased emphasis. This shift over time was statistically significant ($X_1^2 = 7.6$; $p < .01$). Decline in noninteraction was primarily accounted for by the lesser emphasis on a child's appearance. In descriptions of interaction, reports of dominating and aggressive, rebellious and nonconforming behavior increased ($X_1^2 = 19.1$; $p < .001$) and reports of affiliative behavior decreased ($X_1^2 = 9.1$; $p < .01$) on the second interview.

Comparisons of the individual child's reports revealed intra-individual consistency. A child's descriptions on the second interview were by no means repetitions of his first interview; however, if a child used a given dimension of personality on his initial description, he was more likely to report it on the second occasion than was a child who did not mention it

TABLE 1.—Content of Children's Descriptions of Others

CONTENT CATEGORY	ILLUSTRATIVE EXAMPLES	PER CENT OF CHILDREN REPORTING IN INTERVIEW	
		I	II
Interactional content[a]			
(1) domination, direct aggression	"picks fights," "bosses"	31%[b]	49%
(2) indirect aggression	"made fun of me," "chases kids"	15	11
(3) rebellion, non-conformity	"was fresh," "is stubborn"	21	30
1 and/or 2 and/or 3		45%	62%
(4) fearfulness, submission	"scared of everyone," "homesick"	14	16
(5) mild dependence	"asks me for things," "asked for help"	8	6
4 and/or 5		20	21
(6) conformity	"doesn't say bad things," "says 'excuse me'"	50	55
(7) verbal sociability	"talks with us," "laughs at my jokes"	52	47
(8) physical play	"plays all the time," "played games together"	61	55
7 and/or 8		80	74
(9) affiliation	"friendly," "likes to hang around you"	56	47
(10) affection	"likes me," "chose me for a buddy"	32	23
9 and/or 10		69	56
(11) nurturance	"shares," "is a kind girl," "comforted me"	44	51
(12) assertive leadership	"tells me what to do"	18	18
(13) solitary behavior	"sits and watches others," "is quiet"	32	31
Non-interactional content			
(14) abilities, skills, disabilities	"intelligent," "not a good swimmer"	14	15
(15) appearance, features	"has curly hair," "about my size"	35	24
(16) name, age	"got to know his name," "she's ten"	6	6
(17) non-camp contextual factors	"has three brothers," "was a Boy Scout"	10	12
14 and/or 15 and/or 16 and/or 17		51%	42%
Number of children		(247)[c]	(247)

[a] In a check of reliability, two codes independently classified 77 per cent of a sample of 185 units in the identical detailed categories of content.

[b] Percentage indicates proportion of children whose description of another child has any content classified in the designated category. Percentages add to more than 100.

[c] Not included in this tabulation are those children who, instead of describing another child, described their cabin counselor.

225

initially.[3] This self-consistency occurred regardless of whether the same or a different child was being described on the two occasions. Such intra-individual thematic emphasis suggests that each child develops a perceptual framework that for him has general applicability, a possibility that needs testing in further research.

Quality and Complexity of Perceptual Report

Consider these two descriptions of the same child:

I have been with this guy name of Mark. He always talks back to the chief, and gets me to tie his shoes. I wake him up in the morning . . . He is a funny guy, likes to play around a lot. I get along real good. He acts okay . . . Every five minutes he has to be told something. He likes to act simple, too.

He is simple. When he talks, he make me laugh, and he always talks back to the chief (counselor). Yesterday he said that "camp, it looks pretty good, and we look

---

[3]This type of analysis is similar to the procedure earlier mentioned by Hastorf, Richardson, and Dornbusch (1958) for comparing descriptions of the self and of another. The outcome of tests examining the extent to which children were consistent over time in use or non-use of the broad dimensions of action is reported as follows: domination, aggression, rebellion: $X_1^2 = 17.5$; $p < .001$; fearfulness, submission, dependence: $X_1^2 = 2.9$; $.10 > p > .05$; conformity: $X_1^2 = 8.7$, $p < .01$; sociability, play: $X_1^2 = 3.9$, $p < .05$; affiliation, affection: $X_1^2 = 2.8$, $.10 > p > .05$; nurturance: $X_1^2 = 8.7$, $p < .01$; assertive leadership: $X_1^2 = 3.2$, $.10 > p > .05$; non-interactional content: $X_1^2 = 2.3$, $.20 > p > .10$.

like jackasses." He likes for you to have manners. He likes to play with people. He eats a lot. He always wants food passed around the table. Don't want anybody to put their arms across his plate . . . I think he could get along with others all right. He gets along with me, but everybody picks on him. I like to help out people who everybody pick on, something is wrong with them . . . Last night the man say "have your father been pounding on you a lot? I would think that, because something is wrong with him. It might make him worser.

These descriptions have used similar categories of content, yet they differ markedly in how they have organized and synthesized the "parts," and in the extent to which they have attempted interpretation of motives or causes of behavior. The description which arrives at a picture-of-a-person or a "theory" of personality may be regarded as more complex than the description which is an atomistic collection of discrete variables.

A seven-point scale of complexity of organization was used to measure the extent to which children gave systematically organized descriptions. Descriptions rated at the top of the scale painted well-integrated personality portraits involving implicit and explicit inferences about behavior. Those in the intermediate range were typified by more superficial generalizations supported by congruent behavioral detail. At the lower end of the scale of organization were the reports that consisted either of vague global generalizations that were inadequately supported (e.g., "He's Ok." "She's nice." "He's all right.") or a

TABLE 2.—Complexity of Perceptual Organization

RATING[a]	DESCRIPTION OF RATING	INTERVIEW:	
		I	II
7	Interpretive generalization, supported by interweaving of different complicated themes or by complex analyses of "why" of behavior.	8%	8%
6		26%	36%
5		11%	8%
4	Superficial generalization supported by some congruent behavior details	21%	23%
3		20%	16%
2		4%	2%
1	Limited specific details without stated or implied interpretive generalization, or vague global generalization	10%	7%
	(number of subjects)	(261)	(256)

[a]In a reliability check, two codes independently evaluated 49 children's descriptions and identically classified 81 percent of these.

congeries of specific details without a stated or implied theme (Table 2).[4]

The individual child tended to give descriptions at similar levels of complexity on both interviews (*tau* = + .22; $p < .001$), regardless of whether the same or a different peer was described on both interviews. However, there was a significant trend for the

[4]For a more detailed look at complexity of descriptions, explicit inferences were noted on Interview II data. In 37 per cent of the cases, explicit inferences were present. Relatively low-level inferences such as "She doesn't want to make fights," "She likes to make friends with everybody," "He likes me," were more than twice as numerous as the more sophisticated interpretive comments concerning personality, motivating or causal factors, and future consequences, such as "He has the nerve to do things, but he doesn't," "Sometimes he's good so he won't be beat up," and "She probably will have good manners when she grows up."

group toward more highly organized impressions on the second interview ($X_1^2 = 8.5$; $p < .01$). The qualitative superiority of the later descriptions may derive from the fact that the child had more opportunity to collect many diverse bits of information about another child and to observe more occasions of given kinds of behavior in the child which might aid in the synthesizing process.

From the examination of children's perceptions, several conclusions have emerged: (a) Children's descriptions of others were dominated by social relevance; the emphasis on interaction and the very common use of evaluative appraisals gave evidence of this. (b) There was stability over time both in content and quality of the individual child's perceptual report, whether reporting on the same or a different child. (c) Within this stability, there were certain systematic changes over time toward increased emphasis on interaction and more fully organized descriptions.

There were marked individual variations in children's reports. The next portions of this paper attempt to account for some of these variations by examining certain characteristics of the perceiving child and certain characteristics of the child perceived.

CHARACTERISTICS OF THE PERCEIVING CHILD AND HIS PERCEPTION OF PERSONS

In looking for links between the perceiving child and his appraisal of others, variables of age, sex, and the perceiver's behavior have been considered.

Age and Sex

One would anticipate that the child's conceptions of his human world change as greatly with increasing maturity and experience as do his conceptions of the physical world. There have been very few studies, however, concerning the development of the child's sensitivity to phenomena of human characteristics and behavior. Illustrative of these are studies by Gollin (1958), Hunt and Solomon (1942), and Kohn and Fiedler (1961). The present study deals with only a limited cross-section spanning middle childhood (eight to 13 years). By this time most children have had experience with a fairly wide range of personalities in the family, neighborhood and school life; also, the differential roles of boys and girls in society are certainly well defined. To what extent

are age and sex differences related to variability in children's person perceptions?

Age related trends in categories used in describing others did not appear except in reports of aggression and domination, which tended to be more frequent among the older children (Table 3). There was, however, a sex-linked pattern of differences, consistent with the different experiences of boys and girls, and with adult values for boys and girls. Thus, distinctly nurturing behaviors were emphasized more by girls than boys (especially at the end of camp). The boys, on the other hand, were more attentive to acting-out nonconformities and withdrawn behavior. Attending to the conforming actions in the other child ("She's polite." "He doesn't say bad things.") was also more frequent in boys than girls.

When perceptual complexity is considered, there were no consistent sex differences, but age trends appear. Older children tended to give more complex perceptual reports. (For ratings of organization, Interview I: *tau* = + .13; Int. II: + .14. In both instances, $p < .001$). A relevant, but unavailable, measure in the present study is the child's intelligence, which might bear a significant relation to his characteristic ways of perceiving others. The relatively small developmental trends are surprising for functions as complex as the perceiving of persons and interpersonal relations. This may be a reflection of the early development of sensitivities to interpersonal relations. Also, more specific differences by age may have been undetected by the analysis (e.g., concrete *details* of aggressive or nurturant

TABLE 3.—Content of Description Related to Age and Sex of Reporting Child

	INTERVIEW I						INTERVIEW II					
Sex:	Girls			Boys			Girls			Boys		
Age[a]:	8-9	10-11	12-13	8-9	10-11	12-13	8-9	10-11	12-13	8-9	10-11	12-13
Domination, aggression, rebellion[b]	22%	30%	39%	48%	64%	65%	50%	47%	53%	68%	75%	82%
Fearfulness, submission, dependence	24	19	17	21	21	17	29	17	26	15	26	19
Conformity[b]	34	42	39	56	70	48	44	50	42	62	60	70
Sociability, play	80	92	61	73	83	76	74	77	63	74	74	82
Affiliation, affection	71	75	72	60	74	62	62	57	58	45	64	52
Nurturance[c]	39	55	50	46	36	41	68	65	63	34	34	56
Assertive, leadership	15	11	17	19	19	31	18	13	16	19	25	19
Solitary behavior[c]	15	28	11	33	45	52	29	23	32	40	32	40
Non-interactional content[c]	44	36	56	44	72	59	48	38	32	34	54	48
(Number of subjects)	(41)	(53)	(18)	(52)	(53)	(29)	(34)	(60)	(19)	(53)	(53)	(27)

[a]No statistically significant differences between age levels were detected.

[b]Differences between girls and boys are statistically significant on both interviews. Probability of occurrence of X^2 values equal to or larger than those obtained is less than .05.

[c]Differences between girls and boys are significant at the .05 level on one interview only.

229

behavior might be quite different at different age levels, though the generic categories would be the same). A more detailed developmental study is needed.

Personality as Reflected in Behavior Patterns

The personality of the perceiving child, as expressed through his actions, was also examined in relation to cognitive responses. Behavioral records on each child were divided into units of action. Each unit was classed in one of four broad categories: (a) friendly, sociable, and nurturing behavior (49 per cent of all units), (b) aggressive, rebellious, and disruptive actions (20 per cent), (c) assertive and influencing behavior (21 per cent), and (d) submissive, dependent, fearful behavior (10 per cent). Two coders independently classified 89 per cent of 298 units in identical fashion. Each child was scored in terms of the relative frequency with which he initiated these interactions. Combination of the three most frequently occurring kinds of interaction gave behavioral types defined as follows: "active" children scored in the upper third of their cabin group on friendly as well as aggressive interaction, with assertion ranging from high to average; "withdrawn" children rated in the bottom third on at least two of these three dimensions, and high on none; "aggressive" children rated high on aggressive, disruptive, and rebellious action, *not* high on friendliness, and varied from high to low on assertion scores; and "friendly" children ranked high on sociable, affiliative and nurturing interaction and average or below on

both aggression and assertion.[5] Analyses by age and sex revealed no systematic differences in the frequency of these behavior types among boys and girls in the three age groups.

For the analyses that follow, active children were contrasted with withdrawn children on the nature of their perceptions of peers; friendly were contrasted with hostile. Do children who in these respects behave differently give differing cognitive responses? Differences would be predicted either because children of dissimilar personalities may have sensitivities for particular interpersonal phenomena, or because "perceiving" children manifesting contrasting behavior patterns may create differing interpersonal situations. In part the expectation of differences is upheld.

Children differing in behavior showed significant differences in complexity of perceptions, but they showed no stable differences in the categories of content used in describing others.

Active and friendly children gave more complex descriptions of others than did withdrawn or hostile children. (Table 4) Active children made explicit inferences to a greater extent than did the withdrawn (measured only at the end of the session). In comparing friendly with hostile

---

[5]The thirty-two per cent of the observed children not falling in any one of these four types have not been considered in this analysis. There was no systematic or significant relation between age or sex and the occurrence of the several behavior types here considered. This is in accord with reasonable expectations, since measures were relative to the cabin, and cabins were homogeneous with respect to age and sex.

TABLE 4.—Complexity of Perceptual Reports Related to Selected Behavior Types

	ACTIVE	WITHDRAWN	FRIENDLY	HOSTILE
Median organization rating, Interview I	4.33[a]	3.64	4.50	4.12
Median organization rating, Interview II	5.67[a]	4.33	5.25	4.22
Percent using inferences	59%[b]	23%	53%[b]	24%
(number of subjects)	(22)	(38)	(19)	(32)

[a]Difference between "active" and "withdrawn" approaches significance. Probability of occurrence of Mann-Whitney U-values equal to or smaller than those obtained is less than .10.

[b]"Active" differ significantly from "withdrawn"; "friendly" differ from "hostile." Probability of occurrence of chi-square values equal to or larger than those obtained is less than .05.

children, there was a consistent, but nonsignificant, tendency on both interviews for the friendly children to describe others in a more organized fashion, and they were significantly more likely than the hostile children to make inferential statements.

These comparisons suggest that the active participant brings his awareness of others into sharper judgmental focus than does the child who remains on the sidelines. Intentional or not, some degree of manipulation of interaction seems to facilitate obtaining a clear picture—accurate or inaccurate— of the social environment. That descriptions by the more sociable and affiliative children were generally more complex than those of the withdrawn children might be accounted for on similar grounds. That descriptions given by the friendly children are not strikingly superior in quality to those given by the hostile aggressive children might suggest that the general equivalence in their amounts of contact with peers tended to outweigh any possible influences of differences in the affective flavor of their behavior.

BEHAVIOR OF THE PERCEIVED CHILD AND OTHERS' DESCRIPTIONS OF HIM

The portrait of a child reported by his peers would not be expected to reflect his behavior with his peers with complete fidelity, but would be expected to show some correspondence. It was possible in this study to examine the closeness or divergence of these two pictures by comparing peer descriptions with records of behavior on each child made by trained observers, covering four hours of interaction. Descriptions and observations of behavior were both reduced to the four broad classes of action—friendly, aggressive, assertive, and submissive. Presence of a given class of action in a peer's descriptions of a child was compared with relative frequency with which the child initiated such action in his group. In this comparison, peer image and recorded behavior showed a remarkable absence of correspondence. In other words, in the child's synthesized picture of another child, the relevance or salience of a characteristic does not appear to be determined by the sheer frequency of its display in the behavior by the perceived child. This lack of correspondence is open to several possible interpretations. In part, it might be a function of the way in which the data were gathered. Thus, the "sample" of behavior available to the adult observer might not adequately represent the "universe" of peer behavior available to the perceiving child. It is possible, too, that the perceiving child selects from the total behavior of the object child only the direct behavioral interchange between himself and the perceived child, whereas the adult observer is attuned to interactions occurring among all the cabin group. This latter explanation is unlikely—because the reporting child frequently referred to the perceived child's relations with others.

While methodological factors may account for some of the discrepancies between the adult's and the child's "conclusions" about the nature of another child, these discrepancies might also derive from "real" differences in their selection from and interpretation of the same raw materials of children's behavior which are important in the understanding of the perceptions of children and which have importance also as a methodological issue in research with children.

Adults and children, while observing the same actions, might attribute quite different meaning to these actions. The values of scientist-observers and those of children—in this instance children from lower socio-economic groups—may differ. It would not be surprising, therefore, if concomitant differences were also reflected in cognitive interpretation of action. Thus, the adult-as-scientist may impute meaning to particular behavior differing from the interpretation given it by a participating child. Behavioral data may be reliably coded, but still such reliability does not eliminate the possibility of the differential perspective suggested. If such possible differences in cognitive interpretations are real and considerable ones, then this would clearly suggest the need for caution in the utilization of adult observers' reports of children's behavior as suitable "objective" indices in some child development research.

A second potential source of discrepancy between adults' records of behavior and children's perceptual reports is that of selective screening. Here the data shed some light and partially support a hypothesis of perceptual selectivity on the child's part. Feelings of the perceiver enter into the level of organization of his descriptions about the perceived child and into the content of his descriptions. Affect of the reporting child and complexity of organization of description were related curvilinearly ($X_9^2 = 18.32$; $p < .05$, Interview I); disliked children were described in a more systematic fashion than liked children, and liked children were described more systematically than children in a more neutral range of friendship. This relationship was much less pronounced after two weeks of interaction. The interesting qualitative superiority with which disliked children were described may in part reflect the perceiver's personal concern; it may come as the result of intense negative interactions which furnished conspicuous experiences; it may reflect the need to rationalize a negative evaluation.

Content of the reports reflects the affect of the perceiver in the expected manner. Liked children were described in terms that document "good guy" labels; reports of aggressive, fearful and dependent behavior were less often included. Similarly, the least liked children were reported as less affiliative and less nurturant. The extent to which affect is selectively shaping the perception can be seen by considering simultaneously the affect of the reporting child, the content of his report and the adult observer's behavior record of the perceived child. Even when one controls on the amount of recorded friendly behavior of the object child, the more the child is liked by his describer, the more likely is he to be seen as affiliative (Table 5). The amount of reported affiliation decreases systematically, from highest reported on children liked best, to lowest reported on children liked least. In a similar fashion, still controlling on observed friendly behavior of the object child, children most strongly liked are seen as least aggressive; those least well liked, most aggressive. Now controlling on recorded aggressive behavior of the object child, children strongly liked are systematically seen as more affiliative than children less well liked. And those most strongly liked are seen as least aggressive; those least well liked, most aggressive. Affect appears to influence significantly and systematical-

ly the child's selection and interpretation of behavioral information from his peers, resulting in peer assessments quite markedly at variance with the assessments arrived at through the perspectives of scientist observers.

DISCUSSION

We have examined children's perceptions of persons in a new social situation. Their perceptions, as represented by their reports to the investigator, are generally not unrelated congeries of elements but rather syntheses of varied and sometimes disparate characteristics about the other person. Children appraise others in interactional terms, along lines of personal significance. The most highly organized descriptions are given about children who have affective value for the observing child, particularly negative affective value. The sizable variations found in children's cognitive reports, both in content and level of organization, present a dimension of individual differences about which there is relatively little information and relatively little understanding as to its significance for interpersonal relations. Some of the variations in perceptual reports were accounted for in terms of characteristics of the child reporters, such as age and sex differences and differences in the behavioral qualities of the perceivers. Older children and the more active and friendly children were somewhat more likely to give complex person perceptions. Differences in content of descriptions by boys as contrasted with girls are consistent with the differences in the experiences of childhood for the two sexes.

TABLE 5.—Descriptions of Aggression and Affiliation, Related to Affective Value of Perceived Child[a]

A. CONTROLLING ON FRIENDLY BEHAVIOR OF PERCEIVED CHILD

Observed behavior:	High			Average			Low		
Affective value of: perceived child:	Very high	Moderately high	Average or below	Very high	Moderately high	Average or below	Very high	Moderately high	Average or below
Report of: Affiliation	87%	65%	50%	72%	60%	50%	84%	58%	30%
Aggression	30	59	67	34	60	57	32	25	80
(n)	(30)	(17)	(6)	(32)	(5)	(14)	(25)	(12)	(10)

B. CONTROLLING ON AGGRESSIVE BEHAVIOR OF PERCEIVED CHILD

	High			Average			Low		
Report of: Affiliation	76%	63%	31%	85%	60%	50%	81%	63%	60%
Aggression	34	88	77	46	30	67	19	38	40
(n)	(29)	(8)	(13)	(26)	(10)	(12)	(32)	(16)	(5)

[a] Data for this table derive from initial interviews. Interviews conducted at the end of the camp session gave a generally comparable picture.

Momentary and situational factors as well as enduring personality factors undoubtedly account for additional inter-individual variation. The data on the child's tendency to make appraisals in the same dimensions of interpersonal relationships on two occasions of testing, whether or not the same or a different child was being discussed, give one bit of evidence on this point. There is further evidence in the association found between affect of the perceiver and selectivity in his reports on the perceived child.

It would be misleading, however, to point only to differences in children's perceptions. Children's appraisals of their peers in many respects showed shared sensitivities, with repeated thematic emphasis on certain salient relationships, such as sociability, affiliative tendencies, potentially hostile acts. The same themes, with few exceptions, were characteristic of both initial and considered impressions at each age level studied. Thus, the *variations* among children are within this broad common framework. These similar sensitivities (unchanged by age) may possibly be attributable to a common culture of childhood and to similar learning of the significant interpersonal cues, those that are differentially rewarding or punishing in nature.

The particular characteristics of children's person perceptions obtained in this study in unknown ways may derive from the characteristics of the population being studied (children from lower socio-economic classes), and from the particular circumstances under which the testing was carried out. The children were in a new situation in which the other children, the environmental setting, and the adults in charge were all unfamiliar to them. These factors may possibly have heightened children's sensitivities to particular kinds of qualities in other persons. Lack of correspondence between children's reported impressions of another child and adult observers' behavioral records of the child was far greater than one might have anticipated in advance. The children's person perceptions, fashioned, we assume, from expectations, past experiences and personal needs, resulted in "realities" quite different from the assessments of children based on the observations and codings of the researchers. The coexistence of such discrepant "realities" poses a complicated problem in understanding children's responses to interpersonal stimuli, and one calling for more research. It is a truism to state that person perception is a complex process, yet the evidence of the present study indicates the need for emphasizing this fact.

24 *Learning and Reinforcement in Student Pairs*[1]

KENT C. MYERS

ROBERT M. W. TRAVERS

MARY EVE SANFORD

Does an elementary school pupil learn more by studying with another pupil in a teacher-learner relationship than by studying alone? He does not if he plays only the teacher role and the task is rote learning. In such a situation he tends to learn less than when studying alone. However, the child who plays the role of the pupil learns more than when studying alone. The best learning occurs when the pair interchange roles, each serving equally often in the teacher and the pupil role.

Historically, pupils in the classroom have been paired to learn many kinds of tasks, but little evidence has been presented to indicate the amount or quality of learning which takes place under these conditions. Recent work by Durrell and his associates involving pupil teams referred to this phenomenon and attempted to study it in the classroom (Bradley, 1957; Durrell, 1961; McHugh, 1961). These studies generally showed that pupil teams made progress comparable to pupils learning in recitation situations.

This study compares the effectiveness of a number of different learning conditions involving a rote-learning task. Of particular interest to the investigators were the learning conditions which occur when pupils work in pairs, with one pupil in the teacher role and the other in the learner role. The relative amount of learning under these two conditions is a matter of some interest. In addition, a comparison was made with learning by subjects working by themselves with

[1]This is an essential portion of a Doctor's thesis submitted to the Education Department, University of Utah, and was supported by Office of Education Research Contract OE No. 2–10–010.

Reprinted from the *Journal of Educational Psychology*, 1965, **56**, 67–72, by permission of Dr. Travers and the American Psychological Association.

the same task in a self-instruction situation. These subjects received reinforcement from the self-instruction device, but responded covertly to the task as in many of the studies on programed instruction (Goldbeck and Campbell, 1962; Kanner and Sulzer, 1961; Keislar and McNeil, 1962; Michael and Maccoby, 1953; Silverman and Alter, 1961, p. 69; Stolurow and Walker, 1962). The latter studies generally concluded that covert responding produced equal results to overt response modes, and the covert responding was more efficient.

The study was made in an elementary school, but the subjects were removed from their regular classrooms to work with the experimenter in a classroom in the school similar to their regular classroom environment.

METHOD

Task, Tests, and
Task Administration

The learning task was developed by Van Wagenen and Travers (1963) and is described in detail in their paper. The task consisted of 60 German stimulus words (nouns). Each German word was to be correctly associated with one of the two English responses. The task is divided into three sections, each one of which is given on 3 consecutive days.

Subjects learning the task were required to guess which one of the two English words had the equivalent meaning of the German word. After guessing they obtained information concerning the correct answer. Each German word and the two English words were presented on a separate card. The task was prepared in two forms. Both forms were on special

heavyweight, index-size cards. One form was used by pupil pairs, and the other form was used by pupils working alone. The form for pupil pairs consisted of a deck of cards with each item printed on both sides of the card, and each side was identical except that the side exposed to the subject in the teacher role had the correct response marked. The form used by pupils working alone was constructed with one side identical to the form used by pairs, but on the reverse side the reinforcement statement, "The right answer is————," was presented.

The 60-item task was divided into three groups of 20 items each, and learning trials were conducted on 3 successive days, Monday, Tuesday, and Wednesday. On each of these days 20 words were presented with four trials on each word. The 80 presentations required about 15–20 minutes per day to complete.

The Immediate Retention Test was administered on Friday of the same week as the learning trials. This was a multiple-choice test calling for recognition of the English equivalent from four choices. The distractors included the word used in the task as the incorrect choice plus two English words from other task items. This same test was later used as the Delayed Retention Test, which was given to all subjects 3 weeks after the final group of subjects had completed the learning task and the immediate test. This gave delayed retention data at 3-, 4-, 5-, 7-, 8-, and 9-week intervals. The break in continuity of weeks occurred (5–7) because school was dismissed during that week for the state education association convention.

Administration of the task had two major variations, an overt verbal interaction for learning in pairs and covert individual response for learning alone. Pupil pairs were seated in groups of four pairs. Each pair faced one another across a table in a simulated classroom environment with all four pairs within a few feet of another. The teacher subject controlled the cards and presented the task to the pupil subject. Holding the card up, so that the pupil subject could see the task on his side of the card, the teacher subject would say the German word. The pupil subject would then read aloud the German word and the two English words and would then say the English word which he thought was the correct one. The teacher subject would then give the reinforcement feedback statement, "The right answer is ———." The teacher subject would then present the card for the next item.

The subjects working alone were instructed to read the German stimulus and the two English responses and then decide which English word was equivalent to the German word. They then turned the card and read the reinforcement feedback statement and proceeded to the next item.

Learning Conditions

The task was administered to eight subjects at one time. The conditions of learning were:

Condition I: teacher subjects interacting with pupil subjects. This member of the work pair directed the learning of another pupil and was told he was to learn the task along with his pupil. He gave feedback orally to the pupil subject and did not receive feedback orally from another person. The correct answer was available to him on each item, but he made no overt response to the selection of a correct answer. The subject in this condition did, however, interact actively and verbally with the other member of the pair.

Condition II: pupil subjects interacting with teacher subjects. These subjects made active responses to the stimulus and made a choice from two responses as to the correct response. They received the same feedback from the teacher subject, whether they were right or wrong in their choice in the form "The right answer is ———."

Condition III: subjects assigned either the pupil or teacher role at the beginning of the task and the reverse role at the midpoint of the task. These subjects were in a paired situation as in Conditions I and II, but did not continue in the same role throughout the learning trials as the pairs did in Conditions I or II. Halfway through the task, the pupils were stopped and, for the remainder of the task, the roles of the pupils were reversed—the one who had played the learner role now became the teacher and vice versa.

Condition IV: subjects interacted with a self-instruction card to learn the task. The condition was one wherein subjects worked alone on the task and received feedback by reading the feedback statement on the reverse side of the self-instruction card which was always in the form "The right answer is ———."

Sample

Subjects were 192 elementary school pupils in the fourth, fifth, and sixth grades. All subjects were selected on the basis of having had no prior experience with the German language. Metropolitan reading scores were used for equating the groups because the task required some competence in reading and because reading ability and verbal learning measures have been shown to be highly correlated.

TABLE 1.—Means and Standard Deviations for Conditions × Tasks

LEARNING CONDITIONS	TASK[a]					
	A		B		C	
	M	SD	M	SD	M	SD
I (teacher role)	10.25	3.64	7.00	3.09	7.25	3.01
II (pupil role)	12.50	2.97	9.23	2.65	9.38	2.80
III (teacher-pupil)	11.67	3.69	8.67	2.78	8.00	3.10
IV (self-instruction)	13.19	3.28	8.77	2.46	7.40	3.12

[a]Twenty items each.

Twenty-four groups of 8 subjects each were established with 6 groups in each learning condition equally distributed across the three grade levels for a total of 48 subjects per condition. All subjects were in the same elementary school in Salt Lake City. Each experimental session involved 1 group of 8 pupils, who worked either as four pairs of interacting learners or as 8 independent learners depending upon the particular treatment to which the group had been assigned.

RESULTS

The data came from two sources, the Immediate Test and the Delayed Test. The same instrument was used for both tests.

Immediate Test Data

The Immediate Test was given on Friday to all subjects who had completed the learning trials that week.

Means and standard deviations for each Learning Condition × Task were computed and reported. The means in Table 1 show that a decrement across tasks was evident and that subjects in Condition I, teacher role only,

were less effective in learning this task than subjects in other conditions. Condition I subjects had lower mean scores than other subjects on each day's task.

The analysis of variance in Table 2 shows that the main effects, Conditions and Tasks, produced significant effects as did two interactions. Grade Levels gave no significant differences. The total means for the 60 items were computed by grade level and were 28.65, 28.95, and 28.05 for fourth-, fifth-, and sixth-grade subjects, respectively. However, the experimenters observed that the younger children generally required more time to complete the task than did the older children.

In order to further test the significant differences indicated for Conditions on Table 2, the means for all 60 items of the task were computed for subjects in each condition; and these means were 25.35, 31.11, 28.35, and 29.37, respectively, for Conditions I, II, III, and IV. The effect of conditions was treated with an individual degrees-of-freedom test (Li, 1957, p. 226). Table 3 shows the results of this test. Condition II subjects, pupil role only, showed significantly superior learning to all other conditions. Condition III, reversed teacher and pupil roles, and Condition IV, self-instruction, subjects showed superior learn-

ing to Condition I at the .001 level. Conditions III and IV were not significantly different from each other.

Variation among the parts of the total task was highly significant in the analysis of variance (.001 level). The means for Tasks A, B, and C were 11.90, 8.64, and 8.00, respectively.

To investigate the interaction of Tasks × Conditions, which was highly significant in the analysis of variance, the mean scores from Table 1 were plotted graphically. Figure 1 shows that differences in decrement for conditions across the 3 days of the task were not graphically parallel. Learning Condition IV, the self-instruction mode, shows a very sharp decrement from Task A to Task B, and this decrement continued to Task C at a much steeper decline than in any other condition. The differences in decrement between conditions, across the three tasks, appear to account for the significant interaction.

TABLE 2.—Analysis of Variance Table for Immediate Retention Test Data

SOURCE	df	MS	F
Between subjects	191	17.76	
Grades (G)	2	4.50	.27
Conditions (C)	3	93.00	5.58**
G × C	6	17.67	1.06
Residual be-			
tween	180	16.67	
Within subjects	384	10.78	
Tasks (days; T)	2	841.00	141.58***
T × G	4	5.75	.97
T × C	6	22.33	3.76***
T × G × C	12	13.50	2.27**
Residual within	360	5.94	
Total	575		

** $p < .01.$
*** $p < .001.$

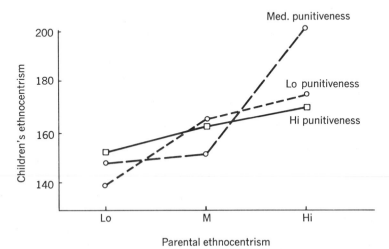

Fig. 1.   Graphical representation of the interaction of tasks and learning conditions.

TABLE 3.—Individual Degrees-of-Freedom Test Comparing Immediate Retention Test Scores of the Four Conditions

SOURCE	df	MS	F
Condition II versus Condition III	1	184.26	11.06***
Condition II versus Condition IV	1	73.50	4.47*
Condition III versus Condition I	1	213.01	12.79***
Condition IV versus Condition III	1	25.01	1.50

Note.—All computations based on 180 degrees of freedom because 180 were involved in the error term from Table 2.

*$p < .05$.
***$p < .001$.

The triple interaction was not examined further because the source was considered to be generally very obscure.

Delayed Retention Test Data

Three weeks after the final group of 32 subjects had completed the experiment, a Delayed Retention Test of the tasks was given to all 192 subjects. Because of the organization of the public school where the data were collected, it was impractical to have the subjects from each grade level participate in the learning task each week; therefore, all subjects learning the task in a given week were from the same grade level. Thirty-two subjects, who completed the task each week, were divided equally into the four conditions of the experiment. The experiment occupied 3 consecutive weeks, and then there was a break of 1 week to allow for the state education association meeting which curtailed school, and then the experiment continued for 3 more consecutive weeks. When the Delayed Retention Test was given to all subjects on the same day, this provided data which showed delayed retention for 3, 4, 5, 7, 8, and 9 weeks. The delayed retention scores were computed for subjects in each condition to allow for comparison with the Immediate Test data. Means for each condition by week of delay were computed and are shown in Table 4. Means for subjects in Condition I were consistently lower than means for subjects in other conditions on the test of delayed retention, but there is little evidence of much decay in the skill over the 9-week period.

An analysis of variance of the data from the Delayed Retention Test was computed and is shown in Table 5.

TABLE 4.—Means for Learning Conditions for Subjects in Each Week of Delay

LEARNING CONDITION	WEEKS OF DELAY					
	3	4	5	7	8	9
I (teacher role)	22.38	18.39	21.75	27.00	19.74	19.50
II (pupil role)	26.64	23.64	21.87	26.01	22.14	23.37
III (teacher-pupil)	23.01	20.49	24.12	25.26	24.87	28.14
IV (self-instruction)	26.88	23.88	29.49	19.26	23.49	23.88

Conditions did not vary as they had on the Immediate Test data. Analysis of variance indicated significance between the .10 and .05 level. The mean scores for all subjects in Conditions I, II, III, and IV on the Delayed Test were 21.46, 23.94, 24.31, and 24.48, respectively. An individual degrees-of-freedom test indicated that Condition I subjects, teacher role only, varied significantly from the others ($df = 1/188$, $M = 147.51$, $F = 11.48$, $p = .001$). The three means scores for Conditions II, III, and IV were very similar; but to be certain that they did not vary significantly an individual degrees-of-freedom test was applied comparing Condition II, pupil role only, with Condition IV, self-instruction. No significant difference was evidenced.

TABLE 5.—Analysis of Variance Table for Delayed Retention Data

SOURCE	df	MS	F
Between subjects	191		
Conditions (C)	3	32.00	2.49
Residual between			
subjects	188	12.85	
Within subjects	384		
Tasks (days; T)	2	516.50	119.00***
T × C	6	7.17	1.65[a]
Residual within			
subjects	376	4.34	
Total	575		

[a]An F of 2.60 was needed at the .05 level.
*** $p < .001$.

The variance across Tasks A, B, and C was still significant at the .001 level of confidence as it had been in the Immediate Test data. Mean scores for each day's task were plotted and the means were 9.56, 7.70, and 6.29 for Tasks A, B, and C, respectively.

DISCUSSION AND IMPLICATIONS

The study of learning by pupil pairs and individual pupils in this experiment indicated that the pupils can be paired to teach one another effectively with materials requiring rote learning in programed form. Evidence from the study produced the following implications:

When pupils are paired to learn a rote-memory task, materials should be so constructed that each pupil receives feedback from the other pupil in the pair. Verbal reinforcement by another person appears to be important in this kind of learning. Pupils in this study who did not receive any feedback from another, but provided this kind of feedback for others produced the poorest results on both immediate and delayed test of the tasks.

Materials which are prepared for use as self-instruction devices probably should be so constructed that these materials offer some variety of experience. Initial, first-day learning by subjects using self-instruction materials in this study was very good but decreased sharply on subsequent days.

The total amount of learning of the task in this study did not seem to be effected by the grade level (age) of the subjects involved. The grades probably differed in the time taken to complete the task.

Condition III in this study, wherein subjects were in both the teacher and pupil role, appears to offer some class-room advantages. Both members of these pairs learned to about an equal degree and maintained high interest and attention throughout the learning task. Additional data should be sought which would give information on what learning takes place when

subjects reverse roles oftener, perhaps on every other item.

Spacing of the trials throughout the week or with rest periods within the learning trials might reduce the decrement across days. Additional data on time distribution for learning trials should be sought.

25 Children's Acquisition of Skill in Performing a Group Task under Two Conditions of Group Formation

MOSES H. GOLDBERG

ELEANOR E. MACCOBY

This study deals with behavior that occurs when children must interact effectively with other children to maximize their own goals. The major question investigated is whether effective interaction is facilitated more by experience with a variety of partners or by continued interaction with a stable group of partners. It is found that children trained under conditions of stable group membership perform more effectively. The groups with constantly changing membership tend more often than constant-membership groups to have high-scoring children who exercise coercive dominance over low-scoring children.

The present study deals with the individual's ability to maximize his own gains in a situation requiring cooperation with others for the achievement of individual goals. Our experiment grows out of the classic earlier work of Mintz (1951), who used a situation

in which several individuals had to pull cones out of a single narrow-necked jar. "Traffic jams" usually developed at the neck of the jar, so that none of the participants could get their cones out, when rewards and punishments were administered to

Reprinted from the *Journal of Personality and Social Psychology*, 1965, **2**, 898–902, by permission of Dr. Maccoby and the American Psychological Association.

each individual on the basis of his own time score. When *groups* of participants received a single score based on the total time for all the cones to be withdrawn from the jar, however, there was efficient cooperative performance. The group worked out a strategy of taking turns and cones were withdrawn smoothly in a relatively short time.

We are interested in the situation of individual rewards and punishments—the situation which resulted in failure for most participants in Mintz' experiment. We assume that even in situations where individuals are motivated to maximize their own gains, they do ultimately acquire the ability to work out cooperative strategies if their individual success depends upon their doing so. We expect that if a game similar to that employed by Mintz is continued over a series of trials, it will be possible to chart the development of these cooperative strategies. We wished to discover how efficiently a group would perform on such a task if, although the group had not previously worked together, they had all previously worked with other groups on the task and thus had an opportunity to acquire certain skills in getting and maintaining group cooperation.

Specifically, we wished to discover whether the acquisition of such skill would be facilitated or hindered by constantly changing group membership during the initial phases of experience with the task. It could be argued that if an individual is to be brought together with a group of strangers to work with them on an individual-reward task with which all are familiar, successful group performance will

be most likely if the individuals involved have all had fairly extensive previous experience in adapting themselves to a variety of partners. Individuals who had previously worked on the task in the company of only one fixed set of partners would presumably be at a disadvantage in interacting with a group of strangers, having had exposure to a lesser range of other individuals to whom they would have had to learn to adapt their own behavior. Putting the issue in terms of acquisition of roles, the individual who has worked in several different groups, composed of a variety of other personalities, will have had experience in taking a variety of roles; a stable group, by contrast, which does not change personnel during the series of training trials, should develop a set of stable role relationships, and the members of such groups may find that the role they have acquired does not transfer easily to a new group setting.

Our hypothesis is: when tested with a group of strangers on a task requiring group cooperation for achievement of individual goals, the individuals who will be most successful will be the ones who have had previous experience in groups of changing composition; those least successful will be those whose previous experience had been with a single unchanging group.

METHOD
Design

CHANGING GROUPS Groups of children performed a cooperative task for eight consecutive trials—the "training period." After each pair of trials, the composition of the groups was changed, so that each of the subjects in these groups worked with four different sets of co-workers during the training trials. The subjects were reassorted once more, after which they performed the task eight more times (test trials) without further shuffling of group membership.

STABLE GROUPS Subjects assigned to this condition had their eight training trials with the same group of co-workers. They were then shifted to new groups, and performed eight test trials.

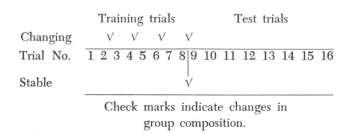

Check marks indicate changes in group composition.

Subjects

The subjects were 64 second-grade children, 32 boys and 32 girls, from two schools in Palo Alto, California. Four groups of 16 were used, and from these pools of 16, four subgroups of four children each were formed. The groups were then designated as follows: 16 boys, stable-membership condition (SB); 16 girls, stable-membership condition (SG); 16 boys, changing-membership condition (CB); 16 girls, changing-membership condition (CG). Groups CG and SB were from one school, SG and CB from the other. An attempt was made to form groups from children who knew each other as little as possible. Cases were randomly assigned to the two conditions.

Procedure

We wished to devise a task which would meet the following criteria:

1. It must require close group cooperation for successful performance, with an uncooperative member able to jeopardize the group's success.

2. It must permit individual differences in performance, and permit reward to be given to the individual on the basis of his

own performance, independent of the total group achievement.

3. It should provide a range of scores, rather than simply a "pass" or "fail" score.

We chose a tower-building task, in which the group of four children working together had to build a single tower of blocks, and build it as high as they could within the 15-second time period allowed for each trial. Each child was given a pile of eight 3-inch blocks of a distinctive color, and his score at the end of the trial was the number of his own blocks that were on the jointly built tower when time was called. No two children could place blocks at the same moment. Even with perfect cooperation (e.g., regularly taking turns placing a block) it was not possible for all the children to place all their blocks. The time allotted was too short, and there was an upper limit to the height of the tower due to the height of the children and the stability of the structure they could build; these factors combined in such a way that the highest tower built during the experiment was 19 blocks. An individual child could reduce everyone's score by knocking over the tower, through carelessness, deliberate negativism, or overzealous addition of blocks to an already wobbly structure. On this task, the potential range of scores for individual children was 0–8 on each trial.

The experimental setting consisted of a large multipurpose room located at the respective schools. Four "stations" were established in the four corners of the room, and a judge was assigned to each station, the senior author serving as coordinator and timer. Also placed at each station was a set of 32 3-inch cubes, 8 each of green, yellow, blue, and red. The 16 children who were to participate in the session were then assembled in the center of the room and the following instructions were read:

> This morning we are going to play a little game—and if you listen carefully and follow the rules, you can win some prizes. Does everybody like M & Ms? . . . OK. . . . Here's what you have to do. Do you see the numbers 1, 2, 3, and 4 in the corners? In a minute I'm going to call all of your names and tell you each one of the numbers. Then you will all go to the number I tell you. But first I'll tell you what you are going to do. When I say "Go" I want everybody at each number to build one tower with blocks. There will be four boys [girls] at each number and all four of you have to build the same tower. I want you to build it as high as you can. There's one thing, though, I want you each to use different color blocks. That way we can see how many blocks each one of you put on the tower. We are going to give you one M & M for each block of your own color that's on the tower. So the more blocks of your color you put on, the more M & Ms you'll get. Be careful, though, if the tower gets knocked

down, it doesn't count and you have to start over. No fair holding the tower, either; it has to stand up by itself. You will have to work quickly because I'm only going to give you a short time. Watch, and I'll show you what I mean. Suppose you build a tower and when I say stop, it looks like this: [blue, red, green; red, blue]. The boy [girl] with the red blocks would get two M & Ms, because there are two red blocks on the tower, the one with blue would get two, the one with green would get one, and the one with yellow wouldn't get anything, because there aren't any yellow blocks on the tower. . . . Does everybody understand? . . .

After this instruction the groups were divided into four subgroups of four children each and these were sent to the four stations. Each group had 16 trials of tower building. The judges distributed rewards (as per instructions to the children) after each trial, and enforced the rules. Each trial was 15 seconds in duration, and there were no rewards for blocks placed after the signal to stop. Towers which collapsed between the signal to stop and the time necessary for the judge to count the blocks were treated as if they had fallen during the trial, and only those blocks still standing erect in the original spot were rewarded.

After the second, fourth, sixth, and eighth trial, the following instructions were given:

> Now before we try it again, I'm going to give you all another number, and I want you to move to the new place. Some of you will stay at the same number, but most of you will have to move.

The subgroups were then reconstituted.
In the changing-membership condition,

complete reconstitution took place. No child ever worked with the same other child again when he moved to a new "station." In the stable-membership condition, all of the children moved, but the subgroups were identical, that is, they moved as a unit of four, except for the last move, the one after Trial 8. At this time they, too, were reconstituted with different partners. The last eight trials (9–16) are regarded as a testing period, and no movements or reconstitutions took place.

RESULTS AND DISCUSSION

We predicted that children who had been trained in subgroups of changing composition would be more successful when placed with still another group in the rest trials than would subjects whose training had oc-

curred in groups of constant composition. The reverse proved to be the case. The mean total number of blocks placed per trial by the 32 subjects in the changing composition groups during their eight test trials was 45.4. That of the constant composition groups was 72. This means that each of the eight four-person changing subgroups built towers averaging 5.7 blocks in height during the eight test trials, while the stable subgroups built towers which averaged 9 blocks in height. This difference is significant, $p < .01$ ($t = 3.02$, $df = 14$). During the eight training trials, the performance of the groups under the two training conditions was not significantly different. The average number of blocks placed per trial by four-man subgroups during training was 7.4 for the stable

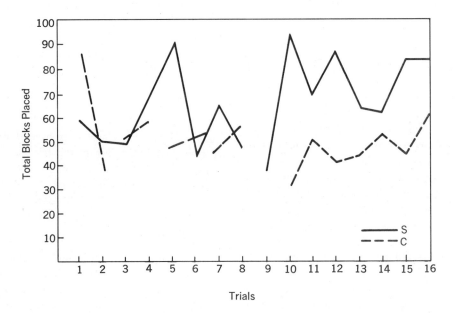

Fig. 1. Changing (C) versus stable (S) groupings. (Total number of blocks placed in each condition trial by trial by 32 subjects in eight subgroups. Break in line indicates reconstitution of membership of four-person subgroups.)

groups, 6.9 for the changing groups. Figure 1 shows the trial-by-trial totals for all of the 32 subjects in each condition combined. Dividing the totals in this graph by 8 will yield the mean performance of four-man subgroups, and dividing by 32 will give the individual mean performance for each trial.

How can we account for the superiority of the constant-composition groups during the test trials? We first entertained the hypothesis that in the constant-membership condition, there was time for the formation of stable role relationships—that some subjects emerged as leaders, others as followers, and that this role acquisition somehow permitted subjects to function more effectively in a new group. It is true that the task permitted the establishment of leadership and followership roles. The situation frequently occurred in which more than one child would place a first block and insist that the tower should be built upon his starting point. The child who succeeded in persuading the group to build on his first-placed block had at least a one-block advantage, of course, but his dominance gave his a greater advantage than this. The number of first blocks placed was significantly correlated with total additional blocks placed. That is, the child who succeeded in establishing the starting point for the tower was able to get more of his blocks on the tower, not counting the first block. It is meaningful, then, to speak of dominance of some individuals in the performance of this task, and we may ask whether leadership or dominance became more polarized, more stably characteristic of specific individuals,

in the constant than in the changing condition.

We can obtain information relevant to this question by examining the variability of scores in each group. If stable dominance patterns were emerging in one of the experimental conditions, this should mean that some individuals would earn consistently high scores and others consistently low scores over a series of trials. If groups were functioning with little polarization, the variance among individual scores should be less.

During the training trials, the scores of individuals were more variable under the changing-composition condition than under the constant-composition condition ($F = 1.97$, $p < .05$). The difference in variability was even more marked during the test trials. For each child, we computed a ratio score—the ratio of the number of blocks he placed during the eight test trials to the total number placed by his group. The average of these ratios was, of course, .25. But in the groups which had been trained under changing-membership conditions, the variability was considerably greater ($F = 2.42$, $p < .01$). There were two children in these groups who clearly exercised coercive dominance over the other children in their groups—one placed 59% of all the blocks placed by his group, the other 50%; there was one child in a group dominated by a high-scoring child who placed no blocks during the test trials, and two others who placed only 7% each of the total being placed by their group. No such extremes were found among the children trained under constant-group condition. Observers' reports on the changing groups indicated that in some instances the dominant child was shouldering others away from the tower. Sometimes he would have a confederate who helped exclude the other two children and in return be allowed to place some of his own blocks.

Several of the groups trained under constant-composition conditions, by contrast, developed smooth cooperative techniques including all group members during the test trials. For example, the four members of a group would each pick up four blocks and stand poised for the starting signal— one child on his knees to place the bottom four blocks, the next child stooped to place the next four just above, etc. At the starting signal, the four sets of blocks would be quickly superimposed; out-of-line blocks would be straightened to stabilize the structure, and then the group would stand back and restrain one another from placing additional blocks so as not to topple the tower. Such a procedure resulted in equal scores for all participants and a high group score. The more equal distribution of scores among the constant-composition group suggests that cooperative techniques of his kind may have been responsible for their high scores during the test trials.

If equalitarian rather than dominance techniques are more effective in maximizing group scores, and constant-composition groups more often employ equalitarian techniques, how does it happen that these groups did not excel during the training trials? We have already seen that in the constant-group condition, different group members obtained more similar scores during this period as well as during

the test trials, yet they did not consistently build higher towers at this time than the changing-membership group. Our observations suggest that it takes time to develop genuinely cooperative processes, because the group must first devise means of controlling would-be coercive individuals. It frequently happened in our control groups that an individual would obtain a high score on early trials by using coercive techniques. But on subsequent trials, he would obtain a score of 0, when other members of the group took measures against him, sometimes by deliberately knocking down the tower. In the groups with constantly changing membership, this mobilization of the group against the bully does not appear to have taken place so readily. We suspect it may have begun to occur during the test trials when the experimental group children continued with the same group of co-workers for a longer period of time than they had done during their training trials, and that the countermeasures which the low-scoring children began to take may be in part responsible for the changing groups' failure to improve their performance during the test trials as much as the stable groups did. It is likely that the course of development of cooperative techniques would be greatly influenced by the characteristic behavior dispositions of group members, for example, whether one was habitually dominant and the others submissive. We suggest that experimental variation of group composition would be a fruitful line of further research, as well as more systematic observation of group process during training and test trials.

In the Community

7

26 Stealing and Temporal Orientation[1]

TIMOTHY C. BROCK

CAROLYN DEL GIUDICE

One approach toward detecting children who may be susceptible to development of delinquent patterns of response is that of focusing on the relationship between time orientation and impulse control, or the capacity to delay immediate gratification of needs. In this study, children who steal money from the experimenter choose fewer temporal concepts and tell stories with shorter time durations than the nonstealers. This relationship between stealing and time orientations is uninfluenced by race, sex, age, IQ, academic achievement, or school and home behavior problems.

The finding that the time spans of stories by middle-class children were longer than those of lower-class led LeShan (1952) to speculate concerning a positive relation between limited time orientation and psychopathy and delinquency.[2] His suggestion has pro-

[1]The invaluable suggestions and comments of W. J. Meyer are gratefully acknowledged. The research was conducted while the first author was at the University of Pittsburgh.

[2]However, from their recent reanalysis of LeShan's data, Greene and Roberts (1961, p. 141) concluded that, "LeShan's findings are equivocal and should not be interpreted as clearly showing a difference in time perspective between middle and lower class children."

Reprinted from the *Journal of Abnormal and Social Psychology*, 1963, **66**, 91–94, by permission of the senior author and the American Psychological Association.

duced uncertain evidence. Barndt and Johnson (1955) found that 17-year-old delinquent boys told stories with shorter temporal duration than matched nondelinquents but Davids and Parenti (1958), in a comparable study, obtained a difference in the opposite direction. In the latter study, employing 11-year-olds, it was concluded that better adjusted children tended to be more present oriented than those judged as less well-adjusted emotionally. Davids and Parenti attempted to resolve their difference with Barndt and Johnson by suggesting that different time orientations are "normal" at different developmental levels. A failure to demonstrate a relationship between frustration tolerance, an intervening explanatory construct proposed by LeShan, and time orientation was reported by Ellis, Ellis, Mandel, Schaeffer, Sommer, and Sommer (1955). Ambiguous results were obtained in studies comparing the time perspectives of adult schizophrenics and matched controls (Wallace, 1956) and of high and low achieving preadolescent boys (Teahan, 1958). In both studies statistically significant differences in the "predicted" direction were obtained for only half the story situations.

In order to provide a clearer test of the hypothesized relation between temporal orientation and psychopathy, an attempt was made to eliminate some of the sources of ambiguity in previous research. A situation was designed to provide unequivocal measures of the occurrence and magnitude of a form of psychopathic behavior, stealing, and of the use of temporal concepts.

METHOD

Subjects

Subjects were 120 children attending an elementary school in a lower-class neighborhood in Pittsburgh. The community consists of 40 city blocks between produce yards and a commercial area; tenements are located among small factories, warehouses, and freight yards. Typical occupations range from chronic unemployment to unskilled laboring jobs, the mean annual income being less than $2,000. Living is substandard with overcrowding and poor sanitation.

In each of three grade levels (2–3, 4–5, 6–8) 40 subjects were recruited, half of whom were males, and half of whom were Negroes. An analysis of variance of IQ and academic achievement ratings in this twelvefold classification yielded Fs less than unity. Within this design, subjects were selected on a random basis except that: children presenting discipline or behavior problems, e.g., truancy, of any kind were excluded; no more than one subject was recruited from the same classroom during the same class period.

Procedure

An opportunity for stealing was devised in the following fashion. The experimenter, officially present in the school with facilities to conduct hearing examinations, sent a message to the teacher of the subject with a note explaining that the subject was needed by the experimenter. Upon entering the room, the subject saw the experimenter standing beside her desk in an apparently flustered fashion. Beside the experimenter and near the desk on the floor was a woman's handbag, overturned, with its contents spilled out. Cards, a comb, assorted papers, and $.65 (2 dimes, 2 nickels, and 35 pennies) were scattered about and nearby was an opened small change purse. The experimenter said:

Look at this mess. I spilled my purse and everything fell out. I have to go up to the kindergarten now [the room most remote from the experimental room] and I don't have time to clean this up. Would you mind getting these things together? I don't care about the change. I don't know how much it is but I think it is only pennies. Most of it rolled away I guess. Just try to get the papers together. I'll be back in about five minutes.

In 5 minutes, the experimenter returned and asked the subject to sit down at the desk opposite her.

A measure of the use of temporal concepts was obtained. The experimenter presented the subject with 20 index cards (3″ × 5″) containing the following words, boldly printed: SCHOOL, MINUTE, DOOR, YESTERDAY, HOUSE, WEEK, SAND, TOMORROW, WINDOW, SECOND, SHOE, HOUR, HOME, DAY, ROOM, MONTH, CHAIR, TIME, DOG, YEAR. Ten of the words, the even numbered in order of presentation, were considered time related concepts and the others, nontemporal. All 20 were matched for Thorndike-Lorge frequency. The experimenter explained:

Now I want you to do something for me. Let's pretend that you are going to tell a story to your teacher or to your mother. What are the most important things you would need to do this? Words, of course. Now, some words you will want more than others, some words will make your story better and easier to understand. I want you to choose ten words that you think are the very best words to tell your story with. Choose them carefully. Let's read them together first to be sure you know them all.

The subject read the words aloud to the experimenter who recorded the subject's choices and put the cards away.

A second measure of temporal orientation was the same as one employed by Barndt and Johnson (1955), Davids and Parenti (1958), Wallace (1956), and Teahan (1958). The experimenter said:

Now I want to see what kind of a story you can tell me. I'll start a story and then you finish it any way you want to. Do you understand? Here is the beginning. About four o'clock one bright sunny afternoon in May, two boys [girls] are walking together down 39th street . . .

The experimenter recorded the story inconspicuously and when the subject finished, inquired, "What time is it now?" or depending on the story material, "How long did this take?" The experimenter recorded the child's estimate and her own. Twelve subjects were either unable or unwilling to tell stories. However, since they did not differ from the others on any of the obtained measures, this loss was not expected to bias the results.

After the subject was dismissed, the experimenter noted the amount of money stolen, if any.

RESULTS

Forty-nine subjects stole; the mean amount was 7.3 cents with a range from 1–55 cents. Negroes and whites were equally represented among stealers and nonstealers and racial background was not related to amount stolen or to differences on the temporal measures. The racial variable was not further considered. The number of temporal words selected is presented in Table 1. The overall average for stealers was 3.63 and for nonstealers, 5.82. Results for the second measure of temporal orientation are presented in Table 2. In six instances where the child's estimate of story time span was different from the experimenter's, the experimenter's estimate was employed. The overall average for stealers was 1.51 hours and

for nonstealers 2.53 hours. The results presented in Tables 1 and 2 were evaluated by analyses of variance (Table 3). The only significant outcome was a main effect of stealing versus nonstealing on both measures of temporal orientation. Subjects who stole selected fewer temporal concepts than nonstealers ($p < .001$) and told stories with shorter time spans ($p < .01$).

It was evident from the cell frequencies in Tables 1 and 2 that the proportion of males to females who stole tended to increase with age (grade). However, the same highly

TABLE 1.—Number of Subjects Selecting Various Temporal Words

	STEALERS						NONSTEALERS					
GRADE:	2–3		4–5		6–8		2–3		4–5		6–8	
	Boys	Girls	Boys	Girls	Boys	Girls	Boys	Girls	Boys	Girls	Boys	Girls
N:	9	7	9	3	16	5	11	13	11	17	4	15
MINUTE	3[a]	2	1	1	8	1	4	7	8	10	2	10
YESTERDAY	6	3	4	1	6	0	9	11	11	13	3	9
WEEK	6	2	3	1	4	2	8	7	6	11	3	9
TOMORROW	7	6	4	1	3	2	6	10	4	11	3	8
SECOND	6	1	5	0	3	2	3	4	7	9	2	6
HOUR	6	2	4	2	8	2	6	6	6	14	2	8
DAY	5	2	2	0	5	3	5	7	4	10	1	7
MONTH	5	3	2	0	4	2	3	8	4	10	2	10
TIME	0	1	3	0	5	2	8	9	8	12	3	9
YEAR	2	4	2	0	3	1	4	7	8	6	3	9
M	5.11	3.71	3.33	2.00	3.06	3.40	5.09	5.85	6.00	6.24	6.00	5.67

Note.—The higher the mean, the greater the number of temporal words chosen.
[a]Three of the nine boys in the second or third grade who stole money picked MINUTE in the word choice situation.

TABLE 2.—Mean Time Spans of Stories Told in Number of Hours

GRADE	STEALERS		NONSTEALERS	
	Boys	Girls	Boys	Girls
2–3	1.66(8)	1.20(5)	2.19(7)	3.79(12)
4–5	2.28(9)	0.35(2)	2.15(10)	2.28(17)
6–8	1.29(15)	1.38(4)	2.38(4)	2.27(15)

Note.—Cell Ns are in parentheses.

significant differences were obtained when separate analyses were made for males and females in the two higher grade categories.

Differences between stealers and nonstealers in their selection of individual temporal concepts were evaluated by computing chi squares for the difference between proportions. For example, from Table 1, MINUTE was chosen by 33% of the stealers and 58% of the nonstealers. For this comparison, $X^2 = 6.35$, $p < .02$. For all temporal concepts, the proportion for nonstealers was greater than that for stealers. Chi square p values for the other words were: YESTERDAY, $p < .001$; WEEK, $p < .02$; TOMORROW, $p < .30$; SECOND, $p < .50$; HOUR, $p < .50$; DAY, $p < .30$; MONTH, $p < .10$; TIME, $p < .001$; YEAR, $p < .001$. These results were used to examine two post hoc hypotheses: nonstealers are more future oriented than stealers, i.e., prefer TOMORROW more than they prefer YESTERDAY; nonstealers, more than stealers, emphasize words denoting long duration (YEAR, MONTH, TIME) rather than short duration (SECOND, MINUTE). The difference between proportions for TOMORROW was not significant but the corresponding difference for YESTERDAY was reliable and it was more than three times that for TOMORROW. Thus, to the extent that YESTERDAY and TOMORROW reflect direction of orientation, differences in past rather than future orientation were more clearly associated with response to the temptation. Evidence on the second hypothesis was equivocal: nonstealers, in comparison with steal-

TABLE 3.—Analyses of Variance of Temporal Words Selected and Time Spans of Stories

SOURCE	TEMPORAL WORDS[a]			STORY TIME		
	df	MS	F	df	MS	F
Stealing (A)	1	16.845	23.47**	1	39.669	9.27*
Sex (B)	1	.242	<1	1	.376	<1
Grade (C)	2	.325	<1	2	.233	<1
A × B	1	.784	1.09	1	12.885	3.01
A × C	2	1.475	2.05	2	.127	<1
B × C	2	.081	<1	2	5.476	1.28
A × B × C	2	.550	<1	2	.426	<1
Error	108	.7177		96	4.2774	

Note.—Because subclass frequencies were unequal, an approximation by Walker and Lev (1953, p. 381) was employed.

[a]The sum of squares for each cell was computed across subjects, not across words.

*$p < .01$.

**$p < .001$.

ers, did choose TIME and YEAR more than SECOND but differential selection of MONTH and MINUTE was about the same for the two groups.

An interesting question concerned magnitude of psychopathic behavior and temporal orientation. Product-moment correlations between amount stolen and the two temporal measures yielded coefficients close to zero ($-.04$ and $-.10$). Hence, the fact of stealing, rather than amount stolen, was a predictor of differences in temporal orientation.

The product-moment correlation between temporal words and story time spans for stealers was $-.08$ ($df = 42$) and for nonstealers $-.21$ ($df = 64$). Thus, the two variables, need for temporal concepts in fantasy production and the time span of such productions, though conceptually similar, were empirically unrelated.

Thirty-three of the 49 stealers made no gesture of redressment to their victim (the experimenter) while 16, on her return, said that the money was all in the purse or that not all the money could be found. The 16 "redressers" differed from the other stealers only in choosing fewer temporal words ($t = 1.81$, $p < .10$, two-tailed). It is unclear how this tendency might be interpreted. Greater concern or guilt over the theft may have motivated relevant verbalization to the returning victim. However, a facile explanation for the money loss would not be unexpected from persons with psychopathic predispositions.

In sum, strong support was found for a positive relation between stealing and limited temporal orientation. This relation was not influenced by race, sex, age, IQ, or academic achievement, and it was obtained for two unrelated measures of time orientation. More importantly, the present subjects were all normal in that they were unknown to have behavior or discipline problems.

DISCUSSION

An empirical generalization linking psychopathic tendency and temporal foreshortening would seem to require few restrictions or qualifications. It might be alleged that, for the present lower-class subjects, proficiency in stealing was a "realistic" mode of adjustment; at least one cannot assume that such behavior elicits the same severity of disapproval and sanction as in middle- and upper-class strata. However, the relation was obtained within lower-class subjects and there was no evidence that magnitude of pressure to steal, as measured by amount stolen, was disproportionately associated with any of the variables studied.

A definitive explanation for the relation between stealing and time orientation is undoubtedly dependent on further experimentation. At present, it may be suggested that stealers cannot take account of the negative consequences of their actions since, to do so, implies an elaborated temporal perspective. When an impulse to violate some norm is aroused, as in the present temptation situation, it is readily acted upon because a foreshortened temporal perspective prevents consideration of sanctions or other negative reinforcements which might occur in the future.

A final issue concerns ambiguity in definition of the dependent variable. In their recent review of research on temporal experience, Wallace and Rabin (1960) emphasized the lack of a consistent theoretical and methodological approach to time perspective and time orientation, "with the meaning of neither concept being explicitly specified." Suggestive psychoanalytic discussions (e.g., Fenichel, 1945, pp. 282, 587; Greenacre, 1945) might be considered in subsequent research focused on experimental manipulation of time orientation in fantasy.

27   *Childhood Social Interactions and Young Adult Bad Conduct*[1]

MERRILL ROFF

Early detection of children who are likely to exhibit later maladjustments is a vital approach toward fostering mental health. This followup study of male child guidance cases and their military service records shows that among young adults who were considered behavior problems in childhood, one of the best indices of adult adjustment is acceptance by peers. Social adjustment to peers during childhood is predictive of two adult maladjustment areas, psychoneurosis and bad conduct.

The present paper describes one part of a larger research project concerned with the relationships between childhood maladjustments, personality problems, and associated background factors—described at the time of their actual occurrence rather than retrospectively—and adjustment in young adulthood. Information contained in child guidance clinic case histories is being compared with personnel and psychiatric information in the Selective Service and military service records of the same persons at a later period. For the total group of male clinic cases from two child guidance clinics in Minnesota, information has been obtained from the Selective Service System, the national Army, Navy, and Air Force Record

[1]This investigation was supported (in part) by USPHS Grant Number M–2218, from the National Institute of Mental Health; by Contract Number DA–49–007 MD–2015 with the Army Medical Research and Development Command; and by Contract AF 18 (600) 454 with the Air Force School of Aviation Medicine.

Reprinted from the *Journal of Abnormal and Social Psychology*, 1961, **63**, 333–337, by permission of the author and the American Psychological Association.

Centers, and the Veterans Administration. Both clinics began during the 1920s; the sample under consideration here includes men who were in service during World War II and after.

An introductory report (Roff, 1956) included a preliminary predictive study, indicating that experienced clinical child psychologists could make significantly accurate predictions of service adjustment, good or poor, on the basis of the case histories. With this demonstration that meaningful predictions could be made on a global basis, it seemed desirable to identify the particular dimensions contributing to prediction. Relevant findings would have both theoretical and practical value and could provide useful leads for appraisal procedures outside the case history situation. Specified dimensions could also be recombined in potentially more effective patterns for predictive purposes.

Criterion subgroups exhibiting various kinds of poor adjustment at the adult level include those diagnosed as psychoneurotic, psychotic, character and personality disorders with and without bad conduct, "psychosomatic" disorders, sexual deviations, etc. One would expect that some case history information may be specifically predictive of only a single type of outcome but that some variables from the childhood period may be more broadly effective in predicting outcomes of more than one kind. The first of these outcome groups to be studied intensively was a sample of persons diagnosed as psychoneurotic while in service. Reports of predictions for this group in contrast to a control group judged to have made

satisfactory service adjustments have been presented elsewhere (Roff, 1957, 1960).

The present paper is concerned with the application of the method developed for the prediction of adult psychoneurosis from childhood histories to a group who exhibited severe bad conduct while in service.

METHOD

The subjects were 164 former child guidance clinic cases who had entered and been discharged from one of the military services. Half of these subjects had a record of severe bad conduct while in service, serious enough to lead to other than an honorable discharge or to a number of days AWOL or days of confinement ("bad time") totaling at least 60. Although most of this behavior occurred in a military setting, a few subjects committed offenses in the civilian community severe enough to result in their discharge from service.

The first major class of offense was repeated periods of AWOL, with or without other violations. A second major type of offense was theft or robbery under a wide variety of circumstances, either in a service situation or while on leave or AWOL. A third category, frequently including repeated offenses or in combination with other types of offense, included disobedience, refusal to obey an order, and violations of this nature, including assault on a superior. Other groups of offenses included repeated drunkenness, forgery, escape from detention, and breaches of regulations governing the possession or use of firearms. In general, this group of men committed violations for which they could have no reasonable hope of escaping detection and punishment. If a man went AWOL for a month, he could expect that this would be detected and that he would be caught and returned (unless he had been placed in civilian confinement in the meantime).

Individuals who had had frequent enough or serious enough offenses in the civilian community to lead to their rejection for military service were not included in the present sample, so some of the most serious offenders were excluded, thus restricting somewhat the range of the group studied. Although the policies regarding rejection varied somewhat from one time to another, a substantial number of serious offenders in all periods were excluded from service altogether.

Many bad conduct subjects were diagnosed by service psychiatrists as having a personality disorder, but not one appropriate for a medical discharge. During World War II, offenders who were sent to disciplinary barracks were carefully studied psychiatrically, partly with a view to determining whether or not they should be returned to duty. More recently, it has been the practice for an offender to be referred to a psychiatrist to assist in determining whether he should receive a medical discharge on psychiatric grounds or an administrative discharge. Since the reports of these interviews give a somewhat more definite picture of the individuals involved than does a simple statement of offenses, abstracts from some of these are presented for illustrative purposes.

This soldier has been in the Army for approximately eight months, and has been under psychiatric evaluation and treatment practically ever since he came into the Army. He is subject to periods of animosity and has developed psychosomatic symptomatology re-

ferred to various parts of the body, which has handicapped him in his duties. He has been convicted by court-martial five times during the past six months.

He is a paranoid personality, chronic, severe, manifested by an habitual inappropriate attitude of being imposed upon or persecuted, nonpsychotic in degree. He has had six periods of AWOL ranging from ten to fifty-nine days.

He is erratic, undependable, and argumentative, with temper tantrums. He has had repeated disciplinary measures taken against him and has been constantly ostracized by the other men because of his laziness, belligerence, and unwillingness to cooperate. He is an anxious, restless, and egocentric individual who has always had phobias and conflicts with others, with a long record of maladjustment in the Navy.

These subjects have been studied without specific reference to combat performance because most of them never reached combat. Beebe and Appel (1958) examined the relationships between various items of information obtained from precombat service records and psychiatric breakdown during combat, finding that men with disciplinary records broke down about twice as often as individuals without such history. The bad conduct of their groups was milder than that of the present subjects.

Control subjects consisted of individuals who had reached and kept a grade of sergeant (or equivalent) or higher without any indications of disciplinary or mental health trouble at any point following entrance into service. They were matched in childhood IQ with the bad conduct cases because intelligence level was sometimes directly related to service career possibilities. Control cases were drawn by taking the nearest appropriate case, in terms of clinic case number, which had not previously been used. While this method provided comparable information for both control and experimental subjects, it meant that the controls differed from a random sample of the general population in having been dealt with by a clinic during childhood. Some subjects had received treatment ranging from minimal to substantial in amount, while others had only been studied.

Procedures for Analyzing Clinic Case Histories

Information in the case histories usually covered the following kinds of items: behavior difficulties; mother; father; grandmother, aunts, etc. (of particular importance if they functioned in place of the parents); siblings; home and family situations; health, including nervous mannerisms and speech; social adjustment outside the family; psychological test data; and psychiatric evaluation.

Readers with no knowledge of the service records of the subjects abstracted all potentially significant information for certain of the categories listed above. These were then evaluated by other readers who had never seen the complete case history. For example, all the information about the mother was abstracted and evaluated by itself. A similar procedure was followed for siblings and sibling relations. Two practices were found desirable in order to lessen a possible loss of information in going from the full case history to these abstracts.

1. Different opinions of the child were sometimes expressed by informants who had had an opportunity to ob-

serve him in different situations. In preparing abstracts, it was found important to identify all abstracted material by the character of the informant who furnished it (teacher, case worker, mother, psychiatrist, etc.).

2. There was sometimes a difference between earlier and later descriptions of a youngster as a result of either treatment or merely the passage of time. It was considered desirable not to lose this chronological information in the course of the abstracting, so the dates were carefully recorded for all items in the abstract.

While this is a highly multivariate situation, it seemed desirable to attempt to develop different single variables on an analytic basis before attempting to put them back together. It would be expected that some simplification of this multivariate situation would result if one or two leading dimensions could be found. Various lines of work, including psychiatric considerations of disturbances of interpersonal relationships in various behavior disorders, the success of nominating techniques and buddy ratings in predicting combat performance (Trites and Sells, 1957; Williams and Leavitt, 1947), and the current use of group procedures as an aid to diagnosis in some child guidance clinics suggested that the boy's social adjustment in relation to other youngsters his own age might be an important area to investigate.

It was thus decided to see what could be accomplished with the general variable of peer group social relationships and related items of information. Abstracts were prepared, including all appropriate material in this category contained in the history, with explicit information about informant and date for each item of information. One class of information, excluded as unhelpful if not actually misleading, covered all statements by the mother indicating good peer group adjustment outside the home situation. Two factors contributed to making this information unsatisfactory. The mother may have had no accurate basis for comparing her child with other children on this score, and sometimes a mother, tiring of contacts with the clinic, reported that everything was fine when information obtained from other sources at the time indicated that this was not so. These observations are in line with the finding of Harris (1959) that for a group of children without serious problems, school personnel and the psychiatrist agreed more closely in the evaluation of children than did the mother with either.

For the peer group adjustment dimension, experience led to the construction of a priority list for the weighting of informants (other dimensions would not necessarily have the same list of priorities). This was related to the opportunities persons in different categories had for actual observation of the youngster in interactions with his associates. Instructions to the readers for the use of this priority list were to examine first the data from informants with the highest priority and to keep working down the list as long as, and only as long as, it was necessary to reach a decision. The priority list is as follows:

1. Persons, primarily teachers, who had an extended opportunity to observe him in a peer group situation when quoted directly.
2. Visiting teachers or case workers when summarizing information from persons in Category 1 without specific quotations; clear and definite formal diag-

nostic statements by psychiatrists which relate to social adjustment.
3. Family members, except for favorable statements by mother.
4. Statements about social adjustment by patient in interview, and statements by psychiatrist except as noted above; comments about personality by psychologists based on impressions obtained during the mental test situation.

Along with the observations of the chronology of statements and the priority list for informants, a guide for evaluating information as positive, neutral, or negative in appraising peer group adjustment was developed. This has been presented in detail elsewhere (Roff, 1957). Among the positive items were such things as all signs of liking by the general peer group, freedom from problems in class or on the playground, successful play with older children (nonsiblings), and indications that girls liked the subject, especially at adolescence. Neutral items are exemplified by a shortage of friends without specific indications of being disliked, playing with younger children, etc. Items to be evaluated as negative included all signs of active dislike by the general peer group, inability to keep friends, and being regarded as "odd," "peculiar," or "queer" by other children.

Working with the abstracts according to the informant priority list and the list of information to be evaluated as positive, neutral, or negative, two graduate students in psychology at approximately the MA level made "blind" evaluations as to good or poor peer group adjustment during the period covered by the case history. Each student evaluated about half the abstracts. Judgments of "good" or "poor" were made only if the reader felt reasonably certain of a judgment. If the information seemed incomplete, a response of "undecided" was made. This required some judgment on the part of the reader, but the area in which judgment was required was narrowed markedly in comparison with global predictions based on the entire case history. This procedure is intermediate between completely global predictions based on the entire case and more atomistic predictions based on a further fragmentation of the case history material.

RESULTS AND DISCUSSION

This procedure for making peer group evaluations was originally developed with subjects diagnosed as psychoneurotic during service. Applied unchanged to a new sample of subjects who showed severe bad conduct while in service and control subjects different from those with which the procedure was developed, it yielded the results shown in Table 1. Those subjects whose earlier peer group adjustment was evaluated as poor showed significantly more bad conduct in service than did subjects whose earlier peer group adjustment was appraised as good.

For purposes of comparison, results obtained earlier with the psychoneurotic subjects are shown in Table 2 (Roff, 1957, 1960). It can be seen that a similar discrimination was obtained for the psychoneurotic group.

The problem of the early detection of individuals who are likely to exhibit later maladjustment of various kinds is generally recognized as an important one. It is commonly assumed in dealing with both physical and psy-

chological difficulties that early treatment would have possibilities of benefit that might be lost if the difficulty were not detected until it had reached a later stage. It is difficult to find detailed results which support this assumption for the problems under consideration in this paper. It remains, however, an important working hypothesis.

The combined results reported here indicate that the level of earlier social adjustment contributes significantly to the discrimination between groups showing adjustment difficulties while in service and "good" groups. This is in line with an impressive amount of evidence that in a situation where there is sufficient mutual exposure to permit thorough acquaintance, appraisal by peers is very effective in predicting subsequent military adjustive reactions of various kinds (Rigby, Sayers, Ossorio, and Wilkins, 1957; Trites and Sells, 1957; Wherry and Fryer, 1949; Wilkins, 1954; Williams and Leavitt, 1947). The school situation is also an appropriate place for effective peer group evaluations, and it has been found that teachers can report accurately on the peer group reactions of children, at least in cases of marked behavior disturbances.

This can be made more concrete by giving illustrations of teachers' comments for the bad conduct subjects. The most frequent descriptions relating to the peer group situation indicate in one set of words or another that the boy is "mean" and is disliked by his associates. Sometimes this is accompanied by attempts to dominate other children. In other cases it is described simply as behavior which is antagonizing to others: "He always wants to be the leader, and if the other children do not do as he says, he is apt to be abusive and ugly to them"; "His conduct is irreproachable in the schoolroom, but he can be very mean when out of sight of authority. The boys in his room do not like him. During the past year, hardly a week went by without someone complaining about him"; "The teacher had known of his hurting children on various occasions. The children disliked him and grew into the habit of blaming him for everything that went wrong"; "He had violent temper tantrums when crossed. He did not get along with any of his classmates and was always in fights with some of them"; and "He feels picked on, wants to dominate, and is often the aggressor in fist fights, and the other boys

are afraid of him." This pattern of overt aggression toward other children was more pronounced than it was in the case of the psychoneurotic group.

In a definitely smaller number of cases, the boy was described as a good-natured nonconformist: "Very much of a problem, just smiled and wanted to do what he pleased"; "There was nothing mean about him, and he was good-natured and generous. He is well-liked by the other children, but all alike consider him as undependable, untruthful, and irresponsible."

Groups who know one another as well as do members of the same grade school class are fairly well aware of disturbed behavior in one of their members, although they may have no clear-cut diagnostic term for it. The peer group reactions employed in the present paper, collected and recorded by clinic personnel, represent a promising if neglected type of data. Further systematizing of such information should lead to an improvement in its predictive value. It seems very likely that a systematic study of antagonizing youngsters, extending over most of the grade school period, would identify, in at least the worst 1 or 2% of the cases, a group which would be of major interest from a long-time mental health point of view. Obtaining appraisals for at least 2 or 3 years would allow both for such real shifts of behavior as do occur and for unreliability in the observations of individual teachers. It seems possible to use this approach to develop a method that may prove more practically effective than any now available for the early location of individuals with mental health problems.

TABLE 1.—Evaluations of Preservice Status in Relation to Outcome in Service: Bad Conduct Group and Controls

OUTCOME	APPRAISAL		
	GOOD	UNDECIDED	POOR
Good	47	14	21
Bad conduct	20	16	46

$X^2 = 10.17; p < .01.$

TABLE 2.—Evaluations of Preservice Status in Relation to Outcome in Service: Psychoneurotics and Controls

OUTCOME	APPRAISAL		
	GOOD	UNDECIDED	POOR
Good	54	32	18
Psychoneurotic	13	29	62

$X^2 = 24.71; p < .001.$

In attempting a solution of the early detection problem, it is not essential that a precise prediction of the specific adult difficulty be made. The finding of the present paper that two major adult adjustment areas, psychoneurosis and bad conduct, can be predicted with the same procedure gives a point of attack for further work on the early identification of individuals who may be expected to show significant maladjustment as adults. While the earlier peer group relations of the psychoneurotic and bad conduct groups are not identical, and preliminary work indicates that they can be differentiated to some extent on the basis of early peer group relations, the discrimination between these two groups is of less practical importance than the finding that there is enough generality in the method to permit the early prediction of later disturbances in both behavioral areas. It is also possible that this same procedure will be effective in locating youngsters who later become psychotic or who as adults exhibit types of personality disturbances other than those discussed here.

SUMMARY

A follow-up study was made of male child guidance clinic cases from two Minnesota clinics in terms of their military service records. A predictive procedure based primarily on peer group adjustment as described in the case histories had been found earlier to discriminate between persons diagnosed as psychoneurotic while in service and controls who were former clinic cases who had made relatively good adjustments in service. This procedure was applied to the prediction of severe bad conduct during service by comparing the peer group abstracts from the clinic case histories of 82 persons who exhibited severe bad conduct while in service with those of controls matched in case history IQ. The procedure based on earlier peer group reactions discriminated between the bad conduct and control groups about as well as it had done with the psychoneurotics. Both these adult problem groups tended as youngsters to have antagonized their associates to an unusual degree. Some implications were discussed.

PART THREE

Personal-Social Development and Behavior: I

Mental Abilities

8

28 *Intelligence: 1965 Model*

J. P. GUILFORD

". . . The structure-of-intellect (SI) model, with its ·five operation categories intersecting with its four content categories, and these, in turn, intersecting with its six product categories . . ." (see Figure 1), was designed in 1958 (Guilford, 1959a). The 1965 model is "an operational model for problem solving in general. . . . Although emphasizing SI concepts, the model also takes into account many of the new findings and new thinking from other sources. The model is presented in Figure 2." An attempt, in progress, to integrate "intelligence into general psychological theory, thus giving intelligence a thorough psychological-theoretical foundation . . . ," is described.

Examination of other American Psychological Association Award Addresses in recent years shows that they are often in the nature of reports of progress. This address will be in that category. When the Program Committee spokesman asked insistently early last spring for a title for my paper, I did not have much idea of what I should say, so I gave a title from which one could take off in a number of directions. I cannot deny that the title is in part a reaction to an address that many of you heard at the APA convention a year ago, in which defenses were offered for a 1937 model of intelligence, which was not very different from a 1916 model (McNemar, 1964).

Being the kind of person who prefers to accentuate the positive, I shall devote the following remarks entirely to new developments with respect to the subject of intelligence. I shall try

Reprinted from *American Psychologist*, 1966, **21**, 20–26, by permission of the author and the American Psychological Association.

quickly to bring you up to date with respect to progress in connection with explorations of intellectual abilities, and also some implications arising from this information. Not to belie the second part of my title, I do have a 1965 model to mention.

STATUS OF THE STRUCTURE OF INTELLECT

Structure-of-Intellect Model

The structure-of-intellect (SI) model, with its five operation categories intersecting with its four content categories, and these, in turn, intersecting with its six product categories, is the same in 1965 as it was when first designed in 1958 (Guilford, 1959a). To refresh your memories, a diagram of the model is given in Figure 1. In this respect there is no change or progress to report. The progress is mainly in terms of demonstration of many new intellectual abilities to occupy cells of the model, with only a very few movings of abilities within the model to give better logical fits to theory.

When efforts were first made in 1955 to organize the known intellectual abilities that had been segregated by factor analysis, 37 distinct abilities were recognized (Guilford, 1956). In 1958, there were 43 such abilities that could be placed within the model. From then on, the model has served as the heuristic source of hypotheses as to what new kinds of abilities for

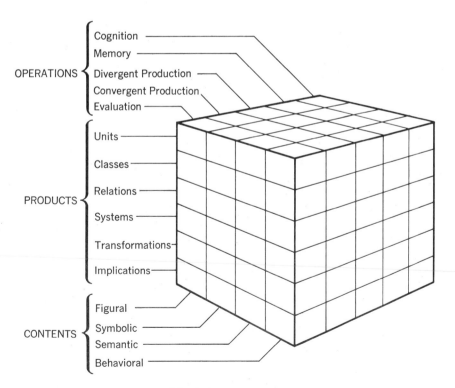

Fig. 1.   Model of the structure of intellect.

which to look. As of today, 80 abilities are believed to have been demonstrated and are placed within the model. Of the 120 cells of the model, five operations times four contents times six products, 75 cells are actually occupied. The discrepancy between 75 and 80 is that 3 cells have been found to contain 2 abilities each and 1 contains 3. The duplications within cells arise from distinctions among parallel visual, auditory, and kinesthetic cognitive and memory abilities. More of such duplications are to be expected when appropriate investigations are made.

To break down these figures more meaningfully, the numbers of demonstrated abilities in the various operation categories are of interest. The differences among operation categories with respect to numbers of known factors reflect the extents to which they have been investigated. Of the 24 theoretical cognitive cells (where cognition is confined by definition simply to comprehension or induction), all 24 are now occupied, with 2 cells having 2 abilities each and 1 having 3 abilities. In the latter instance, the 3 abilities are concerned with cognition of figural systems— visual-spatial orientation, kinesthetic-spatial orientation, and auditory systems (cognition of rhythms and melodies). One cell containing two abilities pertains to cognition of units, visual on the one hand and auditory (such as radio-code signals) on the other. The other cell containing two abilities pertains to symbolic units; the cognition of printed words on the one hand and the hearing of spoken words on the other.

Of 24 projected memory abilities, 12 have been demonstrated, one cell containing 2 abilities. The latter case includes memory for visual systems and memory for auditory systems. The main difference between cognition and memory abilities can be expressed very simply. Cognitive abilities pertain to how much you do know or can know at the time of testing, whereas memory abilities pertain to how much you can remember, given a standard exposure to information. Six memory abilities are currently under investigation in the Aptitudes Research Project (ARP) at the University of Southern California, with the chance of demonstrating some new ones. By the time this paper appears in print, there may be 15 demonstrated memory factors.[1]

In the area of divergent production, which is believed to contain some of the most directly relevant intellectual abilities for creative thinking and creative production, 16 of the 24 potential abilities have been investigated and demonstrated, in both adult and ninth-grade populations; also 6 of them at the sixth-grade level. Lauritzen (1963) has demonstrated a like number at the fifth-grade level. At the present time, 6 additional hypothesized divergent-production abilities are under investigation in the behavioral-content area, by the ARP.

One of the least explored operation

---

[1] I cannot pass by the opportunity to express a deep appreciation for liberal support to the Project from the Personnel and Training Branch, Office of Naval Research; the Cooperative Research Program, United States Office of Education; and the National Science Foundation. I should also like to pay tribute to the many graduate students who have collaborated in this effort.

areas is that of convergent production. Ten of the 24 possible convergent-production abilities have been demonstrated, with 2 more of them being currently under study in an analysis of classification abilities cutting across three operation categories.

Two recently completed analyses aimed at evaluative abilities have brought the number of known factors in the evaluation category to 13, and they have added a great deal to the understanding of this particular class of abilities (Hoepfner, Guilford, and Merrifield, 1964; Nihira, Guilford, Hoepfner and Merrifield, 1964).

BEHAVIORAL-COGNITION ABILITIES Of special note in recent developments is the demonstration of six cognitive abilities for dealing with behavioral information. This is the area marked off years ago by E. L. Thorndike (1920) as "social intelligence." Spearman (1927) was speaking about the same aptitude area under the heading of "psychological relations."

In the 1958 version of the SI model, an entire section involving 30 abilities was hypothesized for this area, with the belief that among the things that we can know, remember, and evaluate, and about which we can do productive thinking, is information about the behavior of other individuals and about ourselves. The major step was in bringing such areas of experience within the general concept of information. The abilities to be expected in this area were thought to be systematically parallel to abilities already found in other information areas—figural, symbolic, and semantic. There were no known abilities found by factor analysis to support such a hypothesis.

According to SI theory, there should

be six abilities in the cognition column for dealing with behavioral information. In the ARP, we proceeded to build tests for each of the six hypothesized abilities, for cognition of: behavioral units, classes, relations, systems, transformations, and implications. With a decision to stay within the context of printed tests as much as possible, the cue information used was in the form of photographs and line drawings of expressions involving the face, hands, arms, head, legs, and combinations of these body parts, also cartoons and cartoon strips, and photographed scenes involving people in pairs and triplets. In three tests, vocalized sound stimuli were also used. We stayed away from tests involving verbalizations on the part of the examinee, but used verbal statements pregnant with social or behavioral meanings as item material in some tests.

With an average of four such tests for each expected factor, the factor analysis demonstrated the six predicted factors, clearly segregated from figural and semantic abilities, with most of the new tests leading on factors where expected (O'Sullivan, Guilford, and deMille, 1965). So far as basic research is concerned, it appears that the large area of social intelligence has been successfully entered. Further work is naturally needed to determine the general significance of these abilities, as measured. We are now in the process of constructing tests for a parallel analysis of abilities predicted in the operational category of divergent production where behavioral information is concerned. Such abilities should be of considerable importance where any person has special need for creative approaches in dealing with others.

SOME RELATED PROBLEMS

Age and Differentiation of Abilities

Because of the Garrett hypothesis there is considerable interest in knowing whether as much differentiation of abilities occurs for children as for adults. Most of our own recent information has come from the testing of senior high school students, for whom the expected differentiations have always thus far appeared, when test batteries have been adequate to check on the hypothesized factors. I have mentioned the fact that ninth-grade students show the usual differentiations among the divergent-production abilities. The same kinds of differentiations are found at the same level for other categories of abilities as well. There is a little less assurance of clear separations at the sixth-grade level, but our experiences have been very limited at that level.

From other sources, it can be noted that some of the factors have been found differentiated at the age of 6 (McCartin, 1963), also at the mental ages 4 and 2, in retarded as well as in normal children (Meyers, Dingman, Orpet, Sitkei, and Watts, 1964). From still other sources (Stott and Ball, 1963), there are suggestions of a number of the SI abilities being detected for preschool and infant populations down to the age of 1. At this time it would appear that when children have reached the level of maturity at which appropriate tests for a factor can be administered and individual differences in scores can be obtained, the factors should be found differentiated. There is thus little to support the Garrett view that factors of intelligence come into being by differentiation from a single, comprehensive ability like Spearman's g.

This is not so strange, when we consider that the four kinds of information—figural, symbolic, semantic, and behavioral — come into the child's sphere of experience at different times, and development in coping with them progresses at different rates. Figural and behavioral information are encountered almost from birth whereas semantic information begins to come later, and symbolic information much later. The early differentiations of abilities must mean that the brain develops naturally different ways of processing the various products of information, as it develops different mechanisms for the five kinds of operations.

Predictive Validity in Mathematics

The ARP has always had a firm commitment to do basic research on the differentiable aptitudes, realizing that the number of investigators who undertake to solve such problems is exceedingly small. We have done one major study devoted to predictive validity, however, in which the criterion was achievement in ninth-grade mathematics (Guilford, Hoepfner, and Petersen, 1965). The study was somewhat premature, since it was realized that some of the potentially relevant SI abilities had not yet been demonstrated, nor were there tests for such hypothesized abilities. But, on the basis of what factors were known, the objective was to determine how well achievement could be predicted from factor tests, singly and in combination, as compared with three traditional academic-aptitude tests and also in combination with them.

Predictions of scores from specially prepared achievement tests in general mathematics and algebra were as good from combinations of factor-test scores as those from standard aptitude tests, or better, with multiple correlations ranging from .5 to .8. The factor tests also added significantly to prediction obtainable from standard aptitude tests in the case of algebra. Discrimination between successful algebra students (above the median in achievement) and successful general-mathematics students could be made with errors of only 10%, using a weight combination of factor tests.

PSYCHOLOGICAL THEORY

The finding of differentiated abilities in the area of intelligence is largely a taxonomic exercise. The outcome is in the form of basic concepts as to kinds of ability, answering the question "What?" Further steps need to be taken in order to answer the questions "How?" and "Why?" The SI theory is a step in these directions, and inferences from that theory lead further toward the goal of general psychological theory.

Role of Information

Of the 15 categories of the structure of intellect, 10 pertain to information, indicating the relative impor-

tance of kinds of information in the economy of intellectual functioning. This has suggested the view that we should regard the organism as a processor of information. A general informational approach to psychological theory is not unique, by any means. The increasing tendency to talk about input and output in place of stimulus and response is very noticeable. It is desirable, then, that we have some systematic categories of information, if we are to have an informational psychology.

Information, of the type with which we deal in psychology, I have defined as that which the organism discriminates. Discrimination is along the lines of the content and product categories, but of course discriminations also occur within each of these categories. The emphasis upon discrimination is in line with the concept of information in the field of communication engineering, but from that point on there is considerable divergence, for by "information" the engineer means *uncertainty,* whereas the psychologist's information must be in terms of probabilities approaching *certainty.* There is not time to go into these issues here.

Principle of Association

Another noteworthy innovation derived from SI theory is the proposal (Guilford, 1961) that we now interpret the ancient and respected concept of association in terms of the six products of information, giving us much more discriminative meaning and extending the possibilities for explanatory effectiveness. This suggestion will be very unpopular, for associationism has been a cornerstone for most psychological theory. The proposal is for a refinement and extension of a concept, not for complete replacement. But it does imply that what is learned and remembered is in the form of acquired products of information rather than stimulus-response connections. And it calls for the reinterpretation of habits or skills also in terms of products of information, largely systems, many of which become units.

Psychoepistemology and Psycho-logic

By his clinical-genetic approach, Piaget has demonstrated efforts working toward the goal of an epistemology empirically derived. I propose that the 24 cells derived from intersecting content and product categories in the SI model can furnish one such an epistemology. The mention of 24 categories, of course, ignores the distinct possibility that there will be more when we see how far auditory, kinesthetic, and perhaps tactual areas of information extend the number. Piaget's efforts have been directed more toward particular concepts, although generalizing somewhat in dealing with classes and relations as generic categories of information. He has by no means covered the whole range of 24 categories.

Piaget also places a great deal of emphasis upon the relation of psychology to modern logic (Inhelder and Piaget, 1964). On the one hand, he emphasizes the principle that the individual's development is in the direction of formal logic in his thinking. On the other hand, he intimates that the application of formal logic should be the goal of the theoretical psychologist and he suggests that as a step in the direction of that goal we need a psycho-logic (Piaget, 1953a). The six product categories are proposed as the basis for such a psycho-logic. Although not chosen with formal logic in mind, the names of the product categories are in fairly good correspondence with concepts of formal logic. Whether formal logic is now adequate for supplying the models for theory in connection with the six products remains to be seen.

A MODEL FOR PROBLEM SOLVING

My title promises a 1965 model, so here it is: an operational model for problem solving in general. Since most behavior readily involves a bit of problem-solving activity, the model could also have applications over wide areas of behavior. Although emphasizing SI concepts, the model also takes into account many of the new findings and new thinking from other sources. The model is represented in Figure 2.

The typical, traditional model for problem solving, since John Dewey (1910), has been a linear time series running through steps such as: seeing the problem, analyzing or structuring the problem, generating solutions, and judging and selecting one of the solutions. Things look more complicated now with respect to problem solving as well as with respect to intelligence. Cybernetics and the computer-simulator people have seen to that.

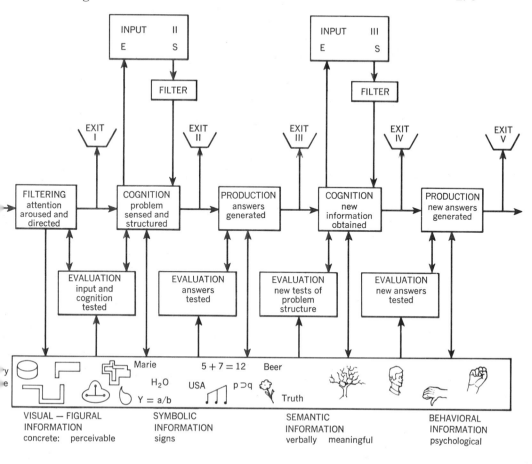

Fig. 2.   Model for problem solving.

The occasion for a problem-solving episode begins with a certain input, mostly through the sense avenues, of course, represented at Input I in the model. The E and S stand for environmental and somatic sources of input, respectively. The somatic source may include both motivational and emotional components, from within the brain as well as from internal receptors. A filtering step determines which input goes further and has any appreciable consequences in behavior. Note that the memory storage underlies and potentially affects all steps, beginning with the filtering operation. "Filtering" is a new and more operational name for "attention." Evaluation is another operation that has to be taken into account at all steps along the way, for the organism is perpetually self-checking and self-correcting. Evaluation is not left to the final stage of problem solving, as commonly supposed in traditional models.

Awareness that a problem exists and identification or structuring of the problem are cognitive operations.

During these operations there is dependence upon memory storage and there is evaluation of cognized information. In the effort to cognize the problem, there may be a seeking for new input information, as at Input II in the model. Filtering of this input also occurs, as well as evaluation.

With the problem reasonably well structured, there is a search for answers, or for information from which answers can be constructed, in memory storage, with the ubiquitous interplay with evaluation. If a solution is accepted, there is an exit from this problem-solving episode at Exit III. Exit I would be a dodging of the problem. Exit II would be a giving up or perhaps a result of distraction before the productive operation got started.

If no good solutions are found to the problem, and if there are doubts about its proper interpretation, a new major cycle begins as shown at the second cognition block. For reinterpretation of the problem, new input may be sought, with steps similar to those already outlined. A number of these major cycles may go on, in what has often been described as trial-and-error behavior. Within each major cycle there are subsidiary loops in the flow of events, each of which might be followed by a number of similar loops. The looping phenomena follow cybernetic principles, with feedback information involved, and evaluation.

The relation of this model to the SI model is fairly obvious. The operation categories have been given prominent roles except that no distinction is shown between divergent and convergent production, both of these kinds of operation being subsumed under the plain heading of "production." Which kind of productive activity occurs will depend upon the kind of search model that is set up consequent to cognition of the problem structure. If the structuring is complete and if enough information is available and is used, the production should be convergent; if there is not enough information for determination of the answer or if the problem is incompletely structured, the production is likely to be divergent.

The information categories are represented by the objects illustrated in memory storage. The four kinds of content are segregated for illustrative purposes. Various examples of products can be found if one looks for them—figural units and systems; symbolic units, relations, and an implication; and units of semantic and behavioral information. Transformations, being changes, are not easily represented in pictorial form, but a modification of either equation would be an example, or an inversion or rotation of any of the figures would be others.

It should be said that the model in Figure 2 is a very general or generic one, and not designed to fit necessarily any particular episode of problem solving. But the basic kinds of operation are there. Modifications would be needed to suit the particular case.

FUTURE DEVELOPMENTS

As indicated earlier, under way and near conclusion is an analysis of symbolic memory abilities. In the test-development stages are an analytical study involving nine abilities dealing with classes in which relations of classification abilities to attainment of concepts will be investigated, and a study of divergent-production abilities in the area of behavioral information. In the stage of planning are analyses of figural-memory and figural-evaluation abilities, also transformation abilities across operation categories. The manuscript for a book on the nature of human intelligence, its development and its decline, is in progress (Guilford, 1067). This effort will include the integration of intelligence into general psychological theory, thus giving intelligence a thorough psychological-theoretical foundation, which it has never had. Another book is planned, which will summarize the findings from the ARP, in preparation for which some reworking of old data will be carried out. As to other future developments, these are very much in the laps of the gods.

29 *The Influence of Experience on the Development of Intelligence*[1]

DAVID P. AUSUBEL

Comments   James J. Gallagher

Nancy Bayley

What effects do environmental deprivation have on intellectual development? To what extent are these effects preventable, reversible, irreversible? Is it possible to accelerate intellectual development and achievement? Are intelligence tests unfair to socially disadvantaged children? These are a few of the questions raised in this report in an effort to understand how the socially disadvantaged can be helped toward full self-realization commensurate with their genetic potentialities.

In considering the impact of experience on the development of intelligence, two issues, in my opinion, are of paramount theoretical and practical significance. First, what effects do environmental deprivation have on intellectual development, and to what extent are these effects reversible? If some retardation is irreversible,

[1] Paper read at a Conference on Productive Thinking in Education sponsored by the NEA Project on the Academically Talented Student, Washington, D.C., May 2–4, 1963.

Reprinted from M. J. Aschner and C. E. Bish (Eds.), *Productive Thinking in Education* (Washington, D.C.: National Education Association, 1965), pp. 45–68. By permission of the authors and the National Education Association.

through what kinds of mechanisms is such irreversibility mediated? Second, is it possible through a program of cognitive enrichment to accelerate both the rate of intellectual development as well as the rate of intellectual achievement?

THE EFFECTS OF ENVIRONMENTAL DEPRIVATION ON THE IQ

What theoretical grounds and relevant evidence do we have for believing that prolonged environmental deprivation induces retardation in intellectual development? It is reasonable to assume, in the first place, that whatever the individual's genic potentialities are, cognitive development occurs largely in response to a variable range of stimulation requiring incorporation, accommodation, adjustment, and reconciliation. The more variable the environment to which individuals are exposed, the higher is the resulting level of effective stimulation. Characteristic of the culturally deprived environment, however, is a restricted range and a less adequate and systematic ordering of stimulation sequences (Deutsch, 1962). The effects of this restricted environment include poor perceptual discrimination skills; inability to use adults as sources of information, correction, and reality testing, and as instruments for satisfying curiosity; an impoverished language-symbolic system; and a paucity of information, concepts, and relational propositions (Deutsch, 1962).

Both the animal and human evidence indicates that early environmental deprivation stunts the develop-

ment of intelligence. Cage-reared rats (Gibson and Walk, 1956; Hebb, 1949) and dogs (Thompson and Heron, 1954) who are deprived of visual and exploratory experience are significantly inferior to pet-reared control animals in later problem-solving ability; and the longer children remain in substandard environmental conditions, *i.e.*, in foundling homes (Freud and Burlingham, 1944; Spitz, 1945, 1949), in orphanages (Dennis and Najarian, 1957; Skeels and Fillmore, 1937; Skeels, et al., 1938), or with mentally retarded mothers (Speer, 1940), the progressively lower their IQ's become in comparison with the IQ's of control children placed in more favorable environments. These findings are consistent with the reports of progressive decline in the intelligence test scores of isolated mountain and canal boat children who also grow up in unstimulating and nondemanding intellectual environments (Asher, 1935; Gordon, 1923; Sherman and Key, 1932; Wheeler, 1942); with the lower IQ's of rural than of urban children (Asher, 1935; Ausubel, 1961; Chapanis and Williams, 1945; Wheeler, 1942); with the social class differential in IQ (Bayley and Jones, 1937; Terman and Merrill, 1937); with the upgrading effect of urban residence on Negro children's IQ's (Klineberg, 1935); and with the high correlation between the intra-pair discrepancies in the IQ's of separated monozygotic twins and the discrepancies in their educational advantages (Newman, Freeman, and Holzinger, 1937). Evidence of depressed IQ, of special retardation in language skills and conceptualization, and of inability to concentrate is found as late as adolescence among children who spend the first three years of life in foundling homes (Goldfarb, 1945).

Language Retardation

It is in the area of language development, and particularly with respect to the abstract dimension of verbal functioning that the culturally deprived child manifests the greatest degree of intellectual retardation. Many factors contribute to this unfortunate developmental outcome. The culturally deprived home, to begin with, lacks the large variety of objects, utensils, toys, pictures, etc., that require labeling and serve as referents for language acquisition in the middle-class home. The culturally deprived child is also not spoken to or read to very much by adults.[2] Hence his auditory discrimination tends to be poor and he receives little corrective feedback regarding his enunciation, pronunciation, and grammar (Deutsch, 1962). Furthermore, the syntactical model provided him by his parents is typically faulty. Later on, when new concepts and transactional terms are largely acquired verbally, *i.e.*, by definition and context from speech and reading, rather than by abstraction from direct concrete experience, he suffers from the paucity of abstractions in the everyday vocabulary of his elders, from the rarity of

---

[2]In this connection it is interesting to note that Anastasi and de Jesus (1953) attribute the relative language superiority of Puerto-Rican nursery school children over comparable white and Negro children in New York City slum areas—in the face of more severe socioeconomic handicaps—to the fact that they enjoy more contact with adults in the home.

stimulating conversation in the home, from the relative absence of books, magazines, and newspapers, and from the lack of example of a reading adult in the family setting.

It is small wonder, therefore, that the abstract vocabulary of the culturally deprived child is deficient in range and precision, that his grammar and language usage are shoddy, that his attentivity and memory are poorly developed, and that he is impoverished in such language-related knowledge as the number concepts, self-identity information, and understanding of the physical, geometric, and geographical environments (Deutsch, 1962). Social class differences in language and conceptual measures also tend to increase with increasing age (Deutsch, 1962), thus demonstrating the cumulative effects of both continued environmental deprivation and of initial deficit in language development.

The culturally deprived child's entire orientation to language is also different from that of the middle-class child. He responds more to the concrete, tangible, immediate, and particularized properties of objects and situations rather than to their abstract, categorical and relational properties (Bernstein, 1958, 1960; Siller, 1957). His speech is instigated more by the objects and actions he sees than by abstract ideas emanating from within, and he makes more ancillary use of nonverbal forms of communication (Riessman, 1962). In short, the language of the culturally deprived child is more concrete, expressive, and informal than that of the middle-class child, showing signs of impoverishment mainly in its formal, abstract, and syntactical aspects (Deutsch, 1962).

However, the most important consequence of the culturally deprived child's language retardation is his slower and less complete transition from concrete to abstract modes of thought and understanding. This transition normally begins to occur in our culture during the junior high-school period. As a result, preadolescent and adolescent children are able to understand and manipulate relationships between abstractions directly, *i.e.*, without the benefit of reference to current or immediately prior concrete-empirical experience (Inhelder and Piaget, 1958). Thus they are no longer limited to semi-abstract, intuitive, and particularized thought, and can formulate more precise, abstract, and general propositions that embody all possible and hypothetical relationships between categorical variables. The transition takes place more slowly and less completely in culturally deprived children for two reasons. First, the culturally deprived child lacks the necessary repertoire of clear and stable abstractions and transactional terms that is obviously prerequisite for the direct manipulation and understanding of relationships between abstractions. Second, for lack of adequate practice, he has not acquired sufficient facility in relating abstractions to each other *with* the benefit of concrete-empirical props, so that he can later dispense with their assistance at the same age as his environmentally more favored contemporaries. Because concrete thought operations are necessarily more time-consuming than their abstract-verbal counterparts, and also because of his

distractibility, unfamiliarity with formal language, impaired self-confidence, and unresponsiveness to time pressure, the culturally deprived child typically works more slowly than the middle-class child in an academic setting (Riessman, 1962).

PREVENTING AND REVERSING INITIAL INTELLECTUAL RETARDATION

The modifiability of children's relative intellectual ability as measured by intelligence tests is no longer seriously in dispute. Once we grant that the IQ represents a multiply determined functional capacity in the development of which experiential and motivational factors play an important regulatory role, it is superfluous to inquire whether it can be modified by significant changes in such factors. The more relevant questions at this point are the extent of the modification that is possible and the conditions under which it occurs, that is, how late in the course of cultural deprivation appropriate experience can reverse intellectual retardation, and what the most suitable kind of experience is for this purpose.

The available evidence indicates that removal from a nonstimulating orphanage to a superior institutional environment (Skeels and Dye, 1939) or to superior foster homes (Freeman, Halzinger, and Mitchell, 1928; Skodak, 1939; Skodak and Skeels, 1949), and the provision of an enriched nursery school environment to orphanage children (Reymert and Hinton, 1940) tend to raise the IQ level. Intensive preschool training even improves the IQ's and educability of children who are mentally retarded on an endogenous basis (Kirk, 1958). It is important to bear in mind, however, that in all of these instances enhancement of intellectual capacity was effected in relatively young children of preschool age. We still lack firm evidence concerning the influence of an optimal learning environment on the intellectual development of culturally deprived elementary-school and adolescent children, especially those who have been subjected for many years to the frustration and demoralization of inappropriate school experience.[3] This is an extremely urgent research problem that should engage our immediate attention. We need to investigate the effects of an optimal learning environment on both IQ scores and on the acquisition of school knowledge, making special efforts to eliminate errors of measurement associated with test content bias, test-taking skills, test rapport, and test motivation. On *a priori* grounds one might anticipate that school knowledge would be more ameliorable than intelligence level to the influence of environmental stimulation.

This discouraging picture of language retardation in the culturally deprived child can be counteracted in at least three different ways. In the

---

[3]Some tangential evidence concerning the ameliorative effect of school experience on intellectual development comes from studies showing that the resumption of regular schooling in Holland after World War II raised the mean IQ of children (de Groot, 1948, 1951), and that long-term improvement in substandard school conditions raised the mean IQ among Hawaiian (Smith, 1942) and East Tennessee mountain children (Wheeler, 1942).

first place, it seems credible that most of the language retardation and its grim consequences for school learning could be prevented by an enriched program of preschool education that would emphasize perceptual discrimination and language acquisition. In addition to the usual preschool activities, much time would be spent in reading and talking to children, in furnishing an acceptable model of speech, in supplying corrective feedback with respect to grammar and pronunciation, in developing listening, memory, and attentivity skills, and in providing appropriate reading readiness, reading, and writing instruction. Concomitantly, of course, an attempt could be made to raise the cultural and intellectual level of the home through a long-range program of involvement in adult education.

Within the regular classroom setting two kinds of ameliorative approaches are possible, especially for those children who have not had the benefit of preschool training. The first approach takes account of the culturally deprived child's slower and less complete transition to abstract modes of thought and understanding during the junior high-school period, and provides more concrete-empirical props and opportunities for direct physical manipulation of objects and situations in the presentation of abstract ideas and relational propositions. Such props, for example, might include audio-visual aids, Cuisenaire rods, the abacus, laboratory material, schematic models and diagrams, and role-playing activities; and in the teaching of mathematics and science, much reliance would be placed on applicability to common problems in the immediate environment and on illustrations drawn from everyday experience. It should be appreciated, however, that these techniques are merely ways of facilitating the transition to a more abstract level of cognitive functioning. We do not want to induce permanent dependence on concrete-empirical props or to be satisfied with this state of affairs as our ultimate objective. In fact, the pursuit of a vigorous program of relational thinking and understanding in the elementary school could help greatly in reducing the later delay in the transition from concrete to abstract thought.

The second needed change within the classroom setting is the long overdue introduction of more imaginative and effective ways of teaching the language arts. More emphasis, for example, needs to be placed on the mastery of the principal syntactical forms in spoken and written discourse, through repetitive practice with feedback, than on the pedantic and essentially trivial labeling and classifying of different varieties of grammatical structure. The culturally deprived child with his pragmatic and nonabstract approach to knowledge couldn't care less, after all, about the different parts of speech and the various esoteric names attached to the different uses of each; and for the most part he is correct insofar as the value or functional utility of such knowledge is concerned.

MECHANISMS MEDIATING IRREVERSIBILITY

The Critical Periods Hypothesis

An increasingly more popular explanation that has been advanced in recent years to account for the apparent irreversibility of certain kinds of behavioral development and developmental retardation is the "critical periods" hypothesis. According to this hypothesis, irreversibility of behavioral development is a function of extreme susceptibility to particular types of stimulation during those brief periods in ontogeny when certain types of behavior are shaped and molded for life. By the same token, if the organism is deprived of the necessary stimulation during the critical period, when he is maximally susceptible to it in terms of actualizing potential capacities or developing in new directions, it is held that some degree of permanent retardation is inevitable.

Numerous examples of the existence of critical periods can be found in the perceptual, motor, and social development of infrahuman mammals. Infant chimpanzees isolated from normal tactual stimulation exhibit defective kinaesthetic learning and cutaneous localization (Nissen, Chow, and Semmes, 1951); and if reared in darkness fail to fixate or recognize familiar objects or to blink in response to a threatening object (Riesen, 1947). Newly born domestic lambs reared on a bottle and isolated from sheep for ten days, experience difficulty later in adjusting to the flock and tend to graze by themselves (Scott, Fredericson, and Fuller, 1951). Similarly, puppies isolated for nine weeks or more are unable to adapt socially to other dogs; and if not removed from the litter by three months of age, are extremely difficult to tame at a later date (Scott and Marston, 1950).

An implicit form of the "critical periods" hypothesis was applied to intellectual development many years ago by Montessori and her followers to justify the particular graded series of learning tasks which children are set in Montessori schools (Rambusch, 1962). More recently it has been invoked by advocates of the proposition that young children can learn many intellectual skills and kinds of subject matter more efficiently than adults can. The argument in both instances is that since there are allegedly optimal (*i.e.*, critical) periods of readiness for all kinds of cognitive acquisitions, children who fail to learn the age-appropriate skills at the appropriate times are forever handicapped in acquiring them later.

Serious difficulties, however, lie in the path of extrapolating the "critical periods" hypothesis to human cognitive development. In the first place, it has been validated only for infant individuals in infrahuman species, and in relation to those kinds of rapidly developing perceptual, motor, and social traits that are largely regulated by genic factors. In human individuals, especially beyond the prenatal period and first year of life, environmental determinants of development are more important, and the rate of maturation is significantly slower. Second, it has never been empirically demonstrated that optimal readiness exists at particular age periods for specified kinds of intellectual activities, and that if adequate conditions for growth are not present during those periods, no future time is ever as advantageous, thereby causing irreparable developmental deficit.

Hence if specific intellectual skills or subject-matter content are not acquired at the earliest appearance of

readiness, this does not mean that they cannot be acquired later just as well or even better. The disadvantage of unnecessarily postponing such learnings inheres rather in the irreparable loss of precious years of opportunity when reasonably economical learning could have occurred if attempted, but did not. When this happens, the individual, in comparison with equally endowed peers, incurs a learning deficit which limits his current and future rate of intellectual development.

The Cumulative Nature of Intellectual Deficit

This brings us to a second, somewhat more credible explanation of the possible irreversibility in cognitive development that results from prolonged cultural deprivation. I refer to the tendency for existing developmental deficits to become cumulative in nature, since current and future rates of intellectual growth are always conditioned or limited by the attained level of development. The child who has an existing deficit in growth incurred from past deprivation is less able to profit developmentally from new and more advanced levels of environmental stimulation. Thus, irrespective of the adequacy of all other factors—both internal and external—his deficit tends to increase cumulatively and to lead to permanent retardation.

New growth, in other words, always proceeds from the existing phenotype, that is, from already actualized capacity, rather than from potentialities inherent in the genotype. It makes no difference in terms of this limiting influence whether the attained deficiency is attributable to inferior genic endowment or to inadequate environment. If, as a result of a consistently deprived environment during the early formative years, superior intellectual endowment is not actualized, the attained deficit in functional capacity significantly limits the extent to which later environmental stimulation, even if normal in quantity and quality, can increase the rate of cognitive growth. Hence, an individual's prior success or failure in developing his intellectual capacities tends to keep his future rate of growth relatively constant.

Differentiation of Intelligence

In addition to the limiting condition of attained level of development or of existing degree of deficiency, we must consider the further limiting factor of the organism's degree of plasticity or freedom to respond developmentally in a given direction in response to appropriate environmental stimulation.

Generally speaking, the plasticity of intelligence tends to decrease with increasing age. At first, intelligence is a relatively undifferentiated capacity that can develop in several different directions. But as children grow older, particularly during preadolescence and adolescence, it becomes increasingly more differentiated as shown by the decreasing intercorrelations among the subtests of a given intelligence scale (Garrett, Bryan, and Perl, 1935). Another indication of the trend toward the progressive differentiation of abilities is the fact that ten-year-old boys of high socioeconomic status make higher scores than ten-year-old boys of low socioeconomic status on tests of both verbal *and* mechanical

ability, but at age 16 are only superior on the verbal tests (Havighurst and Janke, 1944; Janke and Havighurst, 1945). Furthermore, the verbal ability scores of boys who drop out of school at the age of 17 tend to decline whereas their scores on tests of mechanical aptitude continue to improve (Vernon, 1948). Thus by the time an individual reaches adolescence, differential factors of interest, relative ability, specialization of training,[4] motivation, success and failure experience, and cultural expectation operate selectively to develop certain potential abilities and to leave others relatively undeveloped.

Once intelligence undergoes definite relative commitment in the various aforementioned channels, the individual is less responsive to stimulation in areas of minimal development than he was in the original undifferentiated state. Thus, for example, if because of inadequate stimulation during early and middle childhood, genic potentialities for verbal intelligence fail to be adequately actualized, other facets of intelligence (e.g., mechanical, social) which are more satisfactorily stimulated become differentially more highly developed. At this point, therefore, the development of the individual's verbal intelligence is not only limited by his existing de-

---

[4]Additional evidence of the effect of experience on the differentiation of intelligence comes from studies showing that the intelligence test scores of boys who continue longer in school tend to exceed, even twenty years later, the test scores of matched controls with less schooling (Lorge, 1945), and that gains in IQ scores are much more common in college than in non-college populations (Thorndike, 1948).

ficiency in the verbal area, but also by the fact that his once undifferentiated intelligence has been definitely committed in other directions, and is hence less free to respond than previously to an enriched verbal environment. Hence it is evident that the possibility for complete reversibility of environmentally induced retardation in verbal intelligence decreases as children advance in age. This is not to say, of course, that later enrichment is entirely to no avail; but, in my opinion, some of this failure in developmental actualization is irreversible and cannot be compensated for later, irrespective of the amount of hyperstimulation that is applied.

The hypothesis of cumulative developmental deficit implicitly assumes the continued operation of a learning environment the stimulating value of which remains average or below average during the crucial formative years. Hence, despite the twin limiting effects of attained deficit in intellectual development and of increasing differentiation of intelligence on subsequent responsiveness to cognitive stimulation, it is completely consistent with our theoretical analysis to hypothesize that an *optimal* learning environment could arrest and reverse in part the existing degree of retardation. Such an environment must obviously be adequately stimulating, must be specially geared to the deprived individual's particular level of readiness in each subject-matter area and intellectual skill, as well as to his over-all level of cognitive sophistication, and presupposes much individualized attention and guided remedial effort. This, of course, is a far cry from the kind of learning environment that

culturally deprived children typically enjoy. In actual practice their existing intellectual deficit is usually compounded by the fact that not only are they less able than their peers to profit from appropriate new experience, but they are also usually overwhelmed by exposure to learning tasks that exceed by far their prevailing level of cognitive readiness. Hence, since they do not possess the necessary background of knowledge or sophistication required for efficient learning, they typically fail, lose self-confidence in their ability to learn, become thoroughly demoralized in the school situation, and disinvolve themselves from it.

ARE INTELLIGENCE TESTS UNFAIR TO CULTURALLY DEPRIVED CHILDREN?

Liberal educators often unwarrantedly castigate the intelligence test as being unfair to the culturally deprived child, both because it emphasizes verbal ability rather than the mechanical and social kinds of abilities in which lower-class children excel, and because the middle-class environment is more propitious than the lower-class environment for the development of verbal intelligence. Actually, however, the intelligence test is not really unfair to the culturally deprived child on either count. In the first place, it only purports to measure verbal ability and to predict school performance—not ability or performance in the mechanical and social areas. Second, any intelligence test can only hope to measure functional or operating capacity at a given point of development (*i.e.*, degree of actualized genic potentiality) rather than innate potentiality per se. Adequacy of environmental stimulation is always a significant determinant of functional capacity and hence affects performance on an intelligence test. If the environment is inadequately stimulating, then functional capacity is naturally impaired. But this does not mean that our measuring instrument, the intelligence test, is unfair, since its function is merely to identify and measure impaired operating capacity irrespective of the origin of the impairment. The intelligence test, in other words, purports to measure functional capacity rather than to account for it. If the culturally deprived child scores low on an intelligence test because of the inadequacy of his environment, it is not the test which is unfair but the social order which permits him to develop under such conditions.

By the same token we would not say that the tuberculin test is unfair or invalid (a) because the lower-class child really does not have any greater genic susceptibility to tuberculosis but happens to live in an environment that predisposes him to this disease, and (b) because it measures exposure to a particular disease which happens to be related to lower social class status rather than to one which is not so related. In terms of operating functional capacity, an intelligence test is no less fair or valid because a low score is reflective of cultural deprivation than because it is reflective of low genic endowment. Furthermore, to argue that test scores are valid is not to claim that they are necessarily immutable irrespective of future environmental conditions, or to defend those aspects

of the social system that give rise to the culturally deprived environment.

Traditional verbal intelligence tests *are* unfair to culturally deprived children in the sense that such children, in comparison with their middle-class agemates, have fewer test-taking skills, are less responsive to speed pressure, are less highly motivated in taking tests, have less rapport with the examiner, and are less familiar with the specific vocabulary and tasks that make up the content of the test. The tests are unfair in that they do not give the lower-class child a fair opportunity to demonstrate his true attained level of cognitive capacity. When these errors of measurement are eliminated, however, substantial social class differences in IQ still remain (Coleman and Ward, 1955; Haggard, 1954). These may reflect both hereditary and environmental influences.

ACCELERATION THROUGH ENRICHED EXPERIENCE

To what extent can one accelerate the rate of intellectual development in normal or superior nondeprived children by providing enriched or optimal educational experience? If stages of development have any true meaning, the answer to this question can only be that although suitable long-term training could conceivably accelerate to some extent the rate at which the various stages of intellectual development succeed each other, maturational considerations inevitably impose a limit on such acceleration. Also, unlike its effect on children reared under substandard home or school conditions, a program of either preschool

(Goodenough, 1940; Olson and Hughes, 1940; Wellman, 1945) or elementary-school (Goodenough, 1940) enrichment does *not* accelerate the growth of intelligence when provided to children who already enjoy reasonably stimulating home environments and school opportunities.

In general, transitions from one stage of development to another presuppose the attainment of a critical threshold level of capacity that is reflective of extended and cumulative experience which can only be reduced up to a point. Premature practice prior to the onset of readiness in such preschool activities as cube building and cutting with scissors, does not hasten the emergence of these skills (Gesell and Thompson, 1929; Hilgard, 1932, 1933). In other instances, training beyond children's current state of developmental readiness, as for example, practice in extending their memory span for digits (Gates and Taylor, 1925), results in unstable and transitory gains. It was also found that training children in the preoperational stage to appreciate the notion of conservation of mass tends to produce an unstable understanding of this principle which is hardly equivalent to that acquired by older children (Smedslund, 1961). Similarly, young children who receive laboratory training in learning the principle of a teeter-totter (*i.e.*, that the longer side from the fulcrum falls when both ends are equally weighted), are able to learn the principle but fail to acquire any resistance to learning a spurious causal relationship about the operation of a teeter-totter (*i.e.*, that the color of the blocks placed at either end

is the determining factor (Ausubel and Schiff, 1954)). Older children, on the other hand, who are both cognitively more mature and have more incidental experience with teeter-totters resist learning the spurious causal relationship (Ausubel and Schiff, 1954).

But although the possibility of accelerating movement through the stages of intellectual development is at best highly limited, the acquisition of many intellectual achievements that lie within the intrinsic readiness of children can be accelerated by providing suitably contrived experience geared to their cognitive capacity and mode of functioning. Age of readiness for a given intellectual task, after all, is not an absolute, but is always relative, in part, to the method of instruction employed. By taking advantage of the preschool child's extensive reliance on overt manipulative activity in understanding and using symbols, both Montessori and O. K. Moore were able to advance considerably the typical age of reading and writing. Similarly, it is possible successfully to teach the elementary school child many ideas in science and mathematics that were previously thought much too difficult by presenting them at a purely intuitive level. However, one must balance against these possible advantages of early intuitive learning the excessive time cost involved in many instances. In certain cases it may be more feasible in the long run to postpone entirely the introduction of particular subject-matter fields until children are cognitively mature. The decision in each case must be based upon the findings of particularized research. In one progressive school, for example, children who learned no formal arithmetic until the fifth grade equalled matched controls in computation by the seventh grade, and surpassed them in arithmetic reasoning (Sax and Otina, 1958).

In addition it undoubtedly overstates the case to claim that *any* subject can be taught to children in the preoperational stage or in the stage of concrete operations provided that the material is presented in an informal, intuitive fashion with the aid of overt manipulation or concrete-empirical props. It is readily conceivable that some topics, such as "set theory" in mathematics, can be successfully learned by fourth-grade pupils when recast in accordance with their characteristic ways of thinking and conceptualizing experience. This hardly rules out the possibility, however, that the comprehension of many *other* ideas presupposes a certain minimal level of life experience, cognitive maturity, and subject-matter sophistication, or that some ideas simply cannot be expressed without the use of certain higher order abstractions. These latter kinds of concepts would be *intrinsically* too difficult for preschool children irrespective of the method of presentation. Moreover, even assuming that all abstract-verbal concepts could be restructured on an intuitive basis, it would be unreasonable to expect that they could all be made comprehensible to children at *any* age level. Although the intuitive comprehensibility of any given restructured idea is best determined empirically, it would surely be plausible on *a priori* grounds to expect that a certain proportion of these ideas could not be rendered understandable to typical pupils in some of the preschool and elementary grades.

Finally, I think it is necessary to temper the enthusiasm of those educators who believe that children can not only learn everything that adults can but can also do so more efficiently. Adolescents and adults, generally speaking, have a tremendous advantage in learning any new subject-matter—even if they are just as unsophisticated as young children in that particular discipline. This advantage inheres in the fact that they are able to draw on various transferable elements of their *over-all* ability to function at an abstract-verbal level of logical operations. Hence they are able to move through the concrete-intuitive phase of intellectual functioning very rapidly; and unlike the comparably unsophisticated child, who is tied to this latter stage developmentally, they are soon able to dispense entirely with concrete-empirical props and with intuitive understandings. These facilitating transferable elements include the possession of transactional terms and higher-order concepts as well as successful past experience in *directly* manipulating relationships between abstractions (*i.e.*, without the benefit of concrete-empirical props); and research findings suggest that as long as abstract-verbal understandings are meaningfully rather than rotely acquired, they constitute a more complete, explicit, inclusive, and transferable form of knowledge.

In conclusion, therefore, although prior intuitive understanding of many ideas during childhood may greatly extend the elementary-school child's horizon of useful knowledge and facilitate the learning and stabilize the retention of these same ideas when they are taught later at a more formal and abstract level, there is little warrant for believing that children can learn *everything* in this manner, or that this type of learning is more efficient than the verbal-abstract learning that succeeds it. The intellectual achievement of children can only be accelerated within the limits imposed by the prevailing stage of intellectual development. These limitations cannot be transcended through experience. One can, at best, take advantage of methods that are most appropriate and effective for exploiting the existing degree of readiness.

COMMENTS

James J. Gallagher

We have come to realize that what the world appears to be is often determined by the way in which we try to organize our information. It can be no more accurate than the models of reality that we work from. If our models happen to be based on studies using factor analysis, reality appears in one form; if the model is psychoanalysis, then reality takes on a different hue and tone. Dr. Ausubel has pointed out some of the problems that have accrued to us from the use of a particular model of intellectual development built mainly upon popular measuring instruments (i.e., IQ tests).

One such problem is surely illustrated by the contention that IQ tests are unfair to culturally deprived children, a statement that Ausubel quite correctly points out as nonsense. Such an idea, however, could only stem from a conception of intellectual development as being inherently pre-

determined and strongly resistant to environmental modification. There is the further assumption that the IQ test measures such inherent ability.

Another more pervasive example of a distorted picture of reality is the notion of a smoothly continuous nature of mental development which, I believe, stems mainly from the Mental Age concept. We are familiar with Mental Age curves which have been plotted indicating a smoothly accelerated progress of intellectual development from one year to the next. One has to go to European schools of thought to find the concept of stages or levels of development, a somewhat conflicting model which appears to be closer to reality as we know it today.

The interpretations of various events are markedly different depending upon which of these models one accepts. For example, there have been numerous attempts to improve intellectual development through experimental intervention. If one accepts the continuous growth or Mental Age idea, then improvement that can be brought about through experimental means at any point in the developmental scale is as important at one point as at any other point. If one takes the stages or levels of development concept, however, then *when* the training takes place is very important to the final interpretation.

For instance, much of the research cited by Dr. Ausubel, on the effectiveness of environmental change on mental growth, has been done on preschool children or on mentally retarded children at a preschool mental development level. Thus, while it is possible to bring about change within what Piaget might call the preoperational stage (ages 4–8), it does not necessarily follow that this change would pay off in better development at later stages.

A specific example of this is seen in a study conducted under my direction some years ago. Basically, we were attempting to tutor organically injured, mentally retarded children in an attempt to improve their intellectual and educational skills. During the first year of the experiment, some of the youngsters responded quite favorably and gained 15 to 20 Binet IQ points. We looked forward with much enthusiasm to their reaction to the second year of tutoring, but we were dismayed to find that these children only held their own, and in some cases may have lost ground in terms of IQ scores.

A closer examination of the situation, however, revealed that the 15 to 20 IQ point gains during the first year were really on one type of item on the Stanford Binet test and did not involve success at symbolic language or representational language. If the children were to have continued their initial success, they would have had to be successful during the second year at an *entirely different* kind of mental operation. This they were not able to do. Thus, the apparently baffling results of a sharp gain in IQ in one year and no gain in the second year are more easily explained by saying that the children were able to master all the skills necessary at one level of development during the first year but were unable to succeed at a different level of development the second year. Their failure to do this resulted in the peculiar test results.

It is also important to point out that there is an implicit assumption made by Ausubel, that intelligence is what an IQ test measures. If we changed and broadened the definition of intelligence, as many of the persons in this Conference are eager to do, then our findings on whether environmental changes can modify intelligence would have to be changed accordingly.

Ausubel has referred to the importance of the "critical periods" idea. Again, it is possible to have a number of different models of reality. One can view this situation as the "ball rolling off the table" model in which one conceives of the "critical period" passing with a dreadful finality and, once past, the individual losing the opportunity ever fully to develop the skill. Another model, however, would be that, once past the maximum period of development, a slowly eroding process gradually takes place in which the individual loses the ability to build a maximum potential. It does not appear, on present evidence, that this decline in the potential to reach maximum mental growth ever reaches or approaches zero, although Ausubel develops a cogent point when he suggests that children may develop alternative modes of need satisfaction to that of language and abstract conceptualization.

Thus, the culturally deprived child will involve himself with physical activities and the deaf child will learn a low-level system of signing (e.g., using "sign language" and gestures) in preference to the harder road of abstract conceptualization. Once these alternative modes of reacting have been settled upon by the child, it stands to reason that they will be quite difficult to modify.

Finally, Ausubel touches on the "discovery" method controversy which is still much in evidence in education today. Can one teach a child the important elements of set theory or principles of symbolic logic while he is still at a reasonably young age? This is an important question and it is here that I do not believe the issue was fairly met in Ausubel's paper. It is not necessary to maintain that *every* abstract concept can be made comprehensible to young children. One can hold the defensible position that many more abstract concepts can be made comprehensible to young children through good training than has been believed possible in the past, and such a statement would be doubly true for gifted children.

I would dislike to see the door closed on such attempts by the assertion that "the intellectual achievement of children can only be accelerated within the limits imposed by the prevailing stage of intellectual development. These limitations cannot be transcended through experience."

Such a statement would be more meaningful if we knew what such limits might be. I could live much better with the notion presented earlier in the paper that what a child can know is in part a function of the interaction of the child and the instructor and the child's level of intellectual development at that time. It is in the fullest exploration of such interaction that the field of cognition can achieve new excitement and growth and evolve better models of reality than we are capable of producing at the present time.

Nancy Bayley

Dr. Ausubel has done an excellent job of stating the important issues in this area of the influences of early experiences on mental growth, and in reviewing the relevant research. He has pointed out very clearly the importance of the child's general stage of intellectual maturity in determining the kinds of experiences he had and, accordingly, the kinds of stimulation to intellectual growth that are possible for him. He has pointed out that there is ample evidence that change from impoverished to enriched environments will increase the IQ's of very young children, but that we do not understand the mechanisms involved in this change. Furthermore, we have no adequate information about the effectiveness on school-age children of various kinds of efforts to increase mental functioning.

I should like to call attention to another aspect of the effects of early experience on later intelligence. A number of maternal-child behavior correlates have been investigated for the children of the Berkeley Growth Study, for their first 18 years. In one of these studies the behaviors of the mothers toward their children during the testing situations during their first three years and the children's own behaviors have been correlated with their intelligence scores at 39 age points during the period from 1 month through 18 years. We have found systematic changes in correlation, and clear sex differences. The patterns of correlation show that in the first year of life, boy babies with loving mothers tend to be happy, relatively inactive and to earn below-average mental scores, while those with hostile mothers are the reverse of this, showing positive correlations between maternal hostility and sons' mental scores. As they continue through the preschool years, these mother-son correlations drop and then reverse sign (go from positive to negative), so that by 4 and 5 years of age and continuing through 18 years, the correlations are positive between sons' IQ's and loving maternal behavior, and strongly negative between their IQ's and hostile maternal behavior, as observed toward their sons in the first three years of life.

The mother-daughter relations are very different. In the first year, girls with loving, controlling mothers make higher scores; those with hostile mothers make lower scores. In the preschool period this relation is maintained. But by five years of age the correlations drop and remain essentially zero through 18 years, with one exception. There is a persistent negative correlation between girls' IQ and early maternal intrusive behavior.

In searching the correlation tables for some significant relations between the mothers' characteristics and their daughters' IQ's, the one persistent significant r was with an estimate of the mothers' IQ's. A further review showed also higher r's between girls' IQ (5–18 years) and mothers' and fathers' education, and fathers' occu-

pation. A search of the literature in which parent-child intelligence was correlated for sons and daughters separately showed that, though individual pairs of r's are not significantly different, a large proportion of the parent-daughter r's are higher than are the parent-son r's.

These differences have led us to a hypothesis of genetic sex differences in the persistence of the effects of early experience. The girls appear to readjust more readily to current experiences, and thus in the matter of intelligence to earn scores which are relatively more genetically determined than do the boys. The boys' earlier experiences in emotional climate (maternal love-hostility in the first three years) show evidences of lasting effects on their intellectual growth. It appears that in boys there is less likelihood of change from the effects, whether accelerative or depressing, of experiences in the first three years of life. There is supportive evidence in many aspects of physical growth and morbidity.

The point I wish to make is that when we make further studies of the effects of environment and in particular of the reversibility of earlier environmental effects, we should always treat the sexes separately. From this and other studies, there is evidence that the early environment is much more important for the males than for females, in the formation of personality variables and in intellectual functioning—at least into young adulthood.

30 *Cognitive Challenge as a Factor in Children's Humor Appreciation*[1]

EDWARD ZIGLER

JACOB LEVINE

LAURENCE GOULD

This study demonstrates experimentally that an important ingredient in humor is the degree to which the humor makes a cognitive demand on the individual. Cartoons at the upper limit of the child's ability to comprehend evoke the greatest amount of laughter as well as the greatest preference. Cartoons varying in difficulty level from easy to nearly impossible are administered to third-, fifth-, and seventh-grade children of average intelligence. At all three grades mirth and preference scores are peaked at the moderately difficult range. The findings are discussed in relation to the child's motive of cognitive mastery and a motivation-free information-processing approach.

Despite the concern and investigatory efforts of philosophers and psychologists through the ages, no satisfactory comprehensive theory of humor has been forthcoming (see Flugel, 1954, and Levine, in press, for comprehensive historical reviews). Perhaps one reason for this failure is the frequently made assumption that humor is the result of some specific single factor. A more reasonable approach would appear to be one involving the view that humor is a phenomenon reflecting a number of causal factors. This notation of the complexity of the problem surrounding the humor response does not in itself carry us very far towards the problem's solution. What is required

[1]This research was supported by Research Grant MH 06809 from the National Institute of Mental Health, United States Public Health Service, the Gunnar Dybwad Award of the National Association for Retarded Children, and the Veterans Administration. The authors wish to express their appreciation to Inge Winer for running subjects and for her assistance in various phases of this study.

Reprinted from the *Journal of Personality and Social Psychology*, 1967, **6**, 332–336, by permission of the senior author and the American Psychological Association.

is the delineation and investigation of individual variables found to be related to humor, which should then be followed by the study of the interrelationships among such factors.

Some progress along these lines has been made in the body of work that has related the individual's psychodynamics to his tendency to laugh (Levine, in press). This work, for the most part, has emphasized the importance of the content of the humor stimulus, and how such content interacts with the individual's psychodynamics in determining the humor response. Although valuable, this approach has tended to underestimate the importance of cognitive factors in determining the degree of laughter. Whatever the individual's psychodynamic features may be, understanding a joke invariably requires the cognitive capacity to meet the intellectual demands posed by the joke. As obvious as this statement might be, the relation between intellectual level and response to humor stimuli has been far from clear (this literature reviewed in Zigler, Levine, and Gould, 1966a).

This relation was investigated recently by Zigler, et al. in a study with second-, third-, fourth-, and fifth-grade children. For children in grades two through four Zigler, et al. were able to demonstrate that as the children's ability to comprehend a group of 25 cartoons increased, the magnitude of their mirth responses increased. However, contrary to prediction, although comprehension scores continued to go up, mirth scores for fifth graders showed a marked decline from that found for fourth graders. This study indicated that while comprehension is an important factor in determining the mirth response, perfect comprehension does not in and of itself guarantee laughter.

No evidence was found that the lowered mirth response of the fifth graders was due to the particular content of the cartoons. One explanation for this lowered mirth response is that the cartoons were too easy for the fifth graders and represented no intellectual challenge for these older children. It would appear that the child laughs at those cartoons which make appropriate demands on his cognitive structure, and not at those which are either too easy or too difficult. This suggests that an important ingredient in humor is the degree to which the humor stimulus makes a cognitive demand on the individual. Zigler, et al. did find some evidence that cartoons which were at the upper limit of the child's ability to comprehend evoked the greatest amount of laughter. This generates the hypothesis that the mirth response is greatest when the complexity of the humor stimulus and the complexity of the child's cognitive structure are congruent.

Both Freud (1960) and Levine (in press) have also suggested that the sheer pleasure of employing one's cognitive processes in relation to humor stimuli contributes to the experienced gratification. Inherent in this suggestion is the view advanced above that there is a factor influencing the magnitude of the mirth response that is independent of both the psychodynamic features of the individual and the individual's sheer cognitive ability to comprehend the joke. This factor may be related to what White (1959) has referred to as the effectance motive. Employing the effectance concept, one would expect the most laughter when the individual is experiencing the greatest sense of mastery, that is, at the point at which the cognitive demands of the humor stimuli are at the upper limits of the individual's cognitive ability (cognitively congruent). As noted above, some support for this view was obtained by Zigler, et al. (1966a). However, their findings were somewhat equivocal since children at all grades received the same 25 cartoons.

A more direct test of the cognitive-congruence or effectance hypothesis suggests itself. Such a test requires that the difficulty level of the humor stimuli be equated across age groups. One could independently assess the difficulty of cartoons for each age level employed, and then categorize them as easy, moderately difficult, difficult, and nearly impossible. Given this procedure, the particular cartoons in each category would differ for each age level. The cognitive-congruence hypothesis would generate the expectation that the mirth response should peak somewhere in the moderately difficult-difficult range at all age levels. In the present study this prediction was tested with third-, fifth-, and seventh-grade children of both sexes.

METHOD

Selection of Cartoons

This study required groups of cartoons whose difficulty level had been independently assessed on the basis of the comprehension scores of third-, fifth-, and seventh-grade children. The difficulty level of cartoons utilized in an earlier study (Zigler, et al., 1966a) with third- and fifth-grade children was employed to se-

lect the easy, moderately difficult, and difficult groups of cartoons for these two grade levels. Grouping cartoons into difficulty levels for the seventh graders, for whom previous norms were not available, was accomplished by initially administering a heterogeneous pool of 35 cartoons to 20 seventh graders, 10 boys and 10 girls. On the basis of the comprehension scores obtained, groups of easy, moderately difficult, difficult, and nearly impossible cartoons were selected to be employed with the seventh-grade sample. The nearly impossible group of cartoons employed with the seventh-grade sample were also the cartoons classified as nearly impossible in the cartoon sets given to the third and fifth graders. In this way, four groups of four cartoons varying in difficulty level were selected for each grade. In addition to varying the difficulty within a grade level, the following criteria were employed in making the final selections: (a) For each grade the difficulty level within each group of four cartoons would be relatively homogeneous; (b) the difficulty level of any given difficulty grouping of four cartoons would be comparable across grades; (c) there would be no marked differences in the subject matter of the cartoons across grades or across difficulty levels within a grade. This last restriction was included in order to minimize a confounding of subject matter and difficulty. The results of the selection then are three different sets of cartoons for children in the third, fifth, and seventh grade which are comparable in difficulty and content. Each set is composed of four groups of four cartoons each, which on the basis of the children's comprehension scores are categorized as easy, moderately difficult, difficult, and nearly impossible. The order of presentation of each set of cartoons was randomized with the re-

striction that neither of the first two cartoons would be nearly impossible ones,
and that two nearly impossible cartoons
would not appear consecutively. The resultant order of cartoons for each grade
was used for all subjects in that grade.

Subjects

A female experimenter administered
the cartoons individually to 10 boys and
10 girls each in third-, fifth-, and seventh-
grade classes (the mean CAs were 8.7,
10.6, and 12.6, respectively) in predominantly middle-class public schools. Selection of subjects was made by classroom
teachers who were asked to select children who represented the typical or modal
child in the class. They were specifically
asked not to pick the brightest children,
the dullest children, or children with any
type of emotional or physical problem.

Administration

The examiner sat across from the child
at a table with 16 cartoons mounted individually on cardboard lying face down
on the table. The following instructions
were given:

I have a bunch of pictures, and I
want to see if you think they are funny
or not. As I show you each picture, tell
me whether or not you think it is funny.

The experimenter then turned the cartoons over one at a time in constant order
and recorded: (*a*) the spontaneous mirth
response of the child, (*b*) whether or not
the child judged it funny, and (*c*) any
spontaneous comments of the child. Following this initial presentation of the 25
cartoons, the experimenter said: "Now
we'll go through them again, and this

time you tell me about the cartoon. What
is the joke? What is supposed to be funny
about it?" On the second presentation,
the experimenter scored for comprehension.

Following this second run-through the
subjects were asked to select the three
cartoons that they liked best.

Scoring

Three scores were obtained: (*a*) a
facial mirth score employing the categories: 0 = negative response (grimace,
etc.), 1 = no response (blank face, etc.),
2 = inhibited to a half or slight smile,
3 = full smile, 4 = laugh; (*b*) a comprehensive score employing the categories:
0 = no comprehension, 1 = partial comprehension, 2 = full comprehension; (*c*)
preference ranking of cartoons based on
the children's selections.

The interjudge reliabilities for the total
mirth and comprehension scores in the
earlier study (Zigler, et al., 1966a) were
found to be .95 and .94, respectively.

The subjects' comprehension and mirth
scores for each level of cartoon difficulty
are presented in Table 1. A $3 \times 2 \times 4$
(Grade $\times$ Sex $\times$ Difficulty Level) repeated-measures analysis of variance of the
comprehension scores resulted in a significant difficulty effect ($F_{3/162} = 252.39$;
$p < .001$). None of the other main or interaction effects approached statistical
significance. Summing across grade levels,
Tukey tests were run between comprehension scores in adjacent difficulty
groupings. Each of the three comparisons
was found to be significant at beyond the
.001 level. These findings indicate that
the a priori grouping of the cartoons into
difficulty levels accomplished the intended goals.

A $3 \times 2 \times 4$ repeated-measures analysis

**TABLE 1.—Mean Comprehension and Mirth Scores
for Each Level of Cartoon Difficulty**

		CARTOON DIFFICULTY LEVEL							
		Easy		*Moderately difficult*		*Difficult*		*Impossible*	
GRADE	N	Compre-hension	Mirth	Compre-hension	Mirth	Compre-hension	Mirth	Compre-hension	Mirth
3rd	20	1.85	2.16	1.51	2.34	1.15	2.12	.18	1.69
5th	20	1.80	2.12	1.59	2.18	1.15	1.71	.26	1.69
7th	20	1.71	2.22	1.39	2.34	1.08	2.11	.46	1.78

of variance of the mirth-response scores resulted in a significant difficulty level effect ($F_{3/162} = 24.86$; $p < .001$). As can be seen in Table 1, the mirth response peaks at the moderately difficult level and then drops at the two higher difficulty levels at all three grades. A general non-monotonic-trend analysis indicated that this particular pattern is a highly significant one ($F_{1/54} = 96.20$; $p < .001$), and accounted for the bulk of the variance associated with the difficulty level main effect. Individual comparisons run between adjacent mean mirth-response scores revealed that the mean for the moderately difficult cartoons was higher than that for the easy cartoons ($p < .05$); the mean for the moderately difficult cartoons was higher than that for the difficult cartoons ($p < .01$), which in turn was higher than that for the impossible cartoons ($p < .001$). It should be noted that the easy cartoons were not as easy as the impossible cartoons were difficult. Subsequent investigations should employ an easier group of cartoons. However, even lacking this symmetry in the difficulty dimension, the findings were in keeping with the cognitive congruence hypothesis.

**TABLE 2.—Number of Times the Cartoons Were Selected as Preferred,
and Associated Mean Preference Ranks for the
Four Levels of Cartoon Difficulty**

		CARTOON DIFFICULTY LEVEL							
		Easy		*Moderately difficult*		*Difficult*		*Impossible*	
GRADE	N	Prefer-ence	Rank	Prefer-ence	Rank	Prefer-ence	Rank	Prefer-ence	Rank
3rd	20	20	2.18	22	1.98	11	2.85	7	2.95
5th	20	19	2.15	24	1.85	9	3.00	8	3.00
7th	20	12	2.65	22	2.00	16	2.48	10	2.88
Total	60	51	2.33	68	1.94	36	2.77	25	2.94

The number of times that cartoons at each difficulty level were selected by the children as being among the three most preferred are presented in Table 2. If the three cartoons selected by each of the 20 children at a grade level were in the same difficulty category, that category would receive a score of 60. Across grade levels, then, the maximum score would be 180. As can be seen in Table 2, the preference scores are quite parallel with the mirth-response scores, rising from the easy category to peak at the moderately difficult category, and then dropping at the two higher levels of difficulty. The lack of independence of these preference scores precludes a statistical test of significance. In order to perform such a test, each child's preference score was converted to a rank score in the following way: (*a*) If all three of the child's selections were in the same difficulty category, that category would receive a rank of 1. Each of the other three categories would receive a rank of 3; (*b*) if two of the child's selections were in one difficulty category, and a third selection was in a second category, these categories would receive ranks of 1 and 2, respectively. The remaining two categories would receive a rank of 3.5; and (*c*) if the child made one selection from each of three categories, these three categories would each receive a rank of 2, and the remaining category, a rank of 4. The means of these rankings are presented in Table 2. Friedman's analysis of variance of ranks test indicated that the children's preferences differed significantly as a function of difficulty level ($F_{2.03/119.77} = 8.48; p < .001$).

DISCUSSION

A phenomenon appears to have been isolated in this study that has not heretofore been demonstrated in humor research. The magnitude of the mirth response was found to depend upon the degree of cognitive congruence existing between the cognitive demand features of the humor stimulus and the cognitive resources of the individual. It is at the point where comprehending the joke taxes the individual's cognitive structure that the humor response is maximal. Consistent with this thesis and certain data of an earlier study (Zigler, et al., 1966a), the findings revealed that complete and easy comprehension does not result in the greatest amount of laughter. It is in the intermediate range of difficulty that children obtained both the highest mirth response and preference scores. This phenomenon was found at each of the three grade levels, and in both sexes. Furthermore, the striking parallel between the mirth response and the preference findings indicated that the subject's pleasure could be assessed equally well by recording either his spontaneous laughter or requesting a considered judgment of the cartoons.

The findings of the present study are not only consistent with White's effectance notion, but are in keeping with a variety of theoretical views and everyday observations that have emphasized that children enjoy most that which lies at the growing edge of their capacities. The value of the present study would appear to lie in its clear experimental demonstration of this phenomenon, and in the evidence it provides that humor partakes of a phenomenon that has been thought to characterize other more obviously cognitive behaviors. That humor has many features in common with more recognized cognitive creative acts has recently been emphasized by Koestler (1964). On the other hand, it should be clear that there are determinants other than the cognitive-challenge factor which influence the magnitude of the mirth response. The importance of the content of the humor stimulus interacting with the psychodynamic features of the individual has already been noted. Neither the cognitive challenge, nor the psychodynamic factor appears capable of explaining why incomprehensible cartoons evoke as much mirth as was found in this and in earlier studies (Zigler, et al., 1966a, 1966b). What appears to happen in many instances when the child is unable to comprehend the joke correctly is that he sees it as funny for reasons other than the correct one. Often he focuses on a particular feature of the cartoon and finds it uproariously funny. Much of this behavior is probably precipitated by the set involved in the instructions of the task. Once he is told he is to see cartoons and queried about their funniness, the child is confronted with the problem of deducing just why the cartoon is funny. Confronted with such a problem, the child does the very best he can.

Some further speculations concerning the mechanisms mediating the cognitive challenge phenomenon appear to be in order. This study was formulated within a framework that utilized White's concept of effectance. The notion here was that the gratification of the effectance motive occurs when the child uses his cognitive ability to his fullest potential, and that laughter was the emotional expression of this gratification in the same way that satiety would accompany the gratification of the hunger motive. The humor stimuli inducing gratification of the effectance motive should take on reinforcing properties, and thus be preferred by the child when asked to give a preference.

Although this explanation would appear to be consistent with the findings of the present study, a second hypothesis should be entertained. The cognitive-congruence phenomenon found in the present study does not require the type of motivational foundation which inheres in the current thinking on effectance or mastery. One can utilize a motivation-free information-processing orientation and assert that the intrinsic nature of the individual is such that he prefers or enjoys those stimuli which are at a complexity level congruent with his cognitive structure or "channel capacity" (Munzinger and Kessen, 1964). This interpretation is consistent with recent findings obtained on individuals at various age levels (Brennan, Ames, and Moore, 1966; Munzinger and Kessen, 1964).

The distinction between the two hypotheses, though somewhat subtle, is a meaningful one and would appear to generate differential predictions. The effectance hypothesis would generate the prediction that the humor response would depend on two factors: (a) the degree of congruence between the complexity of the humor stimulus and the complexity of the observer's cognitive structure, and (b) the strength of the observer's motive after mastery. The information-processing hypothesis generates the expectation that the magnitude of the humor response and/or preference responses would depend on the first factor alone. It is, of course, possible to test children who are matched in respect to their cognitive complexity (e.g., MA), but who differ on some independent assessment of the motive to be intellectually successful (e.g., underachievers versus overachievers). Such a study would aid in determining which of the two hypotheses discussed is the most appropriate one for encompassing the clear findings of the present study.

Language and Communication

9

31 *The Social Context of Language Acquisition*

VERA P. JOHN

LEO S. GOLDSTEIN

This article on language acquisition in a social context focuses on "the gradual shift in the child's use of words, from labeling specific and often single referents to the use of words for signifying categories of objects, actions, or attributes. The hypothesis advanced here is that the rate and breadth of this shift varies from one social context to another, and that it has differential consequences for cognitive development dependent on the social context in which it occurs." The crucial significance of actively stimulating language growth in the classroom, especially by teachers of the socially disadvantaged, is stressed.

The child, surrounded by a sea of words, sequentially and selectively acquires the nouns, verbs, and phrases of his language as well as the gestures, intonations and dialect of those with whom he interacts. The rate and breadth of this complex acquisition is proportional to the scope of his verbal interactions with those charged with his care.

Language is so pervasive in human behavior, that the process of language acquisition is often taken for granted. A comprehensive treatment of this process is obviously beyond the scope of this paper. There are too

Reprinted from the *Merrill-Palmer Quarterly of Behavior and Development*, 1964, **10**, 265–275, by permission of the senior author and the Merrill-Palmer Institute.

many gaps in our current knowledge to make such an attempt feasible.

In consideration of such limitations, therefore, this paper will focus upon social conditions that affect language acquisition. More specifically, it will focus upon the gradual shift in the child's use of words, from labeling specific and often single referents to the use of words for signifying categories of objects, actions, or attributes. The hypothesis advanced here is that the rate and breadth of this shift varies from one social context to another, and that it has differential consequences for cognitive development dependent on the social context in which it occurs. This hypothesis will be examined and discussed chiefly in terms of the pertinent literature, with occasional reference to empirical studies.

The need to modify the cognitive growth patterns of young children—particularly of those children who live in the slum areas of our major cities—has added new impetus to the search for a clarification of the relationship between language and thought. It is our intention to examine aspects of word acquisition as related to conceptual development, particularly the development of verbal mediation.

The literature on the development of language, structured largely in terms of maturational theory and based on the congruent findings of careful investigators, specifies an approximate sequence and timetable of children's verbal development. The focus of many of these studies has been on the rate of language acquisition, the unit studied being the number of different words elicited from the young child in a standard setting. Here, the social environment is

viewed either as a hampering or enhancing medium in which the development of speech occurs, and the basic process of growth is considered to be neurophysiologically determined.

Although these studies have given us more facts about the increase of the child's active vocabulary, they have failed to deal with language development within the context of modern psychological theories such as those of Hebb and Hunt. Similarities in the quantitative features of overt behavior (i.e., the size of spoken vocabulary) are assumed, by normatively oriented researchers, to be behaviors functionally equivalent for groups of children differing in background. However, studies limited to word-counting afford little insight into the dynamic relationship between social experience and language. While many of these investigators (e.g., Gesell, Templin) may be aware that the content of speech is culturally determined, too often their writings have not reflected this awareness.

In contradistinction to the maturational approach to language development as exemplified by the investigators mentioned above, Osgood's model of language conceptualizes words as abbreviated motor behavior. While his approach permits a simplified description of the complex behavior of language, it focuses on variables which would appear to be tangential to language acquisition. More importantly, motor learning requires little social interaction, but language cannot be acquired in an interpersonal vacuum.

On the other hand, the theoretical writings of Bernstein (1960, 1962), and the recently translated book of Vygotsky (1962), present approaches which are useful in the study of language acquisition in a social context. In his writings, Bernstein emphasized status as a major social determinant of speech patterns within social groups. More centrally related to the approach taken in this paper are hypotheses advanced by Vygotsky three decades ago. He proposed that the conditions which influence the development of speech (overt language) are also related to the development of verbal mediation (covert language). Further, he suggested that a socially determined learning condition of central importance in the acquisition of language is the availability of adults for engaging the child in dialogue.[1]

Consequently, the central theme of this discussion, partially based on Vygotsky's thinking, is that children *develop* and *test* their tentative notions (hypotheses) about the meanings of words and the structure of sentences chiefly through verbal interaction with more verbally mature speakers.

LABEL AND CATEGORIES

The Acquisition of Labels

Social interaction with verbally mature individuals, which affects language acquisition, begins with the occurrence of the infant's earliest vocal responses. Some findings have illustrated the effects of social environment on vocalization in children as young as six months (Brodbeck and Irwin, 1946; Rheingold and Bayley, 1959). The child's language develop-

ment in the first two years of life is primarily in the nature of increasing comprehension of the speech of those around him. By age two, he has developed a speaking vocabulary which may range from 3 to 300 words. In the next two years, the child shifts from using words exclusively as labels with single referents to the use of words which have multiple referents (rudimentary categories).

This process of acquiring and enlarging the use of labels can be sketched in general terms. At an elementary stage of language acquisition, before his first birthday, the child perceives a word as being one of a multitude of attributes of an object (shape, weight, color, name). By the repeated association of seeing and touching the object, and hearing the name of the object, the child acquires a bond between word and referent. Usually, the source of auditory stimulation is the mother. In addition, children engage in communicative interaction with siblings, relatives, other children, teachers and neighbors. The role of more impersonal sources of communication, e.g., television and radio, has become increasingly important in children's acquisition of words.[2]

Put on a more technical level, in describing language acquisition, some researchers rely on the conditioning paradigm. However, such a model presents certain difficulties in that it emphasizes a one-to-one relationship between stimulus and response. In

---

[1]The relationship between children's verbal skills and parental availability has been stressed by McCarthy (1961). She postulates a gradient of verbal proficiency as a function of the amount and kind of contact the child experiences with his mother.

[2]Novel but simple learning is well understood by advertisers. The highly predictable association between the picture of the Coca Cola bottle and its name from the TV sound-track is a fact of great utility in label acquisition.

reality, the word to be learned is usually embedded in a sentence (the verbal context) and its referent (the object which is to be paired with the word) is surrounded by a multitude of extraneous features in the environment. Learning labels requires selective attention—the inhibition of irrelevant aspects of the learning environment.

This learning of new verbal responses, particularly by young children, can be facilitated by a relative invariance in the environment. One of the major characteristics of the home, a natural setting for language acquisition, is its intrinsic variability. This is particularly true of lower-class homes which have been described as lacking in scheduling or predictability for children, and as more crowded, and more transient in their inhabitants than middle-class homes. Children raised in such lower-class homes participated in the studies reported below.

In spite of the complexities and difficulties involved in the process of label acquisition, children do acquire words in the midst of the "noise" of the natural environment. Some accomplish this more readily than others. The abundance of opportunities for hearing the names of objects while seeing and touching them is such that most two-year-olds can understand and use effectively a number of labels.

Receptive Labeling

Children from different social classes vary in their knowledge of words. Some studies of social class differences have recorded systematic variations in verbal indices of children grouped according to father's occupation and/or education. Children from high-income, high-status families have been found to speak in longer sentences, more articulately, and with a more varied vocabulary than do their lower-class peers (Templin, 1957). Thus, in order to understand better the implications of such findings, it is necessary to examine *qualitative* as well as quantitative differences in children's verbal behavior.

One example of qualitative differences in children's verbal behavior emerged from an item analysis of the responses of young Negro children to a receptive verbal task, the Peabody Picture Vocabulary Test (PPVT). Briefly described, the PPVT consists of a series of increasingly difficult items which require the child to display his comprehension of labels, when confronted with four drawings, by pointing to the correct picture-referent. The standardization group for this test consisted solely of white children residing in and around Nashville, Tennessee.

As part of a larger investigation, the PPVT was administered to four-year-old, lower-class Negro children, who had been selected to participate in a pre-school enrichment program.[3] Of

[3]The research and teaching staff of the Institute for Developmental Studies, New York Medical College, is engaged in a variety of projects involving lower-class Negro children. Currently, pre-school enrichment classes are being held in eight Manhattan elementary schools. The Peabody Picture Vocabulary Test (PPVT) protocols of approximately 40 experimental and control children—*before entering enrichment*—was selected for this illustration.

the first 35 words of the test, clusters of items which the children had failed were identified. Three clusters of words were found to be particularly difficult: action words (*digging, tying, pouring, building, pickling*); words related to rural living (*leaf, bee, bush, nest*); and words whose referents may be rare in low-income homes (*kangaroo, caboose, accident*). [Other studies, such as that by Eells (1951), have shown similar trends in that older lower-class children failed to identify words, such as "harp," the referents of which are not usually available in lower-class environments.]

These results raised a question of great interest to us: Why did these lower-class children have such a high percentage of failure with action words? If the environment provides abundant opportunity for the child to hear simple labels, then action words are as likely to be heard by lower-class children as by middle-class children. Perhaps the explanation lies in the learning environment. Children from low-income homes have relatively little opportunity to engage in active *dialogue* when learning labels. Milner (1951) has described the paucity of verbal interaction of children with adults in the low-income as contrasted with the high-income Negro home.

It is our contention, therefore, partially supported by Bernstein's research that the crucial difference between middle-class and lower-class individuals is not in the quality of language, but in its *use*. The functional diversity in language may be a direct result of the occupational and educational experiences of the speaker. Middle-class occupations generally require

and permit verbal interaction with a variety of people. The individual must continually adjust his speech in terms of rate, intonation, vocabulary, and grammatical complexity, in an attempt to provide optimal communication. In contrast to this, the verbal interaction required in lower-class occupations is of a more routine, highly conventionalized nature. The middle-class individual, then, develops a more *flexible* use of language than that found in persons from lower-class backgrounds. The gap between the speaker's verbal skill and the listener's potential for comprehension is greatest in adult-child verbal interactions . Here, the ability to use language flexibly is most important—it permits the adult to adjust his speech to fit the child's level of comprehension.

But if the lower-class child has to rely upon the frequency of co-occurrence of label and referent to a greater extent than the middle-class child, then, for him, the invariance between word and referent must also be greater. Yet, the learning of verbs and gerunds by frequency of occurrence instead of by active dialogue is more difficult than is the learning of labels for specific objects. Gerunds such as "tying" were failed, not because the children were deficient in experience with the referent but rather because they had difficulty in fitting the label to the *varying forms of action observed and experienced*. This fitting process, which consists of selecting the specific connection between word and referent, occurs more easily when there is a variety of *verbal interaction* with adults. The middle-class child learns by feedback; by being heard, corrected, and modified—by gaining "operant control" over his social environment by using words that he hears. The child learns by interacting with an adult teacher who plays an active role in simplifying the various components of word-referent relationships.

In this discussion, the acquisition of labels has been conceptualized as the result of the interaction of two major variables. One, the stability of the word-referent relationship, refers to the specificity of the features of the referent and the degree of its invari-

ance within the learning context in the natural environment. The second variable, derived from the frequency and type of verbal interaction during language acquisition, refers to the amount of corrective feedback the child receives while learning a new label, i.e., the consistency with which his speech is listened to, corrected, and modified.

Figure 1 illustrates the postulated relation of these two variables, in the acquisition of specific labels (A) and of action words (B). Words such as "Coca Cola" and "ball" have char-

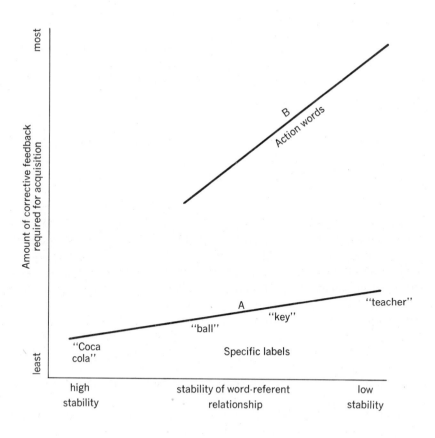

Fig. 1.

acteristics of high stability and physical constancy and they occur within relatively few learning contexts. Such words are easily learned by the mere frequency of co-occurrence of word and referent, and require little corrective feedback. Because of the relatively lower stability of the word-referent relationship for words such as "key" and "teacher," a somewhat greater amount of corrective feedback is necessary for their acquisition. (Line A.)

Most action words occur in contexts of moderate to high variance. As the stability of the word-referent relationship decreases, the amount of corrective feedback required for acquisition increases. (Line B.)

This relationship is postulated for words which are abundant in the natural environment of lower-class as well as middle-class children—but not for words such as "caboose," "accident," and "kangaroo" which may occur infrequently in the lower-class setting. Therefore, the postulated interaction rather than experiential rarity may explain more simply the slower rate of acquisition of labels and action words by lower-class children.

Briefly, our analysis indicates that the child's acquisition of words with shifting and complex referents will be impeded if the required adult-child verbal interaction is insufficient or lacking.

The Acquisition of Categories

While the child is acquiring new labels he also is gaining additional referents for those labels already in his repertoire. Young children, unskilled in the use of words, often reveal their understanding of the nuances of a label, i.e., the multiplicity of their referents, through non-verbal behavior. Long before the two-year-old can correctly pronounce the word "horse," he indicates that he knows several referents for the word when he hears it spoken by pointing to his rocking horse or reaching for his stuffed animal. By the quality and amount of corrective feedback he gives, the actively participating adult determines the breadth of the generalization and the precision of the discrimination the child relies upon while learning multiple referents.

The PPVT data discussed earlier indicate that lower-class children, because of insufficient corrective feedback, have great difficulty in acquiring words which appear in a number of different contexts. The specific context in which a label is first acquired, one characterized by low "noise" or one in which there is frequent reoccurrence of label and referent, is limiting and restrictive. Generalizing a word from one setting to another requires the discovery of the irrelevant variations which accompany the essential constancy. As Brown (1958) has said: ". . . a speech invariance is a signal to form some *hypothesis* [italics ours] about the corresponding invariance of referent."

This process of discovering invariance common to multiple instances of a label is fundamental for the *conceptual* as well as the verbal development of the young child. However, little is known about the mechanics of this process, beyond the recognition that *both* generalizations and discriminations have to be made by the child learning multiple meanings of words.[4]

As part of a larger study designed to gather information about the verbal skills, intellectual performance, and motivational approaches of white and Negro, first and fifth grade, lower and middle-class children in New York City, the Concept Sorting test, developed by the senior author and her co-workers, was used to investigate category formation in young children. The test consists of 16 simple drawings which can be grouped into functional pairs (e.g., *sailor* and *boat*) or into logically consistent piles (e.g., *means of transportation* or *animals*). After the child has finished sorting the cards into piles, the examiner elicits from the child a verbal rationale for each sort. Some examples of the verbalizations of lower-class and middle-class Negro children are given below. (The concept was represented by pictures of four men at work: a policeman, a doctor, a farmer, and a sailor).

Lower-class first-graders

a. "because doctor nurses these other people"
b. "because the man and big Bill (policeman) like each other"
c. "because they look the same"

Middle-class first-graders

a. "because they all **men**"
b. "all the same, all of them are men"
c. "They are both people."

Two hypotheses which were formu-

―――――――

[4]By means of corrective feedback, the child learns that a "dog" is not a horse or cat or some other grossly similar object in his environment (discrimination). He also learns that "dog" is not only that white thing with black spots, but it is also that big brown thing that makes a loud noise, and that other thing with the long floppy ears (generalization).

lated in the major study are relevant here. Verbally less-experienced children were expected to sort the stimulus cards into a larger number of piles. It was also anticipated that middle-class children (as a group, considered to be verbally more-experienced) would offer an explicit statement of a concept, e.g., "they are all animals," while the verbal rationale of lower-class children would reflect a specific aspect of communality, e.g., "they all have legs." These hypotheses were partially substantiated (John, 1963).

The examples given above illustrate the general tenor of responses given by the children. The middle-class (Negro) children tended to produce category labels more often than their lower-class peers who instead were inclined to focus on non-essential attributes. We may say that those children who were successful on this task were those who had developed skills for discovering the crucial, invariant features of objects having the same name.

WORDS AS MEDIATORS

The individual's ability to solve complex problems is related to the use he makes of language in verbal mediation. Jensen (1963b) defines verbal mediation as ". . . verbal behavior which facilitates further learning, which controls behavior, and which permits the development of conceptual thinking." In some of their research, the Kendlers (1956, 1963) have found an increase with age in children's reliance on words as mediators while solving a reversal shift problem. Antecedent conditions necessary for the development of verbal mediation have not yet been explored.

In this paper, we posit, that while the child gains practice in correctly identifying objects having the same name, and while he develops his knowledge about the hierarchy of category-names, he also develops skills of use in verbal mediation. Again, we ascribe a crucial role in the development of verbal mediation to the availability of adults, who serve as language models, and who participate in an ongoing dialogue with the child.

Evidence currently available suggests that some children who can be described as proficient in *overt* verbal skills, also rely upon *covert* language —or verbal mediational processes— when approaching complex problems. Luria's studies of speech-delayed twins (1961) exemplify the parallel development of verbal skills and verbal mediation.

Children from backgrounds of educational retardation have been shown to perform poorly on verbal and conceptual tasks. Jensen (1963a) taught a group of educationally retarded adolescents to use verbal mediation in a task which required the learning of a list of paired associates. These subjects learned to construct a sentence around each pair of meaningful words. A control group of subjects from similar background, who were not instructed in this use of verbal mediation, took five times as long to learn the task. It appears that children who receive insufficient verbal stimulation in early childhood develop deficiencies not only in overt verbal skills but also in verbal mediational behavior.

In our stress on the importance of variety in stimulation, our position is in basic agreement with that of Hebb and other developmental theorists concerned with cognitive processes. However, we have also attempted to specify the demands on the child as he learns. The child, confronted with several disparate objects having a label in common, has to identify those critical and invariant features common to the objects. Similarly, when confronted with two or more non-verbal tasks, the child identifies the common critical features by invoking mediating responses. In both of these learning situations the child is actively searching for invariance among features of his environment. The tools he uses in this search have been sharpened in his verbal communication with others.

Communication and cognition, traditionally treated as separate aspects of language, are posited here as fundamentally interrelated in the early stages of language acquisition. Language is seen as functional behavior for the young child. While he uses his slowly developing communicative skills to inform those who care for him about his needs, he is also organizing his perceptual and social worlds through language. The social environments in which these functions develop are highly complex. Of particular importance is the amount of attention paid to the child's own attempts at early verbalizations: the opportunity made available to the child to learn by feedback, by being heard, corrected and modified—by gaining "operant control" over his social environment as he uses words that he has heard.

In our analysis, the child from a lower socio-economic background may experience a deficient amount of verbal interaction. He learns most of his language by means of *receptive* exposure—by hearing, rather than by the correction of his own active speech. Words acquired with little corrective feedback in a stable learning environment will be of minimum use as mediators, at a later stage of development. In contrast, the child whose language acquisition is characterized by active participation with a more verbally mature individual not only develops greater verbal proficiency—as a result of being listened to and corrected—but also is more likely to rely on, and use effectively, words as mediators.

Language is a socially-conditioned relationship between the child's internal and external worlds. Once able to use words as mediators, the child can effectively change his own social and material reality.

A NOTE ON ENRICHMENT

Can educational implications for pre-school programs be drawn from a theoretical statement on language acquisition? Though some of the ideas presented in this paper may be utilized by the early childhood educator, primarily, this treatment of verbal behavior is presented as a *model* of label acquisition. Ideas developed within the context of a simplified and abstract treatment of language may have to undergo substantial modification in order to be applied in the classroom. However, some general points related to enrichment can be made, based upon the above discussion.

Certainly, the crucial importance of actively stimulating language growth in the classroom is recognized by teachers of the socially disadvantaged.

But the feeling of urgency they bring to the task of increasing the verbal repertoire of children sometimes results in a stress on *quantitative* growth only. This emphasis on vocabulary expansion is not surprising in light of the maturational approach to language.

If the communicative and cognitive functions are significantly related at the beginning of language acquisition, it becomes important to discover ways for these aspects of language to be maintained interrelatedly in enrichment programs. A mechanical approach to vocabulary building will not produce the desired end of developing useful verbal skills. Sylvia Ashton-Warner has vividly described her way of teaching reading to young Maori children. She utilized their deeply personal experiences as basic *content* while imparting the *mechanics* of letters. Similarly, the teacher in the enrichment classroom can discover the interests and concerns of her children by being sensitive to their products.[5]

---

[5] In a summer enrichment program combining instruction and research, the author and her teacher-colleagues worked with kindergarten children. Each child was asked to re-tell a standard story in front of a tape recorder. In studying the modifications of the story made by each child, much was learned about sequential language as well as about the themes of particular interest to young children raised in low-income areas. These children also told a "made-up" story, and in these fantasy products they often related events of concern. Though some of the children spoke with poor articulation and others could not think up their "own" story, many children in this group displayed forcefulness of style and communicative strength in their descriptions.

As was our purpose, this paper has stressed the acquisition of highly developed linguistic patterns as being crucial to young children. Because language is both a highly personal and an objectively necessary tool, however, the educator must be wary lest children learn to resent the acquisition of verbal skills. The teaching of words must be carried out with originality, flexibility, and restraint.

In becoming aware of some of the features underlying label acquisition, the classroom teacher can create a variety of learning contexts built around experiences of significance to the children. The teacher who is aware of the importance of verbal dialogue in the shift from labeling to categorizing, can direct learning not only by her own interactions, but, also, by helping children in the classroom to be effective speakers as well as active listeners.

32   *Cues by Which Children Recognize Words*[1]

GABRIELLE MARCHBANKS

HARRY LEVIN

What cues help children recognize words? According to this study of kindergarten and first-grade children, specific letters, not the shapes of words, are the basis of recognition. The first letter is found to be the most important cue; the final letter is next in importance. The authors conclude, "Theories which propose that beginning readers recognize words as wholes by their shape have not been supported in this study." How may the results of the study relate to the teaching of reading?

Although various theories have been presented, the cues which children use to recognize words are still not well understood. It has been suggested that children recognize words as wholes (Cattell, 1886; Smith, 1928) by geometric shape, outline, or configuration (Bell, 1939; Tinker and

[1]This study was supported in part by a contract with the Cooperative Research Program, United States Office of Education.

Paterson, 1940); by familiarity with grapheme-phoneme correspondences (Gibson, 1962; Gibson, Gibson, Danielson, Osser, and Hammond, 1962); by dominant letters such as ascending or descending letters (Wilson and Fleming, 1938); by initial and terminal letters (Levin and Watson, 1963; Levin, Watson, and Feldman, 1964; Wiley, 1928; Woodward, 1962); or by some combinations of these cues (Davidson, 1931; Gates and Boekker, 1923; Sholty, 1912).

Many of the above investigations used adult subjects, and the trained perception of an adult who is familiar with written language is probably very different from the behavior of a child.

Also, many of the studies used tachistoscopic devices for presenting words, which may produce methods of word recognition somewhat different from those used in ordinary reading.

The basic problem with which this study is concerned is the visual recognition of words by nonreaders and by beginning readers. When a child is confronted with a word he has never before seen and is asked to try to remember it, he must utilize one or several cues—something about the word which he stores in his memory. The purpose of this experiment is to discover which cues are used. The following questions will be asked: (*a*) What are the cues in a word by which nonreaders and beginning readers remember the word? (*b*) Are the same cues utilized in recognizing a long word and a short word? (*c*) Do nonreaders and beginning readers utilize the same cues? (*d*) Do boys and girls use the same cues?

METHOD

Task

A delayed-recognition task was constructed with three-letter and five-letter nonsense words (trigrams and quingrams). Each subject was shown a word on a card (the stimulus card) after which the card was withdrawn from sight. Then the subject was asked to pick out the word he had just seen, or the one most like it, from a group of words which were randomly arranged on a second card (the response card).

The words on the response card were designed to present a systematic series of errors which the subject might make. In other words, each of the word items on the response card contained one cue from the word on the stimulus card. The other cues from the stimulus-card word were either different or exactly the same as the stimulus-card word throughout all the items on the response-card words.

Two intermixed series of words were administered individually to each subject: one series contained trigrams, and the other contained quingrams.

In the trigram series four cues were systematically examined: shape of the word, the first letter, the second letter, and the third letter. *Shape* is here defined by whether the letters are below, above, or on the line. All of the letters were in lower case type. In the quingram series six cues were examined: each of the five letters and shape.

In the trigram series, for example, if the trigram cug was shown on the stimulus card, the items to choose from on the response card were: arp (same shape as cug, but all the letters are changed), che (same first letter as cug, but the second and third letters and the shape are changed), tuk (same second letter as cug, but the first and third letters and the shape are changed), and ILG (same third letter as CUG with all the other cues changed).

If the subject points to ARP on the response card, the assumption is made that the subject is recognizing shape primarily, since ARP is the only response item with the same shape as the original word, and no identical letter cues. Similarly, if the subject points to CHE, he is recognizing on the basis of the first letter.

In the above trial all the cues were varied on the response card, but in order to find out what occurs when the subject does not have the choice of recalling all the cues, but only some of them, certain cues were held the same as the stimulus word in the response word items. For example, if ONG appears on the stimulus card, and the choices ORP, ONT, and OLG are given on the response card, the first letter "o" is the same for all response choices and thus cannot serve as a differentiator among choices. In this case, ORP represents the same shape as the stimulus word, ONT has the same second letter, and OLG the same last letter.

Or, if WEJ is the stimulus word, and the second letter is to be held the same in the response words, the items NEG (same shape), WEL (same first letter), and LEJ (same last letter) were given on the response card.

The combinations of the four cues in the trigram series were varied systematically on the response cards so that each trial represented a different set of items from which the subject might choose. Every cue was presented in combination with every other cue, and each cue was held the same as the stimulus word an equal number of times. The task was constructed so that each subject had an equal opportunity to recognize on the basis of any of the four cues. Each trial

was doubled (i.e., an analogous cue choice with different letters was given in the task) so that reliability of choice could be estimated.

The same system was constructed for the quingrams, in which the combinations of the six cues were systematically varied in the response cards, and each subject had an equal opportunity to recognize words on the basis of any of the six cues an equal number of times. For example, on the trial on which VEJAT was the stimulus word, and the single cue of the first letter was held constant, the response choices and their implications were VOPUF (shape), VETEP (second letter), VHJUO (third letter), VUMAG (fourth letter), and VISHT (fifth letter).[2]

There were 16 doubled trials in the trigram series and 104 doubled trials for the longer words. Altogether, there were 120 items in the task. The trigram and quingram series were intermixed and presented to the subjects in random order. Also, the response choices were randomly arranged on the card. The words were typed on 4 × 6 inch white cards with a special typewriter so that a lower case letter which is "on" the line is one-quarter inch high. Each subject was individually tested.

Subjects

The subjects were 50 kindergarten children (25 boys and 25 girls) with a

---

[2] A 2-page and a 6-page table giving the design of the trigram and quingram tasks have been deposited with the American Documentation Institute. Order Document No. 8250 from ADI Auxiliary Publications Project, Photoduplication Service, Library of Congress, Washington, D.C. 20540. Remit in advance $1.25 for microfilm or $1.25 for photocopies and make checks payable to: Chief, Photoduplication Service, Library of Congress.

mean age of 5.16 years, and 50 first graders (25 boys and 25 girls) with a mean age of 6.54 years. These subjects were drawn at random from the Dryden Central School in Dryden, New York.

There is no instruction in reading or in the alphabet in the kindergarten. First graders were instructed by whole word and sentence methods. New words were generally introduced in sentence context with the first letter of the new word given as a clue. At the time of testing, the first graders had 5 months of this type of training.

TABLE 1.—Reliabilities in Percentage of Consistent Choices

SUBJECTS	%
Kindergarten (boys and girls)	54
First grade (boys and girls)	76
Boys (kindergarten and first grade)	65
Girls (kindergarten and first grade)	66
Trigrams (all subjects)	66
Quingrams (all subjects)	64

RESULTS

Reliability

Reliability was measured by the consistency of choice when the analogous cues were varied on different trials. Average reliabilities are presented in Table 1. The consistency of choice, in all cases, is substantially greater than chance, with the younger children being somewhat less consistent than the 6-year-olds.

Task Results

The number of times the subjects recognized words on the basis of each cue was counted and the totals are shown in Table 2. The first letter of

both the long- and short-word forms was the cue most utilized by both nonreaders and beginning readers in word recognition. The last letter in both word forms was the second most utilized cue for all subjects except the first-grade girls.

In order to test whether there was significant variation among the frequencies with which the various available cues were used, a Friedman two-way analysis of variance was calculated. The variation was significant ($p < .001$) both in the shorter and longer words for kindergarten boys and girls and first-grade boys and girls.

When we knew that the cues were differently used, the Cochran Q test was used to compare each cue with every other within the short and long series. The most informative comparisons are the strong cues with each other and the weak cues with each other, since comparisons between strong and weak cues yield obvious results.

In the comparison of the two strongest cues in the quingram series, the first and the last letters, the first letter was utilized significantly more times than the last in all groups except the kindergarten boys, for whom a great deal of competition between the first and last letters appears to exist in word recognition.

In comparing the two strongest cues in the trigram series (the first and third letters for all groups except the first-grade girls), no significant differences were found. This indicates strong competition between the first and last letters as recognition cues in a short word for all subjects except the first-grade girls.

TABLE 2.—Number of Choices on the Basis of Each Cue[a]

SUBJECTS	QUINGRAMS						TRIGRAMS			
	Shape	1st	2nd	3rd	4th	5th	Shape	1st	2nd	3rd
Kindergarten										
Boys	167	749	260	441	260	712	29	158	73	140
Girls	163	924	280	314	258	653	40	168	67	125
Total	330	1673	540	755	518	1365	09	020	140	265
First Grade										
Boys	47	1137	329	339	185	555	14	200	70	113
Girls	33	1360	428	300	102	375	6	251	76	63
Total	80	2497	757	693	287	930	20	451	146	176
Boys (combined)	214	1886	589	780	445	1267	43	358	143	253
Girls (combined)	196	2284	708	614	360	1028	46	419	93	188

[a]These frequency counts represent the total number of responses less the instances
when the subjects gave no response.

The least used cue in both the trigram and quingram series was shape. Shape was therefore compared with the weakest letter cue. In the comparison of shape with the fourth letter (weakest letter by all groups in the quingram series), the Cochran Q test showed significant differences for all groups except the kindergarten girls. In the trigram series the second letter was least used for all groups except first-grade girls, for whom the third letter was the weakest cue. The comparison of shape with the second letter in the trigrams indicated significant differences for each group. Shape was shown to be significantly weaker than the weakest letter cue for all groups in the trigram series, and for three of the four groups in the quingram series.

DISCUSSION

Although almost all subjects followed the pattern of using the first letter as the most salient and the last letter as second most important cue, there were some who did not follow this pattern. The kindergarten boys often based their judgment of similarity on the last letters of words using the first letter as the second cue. This may be because nonreading boys tend to scan in the opposite direction, i.e., from right to left in a word. Or perhaps they scan from left to right, but tend to remember the most recent cue, i.e., the last letter.

Many first-grade girls used the first letter as most salient, but the second letter as next in importance, and the third letter as third important, etc. These subjects were noted at the time of testing because they tended to say out loud the names of the letters in the original word, in order, from left to right. Then they would appear to search for the letters in that order on the response card. Often, when they had reached the end of the word, they had forgotten the last letters, especially in the quingram series.

Theories which propose that beginning readers recognize words as wholes by their shape have not been supported in this study. The shape of words, offered as a cue next to letter cues, was rejected in favor of letter cues by the subjects in this experiment. Rather, this study indicates that recognition is based on individual letters. Furthermore, the first letter in particular, and also the last letter of a word are the most salient cues used by subjects who are not very familiar with the alphabet.

An explanation of the "first-last" letter phenomenon may lie in the theory of primacy and/or recency of cues. Or, perhaps, the first and last letters of a word stand out in particular because they are isolated on one side by a white space, whereas middle letters are embedded in other letters.

The first-grade girls who recited the letters of the original word obviously show the effects of instruction in the alphabet. These subjects knew the names of the letters well enough to use them as verbal mediators in remembering the original words.

33 *Critical Listening—*
Permanency and Transfer of Gains
Made during an Experiment in
the Fifth and Sixth Grades

SARA W. LUNDSTEEN

Fifth- and sixth-grade children can learn to be more effective listeners. This follow-up study investigates the permanence and transfer of such learning to other in-school and out-of-school activities. The children who receive listening instruction one year later still score significantly higher on the experimental test.

Some studies have been made of general listening ability and critical listening ability (Pratt, 1953; Devine, 1961; Lundsteen, 1963). But the retention of gains made by groups receiving training is seldom investigated. Typically, if transfer or practical significance of such training is noted immediately after instruction, rarely is further investigation of continued transfer made after a lapse of time (Petrie, 1961). If we are to gain

Reprinted from the *California Journal of Educational Research*, 1965, **16**, 210–216, by permission of the author and the California Advisory Council on Educational Research.

assurance of the validity of findings in the field of listening comprehension, it appears necessary to include delayed posttests as a part of adequate experimental design.

In addition, if we are to attribute effectiveness to certain techniques and methods of teaching listening, careful analysis of possible confounding influences must be made. One such variable influencing critical listening ability may be the factor of personality or behavior preferences. This factor has received relatively little assessment in the field of listening (Kelly, 1963; Ross, 1964).

PURPOSE

Accordingly, after a year's lapse of time from the original study, the purposes of this investigation are the following:

(1) To gather data indicating the degree of permanency for gains made by an experimental group who received training in listening critically to verbal spoken materials.

(2) To gather data concerning the transfer or practical significance of training in critical listening to other in-school and out-of-school activities.

(3) To investigate the relationship of scores on a test of behavior preferences to scores on a measure of critical listening ability.

SUMMARY OF THE EARLIER STUDY

In a two group experiment ($N = 287$) in which the control group followed the usual English curriculum, a significant difference (.01 level) was found in favor of the experimental group exposed to nine weeks of lessons (45 minutes, twice weekly) in critical listening. These lessons, described elsewhere in detail (Lundsteen, 1964), dealt with (1) Detecting the Speaker's Purpose, (2) Analyzing and Judging Propaganda, and (3) Analyzing and Judging Arguments. Critical listening was defined as the process of examining ideas, comparing them with some consensual data, and acting or concluding upon the judgment made (Lundsteen, 1963). Factor analysis based on intercorrelations of 16 variables on a 79 item instrument, which was developed for the experiment, yielded four components of critical listening ability. Test-retest reliability for the instrument was .72. Obtained between tests of reading, general listening, thinking, and the experimental test, r's ranged from .26 to .64.

METHODOLOGY

Design

In diagram form, the design of the study follows:

	Pretest	Training	Posttest 1	Posttest 2 (same form as pretest)
Experimental classes (randomly assigned)	X	X	X (one year) interval)	X
Control classes	X	. . .	X	X

The major concern of this report is with the final posttest made after a year's lapse in time. The experimental group consisted of six subgroups or classes taught by the experimental method and the control group consisted of six subgroups or classes exposed to traditional methods of instruction. In addition to being judged as coming from populations that were normally distributed, these groups—experimental and control—were homogeneous in regard to means and variances on all measures used to describe the sample. These descriptions included grade level, sex, and performance on measures of intelligence, reading, thinking, and listening. In effect, the experimental group—comprised of boys, girls, fifth-grades and sixth-grades—and the control group—of like composition—were treated as a homogeneous whole rather than partitioned into blocks. Accordingly, the "t" test was used to test the significance of the difference between the performance of the control and experimental groups.

Sample

Since the population of students in this Texas city was from a relatively stable community, mainly middle to high socio-economic level, there was fortunately little attrition of the sample of 12 volunteer classes. The sample for the present study totaled 222 pupils, 110 of whom had been in the fifth-grade the year before, 112 of whom had been in the sixth-grade and were now in their first year of junior high school.

For the testing on personality variables, permission was secured for only a small sample (N = 30) of two

classes, 15 in each class, all girls. The present investigator had been the English teacher for both groups, one experimental, one control, during the previous year's experimentation. All other classes were self-contained and had been taught by different teachers.

Steps in the Retesting Procedure

During approximately the same month as the year before, the second posttesting was begun by the present investigator using the same taped test of critical listening as was administered the previous year.

Children in the experimental classes were asked to write anonymously describing ways, if any, in which they had used the lessons in critical listening in school or out of school during the past year.

Next, the *Behavior Preference Record*, Form A for grades four through six, by H. B. Wood, published by the California Test Bureau, was administered to the sample of 30 ex-fifth-grade pupils.

RESULTS AND CONCLUSIONS

1. *Maintenance of Superiority by the Group Having Specific Training*

Results from the "t" test between the means of the total experimental group and total control group showed the following: significantly higher scores were still maintained by the experimental group which had 18 lessons in critical listening a year earlier. Control (N = 107) M = 58.4, SD = 7.4; Experimental (N = 115) M = 60.7, SD = 8.1; required t at .05 level = 1.97, computed t = 2.21, p < .05.

Another way to obtain some assurance that the gains made by the experimental group were not of a fleeting nature was to look in a cross-sectional way at the development of critical listening ability. Because there was no significant difference (.01 level) between the mental ability scores of the original fifth-grade sample, experimental group, and the original sixth-grade sample, control group, it may be valid to compare the two groups as to sixth-grade level performance. Results indicate that the sixth-grade class (that had no specific training in critical listening) scored significantly lower than the present sixth-grade class. Control ex-sixth-grade (N = 72) M = 53.1, SD = 7.9; newly promoted experimental sixth-grade (N = 55) M = 58.7, SD = 8.9; required t at .01 level = 2.37, computed t = 3.73, p < .01.

It is interesting to note the progress made, however, by the control groups, ex-fifth-grade, who had no specific training in critical listening. A year earlier, these control groups had gained significantly from their average on original pretest scores. The practice and stimulating effects of merely taking the listening tests as well as the possibility of some inter-class leaking of information and interest, plus general maturation, may account in part for the gains (Lundsteen, 1963). Furthermore, a year later, without any specific training other than the possible haphazard emphasis late in the school year, the control pupils in the earlier grade continued to make significant gains (.01 level). After the original experiment, the control teachers were free to use any of the materials that the experimental teachers had used earlier. Posttest scores for control group (N = 137) M = 54.3, SD = 7.5; retest a year later for control group (N = 107) M = 58.3, SD = 7.37; required t at .01 = 2.34, computed t = 4.29, p < .01. (See Table I.)

TABLE 1.—First Posttest and Second Posttest Differences Comparison of Mean Differences between Fifth- and Sixth-Grades for Control Experimental, and Total Control and Experimental Groups on the First and Second Pottest One Year Apart

GRADE AND POSTTEST GROUP	CONTROL GROUP				EXPERIMENTAL GROUP			
	M	SD	N	t	M	SD	N	t
5th-grade test 1	50.2	7.9	68		57.6	9.8	66	
(ex) 5th test 2	56.2	6.9	55		58.7	8.9	55	
Difference	6.0			4.48*	1.1			.65
6th-grade test 1	58.4	7.0	69		62.8	7.0	74	
(ex) 6th test 2	60.7	7.2	52		62.5	6.9	60	
Difference	2.3			1.76	.3			.25
Total test 1	54.3	7.4	137		60.2		140	
Total test 2	58.4	7.4	107		60.7	8.1	115	
Difference	4.1			4.29*	.5			.49

*Required t at the .01 level is 2.36.

When treated as two different grade levels, this significant improvement was maintained only by the ex-fifth-grade control group (.01 level) and not by the ex-sixth-grade control group. Accordingly, some doubt may be cast upon explaining the control gains by maturation alone.

It should be remembered, however, that the control groups failed to come significantly close to the scores of the experimental group that had had systematic training.

Also it is interesting to note that although the experimental group that had specific training in critical listening continued to outdistance the control group, their superiority was a case of maintaining gains already made with no significant additional gains made after the first posttest. Whether or not attention was turned to the total experimental group or to the separate grade levels, there was no significant improvement of the second posttest scores.

Why did the experimental group fail to make further significant gains on the second posttest of critical listening ability? One reason may lie in the nature of the test used. The experimental group had already mastered a high percentage of the test. Almost all that remained was a relatively small percentage of the most difficult questions. Since the control group in the fifth-grade had the largest portion of the test left to master, this just may be the reason they made the largest gains. Thus a ceiling effect inherent in the test may have prevented measurement of additional progress on the part of the experimental group. Also on the one hand, since the experimental teachers may

have felt a need to cover other materials slighted during the nine weeks of lessons, they may have tended to neglect critical listening for the remainder of the year. The control teachers, on the other hand, possibly curious and eager to try out some of the new materials and ideas, were inclined to indulge in a little incidental teaching of critical listening. Thus the experimental group was measured on knowledge, attitudes and habits taught early in the previous school year, while the control group may have been measured on abilities developed more recently through some incidental exposure.

2. Grade Differences

On the year-later posttest, as on the first posttest, the higher grade was significantly superior in performance to the grade just below it, in both experimental and control groups (.01 level). Test norms generally indicate progressive increase from grade to grade.

Second posttest scores for control groups, ex-fifth-grade (N = 55) M = 56.2, SD = 6.9; ex-sixth-grade (N = 52) M = 60.7, SD = 7.2; required t at .01 = 2.36, computed t = 3.26, $p <$ .01.

Second posttest scores for experimental groups; ex-fifth-grade (N = 55) M = 58.7, SD = 8.9; ex-sixth-grade (N = 60) M = 62.5, SD = 6.9; required t at .01 = 2.36, computed t = 2.49, $p <$ .01.

3. Sex Differences

As was the case the year before, there was no significant difference on the second posttest between control boy and girl scores in either grade level. But, also as on the first posttest, the experimental girls in the earlier grade group continued to significantly surpass the boys, even a year later. Girls in experimental fifth- (now sixth-) grade group (N = 33) M = 61.1, SD = 8.24; boys (N = 22) M = 55.2, SD = 8.91; required t at .05 = 2.00, computed t = 2.50, p < .05.

4.   The Practical Significance of Transfer of the Lessons

The anonymous comments from the experimental pupils gave some interesting evidence of transfer from the lessons over the past year to other in-school and out-of-school activities. As was found in reports collected a year earlier, again the greatest number centered around social relations and communication especially with reference to mass media, to television. Ten reports out of the 107 collected dealt with happenings that had occurred during the summer. The content of the reports dealt with, for example, transfer to voting in school, to debating, to viewing television advertisements, to evaluating hearsay evidence about acquaintances, to recognizing and evaluating facts in content areas such as history, to concentrating upon, unraveling and evaluating the plot of a book, to avoiding daydreaming, and to resisting pressure to follow an undesirable group action.

5.   The Factor of Personality

All correlations between the test of critical listening and the total and part scores of the test of personality, *Behavior Preference Record*, were negligible (range: − .28 to .18) with the exception of the correlation with the scores on integrity (r = .50). Negligible correlations between the *Behavior Preference Record* and the critical listening test might be due to the existence of irrelevant constructs being measured by the former test.

IMPLICATIONS

Results from this study to ascertain the retention of skill in critical listening and the practical significance in terms of transfer of training to other in-school and out-of-school activity appear to favor instruction as practiced in this experiment.

Knowledge and Understanding

10

34 Inducing Children to Ask Questions in Solving Problems

STANLEY S. BLANK

MARTIN COVINGTON

Inducing sixth-grade pupils to ask meaningful questions facilitates their subsequent question-asking behavior, problem solving, and their participation in class discussion. The reading stresses the need for further research on the process of and inducement to asking questions, the place of such instruction in the curriculum, and the use of programmed instruction and other methods to facilitate question asking and problem solving.

A central part of all problem solving is the asking of questions. Questions may be directed at the obtaining of needed information, in cases where the information provided in the statement of the problem is insufficient for its solution. Questions may take the form of the testing of hypotheses, or of seeking clarification and specification of the problem in an effort to get ideas about its solution. Questions may be answered by outside sources of authority (e.g., teachers, books), or by observation and investigation; or questions may be simply reflective in nature, serving to stimulate ideas and further inquiry.

A basic handicap in problem solving suffered by many individuals is the failure to ask questions. This may result in premature and faulty inferences based on insufficient information, and in a paucity of solution ideas.

Reprinted from the *Journal of Educational Research*, 1965, **59**, 21–27, by permission of the authors and Dembar Educational Research Services, Inc.

Our observations of the problem-solving behavior of children in the typical school setting would seem to indicate a widespread deficiency in question asking. The deficiency may stem in part from the atmosphere of the large class which *inhibits* the individual child from freely asking many questions. It also may stem in part from a sheer lack of question-asking practice by the child, and training of the child in *how* to ask questions. That is, in part the deficiency may reflect the absence of a strong enough *set* or readiness to ask questions, and in part it may reflect the absence of an adequate *skill* in question asking.

In light of these critical deficiencies we undertook to develop and to test experimentally a method for inducing greater amounts of question asking by children in solving problems.[1] This procedure was limited to inducing children to ask for additional information when they were given problems with insufficient information for solution. Our primary objective was to see whether the sheer volume of question asking could be appreciably increased by such a method. Also, we were interested to see whether such an increased tendency to ask questions would *transfer* to criterion problems outside of the experimental program, and whether it would manifest itself in the child's general class performance.

Assuming that such positive effects could be obtained, we also wished to determine whether the increased question asking would take the form of relevant questions, that is, questions deemed appropriate to the solution of the problem, and whether children of *different basic ability levels* would benefit differently from such training.

An auto-instructional program was used to induce question asking by the school children. We chose this approach because we were interested to see whether we could succeed in facilitating question asking in an efficient and economical manner, permitting "individualized" instruction within the usual classroom setting. The auto-instructional method appears to us to have significant potential for this and other kinds of training of high-level intellectual skills, though not—to be sure—as used in the usual fashion for the mastery of subject-matter material.

EXPERIMENTAL DESIGN

Fifty-four sixth-grade pupils were studied. These children were enrolled in three summer session general science classes, all taught by the same teacher and all receiving the same kind of instruction on the same general science material.

The pupils, predominantly boys, were divided into three comparable groups of 18 children each. Experimental Group I was given the special auto-instructional program on question asking. It was administered to them during class time by the principal author in conjunction with the regular teacher. Experimental Group II was given an emasculated form of

[1]This study is one part of a current program of research on the facilitation of creative thinking in adults and children, directed by Dr. Richard S. Crutchfield and Dr. Martin V. Covington with the support of a grant from the Carnegie Corporation of New York.

the program. Group III was a control group which received no programmed material at all. All three groups were given question-asking criterion tests before and after the experimental period.

THE QUESTION-ASKING PROGRAM

The auto-instructional program was so designed as to guide the individual through a series of problem solutions in such a way as to demonstrate to him the value and necessity of asking questions in solving the problems and to elicit his own questions. Inasmuch as our aim was to induce a *generalized* question-asking tendency we did not choose to restrict the problems used in the program to any single content area. The problems thus consisted of thought problems having to do with a variety of topics—how to get an overloaded truck through a tunnel; how to travel most rapidly from one point to another; how to best make use of certain natural materials for crossing rivers; how to choose the best of various campsites according to certain criteria.

The program was primarily a branching type in order to offer the child a choice of questions he could ask and to provide feedback appropriate to the question asked. Both multiple choice and constructed responses were involved.

A problem representative of those in the program is:

Page 1

Suppose you are a truck driver. On your truck is a heavy load of big boxes. While driving along the highway you come to a tunnel. The top of the tunnel is 11 feet above the road, but the truck and load are 11 feet 2 inches high. Since it would take too long to unload the truck, drive through the tunnel, and then carry the boxes through and reload the truck, you have to think of another way to get through the tunnel.

You finally think of an idea. Your idea is to let some of the air out of the tires in order to lower the truck so it will go through the tunnel. Then you can drive on to the next town many miles away.

Do you think this idea will work, or do you think it won't work?

After you have thought about this, turn to page 2.

Page 2

Put a check mark in front of the answer you think is best and then turn to the page number given after the answer.

——a) I think the idea will work. (Turn to page 3.)

——b) I don't have enoungh infortion to decide whether or not the idea will work. (Turn to page 6.)

——c) I think the idea won't work. (Turn to page 5.)

Those children who chose alternatives a) or c) were shown reasons why there was not enough information to allow these choices and were instructed to choose again. The pupils who chose alternative b) were shown why this was the best choice and were allowed to proceed with the program.

At later stages in the program the pupil was actually required to formulate questions for himself, after which he saw examples of appropriate questions. For example, the child was given the following problem:

Let's pretend that you are advising a group of African people about things that they can produce and sell to other countries. These products must be made from things that can be found, or grown, in their country. Some ideas are: wool blankets and cotton shirts. Your problem is to decide whether or not the natives will be able to make these things.

Write down the questions you would ask before you decide on the answer. When you have done this, turn to the next page.

On the next page the children saw the following sequence of supplied questions:

Some good questions to ask might be:

1. Can they grow cotton in this part of Africa?
2. Do they raise sheep in this part of Africa?

On subsequent pages the children received feedback to their own constructed questions by means of maps of the country showing such things as the products presently grown, the topography, etc.

At the end of each problem, the children were asked what they had learned from working on the problem. The standard feedback given to the child's answer was: "The main point of this story is: it is a good idea to ask questions when you have a problem. In this way you can often get information which will help you solve the problem."

Altogether the program consisted of ten problems and a total of 233 pages. Some pages included drawings of the problem situation, such as maps. The material was presented in the form of printed booklets, in which the individual wrote his questions. The program was wholly self-administered. The total time allotted for the program was six and three-quarter hours, divided into nine sessions of 45 minutes each. Some children, of course, finished the program sections faster than did others. These children spent the remaining time reading library books available in the classroom.

The emasculated version of the program which was given to Experimental Group II was so designed as *not* to require the individual actively to formulate his own questions. Instead, each of the problems was first presented and the information needed for its solution was then given on subsequent pages, with the statement: "As you can see, certain kinds of information are needed before you can solve a problem like this one." A sample problem from this program is the truck item previously described, but with the crucial difference that instead of having an opportunity to ask questions, the children were merely shown the answer in the following form:

Answer: The idea will work because there is a gas station just beyond the tunnel where you can put the air back in the tires.

As you can see, certain kinds of

information are needed before you can solve a problem like this one.

Thus the Experimental Group II subjects given this emasculated program were exposed to the same set of problems and all the information necessary for solution, but they did not see examples of questions nor were they led to formulate their own questions on these problems. The purpose of this emasculated program was to control for whatever facilitative effect might accrue simply from exposure to the problems and their solutions.

Embedded in both the basic and emasculated programs were five test problems which were designed to evaluate the changes in amount of the individual's question asking as he progressed through the program. These problems were similar in content and format to the problems in the program, except that there was no feedback provided for the questions the children asked.

Both programs were tried out in several pilot studies before the final versions were constructed.

CRITERION MEASURES

Two of the criterion measures were designed to indicate question-asking tendency—an oral criterion test, and a written criterion test. A third criterion measure was performance on a science achievement test requiring problem solving. A fourth criterion measure was the teacher's rating of the child's participation in class discussions of the science material of the course.

Oral Criterion Test

This test was made up in two equivalent forms, one to be used as a pretest and the other as a posttest. Each form consisted of three problems presented with insufficient information for their solution. In order to arrive at a solution the child had to ask questions to get additional information. An example of one of the problems is:

> One day Mr. Jones was out on a hunting trip and got lost. After wandering around he came across a path. He started to follow it. The path led through such heavy bushes that Mr. Jones could see only a little way ahead. Suddenly the path ended at the edge of a small crater. Mr. Jones didn't see the crater and fell in. The walls of the crater were so sheer that he couldn't climb out. After looking around for a while he got an idea, and a few minutes later, he was on his way back to camp. How did Mr. Jones get out of the crater?
>
> You may ask any questions you like and I will try to answer them for you.

The criterion problems were administered to each child in an individual session with an interviewer. The child's responses were tape-recorded and protocols were taken from these tapes. The interviewers, all advanced graduate students in psychology, were trained to be as neutral as possible and to avoid either encouraging or discouraging question asking. The score on this oral criterion test was the total number of questions asked by the child over the three problems.

Written Criterion Test

A series of seven thought problems, containing too little information for their solution, constituted a paper-and-pencil criterion test. These problems were similar in style and content to the oral criterion problems and were presented to the pupils with the instructions that they could write down any questions they wished. However, feedback was *not* provided to these questions. This test was administered as a posttest following the training period. The score on the test was the total number of questions written down by the child over the seven problems.

Science Achievement Test

This written test was specially constructed by the teacher and the experimenters, and consisted of 25 problems. These problems did not directly deal with any of the science materials or concepts presented in the class. For example, a bar-graph of various metals plotted against melting points was presented. The children were asked to determine which of the metals would melt before iron would. The score on this test was the number of problems solved.[2]

Teacher Rating

A form was constructed by which the teacher rated each of the children on a five-point scale as to amount of participation in regular class discussions of the course material.

_____
[2]The coefficients of reliability for this test were 0.72 (Kuder-Richardson formula 21) and 0.86 (split-halves method corrected for length). These coefficients were computed on the data derived from the experimental study.

PROCEDURE

A group IQ test (California Test of Mental Maturity, short-form) was administered to all pupils in the three groups. Two days later, the five interviewers using standard instructions, administered one of the two sets of oral criterion problems to each child individually. Half of the children in each group were randomly assigned one of the sets of problems and half the other set. Two consecutive school days were allotted for this testing. The three groups were checked for comparability of mean IQ scores and mean number of questions asked on the oral criterion pretest; no significant differences were found between the groups in terms of these two variables. The experimental groups were then divided, on the basis of IQ scores, into top, middle and bottom thirds.[3] Five days following the pretests the pupils in Experimental Group I and Experimental Group II began their respective programs. The experimental period lasted for nine school days, 45 minutes per day. The control group was given no special materials, but rather spent this time in regular classwork.

On the tenth and eleventh school days the oral posttests were administered to each pupil individually. Each child was given those oral criterion items not presented to him in the pretest. The procedures used in the posttest were the same as those in the pretest.

Two days after the oral posttest, the written criterion and science achievement tests were administered. The teacher's ratings on all the pupils

_____
[3]The IQ ranges of the three groups were: 81–102, 103–116, 117–135.

in the three groups were obtained at the end of the school term, two weeks after the posttest.

RESULTS

The data indicate that in Experimental Group I there was a steady increase in the tendency to ask questions on the problems embedded throughout the instructional program. Since the Control group was not given the program, there is no opportunity for a control comparison of the performance on the embedded test problems. However, we can compare the performance of Experimental Group II with that of Experimental Group I on these problems. Figure 1 shows the mean number of questions asked on the five successive test problems embedded in the program for both Experimental groups. It is noteworthy that Experimental Group II shows no upward trend in the number of questions asked. Moreover, as the analysis of variance in Table 1 indicates, the differences between the two groups increase significantly as they proceed through the instructional program. In this analysis, the differences between the number of questions asked on test

problem 1 and test problem 5 were computed for both Experimental Groups I and II.

TABLE 1.—Analysis of the Differences between Experimental Groups I and II with Regard to Gains in Question Asking from Test Problem 1 to Test Problem 5

SOURCE	dF	MS	F
Between groups	1	83.72	34.06*
Within groups	34	2.46	

*$P < .01$

Far more important, however, are the data from the oral and the written criterion measures which demonstrate convincingly that the effect of the question-asking experience transfers to test materials outside the program itself. Table 2 shows the mean number of questions asked by the three groups on the oral pretest and posttest, and the mean gains. Note that the volume of question asking is low on the pretest and remains low on the posttest for Experimental Group II and Control Group, while it rises markedly for Experimental Group I.

TABLE 2.—Means and Standard Deviations for the Three Experimental Conditions on Oral Criterion Pre- and Posttests

	NUMBER OF QUESTIONS ASKED					
	Oral Pretest		Oral Posttest		Oral Gain Scores	
	Mean	SD	Mean	SD	Mean	SD
Treatment I	3.61	4.12	13.50	7.51	9.89	7.59
Treatment II	3.06	4.36	2.28	3.64	−0.78	3.61
Control	3.22	6.28	3.67	6.70	0.45	2.01

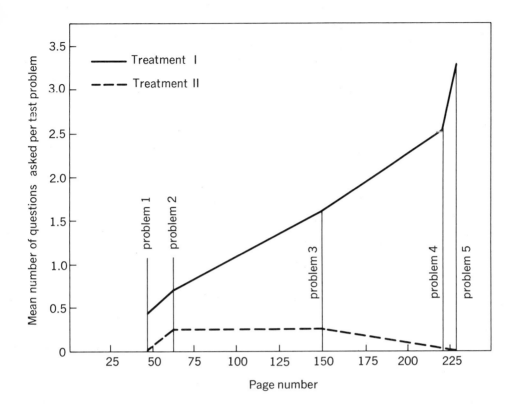

Fig. 1. Mean number of questions asked per problem on the five test problems
imbedded at different points in the programs.*

Analyses of variance for both the oral posttest and mean gain scores, summarized in Table 3, indicate that the effect of training was significant for number of questions asked. For both oral posttest and mean gain analyses, Experimental Group I significantly exceeds both Experimental Group II and the Control Group in number of questions asked (t's significant at the .05 level). The latter two groups do not differ significantly.

Similar results were found on the written posttest (see Tables 3 and 4).

Here again analysis of variance for the written posttest indicates the significant effect of the programmed instruction. And here again the number of questions asked by Experimental Group I exceeds the number asked by Experimental Group II and the Control Group (t's significant at the .05 level), while the latter two groups do not differ significantly.

---

*No test problem was given at the very beginning of the programs. However, since the two groups were equated for number of questions asked on the oral pretest, it may reasonably be assumed that they were comparable in their question-asking tendency at the beginning of the programs.

TABLE 3.—Analyses of Variance of Scores
on Oral and Written Posttests
and of Gain Scores

SOURCE	dF	MS	F
Oral Posttest			
IQ Level	2	14.57	0.32
Treatment	2	673.69	14.93*
IQ Level × Treatment	4	20.57	0.45
Within Groups	45	45.13	
Oral Gain Scores			
IQ Level	2	1.19	0.04
Treatment	2	613.41	22.46*
IQ Level × Treatment	4	4.74	0.17
Within Groups	45	27.31	
Written Posttest			
IQ Level	2	20.39	2.95
Treatment	2	176.39	25.51*
IQ Level × Treatment	4	17.03	2.46
Within Groups	45	6.91	

*$p < .01$

Inasmuch as the three experimental groups had been further subdivided into three ability groups (in terms of IQ test scores), it was possible to examine the relationship of ability level to question asking. Analyses of variance of the oral and written criterion measures (see Table 3) reveal that IQ level was not related significantly either to number of questions asked during posttest or to the facilitative effect of the training program (i.e., gain scores). The interaction was not significant for either the oral, the written or the gain score measures.

The data also provide some evidence that the Experimental I program not only induced a greater volume of question asking but also aided the children to solve problems more effectively in a separate test situation.

Table 5 shows the scores of the three groups on the science achievement test. A one-way analysis of variance reveals a significant effect of the programmed instruction on number of problems solved ($F = 4.44$, significant at the .05 level). As before, Experimental Group I is superior to Experimental Group II and the Control Group (t's significant at the .05 level), whereas the latter two groups do not differ significantly.

TABLE 4.—Means and Standard Deviations
for the Three Experimental Conditions
on the Written Criterion Test

	NUMBER OF QUESTIONS ASKED	
	Mean	*SD*
Treatment I	7.00	4.23
Treatment II	1.72	2.02
Control	1.44	1.65

Finally, it appears that there was even some discernible effect of the question-asking experiences on the readiness of the child to participate in regular class discussions of the material of the science course. A one-way analysis of variance of the teacher's ratings of discussion participation indicates a significant effect ($F = 4.31$, significant at the .05 level). Members of Experimental Group 1 participated to a significantly greater extent than did members of the other two groups (t's significant at the .05 level) whereas the latter two groups did not differ significantly.

It is important to note that the marked increase in question asking in Experimental Group I was not produced at the cost of a loss in relevancy

TABLE 5.—Means and Standard Deviations
for the Three Experimental Conditions
on the Science Achievement Test

	SCORE	
	Mean	SD
Treatment I	16.56	4.63
Treatment II	12.39	4.82
Control	13.61	4.57

of the questions asked. All questions asked by all three groups on the oral posttest were rated for relevancy to the problem.[4] To an overwhelming degree questions were rated relevant in all three groups: Experimental Group I (96%), Experimental Group II (93%), Control Group (88%).

DISCUSSION

Our findings indicate that question-asking behavior can be enhanced among children by means of an auto-instructional program. Suchman (1961) also has demonstrated that question asking can be augmented among school children by instructional procedures. However, in contrast to using standardized programmed instruction, Suchman employed a free teacher-class discussion method in which children were asked to discover the principles involved in simple physics experiments by asking the teacher questions. Evaluation of this instruction was based on the number of questions the child asked and on

---

[4]The questions were rated irrelevant by the raters if they were either redundant with respect to information already provided, or if the information sought had nothing to do with the solution of the problem. The rating was done independently by five raters, with high agreement resulting.

his ability to discover the principles involved in several additional but similar physics experiments. These test problems were administered under conditions similar to those used in Suchman's instructional procedure.

We were interested not only in developing a standard, specifiable instructional method, but also in determining if a question-asking set established by such a method would generalize to test problems presented under different conditions from those used during instruction. The fact that the treatment group exceeded both of the control groups in terms of the number of questions asked on the oral criterion tasks indicates that a question-asking set can transfer to problems presented under conditions which differ from those of the instructional procedure. Another finding is also germane with respect to the transfer effects of the question-asking set. The children in the treatment group increased their participation in class discussion as indicated by the superior ratings these pupils received from the class teacher; it seems a reasonable inference that increased participation in discussion reflects a greater readiness, on the part of the child, to ask questions.

The superior performance of the treatment group on the science achievement test, which was scored for number of correct answers rather than for number of questions asked, indicates that inducing question asking does more than just establish a general question-asking set. It appears to facilitate actual problem solving even though the content and type of problem in the achievement test (e.g., interpreting graphs) differed from that of the treatment program.

It was possible that inducing a question-asking set might result in a large number of irrelevant questions being asked. Such was not the case. Of course, it is possible that the test problems used in the present study may have been too easy to elicit numerous irrelevant questions. It was not feasible in this study to consider the quality of the relevant questions asked. How this variable might be affected by programmed instruction will be a concern in our future research.

The results reveal no relationship between ability level and gains in number of questions asked. Our *a priori* assumption in this regard was that, if anything, there would be a positive relationship. This assumption may in fact actually be correct and the failure to confirm it may be due to certain characteristics of the criterion tests, that is, the criterion problems may not have been challenging enough to induce the abler children to exhibit superior performance. Thus, it is possible that the relationship of gain scores and ability level may depend, in part, on the characteristics (e.g., difficulty level and complexity) of the criterion materials employed by the experimenter.

While the lack of relationship found between ability level and gain scores is consistent with findings of other studies (Stolurow, 1961), there is some indication (Lambert, Miller, and Wiley, 1962) that small sample sizes may conceal a positive relationship between ability level and gain scores. Further research is necessary in this regard.   •

The low incidence in children's question asking may be due, in part, to the absence of a strong enough set or readiness to ask questions and, in part, to the absence of an adequate skill in question asking. The design of the present study was not intended to differentiate between these two factors. However, in light of the brevity of the program, and hence the relatively short opportunity for skill training to occur, our assumption is that an arousal of set most likely accounts for the observed superiority in question asking on the part of the Treatment I group.

There may also be a motivational effect at work here; that is, the program I experiences may have increased the level of problem-solving motivation of the children in this group. This would be reflected in their superior question-asking behavior. It would be difficult to disentangle any such motivational effects from effects of set or skill. This difficulty of disentangling the effects of motivation and set or skill is a problem common in evaluation of all instructional programs.

The general question-asking activity found in problem solving is more complex and serves more functions than just the information-gathering aspects considered in this study. It appears that question asking also involves hypothesis testing and idea seeking as well as information gathering. In addition to these direct functions of question asking, it is possible that inquiry may also serve indirectly to increase the likelihood of problem solution by increasing the time spent by the subject on the problem.

Only further research will clarify these multiple and interacting functions of question asking in the problem solving context. In this regard we believe that there is a need for research instruments which will provide replicable and specifiable experimental conditions. For this reason we have developed the present question-asking program. Although this instrument is, at present, relatively crude, it is undergoing revision for further use.

The findings of the present study point to the need for further research regarding: a) the process and inducing of question asking; b) the place of such instruction in the curriculum; and c) the use of programmed instruction, or other methods, to facilitate such processes as question asking and problem solving.

35   *The Effect of a Program of Guided Learning Experiences in Developing Probability Concepts at the Third Grade Level*[1]

RALPH H. OJEMANN

E. JAMES MAXEY

BILL C. SNIDER

Can a program of guided learning experiences be formulated to develop the concept of probability? In this study third-grade children learn to relate their predictions to the probable outcome when information is available, and tend to wait before making a prediction when only a small amount of information is available and more should be supplied. There is no significant difference between experimental and control groups regarding the gathering of more information to "maximize success," however, "the experimental group was beginning to show a tendency to 'maximize their successes' in the latter three blocks of predictions."

[1]This paper is part of a series designed to investigate segments of an on-going learning program in behavioral science. Appreciation is expressed to the Grant Foundation for their support of this investigation.

In the development of a scientific-causal orientation by a child toward his environment—both physical and social—the ability to think in probability terms plays a significant part.

Reprinted from the *Journal of Experimental Education*, 1965, **33**, 321–330, by permission of the senior author and Dembar Educational Research Services, Inc.

In any complex phenomenon, such as an instance of human behavior, the factors which underlie and produce the behavior are manifold. Furthermore, information about these factors, as is the case with all empirical knowledge of the social and physical world, is characterized by greater or lesser unreliability and this characteristic has to be recognized when using knowledge to estimate the probable way in which the behavior developed or what its effects may be.

When a child is confronted with an instance of behavior, such as when his teacher does something and he has to respond to it, a logical reaction would require him to think of some of the probable reasons for the teacher's action instead of making a snap judgment about it. There is some evidence that children's understanding and appreciation of the dynamics of behavior can be extended through a learning program in behavioral science and that such experiences help them in their daily interactions (Muuss, 1960; Ojemann, 1958; Ojemann, et al., 1955).

In developing an understanding of behavior, however, the concept of probability constitutes an important item. To increase the effectiveness of such programs, it appears helpful to investigate further how the ability to *think in probability terms* can be developed most effectively. The purpose of this study was to devise a program of guided experiences for helping a child learn the elementary aspects of probability and to test the effectiveness of this program at the third-grade level.

In recent years a number of investigators have been interested in probability concepts of children.[2] Most of these have been concerned with the effects of extrinsic rewards on reactions at various input levels.[3] The investigation by Stevenson and Zigler (1958) compared behavior of children coming from two types of environments which differed in the degree of success the children had learned to expect.

The present investigation differs from these in that it is interested in testing the effects of a consciously planned sequence of guided experiences derived from an analysis of the nature of the learning task and of the learners, as will be described later.

DEVELOPMENT OF LEARNING PROGRAM

The development of a program of guided experiences logically requires a theory of planned learning programs (Ojemann and Pritchett, 1963)—a theoretical conception, that is, as to what goes on in the central processes when a sequence of stimuli is applied and how the use of this sequence brings about the development of the concept.

The theoretical considerations used in designing the learning program for this investigation were as follows:

---

[2]Brody, 1963; Craig and Meyers, 1963; Das, 1962; Gratch, 1959; Gruen and Weir, 1964; Jones and Liverant, 1960; Messick and Solly, 1963; Siegel and Andrews, 1962; Stevenson and Weir, 1959, 1963; Stevenson and Zigler, 1958; Yost and Siegel, 1962.

[3]Craig and Meyers, 1963; Jones and Liverant, 1960; Messick and Solly, 1963; Siegel and Andrews, 1962; Stevenson and Weir, 1959; Yost and Siegel, 1962.

When a child is confronted with a situation in which he has to make a choice or decision, the problem is one of selecting the response that has the best chance of producing the result he desires. He thus has to make an estimate or a prediction. If the information he has is in some way incomplete, the logical procedure is to put the prediction in probability terms.

To make a decision in probability terms, the subject has to abstract "completeness of information available" from other aspects of the situation, such as the size, shape, color of the objects with which he is dealing; the appearance of the people involved in the situation; the particular place where the event takes place; what others are doing, and so on. When the request is made to "choose one" or "make a guess," these stimuli should arouse the responses, "What information about this do I have or can I get?"

When a child is placed initially in a situation in which he has to make a decision, a variety of responses may be aroused depending on previous interaction of organism and environment. The responses may be related to various aspects of the situation—the people involved, the nature of the objects, if any, that he must manipulate, the familiarity or strangeness of the situation.

The problem in designing the sequence of experiences is one of using stimuli to intensify the responses represented by "What information do I have?" so that when the child is asked to "make a guess," or "pick one," there will arise the responses represented by "What do I know that will help me?" and responses to other aspects of the situation will be minimized.

MEANING OF INFORMATION AVAILABLE

The concept "information available" includes several items. It includes information about what factors are operating that affect the outcome and what the state of each factor may be. There may be information in the instructions which set the task, there may be information the subject may have gleaned from past experience, and there may be information which can be obtained in subsequent experiences before the opportunity to make a choice has passed. Also, the information may be in a relatively simple form, such as, when the subject is informed that there are two red marbles and six green marbles in the box, or it may be in the form of means and variances, as in the case of date of last killing frost, amount of rainfall, size (tolerances) of a machined casting, and the like.

Furthermore, there may be only one or two factors to consider or there may be many, and the prediction may be for the immediate present or the distant future.

If a child is making a prediction for the immediate present, knowledge of what factors are operating, their present state and how to estimate the resultant are involved.

If a child is making a prediction for some time in the future, the knowledge of the modifiability of each factor is involved, as well as an estimate as to what the chances are that significant modifications will take place in the interval between the present and the future time for which the prediction is made.

An example of the importance of considering the modifiableness of factors when making predictions for some future time is furnished by the predictions relative to population growth made a generation ago in the United States. During the 1930's widespread predictions were made that the population in the United States would remain at a relatively stationary level. Some investigators in the modifiability of attitude toward children at that time, however, pointed out that "the attitudes toward children may change" (Ojemann, 1936) and subsequent developments have indicated the importance of considering the modifiableness of factors.

VARIATIONS
IN SITUATIONS

It thus appears there are several different kinds of situations involving probability thinking. For example, in a situation in which one is called upon to predict what color marble will be drawn from a box, the factors affecting the situation involve primarily the proportion of the respective colors and the care exercised to insure that the selection is random.

However, in a situation in which one is to predict the time of arrival of a plane or train, the number of factors about which information is needed increases. There is the scheduled time, the nature of the weather along the route, the attitude of the persons operating the plane, and so on. "Information available" consists in assessing the "resultant" of the influence of the several factors.

There are situations in which the information available is rather incomplete at the beginning of the task but more information can be gathered as one continues with the activity. The gambler who studies the roulette wheel to determine its bias and then uses this knowledge in placing his bets is a case in point.

In devising a learning program, it appears helpful to recognize the different types of situations in which probability thinking is involved. The discussion above has identified four different dimensions in terms of which situations may vary; namely, number of factors operating to affect result, adequacy of information available, possibilities of gathering more information, and interval elapsing before prediction is applied. Since in the present study the learning program was to be used with third-grade children, it was restricted to three types of situations; namely:

Type A—Situations in which the number of factors influencing the relationship significantly are few in number and the information is available in simple form.

Type B—Situations in which a number of significant factors have to be considered and the resultant of their influences is to be estimated.

Type C—Situations in which little or no information about the significant factors is available but there are some opportunities to make tentative predictions and to observe the results, thus gathering additional information as one proceeds.

In the simplest type of situation, Type A, it appears that two kinds of information are involved. These can best be illustrated by an example. When the subject is confronted with a bag of marbles containing a higher proportion of one color as compared with another and the subject is asked to predict which color will be drawn, he has to consider the information that there is "more of one color than another" and that "when there is more of one color than another, the chances of drawing the former are greater." The latter item may seem so self-evident to the mature reader that he may consider it superfluous. When planning a learning program at the child's level, however, it seems helpful to recognize this.

Thus, in the sequence of experiences in the learning program to be described later, one section appears in which a demonstration is provided to develop the idea that when drawings are made from equally available alternatives, each alternative tends to appear an equal number of times; and when drawings are made from disproportionately available alternatives, the outcome reflects the disproportion.

Situations of Type B involve information as to what factors are involved, information as to the status of each factor and the process of combining the information into a resultant (estimate). The example of the prediction of the arrival of a plane or train cited earlier is a case in point.

In Type C there is the added ability to recognize an opportunity to gain more information when such an opportunity appears and to make use of it.

In developing the learning program with third-grade children, it was assumed that situations of Types A and B and some very simple situations of Type C could be included in the sequence of experiences.

The problem of designing the learn-ing experiences was conceived as one involving the selection of a sequence of stimuli which would tend to produce in the response to a situation calling for a choice, a change from "many diverse responses" (depending on past interaction of organism and environment) to primarily the responses, "What information do I have or can I get that will help?"

In addition to external stimuli, it was recognized that internal stimuli are also operative. The reactions to external stimuli will thus vary somewhat from child to child depending on what internal stimuli are operating at the same time. Interference with learning may occur if strong internal conflicts (feelings of anxiety, inadequacy, or the like) are present, or if the child feels he is devoting his time to something that he does not consider worthwhile. Such emotional reactions may interfere with the arousal of the responses, "What information do I have or can I get?"

In designing the learning program, the first step consisted of raising such questions as the following: Can we be sure the sun will shine tomorrow? What will tomorrow's temperature be? Who will be absent tomorrow? Who will get all the problems right on tomorrow's arithmetic assignment? The purpose was to see where the subjects were in their attitudes towards prediction and in their understanding of such words as *chance, risk, best guess, predict.*

The learning program continued with experiences (selected stimuli) to develop the following abstractions:

a) When a random selection is made from a group of equally available alternatives, each alternative has an equal chance of being chosen. The specific experiences for developing this will be described later.

b) When there are more of one item than another, the former has the greater chance of being selected. This aspect was developed by using a variety of items in several different kinds of situations (different colored marbles, coins of different denominations and number in different hands) so that the information as to relative proportions could be "cut loose" from other characteristics of the objects or situations.

c) More information about how something works often helps. This means information about what factors are operating as well as how each works. If there are several factors, their effect has to be combined.

d) Sometimes it is possible to gather more information as one works with a situation.

As will be seen in the detailed description of the learning program, it was possible in the time available to provide only a very limited experience for developing aspect d. Major attention was given to aspects a to c inclusive.

THE LEARNING PROGRAM

The first session began with a discussion of different types of situations that occur in everyday life in which one has to "make a best guess" or "make a prediction." The children were asked whether they could be sure:

a) that the sun would shine tomorrow.
b) what the temperature would be tomorrow.
c) who will be absent tomorrow.

d) who will get all the problems right on tomorrow's arithmetic assignment.
e) who their teacher will be next year.
f) when it will next snow.
g) what the arrival time of a bus would be.

The seven illustrations appeared to be sufficient to enlist the interest of the subjects; and when it was pointed out that perhaps something could be learned about making better "guesses," the subjects agreed to try.

Then, the meanings of the terms *chance, risk, predict, best guess,* and *maximum* were discussed. The words "chance" and "predict' were familiar to practically all of the class and from this base the meanings of the other terms were introduced.

A bag of six ping-pong balls, numbered one through six, was passed around with each student selecting a ball from the bag, observing its number and then replacing the ball in the bag. The number was recorded on the blackboard. The class was able to generalize from the results that each ball had the same chance of being selected.

E placed five nickles and two pennies in one hand and three nickels and four pennies in the other hand. He asked the question, "Which hand would you choose so that without looking you would have the 'best chance' of getting a nickle?" This situation was varied using different hands as well as different coins (dimes, quarters). The proportion of dimes and quarters were two to one, three to two, even, and two to three. A similar procedure was followed with nickles and dimes. The class formulated the generalization that the best chance occurs when the number of chances of selecting the specified coin is increased.

Six marbles were placed in a bag and the color divisions of the marbles varied (i. e., six yellow; four yellow and two orange; three yellow and three orange; four orange and two yellow; six orange). In each case the pupils were asked to indicate the color that had the best chance of being selected. A drawing was made and discussed. Discussion followed the series to verbalize the idea that as the number of a particular colored marble changes, the chance of that color being selected also changes.

This completed the first 30 minute period.

On the second day the ideas developed the first day were verbally reviewed. The possibility of gathering more information was then introduced. Each subject was supplied with a sheet giving the dates of last "28 degree-low-temperature" day in their locality during the spring of the last 17 years. The data were discussed to insure that each subject was aware of their meaning and to bring out the variability. Then a list of days of last 28 degree temperature for a 36-year period was presented with the date for two years missing. Each pupil was asked to make an estimate of the best guess for the year for which the data were missing. The estimates were compared with the actual data. This was followed by a discussion of the question: "How could we have made a better guess?"

For the next exercise, a bag of eleven checkers was introduced (seven orange and four yellow). The children knew that two colors were represented but did not know the proportions. One checker was drawn and the question was asked, "Are there more orange than yellow in the bag?" The guesses were recorded. Several more drawings were made, replacing the checker each time. The class noted that more "orange ones" than yellow were drawn and they reasoned the best guess was "more orange."

On the third day an additional variable was introduced into the "colored marbles in a bag" situation. Six yellow marbles were thoroughly mixed with three cups of sand. A cupful of the mixture was drawn, and the subjects were asked to estimate how many marbles would be left in the mixture. The mixture was run through a sieve and the marbles counted.

This procedure was repeated five times, each time with different proportions of orange and yellow marbles. Each time the subjects recorded their estimates and each result was discussed.

The procedure was repeated using "copper" and "steel" pennies.

The results were generalized into, "It is harder to guess right when we have to work with more things."

On the fourth day the children were divided into six groups. Each group was supplied with a pair of dice which they "rolled" 36 times, recording the total points obtained in each throw. The object was to determine the point total occurring with highest frequency. Each group reported the observed frequencies. As each group reported, E asked the class what point total they would predict would have the highest frequency when the data from all groups were put together. After all groups had reported E summed the data as the class watched. The highest observed frequency was obtained for the total point of seven. This occurred 29 times. The class verbalized the idea that as more information becomes available, a better guess can be made.

On the fifth day the experiences of the four previous sessions were summarized by E. Then the following demonstrations were conducted.

Three boxes containing two white, one black, and two black marbles respectively, were presented and the class was asked:

a) With which box can we always be sure of selecting a white marble?
b) With which box do we have an equal chance of getting a white and black marble?

The number in the three boxes was then increased to four white, two white and two black, three white and one black. The group was asked, "What do you expect to draw from each box?" The subjects made 20 drawings from each box; the results were tabulated and compared with their predictions.

Finally three opaque boxes with two white and two black; three white and one black; and four black respectively were presented. The group was told that there are four marbles in each box, but that the number of each color varied. They made 50 drawings from each box, each time predicting what color would be drawn. Both predictions and color drawn were tabulated and the question discussed for each box was, "How could we 'be right' most often?"

PROCEDURE

The subjects were two third-grade classes in an elementary school in a midwest community having a population of approximately 30,000. The school was located in a section of the community consisting of slightly above middle-class families. There were 48 pupils in the two classes. Complete data were obtained from 41 subjects—20 in the experimental group and 21 in the control group. Incompleteness of data was the result of absences during the testing and learning periods.

Arrangements were made with the classroom teachers of the experimental group to have E administer the learning program using 30 minutes a day for five successive days. E also visited the class serving as control and indicated to the subjects that they were being used in an experimental study.

For the final testing four tests were used. Tests one and three were administered by E, and Tests two and four by a person unknown to both groups. The final tests were administered the week following the conclusion of the learning program. Each test was given on a separate day.

1. The first post-test consisted of a series of 25 questions. In each question a situation involving two groups of colored objects was described and the subjects were asked, "If I reach into the bag and pull out one of the objects, what color do you think I would get?" Objects different from those used in the learning program were named in the question; such as, blocks, crayons, washers, bolts and "things." As indicated below, a variety of colors was used. The questions were presented orally. The subjects made their responses on a convenient answer sheet, which was provided.

The following proportions of colors were used. A reference was scored correct if the subject chose the higher proportion; or in those cases in which equal proportions were used, such a response as "can't tell" or "not sure" was the correct response. The total possible score was 25. The proportions of colors used in the questions were as follows:

1. 4 red
   3 green
2. 6 black
   6 white
3. 5 orange
   5 green
4. 4 black
   8 white
5. 6 green
   3 black
6. 4 orange
   5 green
7. 5 white
   5 black
8. 6 white
   4 black
9. 4 orange
   4 green
10. 12 white
    11 green
11. 14 orange
    9 red
12. 4 green
    3 orange
13. 3 black
    5 white
14. 7 black
    4 white
15. 7 black
    7 white
16. 5 orange
    4 green
17. 4 orange
    4 green
18. 8 black
    7 white
19. 10 black
    12 white
20. 3 orange
    4 green
21. 2 orange
    4 green
22. 4 red
    6 white
23. 3 red
    2 white
24. 1 red
    2 white
25. 1 red
    1 white

This test yielded a reliability coefficient (KR-formula 21) of .85 using all experimental and control subjects.

2. The second test consisted of two parts with 12 questions in each part. In the first part prior to each question, the subject was presented with a deck of 3 by 5 inch cards. Some cards had a circle drawn on them; some a square. The subject was told the proportions of circles and squares in a given deck. The deck was shuffled, and the subject asked to predict the geometrical shape on the top card. The responses were scored as in the first test. The 12 decks were constituted as follows:

1. 5 squares
   4 circles
2. 3 squares
   5 circles
3. 2 circles
   3 squares
4. 8 circles
   7 squares
5. 7 circles
   5 squares
6. 4 circles
   4 squares
7. 6 squares
   3 circles
8. 4 circles
   3 squares
9. 6 squares
   5 circles
10. 8 circles
    5 squares
11. 3 circles
    3 squares
12. 4 squares
    2 circles

On the second part of this test the same 12 decks were presented. The top card was drawn by the experimenter and shown to the subjects. He was then asked to predict the shape on the next card. In decks one, three, four, eight, and nine the top card was so arranged that the split was even on the remaining cards, so that the correct response would be "can't tell" or "not sure."

The total possible score for parts one and two combined was 24. A reliability coefficient (KR-formula 21) of .72 was obtained for this test using the total experimental and control subjects.

3. The third test was the "Decision Location" test used by Levitt (1953) and by Muuss (1960). The test procedure consisted in presenting a series of 15 slides, beginning with a slide that presented but a small segment of an object, and continuing with each successive slide adding something so that the object was practically com-

plete on the final slide. The subject was asked what he thought the object was or to indicate "don't know." Two types of scores were obtained from this test. Score Number 1 for each subtest was the number of guesses other than "don't know" prior to the point of correct perception of the object. Score Number 2 indicated the slide number at which the "earliest guess" other than "don't know" occurred.

4. In the fourth post-test an opaque box containing nine white washers and three black washers was presented. The subjects were told that there were white and black washers in the box, but nothing was said about the proportion of each. The subjects were asked to predict (indicating their choice on an appropriate answer sheet) the color that would be drawn in eight blocks of 12 predictions each. Each time a drawing was made the washer was replaced before the next drawing was attempted.

RESULTS

Table 1 compares the experimental and control groups as to initial mea-sures. An examination of the data in the table indicates that the two groups did not differ significantly in verbal IQ as measured by the Lorge-Thorndike test nor did they differ significantly on the composite scores of the Iowa Test of Basic Skills or the arithmetic section of this battery. There is a slight edge in favor of the control group on all tests, but the differences are not significant.

The comparisons of the E and C groups on the first two final measures are presented in Table 2. On the first test—predicting the color drawn when information as to proportion is available—the differences between E and C groups was significant well beyond the one percent level of confidence. It will be recalled that in this test, reference was made to a variety of objects not used in the learning program, and a wider variety of colors was included.

In the second test—predicting geometrical forms—the differences between the E and C groups are significant at the one percent level. This test employed geometrical forms. No geometrical forms were included in the learning program.

TABLE 1.—Comparison of Experimental and Control Classes on Initial Measures

	GROUP						
	Experimental (N = 20)		*Control* (N = 21)				
Measure	*M*	*SD*	*M*	*SD*	*Diff.*	*t*	*sig.*
Verbal IQ (Lorge-Thorndike)	117.20	10.14	121.05	13.38	3.85	.994	ns
Arithmetic ITBS	34.80	5.39	36.5	6.59	1.7	.880	ns
Composite ITBS	37.55	6.40	39.33	8.20	1.78	.754	ns

**TABLE 2.—Comparison of Experimental and Control Classes
on First Two Final Measures**

| | GROUP | | | | | | |
| | Experimental (N = 20) | | Control (N = 21) | | | | |
Measure	M	SD	M	SD	Diff.	t	sig.
Predicting color of object drawn when information is available	22.35	2.39	15.38	4.08	6.97	6.46	p < .01
Predicting forms drawn when information is different on two draws	18.05	2.29	14.00	4.53	4.05	3.49	1 < .01

**TABLE 3.—Comprison of Experimental and Control Classes on Mean Number
of Guesses Other Than "Don't Know" Prior to Point of Correct
Perception (Decision Location Test)**

| | GROUP | | | | | | |
| | Experimental (N = 20) | | Control (N = 21) | | | | |
Measure	M	SD	M	SD	Diff.	t	sig.
1. car	3.8	3.97	9.3	4.32	5.5	4.17	p < .01
2. shoe	4.0	4.16	8.48	4.05	4.48	3.40	p < .01
3. kitten	3.95	3.71	9.00	3.78	5.05	4.21	p < .01
4. figure 5	3.25	3.56	7.90	5.11	4.65	3.29	p < .01

The results for the Decision Location Test are given in Table 3 and 4. Table 3 provides the data as to the mean number of guesses other than "don't know" prior to the correct perception. It was hypothesized that the number of incorrect guesses made prior to consistent correct perception would be lower for the experimental group. An examination of the data in Table 3 indicates a significant difference between experimental and control groups on all four series of slides. In other words, the experimental subjects waited for more information than did the control subjects before making a definite closure.

Table 4 provides data as to the slide number on which "earliest guess" other than "don't know" occurred. The data indicate a significant difference between experimental and control groups on three of the four series. These results provide further evidence

TABLE 4.—Comparison of Experimental and Control Classes on Slide Number
at Which "Earliest Guess" Other Than "Don't Know" Occurs
(Decision Location Test)

| | GROUP | | | | | | |
| | Experimental (N = 20) | | Control (N = 21) | | | | |
Measure	M	SD	M	SD	Diff.	t	sig.
1. car	6.90	5.35	2.14	2.34	4.76	4.17	p < .01
2. shoe	5.90	4.47	2.38	2.38	3.52	3.09	p < .01
3. kitten	5.05	4.30	2.09	2.78	2.96	2.56	p < .05
4. figure 5	6.10	5.07	3.57	4.20	2.53	1.70	ns

to support the hypothesis of the tendency to gather more information before a definite closure is made.

In analyzing the results of the final test, the first four blocks of predictions were considered as an opportunity for the subjects to gather information as to the probable proportions of washers in the box. One would not expect a difference to appear between the E and C groups until the subjects had had an opportunity to gather some information that would be of assistance in making a prediction. Accordingly, the results for the first and last four blocks of predictions are presented separately in Table 5. As indicated in the last row in Table 5, the difference between the two groups on the last four blocks of predictions was not significant. The experimental subjects did not show in this test a significant tendency to use the information as it became available. However, an analysis of the graphic representation of the results proved interesting. The data are shown graphically in Figure 1. An examination of this figure shows that as the test progressed, the E group began to "draw away from" the

TABLE 5.—Comparison of Experimental and Control Groups on Predicting
Input Level When Input Information is Unavailable

| | GROUP | | | | | | |
| | Experimental (N = 20) | | Control (N = 21) | | | | |
Measure	M	SD	M	SD	Diff.	t	sig.
Trial Blocks 1–4	28.65	4.74	27.00	6.10	1.65	.94	ns
Trial Blocks 5–8	33.85	5.18	31.52	6.21	2.33	1.27	ns

C group, but this tendency was not sufficient to produce a significant difference. The experimental group did not begin to depart from the control group until the sixth block of predictions. Thus, the results suggest that the E group was beginning to acquire some tendency to "maximize its successes," but it took information acquired in more than four blocks of predictions before they were able to do so. It appears fruitful to consider what effect a strengthening of the learning program would have on this test. It will be recalled in the description of the program that in the time allotted, it was possible to provide only one series of demonstrations for developing this aspect of the concept relating to "maximizing successes." It is planned to develop a more extended learning program in future studies to investigate this aspect further.

DISCUSSION

The several tests taken together indicate that the experimental subjects were acquiring considerable ability to relate their "predictions" to the information available. They showed a significantly greater ability to relate their predictions to the probable outcome when information was available,

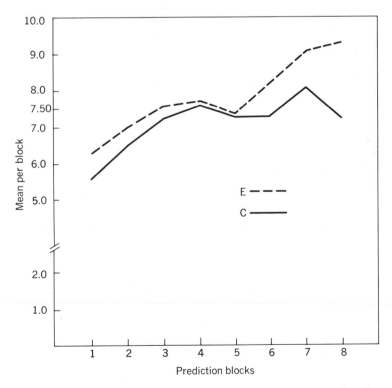

Fig 1. Scores of E and C groups on predicting input level.

and they tended to wait before making a prediction when only a small amount of information was available and more would be supplied.

The task of gathering more information for themselves from a series of attempts so as to "maximize their successes" proved a more difficult task. In making this statement, however, it must be recognized that in the time available it was possible to devote only a small part of the learning program to the development of this aspect of the probability concept. It will be interesting to see what results more extensive learning experiences can produce.

SUMMARY

A program of guided learning experiences was devised for developing several aspects of the concept of probability. In constructing the program, use was made of an analysis of the psychological nature of the learning task and of the nature of the learners. The program was administered to equated experimental ($N = 20$) and control ($N = 21$) classes at the third-grade level. Four tests were used to measure the effect of the program.

The results indicated significant differences between the experimental and control groups as to

1. predictions regarding color of objects drawn when information was available regarding the proportion present of each.
2. predictions relative to geometrical forms drawn from decks of cards when the proportion of forms present was changed from one draw to the other.
3. scores on the Decision Location Test that indicated that the experimental subjects tended to gather more information before making a prediction than did the control subjects.

The fourth test was a test of "maximize successes" on a fixed input two-choice probability situation. No significant differences between E and C groups were found but a graphic analysis of the blocks of prediction suggested that the experimental group was beginning to show a tendency to "maximize their successes" in the latter three blocks of predictions. The results are interpreted as being related to the particular learning program employed. Further work using more extensive learning experiences is being planned.

36   Can First Graders Learn an Advanced Problem-Solving Skill?[1]

RICHARD C. ANDERSON[2]

The general conclusion of this study is that with suitable training, children can acquire, retain, and transfer rather complex and "advanced" problem-solving skills. The trained group, high IQ first graders, solve more problems with fewer unnecessary trials and also solve more transfer problems more efficiently than does the control group.

Though the view has been widely circulated that any child can learn anything any time, the experimental evidence supports only a much less optimistic opinion, indicating that although training can improve the performance of children on tasks that seem to involve "advanced" skills, these skills extinguish quickly, are subject to interference, and do not transfer to other tasks. For instance, Ausubel and Schiff (1954) found that young children taught to predict the operation of a teeter-totter on the basis of the principle that the longer side from the fulcrum falls (when both sides are equally weighted) later showed little resistance to the reasoning that the determining factor was the color of the blocks used as weights. Older children resisted the spurious reasoning. Smedslund (1961) showed that children could be taught the principles of conservation of weight and substance, that is, that changing the shape of an object does not alter its weight or volume. He went on to show (1961b) that children who learned the concept by "external reinforcement" (e.g., they were taught) reverted to nonconservation explanations when by sleight of hand they were presented with evidence that contradicted the principle of conservation. About half of the children who already knew the principle when training began resisted interference. Ervin (1960) taught third and fourth

[1]The project described herein was supported through the Cooperative Research Program of the Office of Education, United States Department of Health, Education, and Welfare.

[2]The author is indebted to the public schools of East Brunswick, New Jersey, and to Peter Buermann, Richard Cummings, Herbert Fraunfelker, and Robert Vojack who assisted in training and testing subjects.

Reprinted from the *Journal of Educational Psychology*, 1965, **56**, 283–294, by permission of the author and the American Psychological Association.

graders a procedure for hitting a target on the rebound by aiming at a backstop but failed to obtain transfer to a task that required aiming a light at a mirror in such a way that the light would reflect on a target. Wohlwill and Lowe (1962) developed three procedures to teach conservation of number. There were no differences among the three procedures and a no-treatment control group, and no transfer to a verbal test of conservation of number.

There are those who argue that studies such as those mentioned in the preceding paragraph should incline one to favor not only Piaget's theory of invariant stages in cognitive development but also a "Piaget-like equilibration-through-internal-cognitive-conflict" model instead of a "conventional-learning-through-external-reinforcement" model (Flavell, 1963, p. 378). As a matter of fact, the results that have been obtained can easily be explained without recourse to an internal equilibration theory. There is little reason for imagining that training will *automatically* result in transfer, resistance to extinction, or resistance to interference. If these qualities are desired, then a behavioral analysis must be made, and the appropriate conditions must be included in the training regimen. The suggestion is that studies showing that children do not readily transfer advanced concepts and problem-solving skills fail as a reason for preferring an internal equilibration model to an S-R model of "cognitive development."

Though there are those with an S-R orientation who are active in the area of problem solving (e.g., Cofer, 1957;

Kendler and Kendler, 1962; Maltzman, 1955, 1960), the majority of the psychologists working in the area are not of this persuasion. Since this is the case, perhaps a brief sketch of a behaviorist view of problem solving is in order. First, it is argued that though it may sometimes be quite complex, problem-solving behavior is essentially the same as other kinds of behavior and can best be understood in the same terms. The belief is that problem-solving behavior, like other forms of complex behavior, can be most profitably conceived as colligations of elemental stimulus-response contingencies.

It is popularly said that people "employ strategies" to solve problems. Terms such as "strategy," "plan," "decision," and "hypothesis" are redolent of volition, conscious ego control, and awareness. These expressions tend to make a person visualize problem solving as a series of deliberate decisions of which the problem solver is aware. It may be that behavior is accompanied by awareness, and a sense of volitional control is different from or even more adaptive than other behavior. But surely people exhibit orderly, "intelligent" adaptive behavior that is not under deliberate control nor necessarily accompanied by awareness. There is, for example, no useful sense in which a native speaker can be said to be "applying" rules of grammar when he utters a well-formed expression in ordinary conversation. Such an ascription is entirely metaphorical. And it can be a very misleading, insidious sort of metaphor for the psychologist attempting a causal analysis. Because of our language habits, those who allow themselves to say that people employ strategies are likely to find themselves trying to discover what strategies people are using by observing people attempting to solve problems. Since any protocol can be produced by an indefinite number of internal mechanisms (see Ashby, 1956; Quine, 1960), the attempt to "see" the latent structure that the observable problem-solving behavior purportedly manifests seems likely to be unproductive. The difficulty is that a strategy should be regarded as an organizing concept that is invented rather than a reality that is discovered.

Unlike some other psychologists with a similar bias, the present author does not object to such concepts as strategy *because* these are theoretical, unobservable, or contain "surplus meaning." Rather, the objection is based on the judgment that this kind of theory has proved unfruitful, lending itself more to ex post facto rationalization than explanation, prediction, and control. Those who have reviewed the rather bulky literature on problem solving argue that it contains a rather meager fund of knowledge, partly because of a preoccupation with the "process tracing" study (Duncan, 1959; Schulz, 1960).

This paper will use phrases such as the *sequence* of problem-solving behavior or the *pattern* of problem-solving behavior. Unlike the term strategy, the term pattern does not beg the question of the most appropriate concepts for comprehending problem-solving behavior. Those who wish may attempt to explain patterns of behavior in terms of strategies, cog-

nitive structures, and the like. Such constructions are not ruled out, but neither is their role preordained by the kind of language used.

Problem-solving behavior can be understood in the following terms. The more or less organized sequences or patterns of behavior, popularly called strategies, that seem to comprise much problem-solving behavior at a molar level of description, are hypothetically under stimulus control of two kinds. First, especially on the part of the good problem solver, behavior is under discriminative control of relevant task and problem cues, those present at the beginning and, depending upon the kind of problem, those cues that emerge during the course of work on the problem. Second, problem-solving behavior is partly controlled by response-produced stimuli, including, perhaps, intraverbals or other forms of mediation. Reinforcers of several kinds—for instance, we might suppose, what Polya (1954) calls "signs of progress" —act to increase the likelihood of certain forms of the behavior that is emitted during the problem-solving episode. If there is an orderly relationship between the contingencies of reinforcement operating during problem solving and the criteria for problem solution, then the problem-solving episode is a sort of microscopic natural-selection process. Presumably, three processes—discriminative control of problem-solving behavior by task cues, control of behavior by response-produced cues, and selection of forms of behavior by reinforcement —are sufficient to account for the co-ordinated, purposeful character of some problem-solving behavior that has seemed so salient to many students of problem solving.

The study described in this report was conducted to demonstrate that when presented with suitable training, children will acquire and transfer a rather advanced, complex problem-solving skill. A procedure was developed to teach children a classical strategy of experimental science: the technique of varying each factor in succession while holding all other factors constant. This skill was chosen for two reasons. First, a training procedure that successfully arranged the skill might have social value. Perhaps the procedure could be adapted for inclusion in school science curricula. As Bruner, Goodnow, and Austin (1956, pp. 81–125) have persuasively argued, the method of varying one factor at a time while holding the rest constant is applicable to a large and important class of problems. Such a skill may, in addition, be subskill in more complex patterns of problem-solving behavior. In other words, it may be a "tactic" in a more sophisticated strategy. Second, the skill is believed to be advanced for first graders. Piaget believes that the technique of varying each factor in succession while holding all other factors constant does not naturally appear until 14–16 years of age. Inhelder and Piaget (1958, p. 335) have stated that:

The adolescent superimposes propositional logic on the logic of classes and relations. Thus, he gradually structures a formal mechanism (reaching an equilibrium point at about 14–15 years) which is based on both the lattice structure and the group of four transformations. This new integration allows him to bring inversion and reciprocity together into a single whole. As a result, he comes to control . . . hypothetico-deductive reasoning and experimental proof based on the variation of a single factor with the others held constant (all other things being equal). . . .

Consider an example of the type of problem the children learned to solve. The task consists of eight plastic cowboys and accessories embedded in a plaster of paris base. The cowboys are either standing or riding horses, either with or without hats, and either with or without rifles. The instructions read to the child were as follows:

In this game, you've got to figure out which kind of cowboy is a friend of the sheriff. I will point to one cowboy who is a friend of the sheriff. You point to other cowboys. Each time you point to a cowboy, I will tell you whether he is a friend of the sheriff. As soon as you are sure you know, tell me which kind of cowboy is a friend of the sheriff.

The concept to be attained might be cowboys who are wearing hats, cowboys without guns who are riding horses, or cowboys with neither horses, guns, nor hats—any of the 27 different conjunctive concepts that can be formed with the cowboy task. The technique of varying each factor in succession while holding the rest constant guarantees a solution to problems such as those from the cowboy task in exactly as many trials (experimental tests, observations) as there are factors being considered. There are three factors to be considered in a cowboy problem; thus it should be possible to solve any cowboy problem in three trials. This was the requirement for children who received training. They were expected to solve each cowboy problem in three trials, that is to say, pick three cowboys and state a concept such that the cowboys selected implied the concept stated and no other. The goal of instruction was to improve the performance of children on a large class of problems identical in form to the cowboy problems.

The training employed the techniques of programed instruction, though it took the form of a script used by a human teacher (with one child at a time) rather than a self-instructional text or teaching-machine program. In the initial phase of training, the program consisted of seven units called "games" that were designed to teach components of the method of varying each factor in succession while holding all other factors constant. The first three games established appropriate "concept-naming" or "conclusion-drawing" behavior. The remaining four games arranged "instance-selection" behavior and integrated conclusion drawing with instance selection. A second phase of training, involving an abbreviated form of the program with each of five additional tasks, was presented to reduce the control of specific task and problem stimuli and bring behavior under the control of relevant abstract or schematic properties of tasks.

The technique for developing the training procedure was a pragmatic one. An a priori analysis of the behavior was made. A program was constructed on the basis of this analysis.

The program was tried with a few children. When a portion of the program functioned badly, the behavior was reanalyzed and the program revised. Eventually, a program was developed that seemed to work.

METHOD

Subjects and Design

A total of 60 first graders from the highest $\frac{1}{3}$ of the mental-age distribution (California Test of Mental Maturity) of all first graders enrolled in five elementary schools in a predominantly middle-class suburban school district in New Jersey were randomly selected and randomly assigned to two groups, with the restriction that there be 15 boys and 15 girls in each group. As a matter of expediency, there was the further sampling restriction that there be exactly six subjects in each group from each of the five schools. One group received the training program, whereas the other group received no treatment or training of any kind. When the first group had completed training, both groups were presented a series of problems, some from tasks that had been employed during training to assess retention, some from tasks none of the children had had experience with before to assess transfer. The transfer tasks were presented in counterbalanced orders. The training group and control group were nearly identical with respect to mental age (MA) and chronological age (CA). At the beginning of the study, the experimental group showed a mean CA in months of 79.2 and a CA standard deviation of 3.8. The control group showed a mean CA of 79.0 and a CA standard deviation of 3.9. The MA mean in months was 105.2 for the training group and 104.5 for the control group. The respective standard deviations were 9.2 and 9.0. A three-factor design (Lindquist, 1953, pp. 281–284) was employed with treatment and sex as between-subjects factors and task as a within-subjects factor.

Training

Each subject (S) in the training group met with an E (experimenters were graduate assistants) for 20-minute individual training sessions three times a week, unless S was ill or there was a special school program being offered. Training continued until S reached training criteria or completed 27 sessions. Training always took place in the morning in such reasonably quiet and private places as the schools were able to furnish. The main features of the training program are outlined below. Some of the detail of the training was created by E as he faced the child. The training may be characterized by saying that the behavior of E was prescribed in considerably more detail than in studies of teaching styles (e.g., discovery versus expository methods) but in less detail than in programed texts or teaching-machine programs. Three form-color-number card-array tasks were used in the first phase of training.

The first card array consisted of a set of eight 2½ × 3¾ inch cards taped in an orderly arrangement on a 16 × 18 inch Masonite panel. The cards had simple geometric figures inscribed upon them that varied with respect to number (one figure or two figures), color (red or green), and form (box or diamond). The other two arrays involved 27 cards that differed with respect to number of figures (one, two, or three), color (red, green, or blue), and form (box, diamond, or racetrack). Each of these arrays was taped to a 20 × 24 inch Masonite panel. The two arrays were identical except that one of them was arranged in an orderly

fashion whereas the other appeared in an irregular arrangement. The boxes, diamonds, and racetracks were ¾ × 1¼ inches and were drawn with felt-tipped pens and an IBM flowcharting template.

The training with the card arrays consisted of seven sections called games that are briefly described below. *Game 1.* E named a concept. S pointed to all of the cards that showed the concept. *Game 2.* E pointed to all of the cards that illustrated a conjunctive concept. S named the concept. *Game 3.* E pointed to a set of cards, some that were examples of the concept and some that were examples of what the concept was *not,* in such a way that a conjunctive concept was defined. S named the concept. For instance, referring to the simplest of the card arrays that have been described, E pointed to the cards exhibiting one red diamond, one red box, and two red diamonds, indicating that each of these "shows my secret" and then indicated that the card with one green diamond on it "does not show my secret." If the child responded "your secret is red," he answered correctly. *Game 4.* E pointed to a card. S picked a card that was different from E's card in just one way—either number, color, or form. At the end of this game, S was expected to be able to pick three cards, one showing a different number, one showing a different color, and one showing a different form, but each otherwise the same as E's card. *Game 5.* E pointed to a card. S selected a set of three cards as in Game 4, then E indicated which of these cards did and did not "show the secret" in such a way as to define a conjunctive concept. Finally, S said the "secret." *Game 6* was identical to Game 5 except that E indicated whether a card showed the secret as soon as it was selected by S. *Game 7* constituted the terminal stage of the program with the card arrays. This game differed from Game 6 mainly in terms of the instructions. The child was not told how to select cards nor was he corrected directly if he selected badly. The practice was to employ each of the three card arrays in each game, beginning with the simplest. When a child could quickly and correctly respond no matter what the concept, he was moved ahead to the next game. The training procedure has been described in greater detail elsewhere (Anderson, 1964, pp. 40–59).

Upon completion of the first phase of training, Ss received training on five additional tasks, namely, the cowboy task previously described, a collection of leaf facsimilies, a switching device, a ball-and-paddle device, and a pegboard game. The cowboy task and the pegboard task will be discussed in the next section. The other three training tasks were as follows.

LEAVES   Eight dittoed leaf facsimilies were attached with cellophane tape to 4½ × 6 inch Masonite blocks. The leaves differed in three ways—pinate versus palmate, simple versus compound, and notched edge versus smooth edge. The problem was to determine "what kind of leaf shows the secret."

SWITCHING DEVICE   A bank of six toggle switches and a master push-button switch faced the subject on one side of an 8 × 6 × 5 inch metal cabinet. Any of the switches could be made relevant or irrelevant by manipulating switches at the rear of the cabinet. The terminal problem was to "find which switches must be up in order for the buzzer to sound when the master button is pushed."

BALL-AND-PADDLE DEVICE   A 14 × 7 × 3½ inch wooden box had a channel through which a small ball could roll and six slots into which paint paddles could be inserted. When pushed in all the way, a solid paddle stopped the ball, whereas a notched paddle permitted the ball to pass. Notched and solid paddles could be placed in the slots in any combination. The terminal problem was to find "which paddles must be out if the ball is to roll through."

Though these five tasks involved different "story lines," different numbers of (stimulus) factors, and a variety of materials and apparatus, the tasks were isomorphic at a certain level of discourse, and problems from any of them could be solved by the method of varying each factor in succession while holding all other factors constant. The training sequence for each of these five tasks consisted of a version of Games 1, 2, 4, 6, and 7. Tasks were employed in counterbalanced orders with random assignment of Ss to orders. When, in E's judgment, S had mastered a certain task, problems were presented from a criterion list of problems for that task until·S reached a criterion of seven of eight consecutive solutions. To be scored as solving a problem, the child had to select a series of instances (equal to the number of factors in the task) and state a conclusion such that the instances that were selected implied the conclusion that was stated and no other. Merely saying the "right answer" was not enough. The child was permitted neither incorrect statements of the conclusion nor poor choices of instances on problems counted toward criterion. If E believed an S was unlikely to reach criterion within a reasonable period of time, S was sometimes skipped ahead to the next task.

Procedures for Presenting and Scoring Problems

Problems were presented in individual sessions according to a standardized procedure by an E who was not acquainted with the child and did not know whether the child was a member of the training group or the control group. S was first *oriented* to the task, meaning that he acquired or demonstrated knowledge of a list of concepts that included the problem concepts. E stated each concept; S pointed to all of the exemplars. The procedure for presenting the problem itself was illustrated with the cowboy task on a preceding page. E presented a "focus instance," that is, an exemplar of the concept. The child then selected or constructed instances until he could name the concept. Each time the child chose an instance, he learned immediately whether the instances showed the concept (positive instance) or did not show the concept (negative instance). On some tasks, the feedback was the physical consequence of the child's action. On others, E gave feedback orally. If an S stopped trying to solve the problem or stated an incorrect conclusion with which he was satisfied, E attempted to keep him going with one of a series of standardized prompts. E was supposed to keep the child performing if he could until either S solved the problem or selected the maximum number of instances allowed on the problem. Listed below is a description of each of the tasks and problems. Appearing first are two tasks employed during training, then five transfer tasks that were presented in counterbalanced orders.

COWBOYS The cowboy task was described in the preceding section. Problems involved determining which kind of cowboy was "a friend of the sheriff." The concept to be attained in the first problem was *hat but no rifle*. The focus was a cowboy on a horse with a hat but no rifle. The second problem concept was *standing with rifle*. The focus instance was a cowboy standing who had a rifle but no hat. S was allowed to select a maximum

of six instances during each cowboy problem.

PEGBOARD A "railroad track," a "road," and a "pond" were painted in white on an 8 × 13 inch piece of green pegboard. Along the track, road, and pond were "trees" consisting of pegs with wooden balls glued to the tops. The trees varied with regard to location, height (tall or short), leaf color (white ball or red ball), and trunk color (yellow peg or green peg). The problem was to find the "kind of tree under which Pirate Pete buried his gold." The concept to be attained in the first problem was *tall with red leaves and green trunk*. The focus instance was a tall tree by the road that had red leaves and a green trunk. The second problem concept was *short by the pond with yellow trunk*. The focus instance for the second problem was a short tree by the pond with white leaves and a yellow trunk. S was allowed to select a maximum of nine instances during each pegboard problem.

SCREWS Materials consisted of 16 screws and bolts that differed in terms of four attributes as follows: short (1½ inches) or long (3 inches), round headed or flat headed, steel or copper, screw or bolt. The materials were placed in a haphazard pile on a table in front of the subject. The experimenter mixed the screws and bolts after the first problem. Each problem involved determining which kind of screws and bolts "showed the secret." The concept to be attained in the first problem was *flat head*. The focus instance was a short, flat-headed copper screw. The concept to be attained in the second problem was *screw*. The focus instance was a long, round-headed steel screw. S was permitted to choose a maximum of eight instances during each screw problem.

SUBURBIA Materials consisted of 16 miniature houses and other fixtures glued to a 16 × 16 inch Masonite panel in a disorderly arrangement. The houses differed with regard to four variables: one story versus two story, north side of the road versus south side of the road, tree versus no tree, car versus no car. Problems consisted of determining which kind of house "showed the secret." The concept to be attained in the first problem was *south side of the street with tree and no car*. The focus instance was a one-story house on the south side of the street with a tree and no car. The concept to be attained in the second problem was *two-story house with a tree and a car*. The focus instance in the second problem was a two-story house on the north side of the street with a tree and a car. S was allowed to select a maximum of eight instances during each suburbia problem.

PENDULUM Materials consisted of a metal stand 40 inches high capable of supporting three pendulums simultaneously. The three pendulums were of different lengths such that the period of the shortest was .5 second, the period of the one of middle length was 1 second, and the period of the longest was 1.5 seconds. Included also were two balls of 1-inch diameter, one of steel, the other of cork. Attached to the back of the stand was a piece of postal board 22 × 28 inches on which were drawn two lines of 30° and 45° from the perpendicular. There were three variables—the length of the pendulum, the amount of weight attached to the pendulum, and the angle from which the pendulum was released. The problem was to "figure out what makes this swing the most times in 10 seconds." The focus instance was the demonstration that the heavy weight on the middle-length string released from a 45° angle swung 10 times

in 10 seconds. S was allowed to try a maximum of six combinations during the pendulum problem.

CHEMICAL Materials consisted of a 4-ounce amber bottle, a watch glass, and two sets of five 1-ounce dropping bottles labeled A, B, C, D, and E. Two of the latter bottles in each set contained water. The other three contained, respectively, diluted solutions of sulphuric acid, hydrogen peroxide, and potassium iodide. The problem was to find "which bottles you have to use to get yellow." The concept to be attained in the first problem was that bottles B, C, and D were necessary. The concept in the second problem was B, C, and E. In each case, the focus instance was the demonstration that when drops from each of the five bottles were placed in the amber jar and the contents were poured on the watch glass, the liquid was yellow. S was allowed to try a maximum of 10 combinations of bottles during each chemical problem.

PENCILS Materials consisted of 12 yellow, hexagonal Number 2 pencils. The pencils displayed three attributes: length (6, 4, or 2 inches), presence or absence of eraser, sharpened or unsharpened. The pencils were arrayed in a disorderly fashion on a table in front of the subject. The problem was to figure out which kind of pencil "shows the secret." The concept to be attained in the first problem was *unsharpened without eraser*. The focus instance was a long, unsharpened pencil without an eraser. The concept to be attained in the second problem was *medium length with eraser*. The focus instance in the second problem was a medium-length, sharpened pencil with an eraser. S was allowed a maximum of seven selections during each pencil problem.

E wrote a protocol recording the instances the child selected, the statements the child made, and the statements *E* made in the sequence in which these occurred. The instances and permissible *E* statements were recorded in coded form. Immediately following a day's administration of problems, the two *E*s working in the same school exchanged protocols to check them for legibility, completeness, accuracy of subject and problem identification, and "legal" use of codes.

Scores on three summary measures of problem solving were obtained in a content analysis of the problem-solving protocols. A "trial" is defined as the selection of an instance. A trial is inefficient if it yields less than the maximum attainable amount of information. A trial is redundant if it yields a conclusion implied by previous trials. Finally, a trial is repetitious if it exactly duplicates a previous trial. The sum of inefficient, redundant, and repetitious trials constituted the first measure of problem solving: *number of unnecessary trials.* Unqualified declarative statements about the concept or the relevance of variables can be classified as inconsistent, consistent but invalid, bizarre, and valid. The sum of inconsistent, consistent, and bizarre statements about the concept comprised *number of invalid conclusions,* the second measure of problem solving. If an *S* selected a set of instances and stated a conclusion such that the instances implied the conclusion and no other, then he solved the problem. *Number of solutions* was the third measure of problem solving. Protocols, identified only by number, were scored by two raters working independently. Interrater reliability coefficients averaged .97, .90, and .91 per problem for unnecessary trials, invalid conclusions, and solutions, respectively. Two similar problems were presented for each of the seven tasks ex-

cept the pendulum task. To estimate reliability correlations between scores on the two problems from each task were extended with the Spearman-Brown formula. The correlations were obtained separately for the training group and the control group and then averaged so as to avoid an overestimation of reliability due to the treatment effect. The mean reliabilities by task were .50, .32, and .53 for unnecessary trials, invalid conclusions, and solutions. Recognize that these coefficients are based on a homogeneous sample of first graders. Higher coefficients probably would be obtained from more heterogeneous samples of first graders or older samples.

TABLE 1.—Cumulative Number of Subjects Reaching Criterion of Mastery on Training Tasks within 27 20-Minute Training Sessions

CRITERION REACHED ON	*CUMULATIVE NO. OF Ss*
Second-phase training	
5 tasks	16
4 tasks	26
3 tasks	28
2 tasks	30
1 task	30
First-phase training	30

Note.—$N = 30$. The criterion for each task was the solution of seven out of eight consecutive problems. An *S* solved a problem if he selected a series of instances and stated a conclusion such that the instances implied the conclusion and no other. Neither unnecessary trials nor invalid conclusions were permitted on problems counted toward criterion.

RESULTS AND DISCUSSION

Acquisition

Table 1 shows the cumulative number of *Ss* reaching criterion of mastery on the several training tasks within the time available. Among those who failed to reach criterion on one or more tasks, there were six instances in which Ss were prevented from reaching criterion for lack of time, and 14 cases in which Ss attempted a task but could not master it. Only one task, the collection of leaf facsimilies, gave Ss appreciable difficulty. Ten Ss attempted this task but could not master it. The reasons are not hard to find. The leaves involved less discriminable stimulus dimensions and less familiar language than the other tasks. The dimensions were pinate versus palmate, simple versus compound, and notched edge versus smooth edge, and precisely these words were used with the children.

TABLE 2.—Frequency of Solutions to Problems by Task and Treatment Group

	NO. OF SOLUTIONS					
TASK	Training group (N = 30)			Control group (N = 30)		
	None	1	2	None	1	2
Retention						
Cowboys	4	8	18	21	7	2
Pegboard	12	11	7	26	3	1
Transfer						
Screws	2	5	23	6	9	15
Suburbia	8	12	10	19	7	4
Pendulum[a]	19	11	—	22	8	—
Chemical	23	5	2	25	5	0
Pencils	2	5	23	9	10	11

[a]Only one pendulum problem was presented.

Retention

Table 2 shows the frequency of solution to the problems presented to measure retention, and Table 3 presents the means and standard deviations of numbers of unnecessary trials and the square root of number of invalid conclusions.

The performance of the training group was distinctly superior to the performance of the control group on problems presented to measure retention. The training group solved more problems ($F = 40.46$, $df = 1/56$, $p < .01$) and solved these problems with fewer unnecessary trials ($F = 52.69$, $df = 1/56$, $p < .01$). At first glance, it appears that the training group did not do as well in absolute terms as might be hoped, particularly on the pegboard task. There were six Ss during training who did not attempt or attempted but could not master the pegboard task. Five of the six children who did not reach the pegboard-training criterion failed to solve either of the pegboard problems, while the remaining child solved one of them. Consider also that, because training tasks were employed in counterbalanced orders, there were intervals of up to 7 weeks between the attainment of the training criterion for a certain task and the presentation of problems to measure retention. When these factors are considered, the performance of the training group on the retention problems was not unsatisfactory, whether viewed relatively with respect to the control group or in absolute terms.

For number of invalid conclusions on retention problems, treatment, task, and the treatment-task interaction were all significant ($p < .01$), largely because the training group emitted *more* invalid conclusions on the pegboard problems than did the control group. This unexpected and undesired result is hard to interpret. The pegboard problems were rather difficult, as can be seen by examining the other two indexes. Perhaps during training some Ss learned to guess when in trouble so as to elicit cues from E.

Transfer

Tables 2 and 3 also present statistics summarizing problem-solving performance on the transfer tasks. The training group solved more transfer problems ($F = 17.33$, $df = 1/56$, $p < .01$) than the control group. Differences favoring the training group were significant for the suburbia problems ($x^2 = 8.36$, $df = 3$, $p < .05$) and the pencil problems ($\chi^2 = 10.36$, $df = 3$, $p < .01$), and the difference approached significance on screw problems ($\chi^2 = 4.84$ $df = 3$, $.10 > p > .05$).

The training group showed fewer unnecessary trials than the control group on the transfer problems ($F = 15.01$, $df = 1/56$, $p < .01$). Also an interaction appeared between treatment and task ($F = 9.84$, $df = 4/224$, $p < .01$). The training group showed fewer unnecessary trials than the control group on the screw problems ($t = 5.59$, $df = 58$, $p < .01$), the suburbia problems ($t = 2.74$, $df = 58$, $p < .01$), and the pencil problems ($t = 4.03$, $df = 58$, $p < .01$).

The training group did *not* show superior performance on the chemical problems or the pendulum problem. What was different about these? For one thing, performance measures for these problems were less reliable. For another, these were the only problems in which the child had to, in a sense, "create" the instances. He had to combine the materials he was given to produce the instance. The instances

TABLE 3.—*Ms* and *SDs* of Number of Unnecessary Trials and Number of Invalid Conclusions by Task and Treatment Group

TASK	UNNECESSARY TRIALS				INVALID CONCLUSIONS[a]			
	Training group		Control group		Training group		Control group	
	M	SD	M	SD	M	SD	M	SD
Retention								
Cowboys	2.60	2.61	6.43	1.38	.65	.77	.70	.79
Pegboard	8.03	4.57	12.57	1.61	1.67	.90	.60	.70
Transfer								
Screws	4.73	2.85	8.20	2.16	1.15	.73	.89	.65
Suburbia	7.10	2.92	8.80	2.58	1.42	.59	.90	.78
Pendulum[b]	8.87	2.86	9.40	2.52	1.10	.78	1.22	.53
Chemical	14.30	2.89	13.30	2.28	1.13	.59	1.43	.35
Pencils	4.27	2.61	6.77	2.34	.94	.57	.85	.65

[a]Square root of number of invalid conclusions.

[b]Twice the (raw) score on the pendulum problem was used in order to make this task comparable with the other tasks in which two problems were presented.

were physically arrayed in front of the child in all of the remaining tasks.

Piaget has reasoned that skill in combining materials to produce instances that are relevant for testing hypotheses involves skill in "conceiving combinatorial possibilities." On the basis of the developmental literature, one would not expect primary-grade children to possess this skill. Hunt (1961, pp. 231–232) has illustrated the point as follows:

Faced with the problem of describing the population of animals on a newly discovered planet, the child with only concrete operations could merely do the empirical task of searching for animals and assigning them to . . . classes . . . On the other hand, if an adolescent with formal operations were faced with such a task, he would be capable of considering all of the various classes of animals that are conceivable, and he might set up a table of these possibilities before he began his exploration.

If the suggestion contained in the present study that children who receive the training program cannot perform well on problems in which instances must be created is confirmed by additional research, then the presumption will be that an additional set of skills is required, perhaps of the sort that is said to involve "conceiving combinatorial possibilities." If such is the case, it may well be possible to design training procedures that arrange these skills.

For all three dependent variables, task was a significant ($p \leq .01$) main effect on both retention and transfer problems. The study was not designed in such a way that a discriminating interpretation of the significant task

effects is possible. Within the constraints imposed by the task analysis, as wide as possible a range of task and problem characteristics was included in order to reflect treatment generality or lack of it.

An interaction ($F = 4.31$, $df = 4/224$, $p < .01$) between treatment and task for invalid conclusions appeared on transfer problems. The training group gave more invalid conclusions ($t = 3.27$, $df = 58$, $p < .01$) on the suburbia problems than the control group. Otherwise, none of the task × task differences was significant. Both suburbia problems involved four (stimulus) factors, three of which were relevant. The pegboard problems, upon which the training group also showed more inappropriate verbal behavior than the control group, also involved four factors, three of which were relevant. Apparently, there was some deficiency in the training procedure with respect to this kind of problem.

Except as already indicated, no significant effects appeared in the study. Specifically, first, sex was nowhere significant as a main effect, and sex did not enter into any significant interactions. Second, order of presentation of tasks proved to be unimportant. There were no differences on unnecessary trials ($F = .11$), invalid conclusions ($F = 2.08$, $df = 4/232$, $p > .05$), or solutions ($F = .54$) as a function of order of presentation of the transfer tasks. Nor did order interact with treatment for any of these measures. The F ratios for the interactions were .05, .55, and .02 for unnecessary trials, invalid conclusions, and solutions. The failure to find differences attributable to order indicates that merely performing on a series of problems was not facilitating and suggests that the effects of training were not transitory.

The exercise in human engineering that has been described in these pages shows that bright children can acquire, retain, and transfer rather complex problem-solving behavior. This finding is noteworthy, especially with respect to transfer, since as a general rule previous research suggests that at best children will achieve a rather tenuous grasp of behavior that seems to involve complex, abstract operations. Since it appears to take about 15 years for the skills that were taught to 6- and 7-year-olds in this project to develop when learning is left to incidental contingencies, it is to be expected that development would take quite a while and involve many steps even under optimum conditions of instruction. Thus, it is not surprising that the "advanced" behavior children acquire in short-term studies such as those of Smedslund (1961a, 1961b), Ervin (1960), or Ausubel and Schiff (1954) is neither permanent, automatically generalized, nor impervious to interference.

No doubt one reason the present effort achieved a degree of success was that the children received a lot of training over a considerable period of time. It must be emphasized, however, that there is no way of telling which features of the complex training procedure were important. For that matter, it is quite possible that better training procedures could be invented for achieving the same ends. Refined versions of the training procedure are currently under development (see Anderson, Boone, and Daniel, 1965).

Many of the prominent figures in child development believe that basic changes in level of intellectual functioning are more matters of "internal equilibration" than of learning as the result of "external reinforcement" (e.g., Bruner, 1961; Smedslund, 1961b). The present project was based on the contrasting presumption that reasoning and problem-solving capabilities are best conceived to consist of repertoires of behavior, modifiable in accordance with principles of learning, instead of inaccessible structures and processes. The results of the project suggest that instruction based on this presumption is feasible.

37 *Children's Creativity in Art: A Study of Types*

ELLIOT W. EISNER

Creativity, according to Eisner, is a capacity common to all that should be developed by the school. This study formulates and tests a theory of creative behavior in the visual arts. Four types of creativity: (1) boundary pushing, (2) inventing, (3) boundary breaking, and (4) esthetic organizing; and two loci of creativity: (1) content and (2) form are proposed. Whereas boundary pushing, inventing, and esthetic organizing are displayed in some degree by almost all the children, boundary breaking is not. No significant relationship is found between IQ and any of the types of creativity. A pertinent research question is how and to what extent can we develop children's art products.

INTRODUCTION

Through research, the conception of creativity has undergone an important change. Once considered an elusive, almost mystical gift belonging to a special few, creativity is now being seen as a capacity common to all —one that should be effectively developed by the school. Once considered a rare type of behavior limited to the arts, creativity is now viewed as penetrating, to some degree, almost all kinds of human activity. Even educators who are usually chary of accepting new responsibilities for an already overloaded curriculum are fascinated by the idea of teaching for the development of creativity.

Reprinted from the *American Educational Research Journal*, May 1965, **2** 125–136, by permission of the author and the American Educational Research Association.

Art education has long been concerned with the development of creativity. Unlocking the creative impulse has been a major function of the teacher of art. Although he may sometimes have confused mere impulsivity with serious creative art, his concern with creativity has been real and sincere. Lowenfeld (1939, 1957), Read (1945), and Shaeffer (1948) are only a few of those who have contributed to both the theory and the practice of developing children's creativity in the arts. The recent flow of creativity research by psychologists is beginning to persuade those working in other academic fields that education for creativity is not solely the responsibility of those working in the arts. Thus, research based largely on scientific grounds is providing new and important directions in American education.

APPROACHES TO THE STUDY OF CREATIVITY

Guilford, Wilson, and Christensen (1952), whose work has been particularly influential, have postulated a set of factors and factorized tests that are theoretically relevant to understanding the structure of the human intellect. He sees creativity as a complex of unitary abilities that are displayed singly or in combination in the creative act. His factor-analysis methods have provided a major approach to the study of creativity, and his tests have been widely used by workers in this area.

A second approach, taken by Blatt and Stein (1957) and others, has been to study individuals known to have high creative ability (as evidenced through patents, discoveries, publications, inventions, and the like) in the hope of finding common personality traits.

A third approach has been the identification of process characteristics through examination of the completed product. This method, developed by Beittel and Burkhart (1963), has been especially valuable in the field of art education, where the product's characteristics are indicative of the methods and modes of action employed by the artist. The constructs *spontaneous, divergent,* and *academic* have proved useful for analyzing the artistic process, and significant personality correlates have been found for individuals displaying these process-strategies.

The research reported here presents a fourth approach to the study of creativity. It represents an effort to formulate and test a typology of creative behavior in the visual arts.

TYPES OF CREATIVITY IN THE VISUAL ARTS

The treatment of *types* of creativity as distinct from that of creativity in general may have advantages. First, kinds of behavior that are now excluded from the conception of creativity in general may be brought into a wider view of creativity. Second, if art works are analyzed with an eye to the different sorts of "creativeness" that they exhibit, it may be possible to arrive at defensible views about the creative competencies of different individuals and, with this knowledge, encourage these competencies more efficiently.

The conception of types of creativity is based upon the various qualities and characteristics that have historically been considered creative in the visual arts. Analyses of children's art works, as well as those of adults, show that their qualities can be classified into a system of types. Some artists make their creative contribution through the treatment of form; others through their selection of subject matter; some in the novel treatment of the conventional; others in the creation of the utterly new. Some children develop unique ways of combining media; others formulate new methods of expression; still others are able to bring aesthetic order to conventional visual elements. Creativity in art does not seem to be a simple unitary trait. Like art itself, creativity has many faces.

The purpose of the present study was to see whether the types of creativity found in the art products of sixth-grade pupils could be systematically identified and, if so, to determine the relationships existing among these types.[1]

Four types of creativity and two loci constitute the typology. The types are 1) *Boundary Pushing,* 2) *Inventing,* 3) *Boundary Breaking,* and 4) *Aesthetic Organizing.* They are described *in general* in the four sections that follow. The loci are 1) content and 2) form. Content is defined as an attempt at representation and is evidenced by the presence of conventional signs. Form is defined as the presence of formal qualities. Thus, every visual art product contains formal

_____
[1]The study also investigated the relationship between each type of creativity and psychological health. These findings are reported elsewhere.

qualities but may or may not contain conventional signs.

Boundary Pushing

In every culture, objects are embedded within various mental fields. These fields are bounded in such a way as to enable members of the culture to place an object in some meaningful context, usually that in which the object is normally found. These fields also act as a sort of psychic economy, a slicing up of the world so that objects within it can be meaningfully and efficiently classified. In addition, they provide the culture with a common set of object-field expectations that act to discourage bizarre actions by individuals within that culture. The fields specify and encourage acceptable, stereotyped, and restricted behavior on the part of individuals who act within the limits of the fields. Some individuals, however, are able to extend these limits. The process of extending or redefining the limits of common objects is called *Boundary Pushing.*

In the area of technology, *Boundary Pushing* was demonstrated by the individual who first thought of installing electric shaver outlets in automobiles, thus extending the usual limits of both the automobile and the shaver. It was also demonstrated by the person who first thought of using rubber for the blades of electric fans and by the individual who first used nylon for the wheels of roller skates. In the classroom, *Boundary Pushing* is displayed by the child who uses numerals to create designs or pictures or who uses an inked eraser as a rubber stamp. *Boundary Pushing* is displayed in the recognition that plywood can be molded into a chair, that a cellophane strip can be used to open a package of cigarettes, and that a key can open a can of coffee. Thus, *Boundary Pushing* is the ability to attain the possible by extending the given.

Inventing

Inventing is the process of employing the known to create an essentially new object or class of objects. The inventor does not merely extend the usual limits of the conventional; he creates a new object by restructuring the known. Edison, to use a classic case, exemplifies the inventor, for his activities were directed not merely toward the novel implementation of known materials or objects but rather toward their combination and reconstruction. His contributions differ markedly from those produced by *Boundary Pushing*. The terminus of *Inventing* is the creation of a new product that may itself be creatively employed, thus being the subject of *Boundary Pushing*. Gutenberg, Bell, and Marconi are only a few of those who have displayed inventive behavior; and our recognition of their contributions, combined with our general reluctance to call them scientists, is indicative of the distinction we make at the common-sense level regarding the ways in which creativity is displayed.

Boundary Breaking

Boundary Breaking is defined as the rejection or reversal of accepted assumptions, thus making the "given" problematic. This type of behavior is probably characterized by the highest level of cognition. In *Boundary Break-*

ing, the individual sees gaps and limitations in current theories and proceeds to develop new premises, which contain their own limits. Copernicus, for example, displayed *Boundary Breaking* in his conceptual (if not theological) rejection of the theory that the earth was the center of the universe. His hypothesis that the earth moves around the sun (and not vice versa) led him to develop a theory that, as far as we know, is valid for the astronomical system. His rejection of the knowledge of the period—theories and beliefs that were limiting—allowed him to contribute significantly to man's understanding of the universe. In the present era, Einstein's notion of simultaneity allowed him to develop new concepts useful for understanding nature through his theory of relativity. His questioning of currently accepted beliefs regarding relationships in time and space led him to propose a theory from which certain natural phenomena can be more accurately predicted.

Another example of *Boundary Breaking* is found in the work of Binet. "Binet's approach was the direct opposite of that of his predecessors. Instead of trying to find a single index of intelligence, he went to the other extreme and deliberately searched for a multiplicity of indexes" (Stephens, 1951, p. 181). By making the "given" problematic and by reversing the approach taken by others, Binet set the pattern for over fifty years of intelligence testing.

Two kinds of behavior characteristically displayed by *Boundary Breakers*—insight and imagination—may function in the following ways. Insight may help the *Boundary Breaker* grasp relationships among seemingly discrete events. It may also enable him to recognize incongruities or gaps in accepted explanations or descriptions. As he recognizes these gaps, his imagination may come into play and enable him to generate images or ideas (or both) useful for closing the gaps. Through the production of these images and ideas, he is able to reorganize or even reject the accepted in order to formulate a more comprehensive view of the relationships among the elements that gave impetus to the initial insight. Insight into gaps in contemporary theory or actions and visions of the possible are probably insufficient to satisfy the *Boundary Breaker;* he must be able to establish an order and structure between the gaps he has "seen" and the ideas he has generated.

Aesthetic Organizing

Aesthetic Organizing is characterized by the presence in objects of a high degree of coherence and harmony. The individual who displays this type of creativity confers order and unity upon matters; his overriding concern is in the aesthetic organization of qualitative components. Decisions about the placement of objects are made through what may be called a qualitative creativity.

Individuals who are able to organize components aesthetically probably obtain a great deal of pleasure from so doing. This inclination towards aesthetic order also seems to be displayed in the way in which forms are *perceived.* Barron (1958) has reported that both creative artists and creative scientists show more preference for designs that are highly complex, asymmetrical, and seemingly disorganized than do less creative individuals. In this sense, the *Aesthetic Organizer* may be an aesthetic see-er as well; that is, he may obtain his aesthetic pleasures by seeing through disorder to identify orderly elements. Some artists and writers report that they are controlled by these urges and drives and admit to following their lead consciously, rather than having and adhering to carefully preconceived plans of execution.

It should be noted that a major difference exists between *Aesthetic Organizing* and the other three types of creativity. In *Boundary Breaking, Inventing,* and *Boundary Pushing,* novelty is a defining characteristic. Either a new use for an object or a new object itself is created. In *Aesthetic Organizing,* this is not necessarily the case; neither a new use nor a new object may have been created. The object upon which creativity was exercised, however, displays a high degree of coherence. Its parts hang together harmoniously. For most artists the aesthetic organization of form is a prime concern, but in children (and they are the subjects of the present study) high aesthetic organizing ability is relatively rare. The preadolescent who is able to organize form to a high degree of coherence and harmony is often said to be gifted; in this study this particular kind of giftedness is considered one type of creativity.

SUBJECTS AND INSTRUMENTS

Once the classes constituting the typology were formulated, the problem shifted to the empirical question: Could this typology be used to identify types of creative characteristics displayed in children's art products?

In order to answer this question, specific criteria were deduced from each general description of a type. These criteria stated the characteristics that would be present in an art product if the subject had displayed a particular type of creativity. For example, a subject who engaged in *Aesthetic Organizing* would produce a work with satisfying formal qualities. Its parts would hang together and it would be unified; balance between figure and ground would be achieved. A subject who engaged in *Boundary Pushing* would produce a work in which either form or content was used in a novel way; his treatment of these aspects of the art product would be original.

Eighty-five sixth-grade pupils—46 boys and 39 girls—in a mid-western private school were the subjects. Their IQ's ranged from 93 to 180, with a median of 128. Where IQ measures other than the Stanford-Binet had been used, scores were converted to Stanford-Binet equivalents.

The subjects were asked to produce two kinds of art works. One was a piece of sculpture made from one-quarter pound of oil-base clay, a handful of colored toothpicks, and a paper plate to be used as a base. To insure privacy, each S worked in an enclosed booth. The instructions were as follows:

In the booth before you, you will find a paper plate, some colored toothpicks, and some oil-base clay. You may build anything you wish out of the clay and toothpicks. The paper plate is to be used as a base so that whatever you make may be moved easily. You will have 45 minutes to complete your work. You may begin.

The second product consisted of a set of nine drawings made in an 8″-by-11½″ booklet. On each page, the Ss found an abstract line, which was to be used as the starting point or stimulus for their drawing. Each page had a border line 1½″ from the edge. The Ss had two minutes to work on each page and were given a signal by the test administrator when the two minutes had elapsed. The instructions were as follows:

On each page of this booklet you will find some simple lines. You are to use your pencil to change each of the lines in any way you wish. You will have two minutes to work on each page so you will have to work rapidly. Wait for the signal before you begin. Once you complete one page, don't turn to the next page until you are told to do so. You may begin.

PROCEDURE AND TREATMENT OF DATA

Three judges were selected to identify the various types of creativity that each art product might display. Each one had had over five years of art-teaching experience with children as well as considerable experience as a practicing visual artist. The judges met daily for two weeks to discuss the criteria and to practice using them in judging the creative characteristics of works similar to those produced in the study. At the end of this time, the judges believed that they adequately understood the criteria and their application and proceeded to the actual evaluation.

The art products of the Ss were arranged in two large rooms. The judges, using a nine-point scale, independently evaluated each product for each type of creativity—one type at a time. As soon as a judge completed one evaluation, he handed in his score sheet and received one for another type; he then selected a different point in the display to begin his next evaluation. This procedure, the purpose of which was to reduce halo effect, was used throughout the judging.

To determine interjudge agreement, the data were treated as follows:

1) For each evaluation[2] the 85 raw scores assigned by each judge were transformed into normalized standard scores. The 14 normalized standard scores from each judge's evaluations were summed for each subject. This procedure yielded three over-all creativity scores for each subject. These three sets of 85 summed scores (one set for each judge) were intercorrelated to determine how well the judges agreed in over-all assessment of creativity.

2) An analogous procedure was followed for *each medium* separately, thus providing individual measures of how well the judges agreed in evaluating structures and how well they agreed in evaluating drawings.

3) The raw scores assigned to the products by each judge in each type and locus of creativity were intercorrelated.

---

[2] The types and loci on which the 14 evaluations were based are listed in Table 1. For obvious reasons, only the locus *form* was used in conjunction with *Aesthetic Organizing.*

Obtaining measures on these three bases—ranging from over-all assessment of creativity to successively more specific assessments—made it possible to locate the points at which interjudge agreement diminished.

On the first basis, over-all assessment of creativity, interjudge agreement was rather high; the coefficients were .82, .78, and .72. When the two media were taken separately, the amount of interjudge agreement dropped slightly; the coefficients for structures were .74, .65, and .61; for drawings, .80, .79, and .71. Finally, when *each type and locus in each medium* was taken individually, the coefficients ranged from .90 to .10, with a median of .59. These data are shown in Table 1.

Once it was decided that the interjudge agreement was high enough to warrant using the data, it became feasible to investigate the relationships existing among the types and between each type and other variables. The following questions guided the investigation:

1) What relationships exist among the scores in the various types of creativity within and between media?

2) When the boys and the girls are grouped separately, are the relationships among the types different in the two groups?

3) When the subjects above the median in intelligence and those below the median are grouped separately, are the relationships among the types different in the two groups?

4) What are the correlations between the scores in each of the types and the Stanford-Binet IQ's?

TABLE 1.—Interjudge Correlations Computed from Raw Scores

| | JUDGES | | |
Type and Locus of Creativity	A vs. B. (N = 85)	A vs. C (N = 85)	B vs. C (N = 85)
Boundary Pushing—Content, Structures	.80*	.70	.90
Boundary Breaking—Form, Structures	.88	.72	.75
Boundary Pushing—Form, Drawings	.74	.58	.68
Aesthetic Organizing—Form, Drawings	.55	.60	.76
Inventing—Content, Drawings	.52	.73	.60
Aesthetic Organizing—Form, Structures	.58	.56	.68
Inventing—Form, Structures	.52	.62	.61
Inventing—Form, Drawings	.55	.56	.65
Inventing—Content, Structures	.51	.47	.54
Boundary Pushing—Content, Drawings	.39	.60	.49
Bourdary Breaking—Form, Drawings	.33	.38	.68
Boundary Breaking—Content, Drawings	.10	.81	.42
Boundary Breaking—Content, Structures	.27	.27	.76
Median	.53	.59	.66

*The smallest product-moment correlation coefficient based upon 85 cases that is significantly different from zero at the .01 level is .25 (one-tailed test).

As mentioned earlier—to make the ratings by the three judges comparable, each set of 85 raw scores was transformed into a set of normalized standard scores. The three corresponding standard scores (one from each judge) of each subject were summed; this provided a *single* score on each type (and locus) of creativity in each medium for each child. The intercorrelations of these summed scores and their correlations with Binet IQ's are presented in Table 2.

The first conclusion to be drawn from the data in Table 2 is that the relationship between creative performance in one medium and creative performance in the other was low. The median coefficient among the 49 *r*'s between media was .11. This finding is consonant with the situation among professional artists. Aside from a few outstanding exceptions, such as Degas, Michelangelo, Picasso, and Moore, most artists display high-level creativity in one or, at best, two media. When they do function creatively in more than one medium, it is most often in media of the same kind—collage and drawing or sculpture and bas relief. The apparent specificity of creative behavior in the visual arts is probably a function of the status of certain skills that are necessary in working in two rather than in three dimensions (or vice versa) or in working in color rather than in black and white (or vice versa). The type of demands a particular medium makes upon an individual probably affects the extent to which he can employ those cognitive abilities that exempli-

TABLE 2.—Correlations among Types and Loci of Creativity and between Types and IQ
(N = 85)

Type and Locus of Creativity	FORM, STRUCTURES				CONTENT, STRUCTURES			FORM, DRAWINGS				CONTENT, DRAWINGS		
	BP	I	BB	AO	BP	I	BB	BP	I	BB	AO	BP	I	BB
IQ	-.02	.05	-.04	-.01	.21	.18	-.09	.05	.16	.03	.07	.15	.01	-.15
Form, Structures BP		.40	-.05	.76	.33	.32	-.03	.25	.19	.17	.25	.13	.27	.20
Form, Structures I			-.30	.39	.02	.20	-.38	.13	.09	.04	.05	.13	.09	.04
Form, Structures BB				.08	-.00	-.05	.64	.11	.16	.01	.18	-.04	-.04	.05
Form, Structures AO					.34	.29	.10	.27	.14	-.03	.25	.07	.17	.04
Content, Structures BP						.83	.22	.09	.06	.11	.18	.28	.18	-.05
Content, Structures I							.05	.06	.07	.11	.16	.29	.21	-.06
Content, Structures BB								-.04	-.03	-.02	.11	-.01	-.09	-.06
Form, Drawings BP									.77	.26	.73	.52	.45	.39
Form, Drawings I										.39	.76	.60	.52	.45
Form, Drawings BB											.26	.33	.39	.50
Form, Drawings AO												.56	.55	.35
Content, Drawings BP													.75	.36
Content, Drawings I														.57
Content, Drawings BB														

BP = Boundary Pushing   I = Inventing   BB = Boundary Breaking   AO = Aesthetic Organizing fy or make possible creative thinking. A person unable to perceive depth might be able to function in a highly creative way in the production of mosaics but surely would be severely handicapped in the production of sculpture. Since the Ss in the present study had had about the same amount of experience in the two media they used, the character of these media and the different kinds of abilities that they elicit may account for the low correlations between them.

Although the relationships indicated by these correlations tend to be slight, seven significant relationships did emerge. Six of these seven occur between types having the same locus. For example, *Boundary Pushing* in content in structures is significantly correlated with *Boundary Pushing* in content in drawings, also *Inventing* in content in structures with *Boundary Pushing* in content in drawings, etc. These relationships may be due to the mental set that each S brought to his work. Those Ss who obtained high creativity scores in the locus of *form* may have sought the stimulation of emerging formal qualities rather than the successful imposition of a preconceived idea or symbol upon the medium. Instead of attempting to master the medium, they may have preferred to treat it as a partner, taking their cues from the unexpected forms that flowed from their actions.

The second conclusion from the correlation table is that the relationships among types of creativity in drawing were higher than those in structures. The fact that the scores in drawing were based on *nine* work samples whereas there was only one structure may partially account for this difference.

The third conclusion is that scores on *Boundary Breaking* in form and content for structures were more highly correlated than were the other types of creativity in form and content. In addition, scores on this type of creativity were least highly correlated with scores in the other types.

The fourth finding from the table isolates a particular type of creative behavior: *Boundary Breaking*, in both form and content, emerged as the most independent of the four types. This may be explained by the nature of *Boundary Breaking*; to engage in this type of creativity, an individual must reject or reverse (or both) the premises upon which the problem rests. Persons able to escape the limits of deeply embedded cultural expectations are rare, and since *Boundary Breaking* is the most dramatic kind of successful escape from such expectations, its rarity (and, therefore, its relatively infrequent occurrence with other types of creativity) is not surprising.

One child who engaged in *Boundary Breaking* in structures used the paper plate, which was intended only as a base, as an integral part of his structure and, in addition, combined torn pieces of cardboard as a functional element. Another child used the colored toothpicks not as a structural element in the clay but as a burden carried by the clay donkey that he built. In drawings, one child carefully punched holes in the several pages so that his drawings had a relief quality. These subjects rejected or reversed the premises on which the problem was built in order to develop novel solutions.

To find out whether different relationships existed among the types of creativity for each sex, the intercorrelations were computed separately for boys and for girls. In 19 of the 91 pairs of coefficients, significance was attained by only one of the coefficients in the pair. However, no pattern could be discerned in these 19 pairs.

The intercorrelations were also computed separately for those Ss above the median IQ and for those below it. All of the 19 significant relationships found were in the matrix based on the scores of Ss in the high-IQ group. In other words, consistency in level of creative performance across media occurred more frequently among high-IQ than among low-IQ subjects.

As has been found in other studies, the relationships between creativity scores and the kind of cognition assessed by Stanford-Binet IQ's were small. In no case did a significant relationship appear between the scores on any type of creativity and IQ.

SUMMARY

Creativity was differentiated according to type and according to the locus (i.e., form or content) at which it was displayed within an art product. The typology was then used to evaluate two art products made by each of 85 sixth-grade pupils. One product was a nine-page booklet of drawings, and the other was a three-dimensional structure of clay and toothpicks. Each product was rated independently by three artistically experienced judges, using a nine-point scale. The degree of interjudge agreement was sufficiently high to warrant investigating the relationships among the ratings.

The relationships between creative performance in one medium and creative performance in the other were low, the median coefficient being .11. However, when significant (.25 or higher) coefficients between two types did occur, they were between types having the same locus. That is, creativity in form in one medium was most likely to be related to creativity in form in the other medium; creativity in content in one medium was most likely to be related to creativity in content in the other medium.

One type of creativity, *Boundary Breaking*, occurred much less frequently than the other types. Whereas *Boundary Pushing*, *Inventing*, and *Aesthetic Organizing* were displayed in some degree by almost all subjects, *Boundary Breaking* was not. The difficulty in achieving this type of creative behavior may account for its rarity.

When correlations were computed for the boys and the girls separately, no differences in the pattern of relationships among the types of creativity were found. However, when the sample was divided in half at the median IQ, those subjects in the upper half were more consistent in their creative performance across media than those in the lower half. No significant relationships emerged between IQ and any of the types of creativity.

38 *Role Replication and Reversal in Play*[1]

BRIAN SUTTON-SMITH

How do fifth-grade children perceive their play behavior within the family and with playmates? The results show changing status relations—first-borns take high power roles with siblings and equal or lower power roles with their friends; later-borns take low power roles with older siblings and high power roles with their friends. A hypothesis for further investigation is suggested: the play behavior with friends of first-borns relicates their responses to their parents; later-borns generalize to play with friends' behavior modeled after the power exercised over them by the first-born.

The present investigations grew out of an intensive analysis of two day-long specimen records on the same boy, one at home and one at camp (Gump, Schoggen and Redl, 1963).[2]

It was apparent in these records that the central character, Wally, who was the oldest in his family, nearly always dominated his younger siblings whether playing with them or not. His play status replicated his sibling status. Yet, when playing with his neighborhood and camp friends, Wally often took an egalitarian or low status role and in some cases even showed remarkable passivity in the face of the playful teasing of his best friend (Gump et al., 1955, p. 117). His play status with friends was the reverse of his status with his siblings. It was the purpose of the present study to inquire whether such changing status relations occurred more generally among children—in particular, whether the play with siblings systematically replicated sibling status relationships while play with friends systematically reversed the re-

[1]This investigation was supported in part by Grant MH 07794-02 from the National Institute of Mental Health.

[2]The author wishes to express his appreciation to Paul V. Gump of the Department of Psychology, University of Kansas, for permission to review these day studies, and to E. F. Morgan, Jr., and Linda Brandt of Clark University for their participation in the analysis of the studies.

Reprinted from the *Merrill-Palmer Quarterly of Behavior and Development*, 1966, **12**, 285–298, by permission of the author and the Merrill-Palmer Institute.

lations which might be predicted from knowledge of the sibling status order. The case study permitted the specific hypothesis that first-borns would dominate their siblings in play but be of equal or lower status with their friends.

The more general significance of this hypothesis is that it is one expression of a recurrent problem in the interpretation of children's play. This problem centers on the nature of the relations between variables antecedent to the play (motivational variables, child training variables, or status variables as in the present case), and variables which are a part of the play structure itself (acts of mock aggression, strategy, or being boss as in the present case). (See Roberts and Sutton-Smith, 1962; Levin and Wardell, 1962.)

The classic position on the relations between antecedent social status and formal play status is that presented by William F. Whyte in *Street Corner Society* (1933). In the young adult group that he studied, Whyte discovered that performance in a favorite game did not depend solely on the player's skill at that game. On the contrary, if that person was playing along with the members of his own gang or clique, his score was determined primarily by his status in that gang. Thus, the leader of the group would tend to get the highest score in the game and the gang member of the lowest status would tend to get the lowest score. This would occur whenever the gang played together even though other tests indicated that from the point of view of pure skill, the players of lower status should have been capable of doing better.

This case study evidence of Whyte's was subsequently paralleled by Harvey (1953) in an investigation of dart playing among well-defined groups of adolescents, in which the expectations that were held for success in game performances were shown to be largely determined by the subject's previous social standing in the friendship group. There are other studies also which indicate that sociometric status outside of a game may interfere with performance, for example, in marksmanship (McGrath, 1962) and basketball (Fielder, 1954). In addition, there are anecdotal materials about children's play which are of similar import. Gesell (1946, p. 121) mentions children who willingly accede to domination in order to be accepted into the play group. And Jones (1943, p. 55) describes a boy who "in spite of almost daily humiliations . . . showed a persistent eagerness to 'belong,' to be a member of groups, and take part in group activities . . ." so always took a lower status in play.

Against such evidence that play status directly replicates sociometric status, it is possible to cite other less well documented evidence which suggests that play status may sometimes have a reverse relationship to sociometric status. Thus Redl and Wineman (1951, p. 288) cite the case of a high-powered boy who took lower powered roles in play: "For him to yield his power in fantasy seems to be acceptable since he is achieving enjoyment out of the other elements of the game, perhaps even his essentially despotic yielding of power." Sometimes because sociometric leaders are of the unassertive and congenial sort mentioned by various investigators

(Jennings, 1947, p. 15; Tryon, 1944, p. 227; Tuddenham, 1951, p. 257), other low status children are permitted to take higher status roles in play. As a grade three boy said of one such sociometric leader in a pilot study carried out by the present investigator:[3] "He does what I like doing. He does anything the other guys want him to do."

Alternatively, there are children of lower sociometric status who so arrange the circumstances of their play that they can reverse the roles within it. Valentine (1948, p. 188) cites the case of the younger sister in a large family compensating for her henpecked family status by exercising an iron control over her peer play group. Lehmann and Witty (1927, p. 146) cite the case of a lower status group of children who were unsuccessful in school achievement playing persistently at a game of high status content, namely, "schools." In the pilot study referred to above, the girl with the lowest sociometric ranking in her class was observed to spend the greater part of her lunch hour playing with children of a lower grade level whom she could dominate. She claimed to have invented the game she played with

_____
[3]In the pilot study, 34 grade three children (19 boys and 15 girls) were given a sociometric to rate them on playmate acceptance, and were observed in their free noon-hour play in order to discover relationships between their group status and their play status. This was done in a Berkeley, California, elementary school while the investigator was a Smith-Mundt research fellow at the Institute of Child Welfare, University of California, 1952–53. A belated appreciation is here expressed for the interest and help of Dr. H. E. Jones, at that time the Director of the Institute.

them, which she called "Witch Pie" and in which she herself took the important role of mother (Gomme, 1964, p. 396).

There are additional reasons for believing that children may sometimes reverse their usual sociometric status in play. These are inherent in the structure of the games themselves, particularly those played by children between the ages of 6 and 12 years. These games usually involve a variety of counting-out, turn-taking, and role-reversal devices which so vary the allocation of status within the game that it would be difficult for children not to get some experience of differential status through playing them (Sutton-Smith and Gump, 1955).

In sum, the literature suggests both that persons may have experiences of status within play which replicate their status with associates outside of play, and that they may have play experiences that are reversely related to their status outside of it. From the above evidence we may derive either that different persons have different types of relations between their status in and out of play, some replicative and some reversed, or what seems more likely, that the *same* persons sometimes have direct and sometimes reversed relations.

In this literature survey a variety of inter- and cross-group relations have been involved. In the present study, the questions being asked refer only to play status within the family and to play status with playmates. The major hypothesis is that first-borns will tend to dominate their play with siblings and be of equal or less power in play with others. While it is not possible to speak with great confidence about the later-borns except to say that they will be dominated in play by their older siblings, there are some indications in the literature to suggest that they may attempt to dominate their best friends. Several studies have indicated that later-borns tend to be more power striving in general (Harris, 1964; Krout, 1939; Veroff, Atkinson, Feld, Gurin, 1960).

METHOD

Subjects

The question of the relations between status in and out of play with siblings and friends was investigated by submitting five copies of a play inventory to 95 children (44 boys and 51 girls) in two fifth grades at Kenwood School, Bowling Green, Ohio.[4] Children in this school are from an upper sociometric housing area and are of predominately middle-class families.

Inventory

The inventory used was an 180-item play inventory (Sutton-Smith and Rosenberg, 1959) which has previously been used extensively in testing masculine-feminine difference (Rosenberg and Sutton-Smith, 1964a), age changes in play preference (Sutton-Smith, Rosenberg, and Morgan, 1963), and relations between play prefer-

ences and play behavior (Sutton-Smith, 1965).

Procedure

The children were asked to write on the first inventory the name and age of their nearest sibling. If they were oldest in the family, this should be the next sibling below them in age; if they were a younger sibling, this should be the sibling immediately older than themselves. Children were asked to check on this 180-item play inventory the games that they had played with that sibling over the past year. They were told also to indicate in each case who had been usually the boss in the play, or whether they were usually equal when they played together. They did this by writing in *me, sib,* or the *equal sign* (=) after the play. Being boss was defined as being in charge of the game, taking the better positions in the game, and being better at the game. The same instructions were followed for the other inventories—only this time the children were instructed to write in respectively, the name of their best friend (*B. F.*), the person in their own class with whom they played most while at school (class playmate: *C. P.*), the person outside of their own class with whom they played most at school (school playmate: *S. P.*), and the person in their neighborhood with whom they played most at home (neighborhood playmate: *N. P.*). They were to fill in the names and the ages of these persons regardless of whether the identity of the various playmates was the same or different.

The forms were administered on two separate occasions, with the sib-

---

[4]A special note of appreciation is also in order here for the assistance provided by Harlan Lehtooma, principal of the Kenwood School, and teachers Mrs. Shaddix, Slebos, Maurer, and Benham.

ling and best-friend forms administered on the first occasion and the other three forms three weeks later. This double administration resulted in slight differences in the size of the N on the separate occasions. In addition, not all the children filled in all the forms properly (omitting names, etc.) which similarly contributed to minor changes in the N (see Table 1). The number of children in each of the eight ordinal groupings is indicated in Table 1. Children were only retained who were in a two-child or larger family and who were within five years of their sibling's age. There was no significant difference in average age difference between first-borns with their younger siblings (2.48 years) and later-borns with their older siblings (2.72 years). First-borns were equally distributed across the two-child, three-child and larger-than-three-child families (11: 13: 10), but the later-borns tended to come more often from the larger size families (10: 26: 38).

These similarities and differences in family size, however, showed no relation to the results that follow. Results for first-borns were uniform irrespective of family size, and results for later-borns varied by type of laterborn positions but not by family size. A check for overlap of persons responded to across the inventories indicated that friend and class playmate were the same in 27% of the cases; friend and schoolmate were the same in 9% of the cases; friend and neighborhood playmate were the same in 23% of the cases; classmate and neighborhood playmate were the same in 9% of the cases; and schoolmate and neighborhood playmate were the same in 9% of the cases.

Reliability

In one grade the sibling form was administered again after the three-week period as a check on the reliability of responses. The form scored as to whether the subject said he or sib was more often the boss ($N = 24$) yielded a 79% agreement between the two occasions.

As an intra-subject check on the reliability of the children's responses to the play inventory, they were also given an open-ended questionnaire (at the end of the second administration of the play scales) in which they were asked the questions: "When playing with your sibling, who gets to be the boss?" "Why?"; "When playing with your friend, who gets to be the boss?" "Why?" Results are to be found in Table 2 and are consistent with those derived from the play inventories in Table 1.

RESULTS

Table 1 shows the number of subjects by ordinal position who say they see themselves or the sibling as more often the boss or equal in the games they play. The determination in a particular case was arrived at by counting the *me* and *sib* references on each play scale (ignoring the "=" references), then deciding whether there were more of the me or sib references or whether these were equal in number. The same procedure was followed for *B. F.*, *C. P.*, etc. The numbers in Table 1 therefore refer to the gross power outcome in each case rather

TABLE 1.—Play-Scale Relations between Ordinal Position and Power in Play

ORDINAL POSITION	N	SIBLING			BEST FRIEND			CLASSROOM PLAYMATE			SCHOOL PLAYMATE			NEIGHBORHOOD PLAYMATE		
		High Power	Equal Power	Low Power	High Power	Equal Power	Low Power	High Power	Equal Power	Low Power	High Power	Equal Power	Low Power	High Power	Equal Power	Low Power
FIRST-BORNS																
MIM	(13)	12	0	1	3	4	6	2	6	5	3	7	2	2	9	2
MIF	(5)	4	0	1	1	1	3	0	4	1	0	4	1	1	3	1
F1F	(9)	9	0	0	3	3	3	0	6	2	1	6	1	2	4	2
FIM	(7)	6	0	1	2	2	3	3	3	1	1	3	2	0	5	1
Totals	*(34)*	*31*	*0*	*3*	*9*	*10*	*15*	*5*	*19*	*9*	*5*	*20*	*6*	*5*	*21*	*6*
LATER-BORNS																
MM2	(20)	3	2	15	10	6	4	1	8	4	0	12	1	6	7	1
FM2	(11)	7	3	1	4	4	3	2	6	2	0	9	0	4	5	1
FF2	(24)	10	4	10	12	6	6	6	8	3	6	9	2	11	5	2
MF2	(19)	2	2	15	4	9	6	3	10	2	4	9	2	4	7	2
Totals	*(74)*	*22*	*11*	*41*	*30*	*25*	*19*	*12*	*32*	*11*	*10*	*39*	*5*	*25*	*24*	*6*

than the frequency within cases. This technique had the virtue of eliminating the effects of different frequencies of response to each inventory by different individuals. There were, however, no significant differences in response frequency of first- or later-borns as a whole, though females as compared with males checked approximately a third more items.

The hypothesis that first-borns would take high power roles with siblings and equal or low power roles with friends was tested by comparing the totals of first-born responses to siblings and to friends across *High Power, Equal,* and *Low Power* (31, 0, 3: 9, 10, 15)—that is, the upper section of the first two columns in Table 1. The data offers overwhelming support ($X^2 = 30.10$, p $<.001$). That is, first-borns see themselves more often

as boss when playing with siblings and more often as equal or not boss when playing with friends. For later-borns, the situation is neatly reversed with later-borns seeing themselves as not being the boss with their older siblings but more often as boss with their friends (22, 11, 41: 30, 25, 19) ($X^2 = 14.74$, p $<.025$).

Results for answers to the questionnaire on who gets to be boss when playing with siblings or friends are similar to those derived from the play inventory, as can be seen from Table 2. First-born responses to siblings and friends (26, 2, 3: 5, 5, 18) yield $X^2 = 26.12$, $p < .001$. Responses of the later-born (16, 2, 39: 22, 17, 16) yield $X^2 = 22.38$, $p < .001$. In short, verbal responses to this questionnaire follow along lines expected from the play scales.

TABLE 2.—Questionnaire Relations between Sibling Position and Power in Play

ORDINAL POSITION	SIBLING			FRIEND		
	High Power	Equal	Low Power	High Power	Equal	Low Power
FIRST-BORNS						
M1M	11	0	1	2	5	6
M1F	4	1	1	0	0	4
F1F	7	0	1	1	0	4
F1M	4	1	0	2	0	4
Totals	26	2	3	5	5	18
LATER-BORNS						
MM2	3	1	11	8	2	2
FM2	4	1	3	3	2	3
FF2	4	0	16	6	6	8
MF2	5	0	9	5	7	3
Totals	16	2	39	22	17	16

Another way of contrasting firsts and later-borns is by directly comparing their respective play with friends. On the inventory, first-borns have a tendency to see themselves as less powerful than friends to a greater extent than do later-borns (9, 10, 15: 30, 25, 19) ($X^2 = 3.94$, $p < .20$). The results for the questionnaire are much more clear cut, resulting in a significant difference between the two groups in their statements about play with friends. Firsts see themselves as bossed, non-firsts as bossing a little more than they are bossed (5, 5, 18: 22, 17, 16) ($X^2 = 9.74$, $p < .01$).

In response to the question "Why?", the majority of first-borns who give reasons (and not all do) say they are the boss of their siblings because they are older or bigger. The majority of later-borns say they are not the boss for the same reason, i.e., that the sibling is older or bigger. The responses to the friend question, however, appear to have a more "projective" character and are interesting because of that. While there is less similarity of answers than with respect to the sibling question, the largest single category of responses from the first-born is that their friend is boss because he is older. Firsts also indicate more compliance with the friend by answers such as: the friend "is bigger," "is bossy," "says things and gets to be boss," "is older," "I do whatever he says," "if my friend doesn't get his own way he won't play," "give the friend a chance," "I let him have his own way," "to be polite," "he knows more." By contrast, the later-borns say they are more often boss with their friends because more often they are older than the friend. But in addi-

tion, there are other statements made by the later-borns which are of an assertive character or indicate compliance with them by their friend. For example: "I can play better," "I think of most games," "I know more," "I do most things right," "the friend doesn't care," "the friend doesn't get mad," "I like to be boss," "the friend lets me be boss," "I am more firm and convincing."

As indicated in Table 1, relations of firsts and later-borns with classmates and schoolmates seem to be less indicative of power relationships. The characteristic pattern appears to be an egalitarian one with equality of relations predominating. This outcome may be due to the intrinsically egalitarian nature of play structure (built-in role reversal, etc.), as indicated in the introduction. Or it may perhaps be due to the nature of game controls existing in the school situation where the play with class playmate and school playmate occurs. That is, it may be understood that everyone is expected to get a turn and bossing is not permitted. The same egalitarianism holds for neighborhood playmates, at least for first-borns. The later-borns persist with their dominating friendship pattern; that is, they claim a higher power over their neighborhood playmates in the same way as they did over their friends. If their sibling and neighborhood playmates are contrasted (22, 11, 41: 25, 24, 6) again there results a $X^2 = 28.92$, $p < .001$.

If the particular ordinal positions within the larger set are examined, it is clear that results are much more consistent for firsts than for later-borns. Later-borns with older and presumably more powerful brothers (the MM2 group) follow the trends observed above most perfectly. The younger child with an older female sibling, however, does not fit the trend. If the younger is a male (FM2) he claims more bossing than his older sister; if a female (FF2), she claims an equal amount. There is a conflict in the evidence here, because the reciprocal older siblings also claim to boss the younger ones. On the direct questionnaire as compared with the game inventory, however, both the younger siblings concede superiority to the older siblings, though this is more marked for the later-born girl. Perhaps it makes sense that the later-born boy with the older sister should be the one most unwilling to concede her superiority.

pared with the number of equal attributions, and each protocol then classified as concerned mainly with power or equality, it is clear that equality dominates throughout most of the play, with one exception. That exception is play with siblings, where power counts at least as much as equality with first-borns and even more so with later-borns. If firsts and later-borns are combined, and their relations in which power is dominant are compared with those in which equality is dominant and comparisons then made between their responses to siblings and friends, (57, 45: 29, 78) the first two columns of Table 3—there results a $X^2 = 17.86$, $p < .001$. In sum, power is the major concern in play with siblings and a minor con-

TABLE 3.—Power and Egalitarian Relations with Different Associates

Relations	Sibling	Best Friend	Classroom Playmate	School Playmate	Neighborhood Playmate	Totals
FIRST-BORNS						
Power	18	9	6	12	5	50
Egalitarian	16	24	36	30	40	156
LATER-BORNS						
Power	39	20	5	7	13	84
Egalitarian	29	54	41	40	34	198

In all the above computations, power or equality is based on the balance of claimed power between subjects and the other player. Equality by that system of reckoning was derived from a balance of claims made for self and other. But the subjects were also asked in the play inventory to indicate the number of games in which they felt relations were equal. If all protocol is rescored for the number of power attributions (*me* or *sib*) as com-

cern in play with friends. Power is also a minor concern in play with class playmates, school playmates and neighborhood playmates, as is clear from Tables 1 and 3.

Yet, another road to the same conclusion is simply to count the total frequency of games over all protocol in which the self is mentioned, the other is mentioned, or equals is mentioned. The totals are: for *me*, 1833; for *other*, 1315; for *equal*, 5375. These totals again show an overwhelming concern with equality rather than with power relations in the responses to these scales.

DISCUSSION

It was the major intent of this paper to investigate the possibility of systematic relations existing between sibling-status and play-status (with siblings and friends), with a view to examining the replicative or reverse character of play structure in general. While results are based only on the children's perception of their own play, the agreement across and between ordinal positions suggests that these responses have consensual validity. Whether real behavior follows the course of these agreements is not dealt with directly. Taken together, however, the self- evidence of the view that older siblings boss younger ones, the case study data cited in the introduction, and the corroborative studies and sociometric references cited below, seem to imply that it does.

The results show that the first-borns' perception of their play with siblings replicates their actual position in the sibling power structure, but that their perception of their play with friends reverses that position. That is, though high powered in the sibling structure, first-borns take equal or lower power positions with friends. Among the later-borns the same duality between replication and reversal of roles in play holds, but with the opposite effect. The later-borns show low power in relation to siblings but high power in relation to friends. In both cases, therefore, replication of sibling power occurs in play with siblings but re-

versal of sibling power occurs in play with friends.[5]

Within sibling relationships where the sociometric relations are fairly rigidly established by age and size differences (and probably long standing differences in parent treatment as well), the current situation parallels that described by Whyte (1933), mentioned in the introduction. The family-group hierarchy is reproduced in the play hierarchy. In the friendship play relations, however, where the engagement in play is presumably of a more voluntary nature, play status relations take on a character which, on the surface, reverses the sibling relations within the family. By implication the methodological usage of relations with "friends" as a "projective" technique is an incidental finding worthy of further investigation.

Nevertheless, it is open to question whether the non-bossiness or compliance of first-borns with their friends is a reversal of relationships with the sib-

---

[5]It was judged that these effects were not produced by a response reversal phenomena on the first administration. It might be argued, for example, that the first-born having said that he was powerful over his sibling might select from among his best friends one who was more powerful than he; or, vice versa, the later-born having said he was less powerful than the first, might select from among his best friends one who was less powerful than he. Both sets of subjects would thus balance out their responses in the direction of an overall socially desirable response. The neighborhood friend responses given on the second administration, however, are similar in direction to the best friend responses, particularly for the later-born, which suggests that the substantive interpretations being made here are the most parsimonious.

lings, or whether it is actually a replication of their existing relationships with the parents. Given the extensive data on the first-borns' compliance, conformity, dependence (Sampson, 1962; Sears, et al., 1957; Goodenough and Leahy, 1927; Becker and Carroll, 1962), the latter interpretation may be the more likely alternative. If so, the conclusion may be that while the firsts strive to keep non-firsts in lower status positions on all possible occasions, thus preserving their own status in the family hierarchy, when in a more voluntary situation among friends they prefer the behavior of being dependent or conforming with another person, which is the relationship they have had with their parents. Thus, their friendship play behavior may be a replication of their responses to their parents rather than a reversal of their attitudes towards their siblings.

Later-borns, on the other hand, who have been characterized in other studies as aggressive and power-striving (Harris, 1964; Krout, 1939; Veroff, et al., 1960), look as if their play relations are a reversal of their responses in sibling relationships. It is not an unreasonable thesis that the power they exercise over friends is a manifestation of the power they seek but cannot obtain with their older siblings, and that their model in this is the power exercised over them by those older siblings. If this is true, it might account for the stronger power-seeking of later-borns. It is a well-established finding in the ordinal literature that firsts tend to be relatively more influenced by their parents than do later-borns, and that later-borns in turn tend to be relatively more influ-

enced by their older siblings (Rosenberg and Sutton-Smith, 1964b). As older children are relatively inexperienced and presumably harsher wielders of power than are their parents, it follows that behavior modeled after theirs by the younger children may have a more assertive character also. It is noticeable in the above results that the later-born claim to assert their power not only over best friends, but also over neighborhood friends. This is not the case with first-borns, although the percentage of overlap between B. F. and N. F. is approximately the same in both cases. That this bossiness of the later born is of a more general nature is supported by a finding in a parallel sociometric study which has shown that classmates more often perceive later-borns, than first-borns as bossy (Sutton-Smith and Rosenberg, 1965).

In sum, while firsts and later-borns replicate their sibling relationships in their play status relations with siblings, their reversal of these status relationships in play behavior with friends appears to be of a quite different origin. The following hypotheses, therefore, seem worthy of further investigation. Namely, that firsts generalize to their play with friends relationships analogous to those they maintain with their parents, but that later borns generalize to play with friends behavior modelled after the power exercised over them by the first-born.

The present finding that the uses of status in play vary by ordinal position, as well as by play associate and presumably by play ecology (neighborhood, school, etc.), contributes towards an understanding of the complexity of the findings in the literature with respect to status and play.

From the finding that about five-eighths of the games checked were characterized as ones of equality not power, a further conclusion may be drawn. That is, normatively speaking, it is not the function of play to systematically replicate or reverse the status relationships found in the family. If we may extrapolate this finding to other dimensions which have been studied in relation to play (aggression, sex, dependency, etc.), and which have been said to bear possible replicative or reverse relations with play, the present data appear to suggest that, again normatively speaking, these matters will not dominate the play behaviors. The fact, however, that they can dominate those behaviors for a considerable portion of the time (three-eighths in the present estimate) helps to explain the predictive power of those play theories which subsume play to concepts which do not derive directly from play phenomena as such. One example in point can be found in psychoanalytic theory, in which play is often explained in terms of affective conflict (Waelder, 1933). Another example is Piaget's play theory, in which play is explained in terms of cognitive disequilibrium (Piaget, 1962; Sutton-Smith, 1966). The present finding that, normatively speaking, children do not perceive their play status relations as dominated by status relations outside the intrinsic economy of play, gives some support to those who view play as a behavior system with a formal character that must be understood in terms of its own intrinsic dimensions (Huizinga, 1949).

39 *Children's Learning from Television*

WILBUR SCHRAMM

JACK LYLE

EDWIN B. PARKER

By comparing two communities, generally alike except for the possession of television, the following selection explores three hypotheses concerning children's learning from television. To what extent are the hypotheses confirmed? What are your answers to the questions in the last paragraph of the article?

Reprinted from E. C. Uliassi (Ed.), *Studies in Public Communication*, Volume 3 (series), Department of Sociology, University of Chicago, 1961, pp. 86–98, by permission of the senior author and Nathan Keyfitz, Professor and Chairman, Department of Sociology, University of Chicago.

No one doubts that children learn from television. Nearly 100 studies (Kumata, 1960) now testify that they learn efficiently in the classroom from instructional television. There is no similar group of studies to prove that they learn in the home from the non-instructional television to which they devote about one sixth of their waking hours from the ages of 3 to 16, but the fact of this learning has been generally accepted. No parent who has watched his children reproduce language and mannerisms, mention names, and beg boxtops, all familiar to him only through television, doubts that his children are learning from television. Indeed, the question of what a child learns from television has been second in the public mind only to the question of what a child learns in school; although whereas the worry has been that the child might not be learning *enough* in school, it is rather that he might learn *too much*, of an undesirable kind of knowledge, from television.

It may be useful, therefore, to try to sketch in some of the dimensions of a child's learning from home television. What does the child tend to learn from television? Does he get an earlier start, thanks to television, in learning about his environment? Does he get an earlier start in learning the skills of communication? Does television really change anything in the amount or nature of his knowledge, from what he would have known without television?

These are not easy questions to answer. For example, the Himmelweit-Oppenheim-Vince (1958, p. 291) team who made a sophisticated study of children's television behavior in England were forced to admit:

"We were not able to find a sufficiently large number of information items (despite careful monitoring of children's and early evening television) which, without being trivial or abstruse, were not also known equally well to the controls (children without television)—a further indication of the essential similarity of the material put over by the different mass media. . . . One or two items of rather specialized information included in the test showed that the viewers do pick up information—but their number was too small to permit more detailed analysis."

We are very fortunate, therefore, as a by-product of a recent study of television behavior, involving 6,000 children in the United States and Canada (Schramm, Lyle, and Parker, 1961), to be able to sketch in, at least tentatively, some of the outlines of children's learning from television. These are the findings we are here reporting.

THE SOURCES OF THE DATA

In the course of the large study mentioned above, we were able to give knowledge tests (along with a great many other instruments and questions) to three fairly large samples of children: (a) 2,196 children sampled from the first six, and the 8th, 10th, and 12th grades in San Francisco; (b) 1,708 children representing the 1st, 6th, and 10th grades in five Rocky Mountain communities; and (c) 913 children, representing the 1st, 6th, and 10th grades in two Canadian communities, one of which did and one of which did not yet have television.

These two latter communities are of special interest to the problem we are discussing. Therefore, let us note about them that they are both cities of about 5,000 persons, in the same general geographical and cultural area, supported by about the same industries and businesses, containing about the same ethnical and religious groups, and served by the same types of school system. But one of them, which we shall call Teletown, is so situated that it receives not only all the Canadian network television, but also most of the United States service. The other, because of the accident of geography and the delayed extension of cables and microwave systems, has no television reception. Teletown has television receivers in more than 75 per cent of its homes, and every child in our sample had regular access to television programs. In the other community, which we shall call Controltown, there was only one television receiver connected, and it received signals, the owners reported, about three nights a year. In these two communities, therefore, we have an opportunity to make comparisons of children's informal learning with the culture held relatively constant, so to speak, except for the presence or absence of television.

THE NATURE OF CHILDREN'S INFORMAL LEARNING FROM TELEVISION

Let us be clear that we are dealing now, not with what children learn from the formal and patterned use of instructional television in the classroom, but rather from the informal use of television in the home. This latter use represents at least 95 per cent of all the television they see.

It is evident that most of a child's informal learning from television will be *incidental* learning. By this we mean learning that takes place when a viewer goes to television primarily for entertainment, and stores up certain items of information without seeking them. Practically all of a child's early use of television is in quest of entertainment. Out of 111 programs named by San Francisco children in the first six grades as programs they liked well enough to try to hear regularly, only four were programs in which the information content, rather than the entertainment content, appeared to be central to the purpose of the program. The act of going purposefully to the media for useful information is behavior that is learned chiefly in school, and more often sends the child to print than to the audiovisual media. The idea of going purposefully to television at home, to seek information, is a relatively uncommon behavior, learned late, and, as we have been able to document in our study, likely to be engaged in, to any considerable extent, only by a relatively small group of children. Therefore, most of the learning that takes place from home television must be incidental to the main purpose of viewing, and we can focus our attention on the presumed characteristics of a child's incidental learning.

The amount of learning, we can suppose, will depend on abilities, needs, and focus of attention. The easiest of these to define and predict upon is mental ability. Bright children, other things being equal, will learn more than less bright ones. So we can suppose that the brightest children, who are likely also to be "achievers," can be expected to make maximum use of *any* opportunity to learn from television.

However, there is also reason to think that television might represent an effective learning opportunity for children of below-average mental ability. This has been found empirically in some of the studies of instructional television (Barrow and Westley, 1959), but it may also be predicted theoretically on the grounds that television obtains from the slower children an extent and degree of attention which they do not commonly give to learning experiences. It supplies motivation they otherwise might not have. This should be especially noticeable in the early years of their lives before they approach the ceiling of their ability to learn.

There are certain other reasons, also, for expecting relatively more learning from television early in a child's life.

For one thing, we should expect a child to be more likely to pay attention to, and store up, some fact or item of behavior, if it is *new* to him. Brodbeck (1955) reports a study of a "Hopalong Cassidy" film which produced considerable learning and behavior change on the part of younger children, but very little on the part of older children. After some investigation, they concluded that this was because the film was a new experience to the young children, but "old stuff" to the older ones. This familiarity effect is especially important in television because of the astonishing repetitiveness of many of the program types. As a child becomes more familiar with the medium, he learns to sort out the material. He sets up a pattern of expectation which keeps him from having to pay too much attention to the familiar items, and allows him to concentrate on the new ones—if they are not *too* unfamiliar.

On this basis, we should expect that the greatest amount of incidental learning from television would take place, let us say, in the ages from three to eight, when television has the least competition. Then the child's slate is relatively clean. Almost any experience is new to him, and therefore absorbing. Later, the competition for attention grows more severe. Every year the memory shelves grow a little more full. But in those years before the child learns to read well, when his horizon is still narrow and his curiosity boundless, when almost everything beyond his home and his little family circle is new—that is the time television has a unique opportunity to contribute to his information and his skills.

Another reason why television should be an especially effective early agent of incidental learning is the matter of its seeming *real*. A number of observers have noted that mass media content has greater impact on children if they believe it "really happened." In the early years of childhood, there is a shadowy border at best between the story world and the real world, and the events of the picture tube, the screen, or the bedtime story often seem terribly real. As children grow older they begin to develop what Dysinger and Ruckmick (1933) call "adult discount," meaning the habit of the adult of looking at an entertainment film or television program as art rather than life. Therefore, during the years when television is still seen as real, and thus transferable to life, we can expect a broader range of learning. But let us be careful not to suggest that learning does not occur, or reality is not perceived, even in the midst of play-acting. We know that many a girl can get suggestions for her love life or her spring wardrobe, even from a program which she knows is drama rather than real life.

Thus far we have been talking about the children's side of the learning. It is obvious, however, that the individuals and organizations who produce programs have something to do with incidental learning from television, because they control what goes into the programs. To be sure, all children do not perceive the same things in the same program, and no program is perceived by the audience precisely as the author or producer conceived it. But on the other hand, television's own focus of attention will obviously have something to do with what is learned from it. Television's focus is overwhelmingly on fantasy and formula programs: westerns, whodunits, situation comedies, and so forth. These programs are quite redundant and repetitive. We have already noted that children typically choose few of the reality programs on television (meaning the programs intended to illuminate public affairs, science, and the like). Therefore, it is highly probable that the average child will be getting a heavy diet of formula and fantasy. In the first years of his viewing, all this

will be new to him and we can expect that his incidental learning from it will be at a maximum. But as he becomes more accustomed to the programs, we can expect him to find fewer and fewer new items to learn. Therefore, on this basis too, we can expect a child to learn relatively less from television as he grows older. And if this program diet is predominantly formula and fantasy, we can predict that his incidental learning will be chiefly from this kind of material. . . .

THE HYPOTHESES

On the basis of what we have been saying, we should expect three relationships to hold, at least in general terms:

(1) Television should give children a faster start at learning useful skills and knowledge about their environments than children typically were given before the age of television (because of the great vividness of the medium, and the amount of time it commands in years when children's memories are least crowded); but that this advantage would be lost after a few years (because of the repetitiveness of television, because children use television relatively little as a source of reality information and because older children without television obtain comparable information from other sources).

(2) In this first advantageous experience with television, the brightest and the slowest children in mental ability, will benefit rather more than the average children, in comparison to children without television (be-

cause the brightest children are "achievers" and will make maximum use of the new medium, and because the very attractiveness of television will provide motivation and command time which the slower children would otherwise not give to a comparable learning experience).

(3) That after the first years of accelerated learning, the effect of television on a child's knowledge will be to increase the levels of knowledge in areas which television, as used by children, chiefly emphasizes (the world of entertainment and fantasy), to decrease for heavy viewers of television the levels of knowledge in areas more easily learned about from other media (such as literature and public affairs), and to make no difference in levels of knowledge in areas which are learned chiefly from sources other than the mass media (for example, science, which is learned chiefly in school).

PROCEDURE

The best setting in which we can test the first part of (1) and (2) is with standardized and special vocabulary tests which we gave in Teletown and Controltown. We can hypothesize, in regard to these, that first grade children in Teletown will have larger vocabularies than first grade children in Controltown. We can also hypothesize that the differences will be larger in the case of the brightest and slowest children than in the case of the average children.

We can test the second part of (1) with information tests we gave the sixth and tenth grades in Teletown

and Controltown on such subjects as science, names in the news, famous authors, famous entertainers, and so forth. Here we hypothesize that there will be no significant difference between Teletown and Controltown children, in corresponding grades, on these tests. In other words, the Controltown children will have caught up with the Teletown children.

Our best opportunity to test (3) is by comparing heavy and light viewers in all three samples (Teletown, San Francisco, Rocky Mountain towns). Here we have numbers that more easily permit a test of significance. Therefore, we hypothesize that in the sixth grade and beyond, in these three samples with mental ability held constant, heavy viewers will score above light viewers on tests that clearly relate to the fantasy content of television, less highly than light viewers on tests that relate clearly to reality material learned more easily from other media than from television, and neither higher nor lower on tests that relate to areas not primarily learned from the mass media or learned equally well from all the media.

TESTS OF THE HYPOTHESES

We gave a Stanford-Binet vocabulary test, standardized on very large North American samples, to first grade children in Teletown and Controltown, in the same week of the school year. [Tables 1 and 2 show] the means of these tests, along with appropriate tests of significance, and an analysis of variance the results of which justify the t tests of significance.

It appears, then, that first grade chil-

TABLE 1.—Mean General Vocabulary Scores for First Grade Children in Teletown and Controltown, by Intelligence Grouping

| INTELLIGENCE | TELETOWN | | CONTROLTOWN | | S^a | t |
	N	MEAN	N	MEAN		
IQ above 115	29	9.10	21	8.19	1.78	1.78*
IQ 100–115	57	7.77	89	7.85	1.63	—
IQ below 100	33	7.52	27	6.33	1.48	3.11**

ᵃUnbiased estimate of standard deviation (within groups).
*Significant beyond the .10 level (.05 by one-tail test).
**Significant beyond the .01 level.

TABLE 2.—Results of Analysis of Variance Calculations for General Vocabulary Scores for First Grade Children in Teletown and Controltown, by Intelligence Grouping

SOURCE OF VARIATION	DEGREES OF FREEDOM	SUM OF SQUARES	MEAN SQUARE	F
Intelligence	2	59.98ᵃ	29.99	11.36***
Television	1	22.05ᵃ	22.05	8.35**
Interaction	2	21.43ᵃ	10.71	4.06*
Individuals	250	659.31	2.64	—

ᵃCorrected for disproportionate subclass frequencies.
*Significant beyond the .05 level.
**Significant beyond the .01 level.
***Significant beyond the .001 level.

dren of high intelligence and low intelligence in a television community do score significantly higher than their counterparts in a non-television community, on general vocabulary. The difference amounts to about one school grade. Between children of average intelligence in the two communities, however, the difference is negligible.

We gave these first grade children also a special vocabulary test made up of five words which they might be particularly likely to encounter on television—the words being *satellite, Prime Minister, pistol, war,* and *cancer.* . . . The results of that test in the two towns [are shown in Tables 3 and 4].

Again, the analysis of variance justifies continuing with the *t* tests. These show that there is a significant difference in favor of the Teletown children among the lowest intelligence group, but that the difference in the high group does not quite reach significance, and, again, that the difference between average children in the two towns is negligible.

To press the analysis further, we also compared the performance of heavy and light viewers in Teletown on the two vocabulary tests. Analysis

TABLE 3.—Mean Special Vocabulary Scores for First Grade Children in Teletown and Controltown, by Intelligence Grouping

INTELLIGENCE	TELETOWN		CONTROLTOWN		S^a	t
	N	MEAN	N	MEAN		
IQ above 115	29	3.10	21	2.71	1.01	1.00
IQ 100–115	57	2.68	89	2.52	1.11	—
IQ below 100	33	2.39	27	1.78	.93	2.52*

[a]Unbiased estimate of standard deviation (within groups).
*Significant beyond the .05 level.

TABLE 4.—Results of Analysis of Variance Calculations for Special Vocabulary Scores for First Grade Children in Teletown and Controltown, by Intelligence Grouping

SOURCE OF VARIATION	DEGREES OF FREEDOM	SUM OF SQUARES	MEAN SQUARE	F
Intelligence	2	—	—	—
Television	1	5.85[a]	5.85	5.32*
Interaction	2	2.37[a]	1.19	—
Individuals	250	276.06	1.10	—

[a]Corrected for disproportionate subclass frequencies.
*Significant beyond the .05 level.

of variance calculations on the general vocabulary test results show a television effect significant at the .05 level, but none of the intelligence groups taken separately attains a significant difference, although the average group is near the .05 level. In the special vocabulary test, however, significant differences are found, and these are recorded in . . . [Tables 5 and 6].

Again we find that the highest and lowest intelligence groups appear to benefit more from television than the average group, and that heavy viewers in both groups do significantly better than light viewers. This result gives us confidence that the differences we are finding are really related to viewing of television.

Therefore, we have considerable support for the hypotheses that first grade children in a town with television will have larger vocabularies than corresponding children in a town without television, and that the differences will be more pronounced in the highest and the lowest intelligence groups than in the middle group.

We are on less firm ground in testing the hypothesis that there will be no difference in knowledge levels in the sixth and tenth grades. Here we did not give vocabulary tests. Six tests and scales are available, however, using the sixth and tenth grade children in Teletown and Controltown. These are on science, ability to name bandleaders and popular singers, knowledge of literature, faraway place names, and statesmen and rulers.

TABLE 5.—Mean Special Vocabulary Scores for First Grade Children in Teletown by
Intelligence Grouping and by Television Viewing
(Heavy viewing = 1 hr. 15 min. or more per
average school day by parents' report)

| INTELLIGENCE | HEAVY VIEWERS | | LIGHT VIEWERS | | S^a | t |
	N	MEAN	N	MEAN		
IQ above 115	13	3.53	16	2.75	.95	2.23*
IQ 100–115	34	2.71	23	2.65	1.05	—
IQ below 100	19	2.68	14	2.00	.95	2.03*

[a] Unbiased estimate of standard deviation (within groups).
*Significant beyond .05 level.

TABLE 6.—Results of Analysis of Variance Calculations for Special
Vocabulary Scores for First Grade Children in Teletown by
Intelligence Grouping and by Television Viewing

SOURCE OF VARIATION	DEGREES OF FREEDOM	SUM OF SQUARES	MEAN SQUARE	F
Intelligence	2	—	—	—
Television	1	5.00[a]	5.00	5.00*
Interaction	2	3.16[a]	1.58	—
Individuals	113	112.61	1.00	—

[a] Corrected for disproportionate subclass frequencies.
*Significant beyond .05 level.

There was no over-all difference between the children of the two communities in these tests, in either of the grades, and very few significant differences in test performance even when the children are divided by intelligence and amount of viewing. This is precisely the experience of Himmelweit, Oppenheim, and Vince (1958), previously referred to, who worked with children bracketing the ages of our sixth graders.

We can report some trends. When the children are divided into groups by school grade and three levels of intelligence, and each of these groups is compared with its corresponding group in the other town, on each of the six tests, we have a possibility of 18 comparisons in each grade, 36 in all. Over 60 per cent of these comparisons, when there is a difference, are in favor of Controltown. Except for one tie, *all* the comparisons in the sixth grade are in favor of Controltown. All the comparisons on the science test, when there is a difference, are in favor of Controltown. To be sure, very few of these differences are significant. However, by sign test, the performance of the Controltown children is significantly superior in the sixth grade, and there is no significant difference in the tenth grade. Thus, we have every reason to believe, at least until better data becomes available, that there is no advantage to sixth and tenth grade children in a television community in the kinds of knowledge here measured. If there is any difference at all, more learning of these kinds would seem to take place among comparable children who do *not* have television.

In order to test the third series of hypotheses, we used the San Francisco, Rocky Mountain, and Teletown samples. Even so, however, it seemed better not to combine the samples, because in San Francisco we had eighth, tenth, and twelfth grades, rather than sixth and tenth, as in the other samples; and furthermore, there were a few slight differences in the tests and scales between samples (for example, in Teletown the Canadian children were not asked to name U.S. Senators, as were the Rocky Mountain and San Francisco children). Therefore, we made comparisons within samples, dividing each grade by heavy and light viewing and by intelligence, and comparing heavy viewers with light viewers in the sixth grade Rocky Mountain sample, and so on. This required us to use sign test statistics rather than more usual comparisons of means.

The results are as predicted. In the case of subject matter closely related to television's central content, the results . . . [appear in Table 7].

With respect to the subject matter which we judged could be learned more easily from media other than television . . . [the results are in Table 8].

Thus we have some evidence that television viewing may contribute to entertainment-related information, and not to information which relates to fine arts or public affairs and is thus more readily learned from print or some other medium.

We have fewer comparisons by which to test the hypothesis that there will be no difference in knowledge of subjects usually not learned from mass media (like science) or learned equally from several media (like faraway place names). Some of the tests were not given in all places, but . . . the results [are shown in Table 9].

On this evidence, at least, we have no basis for believing that there is any real difference related to television in knowledge of this kind.

BRIEF DISCUSSION

The hypotheses hold up, and we have at least a tentative set of propositions for estimating the amount and

TABLE 7.

TEST	RESULT	SIGNIFICANCE*
Ability to name singers	11 out of 13 comparisons favor heavy viewers; 1 is even; 1 favors light viewers	Significant beyond .01 level
Ability to name dance band leaders	8 out of 13 favor heavy viewers; 2 are even; 3 favor light viewers	Significant beyond .05 level

*By sign test: $K = \dfrac{2s + 1}{\sqrt{n}} - \sqrt{n}$

TABLE 8.

TEST	RESULT	SIGNIFICANCE
Ability to name writers	11 out of 13 comparisons favor light viewers; 2 favor heavy viewers	Significant beyond .02 level
Ability to name rulers and statesmen	10 out of 13 favor light viewers; 2 are even; 1 favors heavy viewers	Significant beyond .01 level

TABLE 9.

TEST	RESULT	SIGNIFICANCE
Ability to solve science problems	5 comparisons out of 10 favor light viewers; 2 are even; 3 favor heavy viewers	Not significant
Ability to recognize faraway place names	3 out of 9 favor light viewers; 4 are even; 2 favor heavy viewers	Not significant

kind of incidental learning that goes on as a by-product of children's two or three daily hours of television.

We feel it is necessary to say a word of caution about these results. For one thing, they are a fragmentary report on learning. They contain very little information about many areas of knowledge, or about learning to solve problems or think critically, or about the learning of taste and values, or about stimulation to undertake cultural or scientific or other desirable activities on one's own. To be sure, what we know or conjecture about most of these aspects of learning is not particularly favorable to the television experience, but it is important to know more about them before we close the books on the subject of learning from home television.

However, we have here some suggestive facts. Television *does* apparently send children off to a faster start in the skill they perhaps need most at an early age, although the advantage is chiefly to the brightest and the slowest children and not to the great group of average children. We can suppose, too, with some confidence that the same children who learn more vocabulary from television will also have learned more about their distant environments than comparable children without television. But the faster start is apparently frittered away in a repetitive diet of westerns, whodunits, and situation comedies; and it seems that heavy viewing in the sixth grade or beyond results in more knowledge (than light viewers have) of matters related to entertainment, but less knowledge of public affairs and fine arts.

These facts obviously have implications for public policy, although we have no intention of developing those implications here. However, we should like to suggest a few questions. If these conclusions are indeed broadly applicable, they would suggest that one of the great informative resources for young minds is being used at considerably less than what most observers would consider optimum. Is this necessary, considering the nature of the media and of its support, or can something be done so that the initial advantage of incidental learning from television can be broadened and extended in time? For example, there are many more reality opportunities on television than children make use of. Can parents by example, or schools by precept and interpretation, increase children's use of these reality experiences? To what extent are children's preferences for the richly supported fantasy and formula programs over the weakly supported reality programs inevitable considering the nature of children, and to what extent can they be traced to the support of these programs and the way they are made? With all the talent and resources of broadcasting, and, if necessary, with the resources and talents of foundations and educational institutions, is it possible to find out how to make reality programs skillfully enough that they will be truly competitive for children's interest with formula and fantasy? These are questions which obviously relate to the amount and kind of children's informal learning from television, and we suggest that they are questions with serious import for parents, schools, and broadcasters.

40 *Knowledge and Interests Concerning Sixteen Occupations among Elementary and Secondary School Students*

RICHARD C. NELSON

This study explores the knowledge and interests of third-, fifth-, seventh-, ninth-, and eleventh-grade pupils regarding a series of sixteen occupations. On reactions to occupations, the younger children and those of lower IQ and lower socioeconomic levels tend to respond positively; the older, brighter, and more advantaged children tend to respond negatively. The rejection process occurs as early as the third grade; negative responses outnumber positive responses on a ratio of almost three-and-one-half to one for all of the children in the study. It is suggested that the negative concepts, once learned, may be internalized because no early attempts are made to expose children to the world of work. One may ask: Why do children tend to reject occupations? Should the study of occupations start in the elementary school?

Accurate occupational information is essential to effective occupational choice, which has been explored to some extent in the literature relating to vocational development, but occupational knowledge and related areas of exploration have been insufficiently studied.

One can find material to answer the questions: What single job choice is preferred by each individual in a group at a given point in time? In what areas do young people concentrate their interests at a given point in time?

There is, however, little material to answer such questions as: What do children know about occupations and how does this knowledge develop? How do various age groups compare in their occupational knowledge? What types of occupations have appeal to youngsters of various age groups? Assuming multi-potentiality as a construct, what is the range of occupations given positive consideration at particular points in time by individuals?

PURPOSE AND PROBLEM

In the light of the above questions, this study sought to provide an objective description of some elements of the occupational knowledge and interests of youth, especially at ages prior to high school.

The problem was as follows. Given a stimulus of a group of occupations for identification and reaction, how do children of different age levels and backgrounds compare in naming and describing the occupations, and how do they compare in their reactions to the same occupations?

THE SAMPLE

The 595 students included in the study were selected within the Baltimore County, Maryland, school system. Classroom groups from grades three, five, seven, nine, and eleven were used. Half of the students were selected from a district which is semi-urban in character, the other half were from a semi-rural district. Due to the local practice of homogeneous grouping, it was necessary to select intelligence levels within which to work; the average and slightly above average levels were chosen. Sex and socio-economic subgroups, in addition to the above-mentioned grade level, intelligence level, and urban-rural subgroups, were consistently used as subgroups for which data were analyzed. The Edwards (1927) classification was used to set up socio-economic sub-

Reprinted from *Educational and Psychological Measurement*, 1963, **23**, 741–754, by permission of the author and the Editor, *Educational and Psychological Measurement*.

groups based on occupations of fathers; available school records indicated the occupations. Available school intelligence test scores were used in the formation of intelligence subgroups. Table 1 shows the distribution of subgroups of the sample.

THE INSTRUMENT

In order to widen the scope beyond questions concerning what a child would like to be when he grows up, an instrument was especially constructed for the study. It included colored slides of workers in 16 occupations (the number that could be responded to in a typical class period), and a questionnaire which inquired into both knowledge and interests regarding those same occupations.

Three principles guided the selection of the occupations for which slides were made. First, the occupations had to be available within the geographic area of the study since third grade children might be more limited than older children by geographic factors that would limit potential understanding. Second, the occupations had to illustrate the great breadth of our occupational structure. Merely selecting the occupations on a frequency basis was not sufficient; therefore the varying occupational levels should be illustrated and the jobs included should be distinct in skills required. Third, the selected occupations had to reflect the three to one ratio of men to women in the local occupational structure.

TABLE 1.—Distribution of Subgroups of the Population by Grade Level

SUBGROUPS		GRADE 3	GRADE 5	GRADE 7	GRADE 9	GRADE 11	TOTAL
All Students		68	119	141	146	121	595
Boys		32	65	78	64	52	291
Girls		36	54	63	82	69	304
Socio-economic Levels*							
Professional	0	9	18	18	29	20	94
Managerial	2	12	17	23	21	18	91
Clerical	3	12	24	30	32	21	119
Skilled Labor	4	13	21	30	21	35	120
Semi-skilled	5	13	24	20	21	12	90
Intelligence Quotients							
116 and above		23	35	37	22	23	139
108–115		15	19	39	39	32	144
100–107		18	21	37	38	25	140
99 and below		12	44	28	47	41	172
Urban		34	63	65	76	59	297
Rural		34	56	76	70	62	298

*Based on fathers' occupations. Does not include 81 students whose fathers work as farmers, farm laborers, unskilled workers, or service workers. These 81 students were not utilized in any cases where socio-economic subgroup comparisons were included. They were included in all other comparisons.

Listed in the order maintained throughout the study, the 16 slides were: janitor, assembler (female), bookkeeper, carpenter, manager, teacher (female), farmer, engineer, laborer, sales clerk (female), truck driver, doctor, warehouseman, secretary (female), mechanic, and telephone lineman.

PROCEDURES

Four major areas about each job were explored by each child. These were the title of the job, a description of the job, a reaction, whether "yes," "no," or "not sure," concerning the prospect of entering the job when the child was "through school," and why he responded favorably, unfavorably, or neutrally.

Children from grade three responded to the slides in an interview. Those from grades five, seven, nine, and eleven were surveyed in groups.

After preliminary questions were asked, the lights were turned off, a slide was shown, the lights were turned on, and the child was asked to respond to all four question areas discussed above. The interviewer recorded responses with third grade children. Above that grade the children recorded their own thoughts. Students who omitted or responded inadequately to as many as one-eighth of the questions asked were interviewed briefly. They were asked enough questions to clarify their responses or to ascertain that a lack of information was the cause of the omission.

A subgroup sample of ten per cent (59 students) was restudied 90 to 120 days after their original experience to check reliability. The individual interview procedure was used in the retest.

ANALYSIS OF DATA

The titles and descriptions given to the jobs by students were assigned a value of from three to zero. Three indicated an exact title or insightful description; two indicated a possible title or an adequate description; one an omission, unclear response, less possible title, or a combination of right and wrong factors in the description; zero an incorrect response, one not considered possible, or such immature responses as "It's a man." Three judges achieved consensus on all values assigned. Internal consistency was judged to be the most crucial objective. The *Dictionary of Occupational Titles* (Federal Security Agency, 1949) was used as a major resource in assigning values.

For purposes of coding on Remington Rand data processing cards, values were assigned the reactions or expressions of interest in the job. "Yes" was assigned the number zero, "not sure" was assigned the number one, and "no" was assigned the number two. Except for use in a reliability check, these numbers were not considered to be scores.

Five neutral reasons, 19 positive reasons, and 21 negative reasons for reactions to occupations were classified and were assigned numbers which were used only in the data processing to find out subgroup similarities and differences in reasons.

LIMITATIONS

There were many limitations in the study. As an exploratory, descriptive study, however, it should be expected to raise many questions, more perhaps than it answers. The population sam-

TABLE 2.—Chi-Square Results for Titling of Occupations by Subgroups

	GRADE LEVEL χ^2	SEX χ^2	SOCIO-ECONOMIC LEVEL χ^2	INTELLI-GENCE LEVEL χ^2	URBAN RURAL χ^2
Janitor	63.07**	1.19	6.72	10.58	6.11
Assembler	115.43**	13.69**	16.98	17.13*	7.81*
Bookkeeper	241.57**	2.38	15.35	9.21	11.94**
Carpenter	66.64**	8.93*	14.48	22.92**	10.70**
Manager	71.40**	.00	15.97	11.44	20.81**
Teacher	7.74	2.98	9.57	14.67	10.24**
Farmer	47.60**	2.98	20.81	23.10**	11.71**
Engineer	132.09**	11.31*	21.12*	28.87**	23.36**
Laborer	73.19**	3.57	20.84	44.63**	29.78**
Sales Clerk	128.52**	17.26**	22.86*	11.75	28.92**
Truck Driver	138.04**	3.57	13.48	18.27*	7.69
Doctor	4.76	.00	10.07	5.87	9.01*
Warehouseman	127.33**	.00	12.89	22.94**	17.00**
Secretary	91.04**	2.98	16.51	14.37	14.75**
Mechanic	245.14**	4.76	10.42	15.51	7.66
Telephone Lineman	74.97**	18.45**	26.11*	19.48*	5.86
Degrees of Freedom	12	3	12	9	3

**Significant at one per cent level.
*Significant at five per cent level.

ple was not randomly selected. The occupation sample, while broad, could have been more inclusive, and other ways of selecting such a sample could have been used. Face validity was assumed. There were procedural differences necessary in the reliability substudy.

In essence, however, this study has opened a field of investigation which needs to be explored for vocational development to be understood.

FINDINGS

Reliability

Reliability, after a 90 to 120 day lapse between testings, was significant statistically at the one per cent level of confidence for both knowledge and interest. The reliability coefficient of knowledge scores, which reflected titling and describing consistency, was .74. The reliability coefficient of reactions, reflecting consistency of interests in the occupation, was .58. This is not a high correlation, but when one considers that only 16 jobs were included in the study, it may be hypothesized that a more extensive study might yield higher reliability.

Knowledge

Both chi-square analysis and double entry analysis of variance were utilized to ascertain subgroup and mean differences and as evidence to accept or reject five hypotheses relating to knowledge concerning occupations. A small part of the data is shown in Tables 2 and 3 which display, respectively, chi-square results for titling and describing of occupations by subgroups.

Table 2 is read as follows. For the job of janitor, grade levels were significantly different at the one per cent level of confidence in their titling information. It can be further noted in the table that there was a hierarchy of differences among subgroups; the jobs of mechanic and bookkeeper discriminated most among grade level subgroups in their titling accuracy for these jobs. Add the one other piece of information not shown, that in all grade level comparisons the third and fifth grade children scored low and the ninth and eleventh grade children scored high, and the picture is complete. Thus, older children exceeded younger children significantly in titling accuracy for 14 of the 16 jobs. It was also true that older children were consistently superior to younger in job describing accuracy (see Table 3).

TABLE 3.—Chi-Square Results for Describing Occupations by Subgroups

	GRADE LEVEL χ^2	SEX χ^2	SOCIO-ECONOMIC LEVEL χ^2	INTELLI-GENCE LEVEL χ^2	URBAN RURAL χ^2
Janitor	50.58**	1.19	28.05**	13.93	11.90*
Assembler	118.41**	20.23**	15.01	19.96*	13.30**
Bookkeeper	199.92**	2.98	20.95	17.94*	2.26
Carpenter	87.47**	2.38	28.31**	11.30	29.58**
Manager	55.34**	1.19	21.43*	4.79	9.92*
Teacher	16.66	.00	9.47	4.60	.95
Farmer	14.88	1.19	10.46	10.11	3.34
Engineer	120.79**	3.57	14.36	14.40	.23
Laborer	41.65**	8.93*	12.52	8.65	2.69
Sales Clerk	20.83	3.57	8.12	7.89	3.50
Truck Driver	32.13**	.00	24.05*	19.40*	3.78
Doctor	20.83	.60	14.50	5.26	18.91**
Warehouseman	38.08**	4.17	11.40	18.45*	6.71
Mechanic	23.80*	1.19	15.74	3.56	1.57
Secretary	111.86**	14.88	12.77	6.26	3.21
Telephone Lineman	24.99*	7.23	25.91**	16.27	7.18
Degrees of Freedom	12	3	12	9	3

**Significant at one per cent level.
*Significant at five per cent level.

Neither boys nor girls were consistently superior in titling or describing. Boys titled assembler, carpenter, and telephone lineman and described the assembler significantly more successfully than girls. Girls titled the sales clerk and engineer and described the secretary significantly more successfully than did boys.

The upper socio-economic groups scored significantly higher than the lower socio-economic groups in titling and describing for all jobs on which significant differences appeared. The one exception was that of manager. The occurrence of higher scores for higher socio-economic groups, though not statistically significant for each job, was consistent enough to result in significant mean differences in the double entry analysis of variance when all job titling or describing scores were totalled.

The upper intelligence level groups scored significantly higher than the lower intelligence level groups in all cases in which significant intelligence subgroup titling and describing differences were found.

Urban children scored significantly higher than rural in all but two of the cases in which significant urban-rural subgroup titling and describing differences were found. One exception resulted from the fact that rural children more accurately described the job of manager. For describing the job of doctor the rural children more often received the modal score of two, while the urban children more often scored at the extremes.

Considering all jobs, including the results of both the chi square and analysis of variance, and combining job titles and job descriptions as indicative

of occupational knowledge, the following hypotheses were accepted or rejected as indicated.

Accepted: Differences in amount of accuracy of occupational knowledge possessed by boys, as compared to girls, are due to chance (equal to zero).

Rejected: Differences in amount and accuracy of occupational knowledge possessed (1) by children of different grade levels, (2) by students of various socio-economic levels, (3) by students of various intelligence levels, and (4) by urban and by rural children are due to chance (equal to zero).

The order of the four significant variables from high to low appeared to be grade level, intelligence level, socio-economic level, then urban-rural background.

Jobs most accurately titled were, in order, doctor, teacher, secretary, farmer, truck driver, carpenter, mechanic, sales clerk, janitor, engineer, telephone lineman, laborer, warehouse worker, bookkeeper, manager, and assembler.

Jobs most accurately described were, in order, farmer, secretary, carpenter, janitor, truck driver, teacher, telephone lineman, mechanic, sales clerk, doctor, laborer, warehouse worker, engineer, bookkeeper, manager, and assembler.

Reactions

Both chi-square analysis and analysis of variance were utilized to ascertain subgroup and mean differences and to gather evidence by which to accept or reject five hypotheses relating to reactions toward occupations. Table 4 shows chi-square results for reactions to occupations by subgroups.

TABLE 4.—Chi-Square Results for Reactions to Occupations by Subgroups

	GRADE LEVEL χ^2	SEX χ^2	SOCIO-ECONOMIC LEVEL χ^2	INTELLIGENCE LEVEL χ^2	URBAN RURAL χ^2
Janitor	32.13**	2.74	10.49	12.92	6.06*
Assembler	39.87**	25.49**	7.82	1.82	2.77
Bookkeeper	23.80**	.87	1.80	2.90	8.80*
Carpenter	35.11**	140.29**	12.77	11.70	9.02*
Manager	20.23**	14.70**	5.85	7.17	11.59**
Teacher	50.58**	63.02**	25.17**	3.95	1.46
Farmer	24.40**	42.74**	22.61**	3.75	5.83
Engineer	7.14	41.83**	5.03	6.11	5.99*
Laborer	22.02**	98.66**	15.69*	16.44*	9.12*
Sales Clerk	29.16**	118.65**	26.44**	3.11	13.09**
Truck Driver	14.88	98.36**	25.38**	16.29*	7.21*
Doctor	10.12	.42	14.15	3.21	3.97
Warehouseman	21.42**	59.72**	16.83*	17.59*	11.78**
Secretary	24.40**	229.43**	32.31**	12.10	8.42*
Mechanic	11.31	223.56**	14.76	13.33	7.66
Telephone Lineman	15.47	86.99**	5.63	4.33	.33
Degrees of Freedom	8	2	8	6	2

**Significant at one per cent level.
*Significant at five per cent level.

Table 4 is read much as Tables 2 and 3. In their reactions to the job of janitor, for example, grade level groups were significantly different at the one per cent level of confidence. Again there can be observed a hierarchy in which the greatest differences among grade levels were seen for the jobs of teacher, assembler, janitor, and on through the chi-square differences from high to low.

One factor, the direction of the differences, remains to be discussed since it is not shown in the table.

In all cases where there were significant differences in grade level subgroups in reactions to jobs, the third and fifth grades proved to respond positively more often, while the ninth and eleventh grade children responded positively less often.

The direction of sex differences may be summed up in the fact that boys exceeded girls in numbers of positive reactions for all jobs in which significant differences appeared except those of assembler, manager, teacher, sales clerk, and secretary.

The socio-economic subgroups were consistent in that those from the highest levels responded positively less often, while those from the lowest levels responded positively more often.

Intelligence subgroups reflected a

similar pattern. High groups were less positive; low groups were more positive toward occupations. This pattern was so consistent, although statistically significant for only three jobs, that when double entry analysis of variance was computed for all jobs, mean differences were significant.

In 10 of the 11 cases of significant differences between urban and rural reactions, the rural group exceeded the urban group in number of positive responses. Only for the job of engineer did the urban group exceed the rural in number of positive responses.

Considering all jobs and including the results of both the chi-square analysis and analysis of variance together, the following hypotheses were all rejected as indicated.

Rejected: Differences in the occupational interests held (1) by students of various grade levels, (2) by boys and by girls, (3) by students of various socio-economic levels, (4) by students of various intelligence levels, and (5) by urban and rural children are due to chance (equal to zero).

Numbers of positive reactions or "yes" responses to the idea of holding a job when the child was "through school" were further inspected. The order in which all possible subgroups ranked the occupations were ascertained and rank order correlations were derived. Table 5 reports the correlations for all subgroups.

Table 5 shows that the correlation for boys of grade three and grade five, based on their relative preference for the 16 occupations, was .88. This table shows some extremely important findings. The similarity in ranking the 16 occupations achieved statistical significance in all pairs of subgroups for

which correlation was sought except at two points. Boys and girls in the sex comparison ranked the jobs in a manner that resulted in a low negative correlation. The correlation of .42 in the socio-economic comparisons was not significant. The true import of the table, though, lies in the fact that subgroups tended to rank the occupations very similarly.

One hypothesis had been constructed which dealt with this area of study; on the basis of the information in Table 5 it was reacted to as follows.

Rejected: Correlations among pairs of grade levels in their rank order preferences for occupations are not statistically significant.

Reasons

The fourth question was concerned with why occupations were reacted to positively or negatively. The five positive reasons which were implied or most frequently mentioned by students in explaining why they would like a job, and the number of mentions follow: some positive inherent aspect, or "I like that kind of job," 786; interesting, fun, 170; satisfied with money, 155; satisfied with surroundings, 66; altruism, "can help other people," 63. The ten negative reasons which were implied or mentioned most frequently, and the number of mentions follow: negative inherent aspect, 821; hard work (either mental or physical, often unspecified), 524; not interesting, 424; unsatisfied with money, 367; dislike surroundings, 190; physical danger, 168; prefer other jobs, 138; waste of learning, 135; would not like it, 120; sex inappropriate (boy's or girl's job), 120.

TABLE 5.—Rank Order Correlations of Positive Reactions for All Subgroups

SUBGROUPS		GRADE 5 BOYS	GRADE 7 BOYS	GRADE 9 BOYS	GRADE 11 BOYS
Grade 3 Boys		.88	.79	.70	.79
Grade 5 Boys			.84	.58	.76
Grade 7 Boys				.74	.86
Grade 9 Boys					.82
		GRADE 5 GIRLS	GRADE 7 GIRLS	GRADE 9 GIRLS	GRADE 11 GIRLS
Grade 3 Girls		.82	.79	.84	.79
Grade 5 Girls			.95	.96	.94
Grade 7 Girls				.95	.94
Grade 9 Girls					.96
Socio-economic	Level	Level 2	Level 3	Level 4	Level 5
Professional	0	.87	.78	.42*	.67
Managerial	2		.94	.52	.82
Clerical	3			.57	.80
Skilled Labor	4				.72
Semi-skilled	5				—
Intelligence Quotients		108–115	100–107	99 and below	
116 and above		.93	.92	.78	
108–115			.84	.70	
100–107				.77	
99 and below				—	
Sex		Girls			
Boys		—.23*			
Urban-Rural		Rural			
Urban		.84			

*All correlations significant at the five per cent level of confidence except those so marked.

Frequency of mention of status and pay as reasons for reacting to jobs increased significantly with grade level. Frequency of mention of fear of danger or fear of error decreased significantly as grade level increased. Socio-economic level and intelligence level showed a positive but not significant relationship to frequency of mention of status and pay.

For the most part, however, reasons which were given for reactions to particular jobs at one grade level, socio-economic level, or intelligence level, were similar to the reasons given by other subgroups.

CONCLUSIONS

1. The instrument used was sufficiently reliable to justify its expansion and use in the further study.

2. The techniques used were successful in differentiating amount of occupational knowledge possessed by subgroups. Titling discriminated more than did describing.

3. The techniques used were successful in differentiating interest in the 16 occupations by subgroups.

4. A Vocational Quotient or V. Q. could be established which would point out occupational knowledge needs at varying levels.

5. The children showing more knowledge about occupations tended to be from the higher socio-economic levels, higher intelligence levels, higher grade levels, and urban background. Sex was not a significant factor.

6. Subgroup preferences for occupations varied, but the major difference was that some subgroups were more positive toward the occupations in general, while ranking them similarly.

7. Children showing greater inclination to be positive toward the 16 occupations tended to be from lower socioeconomic levels, lower intelligence levels, lower grade levels, and rural background. Sex differences were inconclusive.

8. Sex was the most important factor in determining reactions toward the individual occupations.

9. Rank order preferences for all occupations by sex were inversely, but not significantly, related.

10. Rank order correlations indicating preferences for occupations were positive and significant for all subgroup pairs based on intelligence level, grade level, urban-rural background, and for all but one of the ten socioeconomic level pairs.

11. Grade to grade ranking of jobs was sufficiently similar to justify questioning the assumption that children in the third and fifth grade are in a fantasy stage in vocational development.

12. There are some sex and grade level differences in reasons given for reacting positively or negatively toward an occupation, but the reasons for which children reacted remained relatively similar from grade to grade. It seemed reasonable to draw the implication that these children reacted toward these occupations in much the same way that adults might be expected to react.

13. Certain reasons tended to be related to particular occupations. For example, altruism related to doctor and teacher; low pay related to janitor. This affinity seemed to help establish the idea that children were responding in ways which might be considered rather mature since most of the connections were ones that logic would dictate.

14. Substantial indication was given that occupational study might profitably be expanded in the elementary school curriculum. This would have the advantage of creating concepts prior to a thorough internalization of sex typing and socio-economic typing of occupations by individuals.

15. When occupations are studied late in the child's school career, much time may be spent by individuals in reconstructing attitudes so that some occupations are acceptable.

16. Because the narrowing process is evident as early as the third grade, vocational adjustment problems may be created when formerly rejected occupations must be reconsidered.

17. It may be hypothesized that an occupation which suddenly appeals to the child rarely rises from among

formerly rejected occupations or consistently rejected levels of work.

18. The groundwork must be laid early if the child is to aspire differently from his peer or parent levels of aspiration. There is probably some bias in the laboring population against the less active occupations, and in the professional level against the occupations requiring heavy work. Early reformation of attitudes may be necessary if distress to the individual is to be avoided when lines are crossed.

19. Walsh (1956) believed that only persons significant to the individual are able to help him alter his self concept. Significant teachers in elementary school might be expected to have an effect by encouraging the child to consider a wide range of what might be called "possible-positives" before he comes close to the occupational choice point.

20. Negatives are of great importance in occupational decision making; negative responses outnumbered positive responses nearly three-and-a-half to one for all of the children in the study. Besides limiting the occupations from which choices may be made, it is likely that they form points of reference to which newly-encountered occupations are compared.

21. "Possible-positives" among occupations also play a referent role. The chances of choices being made from this range and similar occupations would appear to be far greater than from a first and second choice elicited at one point in time. Strong (1931, p. 6) pointed out that, "At any moment, of only one, or at most of a very few, of all these interests can he be conscious."

22. Sex-appropriateness, an activity of interest, and status appear to be the three major referent points by which children evaluate occupations.

23. There would seem to be some basis to hypothesize that the occupational choice question may be an encouragement to fantasy. Asking an elementary school child what he wants to be when he grows up is on a par with asking what college he is going to or whom he plans to marry. All of these questions presuppose more information than most young people have at hand. It would appear to be more important to investigate whether the child is involved in the process of narrowing the field and whether the process of narrowing seems appropriate in relation to the child's intelligence, opportunities, and background.

24. Vocational realism may be better sought, at least through junior high school, by asking a child what occupation he rejects for himself, rather than asking about his choices.

SUMMARY

Much remains to be investigated and written concerning vocational development. This study has attempted to contribute by suggesting and, to some extent, testing a method by which knowledge and interests concerning occupations can be studied. The literature has not previously come to grips with some of the most elementary factors in understanding vocational development.

This study should be utilized as a springboard for research leading to further understanding of vocational development as more than occupational choice. Often the two concepts have been utilized as if they were synonymous.

This study suggests that the occupational elimination process starts early, that occupational attitudes do not await the ninth grade unit on occupations, that fantasy in occupational thinking of younger children comes partly from the questions asked of them, and that relatively irreversible and damaging occupational concepts may be internalized because little effort is made to help children develop an early and objective understanding of the world of work.

PART FOUR

Personal-Social Development and Behavior: II

Social Attitudes

12

41 A Developmental Study of Racial Awareness in Young Children[1]

HAROLD W. STEVENSON

EDWARD C. STEWART

This selection studies the development of children's ability to discriminate the physical differences between Negroes and whites and their preferences and attitudes. The Negro children tend to devalue and reject their own ethnic group. They make fewer own-race choices than do the white children in items involving choices of playmates, companions to go home with, guests for a birthday party, and in selecting own-race dolls that look more like themselves. They also assign negative roles to Negro children more frequently than the white children assign such roles to white children. Is it useful to explore the relationship between such rejection and the development of the self-concept of Negro children?

[1]The study was supported in part by a grant from the Hogg Foundation for Mental Hygiene of the University of Texas.

The writers wish to thank Miss Billye McClendon, Miss Emma Lois Smith, and Mr. Robert Bell, who assisted in testing the children; and the directors and teachers of the following nursery and elementary schools in Austin, Texas, where the study was done: Tarrytown Methodist, All Saints, Jack and Jill, Jeffrey, St. Austin's, Ebenezer, Howson, Twelfth Street, Greater Mount Zion, and Holy Cross.

There have been few studies with young children concerning the development of racial attitudes and awareness. Those published indicate that children as young as three and four are capable of making discriminations between the physical characteristics of Negroes and whites, and that the frequency of discrimination increases with increasing CA.[2] The studies also indicate that racial discrimination by Negro children is dependent upon S's skin color and that among northern children both Negro and white show a preference for the physical characteristics associated with white children (Clark and Clark, 1950; Helgerson, 1943; Landreth and Johnson, 1953). These findings are of great interest. However, further information is necessary for the understanding of the development of racial attitudes. The aim of the present study is to provide information of this type. The study investigates the responses of Negro and white children from three through seven years on a variety of tests concerned with racial awareness and racial attitudes.

METHOD

Subjects

The Ss were 225 children enrolled in private nursery and elementary schools in Austin, Texas, a city with a population of 165,000 whites and 25,000 Negroes. The children ranged in age from 3 through 7 years. There were 25 white Ss of each CA and the number of Negro Ss at each CA from 3 through 7 was 23, 13, 22, 17 and 20, respectively. The groups were approximately evenly divided according to

sex. All the children at the nursery schools who were within the desired age levels were included, and the elementary school Ss were chosen at random from the class roll. In general, the white Ss were of a higher socioeconomic class, based upon parent occupational level, than the Negro Ss. The schools were not integrated and the Ss resided in sections of the city where play and frequent contacts with children of the other race were impossible. The Ss interracial contacts were assumed, therefore, to have been primarily of an incidental nature.

Materials

Four tests were constructed for this study.[3] The purpose of the tests was to investigate children's ability to discriminate the physical differences between Negroes and whites and their racial preference and attitudes. Great care was exercised in constructing the tests so that the materials would not be a source of bias which might distort the results. The materials were reviewed by both Negro and white individuals while they were being prepared. The tests are described below.

1. DISCRIMINATION TEST The test consisted of 20 10 by 20 inch cards; 12 cards were related to race and 8 were used as fillers. The filler cards depicted three objects, such as two chairs and a table; some of the drawings were in color and some were line drawings. The remaining cards were divided into three sets of four cards each. On Set 1 each card contained line drawings of the heads of three children. Two

---

[2]Ammons, 1950; Clark and Clark, 1939a, 1939b, 1950; Goodman, 1952; Horowitz, 1939; Stevenson et al., 1960.

[3]The materials for the study were constructed by Graphic Studios, Austin, Texas.

of the three children were of the same race and two of the same sex; i.e., a Negro boy, a Negro girl, and a white girl. Set 2 consisted of the same type of line drawings as Set 1, but the figures were all of the same sex. Set 3 was identical to Set 2 except that the drawings were in color. The white children had brunette hair and the Negro children had black hair. The faces were painted either a white flesh color or a warm brown, with appropriate highlights and shadows.

Two filler cards were presented first, followed by Set 1. Half of the Ss were then tested on Set 2 followed by Set 3 and half with Set 3 followed by Set 2. The sets were separated by two filler cards.

The S was shown the first filler card and was asked to show E the picture that differed from the other two. If S made an incorrect response, he was instructed concerning the basis of correct response. The same procedure was used with the second card. The instruction, "Show me the one that is different," was repeated before each of the remaining cards was presented and a noncorrectional procedure was used.

On Set 1 S could make a correct response by choosing the child who differed either by race or by sex, while on Sets 2 and 3 a correct response could be made only by choosing the child on each card who differed from the other by race. All of the cards were constructed so that the correct choice varied at random among the three horizontal positions (L, M, R).

2. DOLL ASSEMBLY Four two-dimensional masonite dolls 6 inches high were used. The dolls included a Negro boy and girl and a white boy and girl. The coloring of the dolls was similar to that of the drawings in the Discrimination Test. The girls' costumes consisted of a blouse and a skirt, and the boys', a T-shirt and shorts. The clothing was painted in light pastel shades. Each doll was divided into three pieces by divisions at the bottom of the neck and at the waist. Each section of all four dolls was interchangeable so that all degrees of consistency could be used in assembling the dolls by race and sex.

The pieces were spread in front of S in a random array and S was asked to assemble the dolls to make four children.

3. DOLLS The materials consisted of four small dolls made of a soft, flesh-colored plastic. Only white dolls were available and two of these were modified to create Negro dolls. One doll of each race and sex was used. The boys were clothed in identical shirts and short pants, and the girls in identical dresses.

The S was shown the two dolls of S's sex and was asked, "Which one looks most like you?" After S had made a choice, the four dolls were placed in front of S and S was asked, "Which two children would you rather play with?" The linear arrangement in which the dolls were presented was varied at random among the Ss.

4. INCOMPLETE STORIES The test consisted of seven cards in color depicting play situations. The cards showed one or two central figures, with other figures in the foreground or background. The central figure on most of the cards was drawn in a rear view and was ambiguous with regard to race. The drawings were balanced so that Negroes and whites appeared

equally often on the left and right and children of the same race were not grouped together. The clothing of all figures was in pastel shades, and on each card the color of the clothing differed for each figure. The cards and the stories are described below:

CARD 1.   A child is shown lying on the ground. Four boys, two Negro and two white, are playing in the background. The S was told, "This little boy was playing in the yard. Another little boy was very mean to him and pushed him down." The S was asked, "Which one of these little boys do you think pushed him down?" and then, "Which little boy is going to come over and see if he is all right?"

CARD 2.   Two women, a white and a Negro, are seated in the foreground. Approaching them from the center of the card are two girls, one a Negro and one white. The S was told, "These little girls have been playing in the park. Now this little girl is looking for her mother. Which is her mother?" For half of each racial group the question concerned the Negro girl and for half it concerned the white girl.

CARD 3.   In the foreground a Negro boy and a white boy are pulling on a rope. Each wears cowboy attire and has a gun. In the background a Negro boy and a white boy are playing. The S was told, "These two boys are pulling on the rope, trying to see which one can get it. Which one do you think is going to win and get the rope?" After S made a choice he was told, "This boy (the one who wins) is going to tie up the bad man who is one of these boys. Which one do you think is the bad man?"

CARD 4.   A boy in the foreground is attired in hat, mittens, and jacket. In the background are a white boy and a Negro boy. The S was told, "This little boy is about ready to go home from school and wants a friend to go with him. Which boy do you think he will choose to go home with him?"

CARD 5.   A girl is seated in the left foreground. To her right is a birthday cake on a table. Behind this and to the rear are six girls, three Negro and three white, alternated from left to right according to race. The S was told, "This is Ann. See her birthday cake? Her mother said that she could invite three children to her birthday party. Which three girls do you think that she is going to invite?"

CARD 6.   A boy is seated in the foreground looking at four children, two Negro and two white, playing in the background. The S was told, "This little boy is afraid to go over by these children because one of the boys always hits him. Which of the boys do you think doesn't like him and always hits him?"

CARD 7.   In the center background a Negro boy is seated in a red wagon. A white boy and a Negro boy stand in the background. The S was told, "This little boy has a new wagon and wants someone to pull him. Which boy do you think he will choose to pull him?"

Procedure

The Ss were tested individually at school. The Negro children were tested by a Negro examiner and the white children by a white examiner. Two orders of presentation were used. The order of presentation for half of the Ss was the order in which the tests are described above. For the other half the Dolls and Incomplete Stories preceded the Discrimination Test and the Doll Assembly.

RESULTS

The tests proved to be of interest to the children and in general appeared to be appropriate for the age levels tested. The Discrimination Test and Doll Assembly did, however, appear to be difficult for the 3-year-old Ss. The pretraining on the filler cards on the Discrimination Test was protracted with these children, and although they were eventually able to make the correct choices, it is doubtful that they fully comprehended the nature of the task. In Doll Assembly it was difficult for these Ss to assemble the 12 pieces to form four dolls. There were few instances in which older Ss had difficulty in performing the tasks.

the average numbers of sex choices did increase. At all age levels the average numbers of choices by sex were greater than those by race.

Statistical analysis of the data for Set 1 is facilitated by the use of number of Ss making consistent race or consistent sex responses as the measures of response (see Table 1). There is a significant increase in the number of Ss at each CA making consistent sex responses ($\chi^2 = 35.58$, $df = 4$, $p < .01$), and a significant difference between the proportions of Ss making consistent race and consistent sex responses ($t = 5.81$, $p < .01$). The Negro and white Ss did not differ significantly in frequency of consistent race responses, but a greater number of white, than Negro, Ss did make consistent sex responses ($\chi^2 = 5.71$, $p < .02$).

TABLE 1.—Mean Number of Sex and Race Responses and Number of Ss Making Consistent Sex and Race Responses on Set 1 of the Discrimination Test

CA	CHOICES BY RACE (MEAN)		CHOICES BY SEX (MEAN)		CONSISTENT RACE CHOICES (N)		CONSISTENT SEX CHOICES (N)	
	W	N	W	N	W	N	W	N
3	1.3	1.3	1.3	1.9	0	0	2	0
4	1.4	1.3	1.6	1.8	0	0	2	0
5	.7	1.4	2.8	1.9	0	1	11	2
6	1.2	1.1	2.4	2.1	3	0	11	4
7	1.4	1.4	2.5	2.6	5	5	11	10

Discrimination Test

In Table I are presented the average numbers of choices made on the basis of race and on the basis of sex on Set 1. There were no consistent differences among the choices made by Negro and white Ss. There was no tendency for the average number of race choices to increase with increasing age, but

The results for Sets 2 and 3 are presented in Table 2. For both racial groups there is a consistent rise with increasing CA in the average numbers of correct responses. The average numbers of correct responses for white Ss are higher than those for Negro Ss. There is a significant difference between the number of Negro and white

Ss making consistently correct responses on Set 2 ($\chi^2 = 12.80$, $df = 1$, $p = < .01$) and on Set 3 ($\chi^2 = 31.75$, $df = 1$, $p < .001$).

Dolls

In Table 4 are presented the proportions of Ss at each CA level who chose the doll of S's race as looking more like

TABLE 2.—Mean Number of Correct Responses and Number of S's Making Consistent Correct Responses on Sets 2 and 3 of the Discrimination Test

	SET 2				SET 3			
	Correct Responses (Mean)		Consistent Correct Responses (N)		Correct Responses (Mean)		Consistent Correct Responses (N)	
CA	W	N	W	N	W	N	W	N
3	1.5	2.0	1	1	1.6	1.8	1	0
4	2.9	2.4	11	4	2.8	1.8	11	1
5	3.2	2.4	16	4	3.3	2.7	16	0
6	3.9	3.1	22	7	3.9	2.8	22	3
7	4.0	4.0	25	2	4.0	4.0	25	20

Doll Assembly

The proportion of Ss in each age group assembling all four dolls correctly by race are presented in Table 3. There is a great and relatively consistent increase with age in the proportions in both racial groups. At all CA levels except 4 the proportion of white Ss assembling the dolls correctly by race was greater than the proportion of Negro Ss. An over-all evaluation of the differences between the racial groups yields a χ^2 of 5.54, which is significant at between the .01 and .02 levels of significance.

TABLE 3.—Proportion of Ss Assembling Four Dolls Correctly by Race

CA	WHITE	NEGRO
3	.08	.00
4	.08	.22
5	.44	.18
6	.68	.25
7	.88	.70

S. The proportion of own-race choices of the white Ss begins at a chance level and rises consistently through CA 6. The proportion of own-race choices of the Negro Ss also begins at a near-chance level at CA 3, drops slightly at CA's 4 and 5 and then rises at CA's 6 and 7. At all age levels the proportion of own-race choices was greater by the white Ss than by the Negro Ss. The difference between the total own-race choices in the two groups is highly significant ($\chi^2 = 25.28$, $df = 1$, $p < .001$).

In Table 5 are presented the proportions of own-race choices made when the Ss were asked to choose the dolls with whom they would rather play. The proportions begin at a chance level for both racial groups. The white Ss then show a consistent increase in proportion of own-race choices, while the Negro Ss show a consistent decrease except at CA 7. The over-all proportion of own-race choices was .20

for the Negro Ss and .47 for the white Ss. The difference between these proportions is highly significant ($t = 4.50$, $p < .001$).

TABLE 4.—Proportion of Ss Choosing Own-Race Doll as Looking More Like S

CA	WHITE	NEGRO
3	.52	.43
4	.72	.33
5	.88	.33
6	.96	.53
7	.96	.85

TABLE 5.—Proportion of Choices of Own-Race Dolls as Playmates

CA	WHITE	NEGRO
3	.52	.50
4	.60	.39
5	.64	.35
6	.82	.33
7	.82	.65

Incomplete Stories

On Cards 1 the Ss were asked which of four children, two Negro and two white, pushed a child down. For the white Ss the proportion of own-race choices at all ages was relatively low and did not increase with CA (*see* Table 6). A higher proportion of Negro Ss than white Ss made own-race choices. The proportion of own-race choices increased slightly from CA 3 through 7 for the Negro Ss, but remained relatively constant for the white Ss. The difference between the total number of own-race choices in the Negro and white groups is highly significant ($\chi^2 = 22.67$, $df = 1$, $p < .001$).

On Card 1 S was also asked which child would help the boy who had been pushed down. There were no consistent changes in response with age for either white or Negro Ss. The proportions of own-race choices are lower for Negro Ss than for white Ss except at CA 7; the over-all difference is not significant ($\chi^2 = 3.78$, $p < .05$).

On Card 2 there was an increase with CA in the proportion of correct identification of the child's mother for both the Negro and white Ss. At CA 3 the proportions are below chance, which indicates that the Ss may have tended to choose the mother nearer the child (the Negro mother and white child were on the left of each pair). The total numbers of correct responses do not differ significantly for the Negro and white Ss ($\chi^2 = .17$).

On Card 3 the proportion of white Ss who selected the white child as the winner of the rope was high at all CA levels and showed a general increase from CA 3 through 7. The opposite trend was found for Negro Ss. The choices were at a chance level at CA 3 and were either at or below this level at subsequent ages. The over-all difference between the own-race choices of white and Negro Ss was highly significant ($\chi^2 = 19.63$, $p < .001$).

On Card 3 the Ss were also asked to select a badman. No consistent developmental trends were found for either racial group in the proportion of own-race choices. In general, however, the Negro Ss made own-race choices more frequently than did the white Ss ($\chi^2 = 6.53$, $p < .01$).

The S was asked on Card 4 to select a child who would go home with the child in the story. There is a fairly con-

TABLE 6.—Proportion of Own-Race Choices of Ss on Incomplete Stories

	CARD 1		CARD 2*		CARD 3				CARD 4		CARD 5		CARD 6		CARD 7	
	a		b		a		b									
CA	W	N	W	N	W	N	W	N	W	N	W	N	W	N	W	N	W	N
3	.32	.65	.52	.48	.20	.22	.64	.52	.40	.35	.44	.70	.46	.49	.36	.30	.32	.52
4	.32	.56	.76	.39	.36	.72	.56	.28	.48	.35	.56	.33	.45	.52	.56	.33	.36	.33
5	.40	.45	.56	.41	.92	.73	.72	.30	.32	.64	.92	.23	.65	.48	.42	.82	.40	.45
6	.20	.71	.56	.47	1.00	.76	.72	.41	.40	.35	.88	.35	.66	.41	.44	.59	.32	.29
7	.32	.85	.60	.75	.96	1.00	.88	.45	.20	.50	.88	.40	.85	.31	.20	.80	.32	.90

*Proportion of correct choices.

sistent increase in the proportion of own-race choices for the white Ss. Except for CA 3 the proportion of Negro Ss making own-race choices is low. The difference between the proportions of white and Negro Ss making own-race choices is highly significant ($\chi^2 = 24.42$, $p < .001$).

On Card 5 S was asked to select children to attend a birthday party. Both racial groups made approximately chance selections at CA's 3 and 4. The proportion of own-race choices then increased at successive CA levels for the white Ss and decreased for the Negro Ss. The over-all proportion of own-race choices was .45 for the Negro Ss and .61 for the white Ss. The difference is significant at less than the .02 level ($t = 2.42$).

The S was asked on Card 6 to choose the child the central figure feared. The proportion of own-race choices for the white Ss is at a chance level, except for CA's 3 and 7. There was a general tendency for the own-race choices of the Negro Ss to increase from CA 3 to 7. The difference in the incidence of own-race choices by the two racial groups is significant at between the .01 and .02 levels ($\chi^2 = 5.50$).

On Card 7 S was asked which child the Negro child would choose to pull him. There are no consistent developmental trends in the responses of either racial group. In general, the Negro Ss made more frequent own-race choices than did the white Ss ($\chi^2 = 6.29$, $.02 < p < .01$).

DISCUSSION

The results of this study indicate that the ability to discriminate the physical differences between Negroes and whites develops rapidly during the preschool years. The 3-year-old Ss had difficulty in making discriminations of the types required, but by the seventh year the Ss were capable of making such discriminations with ease. These results corroborate those of previous studies and provide further evidence for the early development of racial awareness.

After the third year, where the responses of both racial groups tended to be made on a chance basis, the frequency of discrimination was rather consistently greater by the white children. This finding is difficult to interpret. The white and Negro Ss represented different socioeconomic groups, and, although the relevance of socioeconomic background in making such discriminations is not clear, it is possible that factors which vary with socioeconomic status, such as intelligence, experience with individual testing, and experience with the types of visual materials used, might provide the basis for the obtained differences. A serious problem is posed in comparative studies of this type because of the near impossibility of matching southern Negro and white children satisfactorily on socioeconomic status, and until more information is available, generalizations from such studies must be extended only to the groups from which the samples are drawn.

Another interpretation of this finding may, however, be made. Young Negro and white children may differ in the degree to which they respond to physical differences associated with race as being relevant in selecting a child as being "different." Negro children live in a predominantly white society. Dolls, books, magazines, and television more frequently depict white than Negro individuals. Negro children have frequent experiences with light-complexioned Negroes. In contrast, white children living in a segregated community have less experience with Negroes and representations of Negroes. If it is hypothesized that young children perceive objects as being "different" to the degree that the characteristics of the objects deviate from those encountered in their everyday experience, it may be predicted that young white children would perceive the physical characteristics of Negroes as being relevant for selecting an individual as being different more frequently than young Negro children would perceive the characteristics of whites as being relevant. The validity of this hypothesis may be tested in further studies employing different types of test materials and subjects who differ in their frequency of contact with members of the other race.

The items related to attitudes towards self and toward race revealed a higher frequency of negative attitudes among the Negro Ss. A greater frequency of own-race rejection on the part of the Negro Ss compared to the white Ss is seen in the lower proportion of Negro Ss making own-race choices in selecting playmates, companions to go home with, and guests for a birthday party, and in selecting own-race dolls as looking more like themselves. The Negro Ss placed the Negro children in negative positions in the Incomplete Stories more frequently than the white Ss placed white children in such positions. The Negro Ss chose Negroes more frequently as being an aggressor (Cards 1 and 6), as being less likely to give aid (Card 1), as losing in a tug of war (Card 3), and as being a badman (Card 3). The surprising thing about these results is that they were obtained with Ss so young; by the ages of 4, 5, and 6 these Ss were responding in a manner which indicated not only awareness of racial differences, but also the use of stereotyped roles. A question of great interest is that of determining how children as young as these acquire such responses to race.

It is not unexpected that the study should raise many questions which cannot be answered with presently available data. It is clear from the results, however, that in order to understand how racial attitudes develop a great deal more information about the responses of young children will have to be obtained.

SUMMARY

A series of tests involving discrimination of physical differences between Negroes and whites and attitudes toward race were presented to 125 white and 100 Negro Ss between the ages of 3 and 7 years. A rapid increase in the ability to discriminate between the races was found in both racial groups between these ages. The white Ss tended to develop such discriminations at a younger age than did the Negro Ss. The Negro Ss made a lower frequency of own-race choices than did white Ss in items involving the selection of a child as a playmate, as looking most like S, etc. The Negro Ss assigned negative roles to Negro children more frequently than the white Ss assigned such roles to white children.

42   Childhood Prejudice as a Function of Parental Ethnocentrism, Punitiveness, and Outgroup Characteristics

RALPH EPSTEIN

S. S. KOMORITA

What are the origins of group prejudice and discrimination? This article suggests that childhood prejudice is a function of at least four factors: children's perceptions of parental prejudice, parental punishment towards aggression, and two characteristics of the group—race and social status. The results indicate that perception of parents as highly prejudiced and moderately punitive is most conducive to the development of prejudice in children.

Reprinted from the *Journal of Personality and Social Psychology*, 1966, **3,** 259–264, by permission of the senior author and the American Psychological Association.

The scapegoat hypothesis, a cornerstone of major conceptualizations regarding prejudice (Adorno, Frenkel-Brunswik, Levinson, and Sanford, 1950; Berkowitz, 1962) is based on the assumptions that severe discipline directed towards aggression may increase the instigation to aggress and anticipation of punishment for aggression directed towards the ingroup results in displacement from the original sources of frustration to outgroups. Equivocal and contradictory results regarding this hypothesis (Masling, 1954; Miller and Bugelski, 1948; Mosher and Scodel, 1960; Stagner and Congdon, 1955) indicate the utility of further research regarding those conditions for which the scapegoat hypothesis may be valid.

According to Allport (1954) and Zawadzki (1948), the predictive value of the scapegoat hypothesis has been limited by its focus on the motivational states of the prejudiced individual and relative neglect of those outgroup characteristics which facilitate their selection as targets for displaced hostility. Insofar as relatively few outgroup characteristics have been studied so far, for example, prior dislike (Berkowitz, 1962) and visibility (Williams, 1947), the major goal of this study was to investigate the development of social distance in children as a function of perceived parental punitiveness towards aggression, perceived parental ethnocentrism, and two major outgroup characteristics—social status and race. Previous research by the authors (Epstein and Komorita, 1965a), carried out on an upper middle-class child population, was based on the assumption that severe parental discipline may sensitize the child to power rela-

tions of strong-weak or superior-inferior, as these dimensions are culturally defined by social status. Assuming that the severely disciplined child may be excessively sensitized to differential status relationships, it was predicted that he would develop greater social distance towards low status rather than middle-class groups and toward Oriental rather than white children. Contrary to prediction, a nonmonotonic relationship between parental punitiveness and social distance was obtained: moderate punitiveness resulted in maximal social distance, and low socioeconomic status of the outgroups elicited greater social distance than their ethnic characteristics.

In order to obtain further clarification of these provocative findings, the current study was carried out. The present study differs from the former in three important respects. Since a significant relationship between parental punitiveness and children's social distance may be based on a third variable, namely, parental ethnocentrism, an attempt was made to obtain children's reports of their parents' ethnic attitudes. Thus, data were obtained in order to clarify the controversy b e t w e e n psychopathological theories of prejudice (Adorno et al., 1950) which focus on parental discipline and social learning theories (Buss, 1961), which emphasize identification with parental attitudes. Furthermore, insofar as religiosity among adults has appeared significantly related to prejudice (Allport and Kramer, 1946), it was decided to replicate the previous research on a parochial school population (Catholic). Finally, since the previous failure to find a significant relationship between social distance and the outgroup's racial characteristics may have been a function of the limited number of ethnic groups studied, a Negro condition was added to the white and Oriental groups.

METHOD
Subjects
The sample consisted of 180 boys and girls who comprised the third through fifth grades at a Catholic parochial school in Detroit, Michigan. This school serves children whose socioeconomic background as determined by residential area is predominantly middle class.

Measure of Parental Punitiveness
The Parental Punitiveness Scale (PPS)[1] was developed by the authors to measure children's perceptions of parental punitiveness towards aggression. A detailed description of the development of this scale is reported elsewhere (Epstein and Komorita, 1965a). Briefly, the scale consists of 45 items which measure parental punitiveness towards physical, verbal, and indirect aggression in each of five major situations: aggression towards parents, teachers, siblings, peers, and inanimate objects. The scale is scorable separately for father's and mother's responses to aggression. However, since the correlation coefficient between father and mother versions was found to be .60, the two scores were pooled to yield a single, average punitiveness scale. The split-half reliability of this average punitive score, with the Spearman-Brown correction, was .81.

Experimental Conditions
Three independent variables were used: race of target group—Negro, Oriental, and white; socioeconomic class of target group—lower versus middle class; and high, medium, and low groups on the

---
[1]Appended to the selection.

basis of scores on the PPS. Thus, a 3 × 2 × 3 factorial design was employed with 10 subjects in each of the 18 experimental conditions.

The basic purpose of the experimental conditions was to create specific cognitions regarding a fictitious group, the "Piraneans." Accordingly, the subjects were presented slides which depicted Piraneans as either middle or lower class, and Negro, Oriental, or white. Race of Piraneans was varied by presenting slides of four Negro, Oriental, or white children, two boys and two girls each, who were representative of the subjects' age range. Socioeconomic class was varied by presenting slides depicting residence and working place of Piraneans. For example, the working-class slides depicted scenes of a ramshackled house, deteriorated slum streets, and street construction, whereas the middle-class slides depicted a new split-level house, suburban streets, and modern office building.

Prior to the group administration of the slides, the following instructions were given:

> There is a group of people whom most of you have never seen. As a matter of fact, you have probably never heard of this group. They are called Piraneans. Would you like to see some slides of the Piraneans?

After viewing the slides, the subjects completed a seven-item social distance scale with regard to Piraneans. These items ranged from, "Would you want to marry these people when you grow up?" (minimal) to, "Would you want these people to visit your country?" (maximal). Each item could be answered by checking one of four alternatives ranging from, "very much yes," to "very much no."

TABLE 1.—Means and Standard Deviations of Piranean Social Distance Scores for Experimental Groups

PARENTAL PUNITIVENESS	WORKING CLASS			MIDDLE CLASS			M SD
	Negro	Oriental	White	Negro	Oriental	White	
High	20.6 (5.34)[a]	15.6 (3.81)	15.5 (4.8)	14.6 (4.98)	14.1 (1.7)	13.1 (2.81)	15.6
Medium	18.5 (4.21)	14.6 (4.92)	14.0 (3.57)	13.2 (3.67)	14.6 (5.02)	12.5 (2.73)	14.6
Low	21.1 (4.76)	16.1 (3.94)	16.3 (4.93)	17.1 (5.86)	14.0 (2.65)	14.5 (3.9)	16.5

Mean social distance

Working class	16.9
Middle class	14.2
Negro	17.5
Oriental	14.8
White	14.3

[a]Standard deviations appear in parentheses.

In order to minimize the potentially confounding factors of differential clarity and brightness, the slides were matched as closely as possible in terms of these variables. The low socioeconomic slides were based on scenes within Detroit slums whereas the middle socioeconomic slides were based on photos of suburban areas. Postexperimental interviews with a sample of subjects indicated that very few were able to state the specific locale of the slides although several subjects believed that the photos were taken within the United States.

In order to determine the children's general ethnocentrism, ratings of the following groups were obtained after the experimental sessions: German, French, Catholic, Italian, Mexican, Negro, Japanese, Jewish, and Russian. Social distance scores for each of these groups were then pooled to obtain a measure of generalized social distance. Three weeks later, the subjects were requested to indicate how they thought their *parents* would rate these same groups on the social distance scales. Thus, measures of the child's and parents' ethnocentrism, as perceived by the child, were obtained.

RESULTS

For the purpose of intergroup comparisons, Table 1 summarizes the means and standard deviations of the social distance scores for the 18 experimental groups.

An analysis of variance of these scores indicated that with regard to main effects, the effect of levels of parental punitiveness was not significant at the .05 level ($F = 2.89$, $df = 2/162$). However, the main effects for social class and race were significant at the .01 level ($F = 8.95$, $df = 2/162$; $F =$

16.99, $df = 1/162$, respectively). These results indicate that the working-class condition elicited greater social distance relative to the middle-class condition and "Negro" elicited more social distance than "Oriental" or "white" conditions.

The interaction between socioeconomic status and race, significant at the .05 level ($F = 3.28$, $df = 2/162$), indicates that the lower class characterization elicited greater social distance towards the Negro relative to the white ($t = 5.73$, $p < .01$) and Oriental ($t = 5.46$, $p < .01$) groups, that is, whereas middle-class status served to minimize differences in attitudes toward the ethnic groups, working-class status enhanced differential social distance toward Negroes on the one hand, and white, Orientals, on the other.

In order to further delineate the antecedents of social distance, the subjects' Piranean social distance scores for each experimental condition were correlated with: the subjects' ethnocentrism, measured by the subjects' reports of their own social distance attitudes towards the 10 nonfictional groups; perceived parental prejudice, as measured by the subjects' reports of parental attitudes toward Negro and Oriental (summation of social distance ratings of Chinese and Japanese); and general parental ethnocentrism, as measured by children's reports of parental attitudes towards the 10 nonfictional groups. These correlation coefficients are shown in Table 2.

Table 2 indicates that social distance toward a fictitious group is significantly correlated with the child's general level of ethnocentrism, and with perceived parental prejudice towards the

TABLE 2.—Correlations between Children's Social Distance towards "Piraneans" and
Children's and Parental Perceived Ethnocentrism

	CHILDREN'S ETHNO- CENTRISM	PARENTAL PREJUDICE TOWARD "NEGRO" AND "ORIENTALS"	PARENTAL ETHNO- CENTRISM
White			
Middle class	.41* (30)	.09 (25)	−.02 (25)
Lower class	.44* (30)	.68** (23)	.25 (23)
Oriental			
Middle class	.27 (30)	.53** (26)	.40* (26)
Lower class	.69** (30)	.60** (30)	.42* (30)
Negro			
Middle class	.47** (30)	.65** (26)	.36 (26)
Lower class	.36* (30)	.59** (27)	.30 (27)
Mean			
Correlations[a]	.45** (150)	.61** (132)	.35** (132)

Note.—Numbers in parentheses denote sample size. Sample size for perceived parental prejudice vary for experimental groups because some subjects were absent for the second experimental session.

[a]Excluding correlation coefficient for "white, middle-class" group.

$^*p < .05.$

$^{**}p < .01.$

specific ethnic groups depicted on the slides. However, for the correlations with perceived parental ethnocentrism, only two of the six correlations are significant at the .05 level. On the other hand, the average correlation, weighted by sample size and pooled over five of the six experimental groups is .35, and 132 df's. This is significant at the .01 level. These average correlations do not include the data for the white, middle-class Piranean condition since there is no theoretical rationale for assuming that parental ethnocentrism would correlate with social distance toward this group. The striking result of the data of Table 2 is that, except for the one correlation of −.02, the correlations are *consistently positive* as well as moderately high. Thus, a moderate proportion of the variance of children's social distance toward the fictitious group can be accounted for by their perception of parental prejudice.

With regard to children's general ethnocentrism as a dependent variable, the correlation between children's and perceived parental ethnocentrism was .48, with 155 df's. This is significant at the .01 level. The correlation between children's ethnocentrism and perceived parental punitiveness on the other hand was only .02. However, there were reasons to believe that this correlation might be nonlinear and that there might be an interaction between the effects of parental punitiveness and parental ethnocentrism on children's ethnocentrism. Accordingly, the data was cast into a 3 × 3 factorial design with three levels of parental punitiveness and parental ethnocentrism. For the 157 subjects for whom complete data were available, 13 subjects were randomly eliminated in order to form equal cell frequencies. This resulted in 16 subjects in each of the nine experimental conditions for a total of 144 subjects. The analysis of variance resulted in a significant main effect of parental ethnocentrism ($F = 18.89$, $df = 2/135$, $p < .01$); this result simply reflects the positive relationship between parental ethnocentrism and children's ethnocentrism found in the previous analysis. The main effect of parental punitiveness was not significant at the .05 level; however, the interaction between the two variables was significant at the .05 level ($F = 2.92$, $df = 4/135$), and the nature of this interaction is depicted in Figure 1.

Application of Duncan's multiple range test (Edwards, 1960) to the data in Figure 1 indicated that if perceived parental ethnocentrism is low or moderate, children's ethnocentrism is independent of parental punitiveness. On the other hand, if a child perceives his parents to be highly ethnocentric, the effects of parental punitiveness are significantly nonmonotonic. Thus, the data suggest that high parental ethnocentrism associated with moderate punitiveness is most conducive to the development of ethnocentrism in children. It should be noted that the same functional relationship was obtained in a previous study on a different population of children (Epstein and Komorita, 1965b).

DISCUSSION

This research suggests that childhood ethnocentrism is related to an interaction between parental ethnocentrism and punitiveness. The striking relationship between parental ethnocentrism and children's social distance attitudes towards fictional as

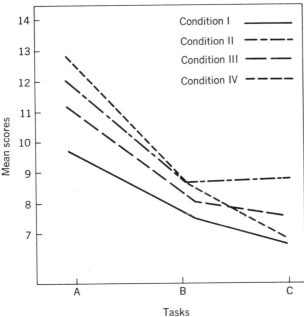

Fig. 1. Children's ethnocentrism as a function of parental ethnocentrism and parental punitiveness.

well as nonfictional groups is consistent with a social learning theory
which focuses upon parental reward
and approval for successful imitation
as the basis for childhood prejudice
(Buss, 1961). This interpretation is
consonant with recent investigations
which have reported that, for specific
populations, childrens prejudices may
directly reflect parental ethnocentrism. For example, Anisfeld, Munoz,
and Lambert (1963) reported that
ethnocentrism among Jewish children
is related to identification with parental beliefs. Mosher and Scodel
(1960) demonstrated that among
middle-class, Protestant children, social distance attitudes were related to
maternal ethnocentrism, but failed to
correlate with authoritarian child-
rearing practices.

Unlike these investigations, however, the current study suggests the
nature of those conditions which facilitate the imitation of parental ethnocentrism, namely, moderately punitive
discipline. The finding that moderate
discipline is more effective than weak
or severe discipline in the transmission
of parental attitudes to the child appears consistent with recent theory
and research regarding the antecedents of identification (Sears, Maccoby, and Levin, 1957; Whiting and
Child, 1953). According to these investigators, "love-oriented" discipline,
which lies midway between permissiveness and punitiveness, is most likely to lead to behavioral similarity between parent and child. Thus, it may
be assumed that a major consequence
of moderate discipline is to orient the
child towards obtaining parental approval and to create some doubt regarding its achievement. The child
may seek to reduce this doubt by inter-

nalizing parental attitudes and values.
On the other hand, the avoidant tendencies and excessive autonomy elicited by high punitiveness or permissiveness, respectively, are likely to inhibit
the process of identification.

These results are compatible with
the results of our previous study on
middle-class children which indicated
that moderate discipline is related to
childhood ethnocentrism (Epstein and
Komorita, 1965b). However, insofar as
the measurement of parental ethnocentrism was not possible, the interpretation of the previous results was
necessarily ambiguous. Furthermore,
our findings suggest that the basic
assumption inherent in the scapegoat
hypothesis of a monotonic relationship
between parental punitiveness and
displaced aggression requires modification. It would seem that given a
population, such as the one employed
in this study, in which a fairly high
level of ethnocentrism is present, it is
probable that training conditions conducive to parental identification, that
is, moderate discipline, are likely to
constitute an important antecedent of
prejudice in children. Moreover, an
important outcome of this study is the
finding that in addition to parental
attitudes and behaviors, the perceived
characteristics of outgroups (race and
socioeconomic status) influence children's social distance attitudes. Whereas both Negro and white groups elicited greater social distance when associated with working- relative to
middle-class status, working-class
status greatly accentuated prejudice
towards the Negro as compared with
the white group. However, middle-
class status served to minimize differential attitudes as a function of ethnic
affiliation.

The assumption that social distance toward working-class Negroes may be primarily a function of stereotypes which elicit emotional and evaluative responses towards this group is supported by Katz and Braly's (1958) report that preferences for foreign groups are determined by the desirability of characteristics previously attributed to these groups, and Negro elicits highly consistent and negative stereotypes compared with other groups. Our findings that prejudice towards the Oriental group is not differentially affected by social status suggests that cultural stereotypes towards Orientals are both less crystallized and less negative as compared with stereotypes regarding Negroes (Katz and Braly, 1958). Stereotypes may contribute to social distance by reducing dissonance associated with rejection of outgroups with whom there has been minimal contact (Festinger,

1957) or facilitating the attribution of dissimilar beliefs and values to outgroups, thereby contributing to the "belief prejudice" (Rokeach, 1960).

This study corroborates previous research by the authors (Epstein and Komorita, 1965a, 1965b) which suggests that the socioeconomic status of the outgroups is a basic variable related to the development of both prejudicial attitudes in children and aggressive acts among adults. Insofar as inferior social status appears to have the most detrimental effects on social distance towards Negroes, increasing opportunities for social mobility may modify hostile attitudes towards Negroes to a significantly greater degree relative to other ethnic groups.

In conclusion, this study points to the utility of investigating childhood prejudice as a joint function of child-rearing attitudes and practices, and stimulus characteristics of outgroups.

PARENTAL PUNITIVENESS SCALE

INSTRUCTIONS: When children do something wrong, their parents may react in different ways. We would like to know what you think would happen if you did something wrong.

Look at the following example:

0. If I hit another child,

MY	a. whip me		a.	MY
FATHER	b. send me to bed without supper		b. *MOTHER*
WOULD	c. have a long talk with me		c.	WOULD
	d. take away television		d.	

Make believe that you hit another child. You parents might react in different ways. Your father might react by: whipping you, sending you to bed without supper, having a long talk with you or taking away television.

Show what you think your father would do by putting a *circle* around the letter a. or b. or c. or d. Then, show what your mother might do by putting a *circle* around one of the letters on the other side. Circle one letter on the "Father" and one letter on the "Mother" side.

Any questions?

1. If I put paint on someone's house,

MY   a. take away my television   a.   MY
FATHER b. have a long talk with me   b. *MOTHER*
WOULD c. whip me   c.   WOULD
             d. send me to bed without supper   d.

2. If I throw a rock at someone's car,

MY   a. send me to bed without supper   a.   MY
FATHER b. take away my television   b. *MOTHER*
WOULD c. whip me   c.   WOULD
             d. have a long talk with me   d.

3. If I lie to my brother (or sister),

MY   a. whip me   a.   MY
FATHER b. have a long talk with me   b. *MOTHER*
WOULD c. take away my television   c.   WOULD
             d. send me to bed without supper   d.

4. If I throw something at my brother (or sister),

MY   a. take away my television   a.   MY
FATHER b. send me to bed without supper   b. *MOTHER*
WOULD c. whip me   c.   WOULD
             d. have a long talk with me   d.

5. If I steal something that belongs to a teacher,

MY   a. send me to bed without supper   a.   MY
FATHER b. take away my television   b. *MOTHER*
WOULD c. whip me   c.   WOULD
             d. have a long talk with me   d.

6. If I lie to another child,

MY   a. take away my television   a.   MY
FATHER b. whip me   b. *MOTHER*
WOULD c. have a long talk with me   c.   WOULD
             d. send me to bed without supper   d.

7. If I scream at another child,

MY   a. send me to bed without supper   a.   MY
FATHER b. take away my television   b. *MOTHER*
WOULD c. have a long talk with me   c.   WOULD
             d. whip me   d.

8. If I break something that belongs to another child,

MY	a. whip me	a.	MY
FATHER	b. send me to bed without supper	b. *MOTHER*
WOULD	c. take away my television	c.	WOULD
	d. have a long talk with me	d.	

9. If I talk back to another child,

MY	a. have a long talk with me	a.	MY
FATHER	b. whip me	b. *MOTHER*
WOULD	c. take away my television	c.	WOULD
	d. send me to bed without supper	d.	

10. If I start a fire on someone's lawn,

MY	a. send me to bed without supper	a.	MY
FATHER	b. take away my television	b. *MOTHER*
WOULD	c. whip me	c.	WOULD
	d. have a long talk with me	d.	

11. If I kick another child,

MY	a. have a long talk with me	a.	MY
FATHER	b. take away my television	b. *MOTHER*
WOULD	c. whip me	c.	WOULD
	d. send me to bed without supper	d.	

12. If I talk back to my brother (or sister),

MY	a. send me to bed without supper	a.	MY
FATHER	b. whip me	b. *MOTHER*
WOULD	c. have a long talk with me	c.	WOULD
	d. take away my television	d.	

13. If I hit my brother (or sister),

MY	a. take away my television	a.	MY
FATHER	b. send me to bed without supper	b. *MOTHER*
WOULD	c. have a long talk with me	c.	WOULD
	d. whip me	d.	

14. If I break a window,

MY	a. have a long talk with me	a.	MY
FATHER	b. send me to bed without supper	b. *MOTHER*
WOULD	c. whip me	c.	WOULD
	d. take away my television	d.	

15. If I scream at a teacher,

MY	a. take away my television	a.	
FATHER	b. send me to bed without supper	b.	MY
WOULD	c. whip me	c. *MOTHER*	
	d. have a long talk with me	d. WOULD	

16. If I put ink on someone's clothing,

MY	a. have a long talk with me	a.	MY
FATHER	b. send me to bed without supper	b. *MOTHER*	
WOULD	c. whip me	c. WOULD	
	d. take away my television	d.	

17. If I hit a teacher,

MY	a. whip me	a.	MY
FATHER	b. take away my television	b. *MOTHER*	
WOULD	c. send me to bed without supper	c. WOULD	
	d. have a long talk with me	d.	

18. If I steal something that belongs to my brother (or sister),

MY	a. send me to bed without supper	a.	MY
FATHER	b. whip me	b. *MOTHER*	
WOULD	c. have a long talk with me	c. WOULD	
	d. take away my television	d.	

19. If I scream at my brother (or sister),

MY	a. whip me	a.	MY
FATHER	b. have a long talk with me	b. *MOTHER*	
WOULD	c. take away my television	c. WOULD	
	d. send me to bed without supper	d.	

20. If I lie to a teacher,

MY	a. take away my television	a.	MY
FATHER	b. whip me	b. *MOTHER*	
WOULD	c. have a long talk with me	c. WOULD	
	d. send me to bed without supper	d.	

21. If I break something that belongs to my brother (or sister),

MY	a. whip me	a.	MY
FATHER	b. take away my television	b. *MOTHER*	
WOULD	c. send me to bed without supper	c. WOULD	
	d. have a long talk with me	d.	

22. If I swear at my brother (or sister),

MY	a. have a long talk with me	a.	MY
FATHER	b. send me to bed without supper	b. *MOTHER*
WOULD	c. take away my television	c. WOULD
	d. whip me	d.

23. If I kick my brother (or sister),

MY	a. send me to bed without supper	a.	MY
FATHER	b. have a long talk with me	b. *MOTHER*
WOULD	c. whip me	c. WOULD
	d. take away my television	d.

24. If I put sand in someone's car,

MY	a. have a long talk with me	a.	MY
FATHER	b. send me to bed without supper	b. *MOTHER*
WOULD	c. take away my television	c. WOULD
	d. whip me	d.

25. If I swear at another child,

MY	a. have a long talk with me	a.	MY
FATHER	b. whip me	b. *MOTHER*
WOULD	c. send me to bed without supper	c. WOULD
	d. take away my television	d.

26. If I pull up the flowers in someone's garden,

MY	a. take away my television	a.	MY
FATHER	b. whip me	b. *MOTHER*
WOULD	c. have a long talk with me	c. WOULD
	d. send me to bed without supper	d.

27. If I swear at my parents,

MY	a. have a long talk with me	a.	MY
FATHER	b. whip me	b. *MOTHER*
WOULD	c. take away my television	c. WOULD
	d. send me to bed without supper	d.

28. If I mess up someone's lawn,

MY	a. whip me	a.	MY
FATHER	b. send me to bed without supper	b. *MOTHER*
WOULD	c. have a long talk with me	c. WOULD
	d. take away my television	d.

29. If I steal something that belongs to another child,

MY	a. send me to bed without supper	a.	MY
FATHER	b. have a long talk with me	b. *MOTHER*
WOULD	c. take away my television	c.	WOULD
	d. whip me	d.	

30. If I throw something at my parents,

MY	a. have a long talk with me	a.	MY
FATHER	b. send me to bed without supper	b. *MOTHER*
WOULD	c. take away my television	c.	WOULD
	d. whip me	d.	

31. If I hit another child,

MY	a. whip me	a.	MY
FATHER	b. send me to bed without supper	b. *MOTHER*
WOULD	c. take away my television	c.	WOULD
	d. have a long talk with me	d.	

32. If I swear at a teacher,

MY	a. whip me	a.	MY
FATHER	b. have a long talk with me	b. *MOTHER*
WOULD	c. take away my television	c.	WOULD
	d. send me to bed without supper	d.	

33. If I steal something that belonged to my parents,

MY	a. take away my television	a.	MY
FATHER	b. send me to bed without supper	b. *MOTHER*
WOULD	c. have a long talk with me	c.	WOULD
	d. whip me	d.	

34. If I tear someone's book on purpose,

MY	a. whip me	a.	MY
FATHER	b. have a long talk with me	b. *MOTHER*
WOULD	c. take away my television	c.	WOULD
	d. send me to bed without supper	d.	

35. If I kick my parents,

MY	a. send me to bed without supper	a.	MY
FATHER	b. whip me	b. *MOTHER*
WOULD	c. take away my television	c.	WOULD
	d. have a long talk with me	d.	

36. If I throw something at a teacher,

MY a. take away my television   a. MY
FATHER b. send me to bed without supper b. MOTHER
WOULD c. have a long talk with me c. WOULD
   d. whip me   d.

37. If I break something that belongs to a teacher,

MY a. have a long talk with me   a. MY
FATHER b. whip me   b. MOTHER
WOULD c. send me to bed without supper c. WOULD
   d. take away my television   d.

38. If I throw something at another child,

MY a. send me to bed without supper a. MY
FATHER b. have a long talk with me b. MOTHER
WOULD c. take away my television   c. WOULD
   d. whip me   d.

39. If I kick a teacher,

MY a. whip me   a. MY
FATHER b. send me to bed without supper b. MOTHER
WOULD c. have a long talk with me c. WOULD
   d. take away my television   d.

40. If I lie to my parents,

MY a. take away my television   a. MY
FATHER b. send me to bed without supper b. MOTHER
WOULD c. have a long talk with me c. WOULD
   d. whip me   d.

41. If I talk back to a teacher,

MY a. send me to bed without supper a. MY
FATHER b. take away my television   b. MOTHER
WOULD c. have a long talk with me c. WOULD
   d. whip me   d.

42. If I hit my parents,

MY a. whip me   a. MY
FATHER b. send me to bed without supper b. MOTHER
WOULD c. take away my television   c. WOULD
   d. have a long talk with me   d.

43. If I scream at my parents,

MY   a. send me to bed without supper   a.   MY
FATHER b. whip me   b. *MOTHER*
WOULD c. have a long talk with me   c.   WOULD
          d. take away my television   d.

44. If I talk back to my parents,

MY   a. take away my television   a.   MY
FATHER b. whip me   b. *MOTHER*
WOULD c. have a long talk with me   c.   WOULD
          d. send me to bed without supper   d.

45. If I break something on purpose that belonged to my parents,

MY   a. send me to bed without supper   a.   MY
FATHER b. whip me   b. *MOTHER*
WOULD c. take away my television   c.   WOULD
          d. have a long talk with me   d.

43 *The Formation of Positive Attitudes toward Group Members*

BERNICE EISMAN LOTT

ALBERT J. LOTT

Positive attitudes toward group members can be formed by experiencing reward in their presence. Three-member groups of children from grades three and five play a game in which some are rewarded and others are not. Those who are rewarded subsequently indicate more positive attitudes toward their fellow group members than do the unrewarded. Would it be useful to study the attitudes of the unrewarded children toward the rewarded? Why?

In an attempt to predict group behavior on the basis of general psycho- logical principles as contrasted with formulations specific to the area, the

Reprinted from the *Journal of Abnormal and Social Psychology*, 1960, **61**, 297–300, by permission of the authors and the American Psychological Association.

concept of group cohesiveness has been re-examined and reformulated within a learning theory framework (Lott, 1961). Within this framework, cohesiveness is defined as *that group property which is inferred from the number and strength of mutual positive attitudes among the members of a group.* The concept of attitude is used, instead of the more usual one of attraction, because of its precise and particular meaning within learning theory, i.e., an implicit anticipatory response having cue and drive properties (Doob, 1947). By defining cohesiveness in terms of mutual positive attitudes among group members, the assumption is made that the members who comprise a group constitute its most significant components.

A number of hypotheses regarding both the antecedents and consequents of cohesiveness, as defined above, have been derived from learning theory (Lott, 1961). The problem of this experiment has been to test the most fundamental of these hypotheses, one which concerns the conditions under which positive attitudes toward group members may be formed.

It is predicted that if a person is rewarded in the presence of others (fellow group members), he will develop positive attitudes toward them. This proposition rests upon the following assumptions:

1. Persons may be conceptualized as discriminable stimuli to which responses may be learned.
2. A person who experiences reinforcement or reward for some behavior will react to the reward, i.e., will perform some observable or covert goal response (R_g or r_g).
3. This response to reward will become conditioned, like any other response, to all discriminable stimuli present at the time of reinforcement.
4. A person (group member) who is present at the time that Individual X, for example, is rewarded thus becomes able, in a later situation, to evoke R_g or, what is more likely, its fractional and anticipatory component, $r_g - s_g$. This latter response, which Hull has called "expectative" (1952, Ch. 5), was earlier interpreted by Doob (1947) as the underlying mechanism of an attitude.

The specific prediction tested by this study is that members of three-person groups who are rewarded for their performance in the presence of their fellow group members will more likely develop positive attitudes toward them than will members of such groups who are not rewarded. Positive attitudes are inferred, here, from choices made on a sociometric test subsequent to, and outside of, the experimental situation.

METHOD

Subjects

Forty-eight children from the University of Kentucky Elementary School, 24 each from Grades 3 and 5, served as Ss.[1]

Procedure

The Ss were divided into 16 three-

---

[1]The authors wish to acknowledge the cooperation of the following persons whose kind assistance made possible both the reported experiment and the pilot work which preceded it: M. Hitch, Principal of Rosenwald Laboratory School, Frankfort, Kentucky; A. Wolfe, intermediate grade teacher at Rosenwald; E. Sasman, Principal of University Elementary School, Lexington, Kentucky; A. Boone, M. Moore, and O. Barrett, teachers at University School of the third, fourth, and fifth grades, respectively.

member groups, following the administration of two sociometric tests. These tests were given, by the regular classroom teachers, on two consecutive days, several days before the actual experimental situation. On the basis of the test results the groups were formed so that each group was made up of children who had *not chosen each other* on either of the tests. Four all male and four all female groups were formed from Grade 3; five male and three female groups were formed from Grade 5.

Omitting the preliminary instructions, the criterion question asked in the first test was as follows:

Test I. Let us suppose that each one of you gets picked to take a trip to the moon in a rocket ship. This is a very special trip . . . . It is important for everyone who is on the same ship to get along well with each other . . . . Because of this you get a chance to pick two children to go along with you. Now, of all the children in this class, which two would you pick to travel in the same rocket with you?

Test II. [For this test the children were asked to think of themselves as visitors from Mars and to choose two classmates whom they would like to have waiting for them when their spaceship landed on Earth.]

For a group situation in which rewards and nonrewards could be manipulated, a board game called "Rocket Ship" was devised. The object of the game, played by groups of three, is to land cardboard rocket ships on planetary objectives. Each objective is reached by traversing a separate path containing four danger zones, at each of which a choice between a white and a striped subpath (one "safe" and the other "dangerous") must be made. By having the children in a group take turns crossing the danger zones first, the *E*s could arrange to have some children succeed and others fail in reaching the plan-

ets safely. The manner in which this was accomplished will be described below.

On the day of the experiment proper (separate days for the two classes), the *E*s were introduced to *S*s as having developed a children's game which they wished to test. One group at a time was called upon (in a predetermined random order) to play the game in a room adjoining the regular classroom.[2] The following instructions, given to each group by one of the investigators (E_1), describe the manner of playing:

. . . You three are rocket ship pilots. Each one of you has your own ship but you are going to take a trip into outer space together, side by side. The first trip you are going to take is to ——. In order to get there you must follow this path which scientists have decided is the safest way to go. The scientists also know that, at a few points along the way on this path, there is great danger. When you get to one of these dangerous points you are going to have to stop and decide whether the striped path or the white path is the dangerous one. One of the paths will get you past the danger safely. If you take the wrong path your rocket ship will be blown up and you'll have to parachute to Earth. . . . When you get to a danger point you'll have to decide which one of the group will take a chance and be the first to try either the striped or white path. If he gets through safely, the other two rockets may follow him. If his ship should get blown up, though, the other two ships will take the other path which you will know to be safe. You'll know that a ship has been blown up when you hear the sound of a bell, like this [sounded

---

[2]Wherever a child, preselected for a particular group, was absent on the day of the experiment, a substitute who met the criterion of nonchoice by, and of, the other group members, was, in all cases, available.

by E_2]. . . . Remember, you must take turns being first.

. . . It's possible for all three of you to get through to a planet safely, but it may be that only two of you will make it, and maybe just one or none of you will make it. . . . If you reach a planet safely you will be able to choose one of these prizes [small plastic auto models] which you may keep. . . . We'll play half the game this morning and half this afternoon.

Each group tried for three objectives in the morning and three in the afternoon. Half the total number of Ss was permitted to land safely on four planets (two at each session) while half was prevented from reaching any of them. "Reward" was thus defined as the receipt of four plastic car models (one for each successful landing). A child was either "rewarded" or "not-rewarded," i.e., made no successful landings at all and received no prizes; there were no in-between conditions. Prizes won in the morning session were held by the Es until the end of the afternoon session at which time the rewarded Ss returned to their classroom with four model cars and the nonrewarded Ss returned with none.

Rewarded and nonrewarded Ss were selected on a random basis prior to the game. A nonrewarded S always had his ship "blown up" when, at his chance to go first at a danger point, he took either the striped or white path.[3] As soon as he made his choice of path, the "blow up" bell was rung by E_2 who sat somewhat apart from the game area.

[3]Each child was in the position of "being first" at a danger point at least once on his way to each of the planets since Ss had been instructed to take turns and there were four danger zones per path and three children in a group. It was always possible, therefore, to "blow up" nonrewarded Ss without interfering with a group's spontaneous behavior regarding which child would go first at which point.

Each group had been randomly assigned, prior to the game situation, to one of the following conditions which describe the number of group members who were to be rewarded during the game: zero, one, two, all. Four groups, two from each class, were assigned to each condition. This aspect of the design was introduced to avoid having the Ss suspect that the game was "rigged." The natural flavor of the game was maintained by having Ss know that it was possible for all three group members to be successful, or only two, etc.

Shortly before the close of the school day, approximately one hour after the last group had played the game, the classroom teacher administered another sociometric test (III), as follows:

Suppose your family suddenly got the chance to spend your next vacation on a nearby star out in space . . . you can invite two children to go on the trip . . . and spend the holiday with you on the star. Which two children in this class would you choose to take with you?

After the choices were collected by the teacher, E_2 appeared before the class to thank the Ss for their cooperation and help. And, because everyone had been such "good sports," four prizes were distributed to each of the youngsters who had not won them during the game.

TABLE 1.—Choices Made by Subjects on Sociometric Test III

SUBJECTS	CHOICES		
	Play-group member	Non-play-group member	N[a]
Rewarded	11	37	48
Nonrewarded	3	45	48

[a]N = number of choices made; each S made two choices.

RESULTS

The results of the final sociometric test (III), which succeeded the play-group experience, are presented in Table 1. The proportion of playgroup members chosen by rewarded Ss was found to be significantly greater than the proportion chosen by nonreward-ed Ss. The obtained critical ratio, corrected for continuity, is 2.14 ($p = .03$; two-tailed). This confirms the prediction that Ss who had been rewarded would choose members of their groups, on the final sociometric test, significantly more often than Ss who had not been rewarded.

DISCUSSION

The present findings indicate that the formation of positive attitudes toward persons is predictable from learning theory principles and can be studied in the laboratory. This study thus extends the applicability of a general S-R framework to significant social behavior.

The prediction that positive attitudes toward persons can be formed by experiencing reward in their presence, was clearly confirmed. Since it is in terms of such positive attitudes among the members of a group that cohesiveness has been defined, the present experiment is seen to be concerned with the antecedents or determinants of cohesiveness even though no attempt was made to measure the variable directly. The specific concern of this first study was with the development of positive attitudes toward group members and not with the

group property that results from such attitudes when they are mutual.[4]

There have been comparatively few experimental attempts to vary group cohesiveness other than by suggesting to the members of a group that they will like each other. One investigation in which determinants were experimentally manipulated (Thibaut, 1950) found a positive relationship between cohesiveness and group status. In another study, more relevant to the present one (Bovard, 1951), a significantly greater level of interpersonal affect was found in group-centered as compared with traditional leader-centered classes. Bovard suggested that this result was due to the fostering, in group-centered classes, of member-to-member interaction which produces greater accuracy in intermember perception, creating, according to Bovard, a situation conducive to "need satisfaction." That the experience of need satisfaction (reward) in the presence of group members can, indeed, result in positive affect toward those group members has been demonstrated in the present experiment.

The results obtained in this study should be evaluated in the light of the following factors which could only have tended to work against substantiation of the hypothesis:

1. Play-group members were, by design, neutral or negative stimuli for one another at the beginning of the experimental situation. This was assured by placing, in a group, only Ss

---

[4] An operational measure of cohesiveness which follows directly from the definition of the concept given earlier has been developed by the investigators and will be reported in connection with its use in another study.

who had not chosen one another on two previous sociometric tests.

2. The amount of reward experience received by rewarded Ss in the presence of others was extremely small when compared with the amount of daily contact our Ss typically had with each other in the classroom, playground, and after school. (Practically all the Ss in each of the classes had been together for their entire schooling, beginning with kindergarten.)

3. The choices made on the two preexperimental sociometric tests (I and II) were found to be unexpectedly stable for third and fifth graders, indicating relatively reliable friendship ties[5] which the experimental experience was able to disrupt, however temporarily.[6]

Despite the above factors the prediction, that positive attitudes toward persons will be developed as a result of the receipt of reward in their presence, was clearly supported. Through the results were obtained with children, there is no reason to expect that they would not hold with adults as well. Such generalization must, of course, await adequate test.

The variable manipulated in the present study was simply reward vs. nonreward. Future research might profitably deal with variations in reward frequency, delay, and schedule, for example, as these affect the conditioning of attitudinal responses, and, consequently, as these affect the development of cohesiveness in small groups. That the results obtained in this study were predicted from general behavior principles increases our confidence in the promise which this kind of an approach holds for the general area of small group behavior.

SUMMARY

Three-member groups of children played a game in which some members were rewarded and others were not. On a later sociometric test, outside of the game situation, rewarded Ss chose a significantly greater proportion of their fellow group members than did the nonrewarded Ss. These results were predicted from general principles of S-R learning theory.

---

[5]Forty percent of the Ss made the same two choices on both tests; another 42% of the Ss repeated one choice on both tests.

[6]No follow-up test was given since there was no reason to expect that the positive attitudes formed during the brief game situation would last, in the absence of continued reward experience in the presence of the same individuals.

44 *The Effects of Experimental Socialization Paradigms upon Two Moral Responses to Transgression*

JUSTIN ARONFREED[1]

This two-part experimental study suggests the complexity of effects in an apparently simple case of adult punishment of child: the specific consequences of punishment determine what the child will learn to do about his own transgressing behavior. Self-criticism by the child relates to the adult's standards of evaluation. Reparative responses of the child depend on whether the adult or child controls the punishment. Several cautions in interpreting the results are noted.

The development of moral behavior has proved to be remarkably refractory to psychological analysis and empirical study, despite the increasing attention that has been given to it. The difficulties in a psychological treatment of the origins of moral responses are undoubtedly related to the virtual absence of experimentation in which the conditions presumed to effect their establishment and maintenance have been systematically varied. There have been some informative assessments (Allinsmith, 1960; Heinecke, 1953;

[1]The author gratefully acknowledges the able assistance and helpful suggestions of Karl Brolein and Sylvia Sandowsky.

Reprinted from the *Journal of Abnormal and Social Psychology*, 1963, **66**, 437–448, by permission of the author and the American Psychological Association.

Sears, Maccoby, and Levin, 1957, Ch. 10; Whiting and Child, 1953, Ch. 11) of moral responses in the context of variations in parental child rearing practices. But despite the theoretical ingenuity exercised in interpreting the results of these surveys, the very limited extent and magnitude of the relationship uncovered make it apparent that we have as yet only a restricted understanding of how such responses are acquired.

Contemporary conceptions of moral development tend to attribute a wide array of relevant phenomena to a unitary psychological structure established through a single process of acquisition. Thus, in the psychoanalytic formulation (Fenichel, 1945, Ch. 6; Freud, 1936, Ch. 8), various aspects of internalized morality are subsumed under the concept of the superego and are viewed as collectively acquired through the mechanism of identification. Even more detailed and behavioral accounts of moral development are inclined to treat different forms of response as more or less equivalent criteria of the "extent of development of conscience" (Sears, et al., 1957, Ch. 10), of the "severity of standards" (Allinsmith, 1960), or of the "strength of superego formation" (Heinecke, 1953).

This assumption of an underlying unity in the forms and sources of moral behavior may obscure some important differences between specific responses and their distinct antecedents. For example, most of the psychological research on moral behavior has focused on its prohibitive and punitive components. Yet people are obviously moral in a broader sense than that of merely avoiding or reacting to transgressions. They also come to find many of their actions intrinsically rewarding, quite aside from any consequent external approval. Even the relatively monolithic psychoanalytic conception distinguishes between the punitive superego and the rewarding ego ideal. And if we think of moral responses as being acquired through social sanctions and becoming, in varying degrees, independent of these sanctions, then it seems clear that the reinforcements which originally define transgressions and their consequences may be very different from those which define actions to be experienced as rewarding or praiseworthy.

Significant distinctions can also be made even among responses which reflect the punitive and prohibitive functions of morality. Many years ago, Hartshorne and May (1928) concluded from their studies of deceit and self-control that moral behavior was highly dependent on the external situation and often did not accord with verbalized moral judgment. More recently, Mowrer (1960b, Ch. 10), in applying learning concepts to socialization, has reproduced a letter from R. L. Solomon that describes work in progress, on internalization in dogs, in terms which suggest that resistance to temptation and reactions to transgression may derive from two patterns of reinforcement which are, to some extent, independent of one another. Hill (1960) has proposed that different types of internalized response to transgression may follow from different learning processes which vary in the temporal relations and reinforcement contingencies between the child's responses and the onset or termination of punishment. And Whiting (1959) has

used cross-cultural observations to infer that effective moral control in the
absence of direct external supervision
need not rest on the experience of guilt
and that a degree of internalization is
possible merely through the fear of
real or imagined external sources of
punishment.

The findings of a survey previously
reported by the writer (Aronfreed,
1961) indicated that children's internalized responses to transgression assume a great variety of forms and
often reveal little evidence of cognitive resources of moral judgment usually associated with the phenomenon
of guilt. The response of self-criticism,
for example, was very circumscribed
in its frequency of occurrence. Confession, apology, reparation, and commit-
ments to modify future behavior were
common, but the greater proportion
of such responses appeared without
the explicit application of a standard
of judgment to the transgression. Furthermore, numerous responses were
characterized by the perception of externally defined consequences of transgression. Although all of the responses
found in the survey were internalized,
in the sense that they occurred without external observation of the transgression and in the absence of any
explicit or threatened punishment,
there was no basis for assuming that
the responses were alternate manifestations of a single, more fundamental
reaction. There was, on the contrary,
striking confirmation that the different
responses were attributable to different patterns of social reinforcement in
that they were predictably related to
the socioeconomic status and sex role
of the child, and, to a lesser degree, to
maternal disciplinary practices.

The two experiments reported in the
present paper are attempts to examine
the specific conditions of reinforcement affecting children's use of two
moral responses, self-criticism and
reparation, in controlled socialization
paradigms. The second experiment,
in replicating the first, introduced certain conceptual and methodological
refinements.

EXPERIMENT I

One of the implications of the survey
described above is that transgressions
may apparently be socially defined
for a child in a minimally cognitive
context. The internalized behavioral
consequences of a transgression would
certainly require discrimination, since
there must be distinct response cues
to which they are attached, but it
would seem that such consequences
encompass a much broader class of
behavior than that for which self-evaluation or judgment is a prerequisite.
There is considerable recent evidence
(Kohlberg, 1963b; MacRae, 1954; Peel,
1959) that a normative framework of
standards for evaluating actions, in
contrast to what are merely expectations about their consequences, is not
simply a natural feature of cognitive
development and social exposure, as
has been suggested by Piaget (1948).
It appears instead to be a variable
function of particular social roles and
cultural settings which the child has
experienced.

Self-criticism, viewed in its bare essentials as a consequence of transgression, is the use of a verbal-symbolic
referent to one's own behavior,
thoughts, or feelings. As such, it represents a response in which the individ-

ual takes action, through the internal mediation of his own cognitive resources, with respect to himself as the object of action. The active quality of the self-critical response was recognized by earlier social-psychological theorists such as J. M. Baldwin (1906) and G. H. Mead (1934), who, while they were primarily concerned with morality as a phenomenon of valuation and consciousness, nevertheless viewed a moral response as being one in which the individual was capable of taking the role of another with respect to himself. The same property of action can be seen to apply to reparation, which uses the individual's own behavioral resources to correct or ameliorate the effects of a transgression. Although reparative responses may simply reduce unpleasant feeling without necessarily implying self-evaluation, they are always constructive or restitutive, and therefore require some kind of manipulation of one's own behavior as well as of the external environment.

The active, self-corrective character of moral responses such as self-criticism and reparation suggests that their establishment might depend on the extent to which a child has been previously socially reinforced for evaluation and acting upon its own behavior. A child who has been encouraged to make corrective or punitive responses to its socially unacceptable behavior would be expected to more frequently resolve subsequent transgressions through its own critical and reparative actions, even in the absence of external sanctions, than a child who has experienced the consequences of transgression in events outside of its own control. One might also expect that a

child's self-mediated resources for responding to transgression would be enhanced by the incorporation of explicitly verbalized standards into its socialization. A cognitive context for punishment would provide evaluative labeling responses for the child to act upon its own behavior with self-criticism. It would also provide, therefore, additional cues for appropriate reparative responses of a kind quite different from those provided by the stimulus of the transgression itself. A number of studies (Allinsmith, 1960; Aronfreed, 1961; MacKinnon, 1938; Sears, et al., 1957, Ch. 10), in which reasoning and the reinforcement of self-punitive reactions were subsumed under the category of "psychological," "love oriented," or "induction" techniques of discipline, have reported a positive relationship between the use of such techniques and the child's self-corrective activity and independence of external events in responding to transgression.

The basic procedure of the experiments reported in this paper was to use mild disapproval and deprivation to punish the child repeatedly for an act of aggression carried out on 10 successive training trials. In the first experiment, two distinct treatments were employed. One treatment maximized cognitive structure through the verbalization of an explicit standard in reference to the aggressive acts, and also gave the child control over the evaluation and punishment of the transgression. In the second treatment, cognitive structuring was minimal, and evaluation and punishment of the child's behavior were entirely in the experimenter's control. A common test trial at the end of both treatments, where a more destructive transgression occurred in the contrived breaking of a doll, was designed to elicit self-critical and reparative responses when the experimenter's punitive socializing role was terminated. The specific moral responses to be observed during the test trial were not made by the child in the course of the experimental treatment, in order that their appearance might be taken to reflect generalized response tendencies and not merely isolated pieces of behavior repeatedly attached to a stimulus situation. The nature of the aggressive acts was purposely made unusual and somewhat removed from ordinary experience, so as to minimize the effects of the child's predispositions and maximize the effects of the procedure.

METHOD

SUBJECTS   The subjects for the first experiment were 57 fifth-grade girls drawn from two public schools in a large urban school system.[2] Both of the schools served fairly homogeneous socioeconomic areas of a working-class character. The children were randomly assigned to the two experimental conditions in roughly equal numbers.

PROCEDURE   Each subject was individually taken by the experimenter, who was a male, from her classroom to the experimental room, where she was asked to sit in front of one end of a rectangular piece of composition board resting upon a small table. The board was roughly 2 × 3.5 feet in size. Twenty-four toy soldiers of the small plastic variety were

---

[2]The author is indebted to a number of administrators and teachers in the Philadelphia public school system, whose cooperation made the experiments possible.

thickly clustered in a triangular formation at the other end of the board. Behind the base of the formation, at the very edge of the board, stood a wooden doll about 6 inches in height, with clearly feminine features and a black uniform not unlike a skiing outfit. A large cloth-padded cardboard box rested on a chair just beyond the far edge of the board and behind the doll. The box was below the height of the board's surface, so that the interior was not visible to the subject when she was seated. The experimenter sat to one side of the board toward the far end. On a table adjacent to the experimenter's right hand were some recording sheets, a box of small Tootsie Rolls, and an instrument to be introduced as the "pusher" (actually a miniature hoe, roughly 2 feet long).

After the experimenter and the subject were seated, the experimenter used one of two procedures which were identical in all aspects not relevant to the experimental treatment, including the specification of the behavior to be punished and the nature of the punishment. The procedures differed only in their degree of cognitive structuring and in the direction of control over evaluation and punishment. In the High Cognitive Structure-High Control condition, the subject's activity was repeatedly put into the context of standards verbalized along the dimensions of careful-careless and gentle-rough, and the subject was also asked to evaluate and punish her own actions. In the Low Cognitive Structure-Low Control condition, only the minimal cognitive framework necessary to clarify the task was used, and evaluation and punishment were under the experimenter's control. The task in which the child was required to engage was arranged so that some degree of aggression was inevitable, since the children might otherwise have made punishment inappropriate by simply inhibiting any action construed as a transgression.

High Cognitive Structure-High Control. The verbal instructions given by the experimenter were as follows (italicized words and statements were used only in this condition):

> I have something here for you to do. The Army uses it to pick people for a special kind of work. *To do this work, you have to be very careful and gentle. Being careful and gentle is the most important thing.*
>
> Here's the way we do it. Back here there is a nurse in a special uniform [experimenter points to doll]. She is important in case anyone gets sick, and all of the soldiers love her because she is so good to everyone. Whenever there's any danger, she has to leave the field by going back into this box [experimenter indicates box by lifting it from chair]. Here's how she goes into the box. You push her off the board with this pusher. You can't lift the pusher; you must keep it down on the board when you push [experimenter demonstrates, then hands pusher to the subject].
>
> Now the soldiers guard the nurse very carefully. They stand all around her like this [experimenter points to soldiers]. Of course, to push her off, you will have to push through the soldiers, and so you will knock some of them over, *even though you're trying to be careful and gentle* [this is, in fact, obviously true, as the spacing between the soldiers is much too narrow to permit the pusher's blade to pass without toppling some of them]. The idea is to see how many of the soldiers you will

knock down. If you knock down just a few, that's good. If you knock down a lot of them, that's not so good. *When you use the pusher, try to be as careful and gentle as you can.*

> Here is a pile of thirty Tootsie Rolls for you [experimenter places pile and small empty box in front of the subject]. When we're all through you may keep however many you have left. Each time, after you push off the nurse, *you* look at the number of soldiers you knocked down, *and you decide how careless and rough you've been*. Then *you decide* how many Tootsie Rolls *you* should take from your pile. *You* take the number of Tootsie Rolls *you* think is right and put them in the box here. Those are the Tootsie Rolls you lose. *You* might take one Tootsie Roll, or two, or three, but not more than three. *The amount you take depends on how careless and rough you think you've been.*

The subject then went through a series of 10 training trials. The experimenter began the first trial by saying:

> Remember to keep the pusher down on the board. Push off the nurse and knock down as few soldiers as you can. *And be as careful and gentle as you can.* All right, go ahead.

The experimenter began all subsequent trials by simply saying:

> Okay, go ahead.

On each trial, after the nurse had been pushed over, the experimenter said:

> All right. You knocked down some soldiers, *so you decide how careless and rough you've been. Take as many Tootsie Rolls as you think is right and put them into the box.*

While the subject was making the Tootsie Roll payment, the experimenter reset the nurse and fallen soldiers. Just as the subject put the Tootsie Rolls into the box, the experimenter casually said:

Good!

This verbal reinforcement was intended to make it somewhat easier for the child to continue the self-depriving behavior.

Low Cognitive Structure-Low Control. The procedure in this condition was initially the same as that indicated in the first three paragraphs of instructions under the first condition described above, except that the italicized portions for maximizing cognitive structure were eliminated here. The experimenter then continued as follows (italicized words and statements were used only in this condition):

Here is a pile of thirty Tootsie Rolls for you [experimenter places pile and small empty box in front of the subject]. When we're all through, you may keep however many you have left. Each time, after you push off the nurse, *I* look at the number of soldiers you knocked down. Then *I* decide how many Tootsie Rolls *I* should take from your pile. *I* take the number of Tootsie Rolls *I* think is right and put them in the box here. Those are the Tootsie Rolls you lose. *I* might take one Tootsie Roll, or two, or three, but not more than three.

The subject then went through the series of 10 training trials. The experimenter began each trial in the same way as indicated above under the first condition, except that the italicized statement (for the first trial) was eliminated. On each trial, after the nurse had been pushed over, the experimenter said:

All right. You knocked down some soldiers, *so I'll have to take—let's see—* [*one, two, three*] *Tootsie Rolls.*

The experimenter then removed the Tootsie Rolls and reset the nurse and soldiers. Since there was always considerable disarray, the experimenter had freedom to vary the number of Tootsie Rolls he took on different trials. This flexibility was used to equate the total loss of Tootsie Rolls for children under this condition with the total loss for children under the first condition, where they controlled their own losses.

Test trial. The eleventh trial of both of the experimental treatments was planned as an apparently unexpected disruption due to the breaking of the nurse doll. The bottom half of one leg of the doll was detachable, having been prepared so that it was attached only by a tiny screw and could be unobtrusively removed by the experimenter with only a few gentle turns. Since the experimenter had to be present during the test trial to observe the child's responses, some change in the situation had to occur to indicate to the child that the previous punitive consequences of transgression were no longer forthcoming. Accordingly, the experimenter terminated his role as a socializing agent on this trial and used nondirective, apparently casual verbal stimuli to make the situation more appropriate for the child to show her own overt reactions to transgression.

When the subject pushed off the nurse on this trial, the experimenter looked into the box with a surprised expression and said:

Oh, my—it's broken.

While making this statement, the experimenter reached into the box with both hands, as though slowly picking up the doll, and quickly removed the leg. This procedure took only 2 or 3 seconds, and the child could not see the interior of the box. The experimenter held up the doll in one hand and the detached leg in the other, and, looking at them (but not directly at the child), added:

And we don't have another nurse here to use for this—[1] I wonder why it broke.

This last query, spoken reflectively as though the experimenter were thinking to himself, was an indirect verbal stimulus to elicit a self-critical response in those subjects in whom it might be prepotent.

If the subject gave any response to Stimulus 1 that was relevant to the cause of the doll's breaking, whether or not it was self-critical, the experimenter went on to the third stimulus (given below). If the response was not clearly relevant to the doll's breaking, or if the subject gave no response, the experimenter presented Stimulus 2:

Why do you think it broke?

This second question was meant to provide a stronger eliciting stimulus for self-criticism. Then, regardless of the responses to the first two stimuli, Stimulus 3 was:

Well, now that it's broken, I wonder what we should do.

This third comment was spoken reflectively and was the first indirect stimulus intended to elicit reparative responses. If the subject offered any response that was relevant to the implied question, whether or not it was reparative, the experimenter terminated the test trial procedure. If the subject gave no response, or one that was not relevant to the question, the experi-

menter then presented the final, stronger eliciting Stimulus 4:

What do you think we should do now?

Then, regardless of the subject's response to this last question, the test trial procedure was always terminated. The subject's responses to all of the experimenters verbal stimuli were written down verbatim as they occurred.

CLOSING PROCEDURE A closing procedure was used to put the subject at ease about her performance and to invoke her cooperation in not discussing the experiment with other children. Informal checks, as well as the children's behavior during the experiment, indicated that excellent security was maintained.

Results and Discussion

It was apparent that all of the children took the experimental situation seriously and that, without respect to treatment, they uniformly paid close attention to the loss of Tootsie Rolls and exercised care in pushing over the nurse. Almost all of the children were visibly concerned about the breaking of the doll, though their responses were quite variable. Some self-critical responses were given to the experimenter's first, rhetorical verbal stimulus (1), but the majority appeared only when the second, more direct stimulus (2) was presented. Likewise, most of the reparative responses occurred to the direct question (4) rather than to the indirect stimulus (3). Frequency counts were taken of the number of children who showed any instance (one or more) of each of the two types of response, to either the direct or indirect stimuli, and the number of children who showed no evidence of the response.

Self-critical and reparative responses were independently identified by highly specified criteria which required virtually no judgment or interpretation. A response was classified as self-critical if the child, in accounting for the doll's breaking, referred to her behavior in pushing it—for example, any response indicating that she had not pushed the nurse "the right way," had pushed it too hard, had pushed it so that it did not hit the box properly, etc. The fact that only four of the children actually used the words "careless" or "rough" suggests that self-critical responses did not represent merely what the child regarded as appropriate verbalizations of the experimenter's words and that they followed from a more general self-evaluative orientation induced by the procedure. Responses were classified as reparative when they indicated the child's perception that the effects of transgression could be corrected or ameliorated through her own resources for constructive action. These responses invariably took the form of suggestions for repairing the doll or continuing the procedure, even without the doll, in some alternative way.

Table 1 shows the frequency of self-critical and reparative responses under each of the experimental conditions. Both types of responses were significantly more likely to occur when cognitive structure and the child's control over punishment had been maximized than they were when there had been minimal cognitive structure and control. It is interesting to note that children who gave no self-critical responses, particularly those in the Low Cognitive Structure-Low Control condition, often attributed the

TABLE 1.—Frequency of Self-Critical and Reparative Responses under Conditions of High Cognitive Structure—High Control and Low Cognitive Structure—Low Control

TYPE OF RESPONSE	HIGH COGNITIVE STRUCTURE –HIGH CONTROL (N = 29)	LOW COGNITIVE STRUCTURE –LOW CONTROL (N = 28)
Self-criticism		
Present	18	7
Absent	11	21
Reparation		
Present	16	8
Absent	13	20

Note.—Frequencies represent number of subjects who show any instance (one or more) of a given response and number of subjects who show no evidence of the response. Chi square values for 2 × 2 contingency tables (employing correction for continuity) are as follows: Self-criticism, $x^2 = 6.52$, $p < .01$, one tailed test; Reparation, $x^2 = 3.15$, $p < .05$, one tailed test.

breaking of the nurse to factors external to their own actions. Thus, they might indicate that the nurse was poorly constructed, that it was broken by the physical impact with the cloth-padded box, or that it had been given too much use. Analogously, children who did not make reparative responses sometimes simply indicated their inability to make any constructive suggestion. Some made comments to the effect that the experimenter should decide what ought to be done.

While the experimental effects confirmed expectations, they were limited to indicating that, in response to a transgression in the absence of external punishment, the children's use of cognitive and behavioral resources to act upon either their own actions or the external environment was a function of the extent to which they had previously been provided with such resources and encouraged to use them. The design of the experiment reflected a conceptualization of the antecedents of self-criticism and reparation that obscured certain more detailed and explicit interpretations of the findings. The socialization paradigms were constructed in a manner that made it impossible to separate the effects of cognitive structuring from those of control over punishment. Since the two moral responses bore a parallel relationship to the experimental treatments, it could not be ascertained whether contingencies existed between them or whether they had independent antecedents which had been subsumed together in the treatments. For example, the two responses might be viewed as interchangeable variants of a single generalized response tendency or, alternatively, as separate response tendencies induced by common features of treatment. It was even possible that one of the responses was induced only secondarily through the mediation of the other.

In order to examine the antecedents of the two moral responses more closely, a second experiment was designed to permit cognitive structure and control over punishment to vary independently of one another and to go beyond merely drawing a parallel between the properties of the responses and the resources provided by the socialization paradigms. Conceptual changes were introduced which emphasized the functional significance of the responses and outlined the specific me-

chanisms through which the two antecedent variables might have different behavioral consequences. Self-criticism and reparation, while they might both be instances of the child's active use of its own resources, were clearly distinct responses, and it was difficult to imagine that they did not have distinct determinants. One obvious possibility that suggested itself was that self-criticism, a cognitive and evaluative response, might be more affected by the articulateness of standards provided for the child than by the degree of control over punishment. Conversely, a reparative response, oriented toward actively correcting the effects of transgression, would seem more closely related to whether a child was given responsibility for its own deprivation than to the amount of cognitive structuring present.

The second experiment also utilized a different kind of sample in order to expand the generality of the expected findings. Previous evidence (Aronfreed, 1960, 1961; Sears, et al., 1957, Ch. 10) of the relationship of moral responses to socioeconomic status and sex role suggested the desirability of using middle-class boys as subjects, in contrast to the working-class girls used in the first experiment. Replication of the findings, under such a sampling variation, would indicate that the experimental effects could not be attributed to an interaction of the procedures with predispositions already attached to particular social roles.

EXPERIMENT II

The conceptual framework of the second experiment proceeded from the view that a behavior may be defined as a transgression to the extent that it has been exposed to negative (punitive) sanctions. The social punishment results in the behavior itself becoming a cue for an affective response that may be given the general designation of anxiety, though it might well have various qualities dependent on the nature of the punishment. When the anxiety is no longer contingent on the actual presence of punishment, it may be regarded as the first and invariant component of any internalized moral response to transgression. The anxiety is reducible by a number of different responses which acquire instrumental value because they reproduce certain significant cues which are often associated, in the original socializing situation, either with the avoidance or termination of punishment or with the attenuation of the anticipatory anxiety that precedes punishment. The child may then make the relevant cue producing responses to reduce the anxiety aroused by subsequent transgressions, even in the absence of external punishment. The use of the term guilt, in this framework, would be appropriate only when the moral responses have a self-evaluative, cognitive component.[3]

The cues associated with anxiety reduction may, in certain instances, be

---

[3]What is being described here, of course, is nothing more than a learning process having two aspects which correspond to varieties of classical and instrumental conditioning. Mowrer (1960a) has described the reinforcement value of cues associated with the termination of punishment (and anxiety) as being crucial to a complete account of secondary reinforcement. A number of animal studies relevant to this phenomenon have recently been summarized by Beck (1961).

stimulus aspects of the child's own responses which were originally effective in arresting or terminating punishment. Children frequently learn that their raparative responses (as well as other responses, such as confession) are followed by this kind of direct external reinforcement. In the self deprivation condition of the first experiment, the child made a reparative response, on each training trial, that terminated a punitive situation and the anxiety aroused by it. Presumably, such training might well have induced a corrective or ameliorative disposition of the test trial, when there was no punishment, even if explicit standards of evaluation had not been provided. In naturalistic socialization, of course, reparation may also be followed by positive reinforcement, and the experimenter's saying the word "Good!" when the child removed her own Tootsie Rolls might be taken as analogous to such a reinforcement.

Direct external reinforcement of a moral response does not provide, however, a very satisfactory account of the origins of self-criticism. The self-critical response is not easily open to observation by others (it is not ordinarily verbalized). Its initial appearance in very young children, among whom it is more often overt, is frequently quite vigorous and sudden. Furthermore, it actually reproduces an aspect of the socializing agent's punitive behavior, and the manner in which its external reinforcement could be controlled by the agent is not readily apparent. For example, in the experimental socialization paradigm with high cognitive structure, only the experimenter had used evaluative labels during training to refer to the children's behavior. The appearance of a self-critical response on the test trial may be viewed, then, as an adoption of the experimenter's role, a phenomenon with many of the properties commonly referred to as imitation or identification.

Freud (1933a, Ch. 3; 1936, Ch. 8) at various times attributed the child's adoption of a model's behavior both to the desire to reproduce the characteristics of a loved object and to the desire to defend against the anxiety aroused by the threatening or aggressive aspects of the model. These two motive sources have been elaborated and modified by others (Bronfenbrenner, 1960; Freud, 1946, Ch. 9; Mowrer, 1950, Ch. 21; Sanford; 1955), but without a description of the specific reinforcement mechanisms through which the modeling takes place. Direct external reinforcement has been suggested to explain certain forms of imitation (Church, 1957; Miller and Dollard, 1941), and Hill (1960) has recently attempted to use it to derive the origins of self-criticism. Other theorists (Mowrer, 1960b, Ch. 3; Sears, et al., 1957, Ch. 10; Whiting and Child, 1953, Ch. 11) have taken the view that the child reproduces stimulus properties of a model's behavior which are already secondary reinforcers because of their association with the model's affection and nurturance. A form of observational learning has also been proposed (Darby and Riopelle, 1959; Maccoby and Wilson, 1957), in which reinforcements or their affective consequences are somehow vicariously generalized from model to subject. Finally, a number of recent theoretical treatments specify that, because of the resources or goal states controlled by the model

but desired by the subjects, it becomes self-reinforcing for the subject to maximize the perceived similarity between self and model (Kagan, 1958) or to covertly practice (toward the self and others) role actions of the model which occur in close contiguity to the subject's own responses (Maccoby, 1959b) or which maintain drive reducing effects through their translation into control over the resources in fantasy (Whiting, 1960).

The reinforcement mechanisms outlined above are awkward in their application to the experimental paradigm in question here (and to the ordinary socialization situation), where the child makes a response that is previously made only by the socializing agent and that is clearly associated with punishment. It is difficult to see how the self-critical response could have been directly reinforced during the training trials, why the child would reproduce aspects of a nonnurturant experimenter's role which obviously do not result in pleasurable experience, or why the child would receive vicarious satisfaction in perceiving the experimenter's criticism of its actions. Likewise, the motivation for reproducing the experimenter's control of punitive resources is not apparent. The child may, of course, have been making implicit self-critical responses during training, but we are still left with the problem of why the responses are made at all and of how they are reinforced.

A solution to the problem is made possible by considering that moral responses may acquire instrumental value for reducing the anxiety aroused by a transgression through more than one pattern of reinforcement. Not only may they reproduce cue aspects of those behaviors of the child which were originally associated with avoidance or termination of punishment, as in the case of reparation, but they may also reproduce cue aspects of the previous punitive behavior of a socializing agent. After a child has had some experience with a transgression, punishment itself may come to serve as a cue signifying the attenuation of the anxiety that accompanies its anticipation. When a child's punishment incorporates the verbalization of evaluative labels in reference to its actions, the labels, like any other component of punishment, may become cues for the termination of the anxiety that comes to be directly attached to the transgression. The child can then subsequently itself make the evaluative response, even in the absence of external punishment, and thus reproduce the anxiety reducing cues in its own behavior.[4]

We may assume that, as a result of the training procedures, the child begins to experience anxiety each time the soldiers are knocked down. Under high cognitive structuring, the experimenter's critical evaluation ("careless" and "rough") becomes part of the anticipated punishment associated with the termination of the anxiety. The place of the verbal criticism in the punishment, and its timing with respect to onset and termination of anxiety, would therefore be expected to

_____

[4]An appreciation of this cue value of punishment is useful in understanding why some children's predominant response to transgression might lie in the perception of punishment in the actions of other people or in impersonal fortuitous events.

motivate the child to reproduce the critical responses during the test trial, regardless of the degree of direct control that the child has exercised over the loss of Tootsie Rolls.

METHOD

SUBJECTS The subjects for the second experiment were 68 fifth-grade boys from another public school in the same urban school system from which the girls for the first experiment had been drawn. The school was in a residential area having an entirely middle-class population. Seventeen children were randomly assigned to each of four experimental conditions.

PROCEDURE The second experiment used the same experimenter used in the first one. The procedures were also, in most essential respects, the same as those of the first experiment. They differed from the original procedures primarily in using four rather than two distinct conditions, and in introducing minor changes of instruction and treatment into two of the four conditions, in order to permit cognitive structuring and control over punishment to vary independently of one another. There were now two conditions in which explicit standards of evaluation were presented. The initial portion of the instructions for both of these conditions was identical to that described under the first three paragraphs of general instructions for the first experiment, including the italicized sections for maximizing cognitive structure. There were, likewise, two conditions of low cognitive structure using the same initial instructions, but with the italicized sections removed. The procedure within each of the two sets of conditions then bifurcated so as to introduce variation in the degree of control over punishment.

High Cognitive Structure-High Control. The instructions continued here as shown in the fourth paragraph of instructions under the original High Cognitive Structure-High Control condition.

High Cognitive Structure-Low Control. Here the experimenter continued the procedure as follows (italicized words and statements were used only under the condition with low control):

Here is a pile of Tootsie Rolls for you [experimenter places pile and empty box next to the subject's right hand]. When we're all through, you may keep however many you have left. Each time, after you push off the nurse, *I* look at the number of soldiers you knocked down, and *I* decide how careless and rough you've been. Then *I* decide how many Tootsie Rolls *I* should take from your pile. *I* take the number of Tootsie Rolls *I* think is right and put them in the box here. Those are the Tootsie Rolls you lose. *I* might take one Tootsie Roll, or two, or three, but not more than three. The amount *I* take depends on how careless and rough *I* think you've been.

The experimenter's statements in initiating trials were again the same as those described for the original High Cognitive Structure-High Control condition (initiation of trials did not carry any manipulation of the Control variable). The experimenter's procedure in terminating each trial was to say:

All right. You knocked down some soldiers, so *I* decide how careless and rough you've been. *I'll have to take— let's see—|one, two, three| Tootsie Rolls.*

Low Cognitive-High Control. After the common initial portions of the instructions, the procedure here continued as follows (italicized words and statements were used only under the condition with high control):

Here is a pile of thirty Tootsie Rolls for you [experimenter places pile and empty box next to the subject's right hand]. When we're all through, you may keep however many you have left. Each time, after you push off the nurse, *you* look at the number of soldiers you knocked down. Then *you* decide how many Tootsie Rolls *you* should take from your pile. *You* take the number of Tootsie Rolls *you* think is right and put them in the box here. Those are the Tootsie Rolls you lose. *You* might take one Tootsie Roll, or two, or three, but not more than three.

The experimenter initiated trials in the way described under the original Low Cognitive Structure-Low Control condition (initiation of trials did not carry any manipulation of the control variable). In terminating each trial, the experimenter said:

All right. You knocked down some soldiers. *Take as many Tootsie Rolls as you think is right and put them into the box.*

Low Cognitive Structure-Low Control. The remainder of the instructions and procedure in this condition was the same as that described for the original Low Cognitive Structure-Low Control condition in the first experiment.

For all four of the experimental treatments summarized above, the test trial and closing procedures were identical to those used in the first experiment.

Results and Discussion

The criteria for establishing the presence of self-critical and reparative responses were the same as those described in the report of the first experiment. Table 2 shows the frequencies of occurrence and nonoccurrence of the two types of response under each of the four experimental conditions. Chi square values for the comparisons evaluating the effect of each independent variable upon each of the two responses are presented in Table 3. The two tables indicate a series of significant differences which are almost entirely those expected. Self-critical responses are more likely to appear when the socialization paradigm provides explicit standards of evaluation than when cognitive structure is minimal. It is also clear that the effect of cognitive structuring on self-criticism is in no way contingent on the degree of control over punishment

given the child, since the effect is equally apparent under conditions of both high and low control. Control over punishment alone, when separated from any variation in cognitive structure, obviously has no effect whatsoever on self-criticism. It seems reasonable to conclude, therefore, that a socialization situation in which the child actively uses its own resources in responding to transgression, as happens under conditions of self-deprivation, does not in itself evoke a generalized response tendency of action with respect to one's own behavior, of which self-criticism is one form. It would appear that the reinforcement of a self-critical response requires that punishment be associated with the verbalization of specific cognitive labels.

The effects of the experimental treatments on reparative responses, while generally in the anticipated direction, are not quite as definitive as

TABLE 2.—Frequency of Self-Critical and Reparative Responses under Four Conditions of Cognitive Structure and Control of Reinforcement at Punishment Termination

TYPE OF RESPONSE	HIGH COGNITIVE STRUCTURE		LOW COGNITIVE STRUCTURE	
	High Control	Low Control	High Control	Low Control
Self-criticism				
Present	11	10	5	4
Absent	6	7	12	13
Reparation				
Present	14	4	10	6
Absent	3	13	7	11

Note.—$N = 17$ in each of the experimental groups. Frequencies represent number of subjects who show any instance (one or more) of a given response and number of subjects who show no evidence of the response.

TABLE 3.—Chi Square Values for Frequency Comparisons of Self-Critical and Reparative Responses under Four Conditions of Cognitive Structure and Control of Reinforcement at Punishment Termination

COMPARISON	CHI SQUARE VALUE	
	Self-criticism	Reparation
High Cognitive Structure versus Low Cognitive Structure		
High Control	2.95*	1.28
Low Control	3.04*	0.14
Both groups	7.22**	0.06
High Control versus Low Control		
High Cognitive Structure	0.00	9.56**
Low Cognitive Structure	0.00	1.06
Both groups	0.06	9.94**

Note.—Chi square values for 2 × 2 contingency tables (employing correction for continuity) based on frequencies in Table 2.
*p < .05, one-tailed test.
**p < .01, one-tailed test.

the effects on self-criticism. Control over punishment, rather than cognitive structuring, is the major source of variation. But its effect is clearly apparent only under the condition of high cognitive structure. There is some tendency for control over punishment to affect reparative responses even when cognitive structure is minimal, but the tendency does not attain statistical significance. Since cognitive structure per se does not significantly affect reparative responses, its effect on these responses might be interpreted as a secondary or modifying one. Reparation seems to be reinforced primarily by giving the child active control over the corrective or punitive consequences of transgression. It is quite possible, however, that explicit cognitive labeling adds another dimension to this control, and facilitates reparation through the additional cue values which it provides. Such an interpretation might find some tentative support in the fact that, given the condition of high control over punishment, there is a tendency for reparative responses to be more frequent when cognitive structure is maximized. It is obvious, in any case, that self-criticism and reparation cannot be thought of as alternative or equivalent responses to transgression deriving from a single pattern of socialization. Nor can either one of the responses be viewed as a fundamental reaction to transgression through which the other is only secondarily mediated. The two responses must be regarded as outcomes of distinct patterns of social reinforcement, even though these patterns may happen to be intimately interwoven in the ordinary course of child rearing relationships.

Certain restraints need to be recognized in interpreting the results of these experiments. While there was no punishment on the test trial, so that the moral responses observed showed internalization in the sense of being independent of the original negative reinforcements on which they were based, some ambiguity remains as to the degree of internalization, since the experimenter had to be present in order to observe the children's responses. Further, the effect of the punishment itself, being compounded of disapproval and deprivation, is difficult to evaluate precisely. The use of terms like "careless" and "rough" might have created a greater perceived intensity of punishment, a possibility conceivably reflected in the fact that minimal cognitive structuring seemed to depress even the impact of high control over punishment on reparative responses. Finally, the treatments are not entirely divorced from the child's previous socialization, and generalization or transfer may have entered into their inducement of moral responses. An unequivocal demonstration of the conditions necessary to establish a new moral response tendency would require the use of symbolic referents with no previous evaluative connotation and a more exact control over the timing of punishment with respect to the behavior of both the child and the socializing agent.

45 Resistance to Temptation in Relation to Sex of Child, Sex of Experimenter, and Withdrawal of Attention

ROGER V. BURTON

WESLEY ALLINSMITH

ELEANOR E. MACCOBY[1]

Four-year-old children are tested for cheating while playing a game. They conform to the rules more with an adult of the opposite sex and withdrawal of attention increases boy's cheating but has no effect on girl's cheating. Several interpretations of these findings are discussed. The study concludes also that desire to please a cross-sex adult, arousal of achievement motivation by a same-sex adult which may increase in boys by withdrawal of attention, and resentment at withdrawal of attention by boys, could influence resistance to temptation either singly or in combination.

[1] We express our appreciation to the staff of the Laboratory of Human Development of Harvard University, especially to John W. M. Whiting, for many constructive comments on this study.

This experiment is part of a larger study designed to investigate the factors influencing resistance to temptation. A paper has already reported the

Reprinted from the *Journal of Personality and Social Psychology*, 1966, **3**, 253–258, by permission of the senior author and the American Psychological Association.

relationships between child-rearing practices and temptation behavior and indicated the complex nature of this area of study (Burton, Maccoby, and Allinsmith, 1961).

The theoretical bases for this experiment came mainly from modifications of Freudian identification theory as delineated by Allinsmith (1954), Maccoby (1959a), Sears, Maccoby, and Levin (1957), and Whiting (1954b, 1959), and the work on nurturance-withdrawal of Hartup (1958). Sears, et al., proposed a theory of identification which predicts that girls will be more strongly identified with their mothers than boys will be with their fathers. The rationale for this theory is that the mother is the main agent for important resources, especially for nurturance and discipline, during infancy and early childhood regardless of the sex of the child, and is therefore the first object of identification for both boys and girls. She continues in this role for her growing daughter; but the father becomes more and more the boy's model for identification as he takes a more active disciplinary role in his son's life, and as he possesses more of the skills his maturing son wants to have. From this theory the prediction was that girls would conform to standards established by an adult experimenter more than would boys and that this would be especially so when the experimenter was a woman. Furthermore, a female experimenter should produce more conformity than a male experimenter in both boys and girls who are only 4 years old.

Using the work of Hartup (1958) as a basis, we also hypothesized that withdrawal of attention by a formerly nurturant experimenter would arouse dependency anxiety which would mediate the motive to reestablish a nurturant relationship with the experimenter. We would expect, from this reasoning, that interrupting the attention the experimenter paid to the subject would produce greater identification with the experimenter's rules and thus greater conformity to such rules than would continuous attention.

These predictions assume that: acceptance of adult standards will be mediated by the identification process; at this early age there has been enough time for the boy to shift his main object of identification to his father; there will be generalization from the child's mother and father to the female and male experimenters, respectively.

The standards established in the experimental situation were rules of a very simple game. The adult experimenter taught the child subject these rules and the child was then tempted to deviate from these rules in order to get a "good score." This experiment was designed to answer the following questions concerning the sex of the child subject, the sex of the experimenter, and withdrawal of attention:

1. Is there an overall difference between 4-year-old boys and girls in conforming to the rules of a game?
2. Does the sex of the experimenter affect the behavior of the child in a resistance to temptation setting?
3. Does the sudden withdrawal of attention just prior to the temptation test affect the child's behavioral tendencies to resist temptation or to deviate from the rules?
4. Are there any interaction effects from sex of the subject, sex of the experimenter, and withdrawal of attention on resistance to temptation?

METHOD

Subjects

The 112 children in this study were all 4 years old and enrolled in private nursery schools. They came from well-established, middle-class homes, with well-educated parents. The fathers were professional men, executives in business, or graduate students. None of the children showed any noticeably "abnormal" characteristic.

Procedure

The experimenter brought the subject, individually, from the classroom to the room used for the experiment, telling him, "We have a game for you children to play, and it is your turn." The experimenter talked with the subject while walking to the experimental room and tried to be warm and friendly during this time. In a few cases, the teacher had to accompany the child to the testing room, but she remained only a minute or two until the subject became fascinated with operating the game.

The game consisted of a 1 × 4 foot board with five lights which came on, accompanied by a chime, whenever a string behind the board was hit. One light came on at a time and remained lit until the experimenter reset the game. The rules of the game were to stand on a foot marker, placed about 5 feet from the game, and to try to hit the string with bean bags which were to be thrown only once over the front board. The game was placed against a backstop so that all bags which went over the 1 foot high board would land somewhere near the string. Since the string was behind this front board, the subject could not see whether or not his bag actually hit the string when he was standing on the marker. In fact,

a hidden experimenter (E_2) completely controlled these lights and chimes. He was behind a one-way mirror in a portable observation booth which could be installed in whatever room the school let us use for testing.

A standardized script was followed in showing the subject how the game "worked" and in teaching him the rules of standing on the marker when throwing and of throwing each bag only once over the board. All subjects received the same schedule of three "hits," out of the possible five, for two practice games. After the subject clearly demonstrated he understood the rules, E_1 took the subject to a nearby table and said, "We'll play with this again later. Now I have another game to show you." This new activity, with which the child was to be engaged for a 3-minute period, consisted of little plastic pieces which could be fitted together by their ball-and-socket connections to make Walt Disney animals.

After 1 minute of play during which E_1 was very nurturant and attentive to the subject, E_2 signaled E_1 in the event that this subject was to receive interrupted instead of continuous attention. The treatment for the subject was kept from E_1 to avoid any influence such knowledge might have had on his behavior during the first part of the procedure. E_2 tapped his pencil once against the wall to signal interrupted attention. E_1 would then go to another table, without any explanation to the subject, and start to fill out a rating form on the subject's behavior. In response to the subject's questions or requests, E_1 said, "You go ahead and play. I'm busy," or "I have some work to do now." The attempt was to make as much contrast as possible between the "warm" and "cold" relationships during this interrupted play treatment.[2] At the end of 2 minutes, E_1 said, "Well, that's done," and returned to the subject. For the continuous attention treatment, no signal was given to E_1 so that he continued to play very nurturantly with the subject for the 3 minutes.

At the end of this period, for both interrupted and continuous attention treatments, E_1 put the construction toys on a box and out of sight and reach of the subject while saying, "Now we'll play the bean bag game again." A tray of toys, pretested for attractiveness, and including items of appeal to both sexes as well as sex-neutral toys, was uncovered and the subject was told that he could win the toy of his choice if he "got enough lights on." The subject was then asked which one he would choose if he should get enough lights to win the prize. This was done to insure that all subjects focused on a toy they would really like. This was our method of maximizing temptation in order to control for differential arousal to deviate from the rules. E_1 tested the subject on whether he knew

---

[2]We thank Judy F. Rosenblith who gave us suggestions about the design of the study in regard to withdrawal of attention.

the rules for the game, and, if necessary, reviewed them with him. Just as the subject was about to play the game, E_1 looked at his watch and said, "I have to go out to make a telephone call, but you go ahead and play the game according to the rules while I'm gone." To eliminate fear of being caught, E_1 took the subject to the door and showed him how he was to hook the door so that no one could come in and "bother" him while he was playing the game. E_1 said he would knock when he returned. All children understood the instructions and locked E_1 out as we intended.

Only one light, after the second throw, was given to the subject during the 3-minute test period if he followed the rules. Additional lights were given for each act of breaking the rules: stepping forward, moving the foot marker, retrieving bags that had already been thrown and rethrowing them, and hitting the string with the hand. During this test period, E_2 recorded the subject's behavior and controlled the lights.

After the 3 minutes, E_1 returned, knocked on the door for admittance, and said to the subject "Let's play the game again and this time will be for the prize." E_1 ignored the lights the subject obtained

---

TABLE 1.—Mean Number of Bags Correctly Thrown before Deviation (Total Sample)

SEX OF SUBJECTS:	BOYS		GIRLS	
Sex of experimenter:	*Male*	*Female*	*Male*	*Female*
Treatment				
Continuous attention	5.3 $(n = 11)$	6.1 $(n = 24)$	5.8 $(n = 10)$	4.4 $(n = 26)$
Interrupted attention	3.7 $(n = 11)$	4.9 $(n = 10)$	5.6 $(n = 10)$	4.5 $(n = 11)$

during the test period. If the subject indicated he wanted E_1 to consider that score for the prize or for some sign of approval, E_1 said, "You certainly know how to play the game now, and this time will be for the prize." This last game was played to have a check on whether the subject really understood and would follow the rules with E_1 present, to eliminate any guilt or feelings of failure which might have resulted from the subject's behavior during the test period, and to avoid reinforcing any cheating.[3]

Resistance to Temptation Measure

The resistance measure was a 7-point scale based on a count of the number of bags the subject threw correctly before deviating from the rules. If the subject deviated immediately, he received a score of 1. His score was 2 if he threw one bag correctly and then deviated. If he threw all five bags correctly and then cheated, he had a score of 6. If he never deviated during the test period, his score was 7. The scoring reliability of this measure was almost perfect.[4]

RESULTS

Table 1 gives the means and n's for each group in the experimental design.

[3]For discussions of differences in ability, of the different motives which might be aroused and which might produce individual differences in temptation, and of our attempt to control for such differences by the described procedures, see Burton, et al. (1961).

[4]Later research has shown that this test has very high test-retest reliability: 19 of 20 children, tested 1 week apart, either conformed to the rules or deviated both times. Among those who deviated, there is a tendency (not statistically significant) upon second testing to deviate faster in actual time and in fewer bags correctly thrown before first deviation.

Bartlett's (1937) test indicated there was nonhomogeneity of variance among the cells, which, with unequal n's, precluded a straight analysis of variance with appropriate weightings for each cell. Table 2 shows the means of a reduced sample with each group having 10 subjects.

Table 3 presents the results of an analysis of variance of the reduced sample.

It can be seen that none of the main effects were significant by themselves. The only significant F ratio is the interaction between sex of subject and sex of experimenter. An inspection of the means shows that this result is due to greater resistance in the cross-sex groups.

TABLE 2.—Mean Number of Bags Correctly Thrown before Deviation (Reduced Sample)

SEX OF SUBJECTS:	BOYS		GIRLS	
Sex of experimenter: Treatment	*Male*	*Female*	*Male*	*Female*
Continuous attention	5.6	5.9	5.8	4.3
Interrupted attention	3.7	4.9	5.6	4.4

Note.—$n = 10$ in each group.

The means of the different groups in Tables 1 and 2, however, indicated that boys and girls should be analyzed separately, especially in regard to any treatment effects. As there is no indication from these means of any interaction between sex of experimenter and type of treatment, we have returned to the full sample to make two-way comparisons of the groups controlling on sex of subjects. Table 4 summarizes these contrasts. These contrasts indicate there is a cross-sex effect for both boys and girls—such that there is more cheating with a same-sex experimenter and more conformity to the rules with an opposite-sexed adult. Furthermore, the treatment effect remains significant for boys and, though in the opposite direction, is clearly not significant for girls. Continuous attention for boys produced a greater abiding by the rules and interrupted attention produced deviation from the rules.

TABLE 3.—Analysis of Variance of Number of Bags Correctly Thrown before Deviation (Reduced Sample)

SOURCE	df	SS	MS	F
Sex of subject (A)	1	.00	.00	.000
Sex of experimenter (B)	1	1.80	1.80	.392
Treatment C	1	11.25	11.25	2.449
A × B	1	22.05	22.05	4.799*
A × C	1	9.80	9.80	2.133
B × C	1	1.80	1.80	.392
A × B × C	1	.45	.45	.098
Error	72	330.80	4.5944	
Total	79	377.95		

*$p < .05$.

In order to assess the effect of individual experimenters, comparisons were made for the three male experimenters and the seven female experimenters. There were no significant differences among any of these within-sex experimenter comparisons.

DISCUSSION

Referring to our original predictions, it is clear that 4-year-old girls did not

TABLE 4.—Differences between Means of Groups in Total Sample

CONTRAST (MEANS)	t	df
Boys		
Male experimenter (4.524) versus female experimenter (5.735)	2.289*	53
Continuous (5.829) versus interrupted (4.300)	2.715**	53
Girls		
Male experimenter (5.700) versus female experimenter (4.459)	2.07*	55
Continuous (4.806) versus interrupted (5.048)	0.405	55

*$p < .05$.
**$p < .01$.

abide by rules more than boys, and that the sex of experimenter was significant only in interaction with the sex of subject. Further, withdrawal of attention had an effect only on boys and this effect was opposite to what would be expected were dependency arousal to increase identification with—and consequently, conformity to—the experimenter's standards.

Sex Interaction

A reexamination of the assumptions underlying the derivations of our hypotheses indicates that conformity with the rules would be related to the degree to which the subject identified with the experimenter. It is clear, post hoc, that this assumption may not have been correct, and that the data are more in line with predictions reasoned from a theoretical scheme of the stages in the identification process as originally depicted by Freud (1933a). According to this picture, the child of 4 would not yet have identified with the parent of the same sex but would be experiencing increasing libidinal attachment toward the parent of the opposite sex. Identification with the same-sex parent should occur with the Oedipal resolution around 6 years of age. From such a theoretical position, one could derive the hypothesis that resistance to temptation in 4-year-olds would be greater with opposite-sex adults in order to please them. Our results are certainly more in line with such considerations. However, if we are dealing with pre-Oedipal-resolution children who have a greater cathexis for the opposite-sex parent, the predictions regarding conformity to the rules of our game would not be based on "internalization" of parental strictures. The issue of pleasing the no-longer-present experimenter in our test situation becomes ambiguous in that obtaining a good score to please the experimenter is as likely as conforming to his rules. Thus, to make precise differential predictions from either the pre-Oedipal-resolution or postresolution psychoanalytic conceptions is difficult. Data on 7-year-olds are now necessary for a more complete test of this theory since after the Oedipal resolution the significant interaction should be for greater compliance with the rules established by a same-sex experimenter.

Other experiments investigating sex of experimenter and of child as independent variables demonstrated their effect on performance and are relevant for our post hoc considerations. Stevenson (1961) found that a female experimenter was more effective than a male experimenter as a dispenser of social reinforcements to increase performance in 3–4 year olds. But for ages older than 4, the results often indicate that reinforcements dispensed by an opposite-sex experimenter are more effective than those by an experimenter of the same sex as the subject (Gewirtz and Baer, 1958a, 1958b; Gewirtz, Baer and Roth, 1958; Stevenson, 1961). The results of these studies and our experiment all conform to the hypothesis that young children are motivated to please an opposite sex adult more than an adult of the same sex.

This interpretation of our results is based on the assumption that, in order to please an adult of the opposite sex, the child will conform to the rules, rather than cheat to obtain a high score in order to please an adult of the same sex. In fact, however, each of these motives may be contributing to our findings if conforming behaviors are more associated with gaining love from the opposite-sex parent and achievement behaviors are more often instigated by the relationship with the same-sex parent. It is also possible that the wish to please, though operating in our results, is different for boys and girls. In the case of boys, it is the desire to please a father figure by achieving; hence, by contrast, conformity would be associated with an opposite-sex experimenter. For girls, it is the wish to please a father figure by conforming compared with less conformity with a same-sex adult. Though less parsimonious than a single factor model in positing a different basis in boys from that in girls, this interpretation—that both conformity to restrictions of opposite-sex adults and achievement arousal by same-sex adults produce an association of conformity with having an opposite-sex experimenter—does seem reasonable for our results and would be consonant with the results of other research cited above and below.

Withdrawal of Attention

Manipulating the relationship of the child to the experimenter has also produced differential performance in other studies. Withdrawal of attention (Hartup, 1958; Rosenblith, 1959, 1961) and complete isolation from social contacts (Gewirtz and Baer, 1958a, 1958b; Gewirtz et al., 1958; Stevenson and Odom, 1962; Walters and Ray, 1960) have tended to increase performance, although these results are inconsistent in regard to whether withdrawal is more effective when the experimenter is the same or opposite sex as the subject. These results were interpreted as supporting dependency arousal (Hartup, 1958; Rosenblith, 1959, 1961), social deprivation and drive (Gewirtz, 1958a, 1958b; Gewirtz, et al., 1958; Stevenson and Odom, 1962), and anxiety arousal (Walters and Ray, 1960).

If performance in these experiments is increased in order to please the experimenter, then the results just reviewed might suggest that withdrawal or isolation would increase this motive. Our data conform to this interpretation if one assumes that for boys a motive to please the experimenter by getting a high score is operating (Table 4). For the effect found is that in boys withdrawal increases cheating. If conformity to the rules of the game is increased in boys by wanting to please a female (opposite-sex) adult, then withdrawal seems to decrease this motive. Perhaps there is some feeling of being rejected which re-

duced any motive to need to conform to the rules to please the experimenter. Were this the case, the motive to resist temptation would be decreased in the subject by withdrawal of attention, leaving as a greater influence on his behavior the motive to cheat in order to win a prize for himself. In the case of girls, there is a very slight difference in favor of withdrawal to increase conformity, but this is mainly due to the larger number of girls in the continuous attention cell to have had a female experimenter.

Arousal of Achievement

In our post hoc discussion we have repeatedly felt the need to consider the arousal of achievement in accounting for our findings. The temptation test used appears to be strongly loaded with components relevant for achievement motivation. This consideration was given support in the somewhat parallel study by Grinder (1960) which produced its clearest results when he analyzed the resistance to temptation data in such a way as to control for achievement motivation. If the degree of achievement motive aroused in the subject were increased by withdrawal of attention, and the amount of cheating were correlated with this increase in motivation to obtain a high score, then the increase in cheating in boys under the withdrawal of attention is understandable. The lack of this effect on girls would be consistent with other failures to obtain increased achievement motivation in girls (McClelland, Clark, Roby, and Atkinson, 1958).

With such different interpretations possible, it seems that no single explanation presently available can account for the results of studies such as this. Clearly, additional studies investigating the motives involved in temptation tests are required to assess the extent to which these and possibly other motivational components determine whether a person will cheat or not.

46 *Attitudes of Children from a Deprived Environment toward Achievement-Related Concepts*

JUDITH W. GREENBERG

JOAN M. GERVER

JEANNE CHALL

HELEN H. DAVIDSON

The findings indicate that a group of fourth graders from a depressed urban area score high in value orientation (that is, expressing adherence to the prevailing values of society) and score low in self-concept (that is, rating of "myself"). The children show generally favorable attitudes toward school and authority figures, and interestingly, the poor achievers, particularly the boys, express more favorable attitudes than the good achievers. Several theoretical issues are discussed: the inverse relationship between achievement and attitudes toward school and authority concepts, and the need for further research into psychological variables associated with achievement.

The academic achievement of children from deprived environments has aroused increasing concern and interest in recent years. Lower-class children as a group fall below national norms in achievement and it is widely believed that they have negative attitudes toward academic learning. However, there has been relatively little attention given to the variability within the lower-class group itself. In academic achievement there is a wide range, with some children achieving success despite economic and cultural handicaps. Is there a corresponding range in the feelings and meanings attached to concepts that are related to school achievement?

Reprinted from the *Journal of Educational Research*, 1965, **59**, 57–62, by permission of the authors and Dembar Educational Research Services, Inc.

The purposes of this study were, first, to investigate the attitudes of a group of Negro children from a severely deprived environment toward a number of concepts presumed to be important for school learning, and second, to determine whether there were variations in attitudes associated with differences in school achievement and with sex.[1]

Procedure

SUBJECTS The subjects were 115 fourth-grade Negro children from one public school in a severely depressed urban area. Subjects were classified into three groups on the basis of grade equivalent scores on the Metropolitan Primary Reading Test administered at the end of third grade: "Good Achievers"—3.9 to 5.2; "Average Achievers" —3.0 to 3.8; "Poor Achievers"—1.7 to 2.9. Table 1 presents the mean reading scores for boys and for girls at each achievement level.

INSTRUMENT A semantic differential instrument was developed using Osgood's et al., (1957) technique. It consisted of 13 concepts to be rated on eight three-point adjective scales. The concepts included people who may be important in achievement behavior as well as specific aspects of school. Several nonschool items were included for comparison and to mask the purpose of the instrument. The concepts, in order of presentation, were Best Friend, Myself, Smart Child, Mother, Father, Teacher, School, TV, Reading, Homework, Playing, Arithmetic, Dumb Child.

The adjective scales were chosen chiefly from those that had been found in the past to have high loadings on the evaluative factor, the primary component in meanings and attitudes (Osgood et al., 1957). Six evaluative adjective pairs were used. Good-Bad, Clean-Dirty, Rich-Poor, Happy-Sad, Nice-Mean, Smart-Stupid. In addition, there were two potency scales: Big-Little and Strong-Weak. The vocabulary was modified to adapt it to the level and familiar usage of the children. The use of three-point scales constituted another adaptation. Osgood suggested that the seven-point scale used with adults be reduced to a five-point scale for children. However, it was felt that for this group of children additional simplification was required.[2] The instrument was pretested with individuals and with a school class.

The semantic differential was chosen over other types of attitude assessment for several reasons: it has a well-formulated theoretical rationale; considerable work has been done with it which indicates that it can be used for attitude measurement, for investigating meanings within a culture and for making comparisons among groups; it does not require extensive reading by the subjects, and it can be administered to groups and scored objectively; finally, its semi-projective nature should enable it to probe more

---

[1] This report is part of an ongoing investigation of achievement functioning in lower-class children undertaken in co-operation with the Board of Education of New York City (Assistant Superintendent Charles M. Shapp).

[2] The range of responses obtained, both in individual scores and in mean values, indicates that the simplified instrument did elicit differential responses and that it can be a useful device with young children.

TABLE 1.—Mean Reading Achievement Scores for the Three Achievement Groups, by Sex

	GOOD ACHIEVERS	AVERAGE ACHIEVERS	POOR ACHIEVERS
Boys	$N = 12$	$N = 26$	$N = 18$
	4.3	3.4	2.2
	(0.32)*	(0.27)	(0.33)
Girls	$N = 16$	$N = 27$	$N = 16$
	4.4	3.5	2.5
	(0.40)	(0.25)	(0.27)

*Standard Deviations are shown in parentheses.

deeply than a direct question technique.

The semantic differential has been used successfully with college students to investigate areas related to this study. For example, Husek and Wittrock (1962) studied attitudes toward "School Teachers" using 117 scales; another study by Winter (1961) included a comparison of teachers' and students' attitudes towards a number of concepts related to school learning.

The instrument was administered by a psychologist in five fourth-grade classrooms. The children received booklets containing thirteen identical pages. Each page had a blank line at the top on which the child was to write the concept to be rated; the eight adjective scales were listed on each page in the same fixed random order, with some positive adjectives appearing on the left and some on the right side of the scale. Directions were given orally so as not to penalize the poor readers. The examiner printed each concept on the blackboard and repeated the instructions to pace the group as they checked the eight scales for each concept.

SCORING AND ANALYSIS OF DATA   For

each scale a positive adjective checked was scored "plus 1," a negative adjective, "minus 1" and the neutral position, "zero." Evaluative and potency scales were summed separately and scores handled independently throughout. The possible range of evaluative scores was from −6 to +6. Since there were only two potency scales, each child's potency score was multiplied by three to give a range comparable to the evaluative ratings. Thus, each child had an evaluative and a potency score for each of the thirteen concepts with a possible range of from −6 to +6 for each score, the more positive scores indicating more positive attitudes.

Mean ratings were calculated for the total group of subjects and for boys and girls separately within each of the three achievement levels. An analysis of variance was performed using sex and achievement as the classifying variables.[3]

[3]We are indebted to Dr. Donald M. Medley (Division of Teacher Education of the N.Y.C. Board of Higher Education) for suggesting the method employed for handling unequal frequencies in cells as described in Walker and Lev (1953, p. 381).

TABLE 2.—Mean Ratings and F-Ratios for Each Concept on Evaluative Scales by Achievement Level and Sex

CONCEPT	MEAN RATINGS‡							F-RATIOS		
	Total Group (115)	Good Achievers		Average Achievers		Poor Achievers		Source of Variation		
		Boys (12)	Girls (16)	Boys (26)	Girls (27)	Boys (18)	Girls (16)	Achievement	Sex	Interaction
Mother	5.1	5.0	3.9	5.2	5.3	5.4	5.4	7.09**	2.62	2.56
T.V.	4.9	4.8	4.9	4.8	4.7	5.2	5.2	0.69	0.01	0.03
Father	4.8	4.8	4.0	4.6	5.0	5.1	5.4	2.52	0.03	1.15
Teacher	4.6	3.9	4.4	4.0	5.0	5.3	4.7	1.48	0.39	1.32
Reading	4.4	5.2	3.5	4.3	4.5	5.1	4.4	0.53	4.48*	2.80
Smart Child	4.3	4.8	4.1	4.3	4.4	4.7	3.8	0.10	1.64	0.76
Playing	4.2	3.9	3.9	4.2	4.6	4.2	4.3	0.44	0.11	0.04
Arithmetic	3.9	4.7	3.3	3.8	3.6	4.2	4.4	0.34	1.00	1.11
Best Friend	3.9	3.8	3.8	3.6	3.6	4.5	4.2	1.82	0.13	0.08
Myself	3.6	3.9	2.6	3.7	3.8	3.7	4.2	1.11	0.40	2.19
Homework	3.5	3.8	3.4	2.5	3.6	4.5	3.6	1.20	0.03	1.25
School	1.4	-0.2	0.0	1.5	1.3	4.0	1.2	6.07**	1.81	2.10
Dumb Child	-1.9	-2.8	-2.9	-2.0	-1.9	0.5	-2.8	1.92	2.39	2.46

‡Possible range of ratings: −6.0 to +6.0 with +6.0 indicating the most favorable rating.

*p = < .05.
**p = < .01.

FINDINGS

THE TOTAL GROUP An overview of
the findings for the entire group of
subjects may be obtained by examining the total group means for each concept shown, in their respective rank
orders, in the first column of Table 2
for the evaluative scales and in the first
column of Table 3 for the potency
scales. The three authority figures
(Mother, Father, Teacher)—along
with "TV"—received high positive ratings on both evaluative and potency
scales. All other concepts, except
"Dumb Child," also received positive
ratings. On the other hand, negative
ratings were assigned to "Dumb
Child," the one specifically unfavorable concept, which ranked lowest on
both factors. The very high potency
rating for "Father," close to the maximum possible value, is of particular
interest in view of the fact that many
of these children come from homes
where the father is absent and where
there is a strong matriarchal tradition.
The relatively low position of "Myself"
on the evaluative scales is also worth
noting. In general, these children, despite their deprived status, displayed
sensitivity to prevailing cultural values
and expressed attitudes that seem in
keeping with their age level. However,
it should be borne in mind that there
are no norms available and that any
interpretations of findings are advanced more as hypotheses than as
conclusions.

The overall evaluative ratings of the
concepts were, for the most part, higher than the potency ratings, suggesting
that while the children considered
most of the concepts "good" they did
not see them as equally "strong." In
the case of "Reading" the discrepancy
was especially marked. Although
"Reading" ranked fifth on the evaluative factor, it was next to the lowest
on potency. Are these children saying,
"We know that reading is something to
be admired and valued, but we don't
see it as an influential force in our
lives"?

In contrast to most other concepts,
the mean potency rating for "School"
exceeded the mean evaluative rating,
and, in addition, the mean evaluative
rating for "School" was relatively low
in comparison to the evaluative ratings for specific school subjects. These
discrepancies may have arisen from a
misinterpretation by the children of
the word "School" as referring to the
school building itself, an old and un-
attractive slum structure.

ACHIEVEMENT AND SEX VARIATION
When the findings were analyzed by
sex and three achievement levels, a
number of significant differences were
found. The mean ratings of each concept for the six sub-groups, along with
F-ratios, are presented in Table 2 for
the evaluative scales and in Table 3
for the potency scales.

The significant differences resulted
chiefly from achievement variation,
specifically, in the ratings of "Mother"
and "School" on the evaluative scales
and "Mother," "TV" and "Dumb
Child" on the potency scales. There
was one significant sex difference in
the evaluative ratings of "Reading"
and one significant interaction effect
in the potency ratings of "Reading."

In the ratings of the concept
"Mother," it was the poor achievers
who assigned the most favorable ratings on both the evaluative and potency scales. Of particular interest

TABLE 3.—Mean Ratios and F-Ratios for Each Concept on Potency Scales by Achievement Level and Sex

| CONCEPT | MEAN RATINGS‡ | | | | | | | F-RATIOS | | |
| | Total Group (115) | Good Achievers | | Average Achievers | | Poor Achievers | | Source of Variation | | |
		Boys (12)	Girls (16)	Boys (26)	Girls (27)	Boys (18)	Girls (16)	Achievement	Sex	Interaction
Father	5.5	6.0	5.2	5.2	5.8	5.5	5.6	0.08	0.00	1.84
Mother	4.6	4.2	3.4	4.3	5.2	4.8	5.6	3.82*	0.46	1.86
Teacher	4.1	3.5	3.9	3.5	4.2	4.8	4.9	1.46	0.47	0.11
T.V.	3.5	4.0	3.9	3.5	4.9	3.0	1.3	4.83**	0.05	2.38
Playing	3.4	2.8	3.0	4.0	3.1	3.3	3.6	0.62	0.08	0.50
Myself	3.2	2.8	3.4	3.4	3.1	3.4	2.1	0.23	0.26	0.84
School	3.1	2.0	3.6	2.5	3.3	4.0	2.9	0.40	0.42	1.39
Arithmetic	2.7	2.5	2.2	2.5	2.6	3.7	2.4	0.40	0.58	0.35
Best Friend	2.6	2.2	1.7	2.5	3.0	2.7	3.0	0.73	0.01	0.23
Smart Child	2.5	3.0	2.6	2.8	1.9	3.2	1.9	0.17	1.50	0.15
Homework	2.3	1.0	1.9	2.8	2.0	2.8	3.0	1.55	0.00	0.47
Reading	0.9	1.0	−0.2	0.0	1.2	3.7	0.0	1.59	2.99	6.87**
Dumb Child	−1.9	−3.2	−3.0	−1.7	−2.6	1.0	−2.2	3.95*	3.03	2.01

‡Possible range of ratings: −6.0 to +6.0 with +6.0 indicating the most favorable rating.
*p = ∨ .05.
**p = ∨ .01.

were the low ratings of "Mother" given by the good-achieving girls in comparison to the other groups. (It is interesting to note that these girls were lowest in their self-evaluative ratings too.) The concept "School" was also evaluated most favorably by the poor achievers, particularly the boys.

For the concept "Dumb Child" the good achievers were the most strongly negative and assigned the lowest potency ratings. The same pattern of responses was observed for the evaluative ratings of "Dumb Child" although the differences did not reach the level of significance there. On both factors, the poor-achieving boys gave "Dumb Child" slightly positive ratings. Thus, the poor achievers, who may find the concept more threatening personally, did not reject "Dumb Child" as strongly as the better achievers.

In the case of "TV," the average achievers assigned the most favorable potency ratings, followed by the good achievers. The poor achievers gave "TV" much lower potency ratings than the other groups. This finding does not seem to contribute to conceptualization of the data. (One possible interpretation is that the importance of "TV" has been denigrated by teachers and that the poor achievers gave what they perceived as the socially most desirable response.)

The ratings of "Reading" provided two significant differences. The sexes differed on the evaluative scales, with the boys assigning the higher ratings. In the potency ratings of "Reading," there was a significant interaction of sex and achievement arising from the highly favorable ratings of the poor-achieving boys. "Reading" ranked fifth among the 13 concepts in the mean

potency ratings of the poor-achieving boys; for the five other sub-groups, "Reading" ranked next to the lowest.

In general, it appears that the poor-achievers tended to assign the most favorable ratings, particularly to concepts which have high social value.[4] It may be that they were less able than the better achievers to express critical attitudes. The poor-achieving boys showed the most global favorability of response.

Discussion and Conclusion

Although it is often assumed that lower-class children have negative attitudes toward school-related and authority concepts, the young Negro children studied here expressed favorable attitudes. We realize that this result may in part be due to the general tendency to give favorable and socially acceptable responses on rating instruments. However, for this group of children the indication that they are aware of what is socially acceptable and what should be valued is in itself important to note.

The fact that there was a discrepancy between the evaluative and potency ratings may be related to the

------

[4]The possibility that the higher ratings of the poor achievers represented an artifact of the instrument was investigated. It has been found (Osgood et al, 1957) that less able subjects tend to be more polarized in their judgments and it is well known that individuals tend, in general, to rate more positively than negatively. Since the good achievers did use the neutral position more frequently than other subjects, it was decided to re-score papers for some of the concepts eliminating those scales which were assigned a neutral rating. The results obtained from this re-scoring procedure did not change the direction of the differences.

observation by Rosen (1959) that Negro subjects may score high in value orientation, i.e., expressing adherence to the prevailing values of society, while scoring low in personal achievement motivation. The relatively low ratings of "Myself" provide additional evidence for this interpretation.

It is generally taken for granted that good achievers have more favorable attitudes toward school than poor achievers and that girls are more favorable than boys. This study did not find these relationships, and other studies too have reported conflicting evidence suggesting that findings may be influenced by such factors as the criterion of achievement used. For example, Malpass (1953) using eighth-grade children, found that a number of attitude measures were positively correlated with achievement as measured by teachers' grades but not with achievement as measured by standardized tests. The study cited previously (Winter, 1961) which used a semantic differential with college students, found a correlation between grades achieved and the degree of similarity in values between teacher and student. It is quite possible that in the present study, if teachers' grades instead of achievement test scores had been the criterion used to form the achievement sub-groups, a different pattern of relationships might have emerged.[5] Inconsistent findings in studies of the relationship between attitudes and achievement may also stem from the nature of the setting and composition

of the group studied. The findings reported here may be specific to a homogeneous, lower-class group and similar children in a heterogeneous socioeconomic setting might have expressed different attitudes.

A number of theoretical questions may be raised regarding the inverse relationship observed in this study between achievement and favorability of expressed attitudes toward certain school and authority concepts. It is quite possible that the higher ratings of the poor achievers may be symptomatic of rigid defenses that mask underlying anxiety or hostility. The good achievers seemed to demonstrate greater critical ability, independence, self-confidence and reality orientation which may be related to their success in school. Similar interpretations may be adduced regarding the instances in which the boys' ratings were more favorable than those of the girls. The particularly high ratings assigned by the poor-achieving boys tend to reinforce these interpretations. Lower-class Negro boys are apt to face special difficulties in identification and other important aspects of development and maturation. The poor-achieving boys, with their psychological and educational burdens, may well be the sub-group with the strongest defensive needs.

One may also speculate on the extent to which the findings depend upon the projective level of this instrument. Would a direct set of questions elicit more similar responses from good and poor achievers in that both would give the expected favorable surface replies? Would a deeper projective instrument perhaps reverse the direction of the findings if, in penetrat-

---

[5] It has been observed that even as low as fifth grade, interpersonal perceptions of teachers and children are an important factor in achievement behavior (Davidson and Lang, 1960).

ing the defenses of the poor achievers, it revealed that their basic attitudes were more negative? In fact, it was observed that in "self" drawings obtained from this same group of subjects, the poor-achieving boys displayed more negative characteristics than the other sub-groups (Lourenso, Greenberg, and Davidson, 1965). Also, in a TAT-type task used with a small selected sample, the stories of the poor achievers included more often than those of the good achievers, instances of punishment, hostile emotions, unhappy endings and authority figures cast in negative roles (Davidson, Greenberg, and Gerver, 1962).

The development of further insights into the psychological variables that are associated with achievement should be helpful in current efforts to improve academic attainment among children from deprived environments.

Summary

This study sought to investigate the attitudes of children from a severely deprived environment toward a number of concepts presumed to be important for school learning and to determine whether there were variations in attitudes associated with differences in school achievement and with sex.

Subjects were 115 fourth-grade Negro children from one public school in a severely depressed urban area. Subjects were classified as "Good," "Average" or "Poor" achievers on the basis of scores on the Metropolitan Primary Reading Test administered at the end of the third grade.

A semantic differential instrument was developed using Osgood's technique. It consisted of 13 concepts to be rated on eight three-point adjective scales, six evaluative and two potency. The concepts, in order of presentation, were: Best Friend, Myself, Smart Child, Mother, Father, Teacher, School, TV, Reading, Homework, Playing, Arithmetic, Dumb Child.

Each child received an evaluative and a potency score for each of the 13 concepts with a possible range of from -6 to $+6$ for each score, the more positive scores indicating more positive attitudes. An analysis of variance was performed using sex and achievement as the classifying variables.

The findings revealed that this group of Negro children from a deprived environment expressed generally favorable attitudes, particularly toward important authority figures. Their ratings on evaluative scales of the semantic differential were somewhat higher than their potency scale ratings. In most instances, the poor achievers assigned more positive ratings than the better achievers, producing significant achievement differences in the ratings of "Mother" and "School" on the evaluative scales and "Mother" on the potency scales. The only unfavorable concept, "Dumb Child" evoked chiefly negative responses; on the potency scales there was a significant achievement difference with the good achievers assigning the most strongly negative ratings. One significant sex difference emerged for "Reading" on the evaluative scales, where the boys' ratings were more favorable than those of the girls. There was also a significant interaction effect for the potency ratings of "Reading" where the poor-achieving boys assigned the most favorable ratings.

It was suggested that the relatively

high favorable ratings of the poor achievers, particularly the boys, might stem from their greater defensive needs. The good achievers, on the other hand, seemed to demonstrate greater critical ability, self-confidence and reality orientation which may be related to their success in school.

Motivation and Emotion

14

47 Effects of Different Reinforcers: A Comparison across Age Levels[1]

MADGE NICKELL

ROBERT M. W. TRAVERS

The relative effectiveness of two reinforcing conditions, verbal and physical, are compared as a function of age and sex. Physical reinforcement is found more effective than verbal reinforcement at all age levels. Verbal reinforcement even in combination with physical reinforcement results in no greater response than does physical reinforcement alone. The reading briefly discusses why adult verbal approval of a child's behavior tends to be a weaker reinforcer than physical reinforcement.

While many kinds of events and objects are commonly used as reinforcers of behavior in children, little is known about the relative effectiveness of different reinforcers at various age levels. Some reinforcing events involve praise or other words of encouragement, while other reinforcers involve the delivery of physical objects such as small toys, candy, and other objects. The former are referred to here as verbal reinforcers and the latter as physical

[1]This study is adapted from a Master's thesis submitted to the Department of Educational Psychology at the University of Utah by the first author (Nickell, 1962). Support is acknowledged from a Graduate Research Fellowship awarded by the University of Utah and from a United States Office of Education grant (Contract No. OE–2–10–010).

Reprinted with permission of author and publisher: Nickell, Madge and Travers, Robert M. W. Effects of different reinforcers: a comparison across age levels. *Psychol. Reps.*, 1963, **13**, 739–746.

reinforcers. McCullers and Stevenson (1960) compared the effectiveness of verbal and physical reinforcements with groups of prekindergarten and 8- to 10-yr.-olds, using a marble-dispensing device. Marble reinforcement was available upon the depression of any of three knobs. Verbal reinforcement was added to the physical reinforcement on one knob. The effectiveness of verbal reinforcement was demonstrated by an increase in frequency of response to the knob delivering both physical and verbal reinforcement in the prekindergarten group. However, adding verbal to physical reinforcement was no more effective than physical reinforcement alone in the 8- to 10-yr.-old group, suggesting that verbal reinforcement is relatively ineffective at this older age. With slightly older age groups, Page (1958) compared the improvement in the test scores of high school Ss and junior high school Ss resulting from spontaneous comments of approval from teachers. The difference was not significant. However, in another study comparing the effectiveness of reinforcement between older and younger groups, Stevenson and Cruse (1961) found approval less reinforcing among a group of 12-yr.-olds than among a group of 5-yr.-olds who worked on a marble-insertion task.

The sex of Ss and Es was not controlled in the foregoing studies. A more recent study (Stevenson, 1961) involving comments of approval controlled these two variables and reported significant differences in response as a result of interactions between the sex of S and E. Thus, sex is to be controlled.

The present study differs from the previous studies in another respect also, namely, that it permits a direct comparison of the magnitude of the effect of two reinforcing conditions. Previous research has typically superimposed some form of verbal reinforcement on a physical reinforcement and measured the increment thus produced.

On the basis of the foregoing findings, the present study advances the following hypotheses: (a) verbal reinforcement will be more reinforcing than will physical reinforcement with prekindergarten children; (b) physical and verbal reinforcement will be equally effective with intermediate grade children; (c) a low level of dependence on adult approval at the junior high school level will be reflected by greater responsiveness of this group to physical than verbal reinforcement; and (d) verbal reinforcement will be more effective at the prekindergarten than at higher age levels, specifically at the third grade level as found by McCullers, *et al.* (1960).

The assumption is made in stating the hypotheses that the effect of changing the magnitude of either one of the reinforcing contingencies would be small compared with the effect of differences in age and sex. For example, it is assumed that a change from E's saying "good" to saying "very good" would be small in comparison with the main effects and interactions considered in the study.

METHOD

Subjects

Ss were 80 males and 80 females selected on the basis of chronological age and sex. Twenty males and 20 females were selected within each of the following four age ranges: (a) 3–11 to 5–8, (b) 8–11 to 9–7, (c) 12–5 to 13–3, and (d) 14–8 to 15–8. The age levels are representative of students in prekindergarten and grades 3, 6, and 9. Ss in the prekindergarten group were obtained from private nursery schools and the remainder from two public schools in metropolitan Salt Lake City.[2]

Apparatus

A device which delivered different kinds of reinforcement upon the depression of each of four knobs was selected as a task which could be administered at the various age levels. The panel which fronted the apparatus was a square, 23½ in. across. Centered 8¼ in. from the top edge was a round, red light which served as a signal to S for another trial. The light was turned on from behind the panel and extinguished automatically following the depression of a knob. A row of four knobs was centrally placed 7½ in. below the red light. A glass-covered, enclosed box located 3½ in. below the knobs served as a receptacle for the marbles which were dispensed upon the activation of a solenoid behind the panel. The contents of the receptacle were not accessible to S but entry of the marbles into the box was audible and the marbles were visible.

Procedure

Ss were tested individually in an experimental room established in the school. The female E addressed each S by his first name and gave these instructions:

———

[2]The writers wish to express appreciation to the faculties and students of the schools involved for their cooperation.

———, this is a game, I can turn a light on like this (light on), and you can turn it off (depress knob). Now, you try it (light on). Now, try another one (light on). Try all of them. (Allow a total of four trials.) But, not all of the knobs are the *right* knob. Sometimes I will tell you that you have pushed the right knob. I'll say "good" or "that's good." Sometimes you'll get a marble here (pointing) when you push the right knob. If you push the right knob most of the time, you may choose one of these toys (point to display) when we're through. Now, how will you know if you've pushed the right knob?" (Continue with this until they say "get a marble" and "you say good".)

Practice was given under actual reinforcement conditions until S had depressed each of the four knobs once. Following this, S was given 120 trials.

The conditions assigned to the four knob positions were marble only, verbal only, marble and verbal simultaneously, and no reinforcement. To counterbalance knob position effects, the relationship of the reinforcing contingency to knob position was changed from S to S so that each reinforcement was delivered from each knob position an equal number of times within each age group. Reinforcement was delivered on 50% of the trials and was assigned so that it occurred in random, rather than systematic order.

Incentive items were provided for participation in the task and were displayed approximately 6 ft. from S. A bag of candy, a toy suitable for a male, one suitable for a female, and another which might be chosen by either sex constituted the four-item display. Objects which were appropriate to S's age were selected at the four age levels. The objects were held constant within each age group.

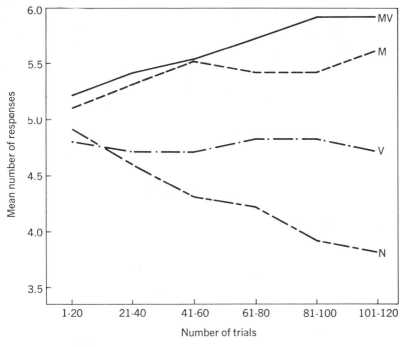

Fig. 1.   Learning curves derived from the responses of all Ss (M = marble, V = verbal, N = no reinforcement).

RESULTS

Figure 1 shows the mean number of responses made to the reinforcers by blocks of 20 trials for the total sample.

The data are not as amenable to treatment by analysis of variance as they might appear to be at first sight. While one may be tempted to undertake an analysis of variance involving four reinforcing conditions, two sexes, and five age levels, limitations are placed on this procedure by the fact that the number of responses per S across reinforcing conditions is always 120. This means that scores for reinforcing conditions are not independent as they should be to use analysis of variance. Least violence is probably done to the assumptions of analysis of variance when making direct comparisons if the fewest possible reinforcing conditions are considered at a time.

For this reason, after an initial overall F test, an analysis of variance involving only two of the reinforcing conditions was undertaken before one involving three.

Initially, an F test was computed including all the reinforcing conditions but involving no test of age or sex differences (Table 1). This analysis revealed a difference among the reinforcing conditions which was significant beyond the .001 level. In order to determine the effect of age or sex differences, an additional analysis, a 2 × 2 × 4, was undertaken. The two reinforcing conditions used in the latter analysis (Table 2) were verbal and physical only. The difference between the two reinforcing conditions was significant, with the physical reinforcement having the greater mean number of responses.

TABLE 1.—Analysis of Variance of Number of Responses for the Four Reinforcing Treatments for All Ss

SOURCE	df	MS	F	p
Reinforcing Conditions	3	2106.65	38.08	$< .001$
Within	636	55.32		
Total	639			

TABLE 2.—Analysis of Variance of Response Frequency Under Verbal and Physical Reinforcements with Four Age Levels and Two Sexes

SOURCE	df	MS	F	p
Reinforcing Conditions	1	1202.22	24.46	.001
Age	3	1.49		
Sex	1	5.00		
R × A	3	48.88		
A × S	3	33.31		
R × S	1	167.23	3.40	$.10 < p > .05$
R × A × S	3	31.63		
Within	304	49.15		
Total	319			

The latter analysis revealed that age was not a variable which was influential in affecting response to the two reinforcements in this comparison. This finding resulted in the rejection of the hypotheses that verbal reinforcement would be more effective than physical among the prekindergarten students and that the two reinforcements would be equally reinforcing with the intermediate group (Ages 8–11 to 9–7). The hypotheses stating that physical reinforcement would be more effective than verbal in the two older age groups were confirmed.

An interaction between the rein-

TABLE 3.—Analysis of Variance of Mean Response Frequencies for Physical, Verbal, and Physical + Verbal Reinforcements with Four Age Levels and Two Sexes

SOURCE	df	MS	F	p
Reinforcing Conditions	2	1171.12	19.30	.001
Age	3	3.21		
Sex	1	15.69		
R × A	6	66.46	1.10	
R × S	2	79.76	1.31	
A × S	3	36.99		
R × A × S	6	23.50		
Within	456	60.69		
Total	479			

TABLE 4.—Scheffe's Test between Means: Comparison between Mean Response to Verbal
and Physical Reinforcement and between Mean Response to Physical
and Verbal + Physical Reinforcement

	PHYSICAL REIN- FORCEMENT	VERBAL REIN- FORCEMENT	K	p
Mean Response	32.29	28.41	3.15	$<.05$

	PHYSICAL REIN- FORCEMENT	PHYSICAL + VERBAL REIN- FORCEMENT		
Mean Response	32.29	33.62	1.08	n.s.

forcing conditions and sex was significant at approximately the .05 level in the $2 \times 2 \times 4$ analysis. This interaction was the product of two factors: (a) the greater responsiveness of males to physical reinforcement as compared with verbal reinforcement and (b) the responsiveness of prekindergarten females to verbal reinforcement.

Another analysis was made (Table 3), including three of the reinforcing conditions—verbal, physical, and physical-verbal. There was, again, a difference among the conditions of reinforcement which was significant beyond the .01 level. Scheffe's test among the means of the reinforcing conditions in this analysis demonstrated that physical reinforcement alone was significantly more effective than verbal alone. A comparison of the means of the physical reinforcement and the verbal-physical combination was also made to determine the effect of offering verbal and physical reinforcement simultaneously. No significant difference was found between the two which indicates that, statistically, physical reinforcement alone is as ef-

fective as physical reinforcement when it is offered simultaneously with verbal reinforcement (see Table 4).

To determine whether verbal reinforcement was more reinforcing in the prekindergarten than the third grade group, the mean frequencies of response were compared by t tests (see Table 5). The difference in response frequency between females in the prekindergarten and in the intermediate groups was significant at the .01 level. The prekindergarten females had a higher frequency of response to verbal reinforcement than did those in the intermediate group; the responses of the males did not differ significantly. This indicates that verbal reinforcement is more effective among prekindergarten females than among intermediate group females; it is equally effective with males in the two groups.

DISCUSSION

Perhaps the most general finding of the study is the extraordinarily poor effect which approval has as a reinforcer compared with physical reinforcement, except for girls at the

TABLE 5.—Mean Responses to Verbal Reinforcement by the Prekindergarten
and Intermediate Groups

	PREKINDER- *GARTEN*	*INTERMEDIATE*	*t*	*p*
Female	31.05	26.8	2.84	.01
Male	27.3	28.15	0.43	

prekindergarten level. This finding
runs counter to the conception of reinforcement provided in most textbooks
on elementary education which generally take the position that adult approval is perhaps the most powerful
influence on child behavior. In the case
of girls at the prekindergarten level,
this may be true but it can hardly
stand as a generalization. There seem
to be many reasons why approval may
well be a much weaker reinforcing
contingency than many writers suppose it to be. Some of these need to be
given brief consideration.

First, approving remarks are very
common events in the life of most
children. Teachers can be observed
whose stream of behavior in the classroom consists of a flow of comments
or gestures of approval. The common-
place nature of such comments may
weaken their reinforcing effect. Second, since the behavior of pre-school
girls is generally more acceptable to
the mother than is the behavior of preschool boys, one might well expect
that approval would be less effective
for young boys than for young girls.
Third, there is the possibility that expressions of approval toward children
may be much more satisfying to the
adult who gives them than to the child
to whom they are directed.

Another matter of interest is the
relatively high level of effectiveness
of the so-called physical reinforcement
in this study. This effectiveness could
be accounted for in a number of different ways.

First, the delivery of the marble by
mechanical means is a novel event.
There is an overwhelming amount of
evidence that novel events have reinforcing properties on the behavior of
a wide range of organisms. The novelty of the event may, in this particular
case, account for its effectiveness as a
reinforcer. Second, in the case of the
delivery of a marble, S has the experience of acting directly on the environment and of being the cause of an
event. Such a relationship to the environment is considered by many
psychologists, including Woodworth
(1958), to be one characteristic of
most higher organisms.

Finally, the point must be made
that the highly sophisticated interpretations of the effect of reinforcers on
child behavior, such as those which
invoke Freudian concepts, appear to
involve constructs which are too re-
motely related to be of value at this
time. A much simpler theory accounting for the nature of events that reinforce child behavior seems to be
needed.

48　*Effects of Probability of Reward Attainment on Responses to Frustration*[1]

WALTER MISCHEL

JOHN C. MASTERS

The hypothesis that blocking or delaying a reward increases its value is supported. Sixth-grade children view a film, which is interrupted near the climax under the pretext of a damaged fuse. The probability that the film could be resumed is either 1, .5, or 0. Thereafter, the fuse is "fixed" and all children see the remainder of the film, with final value ratings obtained at the end. Children who are given a 0 probability for seeing the remainder of the film increase their valuation of it more than those in the other groups, and this increase is maintained even after the entire film is shown.

Frustration may be defined as an imposed delay of reward and is typically operationalized by interrupting or blocking the organism's progress towards a valued goal. Various determinants of the ensuing responses have been investigated, with the speed and pressure of plunger-pushing frequently used as measures of the intensity of responses to frustration in human studies (e.g., Ford, 1963; Haner and Brown, 1955). There is considerable evidence from these studies, as well as from animal investigations, that the expectancy of goal attainment, *before* the imposed delay of reward, affects the amplitude of responses to frustration monotonically (Amsel, 1958; Ferster, 1958). That is, when subjects with a high expectancy of goal attainment are frustrated they respond more vigorously than those with lesser expectancies for reward.

Surprisingly, a quite different aspect

[1]This study was supported by Research Grant M-06830 from the National Institutes of Health, United States Public Health Service. Grateful acknowledgement is due to the administrators and teachers of the Whisman School District who generously cooperated in this research.

Reprinted from the *Journal of Personality and Social Psychology*, 1966, **3**, 390–396, by permission of the authors and the American Psychological Association.

of expectancy in the frustration situation has been relatively ignored. Namely, *after* the onset of frustration, how does the subject's expectancy for ultimately obtaining the blocked reward affect his responses? Especially when the objective probability for eventual goal attainment is ambiguous, subjective probabilities for obtaining the delayed goal may range from the definite anticipation of goal attainment to the expectation that the reward is lost irrevocably. It seems likely that such expectancies are potent determinants of responses to frustration and the systematic manipulation of these expectancies is the focus of the present study. Change in the evaluation of the blocked reward is the reaction to frustration of main interest in this study.

In this experiment children were subjected to a frustration, in the form of an externally produced delay-of-reward. The experimental treatments involved variations in the probability that the frustration would be terminated and the blocked reward attained. More specifically, elementary school children viewed an exciting motion picture film which was interrupted near the climax on the pretext of a damaged electrical fuse. The experimentally presented probability that the fuse could be repaired and the film resumed was either 1, .5, or .0. A control group viewed the film without interruption. Response measures of the perceived value of the film, and the children's delay of reward behavior with other goal objects, were administered before and after the imposed delay period. Thereafter the fuse was "fixed" and the remainder of the movie was shown to all subjects, with another

rating of its value and attractiveness obtained at the end.

There is some suggestive indirect evidence that the nonavailability of a reward increases its attractiveness or value (e.g., Aronson and Carlsmith, 1963). However, the relationship between expectancy or subjective probability and reward value or utility remains unclear. For example, Lewin, Dembo, Festinger, and Sears (1944) and Atkinson (1957) assume an inverse relationship between subjective probability and reward value, whereas Rotter (1954), Edwards (1954), and others argue for the independence of these constructs.

In a cogent discussion of this issue, Feather (1959a) has reasoned that, at least in our culture, persons learn to place greater value on the attainment of goal objects which are difficult to get because of the relatively consistent occurrence of sizable rewards for the successful achievement of difficult goals and deprecation or punishment for failure to attain easy goals. Moreover, achievement of the difficult is probably more typically and highly rewarded when it was due to the person's own efforts or skill, rather than to chance factors beyond his control, and likewise failure to achieve the easy is chastised more when it was due to the person's lack of skill than when it was a chance occurrence. In view of this, Feather hypothesized that an inverse relationship between attainment attractiveness (goal value) and success probability would be more apparent in "ego-related" than in chance-related situations, and in achievement-oriented as opposed to relaxed conditions. Feather's (1959b) empirical results supported an inverse relationship between attainment attractiveness and success probability and indeed suggested that the independence assumption may be an oversimplification even for chance-related situations under achievement-oriented conditions. Similarly, Atkinson (1957) suggests that

the incentive values of winning qua winning, and losing qua losing, presumably developed in achievement activities early in life, generalize to the gambling situation in which winning is really *not* contingent upon one's own skill and competence [pp. 370–371].

In the present experiment, it was reasoned that the learned inverse association between reward value and attainment probability in achievement-related situations generalizes to non-achievement-related frustration conditions in which goal attainment is not in the subject's control and is not contingent on his behavior. If in our culture persons acquire the generalized expectation that unlikely or unavailable positive outcomes are more valuable than likely or assured positive outcomes, then the value ascribed to an unattainable reward should be greater than that attributed to a reward that either may be attainable or whose attainment is assured. Accordingly, it was predicted that the perceived value of the delayed reward (film) would be greater when it is ultimately unattainable ($P = 0$) than when its attainment is assured ($P = 1$). Moreover, it was anticipated that certainty of reward attainment minimizes the effects of the imposed delay or frustration and therefore no differences were expected between the $P = 1$ treatment and the control group.

Likewise, it was anticipated that the perceived value of the reward would be greater in the $P = 0$ condition than in the $P = .5$ group and that subjects in the latter would value the reward more than those in the $P = 1$ treatment or the control group. A posttest was included to determine whether differences between treatments in the perceived value of the delayed reward are maintained even after the frustration is terminated and the delayed reward is obtained.

It also seemed plausible that when the perceived frustration is greater subjects will more frequently self-administer other available immediate rewards. Therefore, when the delayed reward is permanently unattainable, immediate self-reward (in the form of increased preference for immediate smaller as opposed to delayed larger rewards) should be greater than when it is ultimately attainable ($P = 0 > P = 1$). This was not hypothesized on the basis of any "compensatory mechanisms," but on the assumption that individuals in our culture learn that immediate self-reward is more acceptable following strong frustration than following minimal frustration.

METHOD

Subjects

The subjects were 56 boys and 24 girls, all sixth-grade students at two public schools in Mountain View, California.

Design and Procedure

PREEXPERIMENTAL ASSESSMENT OF DELAY-OF-REWARD RESPONSES In a preexperimental session the children were administered in their classroom groups a series of 14 paired rewards, in each of which they were asked to select either a small reward that could be obtained immediately, or a more valued item contingent on a delay period ranging from 1 to 4 weeks. The group administration (Mischel and Gilligan, 1964) proceeded in the following manner. Children were provided individual booklets containing on each page a brief description of a given set of paired objects and the associated time interval. After the experimenter had displayed both rewards and explained the temporal contingency, the children were instructed to record their choice and to turn the page in preparation for the next set of items. The subjects were also advised to choose carefully and realistically because in one of the choices they would actually receive the item they selected, either on the same day or after the prescribed delay period, depending upon their recorded preference. This promise was indeed kept.

Half of the sets of paired rewards involved small amounts of money (e.g., $.25 today, or $.35 in 1 week), while the remaining items included edibles (e.g., small bag of salted peanuts today, or a can of mixed nuts in 2 weeks), children's magazines, and various play materials (e.g., small rubber ball today, or a large rubber ball in 2 weeks).

ASSIGNMENT TO TREATMENTS The total pool of subjects was divided into quartiles on the basis of the distribution of delay-of-reward responses. An equal number of children from each quartile was randomly assigned to each of the three experimental groups and the control group, thus producing groups similar in their initial willingness to defer immediate rewards for the sake of delayed, larger gratifications. The same proportion of boys and girls was assigned to each group.

At each of the two schools each of the four experimental conditions was administered once, with an approximately equal number of children from each school in each condition. Two new experimenters, unconnected with the preexperimental session, were used and each administered one half the treatments in one school and the other half in the second school. The temporal sequence of treatments at the two schools was balanced, the sequence in the second school being the reverse of the one in the first school.

EXPERIMENTAL TREATMENTS Approximately 4 weeks after the assessment of delay-of-reward responses, the experimental sessions were conducted in a research trailer stationed at the school. From 8 to 12 subjects participated in each session. The experimenter was introduced as coming from "Deluxe Movie Studios" to prescreen an "exciting space movie" and to obtain the children's opinions about it. The film was a 20-minute documentary on space exploration. The children were told that they would fill out "audience estimate and opinion sheets" several times to determine their "feelings at different points." These sheets contained the value ratings described below. The experimenter explained that he was also interested in children's expectations about how attractive the film would be and therefore they would be asked to rate it before it actually commenced. This rationale was used to obtain a base level of attractiveness ratings in all groups to serve as a comparison point for any subsequent changes in the rated value of the film.

In the experimental groups the movie began as soon as the first value ratings were completed and collected. After 5 minutes, at a predetermined climactic point in the film (just as the space ship was being launched) the projector failed. A confederate, posing as the "district electrician," entered and explained that the power failure was due to his overloading the circuits with electrical tools. This rationale was used to avoid connecting the cause of frustration with either the experimenter and his procedure or with the subjects' own behavior. The experimental treatments consisted of the following variations in the probability of resuming the interrupted film, announced by the confederate:

[$P = 1$]: I'm positive I can fix it—I've had things like this happen in the past, and I've always managed to fix them.

[$P = .5$]: I've had things like this happen before—sometimes I was able to fix them, sometimes I wasn't. I never know for sure . . . there's probably about a 50–50 chance.

[$P = 0$]: It takes a special fuse for this circuit, and there are none around here . . . I can't possibly fix it . . . there's no chance.

To increase credibility, the experimenter asked if the confederate was sure of his evaluation and the confederate reiterated his initial statement confidently in paraphrased form and left. The experimenter expressed his regret at the interruption but reminded the subjects that repeated "audience estimate" sheets were

needed and circulated the second set of value ratings.

In the control group the movie was not interrupted and both sets of ratings were obtained before the movie began. The second set of ratings was administered approximately 5 minutes after the first set, and during the intervening period the experimenter prepared the film and projector. The rationale given to the children for readministering the ratings was in terms of the need for repeated measurements of their feelings at different times.

Following these second value ratings the children in all groups were administered a measure of immediate or delayed self-reward (described below).

Approximately 10 minutes after his first entry, and after the second ratings of the film and the delay-of-reward measures were completed, the electrician returned to all experimental groups, announcing that he had been able to fix the fuse and the movie would continue. The remainder of the film was shown and, when it ended, ratings of the movie were obtained for the third and final time. Table 1 summarizes the design and measures for all conditions.

ASSESSMENT OF REWARD VALUE   A four-item measure of reward or goal value was

TABLE 1.—Summary of the Experimental Design

EXPERIMENTAL GROUPS	PHASE 1: FIRST MEASURE OF FILM VALUE[a]	EXPERIMENTAL TREATMENTS	PHASE 2: SECOND MEASURE OF FILM VALUE AND RE-ADMINISTRATION OF DELAY MEASURE[b]	FILM COMPLETED	PHASE 3: THIRD MEASURE OF FILM VALUE
I ($N = 20$)	Same	Film interrupted; $P = 1$ for resumption	Same	Same	Same
II ($N = 20$)	Same	Film interrupted; $P = .5$ for resumption	Same	Same	Same
III ($N = 20$)	Same	Film interrupted; $P = 0$ for resumption	Same	Same	Same
IV ($N = 20$)	Same	No interruption; film not yet begun	Same	Same	Same

[a]Following this, film begins in all groups except IV.
[b]Following this, film begins in Group IV.

administered in printed booklets, the subject checking his response to each item on a 7-point intensity scale. The items were:

(a) Let's pretend that you are the manager of a movie theatre. Instead of charging a set price for letting people see the movies you have, you do things differently—when you have a movie that you think is very good, you charge a lot for them to get in; when you think a movie is bad, you don't charge very much at all. Now let's pretend that the movie I have today is at your theatre—check about how much you would charge for tickets [0 to $1.00].

(b) Let's pretend that you have a month's allowance of $1.00 to spend on movies. Suppose the movie I have with me today is showing at a theatre you usually go to. Remember, you have $1.00 to pay for movies for a whole month, and if you go to see a show, part of your money will be gone. Now, let's also pretend that they *don't* have the regular prices at the theatre for this movie, but they have special ones—and you don't know exactly how much they are. How much would you pay [0 to $1.00], out of your dollar, to see the movie I have here today if it were at that theatre?

(c) We all go to see movies. Let's compare the movie I have here with some of the movies you have seen in regular theatres. Check above the words [from "much better" to "much worse"] that tell how well *you* feel this movie compares [or will compare] with others.

(d) We are interested in how good you think the movie is going to be [or is]. You are to put a check mark above the words [from "really good" to "aw-

ful"] which say how good *you* feel the movie is [or will be].

The above measures were given in the same random sequence to all subjects, with a different sequence used in each of the three administrations.

ASSESSMENT OF CHANGES IN DELAY BEHAVIOR Immediately following the second set of ratings the children were administered a new series of 14 paired choices between immediately available smaller rewards and delayed larger rewards. The rewarding objects differed from those employed in the preexperimental sessions, but the money items were the same since pretesting revealed that subjects were unable to recall the exact amounts and temporal intervals involved. The experimenter indicated at the outset that these choices were unconnected with his own project and were being administered for a Stanford researcher during the available period in order to save time.[2]

RESULTS

Prior to the experimental manipulations the groups did not differ appreciably in their initial evaluation of the film. The first (Phase 1) mean value

---

[2]At the end of each experimental session the children were informed of the importance of not communicating with others about the experiment because it would "spoil things for us and take the fun out of it for the other children." All subjects agreed to this and were given the rewards they had been promised, either at this time or after the specified delay period, depending on the choice they had made. Informal postexperimental interviews indicated that there had been no communication about the particulars of the experiment.

ratings of the movie in the control, $P = 1$, $P = .5$, and $P = 0$ groups, respectively, were 16.85, 16.90, 16.75, and 16.55. Figure 1 shows the mean value rating of the film at each of the experimental phases for each group.

To assess the effect of the independent variable, change scores were computed for the difference between each pair of value ratings in each group. Analysis of variance of the mean change in value ratings immediately after interruption of the film (difference between Phase 2 and Phase 1 ratings) revealed a significant effect ($F = 5.91$, $df = 3/76$, $p < .005$). Table 2 summarizes the results of t tests for differences between groups in mean value change. It is evident (Row 1 of Table 2) that subjects who were told they would definitely not see the remainder of the film ($P = 0$) increased their evaluation of it significantly more than those in all other conditions.[3] None of the other groups ($P = 1$, $P = .5$, control) differed from each other.

_____

[3] As a partial check on the internal consistency of the four items measuring the value of the film, the effects of the independent variable were examined separately for the first two items combined and the last two items combined. Since the results revealed highly similar trends the final analyses were based on all four items combined.

Moreover, as Figure 1 indicates, the increased evaluations of the film in the $P = 0$ condition was maintained even after the interruption was terminated and the movie completed. Analysis of variance of changes in value ratings from Phase 2 to Phase 3 indicated no significant differences between groups ($F < 1$). However, analysis of variance of change from the first preexperimental value measure to the terminal rating after completion of the film indicated significant treatment effects ($F = 2.74$, $df = 3/76$, $p < .05$). The between-group comparisons of these change scores (Table 2) show that subjects in the $P = 0$ condition tended to maintain their overevaluation of the movie even after they viewed the entire film, although the difference between the overall increment in the $P = 0$ group and the $P = 1$ condition falls short of acceptable significance.

The data clearly showed an increase in the evaluation of an unattainable goal but there was no evidence for a linear inverse relationship between the probability of attaining a goal and the value attributed to it. Value changes in the $P = .5$ condition were not significantly different from those in the $P = 1$ or control groups. Indeed, the mean terminal value rating was slightly (not significantly) higher in the

TABLE 2.—Between-Group Comparisons of Mean Changes in Value of Film

MEAN CHANGE BETWEEN	$P = 0$ VERSUS CONTROL t	$P = 0$ VERSUS $P = 1$ t	$P = 0$ VERSUS $P = .5$ t	$P = .5$ VERSUS $P = 1$ t	$P = .5$ VERSUS CONTROL t	$P = 1$ VERSUS CONTROL t
1. Phase 1 and 2 (Preprobability to postprobability)	3.88**	3.12**	2.94**	.18	.94	.76
2. Phase 1 and 3 (Preprobability to postfilm)	2.69*	1.70	2.20*	.49	.49	.98

*$p < .05$.
**$p < .01$.

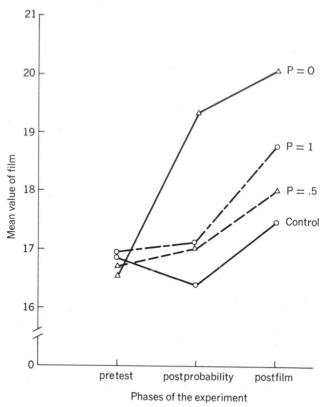

Fig. 1.   Mean value of film at each phase of the experiment.

$P = 1$ treatment than in the $P = .5$ condition.

The effects of treatments on changes in delay-of-reward behavior were examined by comparing the number of preexperimental and postexperimental immediate reward choices made in each condition. The control, $P = 1$, and $P = 0$ groups showed mean increases in immediate reward choices of 1.1, 1.5, and 1.3, respectively, whereas in the $P = .5$ condition there was a fractional decrease $(-.3)$. Analysis of variance of these data yielded no significant effect $(F < 1)$.

DISCUSSION

The results show that the value of a blocked or delayed reward can be affected by the expectancy for its ultimate attainment. When the probability for seeing the interrupted film was stated as 0, its rated value increased significantly more than when it was 1 or .5. When resumption of the film was presented as a certainty, children evaluated the film no differently than those who saw it without interruption.

Although the value of the film increased most when its completion seemed nonattainable, and this change was maintained even after the film was completed, significant increases did not occur when an intermediate probability ($P = .5$) was given. Subjects given an intermediate probability did not differ from those in the $P = 1$ and control conditions. An extension of the present study, using a large number of probabilty levels, would clarify whether the obtained effect of probability on value is restricted to unattainable outcomes ($P = 0$) or holds for highly unlikely outcomes (e.g., $P = .10$).

Since subjective probability does not necessarily match experimentally presented probability statements, it would also be interesting to assess the subject's expectancies for attaining the delayed reward and to examine the relationship between subjective probability and reward value in the present situation. For example, in the $P = .5$ treatment, most children may have had subjective expectancies for seeing the film which exceeded .5 considerably. Such effects may account for the lack of difference obtained between the $P = 1$ and $P = .5$ manipulations.

The present results indicate that in our culture unattainable positive outcomes may be more valued than those which are attainable and that the unavailability of a positive outcome enhances its perceived desirability. Moreover, the findings support the view that the higher value attributed to unlikely outcomes in achievement-related situations generalizes very broadly even to non-achievement-related situations in which the probability for goal attainment is clearly independent of difficulty level and in which goal attainment is entirely outside the subject's own control. These results have direct implications for understanding responses to frustration. If the nonattainability of a reward increases its desirability, persons who, on the basis of their previous histories, expect that delayed or blocked rewards are lost irrevocably will respond quite differently from those who anticipate their ultimate attainment. The individual who has learned that blocked goals tend to be unattainable may remain on the unhappy treadmill, expecting that what he wants cannot be obtained and overevaluating and wanting what he cannot have. Certainly this is not an unfamiliar clinical phenomenon. In contrast, the person who has learned that frustrated goals ultimately tend to become available may respond to delay of reward with equanimity.

The treatments did not significantly affect self-reward behavior in the form of changes in willingness to defer immediate rewards for the sake of larger but delayed outcomes. Unexpectedly, there was a slight, nonsignificant trend towards increased *delay* behavior in the $P = .5$ condition, whereas in all other treatments subjects tended to increasingly choose immediate rewards. It may be speculated that when the ultimate attainment of the blocked reward is uncertain children try to be especially "good," deferring immediate gratification in the irrational hope that their "good" behavior will increase the probability of obtaining the blocked goal. This is sheer speculation but may be interesting to pursue.

The present experiment was designed to minimize the occurrence of cognitive dissonance at the onset of frustration and therefore the frustration was deliberately unconnected with the subject's own behavior and not contingent on his own decisions. In contrast, when a temporary or permanent delay of reward is a consequence of the subject's own behavior, dissonance theory (Festinger, 1957) might generate predictions opposite to those of the present study. In a recent study by Carlsmith (1962), subjects were exposed to the possibility of electric shock with variations in the probability that they would actually receive the shock. The probability was ostensibly determined by the subject's performance on a fictitious personality test. Carlsmith's prediction of an increase in the rated "pleasantness" of the shock as a function of the probability of receiving it was supported and is consistent with dissonance theory. Comparisons betwen the present study and the Carlsmith experiment are precarious because they differ in several critical ways; for example, the latter was not a frustration paradigm, involved aversive rather than positive outcomes and presented probabilities ostensibly determined by the subject's own performance.

In a very recent study by Turner and Wright (1965) children rated the attractiveness of toys before and after a number of experimental manipulations. In one condition they were informed that they could "never" play with one of the toys they had just rated and in another that they could play with it "later." The rated value of the toy decreased in the "never" condition and increased in the "later" condition. These findings appear inconsistent with the present results but again there are numerous problems that prevent clear comparisons. For example, in the Turner and Wright study the children may have interpreted the "never" condition as the punishing consequence of their own rating behavior. Perhaps even more important, in both the Carlsmith (1962) and the Turner and Wright (1965) studies, the post-manipulation ratings were obtained after brief temporal delays (15 minutes and 5 minutes, respectively) whereas in the present experiment the reevaluation occurred almost immediately after the announced probabilities. It may be that such temporal effects are critical determinants of the relationship between expectancy and value. The initial response to an unattainable positive goal may be to overevaluate it (as in this study) but after being faced with its unattainability for some time justification processes commence and the value of the reward becomes minimized. It would be interesting to test for a positive relationship between probability of goal attainment and reward value under dissonance-producing conditions (in which the frustration is the consequence of the subject's own behavior) using an extension of the present experimental design, and including a temporal variation in the amount of time elapsing between the onset of frustration and the measurement of reward value.

49   *Effects of Severity of Threat and Perceived Availability on the Attractiveness of Objects*[1]

ELIZABETH ANN TURNER

JOHN C. WRIGHT

Two experiments relate changes in children's evaluation of play objects to several types of interference with free play. The first experiment repeats a previous study in which coercion not to play with a desirable toy produces relative increases or decreases in attractiveness, depending on whether a strong or mild threat, respectively, is used. In the second experiment the effects of five ways of preventing play with the critical toy are investigated. When the toy is secretly removed and returned, when it is removed in order to fix it for the child, and when it is removed with the promise to return it, its attractiveness increases. When the toy is removed without explanation, or when it is removed and the child is told it never will be available for play, its relative attractiveness declines. The results are interpreted in terms of satiation-novelty and cognitive-dissonance processes.

In a recent study, Aronson and Carlsmith (1963) found that mild, but successful coercion was more effective than strong coercion in inducing a child to devalue an object previously rated as attractive. Preschool children ranked several toys by a paired-comparison procedure. Each child was then threatened with either mild or severe consequences if he played with the second ranked toy during the play session. After leaving the subject alone for 10 minutes to play with the' toys, the experimenter had the child rank the toys again. Each child was tested in both strong and weak conditions, with a period averaging 45 days between the two conditions. It was hy-

[1] Experiment I is a portion of an honors thesis submitted by the senior author to the Institute of Child Development, University of Minnesota. Experiment II was supported by Grant NSF-GS-202 from the National Science Foundation to Elliot Aronson. The authors wish to thank Elliot Aronson for his advice and assistance in the design of Experiment II.

Reprinted from the *Journal of Personality and Social Psychology*, 1965, **2**, 128–132, by permission of the authors and the American Psychological Association.

pothesized that mild threat as compared with strong threat would arouse greater dissonance between the rated attractiveness of the critical toy and the subject's avoidance of it during the play session and, therefore, that subjects would tend more to devalue the critical toy in the postexperimental ranking. This hypothesis was confirmed.

Much of the difference found between the strong and weak conditions, however, was due to the fact that for many subjects the strong threat produced an increase in the rated attractiveness of the critical toy. This portion of their results is not readily explained by dissonance theory. Aronson and Carlsmith suggested that the tendency of the critical toy to increase in attractiveness was not attributable to the strong threat but rather to some other base-line factor present in the general experimental situation. As a test of this hypothesis a "no-threat" control condition was added in which the experimenter simply took the critical toy with him when he left the room, without issuing any threat. In this condition, as predicted, the attractiveness of the critical toy increased about as much as in the strong-threat condition, indicating that the increase could not be attributed to the strong threat itself. The dissonance-produced derogation of the critical toy in the mild-threat condition may be seen as overriding a general baseline tendency for the critical toy to increase in attractiveness.

The present study was designed primarily to investigate what factors might be responsible for the general increase in attractiveness of the critical toy. As a preliminary investigation, an attempt was made to replicate the Aronson and Carlsmith results using separate groups of subjects under strong- and mild-threat conditions (Experiment I). In Experiment II three alternative explanations for the general tendency of the critical toy to rise in the strong-threat and no-threat conditions were investigated.

One explanation proposed by Aronson and Carlsmith was that in the absence of dissonance, subjects had an opportunity of becoming satiated with the more atttractive toys during the play period, but not with the critical toy, since the latter was either avoided (strong-threat condition) or unavailable (no-threat control). Data consistent with this hypothesis have been obtained by Harris (1965), Maddi (1961), and Berlyne (1960) in studies of the incentive value of "relative novelty." This explanation will be referred to as the *satiation-novelty hypothesis.*

A second possibility suggested by Aronson and Carlsmith is that the distinctiveness and attractiveness of the critical toy may be enhanced merely by an adult's calling special attention to it or treating it as exceptional. This explanation will be referred to as the *attention hypothesis.*

A third explanation would suggest that an object becomes attractive in proportion to its unavailability. As something becomes unavailable, its desirability correspondingly increases if one assumes that the unavailability results from the object's having been selected by someone else. If the experimenter removes something from the subject's choice array, the subject may assume that the experimenter wants it for himself. An alternative set of assumptions leading to the same conclusion has to do with restriction of free-dom of choice (see Brehm, 1961). If one believes he has freedom of choice and this freedom is unexpect-edly reduced, a possible consequence is motivation to regain that freedom, or to demonstrate that it has never been lost, by an increased evaluation of the unavailable or prohibited alter-native.

In the strong-threat and control con-ditions the critical toy is made unavail-able and hence more attractive. In the mild-threat condition, however, the toy is not so definitely unavailable; freedom of choice is not so forcibly restricted; and dissonance, which would have opposite effects, is aroused. This explanation is referred to as the *unavailability hypothesis.*

EXPERIMENT I

METHOD

SUBJECTS   The subjects, 33 girls from the nursery school of the Institute of Child Development at the University of Minnesota, ranged in age from 3.9 to 5.1 years. They were randomly divided into two experimental groups, a mild-threat condition and a strong-threat condition, with 16 subjects in each experimental group.[2]

PROCEDURE   The experimental room contained a one-way mirror and a low table. Along the wall opposite the door eight toys were placed in a row. They were: a gun with rubber darts, a stiff

_____

[2]One subject in the strong-threat con-dition was replaced because she played with the forbidden toy while the experi-menter was absent from the room.

plastic doll with no accessories, battery-powered Army tank, a puzzle with 100 pieces, a large truck carrier with four smaller trucks, a homemade stuffed cat, a plastic rocket ship, and a ball and jacks. As a part of a separate research design the four most attractive toys were mas-culine, and all the subjects were female. However, these considerations do not in-validate the test of the present hypothesis which concerns the effects of strong versus mild threat on the child's attitude toward the critical toy. Before the study was initiated, the experimenter spent 3 weeks playing with the children in the nursery school so that they would be familiar with the experimenter, an adult female, when the study began.

The experimenter led the subject into the experimental room and pointed out the toys on the floor. The subject was in-vited to kneel on the floor next to the experimenter as she demonstrated each of the toys. Then the subject was allowed to manipulate each toy very briefly. The experimenter pointed out each toy again and said: "Look at all the toys very care-fully. Now of all these toys which one would you like to play with best of all? Which one do you like the very best?" When the subject made a choice, she was requested to pick it up and to put it on the other side of the room. The experi-menter said: "Now of all the toys that are left, which one would you like to play with best of all? Which one do you like the very best?" This procedure was re-peated until the child had chosen seven out of eight toys. In this way a rank order of preference of the toys was obtained.

The experimenter then randomly placed the toys around the room, except for the second ranked toy, if it were a masculine toy, or if the second choice were nonmasculine, the next highest ranked masculine toy.[3] As in the Aronson and Carlsmith study, the second ranked toy instead of the first ranked toy was chosen as the critical toy on which the prohibition was placed, because this permitted the subject to change the evaluation of the toy in either direction. The toy was placed on the table as the experimenter said, "I have to leave the room for just a minute to do an errand. While I'm gone you can play with any of these toys you want except this boy toy [indicating the toy on the table]." In the mild-threat condition the experimenter added: "You shouldn't play with the —— [naming the toy]. I'll be right back—goodbye." In the strong-threat condition, the experimenter substituted: "If you play with it, it would be very naughty and you wouldn't be able to play with any of the toys again. Remember it would be very naughty to play with the —— [naming the toy]. I'll be right back—goodbye." If the subject asked why she could not play with the toy on the table, the experimenter said that they would talk about that when the experimenter got back.

---

[3]In eight instances the critical toy was one ranked third or lower instead of the one ranked second. This variation stemmed from the requirement for other purposes that the critical toy be also a masculine toy. Three of these instances occurred in the mild-threat condition and five in the strong-threat condition.

When the subject asked specifically if she could play with a toy other than the critical toy the experimenter said, "Yes."

The experimenter then left the room and observed the subject for 5 minutes from behind the one-way mirror. When the experimenter returned, the forbidden toy was taken from the table and placed on the floor with the comment, "Now, let's play with all the toys." After allowing the subject to play briefly with all the toys, including the forbidden toy, the experimenter suggested that the "game" be played again. The order of placement of the toys along the wall was reversed and the subject was asked to choose the toys again according to her preference. After this ranking, the subject was allowed to play with all the toys again before returning to the nursery school.

Results

Table 1 shows the number of subjects who decreased their liking for the critical toy, increased their liking for it, or did not change their liking for the critical toy from the first ranking to the second, together with comparable frequencies from the Aronson and Carlsmith study. In the mild-threat condition there was a tendency for the subjects to decrease their liking for the critical toy, while in the strong-threat condition subjects tended to increase

TABLE 1.—Changes in Rerating the Attractiveness of the Critical Toy (Experiment I)

CONDITION	INCREASE	NO CHANGE	DECREASE	TOTAL
Mild threat				
N	2 (4)	5 (10)	9 (8)	16 (22)
%	12.5 (18.2)	31.2 (45.4)	56.3 (36.4)	100 (100)
Strong threat				
N	8 (14)	5 (8)	3 (0)	16 (22)
%	50.0 (63.6)	31.2 (36.4)	18.8 (0)	100 (100)
Total				
N	10 (18)	10 (18)	12 (8)	32 (44)
%	31.3 (40.9)	31.2 (40.9)	37.5 (18.2)	100 (100)

Note.—Comparison data from Aronson and Carlsmith (1963) are shown in parentheses.

their evaluation, as predicted. By a chi-square test the difference between the strong- and mild-threat conditions was found to be significant at the .05 level ($\chi^2 = 6.60$, $df = 2$). Excluding the cases in which there was no change in either direction in the position of the critical toy, on the assumption that the experimental manipulation had no effect on these subjects, the chi-square was 6.60 ($df = 1$), significant at the .01 level.

These results are very close to those of the Aronson and Carlsmith study and confirm the dissonance explanation of the difference between the effects of mild and strong threat. Again however, some of the obtained difference between the strong- and weak-threat conditions was due to the tendency of subjects in the strong-threat condition to increase their evaluation of the critical toy.

EXPERIMENT II

The conditions in Experiment II were designed to test the satiation-novelty hypothesis, the attention-distinctiveness hypothesis, and the unavailability hypothesis as explanations of the rise in attractiveness of the critical toy. In one condition (disappear) the toy was removed and returned secretly so that a rise would be predicted only by the satiation-novelty hypothesis. A second condition (fix) called attention to the toy, but did not imply restriction of the child's freedom of choice. Here a rise would be predicted by both the satiation-novelty and the attention-distinctiveness hypotheses, but not by the unavailability hypothesis. In the third condition (removal, there was a moderate restric-

tion of the subject's freedom of choice. In this condition a rise would be predicted by all three hypotheses.

The inclusion of the last two conditions (never and later) represented an attempt to clarify the removal manipulation, which it was believed could be interpreted by the child as either that he could never play with the critical toy or that he could definitely play with it later.

METHOD

Subjects

The 82 subjects, ranging in age from 6.0 to 8.3 years, attended art classes at the Institute of Child Development during a special summer session.[4] They were randomly divided into five experimental groups without regard to the sex distribution.

Procedure

The study was conducted in an experimental room in which six toys were placed along one wall. The toys were: a plastic tennis racket with ball attached, a power-operated robot, "slinky," a ball and scoop, a four-way periscope, and a "wheel-lo." The ranking procedure was essentially the same as in Experiment I. After the child had ranked five of the six toys, the experimental conditions were introduced. The five conditions were called: disappear, fix, removal, never, and later. In all five conditions the experimenter left the room for 7 minutes carrying with her the third ranked toy. The third ranked toy was designated as

---

[4]Two subjects were replaced, one because she cried when the experimenter left the room, and the other as a result of the experimenter's failure to remove the toy without detection in the disappear condition.

the critical toy instead of the second ranked toy used in previous experiments in order to allow a wider margin for increases in relative attractiveness.

In the disappear condition the experimenter removed the critical toy from the room in the pocket of her smock, making sure that the subject did not see her do so. When she returned, she restored the critical toy, again with secrecy. In the fix condition, the experimenter picked up the critical toy and said, "This looks kind of dusty. I think I'll go clean it up *for you.* I'll be right back." Before leaving in the removal condition the experimenter said, "You can't play with this toy now, maybe later."

TABLE 2.—Changes in Rerating the Attractiveness of the Critical Toy (Experiment II)

CONDITION	INCREASE	NO CHANGE	DECREASE	TOTAL
Disappear	10	4	2	16
Fix	9	5	2	16
Removal	2	4	10	16
Never	2	1	13	16
Later	10	3	3	16
Total	33	17	30	80

In the never condition the experimenter left the room carrying the critical toy, after telling the child that he could play with any of the toys except the critical toy, which he could not ever play with. In the later condition the experimenter said, "You can't play with this toy now, but when I come back and we finish the game, I promise that you'll get a chance to play with it."

When the experimenter returned to the room the child was told that he would get a chance to play with the toys again a little later, but first they would play the "choosing game" again. In the never condition, the instructions varied: the child was told that after he had reranked the toys he could have another chance to play with the toys except, of course, the forbidden toy. In all conditions after the second ranking, the child was given an opportunity to play with all the toys for a few minutes before he returned to class.

Results

As shown in Table 2 the data from the disappear, fix, and later conditions were similar. In these conditions the subjects tended to increase the position of the critical toy from the first ranking to the second. In contrast to these three conditions, the removal and never conditions showed a tendency for the critical toy to decrease in the ranking. By a chi-square test these condition differences were found to be highly significant ($x^2 = 31.18$, $df = 8$, $p < .001$). Excluding the cases in which there was no change in ranking did not affect the significance of the test.

Table 3 shows the mean change of the critical toy for each of the five conditions. The pattern of the results is the same as in Table 2. The difference between the disappear and fix conditions was not significant ($t = .133$, $df = 30$). However, the difference between the disappear and removal conditions ($t = 3.64$, $df = 30$, $p < .001$) and the difference between the fix and removal conditions ($t = 3.76$, $df = 30$, $p < .0005$) were highly significant. Finally, the difference between the never and later conditions was found to be very significant ($t = 3.52$, $df =$ 30, $p < .005$).

TABLE 3.—Mean Change in Attractiveness of Critical Toy (Experiment II)

CONDITION	N	M	SD
Disappear	16	+ .75	1.34
Fix	16	+ .09	1.20
Removal	16	−1.00	1.37
Never	16	−1.38	1.31
Later	16	+ .38	1.50
All conditions	80	− .11	

DISCUSSION

The results of Experiment I were quite consistent with those obtained by Aronson and Carlsmith (1963). The tendency of subjects to devalue the critical toy in the mild-threat condition of both studies is in accord with the dissonance-theory prediction. Moreover, the effect operates in spite of a general tendency for the critical toy to rise as seen in the strong-threat and control conditions.

In Experiment II it was expected that subjects in the disappear, fix, and removal conditions would show an increase in the position of the critical toy if the satiation-novelty hypothesis were correct. If the general rise were due primarily to the special attention called to the critical toy by the experimenter, then only the fix and removal conditions would produce a rise. Finally, it was expected that only the removal and never conditions would produce a rise if the increase could best be explained on the basis of the unavailability hypothesis (loss of freedom of choice).

Subjects in the disappear and fix conditions tended to increase their liking for the critical toy while subjects in the removal condition tended to decrease their liking for the toy. Although there was not a tendency for the critical toy to rise in the removal condition, the rise in the disappear and fix conditions still seems to suggest that satiation with respect to the noncritical toys, producing relative novelty for the critical toy, is primarily responsible for the rise. The "attention" hypothesis is weakened by the failure of the fix condition to elicit a greater rise than the disappear condition, and the unavailability hypothesis is directly contradicted by the decline obtained in the removal condition. There remains only the problem of explaining the decline in the removal condition, since the satiation-novelty hypothesis tentatively accepted above, predicts a rise.

The devaluation of the critical toy found in the removal condition resembles the dissonance effect found in the mild-threat condition of Experiment I. It is possible that the removal condition also aroused dissonance, in this case between the high rating and the unavailability of the critical toy. Because of the ambiguity of the instructions concerning future availability of the toy in the removal condition, the never and later conditions were devised. The results clarify the findings for the removal condition. When the subject knows with certainty that a highly evaluated toy is permanently unavailable (never condition) he tends strongly to devaluate it. This devaluation may be attributed to the attempt by the subject to reduce dissonance between the desirability and the unavailability of the critical toy (the sour-grapes effect). Finally, the later condition, like the fix condition, fails to arouse dissonance and is hence susceptible to the satiation-novelty effect—a rise in evaluation of the critical toy.

It is concluded that the temporary unavailability of a desired object tends to increase its desirability in relation to other available objects as predicted by the satiation-novelty hypothesis. However, if the unavailability is clearly permanent or if the object is voluntarily avoided as a result of barely sufficient coercion, then cognitive dissonance is aroused which can only be reduced by devaluation of the desired object.

50 A Study of Social Stereotype of Body Image in Children[1]

J. ROBERT STAFFIERI

The body type (that is, fat, muscular, thin) of a child may be a determiner of his behavior and personality traits through social learning from peers, adults, and the mass media. The results of this study indicate that boys between the ages of six and ten expect certain behavior from persons with a particular body type, show a clear preference for the mesomorph (muscular) image, and are reasonably accurate in perception of their own body types.

The role of an individual's body configuration in social interactions and the effects of these interactions on self-concept is an important part of the total process of personality development. It is not uncommon to be the initiator or recipient of such statements as "He certainly is a crafty, wiry little thing," or "He is all skin and bones—must worry a lot." It is reasonable to assume that the individual who is the recipient of statements which are based on another person's perception of his body is likely to incorporate these perceptions into his own body concept. As a direct result of an individual's body configuration, he typi-

[1]This article is based on a dissertation submitted in partial fulfillment of the requirements for the degree of Doctor of Education at Indiana University. The author wishes to express his appreciation to Boyd R. McCandless, under whose direction the investigation was conducted.

Reprinted from the Journal of Personality and Social Psychology, 1967, 7:1, 101–104, by permission of the author and the American Psychological Association.

cally receives rather consistent reactions from others. These reactions thus provide a framework for his body concept, which becomes a significant part of the total self-concept.

One implication from this process is central to the concerns of this investigation. Since body configuration is objectively definable (e.g., tallness versus shortness, fatness versus thinness), it is reasonable to hypothesize a definable range of consistent and stable reactions to a particular body configuration.

Evidence linking body build and personality is at best tenuous. Perhaps the etiology of such a relationship (if it exists) lies in the realm of social learning rather than physical constitution per se. McCandless (1960) stated that ". . . there are suggestions that if substantial and consistent personality-body type relations should be demonstrated, patterned types of social response may constitute the responsible factor as reasonably as genetics [p. 47]."

Evidence suggests that individuals will behave to some degree in a manner consistent with the expectations of others. If these expectations are consistent over people and time, it is reasonable to expect emitted behavior consistent with the expectations. Once the individual accepts an expectation as being true of himself, the literature suggests that he will act in a manner to fulfill the belief, thus providing added continuity to behavior which was originally emitted because of expectation (e.g., Payne and Farquhar, 1962).

Most investigations relating body build to social-personal behaviors suggest that, although the magnitude of the correlations is not high and the proportion of correlations is not much

higher than would be expected by chance, some support exists for acceptance of the concept of body-built-personality interrelations (e.g., Hanley, 1951; Walker, 1962, 1963).

Previous research has provided some evidence to suggest that a body type is capable of eliciting rather common reactions from adults in the form of descriptions of personality/behavior traits. Is the role of body type as a stimulus in social situations limited to the adult population? What is the relation of age to this process? Is there a relationship between body image stereotype and individual process of perceiving? What part does body type play in social interactions? The purpose of this study was to investigate the role of body-image stereotypes in children with general reference to three areas: development, interpersonal functions, and social functions.

METHOD

Subjects

The subjects for this study were 90 male children from 6 to 10 years of age in the elementary division of the University School, Indiana University. The sample population consisted of 18 subjects at each age level (6 to 10 years), who were grouped (according to their relative fatness, muscularity, and thinness) on the basis of the ponderal index

$$\left(\frac{\text{height in inches}}{\sqrt[3]{\text{weight in pounds}}} \right)$$

and teacher rating of body type. Although these groups (six subjects in each group at each age level) are referred to in the study as endomorph, mesomorph, and ectomorph, these are meant as descriptive characteristics of typically fat, muscular, and thin boys, respectively,

TABLE 1.—Frequency of Assignment of
Adjectives to Silhouettes by Subjects
6 to 10 Years Old

ADJECTIVES	SILHOUETTES			
	En	M	Ec	χ^2
Strong	15	74	1	100.067***
Best friend	9	67	14	68.867***
Quiet	21	10	59	44.067***
Fights	40	45	5	31.667***
Kind	24	35	31	2.067
Cheats	63	9	18	55.800***
Clean	3	54	33	43.800***
Worries	30	11	49	24.067***
Lots of friends	8	69	13	74.467***
Nervous	42	5	43	31.267***
Happy	19	54	17	28.867***
Helps others	17	55	18	31.267***
Polite	13	50	27	23.267***
Argues	58	17	15	39.267***
Remembers	10	26	26	26.400***
Gets teased	60	4	26	53.067***
Lonely	33	9	48	25.800***
Sick	41	7	42	26.467***
Forgets	51	14	25	24.067***
Lazy	67	5	18	71.267***
Healthy	4	77	9	110.867***
Lies	56	10	24	37.067***
Sneaky	25	24	41	6.067*
Honest	13	61	16	48.200***
Sloppy	72	9	9	88.200***
Brave	8	68	14	72.800***
Teases	35	30	25	1.667*
Naughty	46	18	26	13.867***
Good looking	1	74	15	100.067***
Mean	54	19	17	28.867***
Afraid	27	7	56	40.667***
Ugly	77	4	9	110.867***
Sad	31	11	48	22.867***
Smart	5	67	18	71.267***
Dirty	60	16	14	45.067***
Tired	39	12	39	16.200***
Stupid	58	8	24	43.467***
Weak	21	0	69	83.400***
Neat	2	73	15	95.267***

Note.—En = Endomorph; M = Mesomorph; Ec = Ectomorph.
   *$p < .05$.
   ***$p < .001$.

and do not stringently represent a particular method of body typing. In addition, there was a sample of 12 4-year-old
and 12 5-year-old subjects included in a
part of the study, but the results utilized
from this group are considered as a tentative pilot investigation.

Measures

Three measures were obtained for each
subject who participated in the study:
(*a*) assignment of adjectives to silhouettes representing three variations of body
type, (*b*) determination of body type
preference of each subject, and (*c*) a
sociometric measure of each class.

ADJECTIVES   A list of 39 descriptions
(primarily one-word adjectives) was developed, each of which could be applied
to any of the silhouettes. The descriptions,
hereinafter referred to as adjectives, were
selected on the basis of (*a*) a prior pilot
study, (*b*) apparent relatedness to be-
havior/personality variables, and (*c*) the
likelihood of their meaning being known.
The adjectives were not designed to survey all possible descriptions which could
be applied to individuals, but were intended to be a reasonable sample of a
more extensive universe.

SILHOUETTES   The stimuli to which the
above-mentioned adjectives were applied
were three full-body silhouettes (black
on white). Each silhouette profile was approximately the same height (13 inches),
head shape, and facial outline. The dis-
tinguishing features were those which are
commonly associated with the three gross
bodily characteristics of extreme endomorph, mesomorph, and ectomorph. Essentially, the body curvatures represented
fat, muscular, and thin body types. In this
study, there were two sets of three silhouettes each. One set was designed to
represent adult figures, the other to represent child figures. The silhouettes were

counterbalanced for both order in body-types presentation and child-adult form. This was also done for assignment of adjectives and body-type preference. In each age level, half of the subjects (nine) responded to child forms and half to adult forms. With three silhouettes, there were six possible orders of presentation, so that each subject of a particular body type in each age group responded to a different order of silhouettes. All three silhouettes were hung on a white background card (30 × 20 inches). They were clearly discriminable.

TABLE 2.—Body Type Preference of Subjects by Age

| | SILHOUETTES | | | |
AGE	Endo-morph	Meso-morph	Ecto-morph	χ^2
4–5	8	6	10	1.000
6	5	7	6	.333
7	6	12	0	12.000**
8	1	16	1	26.833**
9	4	11	3	6.333*
10	0	16	2	23.333**

*$p < .05$.
**$p < .01$.

TABLE 3.—Accuracy of Self Perception of a Selected Group of Subjects

| SELF RATINGS | SUBJECTS | | | |
	1–2	3	4–5	ε
1–2	7	4	3	14
3	3	10	8	21
4–5	0	1	4	5
ε	10	15	15	40

Note.—$\chi^2 = 10.367$ ($< .05$), C = .454.

BODY-TYPE PREFERENCE   In order to determine the body type preferred, each subject was presented with five variations of body-type silhouettes. In addition to the three used in the assignment of adjectives, two silhouettes were cut representing endo-mesomorph and ecto-mesomorph. These five silhouettes represented a range of body type and were also counterbalanced for order in presentation and child-adult form.

SOCIOMETRY   The sociometric measure used in this study was responded to by most boys and girls in all classes from Grades 1 through 5. It was administered to all classes separately. The children were asked to indicate (in writing) who, in that class, were their five best friends and who were the three children that they "did not like so well." The instructions were constant for all classes and the list was ordered from their "very best friend" (first choice) to their fifth best friend (fifth choice), and from the person whom they disliked most (first choice) to the person that they disliked, but did not dislike as much as the first or second choice (third choice). The sociometric data for 6, 7, and 8-year old children were collected (using the same procedure) about 5 months prior to this study, and were available to the investigator. This measure provided data from each child in the class which indicated the number of times each subject was chosen as first best friend, second best friend, and so on, and most disliked, second most disliked, and third most disliked.

RESULTS

The results of the study indicate that:

1. Boys from 6 to 10 years old demonstrated a common concept of be-

havior/personality traits which were associated with various body types. These stereotypes began to appear in children 4 and 5 years old, but the evidence is tentative (Table 1).

2. All the significant adjectives assigned to the mesomorph image were favorable (16); the adjectives assigned the endomorph were unfavorable (socially) and primarily socially aggressive; the adjectives assigned to the ectomorph were primarily unfavorable (personally) and of a generally socially submissive type.

3. The assignment of adjectives to the images was not related to the body type of the subject who assigned them.

4. Subjects showed a clear preference to look like the mesomorph image. This preference became apparent between 6 and 7 years (Table 2).

5. A selected group of subjects demonstrated reasonable accuracy in perception of their own body types (Table 3).

6. Mesomorph subjects received a consistently high number of acceptance choices and endomorph subjects received a consistently low number of acceptance choices (Table 4).

TABLE 4.—Number of Acceptance Choices Received by Subjects

| | *SUBJECTS* | | | |
ORDER	*Endo-morph*	*Meso-morph*	*Ecto-morph*	χ^2
1st	59	76	11	10.443**
2nd	76	101	58	11.906**

**$p < .01$.

DISCUSSION

The results of this study indicate a rather clear stereotype pattern for the three body images within age levels and across age levels. The mesomorph image is perceived as entirely favorable. The ectomorph image is basically unfavorable, but different from the unfavorable concept for endomorph.

It is clear that the mesomorph body type for both children and adults is representative of an ideal male physique. The favorable stereotype of the mesomorph is evident at 6 years of age. However, the preference to look like the mesomorph does not appear until 7 years and is not clearly established until 8 years. Although the data are not sufficiently clear to warrant a firm conclusion, this difference may tentatively be attributed to inaccurate self-perceptions by the subjects at 6 and 7 years. Data suggest reasonable accuracy of self-perception of body type from 40 subjects, mostly 7- and 10-year olds. The 10-year-old boys were more accurate in their self-perceptions than the 7-year-old boys. If the younger boys do not perceive themselves accurately, there may not be sufficient motivation for them to report a preference to look differently. Subjects 8 years and older appear to report self-perceptions quite accurately, and clearly prefer to look like the mesomorph image. The point at which accuracy of self-perception becomes apparent (probably 8 to 9 years of age) may also be the beginning of dissatisfaction with one's body, and the degree of dissatisfaction may well be proportional to the extent that one's body differs from the mesomorph image.

While the results of this investigation do not provide an answer to the problem of whether body type constitutionally determines personality, or that body type is a determinant of personality through the process of social learning, there are some implications which support the latter point of view. Most authors would agree that, at least minimally, an individual's physical constitution determines certain behaviors which can be emitted. Beyond this point, however, the results of this study suggest that personality correlates of body type may be reasonably explained on the basis of expected behavior. Thus social expectation could explain the low but rather consistently found correlations between body type and behavior/personality traits.

If children behave in a manner consistent with expectations, even to a minimal degree, some reinforcement of the expectations occurs and gives continued support to the stereotype.

51 *Pupil Perceptions of Parental Attitudes toward School*[1]

MARGARET BARRON LUSZKI

RICHARD SCHMUCK

The focus of this selection is, in part, on the self—perception of self and perception of parental attitudes toward school. Pupils who perceive their parents as holding supportive attitudes toward their school life have more positive attitudes toward school, utilize their abilities more fully, have higher self-esteem, and make a more positive psychological adjustment, than pupils who perceive less parental support. Noted are a number of ideas for the teacher to help parents assume more supportive roles in relation to their children and to help the child achieve more insight into the behavior of his parents.

[1]This study is a continuation of the same research reported in part in Schmuck, Luszki, and Epperson (1963). The total project, which concerns mental health in the classroom, is part of the Inter-Center Program of Research on Children, Youth and Family Life of the Institute for Social Research at the University of Michigan. It was supported by grants from the National Institute of Mental Health (Grant OM–376) and the U.S. Office of Education (Co-operative Research Project No. 1167).

The authors wish to express special thanks to Raymond Brant, Ann Arbor Veterans Administration Hospital, and James Wigle, Institute for Social Research, for their statistical assistance; and to Ronald Lippitt and Robert Fox, principal investigators.

Reprinted from *Mental Hygiene*, 1965, **49**, 296–307, by permission of the authors and the National Association for Mental Health, Inc.

Family characteristics and living styles are receiving increased attention as factors related to school adjustment as well as to mental health in general. Deutsch (1960, 1963) and Curry (1962), for example, have found that children from lower class families are considerably more deficient in language skills and cognitive development than middle class youngsters.

One family characteristic related to social class which has received extensive study is maternal employment (Burchinal and Rossman, 1961; Hoffman, 1964; Stolz, 1960). Although it is often assumed that children of working mothers perform more poorly in school than children of nonworking mothers, few studies have clearly validated this assumption. Indeed, as Sussman (1961) pointed out, the important variables appear to be the mother's motives for working and her attitudes both about the child and the school, rather than the fact of her employment.

In research focused specifically on parental attitudes, Armstrong (1958) and Morrow and Wilson (1961) showed that negative parental attitudes toward school were related to children's poor academic performance. Gildea, Glidewell and Kantor (1961) found that such parental attitudes were class-related, with middle class parents asserting demands for individual success more often than working class parents.

The quality of interpersonal relations within the family is a related factor influencing pupil classroom adjustment. In a study of families including adults living in the home in addition to the parents, Clark and Van Sommers (1961) found that unsatisfactory relations among the adults in the family contributed to poor relations between parents and children, to contradictory demands on the children, to withdrawal of the father from family activities, and to subsequent maladjustment of the children in school. This latter finding was supported also by Morrow and Wilson (1961) and Easton (1959), who established an association between dissident parent-child relationships and low school achievement.

One of three explanations is usually presented for findings which show a relation between family characteristics and pupil mental health in the classroom. The first emphasizes the material environment in the home. As Hunt (1961) and others have pointed out, a varied environment and a variety of stimuli during early development, conditions more likely to be found in middle class than in lower class homes, are conducive to higher ultilization of a child's intellectual potential than impoverished and monotonous environments.

A second and more social psychological explanation emphasizes the lack of orientation to education of lower class parents and the discontinuity between the values and requirements of the lower class family and the demands and expectations of the school. This explanation is supported by Bertrand (1962), who argued that when the values of the family and the school are contradictory, the children have little incentive for school achievement. When the values of home and school are harmonious, however, achievement in school leads to recognition and praise at home. Such supportive experiences in the home increase both a child's academic motivation and his classroom mental health by building positive attitudes toward school, which, in turn, lead to fuller utilization of his intellectual potential.

A third explanation, supported by Serot and Teevan (1961) and complementary to the second, is that general parental affective support of the child and of his role as a pupil, when these positive attitudes are perceived by the child, help him to develop both a high level of personal esteem and positive attitudes toward school. These positive feelings, in turn, facilitate the child's utilizing his abilities at a high level, and his better performance in school further enhances his self-evaluation and feelings about school.

In further development of the third explanation, we postulate a circular process between the parents' attitudes toward school and their child's achievement efforts in school, mediated by the child's perception of his parents' attitudes. We assume that in most cases a child learns his initial attitudes toward school from his parents, and that these attitudes have their roots in the parents' social class, personal background, and day-to-day interaction with each other. Parents' attitudes about school are also influenced to some degree by their child's first reactions to school and his early performance in the classroom. Sometimes, for instance, a child's success in school reflects credit on the parents, making them feel more positive toward school, and these feelings may be reflected in the child's perception of his parents' attitudes.

On the other hand, a child's lack of immediate success in school, particularly for those parents who are not academically oriented in the first place, could result in the parents feeling increasingly more negative toward the school, and also toward the child as a pupil. This is especially true of parents whose own school experiences were unpleasant. In any case, a stable relationship develops between parents and child with the parents' attitudes and conceptions about school dovetailing with the child's. In this way a child's school adjustment is influenced by his parents.

Although parental attitudes toward school are important, the child's perception of these attitudes is more crucial for his behavior as a pupil than the attitudes themselves. Of particular relevance here is the work of Serot and Teevan (1961), which indicated that a child's personal adjustment is related to his perception of his relationship with his parents, that the child's perception of this relationship is not necessarily related to his parents' conception of that same relationship, and that the parents' conception of the parent-child relationship is often unrelated to the child's adjustment. *The intervening variable, a pupil's perception of his parents' attitudes toward school, is the focus of the research reported here.*

METHODS

The data reported in this study came from 27 public school classrooms, drawn from a pool of rural, industrial, suburban and university communities in the Middle West. These classrooms, with a total of 727 pupils, included 18 elementary, 4 junior high, and 5 senior high school groups. The fathers' occupations for the pupils in the sample differed significantly from classroom to classroom. For instance, in one classroom 90 per cent of the fathers were professional while in another, 97 per cent were classified as unskilled. The racial composition ranged from predominantly Negro in two classes to all Caucasian in others, with an over-all total of 10 per cent non-white.

Data for three family characteristics were derived from a short information form.

Familial Social Class

Occupation of the father was used to assess the social class background of a pupil's family. Occupations were identified by three questions answered by the pupils, i.e., "Where does your father work?" "What is the name or title of his job?" and "What exactly does he do on the job?" Occupations were coded on the basis of a modified census classification, but for purposes of this analysis were grouped into three social classes as follows: (a) upper middle class, consisting of upper professional and upper white-collar occupational categories (26 per cent); (b) lower middle class, consisting of lower white-collar and skilled workers (47 per cent); and (c) working class, including the semiskilled and unskilled categories (27 per cent).

Parental Education

Information regarding educational attainment of parents was obtained from a multiple choice question: "How far did your father (mother) go in school?" For father's education, the sample was equally divided between college graduates and those who had not finished high school (25 per cent in each category), with 31 per cent who had completed high school, a few of whom had, in addition, some college work. The pattern for mothers was similar, except that there were more falling in the middle category (40 per cent) and fewer in the lower category (20 per cent). Many pupils (19 per cent) answered "Don't know" with regard to their father's education and 17 per cent with regard to their mother's.

Maternal Employment

Each pupil was asked whether his mother was employed, and if so, whether she worked full or part-time.

Two classroom variables were obtained as indicated below.

Peer Interpersonal Affective Relations

Every pupil nominated four classmates he liked most and four he liked least. A pupil was awarded one acceptance score for each positive nomination. Pupils in each class were rank-ordered according to their acceptance scores. This distribution was used in designating high, medium and low status pupils on the "popularity" dimension.

Utilization of Abilities

Each class was split at the median into a high intelligence and a low intelligence group by scores from standard intelligence tests. The teacher then divided each of these groups into high achieving and low achieving subgroups. Thus, the class was divided into four ability—achievement groups: high ability—high achievement, high ability—low achievement, low ability—

high achievement, and low ability—
low achievement.

The two high achieving groups were
considered to be utilizing their abilities more completely and were designated "high utilizers," while the two
low achieving groups were considered
to be "low utilizers." This ability-
achievement measure, as indicated by
the way each class was divided, represented the pupil's *relative* position in
his class, not his ability or achievement in relation to all pupils of a particular age or grade. A comparison of
the I.Q. scores for the total sample
yielded no significant difference between high and low utilizers; e.g., I.Q.
mean for the "high utilizers" was
109.38, while that for the "low utilizers" was 109.00.

A sentence completion test, prepared for this research, provided data
for three pupil perceptual variables.[2]
The test as a whole consisted of 46
sentence stems, relating to different
aspects of the child's life. Two indices
were developed from clusters of stems,
and two stems were used individually.[3]

---

[2]The authors are indebted to Malpass
and Tyler (1961) for providing the basis
for the coding and scoring principles
used.

[3]For the sentence stems reported, single item per cent agreement with the total
indices ranges from 68 per cent to 78 per
cent, while inter-item correlations range
from .36 to .58. These moderately high
and consistent percentages and correlations indicate a fair amount of internal
consistency and imply that each item is
contributing in its own right to the total
index. Analysis of rater reliability indicated at least 95 per cent agreement for
high-low scoring for each index. On the
qualitative coding for the parental support index, with a total of 27 categories,
there was 84 per cent agreement between
two raters.

Self-Esteem

An index of the pupil's attitude toward himself was based on three sentence completion items, each of which
was rated on a seven-point scale, according to its degree of positiveness.
The mean of the three ratings provided a "self-esteem index."[4] Following
are the three sentence stems, with a
few typical responses showing high
and low self-esteem.

High self-esteem:

"When I look in the mirror, I
   like what I see . . .
   feel happy . . .
   *am pretty well satisfied with what
   I see.*"
"Sometimes I think I am
   very smart . . .
   *lucky to have such a nice fam-
   ily . . .*
   quite mature for my age."
"When I look at other boys and girls
and then look at myself, I feel
   glad I'm what I am . . .
   *good because I have so many
   friends . . .*
   right at home."
Low self-esteem:
"When I look in the mirror, I
   *am disgusted with my appear-
   ance . . .*

---

[4]The self-esteem index was consistent
with a different kind of self-evaluation.
On an attitude questionnaire pupils were
asked to rate each of their classmates and
themselves on a nine-point scale, ranging
from "a person who has only things about
him you like" to "a person who has only
things about him you don't like." A chi-
square analysis showed an association between the self-evaluation on this nine-
point scale and the self-esteem index
based on the three sentence completion
stems ($p < .001$).

*wonder how anyone could love
me . . .
don't like what I see."*
"Sometimes I think I am
*not wanted in school because no
one wants to work or play with
me . . .
the only one in the family they
hate . . .
left out of things."*
"When I look at other boys and girls
and then look at myself, I feel
*that I'm not wanted around this
school . . .
ashamed . . .
that I'm an ugly creep . . ."*

It is generally recognized that positive attitudes toward the self are an important aspect of mental health (Schmuck, Luszki, and Epperson, 1963). An inspection of the above responses bears this out.

School Adjustment

A similar method was used to compute a "school adjustment index," which was based on the five sentence completion stems shown below. For each stem, examples are given to show what was rated as high and as low school adjustment.

High school adjustment:

"My schoolwork
*is a lot of fun . . .
is improving a lot."*
"Studying is
*a chance to learn what you need
to know . . .
very important."*
"Homework is
*interesting . . .
important to do."*
"Learning out of books is

*fun and I learn a lot . . .
the easiest part of school."*
"This school
*is my idea of a good school . . .
is one I like a lot."*

Low school adjustment:

"My schoolwork
*is very dull and boring . . .
is not important because I'm quitting school."*
"Studying is
*too hard . . .
a waste of time."*
"Homework is
*something I hate . . .
stupid."*
"Learning out of books is
*not a good way to learn . . .
for the birds."*
"This school
*is awful . . .
is pretty bad—I hate it."*

Pupil Perceptions of Parental Attitudes toward School

A measurement of the pupil's perception of each of his parent's attitudes toward school was obtained from the following two sentence completion stems:

"When I talk about school, my mother . . . . ."
"When I talk about school, my father . . . . ."

These stems were widely separated by ones dealing with other subject matter. Responses were rated on a seven-point scale ranging from strong approval, affective support, and interest in what the pupil has to say about school ("is proud of me," "says I'm doing fine," "enjoys hearing about school"), to strong disapproval or negative affect ("makes wise-cracks about school," "says the school isn't any good," "wants me to quit school"). The coding of responses also included certain qualitative aspects. Supportive answers were divided into approval or affective support, active help with schoolwork, and achievement emphasis. On the nonsupportive side, categories such as lack of interest, threat, and lack of understanding were used. When an hypothesis refers to "parents" rather than to mother or father, an average of the two measurements is used.

RESULTS

Family Characteristics

The clearest difference found in this study was associated with the parents' educational level. Parents who were seen as supportive of school by their children had more formal education than those seen as indifferent or nonsupportive ($p < .01$ for fathers and $p < .005$ for mothers). Among the highly supportive fathers, 39 per cent were college graduates, many with additional graduate work. Among the nonsupportive fathers, only 23 per cent had this degree of educational attainment. In contrast to this, among the fathers who failed to finish high school, 37 per cent were seen as not supportive, and 27 per cent as supportive. Looking at the most educated fathers as a group, 55 per cent were seen as highly supportive and only 16 per cent as not supportive.

The results were even more significant in relation to mothers. Among the highly supportive mothers, 32 per cent were college graduates and 17 per cent

had not completed high school. Among the nonsupportive mothers, on the other hand, 34 per cent had not completed high school and only 21 per cent had graduated from college. Looking at the most educated mothers as a group, 61 per cent of them were seen by their children as highly supportive of school, and only 11 per cent as nonsupportive.

Despite the clear association between a pupil's perception of his parent's interest in school and that parent's educational level, no statistically significant relationship was found in our sample between the father's occupational status and the pupil's perception of his parents' interest in school. There was, however, a trend suggesting that parents in the upper middle class tended to be more supportive of school than parents in the lower middle and working occupational categories. The data showed that 58 per cent of the upper middle class parents were viewed as being highly supportive of school, while only 47 per cent and 48 per cent of the parents in the lower middle and working classes respectively were perceived as highly supportive.

Further, children of mothers who work full-time were likely to see their mothers as less supportive of school than did other children. The data supported this generalization ($p < .01$). The difference was highlighted in the findings for mothers who were seen as nonsupportive. Twenty-two per cent of the working mothers compared to 12 per cent of the nonworking mothers were viewed by their children as nonsupportive of school. The social status of these working mothers tended on the whole not to differ from that of other women in the sample and did not account for this result. These results, in summary, indicate that maternal education and employment, though not father's occupation, are associated with the child's perceptions of parental attitudes toward school.

Pupil Age and Sex

Age and sex have been shown to have a bearing on children's parental perceptions. Kohn and Fiedler (1961), for example, reported that younger pupils differentiated between others less than older pupils, and females were somewhat more positive than males in their perceptions of others. Kagan (1956) and associates (Kagan and Lemkin, 1960; Kagan, Hosken, and Watson, 1961) made rather extensive studies of children's perceptions of parental attributes. None of the attributes studied was related directly to attitudes toward school, but the results showed that boys viewed their parents somewhat differently than girls.

Our data indicated that younger pupils perceived their parents as supporting academic striving more than older pupils. There was clearly an inverse relationship between a pupil's age and his perception of positive parental support of school ($p < .005$). The data showed that over 56 per cent of the elementary level pupils in the sample indicated very positive parental support of school, while only 38 per cent of the senior high school pupils indicated such support. In both the neutral and the nonsupportive categories, on the other hand, there was an increasing percentage as one ascended the educational ladder.

Chi-square analysis of the data indicated that sex of pupil and strength of perceived parental support of school were not related.

Types of Perceived Parental Support of School

The data reported above all relate to quantitative aspects, or the strength of perceived parental support. Some differences were found also on the qualitative side. Three general types of pupil perceptions of parental attitudes toward school were isolated: (a) *affective support and approval;* e.g., "is proud of me," "thinks I'm doing well," "is pleased with my school work"; (b) *offer of help and active support;* e.g., "wants to help me," "asks questions and tries to help me," "wants to know and help," and (c) *emphasis on academic achievement;* e.g., "wants me to do my very best," "wants me to learn more," "wants me to stay in school and get a diploma."

In an analysis of these data, four findings emerged.

1. Mothers and fathers did not differ significantly in the type of support the pupils viewed each as offering.

2. Lower middle class pupils, both boys and girls, perceived more *affective support and approval* from both parents than upper middle and working class pupils.

3. Upper middle class pupils, primarily girls, perceived more *parental helping and active support* than working class pupils—who in turn perceived more than lower middle class pupils.

4. Boys perceived more *parental academic achievement pressure* than girls. Furthermore, boys in the working and lower middle classes perceived more parental achievement pressure than boys in the upper middle class.

Self-Esteem, School Adjustment and Classroom Performance

The data generally indicated that pupils who viewed their parents as actively interested and supportive of what they were doing in school made a more positive psychological adjustment to school than pupils who saw their parents as less supportive. First, pupils who perceived their parents as holding supportive attitudes toward their school life felt more positive about themselves than pupils who perceived less parental support. Indices for parental support of school and self-esteem showed that pupils who viewed their parents as supporting school had more positive self-feelings than pupils who viewed less parental support of school ($p < .005$).

Secondly, pupils who perceived their parents as holding supportive attitudes toward their school life felt more positive about school than pupils who perceived less parental support. Seventy-seven per cent of the pupils perceiving very high parental support had positive attitudes toward school, whereas only 6 per cent of the pupils with highly supportive parents had negative attitudes toward school. When the pupils with positive attitudes toward school are viewed as a group, it will be seen that 57 per cent saw their parents as highly supportive, whereas only 9 per cent saw their parents as nonsupportive.

Finally, pupils who perceived their parents as holding supportive attitudes toward their school life utilized their abilities more completely than pupils who perceived less parental support. The data confirm this statement for elementary pupils ($p < .025$) and for junior high school pupils ($p < .05$), but not for those in tenth through twelfth grades. Generally speaking, the younger the pupil, the more impact his perception of parental support of school has on his classroom performance. This finding is consistent with those of Coleman (1961) and others which show the greater impact of the peer group and reduced influence of the parents during adolescence.

About 53 per cent of the elementary pupils with very supportive parents were utilizing their abilities quite adequately. Over 62 per cent of those elementary pupils with nonsupportive parents, on the other hand, were utilizing their abilities at a low level. In the junior high, 70 per cent of those pupils who perceived their parents as nonsupportive of school were low utilizers. There was some trend for this to be the case in senior high also, but the chi-square analysis did not reach a high enough level to be significant.

Nevertheless, 59 per cent of senior high pupils who perceived their parents as not supporting school were underutilizing their abilities. Since the high and low utilizers in the sample were equal in intelligence, these results point to the important associations between (a) a pupil's perception of his parents' support of school life, and (b) a pupil's attitudes toward self and school as well as his academic achievement.

Perhaps some examples taken from our data will help make these findings more concrete. Consider, for instance, this fourth-grade boy who saw his parents as unsupportive of school. When presented with the incomplete sentence, "When I talk about school, my father," he answered, *"doesn't like it."*

For his mother, he wrote, "*Says I am doing bad.*" He had an I.Q. of about 106 which was rather high according to the ability range of this particular class. However, his teacher said he was achieving at quite a low level. Furthermore, he manifested a very negative attitude toward himself and rather negative feelings toward school. He filled out the self items in the following ways: "Sometimes I think I *am nuts,*" "When I look at other boys and girls and then look at myself I feel *like a smart aleck,*" "When I look in the mirror, I *see a bad boy.*" On another self-related incomplete sentence, he wrote, "When I am by myself I *feel stupid.*"

On some of the incomplete sentences for assessing his attitudes toward school, he answered: "My schoolwork is *hard,*" "Studying is *not easy,*" "Homework is *stupid,*" "Learning out of books is *dum*" (sic).

This boy had a few friends his own age, but by and large he appeared to be isolated from his peers. His life as a pupil was not a happy one. His teacher saw him as a boy who was generally uninterested in school. She added that sometimes he tried hard, but that he was not able to concentrate for long periods.

Let us contrast him with another fourth-grade boy who was achieving very highly considering his intelligence level. He had about as many close friends as his classmate described above, but showed a much different pattern of perceived parental support for school and attitudes toward school. This boy wrote: "When I talk about school, my father *likes to know what I have done in school,*" and ". . . my mother *listens very carefully.*" On another item he wrote, "A father is nice

when *I talk about school,*" indicating again his perception that his father was very supportive of him as a pupil.

In revealing his attitudes toward school, he answered: "Studying is *fun,*" "Homework is *fun when it is easy,*" "This school is *nice.*" He also viewed his teacher as reflecting general satisfaction with his behavior as a pupil, writing: "My teacher thinks I am *nice most of the time.*"

Consider a third pupil, this one a fifth-grade girl, who perceived her parents as being very supportive of her academic behavior. She answered, "When I talk about school, my father *likes me to talk about school,*" and ". . . my mother *wants to know about it.*" She had an I.Q. of 100 which was low according to the ability range of this particular class, but she was achieving at quite a high level. Furthermore, her score on the self-esteem index was very positive. She filled out the self items as follows: "Sometimes I think I am *pretty good,*" "When I look at other boys and girls and then look at myself, I feel *that I like me and the others.*" "When I look in the mirror, I *feel that I look OK.*" About school she wrote, "This school *is nice,*" and "Studying is *fun most of the time.*"

Finally, contrast this pupil with a fifth-grade girl who viewed her parents as being very unsupportive of school. She wrote, "When I talk about school, my father *gets mad,*" and ". . . my mother says *how many bad things do you do in school?*" Even though her I.Q. score was average for her class, she was achieving at a very low level. Her negative attitude toward herself was revealed in the following responses: "Sometimes I think I am *really dumb,*" "When I look at other boys and girls and then look at myself, I feel *that they are more pretty and smart*," "When I look in the mirror, I *think how I can change myself*."

Sociometric Status
in the Peer Group

The results indicated that sociometric status in the peer group and perceived parental support of school were unrelated, but, when taken together, were powerful predictors of a pupil's classroom performance.

The data indicate that at three levels of perceived parental support, very supportive, moderately supportive, and nonsupportive, sociometric liking status in the peer group was positively associated with utilization of abilities. In the very supportive condition, for instance, 65 per cent of the pupils with high liking status were high utilizers, 53 per cent with medium liking status were high utilizers, and only 37 per cent with low liking status were high utilizers ($p < .001$).

Conversely, pupils with moderate parental support and low sociometric position were utilizing their abilities at a low level in 60 per cent of the cases. Fewer than 54 per cent of the pupils with moderate home support and medium peer group status were low utilizers, while only 38 per cent of the pupils with moderate parental support and high peer group status were low utilizers. Finally, it appeared that even in the nonsupportive home conditions, there was a trend, though not significant, for pupils with high liking status in the peer group to be higher utilizers of their abilities than those with lower status ($p < .10$). The results suggest that peer support may serve

as a substitute source of personal gratification, especially as the pupil grows older.

IMPLICATIONS
FOR TEACHERS

If the direction of causality postulated in our introduction is correct, the findings reported here show how important it is for children to feel that their parents are interested in and supportive of their school life. In our sample, such feelings are associated with favorable classroom performance, positive attitudes toward school, and a healthy level of self-esteem. This implies that administrators and teachers should try to increase every pupil's chance to obtain parental support by attempting actively to educate parents in the significant role they play in the life of a child in school.

The problem of working with parents is a complex one, beyond the scope of this research. The following ideas, however, suggest a few things that might be done. First is the job of obtaining information about the home. Some states have records of pertinent home information about each pupil which are easily accessible to the teacher. A teacher may want to secure additional information. Some teachers, in the context of getting acquainted with a new class, ask pupils to fill out questionnaires covering family background information. Sentence completion stems such as those used in this research are also useful. Institutional means available to teachers, such as parent-teacher associations and the services of visiting teachers should be used as fully as possible. Occasionally, the teacher himself may make a home visit, after a conference with one of the parents, to get a better idea of the home life of the pupil. Whatever information gathering and diagnostic techniques are employed, it is important for the teacher to get some valid idea early in the year about the state of affairs in each of his pupils' homes.

If the information about a home suggests that some changes are desirable, the teacher may be able to establish a positive enough relationship with the parents so that through conferences and visits he will be able to help them assume more supportive roles in relation to their child's school life.

Through meetings with groups of parents, too, teachers can engage parents in discussions of how they treat their children in relation to school, make suggestions about alternative actions, and gain some commitment to action by setting up a later date for evaluation and discussion. A teacher might, for instance, attempt to enhance parental support by discussing individual differences. An understanding of differences among pupils relative to sex, cultural background, abilities and interests increases the opportunity for parents to be more accepting and tolerant of their children. In addition to producing greater acceptance of their own child as a pupil, a family standard of acceptance of differences may emerge from trying out new ways of relating to the child.

Approaches such as these have proved successful in changing behavior and attitudes. Teachers often find parents eager for information and guidance because their lack of support stems primarily from their failure to understand child behavior. In some parents, however, negative feelings to-ward the child and toward school are deep-rooted, and even a highly skilled teacher may be unable to enlist cooperation. Perhaps such parents should be referred to a visiting teacher who could try to understand and alleviate the nonsupportive attitudes. In such work, both teacher and visiting teacher must be careful not to put further pressures and strains on what may be already a difficult home situation.

The finding that the parents who are less supportive of their children's school life have less education on the whole than the more supportive parents suggests that at times the problem is one which spans the generations. In some parents, the mere mention of school brings out their own feelings of frustration and failure, and the personal threat aroused by any approach from the teacher may be so strong that little can be done to gain their cooperation.

Other parents may lack the skill needed to communicate an attitude of support for either the educational institution or their child's academic efforts. Children in such families are suffering because their parents have not received adequate preparation for the complex task of child-rearing in an increasingly industrialized society. Family life education on a large scale is needed. Parent-teacher conferences alone cannot supply the background necessary to understand child behavior. Programs of family life and child development education must become more easily available to parents, and mental health consultants and social workers should be more accessible for parent consultation. Sometimes family counseling is in order, especially where pupil maladjustment in school is symptomatic of family strains and conflicts.

Despite the relationship between parental attitudes and pupil school adjustment, there are many pupils who do not follow this pattern, pupils who like school and do well in school despite lack of support at home for their school endeavors. Many such cases can be attributed to positive child-teacher relationships. The teacher's own feelings about and behavior toward individual pupils can go a long way toward making school a place where security and respect are found. Thus, it is possible that a child's desire for personal worth, although threatened by nonsupportive parents, may find some opportunity for fulfillment in the classroom.

The teacher can also help the child achieve some insight into the behavior of his parents. Informally, in his day-to-day relations with pupils, and formally through the social science curriculum, the teacher can stimulate pupils to think about the reasons for behavior in general and parental behavior in particular. Through human relations skills gained in the classroom, the pupil can be helped to handle his own family situation better.

SUMMARY

This study substantiates the general proposition that family characteristics and living styles are related to a child's perception of his parents' attitudes toward school. Specifically, parents who are seen as supportive of school life have more formal education than those who are indifferent or nonsupportive. Also, children of mothers who work fulltime see their mothers as less supportive than do other children. Younger pupils view their parents as supporting their school life more than older pupils.

Three types of pupil perceptions of parental attitudes toward school are isolated: (a) affective support, and approval, (b) help and active support, and (c) academic achievement pressure. These three types of perceived support are differentially related to the familial social class and sex of the pupils.

This research shows further that pupils who perceive their parents as holding supportive attitudes toward their school life utilize their abilities more fully and make a more positive psychological adjustment to school than pupils who perceive less parental support. Indices for parental support of school, self-esteem, and school adjustment show that pupils who view their parents as supporting school have higher self-esteem and more positive attitudes toward school than pupils who view less parental support of school. Finally, sociometric status in the peer group and pupil perception of parental support of school, taken together, predict a pupil's utilization of his abilities better than one of these alone.

The paper concludes with some suggestions for teachers.

52 *The Process of Learning Parental and Sex-Role Identification*[1]

DAVID B. LYNN

This selection presents a theory of the process of learning sex-role identification. It attempts to provide a coherent and comprehensive framework, and it presents research evidence in support of a sequence of hypotheses.

The purpose of this paper is to summarize the writer's theoretical formulation concerning identification, much of which has been published piecemeal in various journals. Research relevant to new hypotheses is cited, and references are given to previous publications of this writer in which the reader can find evidence concerning the earlier hypotheses. Some of the previously published hypotheses are considerably revised in this paper and, it is hoped, placed in a more comprehensive and coherent framework.

Theoretical Formulation

Before developing specific hypotheses, one must briefly define identification as it is used here. *Parental*

identification refers to the internalization of personality characteristics of one's own parent and to unconscious reactions similar to that parent. This is to be contrasted with *sex-role identification*, which refers to the internalization of the role typical of a given sex in a particular culture and to the unconscious reactions characteristic of that role. Thus, theoretically, an individual might be thoroughly identified with the role typical of his own sex generally and yet poorly identified with his same-sex parent specifically. This differentiation also allows for the converse circumstances wherein a person is well identified with his same-sex parent specifically and yet poorly identified with the typical same-sex role generally. In such an instance the parent with whom the individual is well identified is himself poorly identified with the typical sex role. An example might be a girl who is closely

[1] Presented at the Annual Meeting of the American Orthopsychiatric Association, 1966.

Reprinted from the *Journal of Marriage and the Family*, 1966, **28**, 466–470, by permission of the author and the National Council on Family Relations.

identified with her mother, who herself is more strongly identified with the masculine than with the feminine role. Therefore, such a girl, through her identification with her mother, is poorly identified with the feminine role (Lynn 1962).

Formulation of Hypotheses

It is postulated that the initial parental identification of both male and female infants is with the mother. Boys, but not girls, must shift from this initial mother identification and establish masculine-role identification. Typically in this culture the girl has the same-sex parental model for identification (the mother) with her more hours per day than the boy has his same-sex model (the father) with him. Moreover, even when home, the father does not usually participate in as many intimate activities with the child as does the mother, e.g., preparation for bed, toileting. The time spent with the child and the intimacy and intensity of the contact are thought to be pertinent to the process of learning parental identification (Goodfield, 1965). The boy is seldom if ever with the father as he engages in his daily vocational activities, although both boy and girl are often with the mother as she goes through her household activities. Consequently, the father, as a model for the boy, is analogous to a map showing the major outline but lacking most details, whereas the mother, as a model for the girl, might be thought of as a detailed map.

However, despite the shortage of male models, a somewhat stereotyped and conventional masculine role is nonetheless spelled out for the boy, often by his mother and women teachers in the absence of his father and male models. Through the reinforcement of the culture's highly developed system of rewards for typical masculine-role behavior and punishment for signs of femininity, the boy's early learned identification with the mother weakens. Upon this weakened mother identification is welded the later learned identification with a culturally defined, stereotyped masculine role.

(1) *Consequently, males tend to identify with a culturally defined masculine role, whereas females tend to identify with their mothers* (Lynn, 1959).

Although one must recognize the contribution of the father in the identification of males and the general cultural influences in the identification of females, it nevertheless seems meaningful, for simplicity in developing this formulation, to refer frequently to *masculine-role identification* in males as distinguished from *mother identification* in females.

Some evidence is accumulating suggesting that (2) *both males and females identify more closely with the mother than with the father.* Evidence is found in support of this hypothesis in a study by Lazowick (1955) in which the subjects were 30 college students. These subjects and their mothers and fathers were required to rate concepts, e.g., "myself," "father," "mother," etc. The degree of semantic similarity as rated by the subjects and their parents was determined. The degree of similarity between fathers and their own children was not significantly greater than that found between fathers and children randomly matched. However, children did share a greater semantic similarity with their own mothers than they did when matched at random with other maternal figures. Mothers and daughters did not share a significantly greater semantic similarity than did mothers and sons.

Evidence is also found in support of Hypothesis 2 in a study by Adams and Sarason (1963) using anxiety scales with male and female high school students and their mothers and fathers. They found that anxiety scores of both boys and girls were much more related to mothers' than to fathers' anxiety scores.

Support for this hypothesis comes from a study in which Aldous and Kell (1961) interviewed 50 middle-class college students and their mothers concerning childrearing values. They found, contrary to their expectation, that a slightly higher proportion of boys than girls shared their mothers' childrearing values.

Partial support for Hypothesis 2 is provided in a study by Gray and Klaus (1956) using the Allport-Vernon-Lindzey Study of Values completed by 34 female and 28 male college students and by their parents. They found that the men were not significantly closer to their fathers than to their mothers and also that the men were not significantly closer to their fathers than were the women. However, the women were closer to their mothers than were the men and closer to their mothers than to their fathers.

Note that, in reporting research relevant to Hypothesis 2, only studies of *tested similarity*, not *perceived similarity*, were reviewed. To test this hypothesis, one must measure tested similarity, i.e., measure both the child and the parent on the same variable

and compare the similarity between these two measures. This paper is not concerned with perceived similarity, i.e., testing the child on a given variable and then comparing that finding with a measure taken as to how the child thinks his parent would respond. It is this writer's opinion that much confusion has arisen by considering perceived similarity as a measure of parental identification. It seems obvious that, especially for the male, perceived similarity between father and son would usually be closer than tested similarity, in that it is socially desirable for a man to be similar to his father, especially as contrasted to his similarity to his mother. Indeed, Gray and Klaus (1956) found the males' perceived similarity with the father to be closer than tested similarity.

It is hypothesized that the closer identification of males with the mother than with the father will be revealed more clearly on some measures than on others. (3) *The closer identification of males with their mothers than with their fathers will be revealed most frequently in personality variables which are not clearly sex-typed.* In other words, males are more likely to be more similar to their mothers than to their fathers in variables in which masculine and feminine role behavior is not especially relevant in the culture.

There has been too little research on tested similarity between males and their parents to presume an adequate test of Hypothesis 3. In order to test it, one would first have to judge personality variables as to how typically masculine or feminine they seem. One could then test to determine whether a higher proportion of males are more similar to their mothers than to their fathers on those variables which are not clearly sex-typed, rather than on those which are judged clearly to be either masculine or feminine. To this writer's knowledge, this has not been done.

It is postulated that the task of achieving these separate kinds of identification (masculine role for males and mother identification for females) requires separate methods of learning for each sex. These separate methods of learning to identify seem to be problem-solving for boys and lesson-learning for girls. Woodworth and Schlosberg (1954) differentiate between the task of solving problems and that of learning lessons in the following way:

> With a problem to master the learn-er must explore the situation and find the goal before his task is fully present-ed. In the case of a lesson, the prob-lem-solving phase is omitted or at least minimized, as we see when the human subject is instructed to memorize this poem or that list of nonsense syllables, to examine these pictures with a view to recognizing them later.

Since the girl is not required to shift from the mother in learning her iden-tification, she is expected mainly to learn the mother-identification lesson as it is presented to her, partly through imitation and through the mother's selective reinforcement of mother-sim-ilar behavior. She need not abstract principles defining the feminine role to the extent that the boy must in de-fining the masculine role. Any bit of behavior on the mother's part may be modeled by the girl in learning the mother-identification lesson.

However, finding the appropriate identification goal does constitute a major problem for the boy in solving the masculine-role identification prob-lem. When the boy discovers that he does not belong in the same sex cate-gory as the mother, he must then find the proper sex-role identification goal. Masculine-role behavior is defined for him through admonishments, often negatively given, e.g., the mother's and teachers' telling him that he should not be a sissy without precisely indicating what he *should* be. More-over, these negative admonishments are made in the early grades in the ab-sence of male teachers to serve as models and with the father himself often unavailable as a model. The boy must restructure these admonishments in order to abstract principles defining the masculine role. It is this process of defining the masculine-role goal which is involved in solving the masculine-role identification problem.

One of the basic steps in this formu-lation can now be taken (4) *In learn-ing the sex-typical identification, each sex is thereby acquiring separate methods of learning which are subse-quently applied to learning tasks gen-erally* (Lynn, 1962).

The little girl acquires a learning method which primarily involves (a) a personal relationship and (b) imita-tion rather than restructuring the field and abstracting principles. On the other hand, the little boy acquires a different learning method which pri-marily involves (a) defining the goal (b) restructuring the field, and (c) abstracting principles. There are a number of findings which are consistent with Hypothesis 4, such as the frequently reported greater problem-solving skill of males and the greater field dependence of females (Lynn, 1962).

The shift of the little boy from mother identification to masculine-role identification is assumed to be frequently a crisis. It has been observed that demands for typical sex-role behavior come at an earlier age for boys than for girls. These demands are made at an age when boys are least able to understand them. As was pointed out above, demands for masculine sex-role behavior are often made by women in the absence of readily available male models to demonstrate typical sex-role behavior. Such demands are often presented in the form of punishing, *negative* admonishments, i.e., telling the boy what not to do rather than what to do and backing up the demands with punishment. These are thought to be very different conditions from those in which the girl learns her mother-identification lesson. Such methods of demanding typical sex-role behavior of boys are very poor methods for inducing learning.

(5) *Therefore, males tend to have greater difficulty in achieving same-sex identification than females* (Lynn, 1964).

(6) *Furthermore, more males than females fail more or less completely in achieving same-sex identification, but they rather make an opposite-sex identification* (Lynn, 1961).

Negative admonishments given at an age when the child is least able to understand them and supported by punishment are thought to produce anxiety concerning sex-role behavior. In Hartley's (1959) words:

This situation gives us practically a perfect combination for inducing anxiety—the demand that the child do something which is not clearly defined to him, based on reasons he cannot possibly appreciate, and enforced with threats, punishments and anger by those who are close to him.

(7) *Consequently, males are more anxious regarding sex-role identification than females* (Lynn, 1964). It is postulated that punishment often leads to dislike of the activity that led to punishment (Hilgard, 1962). Since it is "girl-like" activities that provoked the punishment administered in an effort to induce sex-typical behavior in boys, then, in developing dislike for the activity which led to such punishment, boys should develop hostility toward "girl-like" activities. Also, boys should be expected to generalize and consequently develop hostility toward all females as representatives of this disliked role. There is not thought to be as much pressure on girls as on boys to avoid opposite-sex activities. It is assumed that girls are punished neither so early nor so severely for adopting masculine sex-role behavior.

(8) *Therefore, males tend to hold stronger feelings of hostility toward females than females toward males* (Lynn, 1964). The young boy's same-sex identification is at first not very firm because of the shift from mother to masculine identification. On the other hand, the young girl, because she need make no shift in identification, remains relatively firm in her

mother identification. However, the culture, which is male-dominant in orientation, reinforces the boy's developing masculine-role identification much more thoroughly than it does the girl's developing feminine identification. He is rewarded simply for having been born masculine through countless privileges accorded males but not females. As Brown (1958) pointed out:

The superior position and privileged status of the male permeates nearly every aspect, minor and major, of our social life. The gadgets and prizes in boxes of breakfast cereal, for example, commonly have a strong masculine rather than feminine appeal. And the most basic social institutions perpetuate this pattern of masculine aggrandizement. Thus, the Judeo-Christian faiths involve worshipping God, a "Father," rather than a "Mother," and Christ, a "Son," rather than a "Daughter."

(9) *Consequently, with increasing age, males become relatively more firmly identified with the masculine role* (Lynn, 1959).

Since psychological disturbances should, theoretically, be associated with inadequate same-sex identification and since males are postulated to be gaining in masculine identification, the following is predicted: (10) *With increasing age males develop psychological disturbances at a more slowly accelerating rate than females* (Lynn, 1961).

It is postulated that as girls grow older, they become increasingly disenchanted with the feminine role because of the prejudices against their sex and the privileges and prestige offered the male rather than the female. Even the women with whom they come in contact are likely to share the prejudices prevailing in this culture against their own sex (Kitay, 1940). Smith (1939) found that with increasing age girls have a progressively better opinion of boys and a progressively poorer opinion of themselves. (11) *Consequently, a larger proportion of females than males show preference for the role of the opposite sex* (Lynn, 1959).

Note that in Hypothesis 11 the term "preference" rather than "identification" was used. It is *not* hypothesized that a larger proportion of females than males *identify* with the opposite sex (Hypothesis 6 predicted the reverse) but rather that they will show *preference* for the role of the opposite sex. *Sex-role preference* refers to the desire to adopt the behavior associated with one sex or the other or the perception of such behavior as preferable or more desirable. *Sex-role preference* should be contrasted with *sex-role identification*, which, as stated previously, refers to the actual incorporation of the role of a given sex and to the unconscious reactions characteristic of that role.

Punishment may suppress behavior without causing its unlearning (Hilgard, 1962). Because of the postulated punishment administered to males for adopting opposite-sex role behavior, it is predicted that males will repress atypical sex-role behavior rather than unlearn it. One might predict, then, a discrepancy between the underlying sex-role identification and the overt sex-role behavior of males. For females, on the other hand, no comparable punishment for adopting many aspects of the opposite-sex role is postulated. (12) *Consequently, where a discrepancy exists between sex-role preference and identification, it will tend to be as follows: Males will tend to show same-sex role preference with underlying opposite-sex identification. Females will tend to show opposite-sex role preference with underlying same-sex identification* (Lynn, 1964). Stated in another way, where a discrepancy occurs both males and females will tend to show masculine-role preference with underlying feminine identification.

Not only is the masculine role accorded more prestige than the feminine role, but males are more likely than females to be ridiculed or punished for adopting aspects of the opposite-sex role. For a girl to be a tomboy does not involve the censure that results when a boy is a sissy. Girls may wear masculine clothing (shirts and trousers), but boys may not wear feminine clothing (skirts and dresses). Girls may play with toys typically associated with boys (cars, trucks, erector sets, and guns), but boys are discouraged from playing with feminine toys (dolls and tea sets). (13) *Therefore, a higher proportion of females than males adopt aspects of the role of the opposite sex* (Lynn, 1959).

Note that Hypothesis 13 refers to *sex-role adoption* rather than *sex-role identification* or *preference. Sex-role adoption* refers to the overt behavior characteristic of a given sex. An example contrasting sex-role adoption with preference and identification is an individual who *adopts* behavior characteristic of his own sex because

it is expedient, not because he *prefers* it nor because he is so *identified.*

SUMMARY

The purpose of this paper has been to summarize the writer's theoretical formulation and to place it in a more comprehensive and coherent framework. The following hypotheses were presented and discussed:

1. Males tend to identify with a culturally defined masculine role, whereas females tend to identify with their mothers.

2. Both males and females identify more closely with the mother than with the father.

3. The closer identification of males with their mothers than with their fathers will be revealed most frequently in personality variables which are not clearly sex-typed.

4. In learning the sex-typical identification, each sex is thereby acquiring separate methods of learning which are subsequently applied to learning tasks generally.

5. Males tend to have greater difficulty in achieving same-sex identification than females.

6. More males than females fail more or less completely in achieving same-sex identification but rather make an opposite-sex identification.

7. Males are more anxious regarding sex-role identification than females.

8. Males tend to hold stronger feelings of hostility toward females than females toward males.

9. With increasing age, males become relatively more firmly identified with the masculine role.

10. With increasing age, males develop psychological disturbances at a

more slowly accelerating rate than females.

11. A larger proportion of females than males show preference for the role of the opposite sex.

12. When a discrepancy exists between sex-role preference and identification, it will tend to be as follows:

Males will tend to show same-sex role preference with underlying opposite-sex identification. Females will tend to show opposite-sex role preference with underlying same-sex identification.

13. A higher proportion of females than males adopt aspects of the role of the opposite sex.

53 *Child Anxiety: Self-Estimates, Parent Reports, and Teacher Ratings*

ARMIN GRAMS

A. JACK HAFNER

WENTWORTH QUAST

To what extent do two widely used scales measuring anxiety in children agree? Are there sex differences in anxiety scores? Do mothers and fathers agree on their ratings of their children's anxiety? How similar are parent's estimates to their children's self-reports? How do children's anxiety scores and parents' assessments of the anxiety of their children compare with teachers' ratings of child adjustment? These are some of the complex questions explored in the following experimental study of fourth-, fifth-, and sixth-grade children.

Considerable research has been done with the Children's Manifest Anxiety Scale (CMAS) and the General Anxiety Scale for Children (GASC). Although derived from different theoretical assumptions concerning anxiety (Castaneda et al., 1956; Sarason et al., 1958; Sarnoff et al., 1958), the two scales purportedly deal with some general characteristics of anxiety in children. One of the questions the present study was designed to investigate was how the CMAS and GASC agree when administered to the same children. Because sex differences in anxiety score are reported for both

Reprinted from the *Merrill-Palmer Quarterly of Behavior and Development,* 1965, **11,** 261–266, by permission of the authors and the Merrill-Palmer Institute.

instruments, such differences were examined here as well.

Secondly, we were interested in the congruence of parents' estimates of children's anxiety with the children's self reports. Davidson et al. (1958) report that mothers' ratings fail to discriminate between children categorized as High-Anxious or Low-Anxious on the basis of their scores on the Test Anxiety Scale and the General Anxiety Scale for Children, but that fathers' ratings do discriminate the groups in the predicted direction. In the Davidson study the parents' ratings were obtained during a home interview in which the parents filled out a personality check list. In the present study the parents rated the child's anxiety on a parent form of the CMAS and the GASC prepared especially for this purpose.

Finally, the present study compares both the children's anxiety scores and the parents' anxiety assessments with teachers' ratings of the adjustment of the children. L'Abate (1960) has shown some limited relationship between the CMAS and other measures of adjustment.

POPULATION AND PROCEDURE

A group of 110, fourth, fifth, and sixth grade children (47 boys and 63 girls) in a large middle-class suburban public school and their parents served as subjects. The anxiety scales were administered by the first author to the children in their classroom. The parents filled out their questionnaires at home, having been provided with a special parents' form which was worded exactly like the children's scales except that the phrase "My child" was

submitted for "I" in the CMAS and "Does your child" for "Do you" in the GASC. The order in which the two subjects completed the two forms was counterbalanced.

Teachers evaluated the personality adjustment of all children in their respective classrooms in a separate rating scale which Anderson (1960) devised for use in a longitudinal study of personality development. Nine specific traits and one general assessment were evaluated on a five point scale, so constructed that high scores indicated better adjustment, low scores, poorer. Teachers had no knowledge of which children were being selected for further study and no information about subjects' scores on the anxiety scales.[1]

RESULTS

On the two anxiety scales, inter-test agreement between the children's scores was substantial for both boys ($r = .79$; $p < .01$) and girls ($r = .78$; $p < .01$).

The mean scores for boys and girls on the two tests appear in Table 1. We find sex differences on the GASC but not on the CMAS. This finding agrees with the report of Sarnoff et al. (1958) with regard to the GASC and with the findings of Hafner and Kaplan (1959) and Levitt (1957). It is not consistent with that of Castaneda et al. (1956), however, who found significantly lower scores for boys on the CMAS.

---

[1]Appended to the selection are the four anxiety scales (two for children and two for parents) and the scale for teacher evaluation of the personality adjustment of children.

TABLE 1.—Sex Differences on the CMAS and GASC

TEST	MEANS		t
	Boys	Girls	
CMAS	15.3	14.7	.10
GASC	10.2	15.2	3.38**

**p < .01.

The inter-test agreement is considerably lower for mothers and fathers than for children (Table 2). We also find the fathers' inter-test agreement is greater for sons than for daughters. That this is not necessarily an indication of greater validity, however, is suggested by the lack of relation between the ratings of fathers and either sons or daughters (Table 3). Referring again to Table 2, the correlations between ratings on the two tests by sex of child are more similar when the rater is mother. Both parents' responses on the two measures, however, show greater inter-test agreement when thy are rating a child of their own sex.

TABLE 2.—Inter-test Agreement in Parent's Appraisal of Child's Anxiety on CMAS and GASC

		N	r
Fathers CMAS–GASC	(When rating sons)	45	.41**
	(When rating daughters)	62	.27*
Mothers CMAS–GASC	(When rating sons)	46	.42**
	(When rating daughters)	64	.52**

*p < .05.
**p < .01.

We next ask how well mother and father agreed on their ratings of their children. On the CMAS the correlation was .52, on the GASC it was .57, both figures proving significant at the .01 level. Although these correlations are rather high, we find (Table 3) that on either scale, and for both boys and girls, mothers predicted their children's anxiety scores with greater accuracy than did fathers. The correlations for mothers were significant for both boys and girls, whereas neither correlation for fathers was significant. (When the entire sample is used, however, a father-child agreement of .25 was obtained on the GASC and this is significant at the .01 level.)

TABLE 3.—Parent-Child Agreement on Child's Anxiety

	N	r	
		CMAS	GASC
Father-son	46	.05	.00
Father-daughter	62	.12	.21
Mother-son	47	.60**	.31* (N = 47)
Mother-daughter	63	.52**	.43**

*p < .05.
**p < .01.

The results indicate that the CMAS and the GASC are measuring something similar. If we had presented data on children alone, we might still be left with the question raised by Wirt and Broen (1956), namely, that these instruments may only be measuring willingness to admit to difficulties. Faced with the obtained degree of father-mother, and mother-child agreement, however, it is difficult to deny that the tests have some validity. There are some disconcerting findings, however, which we are obliged to consider, and which may indeed require further investigation before we have any substantial understanding of the factors involved.

One such finding is that almost no relationship exists between the father's estimate of the child and the child's own report. The mother-child agreement, on the other hand is substantial. We investigated the possibility that fathers may be more defensive, and thus less willing than their wives to admit to "shortcomings" they may observe in their children. In line with what Sarason et al. (1960) have reported, we found no mean difference between fathers and mothers in the

ratings they gave their children on the two scales. Another explanation may be that mothers are more accurate in their perception because they spend more time with their children than do fathers. This would be more plausible if we were discussing younger children, especially pre-schoolers, but because these are children 10–12 years of age there is probably little difference in the actual amount of time spent with each parent. A somewhat more subtle consideration is that a greater proportion of the time which mother spends with children this age may be spent dealing with the kind of problems surveyed by these scales. The speculation here is that a child with fears, worries and feelings of inadequacy will, if he shares them with his parents at all, be more likely to do so with mother rather than with father. Actually, if such sharing is a means whereby parents are apprised of their children's emotional inner world, then our data indicate quite definitely that it is the mother and not the father with whom the majority of such personal matters are shared.

Davidson et al. (1958) report that fathers' descriptions of children selected as high anxious or low anxious on the basis of the anxiety scales were more congruent with the criterion than mothers' descriptions. When we restricted our sample to the high anxious and low anxious children we did not find similar results. We noted only the generally lowered parent-child correlations which restricted variance imposed. In the Davidson study, however, the parents did not fill out a form of the anxiety questionnaire, but rather were interviewed in their home, completed a parent attitude inventory, and a personality check list. It is on the basis of the latter that they report their results. We think that our findings arc different because our parent instruments were different and the method of analysis was different. Furthermore, it is possible that our findings, based on data gathered from parents who were willing to participate, lack the dimensions which might have characterized the data had we been able to obtain scores from all or even most of the parents of high anxious and low anxious children. We are continuing to investigate achievement and adjustment differences in the children of cooperative and non-cooperative parents in an attempt to study this problem more closely.

At this point we turn to data obtained from the teachers. Although it is occasionally suggested that teachers' ratings of pupil adjustment are more favorable to girls than to boys, in this study no such sex bias emerged. Teacher ratings of boys and girls did not differ. Comparing teachers' ratings with the children's self-reports of anxiety (Table 4), we found only one r to be significant and that one is quite low. The lack of substantial agreement between teacher ratings of adjustment and the children's own anxiety scores is consistent with the finding of L'Abate (1960), and suggests that teachers' perception of classroom adjustment is independent of the way in which a child admits to the presence or absence of anxiety.

Some differences in the CMAS and GASC are suggested by the lack of consistency in the amount of agreement between teacher ratings of adjustment and parents' ratings of anxiety on the CMAS as compared with the GASC. When teachers' ratings are correlated with parents' estimates of their children's anxiety on the CMAS a high degree of agreement exists when they are rating girls (.69 and .82), but not when they rate boys. There is no agreement of this sort at all when the teachers' ratings are compared with the parents' estimates on the GASC. One correlation (teacher-father: girls .27) is significant at the .05 level, but

TABLE 4.—Teacher-Child Agreement on Child's Anxiety

	N	CMAS	N	GASC
Teacher-boy	46	.20	46	.07
Teacher-girl	63	.19	64	.29*

*p < .05.

TABLE 5.—Teacher-Parent Agreement on Child's Anxiety

		CMAS		GASC	
		N	r	N	r
Teacher-father:	Boys	44	.10	45	−.28
	Girls	64	.69**	63	.27*
Teacher-mother:	Boys	45	.08	46	−.23
	Girls	65	.82**	64	.22

*p < .05.
**p < .01.

its magnitude is relatively low. The difficulty here is the lack of relationship between teachers' ratings and parents' estimates of anxiety on the GASC for girls.

Since all correlations for boys are low, we might suggest that the criteria teachers use to evaluate the adjustment of boys are not related to the descriptions contained in the anxiety scales to which the parents responded. The problem in the case of girls is that when parents react to CMAS items they come up with evaluations which are quite similar to the ratings the teachers make, but the similarity all but disappears when the parents respond to the GASC. The solutions to these complexities must await further research.

CHILDREN'S MANIFEST
ANXIETY SCALE (CMAS)

1. It is hard for me to keep my mind on anything.
2. I get nervous when someone watches me work.
3. I feel I have to be best in everything.
4. I blush easily.
5. I like everyone I know. L
6. I notice my heart beats very fast sometimes.
7. At times I feel like shouting.
8. I wish I could be very far from here.
9. Others seem to do things easier than I can.
10. I would rather win than lose in a game. L (no)
11. I am secretly afraid of a lot of things.
12. I feel that others do not like the way I do things.
13. I feel alone even when there are people around me.
14. I have trouble making up my mind.
15. I get nervous when things do not go the right way for me.
16. I worry most of the time.
17. I am always kind. L
18. I worry about what my parents will say to me.
19. Often I have trouble getting my breath.
20. I get angry easily.
21. I always have good manners. L
22. My hands feel sweaty.

23. I have to go to the toilet more than most people.
24. Other children are happier than I.
25. I worry about what other people think about me.
26. I have trouble swallowing.
27. I have worried about things that did not really make any difference later.
28. My feelings get hurt easily.
29. I worry about doing the right things.
30. I am always good. L
31. I worry about what is going to happen.
32. It is hard for me to go to sleep at night.
33. I worry about how well I am doing in school.
34. I am always nice to everyone. L
35. My feelings get hurt easily when I am scolded.
36. I tell the truth every single time. L
37. I often get lonesome when I am with people.
38. I feel someone will tell me I do things the wrong way.
39. I am afraid of the dark.
40. It is hard for me to keep my mind on my school work.
41. I never get angry. L
42. Often I feel sick in my stomach.
43. I worry when I go to bed at night.
44. I often do things I wish I had never done.
45. I get headaches.
46. I often worry about what could happen to my parents.
47. I never say things I shouldn't. L
48. I get tired easily.
49. It is good to get high grades in school. L (no)
50. I have bad dreams.
51. I am nervous.
52. I never lie. L
53. I often worry about something bad happening to me.

CHILDREN'S MANIFEST ANXIETY SCALE (CMAS)— PARENT FORM

Parent's Name_____ Mother_____ Father_____

Child's Name _____

Following are some statements telling how children sometimes feel. Read each statement carefully. Put a circle around the word Yes if you think it is true about your child. Put a circle around the word No if you think it is not true about your child. Be sure to answer *every* statement.

1. It is hard for my child to keep his mind on anything.
2. My child gets nervous when someone watches his work.
3. My child feels he has to be best in everything.
4. My child blushes easily.
5. My child likes everyone he knows.
6. My child notices his heart beats very fast sometimes.
7. At times my child feels like shouting.
8. My child wishes he could be very far from here.
9. Others seem to do things easier than

my child can.

10. My child would rather win than lose in a game.
11. My child is secretly afraid of a lot of things.
12. My child feels that others do not like the way he does things.
13. My child feels alone even when there are people around him.
14. My child has trouble making up his mind.
15. My child gets nervous when things do not go the right way for him.
16. My child worries most of the time.
17. My child is always kind.
18. My child worries about what his parents will say to him.
19. Often my child has trouble getting his breath.
20. My child gets angry easily.
21. My child always has good manners.
22. My child's hands feel sweaty.
23. My child has to go to the toilet more than most people.
24. Other children are happier than my child.
25. My child worries about what other people think about him.
26. My child has trouble swallowing.
27. My child has worried about things that did not really make any difference later.
28. My child's feelings get hurt easily.
29. My child worries about doing the right things.
30. My child is always good.
31. My child worries about what is going to happen.
32. It is hard for my child to go to sleep at night.
33. My child worries about how well he is doing in school.
34. My child is always nice to everyone.
35. My child's feelings get hurt easily when he is scolded.
30. My child tells the truth every single time.
37. My child often gets lonesome when he is with people.
38. My child feels someone will tell him he does things the wrong way.
39. My child is afraid of the dark.
40. It is hard for my child to keep his mind on his school work.
41. My child never gets angry.
42. Often my child feels sick to his stomach.
43. My child worries when he goes to bed at night.
44. My child often does things he wishes he had never done.
45. My child gets headaches.
46. My child often worries about what could happen to his parents.
47. My child never says things he shouldn't.
48. My child gets tired easily.
49. It is good for a child to get high grades in school.
50. My child has bad dreams.
51. My child is nervous.
52. My child never lies.
53. My child often worries about something bad happening to him.

GENERAL ANXIETY SCALE
FOR CHILDREN (GASC)

Name_____ Age_____ Boy_____ Girl_____

School_____ Grade_____

Following are some questions which are different from the usual school questions because there are no right or wrong answers. You are to read each question and then put a circle around either "Yes" or "No." These questions are about how you think and feel and, therefore, they have no right or wrong answers. People think and feel differently. One person might put a circle around "Yes" and you may put a circle around "No." For example, if you were asked this question: "Do you like to play ball?" Some persons would put a circle around "Yes" and some would put it around "No." Your answers depend on how you think and feel. These questions are about how you think and feel about school and a lot of other things. Remember, read each question carefully and then answer it "Yes" or "No" by deciding how you think and feel. If you don't understand a question, ask about it.

1. When you are away from home, do you worry about what might be happening at home?
2. Do you sometimes worry about whether your body is growing the way it should?
3. Are you afraid of mice or rats?
4. Do you ever worry about knowing your lessons?
5. If you were to climb a ladder, would you worry about falling off it?
6. Do you worry about whether your mother is going to get sick?
7. Do you get scared when you have to walk home alone at night?
8. Do you ever worry about what other people think of you?
9. Do you get a funny feeling when you see blood?
10. When your father is away from home, do you worry about whether he is going to come back?
11. Are you frightened by lightning and thunderstorms?
12. Do you ever worry that you won't be able to do something you want to do?
13. When you go to the dentist, do you worry that he may hurt you?
14. Are you afraid of things like snakes?
15. When you are in bed at night trying to go to sleep, do you often find that you are worrying about something?
16. When you were younger, were you ever scared of anything?
17. Are you sometimes frightened when looking down from a high place?
18. Do you get worried when you have to go to the Doctor's office?
19. Do some of the stories on radio or television scare you?
20. Have you ever been afraid of getting hurt?
21. When you are home alone and someone knocks on the door, do you get a worried feeling?
22. Do you get a scary feeling when you see a dead animal?
23. Do you think you worry more than other boys or girls?
24. Do you worry that you might get

hurt in some accident?

25. Has anyone ever been able to scare you?
26. Are you afraid of things like guns?
27. Without knowing why, do you sometimes get a funny feeling in your stomach?
28. Are you afraid of being bitten or hurt by a dog?
29. Do you ever worry about something bad happening to someone you know?
30. Do you worry when you are home alone at night?
31. Are you afraid of being too near fireworks because of their exploding?
32. Do you worry that you are going to get sick?
33. Are you ever unhappy?
34. When your mother is away from home, do you worry about whether she is going to come back?

35. Are you afraid to dive into the water because you might get hurt?
36. Do you get a funny feeling when you touch something that has a real sharp edge?
37. Do you ever worry about what is going to happen?
38. Do you get scared when you have to go into a dark room?
39. Do you dislike getting in fights because you worry about getting hurt in them?
40. Do you worry about whether your father is going to get sick?
41. Have you ever had a scary dream?
42. Are you afraid of spiders?
43. Do you sometimes get the feeling that something bad is going to happen to you?
44. When you are alone in a room and you hear a strange noise, do you get a frightened feeling?
45. Do you ever worry?

GENERAL ANXIETY SCALE FOR CHILDREN (GASC) — PARENT FORM

Parent's Name _____

Child's Name _____

Following are some questions about your child which differ from the usual questions because there are no right or wrong answers. You are to read each question carefully and then put a circle around either "Yes" or "No." These questions are about how your child thinks and feels and, therefore have *no* right or wrong answers. Put a circle around the word "Yes" if you think it is true about your child. Put a circle around "No" if you think it is not true about your child. Be sure and answer *every* question.

1. When your child is away from home, does he worry about what might be happening at home?
2. Does your child sometimes worry about whether his body is growing

the way it should?
3. Is your child afraid of mice or rats?
4. Does your child ever worry about knowing his lessons?
5. If your child were to climb a ladder,

would he worry about falling off it?

6. Does your child worry about whether his mother is going to get sick?

7. Does your child get scared when he has to walk home alone at night?

8. Does your child ever worry about what other people think of him?

9. Does your child get a funny feeling when he sees blood?

10. When his father is away from home, does your child worry about whether the father is going to come back?

11. Is your child frightened by lightning and thunderstorms?

12. Does your child ever worry that he won't be able to do something he wants to do?

13. When your child goes to the dentist, does he worry that the dentist may hurt him?

14. Is your child afraid of things like snakes?

15. When your child is in bed at night trying to go to sleep, does he often find that he is worrying about something?

16. When your child was younger, was he ever scared of anything?

17. Is your child sometimes frightened when looking down from a high place?

18. Does your child get worried when he has to go to the Doctor's office?

19. Do some of the stories on radio or television scare your child?

20. Has your child ever been afraid of getting hurt?

21. When your child is home alone and someone knocks on the door, does he get a worried feeling?

22. Does your child get a scary feeling when he sees a dead animal?

23. Does your child think he worries more than other boys and girls?

24. Does your child worry that he might get hurt in some accident?

25. Has anyone ever been able to scare your child?

26. Is your child afraid of things like guns?

27. Without knowing why, does your child sometimes get a funny feeling in his stomach?

28. Is your child afraid of being bitten or hurt by a dog?

29. Does your child ever worry about something bad happening to someone he knows?

30. Does your child worry when he is home alone at night?

31. Is your child afraid of being too near fireworks because of their exploding?

32. Does your child worry that he is going to get sick?

33. Is your child ever unhappy?

34. When his mother is away from home, does your child worry about whether she is going to come back?

35. Is your child afraid to dive into the water because he might get hurt?

36. Does your child get a funny feeling when he touches something that has a real sharp edge?

37. Does your child ever worry about what is going to happen?

38. Does your child get scared when he has to go into a dark room?

39. Does your child dislike getting in fights because he worries about getting hurt in them?

40. Does your child worry about whether his father is going to get sick?

41. Has your child ever had a scary dream?

42. Is your child afraid of spiders?

43. Does your child sometimes get the feeling that something bad is going to happen to him?

44. When your child is alone in a room and hears a strange noise, does he get a frightened feeling?

45. Does your child ever worry?

Teacher Rating of Child Adjustment

School _____ Name _____ Grade _____

Instructions: On the line at the left of each item, write the number of the word or phrase that corresponds to your rating of the child.

_____ 1. IN MY OPINION, THIS CHILD'S GENERAL ADJUSTMENT IS

Poor	Fair	Average	Good	Excellent
1	2	3	4	5

_____ 2. HOW REALISTIC IS HE?

Knows his own faults and good points	Fairly realistic about himself	Somewhat realistic	Doesn't seem to know the score about himself	Completely unaware of what he is like
5	4	3	2	1

_____ 3. HOW WELL DOES HE PERSIST AT A TASK?

Gives up very easily	Gives up when he has a little trouble	Takes quite a bit to make him give up	Sticks to a job when it is very troublesome	Won't give up in spite of everything
1	2	4	5	3

_____ 4. HOW WELL DOES HE TAKE RESPONSIBILITY FOR WHAT HE DOES?

Takes responsibility for what he does	Seldom makes excuses	Sometimes alibis	Tries to pass the buck	Definitely blames others when he is in the wrong
5	4	3	2	1

_____ 5. HOW ATTENTIVE IS HE IN SCHOOL?

Inattentive most of the time	Tends to be inattentive	Moderately attentive	Usually attentive	Very attentive
1	2	3	4	5

6. HOW DEPENDENT IS HE?

Tackles problems very much on his own	Independent	Uses own skill first, then seeks help	Dependent	Seeks help at slightest difficulty
5	3	4	2	1

7. HOW FLEXIBLE IS THIS CHILD?

Very easily led or influenced	Tends to "drift" with the tide	Takes sensible suggestions, rejects others	Slow to adapt to new ideas	Rigid inflexible
1	4	5	2	3

8. HOW MUCH AT EASE IS HE?

Passive	Relaxed	Settles down after excitement	Nervous	Tense
2	5	4	1	3

9. HOW WELL CAN HE TAKE IT?

Tough, nothing offends him	Insensitive, hard to hurt	Has feelings, but controls them	Soft, sometimes can't take it	Touchy, very easily hurt
4	2	5	3	1

10. HOW COMPLIANT IS HE?

Does opposite of what he is told	Often contrary, resistive	Agrees to sensible requests	Goes out of his way to please	Too anxious to please; apple-polishes
2	1	5	4	3

54 *Modifiability of an Impulsive Tempo*[1]

JEROME KAGAN

LESLIE PEARSON

LOIS WELCH

Impulsive first-grade children are trained to be reflective under two tutoring conditions: (1) the trainer informs the child and (2) the trainer does not inform the child that they share some interests and attributes. Both groups show longer response latencies after training. However, the hypothesis concerning the facilitating effect of perceived similarity does not receive convincing support. Also, the training does not have a strong effect on error scores and does not generalize to the inductive reasoning test. How would you set up an experiment to teach children to be less impulsive?

An extended series of investigations on a conceptual tempo dimension called reflection-impulsivity has demonstrated impressive stability over both time and tasks, and meaningful predictions to a variety of problem-solving tasks (Kagan, 1965a, 1965b, Kagan, Rosman, Day, Albert, and Phillips 1964). Impulsive children, in contrast to reflective children of similar age and verbal skills, make more errors in reading prose when in the primary grades, are more likely to offer incorrect solutions on inductive reasoning problems and visual discrimination tasks, and make more errors of commission on serial recall tasks. Impulsive children do not seem to care about making mistakes for they offer answers quickly and without sufficient consideration for the probable accuracy of their solution. This disposition is often a handicap in the typical school situation, for most teachers do not have a high tolerance for incorrect replies, and the peer group is prone to jeer at the child who impulsively blurts out obviously incorrect answers.

Although existing evidence suggests that an impulsive attitude begins its

[1]This research was supported in part by research grant MH–8792 from the National Institute of Mental Health, United States Public Health Service.

Reprinted from the *Journal of Educational Psychology*, 1966, **57**, 359–365, by permission of the senior author and the American Psychological Association.

growth during the preschool years and may be a deeply entrenched habit (Kagan, Rosman, Day, Albert, and Phillips, 1964), it is worthwhile, nevertheless, to inquire into the modifiability of an impulsive tendency. This report summarizes one attempt to train impulsive children to be more reflective.

There are at least four major motives that mediate behavior change: (a) the desire for an external reinforcement, such as praise, love, money, toys, candy, etc., (b) the desire to avoid an unpleasant experience, (c) the desire to be correct and/or to be competent at a task, and (d) the desire to maximize similarity to a model.

The most popular incentives used by teachers, parents, employers, and psychologists to effect a change in response hierarchies capitalize on the first two motives, the child's desire for a positive social response and his desire to avoid a punishment. Some students of the tutorial process insist that the mere attainment of a correct answer is sufficient reward, and they remove all human agents from the learning situation.

The incentive least likely to be exploited is subject to controversy; namely, the child's desire to maximize similarity to a desirable adult. It is acknowledged that children spontaneously imitate and adopt selected responses displayed by particular adults. There is disagreement, however, as to the reasons for this imitation. It has been argued (Kagan, 1958) that the child wishes to maximize similarity to a desirable adult in order to share vicariously in his resources. This process eventually leads to an identification with the model. The motive to maxi-

mize similarity to a model appears to be of major importance in the establishment of unusually strong motivations for a career, especially intellectual careers. It was decided, therefore, to compare the differential effectiveness of training in reflection under two conditions, a normally nurturant condition between child and tutor, and one in which the child was persuaded to believe that he shared some attributes with the tutor and by becoming reflective he could increase the pool of shared characteristics. It was assumed that the initial belief in similarity to the tutor would act as an incentive to motivate the child to add to the number of shared similarities. If a child believed that the tutor valued reflection he should be more highly motivated to adopt this attitude than the child who perceived no initial similarities to the trainer.

This investigation asked two questions: Can an impulsive attitude be modified through direct training in reflection? Is there any training advantage when the child initially perceives some basis of similarity to the trainer?

METHOD

Procedure

SUBJECTS A group of 155 first-grade children was administered the Matching Familiar Figures (MFF) and two verbal scales from the Wechsler Intelligence Scale for Children, along with inductive reasoning tests, in the fall of the first grade. The MFF is a visual discrimination task in which pictures of familiar objects are presented along with six similar variants. The child must select the one variant that is identical with the standard. The child's response latency to the first solution hypothesis and errors are the major variables studied. Figure 1 illustrates a sample item from the test.

The subjects (Ss) were classified as impulsive or reflective on the basis of their performance on the 12 MFF test items. Impulsive children were above the median on total errors and below the median on average response latency (for all 12 items) for their sex (that is, they responded quickly and made many errors). Reflective children were below the median on errors and above the median on response latency. The impulsive Ss were assigned to one of three groups: trained under conditions of perceived similarity to the trainer (Group I-Id); trained under low perceived similarity to the trainer (Group I-non Id); and no training group (Group I-C). The assignment of children to the three groups was such that the profile of verbal ability was close to identical across the groups. There were 10 boys and 10 girls in each of the three groups of impulsive children. In addition, 20 reflective children (10 boys and 10 girls) were selected from the total pool of 75 reflective children. These Ss were not given any training and were treated as Group I-C.

Training

Each of the 40 children in the two training groups was seen by an adult the same sex as the child[2] and each trainer worked with children in both Groups I-Id and I-non Id. Each child was seen for three sessions, each session lasting about 40–50 minutes. The sessions were separated by 2 or 3 days.

---

[2]The trainers were Leslie Pearson, Lois Welch, David Cohen, and Robert Stewart.

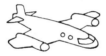

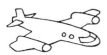  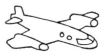

  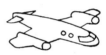

Fig. 1. Illustrative item from the MFF test administered after training.

TRAINING SESSION 1: GROUP I-ID During the first part of the session the experimenter (E) began to persuade the child that E and S shared interests and attributes. This was accomplished by having E ask S a set of standard questions. After the child had answered E would answer in a similar way and comment on the similarity between adult and child. A sample of dialogue in Session 1 follows.

How many brothers and sisters do you have? [After the child answers, E answers in a way consonant with the child and adds:]

Gee, we are the same, we both have a (brother, sister). Let's see if we are the same in other ways. What are your favorite foods to eat? [After S answers, E responds in a consonant manner for one of the items and adds:]

Oh, we're the same on foods, too. What's your favorite game? [After S's answer, E answers in a consonant manner and remarks on the similarity and then asks:]

What other games do you like to play? [E notes one consonance after these answers].

Let's see how else we might be the same. What's your favorite animal? [After S answers, E answers consonantly, then brings out a leaflet of animal pictures with three pictures to a page].

Let's look at some animal pictures that I have here and we will pick our favorites. [E then shows S three pictures, of a sea otter, squirrel, and giraffe. After the child picks a favorite animal E picks the same one and remarks on the similarity].

Following the first phase of similarity training, which took about 20–30 minutes, the specific training in reflection was initiated. The E first commented that he was reflective and valued reflection on tasks. His actual comments were:

We're so much the same on so many things that I'm going to tell you something about myself. Maybe we can be the same on that, too. I think it's important not to make mistakes and to be right. So I take my time and always check my answers. One of the things we're going to do together is some other kinds of games a little bit like what you did just before vacation. The important thing in these games is to try not to make a mistake. I want you to get them right every time on your first try and one way to get them right is to think about your answer. [The E then demonstrated how he behaved reflectively on tasks with response uncertainty. The training then began].

The training tasks were the same in all three sessions and included parallel items. The three training tasks were a haptic-visual matching task, a design-matching task, and an inductive reasoning test.

In the design-matching task the child was shown a geometric design and an array of similar variants and was asked to select the variant that was exactly like the standard. This task had the same requirements as MFF except that all of the stimuli were geometric designs and none was a familiar figure. The second task was an inductive reasoning task in which the child was told three characteristics of an object and had to guess what the object was (e.g., What is cold, white, and round?). The third task was a haptic-visual matching task in which the child haptically explored a letter of the alphabet that was made from discrete tacks placed in a board. The child had to select from a visual display of letters the letter that was represented by the tack display he had explored haptically. The visual array was exposed while the S was exploring the tacks. During the training session S was given six items from each of these three tasks.

The training procedure for delay was direct. The E told the child that he was not allowed to offer an answer for a fixed period of time (10 or 15 seconds). The E said that he would look at his watch and tell the child when he was allowed to answer. The E instructed the child to study the stimuli in the task and to think about his answer during the enforced period of delay. The 15-second delay was imposed for all items on the visual matching and haptic-visual tasks; a 10-second delay was imposed for the inductive reasoning items. The child was only allowed one response per item and was not told if that response was correct or incorrect. All of the children delayed their responses most of the time. On the few occasions when a child did not delay, the E accepted the response and proceeded to the next item.

TRAINING SESSION 1. GROUP I-NON ID The E administered the same pretraining interview as described for Group I-Id, with one difference. The E never indicated that he shared interests or attributes with the child. He merely commented positively on the child's choice. The specific training in reflection proceeded exactly as was described for Group I-Id.

TRAINING SESSION 2. The format for training sessions 2 and 3 was similar to the one described for Session 1. The Ss in groups I-Id and I-non Id were asked the same questions in the same order. However, the Ss in Group I-Id were reminded how similar E and S were; the children in Group I-non Id were not given this information. The E spent the opening part of the interview asking new questions about

S's interests and, according to a fixed schedule, either commented that S and E were similar in their answers to selected items (for Group I-Id) or merely noted the child's answer without indicating consensual agreement. The direct training for reflection followed and the tasks included six additional items from the visual matching, haptic-visual matching, and inductive reasoning tests. As in Session 1, E insisted that the child delay a fixed period of time before answering.

TRAINING SESSION 3. The final session devoted a shorter time to pretraining matters. The training tasks included a final set of six items from the three training tasks.

In sum, the training procedure emphasized inhibition of impulsive answers, but placed no emphasis on more efficient visual scanning techniques or more analytic reasoning. The children were trained only to delay their answers; they were not given better ways of solving the problem.

Evaluation of Training

Each S was seen for a final evaluation session between 6 and 8 weeks after the third training interview. The examiners were two new adult females[3] who were complete strangers to the children. Moreover, the examiners did not know whether the children were impulsive or reflective nor to which training group they belonged. Each S was given an entirely new version of MFF under standard instructions and an inductive reasoning test. The items in the inductive reasoning test illustrated three pictures that described the beginning of a story or sequence. The child was also shown four additional pic-

---

[3] Janet Levine and Marion Cleveland were the examiners for this evaluation phase.

Fig. 2.   Illustrative item from the Picture Completion Reasoning Test.

tures and was asked to select the one picture from the four alternatives that illustrated best "what happened next." Figure 2 illustrates a sample item from this test.

Data Analysis

Each S had been given different forms of the MFF and Picture Completion Reasoning Tests six months earlier, in the fall of the first grade. The major variables analyzed were: (*a*) the raw response time and error scores following training, and (*b*) change scores for response time and errors pre- and posttraining. The MFF variables included absolute and percent-change scores for response time and er-

rors (percent-change score was obtained by dividing the difference between the values on the first test session and the second test session by the first test session score). For the Picture Completion Reasoning Test the variables were mean number of errors made after training, response time to the incorrect choices, response time to all items, and the percent-change score for response time to the incorrect items.

RESULTS AND DISCUSSION

Table 1 contains the mean scores for each of the groups on the major variables. *The only important effect of training was to lengthen the response times to MFF.* The children in each training group showed longer response times to MFF than the impulsive controls ($p < .05$, two-tailed test for each group). Moreover, the trained group showed larger percent increases in response time, when the current response time measure was compared with the one obtained 6 months earlier ($p < .05$, t test for Group I-Id; $p < .10$ for Group I-non Id). It is of interest that the response times for the reflective children who were not seen between fall and spring were not significantly longer than those of the impulsive children who were trained in delay. The training produced response latencies that matched those of normal reflectives.

The variability of the MFF response time scores was much greater after training than it was in the fall, but this increase was due, in part, to the large increase in mean response times for Group I-Id and Group I-non Id. The coefficient of variation (100 SD/M) on the early fall test was 30; the average coefficient of variation after training was 63 for Group I-Id, 64 for Group I-non Id, and 53 for the control group (Group C).

Although both the absolute and relative variability of response times were greater in the spring, there was no marked difference in variability among the three groups of impulsive children.

Unfortunately, error scores were not much affected by the training. The results were in the anticipated direction, for both training groups made fewer errors than the nontrained controls, but the differences did not reach acceptable levels of significance. Percent-change in errors revealed that the

girls showed an average decrease in errors, whereas the boys' average change score was low, but positive. In sum, training had a marked effect on response delay, but a minimal effect on quality of performance. Since the primary focus of the training was on inhibition of a fast response rather than improved strategies of visual detection, it is reasonable that response latency should be affected more dramatically than recognition errors.

Effect of Training on Inductive Reasoning

The Ss were not given any training specific to the items in the Picture Completion Reasoning Test, but it was hoped that the training would affect performance on this task. As with MFF, the training produced increased response times to incorrect choices, but the differences were not statistically significant. Errors were not affected by the training.

Effect of Perceived Similarity to the Trainer

The differential effect of training under high or low perceived similarity was of borderline significance. It will be recalled that the children were trained by an adult the same sex as themselves, but it was only possible to use female adults as the assessors in the final evaluation. This condition of testing should lead, a priori, to an attenuation of the effect among boys and a maximization of the effect for girls, since the girls were trained and tested by an adult of the same sex. The results are congruent wih this expectation, for the effects of high or low perceived similarity during training were more dramatic for girls than for boys

TABLE 1.—Mean Scores on MFF and Picture Completion Reasoning Tests

VARIABLES	GROUP I-Id		GROUP I-NON Id		GROUP I-C		GROUP-REFLECTIVE	
	Boy	Girl	Boy	Girl	Boy	Girl	Boy	Girl
MFF								
Response time								
M	15.2	32.7	13.2	21.6	7.2	14.0	13.8	28.8
SD	7.8	21.2	8.8	13.8	3.4	8.0	7.3	16.4
Errors								
M	28.0	16.6	25.1	18.3	27.6	23.9	22.6	17.8
SD	7.6	4.7	7.1	5.5	7.6	8.8	5.4	5.6
% increase response time	133.4	460.0	127.1	236.6	36.2	137.3	19.3	65.1
% increase errors	5.7	−25.8	4.0	−19.3	22.0	−4.5	165.7	102.1
Picture completion								
Errors								
M	8.0	4.8	7.4	5.5	8.4	5.3	5.0	4.0
SD	2.8	2.8	3.5	2.9	2.5	2.8	2.6	3.4
Response time to incorrect								
M	11.7	17.9	15.1	18.9	12.2	16.5	15.8	16.3
SD	4.6	8.5	5.9	6.6	4.8	5.0	5.7	12.4
Response time, all items								
M	10.9	14.9	13.5	16.0	11.8	15.0	12.8	15.5
SD	3.4	3.6	3.7	4.0	4.6	4.0	4.7	3.8
% increase in response time to incorrect	37.4	70.7	70.3	110.2	0.1	86.2	27.3	−2.8

on both tests. The mean percent increase in response time on MFF was 460% for Group I-Id girls, in contrast to 237% for Group I-non Id girls. Although these means were not significantly different, the girls at either extreme supported the major hypothesis. Of the total of 20 impulsive girls in Groups I-Id and I-non Id, 4 of the 5 who manifested the greatest increase in response time after training were in Group I-Id; whereas 4 of the 5 who decreased the most in response time were in Group I-non Id. This 4–1–1–4 distribution yielded a one-tailed p value of .103 by the Exact Test. The magnitudes of response time increases shown by these four girls in Group I-Id also furnish some support for the hypothesis. The actual change scores in Group I-Id were as follows: from 4 to 80 seconds, from 5 to 58 seconds, from 6 to 31 seconds, and from 6 to 29 seconds.

In sum, the brief training (about 60 minutes total) in delay produced larger response latencies among impulsive children. Unfortunately, the training did not have a strong effect on error scores and did not generalize to the inductive reasoning test. Since the adult who administered the posttraining MFF was not the trainer, the results cannot be attributed to a desire to please the trainer. The tendency to delay did generalize to another adult. The study demonstrates that impulsive children can be taught to modify their behavior and the effect can last a few weeks. The hypothesis concerning the facilitating effect of perceived similarity did not receive convincing support. The effect was manifest for only a few of the girls. However, the authors believe that these minimal trends warrant continued study of the psychological significance of perceived similarity between tutor and tutee.

PART FIVE

Understanding and Helping the Child

Individual Approaches

16

55 *An Infant's Phobia Treated with Reciprocal Inhibition Therapy*[1]

PETER M. BENTLER

A year-old child's aversion to water and bathing is treated by toys and contacts with the mother, aimed to elicit pleasurable responses incompatible with anxiety. After a month of treatment and a follow-up of six months, the girl shows no averse reactions to water.

Phobias which are complex to unravel often have simple beginnings as conditioned emotional reactions. This paper reports a successful attempt to apply reciprocal inhibition psychotherapy to a female infant child whose primary phobia consisted of a fear of water.

[1]This investigation was supported in part by a Public Health Service fellowship number MPM–15,840 from the National Institute of Mental Health, U.S. Public Health Service. I am indebted to Martha F. Newman and Professors Albert Bandura and Ernest R. Hilgard for their advice in relation to a critical reading of the manuscript.

According to some recent interpretations of the origins of phobias, a traumatic fear-producing event occurring temporally and spatially with neutral stimuli may suffice to initiate phobic reactions to these stimuli. In this view, a phobia is a learned response, following the same laws of learning and unlearning as other responses (Wolpe, 1958). This etiological explanation is used for adults, and applies to children as well (Rachman and Costello, 1961).

Psychotherapy aimed at treating phobias should, therefore, be consistent with principles of learning theory

Reprinted from the *Journal of Child Psychology and Psychiatry*, 1962, **3**, 185–189, by permission of the author and Pergamon Press Ltd.

relevant to the unlearning of responses. The theory upon which reciprocal inhibition therapy is based states that conditioned fear or anxiety is the central constituent of neurotic behaviour, such as is evident in phobic reactions. Since conditioned fear is the product of learning, removing the fear through extinction or counter-conditioning procedures consistent with learning theory should remove the phobia (Wolpe, 1961). The fear is removed on the principle that a response inhibitory to anxiety or fear occurring in the presence of anxiety-provoking stimuli weakens the bond between the stimuli and the anxiety response.

A variety of procedures have been developed for treating phobias with reciprocal inhibition therapy. The most extensive application of reciprocal inhibition has been to adult neuroses, where hypnotically induced relaxation is usually used to counteract the anxiety created by having the patient imagine phobic objects. Treating children's phobias has not been as popular, though the earliest work had been with children. M. C. Jones (1924), in her classic study directly foreshadowing current emphasis in this area, successfully treated a 34-months-old boy for fear of a white rat, rabbit, and other furry objects by presenting food and the fear-object simultaneously. Jones also mentioned other techniques which appear to be practicable with children and at the same time to be in accord with current learning theory—social imitation and systematic distraction. Lazarus (1960) has reported cases of children treated with systematic desensitization based on relaxation, deconditioning aided by the use of drug-induced sedation, and

deconditioning obtained by conditioned avoidance responses. Rachman and Costello (1961) point out that assertive responses and pleasant responses in the life situation can also serve, among others, to aid treatment of children's phobias.

Many of these techniques are not feasible with very young children or infants. It is difficult to arrange therapy in such a way that social imitation of approach responses occurs when desired. While distraction aimed at offering the infant a substitute activity will lead to non-practice of the phobic reaction, the necessary reciprocal inhibition of anxiety may not occur. Getting a small child to cooperate sufficiently for the use of relaxation with imagined phobic scenes also presents a problem. Conditioned avoidance responses in conjunction with deconditioning present a situation potentially useful with infants, but this procedure generally requires a stationary, non-active, and cooperating child. Such a child may be difficult to obtain.

The use of drugs for the purpose of relaxation along with the gradual introduction of fear-producing stimuli, as described by Lazarus, should be possible with infants. This method presents an advantage over treatment of adult patients with imagined scenes in that the real objects of fear can be presented instead of such imagined scenes. The feeding situation represents a more easily manipulable situation. Fear-object and food can be presented simultaneously, with the food serving to inhibit anxiety created by the phobic object. The recent work of Harlow (Harlow and Zimmerman, 1959) demonstrating the importance of a soft and cuddly terry-cloth monkey mother in allaying infant monkeys' fear, such as that produced by a strange environment, would lead one to expect that body-contact with a warm mother can serve to inhibit phobic reactions in human infants. In addition to any innate reciprocally-inhibiting effects stemming from body-contact, the association of mother and child in the feeding situation should result in learned fear inhibition with contact, if the mother-child relationship has been normal. These secondary rewarding and fear-reducing responses should, with time, become associated not only with the contact, but also with the sight and sound of the mother. Another method of inducing reciprocal inhibition in infants would be the simultaneous presentation of attractive toys and the phobic object, since these toys could evoke positive affective responses which may be inhibitory to anxiety.

In the case reported in this paper, distraction, affective responses towards attractive toys, and body-contact with the mother as well as other mother-related stimuli, were used to elicit responses incompatible with anxiety. This year-old infant represents the youngest reported case treated with the method of reciprocal inhibition.

CASE HISTORY

Description

At approximately 11½ months of age Margaret gleefully waded in a small swimming pool, bathed with evident delight, and never objected to being washed when her diaper was changed. At this time she was placed with a baby-sitter for daily care while her mother went to work for several days. At the end of this time, Margaret's mother attempted to bathe her again in the bathroom. During the first few moments of the bath, Margaret was happy. She tried to stand up in the bathtub, slipped, and began screaming. She refused further bathing with violent screams and had to be removed from the tub.

Testing during the next few days indicated Margaret reacted with violent emotion not only to the bathtub, the faucet, and water in the tub, but also to being washed in the handbasin, to faucets or water in any part of the house, and to the wading pool. It is clear that slipping in the tub plus other possible unknown prior circumstances (e.g. at the baby-sitter's) or concomitant events (e.g. soap in the face) caused a great change in Margaret's emotional responsiveness to a wide range of situations.

During the next week it became apparent that Margaret would continue this behaviour unless systematic steps were taken to overcome her fear. Being cleaned in the washbasin brought only further screams and Margaret refused to play with water.

Interpretation

Here were the beginning stages of a phobia. The initiating traumatic event was in view. Generalization had already occurred, since Margaret was now afraid of water, not only in the bathtub, but anywhere around the house, as described above. Defence mechanisms were still clearly limited to physical avoidance of the traumatic situation and its generalized stimuli. The problem appeared to be one of eliminating or extinguishing a conditioned fear or phobia, so the technique of reciprocal inhibition was applied.

Treatment

As mentioned above, distraction, affective responses toward toys, body-contact, and other mother-related stimuli were used to elicit responses incompatible with anxiety. Since the author was not an expert in reciprocal inhibition therapy, use of the feeding situation to inhibit fear was considered inadvisable, since inappropriate handling of the case could result in the transfer of the fear to feeding rather than transfer of pleasant emotional responses to the phobic object. No specific schedule was followed; the mother was instructed in the course of treatment, but could be lax about applying it. The basic rule was that Margaret should be exposed only to small amounts of anxiety.

Treatment consisted of four parts and lasted approximately a month. First, toys were placed in the empty bathtub and Margaret was given free access to the bathroom and the toys. She would enter the bathroom and remove a toy from the tub occasionally, but she did not stay near the tub and refused to play with the toys while leaning over the tub. She continued to scream if any washing was attempted, but became less emotional toward the tub. Free access of this type was allowed throughout the duration of treatment. Second, Margaret was twice placed on the kitchen tables surrounding the sink while the sink was filled with water and toys were floating in it. At first Margaret screamed when near the water. She started to play with the toys on the table, but these toys were gradually moved towards and into the water, so that she had to move towards it in order to play. She refused to enter the water. All toys were then placed on the other side of the basin, and onto a ledge above it so that Margaret would have to walk through the basin in order to reach them. After several vacillations, Margaret entered the water reluctantly. Some minor crying resulted from wetting her buttocks, but the kitchen sink helped desensitize Margaret to water. The third step consisted of washing Margaret, at diaper-changing time, in the bathroom sink. She was generally given a favourite toy to play with, but the mirror hanging over the sink proved more interesting, and initial crying soon turned to happy squeals. Margaret also started playing with the water, and during this time she again learned to play with the sprinkler in the yard. The fourth and final step was washing Margaret at diaper-change time in the tub, with water running. To this she objected at first, with screams, but parental hugging and firmness caused her to stop crying after two days.

Behavioural Changes
Resulting from Treatment

At age 12¾ months Margaret was thoroughly recovered and played normally though cautiously in the tub while taking baths. She had no more fear of faucets, tubs, or water anywhere around the house. Her behaviour had undergone extensive changes. At 13 months she was not only willing to take baths or to be washed, but she gleefully initiated approach responses to water. On warm days Margaret would rush madly towards the wading pool in the backyard, enter it, and splash about joyously while playing. A follow-up study conducted at age 18 months indicated that these changes were quite permanent. She gladly played in the bathtub and showed no aversive reactions to water anywhere in or near the house.

DISCUSSION

While treatment of Margaret's case appears to be successful, it is also evident that several procedures could have accelerated the treatment process. More careful sequencing of anxiety-related cues should have been advantageous. For example, a play session with toys floating in a small pail far removed from the bathroom might have been a good first step to be followed by playing with toys floating in larger quantities of water. The play scene could have gradually been

moved closer and closer to the bathroom until it was finally inside the tub itself. This routine should be executed regularly and not as laxly as the parents applied the methods in this case. Furthermore, the addition of attractive food would seem to be a most important therapeutic tool in reducing the anxiety and treating the phobia.

SUMMARY

A year-old female child acquired phobic reactions to water when slipping in a bathtub. She was treated with reciprocal inhibition psychotherapy. Attraction towards toys and body-contact with the mother were used to elicit responses which were presumed to be incompatible with anxiety. One and a half months after the traumatic incident the infant gleefully initiated approach responses toward the formerly phobic object. A follow-up study conducted at age 18 months indicated these changes were quite permanent.

56   *Effects of Adult Social Reinforcement on Child Behavior*[1]

FLORENCE R. HARRIS

MONTROSE M. WOLF

DONALD M. BAER

Adults can try to help many children by systematic adult social reinforcement. This article shows the effects of adult attention on several problem behaviors of normal preschool children: excessive crawling, crying, solitary play, passivity. The procedure is to withdraw or withhold attention for undesirable behavior and to give immediate attention for desirable behavior.

There is general agreement among educators that one of the primary functions of a nursery school is to foster in each child social behaviors that contribute toward more pleasant and productive living for all. However, there is no similar consensus as to precisely how this objective is to be attained. Many writers subscribe to practices based on a combination of psychoanalytic theory and client-centered therapy principles, usually referred to as a mental hygiene approach. Yet there are considerable variation and vagueness in procedures recommended, particularly those dealing with such problem behaviors as the child's hitting people, breaking valuable things, or withdrawing from both people and things. Read (1955), for example, recommends accepting the child's feelings, verbalizing them for him, and draining them off through vigorous activities. Landreth (1942) advises keeping adult contacts with the child at a minimum based on his needs, backing up verbal suggestions by an implicit assumption that the suggestion will be carried out and, when in doubt, doing nothing unless the child's physical safety is involved. In addition to some of the above pre-

[1]These studies were supported in part by research grants from the National Institute of Mental Health (MH–02208–07) and the University of Washington Graduate School Research Fund (11–1873). The authors are also indebted to Sidney W. Bijou for his general counsel and assistance.

cepts, Taylor (1954) counsels parents and teachers to support both desirable and undesirable behaviors and to give nonemotional punishment. According to Standing (1959), Montessori advocates that teachers pursue a process of nonintervention, following careful preparation of a specified environment aimed at "canalizing the energy" and developing "inner command." Nonintervention does not preclude the "minimum dose" of instruction and correction.

Using some combination of such guidance precepts, teachers have reported success in helping some nursery school children who showed problem behaviors; but sometimes adherence to the same teaching principles has not been helpful in modifying the behavior of concern. Indeed, it is usually not at all clear what conditions and principles may or may not have been operative. All of these precepts have in common the adult behaviors of approaching and attending to a child. Therefore, it seemed to the staff of the Laboratory Preschool at the University of Washington that a first step in developing possible explicit criteria for judging when and when not to attend was to study the precise effects that adult attention can have on some problem behaviors.

This paper presents an account of the procedures and results of five such studies. Two groups of normal nursery school children provided the subjects studied. One group enrolled twelve three-year-olds and the other, sixteen four-year-olds. The two teachers of the younger group and the three teachers of the older group conducted the studies as they carried out their regular teaching duties. The general methodology of these studies was developed in the course of dealing with a particularly pressing problem behavior shown by one child at the beginning of the school year. It is worth considering this case before describing the procedures which evolved from it.

The study dealt with a three-year-old girl who had regressed to an excessive amount of crawling (Harris, Johnston, Kelley, and Wolf, 1964). By "excessive" is meant that after three weeks of school she was spending most of her morning crawling or in a crouched position with her face hidden. The parents reported that for some months the behavior had been occurring whenever they took her to visit or when friends came to their home. The teachers had used the conventional techniques, as outlined above, for building the child's "security."

Observations recorded in the third week at school showed, however, that more than 80% of the child's time was spent in off-feet positions. The records also showed that the crawling behavior frequently drew the attention of teachers. On-feet behaviors, such as standing and walking, which occurred infrequently, seldom drew such notice.

A program was instituted in which the teachers no longer attended to the child whenever she was crawling or crouching, but gave her continuous warm attention as long as she was engaging in behavior in which she was standing, running, or walking. Initially the only upright behaviors that the teachers were able to attend to occurred when the child pulled herself almost to her feet in order to hang up or take down her coat from her locker, and when she pulled herself up to wash her hands in the wash basin. Within a week of the initiation of the new attention-giving procedure, the child acquired a close-to-normal pattern of on-feet behavior.

In order to see whether the change from off- to on-feet behavior was related to the differential attention given by the teachers, they reversed their procedure, making attention once again contingent only upon crawling and other off-feet behavior. They waited for occasions of such off-feet behavior to "reinforce" with attention, while not attending to any on-feet behavior. By the second day the child had reverted to her old pattern of play and locomotion. The observational records showed the child was off her feet 80% of the class session.

To see whether on-feet behavior could be re-established, the teachers again reversed their procedure, giving attention to the child only when she was engaging in behaviors involving upright positions. On-feet behavior rose markedly during the first session. By the fourth day, the child again spent about 62% of the time on her feet.

Once the child was not spending the greater portion of her day crawling about, she quickly became a well-integrated member of the group. Evidently she already had well-developed social play skills.

As a result of this demonstration that either walking or crawling could be maintained and that the child's responses depended largely upon the teachers' attending behaviors, the teachers began a series of further experimental analyses of the relationship

between teacher attention and nursery school child behavior.

PROCEDURES

A specified set of procedures common to the next studies was followed. First, a child showing problem behavior was selected and records were secured. An observer recorded all of the child's behavior, the environmental conditions under which it occurred, and its immediate consequences under conventional teacher guidance. This was done throughout the 2½-hour school session, daily, and for several days. The records gave detailed pictures of the behavior under study. In each case, it became apparent that the problem behavior almost always succeeded in attracting adult attention.

As soon as these records, technically termed "baseline" records, of the typical behavior of the child and teachers were obtained, teachers instituted a program of systematically giving differential attention to the child. When the undesired behavior occurred, they did not in any way attend to him, but remained absorbed in one of the many necessary activities of teachers with other children or with equipment. If the behavior occurred while a teacher was attending to the child, she at once turned to another child or task in a matter-of-fact and nonrejecting manner. Concurrently, teachers gave immediate attention to other behaviors of the child which were considered to be more desirable than the problem behavior. The net effect of these procedures was that the child could gain a great deal of adult attention if he refrained from engaging in "problem behavior." If under this regime of differential attention the problem behavior diminished to a stable low level at which it was no longer considered a problem, a second procedure was inaugurated to check out the functional relationship between changes in the child's behavior and the guidance procedures followed.

The second procedure was simply to reverse the first procedure. That is, when the problem behavior occurred, the teacher went immediately to the child and gave him her full, solicitous attention. If the behavior stopped, she turned to other children and tasks, remaining thus occupied until the behavior recurred. In effect, one sure way for the child to secure adult attention was to exhibit the problem behavior. This procedure was used to secure reasonably reliable information on whether the teachers' special program had indeed brought about the changes noted in the child's behavior. If adult attention was the critical factor in maintaining the behavior, the problem behavior should recur in stable form under these conditions. If it did so, this was evidence that adult attention was, technically speaking, a positive social reinforcer for the child's behavior.

The final stage of the study was, of course, to return to procedures in which attention was given at once and continuously for behaviors considered desirable. Concurrently, adult attention was again withheld or withdrawn as an immediate consequence of the problem behavior. As the problem disappeared and appropriate behaviors increased, the intense program of differential adult attention was gradually diminished until the child was receiving attention at times and in amounts normal for the teachers in the group. However, attention was given only on occasions of desirable behavior, and never (or very seldom) for the undesirable behavior.

CRYING AND WHINING

Following the above procedures, a study was conducted on a four-year-old boy who cried a great deal after mild frustrations (Hart, Allen, Buell, Harris, and Wolf, 1964). This child averaged about eight full-fledged crying episodes each school morning. The baseline observations showed that this crying behavior consistently brought attention from the teachers, in the form of going to him and showing solicitous concern. During the following days, this behavior was simply ignored. (The only exceptions to this were to have been incidents in which the child had hurt himself considerably and was judged to have genuine grounds for crying. Naturally, his hurts were to be attended to. Such incidents, however, did not occur.) Ten days of ignoring the outcries, but giving approving attention for verbal and self-help behaviors, produced a steady weakening of the crying response to a nearly zero level. In the final five days of the interval, only one crying response was recorded. The number of crying episodes on successive days is graphed in cumulative form in Figure 1.

During the next ten days, crying was again reinforced whenever it occurred, the teachers attending to the boy on these occasions without fail. At first, it was necessary to give attention for mere grimaces that might follow a bump. The daily crying episodes

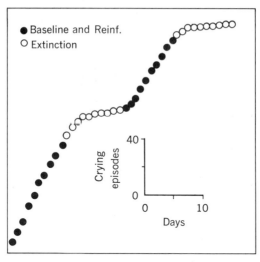

Fig. 1. Cumulative record of the daily number of crying episodes.

quickly rose to a rate almost as high as formerly. A second ten-day period of ignoring the outcries again produced a quick weakening of the response to a near-zero level, as is apparent in the figure. Crying remained at this low level thereafter, according to the informal judgment of the teachers.

The same procedures were used in another study of "operant crying" of a four-year-old boy, with the same general results.

ISOLATE PLAY

Two studies involved children who exhibited markedly solitary play behavior. Extremely little of their morning at nursery school was spent in any interaction with other children. Instead, these children typically played alone in a quiet area of the school room or the play yard, or interacted only with the teachers. For present purposes, both of these response patterns will be called "isolate play." Systematic observation showed that isolate play usually attracted or maintained the attention of a teacher, whereas social play with other children did so comparatively seldom.

A plan was initiated in which the teacher was to attend regularly if the child approached other children and interacted with them. On the other hand, the teacher was not to attend to the child so long as he engaged in solitary play. To begin with, attention was given when the child merely stood nearby, watching other children; then, when he played beside another child; and finally, only when he interacted with the other child. Teachers had to take special precautions that their attending behaviors did not result in drawing the child away from children and into interaction solely with the teacher. Two techniques were found particularly effective. The teacher directed her looks and comments to the other child or children, including the subject only as a participant in the play project. For example; "That's a big building you three boys are making; Bill and Tom and Jim (subject) are all working hard." Accessory materials were also kept at hand so that the teacher could bring a relevant item for the subject to add to the play: "Here's another plate for your tea party, Ann." In both isolate cases this new routine for giving adult attention produced the desired result: Isolate play declined markedly in strength while social play increased two- or threefold.

After about a week of the above procedure, the consequences of nonisolate and isolate play were reversed. The teachers no longer attended to the child's interactions with other children, but instead gave continuous attention to the child when he was alone. Within a week, or less, isolate play became the dominant form of activity in both cases.

The former contingencies were then reinstated: The teachers attended to social interactions by the child, and ignored isolate play as completely as they could. Again, isolate play declined sharply while social interaction increased as before. The results of one of these studies (Allen, Hart, Buell, Harris, and Wolf, 1964) are summarized in Figure 2.

Figure 2 shows the changes in behavior of a 4½-year-old girl under the different guidance conditions. The graph shows the percentage of play time that she spent in interaction with other children and the percentage of time spent with an adult. The remainder of her time was spent alone. It is apparent that only about 15% of this child's play time was spent in social play as long as the teachers attended

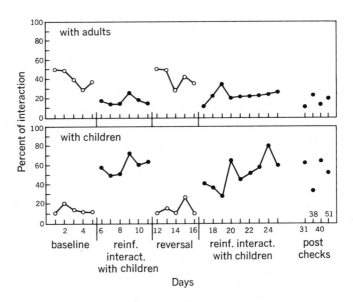

Fig. 2.   Daily percentages of time spent in social interaction with adults and with children during approximately two hours of each morning session.

primarily to her solitary play. But interacting behaviors rose to about 60% of total play time when the teachers attended only to her social play. At the same time, her interactions solely with teachers, not being reinforced, fell from their usual 40% of the child's playtime to about 20%. These were considered reasonable percentages for this nursery school child. During Days 17 through 25 the schedule of adult reinforcement of social play was gradually reduced to the usual amount of attention, given at the usual irregular intervals. Nevertheless, the social behavior maintained its strength, evidently becoming largely self-maintaining.

After Day 25, the teachers took care not to attend too often to the child when she was alone, but otherwise planned no special contingencies for attending. Four checks were made at later dates to see if the pattern of social behavior persisted. It is apparent (Figure 2, Post Checks) that the change was durable, at least until Day 51. Further checks were not possible because of the termination of the school year.

A parallel study, of a three-year-old isolate boy (Johnson, Kelley, Harris, Wolf, and Baer, unpub.) yielded similar results showing the same pattern of rapid behavioral change in response to changing contingencies for adult attention. In the case of this boy, post-checks were made on three days during the early months of the school following the summer vacation period. The data showed that on those days his interaction with children averaged 55% of his play time. Apparently his social play was well established. Teachers reported that throughout the remainder of the year he continued to develop ease and skills in playing with his peers.

The immediate shifts in these children's play behavior may be partly due to the fact that they had already developed skills readily adapted to play with peers at school. Similar studies in progress are showing that, for some children, development of social play behaviors may require much longer periods of reinforcement.

EXCESSIVE PASSIVITY

A fifth case (Johnston et al., 1966) involved a boy noted for his thoroughgoing lack of any sort of vigorous play activity. The teachers reported that this child consistently stood quietly about the play yard while other children ran, rode tricycles, and climbed on special climbing frames, trees, fences, and playhouses. Teachers also reported that they frequently attempted to encourage him, through suggestions or invitations, to engage in the more vigorous forms of play available. Teachers expressed concern over his apparent lack of strength and motor skills. It was decided to select a particular form of active play to attempt to strengthen. A wooden frame with ladders and platforms, called a climbing frame, was chosen as the vehicle for establishing this activity. The teachers attended at first to the child's mere proximity to the frame. As he came closer, they progressed to attending only to his touching it, climbing up a little, and finally to extensive climbing. Technically, this was reinforcement of successive approximations to climbing behavior. Figure 3 shows the results of nine days of this procedure, compared to a baseline of the preceding nine days. In this figure, black bars represent climbing on the climbing frame, and white bars represent climbing on any other equipment in the play yard. The height of the bars shows the percentage of the child's play time spent in such activities. It is clear that during the baseline period less than 10% of the child's time was spent in any sort of climbing activity, but that during the course of reinforcement with pleased adult attention for climbing on the frame, this behavior greatly increased, finally exceeding 50% of the child's morning. (Climbing on other objects was not scored during this period.) There then followed five days during which the teachers ignored any climbing on the frame, but attended to all other appropriate activities. The rate of climbing on the frame promptly fell virtually to zero, though the child climbed on other apparatus and was consistently given attention for this. Another five

days of reinforcement of use of the climbing frame immediately restored the climbing-frame behavior to a high stable level, always in excess of 40% of the boy's play time. After this, the teachers began an intermittent program of reinforcement for climbing on any other suitable objects, as well as vigorous active play of all sorts, in an effort to generalize the increased vigorous activity. Frame-climbing weakened considerably, being largely replaced by other climbing activities, which were now scored again as data. Activities such as tricycle-riding and running were not systematically recorded due to difficulties in reliably scoring them. It is clear from the data obtained, however, that climbing activities were thoroughly generalized by this final procedure. Checks made the following school year in another play yard indicated that vigorous climbing had become a stable part of his behavior repertoire.

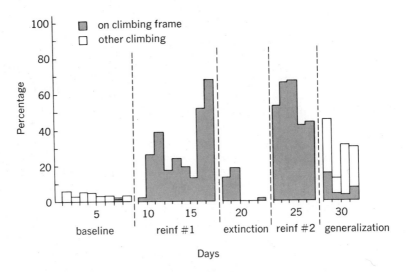

Fig. 3. Daily percentages of time spent in using a climbing-frame apparatus. Open bars indicate time spent in climbing on other equipment.

SUMMARY AND DISCUSSION

The above studies systematically examined effects of adult attention on some problem behaviors of normal preschool children. The findings in each case clearly indicated that for these children adult attention was a strong positive reinforcer. That is, the behavior which was immediately followed by a teacher's giving the child attention rose rapidly to a high rate, and the rate fell markedly when adult attention was withheld from that behavior and concurrently given to an incompatible behavior. While it seems reasonable that for most young children adult attention may be a positive reinforcer, it is also conceivable that for some children adult attention may be a negative reinforcer. That is, the rate of a behavior may decrease when it is immediately followed by the attention of an adult, and rise again as soon as the adult withdraws. Actually, for a few children observed at the preschool, it has been thought that adult attention was a negative reinforcer. This seemed to be true, for instance, in the case of the climbing-frame child. Before the study was initiated, the teachers spent several weeks attempting to make themselves positively reinforcing to the child. This they did by staying at a little distance from him and avoiding attending directly to him until he came to them for something. At first, his approaches were only for routine help, such as buttoning his coat. On each of these occasions they took care to be smilingly friendly and helpful. In time, he began making approaches of other kinds, for instance, to show a toy. Finally, when a teacher

approached him and commented with interest on what he was doing, he continued his play instead of stopping, hitting out, or running off. However, since his play remained lethargic and sedentary, it was decided that special measures were necessary to help him progress more rapidly. It was the use and effects of these special measures that constituted the study. Clearly, however, adult attention must be or become positively reinforcing to a child before it can be successfully used to help him achieve more desirably effective behaviors.

Studies such as those reported here seem to imply that teachers may help many children rapidly through systematic programming of their adult social reinforcements. However, further research in this area seems necessary. Some of our own studies now in progress suggest that guidance on the basis of reinforcement principles may perhaps bring rapidly into use only behaviors which are already available within the repertory of the child. If the desired behavior requires skills not yet in the child's repertory, then the process of developing those skills from such behaviors as the child has may require weeks or months. For example, a four-year-old child who could verbalize but who very rarely spoke was helped to speak freely within several days. On the other hand, a child of the same age who had never verbalized required a lengthy shaping process that involved reinforcing first any vocalization, and then gradually more appropriate sounds and combinations of sounds. The latter study was still incomplete at the close of a year of work. The time required to develop social behaviors in isolate children has likewise varied considerably, presumably for the same reasons.

Although the teachers conducted these studies in the course of carrying out their regular teaching duties, personnel in excess of the usual number were necessary. The laboratory school was staffed with one teacher to no more than six children, making it possible to assign to one teacher the role of principal "reinforcer teacher" in a study. This teacher was responsible for giving the child immediate attention whenever he behaved in specified ways. In addition, observers were hired and trained to record the behavior of each child studied. Each observer kept a record in ten-second intervals of his subject's behavior throughout each morning at school. Only with such staffing could reinforcement contingencies be precisely and consistently administered and their effects recorded.

Unless the effects are recorded, it is easy to make incorrect judgments about them. Two instances illustrate such fallibility. A boy in the laboratory preschool frequently pinched adults. Attempts by the teachers to ignore the behavior proved ineffective, since the pinches were hard enough to produce at least an involuntary startle. Teachers next decided to try to develop a substitute behavior. They selected patting as a logical substitute. Whenever the child reached toward a teacher, she attempted to forestall a pinch by saying, "Pat, Davey," sometimes adding, "Not pinch," and then strongly approving his patting, when it occurred. Patting behavior increased rapidly to a high level. The teachers agreed that they had indeed succeeded in reducing the pinching behavior

through substituting patting. Then they were shown the recorded data. It showed clearly that although patting behavior was indeed high, pinching behavior continued at the previous level. Apparently, the teachers were so focused on the rise in patting behavior that, without the objective data, they would have erroneously concluded that development of a substitute behavior was in this case a successful technique. A second example illustrates a different, but equally undesirable, kind of erroneous assumption. A preschool child who had to wear glasses (Wolf, Risley, and Mees, 1964) developed a pattern of throwing them two or three times per day. Since this proved expensive, it was decided that the attendants should put him in his room for ten minutes following each glasses-throw. When the attendants were asked a few days later how the procedure was working, they said that the glasses-throwing had not diminished at all. A check of the records, however, showed that there was actually a marked decrease. The throwing dropped to zero within five days. Presumably, the additional effort involved in carrying out the procedure had given the attendants an exaggerated impression of the rate of the behavior. Recorded data, therefore, seem essential to accurate objective assessments of what has occurred.

The findings in the studies presented here accord generally with results of laboratory research on social development reviewed in this journal by Horowitz (1963). The importance of social reinforcement was also noted by Bandura (1963) in his investigations of imitation. Gallwey (1964) has replicated the study of an isolate child discussed here, with results "clearly confirmatory of the effectiveness of the technique." Further studies in school situations that can combine the function of research with that of service seem highly desirable.

57 *Interpersonal Assessment of Play Therapy Outcome*[1]

JULIUS SEEMAN

EDYTH BARRY

CHARLOTTE ELLINWOOD

In this controlled study on psychotherapy with children, classmates and teachers perceive the children who receive individual play therapy as significantly less maladjusted after therapy.

Research in outcomes of psychotherapy has begun to gain a secure scientific footing. However, most of the research developments concern therapy with adults, and the province of therapy with children has seen much less research advance. This paper reports a study of therapy with children.

A study by Cox (1953) appears to be the first in which the concept of controls was fully realized. Cox chose two equivalent groups of children living within an institutional setting and provided play therapy for the children in one of the groups. Pretest-posttest comparisons on TAT and sociometric measures showed significant changes in favor of the experimental group.

Controlled studies by Bills (1950) and by Seeman and Edwards (1954) investigated the effect of play therapy upon reading performance. Both studies showed positive effects of therapy upon performance.

Dorfman (1958) studied personality outcomes of client-centered play therapy, using both the own control and matched control techniques. Her results indicated significant positive changes associated with therapy.

Three reviews have summarized research in play therapy (Dorfman,

[1]Appreciation is expressed to Lois DeLattre, Leonard Hersher, Sophie Fox Kirtner, and Leo Subotnik for their help in the study.

Thanks are due to the U. S. Public Health Service, Institute of Mental Health (projects M–593 and M–707), for grants in support of this study.

Reprinted from *Psychotherapy: Theory, Research, and Practice*, 1964, **1,** 64–66, by permission of the senior author and Dr. Eugene T. Gendlin, Editor.

1951; Lebo, 1953; and Levitt, 1957b, 1963). Levitt used Eysenck's method of deriving a base point of improvement without therapy and then comparing reported changes brought about by therapy. He found that the proportion of children reported as improved by therapy was no higher than the proportion reported as improved in the nontherapy groups. There are a number of weaknesses conceded in this method, most of which concern questions about comparability of the groups and adequacy of the criterion measures. The issue, however, is a basic research issue.

The history of therapy research reveals that most studies founder on the problem of adequate controls. The variables of self-initiated request for therapy, motivation for change, and personality organization have not often been adequately accounted for, and have risen to obscure the effect of the therapeutic process itself. The present study was designed to come to terms with these variables.

From the standpoint of criterion measures, the study chose to utilize interpersonal assessment of change. These criteria make sense on both practical and theoretical grounds. Interpersonal judgments have a demonstrated validity (Gronlund, 1959); they are readily interpretable; and they are in accord with predictions from the theory of therapeutic outcome.

METHOD

Selection of Samples

The locale of the study was a predominantly upper middle class school in a large city. The second and third grades, consisting of about 150 children, were given a modified version of the Tuddenham reputation test (Tuddenham, 1952), and the teachers completed a teacher rating scale (Radke-Yarrow, 1946) for each child. Both of these instruments contain behavior ratings of a personality assessment type, and permit classification of the children into categories of high adjustment, aggression, and withdrawal.

All scores were converted to standard scores so that a composite adjustment rating could be devised. The sixteen children rated lowest in adjustment on these scales comprised the children in the study. Eight children were designated as the therapy children and eight as the controls. There was equal representation in the groups among boys and girls, and among aggressive and withdrawn children. The experimental and control groups were thus equivalent in age, sex, total adjustment scores, and type of maladjustment. There was no differential selection in terms of the crucial variable, motivation for therapy, since the subgroups were selected randomly.

During the course of the experiment, two children each in the experimental and control groups transferred out of the neighborhood; all data analyses omit these children. By a fortunate coincidence all of these children were from the withdrawn groups. The experimental vs. control balance thus remained intact.

Procedure

Each child in the experimental group was brought to a clinical facility once a week for individual play therapy. Length of therapy was determined by therapist judgment of need in conjunction with the children's attitudes toward continuing, without reference to test data. Median length of therapy for the group was 37 sessions.

In order to provide for a clear-cut test of the effect of therapy upon the children, no differential contact was made with the parents of the experimental and control groups. Mothers of the experimental group were seen once before therapy and once after therapy. Control group mothers were also seen twice, at time intervals equivalent to those of the experimental group.

Testing Intervals

The teacher rating scale and reputation tests were administered on three occasions: once before therapy, once at the end of the school year (seven months after the first administration), and finally one year after the second testing. The interval from first to last testing was thus 19 months.

By the time of follow-up testing, the classes had been reorganized and were taught by different teachers, so that we may consider this testing period the most removed from the experiment. Although the second testing interval is referred to in Table 1 as *posttest*, two of the children had not completed therapy at that point. For these children this might be considered a "late therapy" testing point.

A *priori* directional hypotheses specified that score changes for the experimental group would exceed significantly those of the control group.

RESULTS

Table 1 presents the results. Difference scores were derived by comparing directly the standard scores of a given child at each testing interval.

It will be noted from the table that score changes on the reputation test favored the experimental group. On the teacher rating scale the experimental group showed marginally significant improvement as compared to the control group on the posttest vs. follow-up. However, the overall teacher rating scores conceal more decided differences between the groups. Since the aggressive experimental and control subgroups remained intact throughout the study, it was possible to compare the two groups with respect to changes in aggression scores, according to *a priori* hypotheses. Table 2 presents the results. It will be seen that at pretherapy time all children had positive aggression Z scores, indicating that all of them were more aggressive than the class average. This is of course to be expected, since they were chosen on this basis. By follow-up time, all children in the experimental group had lower aggression scores than the average child in the class, while all control children still had higher-than-average aggression scores.

Statistical comparison of the two groups with respect to change scores yielded a *t* ratio of 4.86, thus indicating a significant contrast between the groups.

It is clear from the foregoing results that children who are involved in a therapy experience are perceived by others as significantly less maladjusted after therapy. Comparable shifts in interpersonal judgments do not occur in the absence of therapy.

It is pertinent to point out one incidental statistical finding here. When groups are chosen from the extremes

TABLE 1.—Score Changes for the Groups

TEACHER RATING

Interval	Experimental		Control		Diff.	t	pᵃ
	$\bar{D}$	Sigma	$\bar{D}$	Sigma			
Pretest vs. posttest	−.33	8.71	.83	8.57	−1.16	.23	n.s.
Pretest vs. follow-up	5.17	13.24	−1.00	8.85	6.17	.95	n.s.
Posttest vs. follow-up	5.50	10.18	−1.83	3.54	7.33	1.67	.10>P>.05

REPUTATION TEST

Interval	Experimental		Control		Diff.	t	pᵃ
	$\bar{D}$	Sigma	$\bar{D}$	Sigma			
Pretest vs. posttest	2.67	5.89	2.00	10.12	.67	.14	n.s.
Pretest vs. follow-up	9.17	5.88	−1.83	7.71	11.00	2.78	<.05
Posttest vs. follow-up	6.50	6.32	−3.83	10.38	10.33	2.08	<.05

ᵃ$t_{.05}$ = 1.81 for 10 d.f. on one-tailed test of directional hypothesis.

TABLE 2.—Teacher Ratings of Aggressive Behavior

EXPERIMENTAL AGGRESSIVE	GROUP Z SCORES[*]			CONTROL AGGRESSIVE	GROUP Z SCORES		
Child	Pre-therapy	Follow-up	Difference	Child	Pre-therapy	Follow-up	Difference
A	2.87	− .67	−3.54	W	1.94	2.28	.34
B	.47	−1.29	−1.76	X	.87	1.74	.87
C	1.38	− .52	−1.90	Y	.17	1.56	1.39
D	1.60	− .23	−1.83	Z	1.79	1.37	− .42

[*]Negative Z scores denote aggression ratings lower than the class mean.

of a distribution, as these groups were, a statistical regression effect may complicate the results. It is of interest to note that in none of the control group analyses does a regression effect appear.

DISCUSSION

Two points may be worthy of special note in this study. The first point relates to the findings with regard to the aggressive groups. Parents and educators sometimes express concern at the behavior latitude permitted in play therapy, particularly with regard to aggressive children. The view sometimes expressed is that such children need a controlled environment rather than a permissive one. The findings in this study are of interest in this connection, since they indicate that a striking reduction in aggressiveness may result from a permissive therapeutic climate. Such an outcome is predicted from therapeutic theory. The second point is that behavior changes occurred without work with parents. This finding suggests that children as young as seven or eight years old may change even in the absence of systematic environmental alteration. There

may be implications here for degree of autonomy in children of this age level.

The final point concerns the cumulative implications of this study when taken in conjunction with the ones previously cited by Cox (1953), Bills (1950), Dorfman (1958), and Seeman and Edwards (1958). All of these studies of therapy used control techniques and all showed that the experimental groups registered changes not observable in the control groups. It seems reasonable to state that the conclusions of Levitt (1957b, 1963) concerning the absence of evidence for change due to therapy no longer hold categorically.

SUMMARY

Two equivalent groups of children relatively low in adjustment were selected from a larger sample. Members of the E group came for individual play therapy. Reputation test scores for the E group showed significant positive contrasts with the control group. Overall teacher rating changes were marginal. Teacher ratings of aggression for the aggressive therapy group were significantly lower than those for the control groups at follow-up.

58 *Psychotherapy Research and the Expectation-Reality Discrepancy*[1]

EUGENE E. LEVITT

It is hypothesized that "the more the patient finds that the therapeutic situation fails to conform to his preconception of it, the less it is likely to effect him favorably. . . . expectations concerning the psychotherapy process are often misconceived. . . . The patient sees himself as relatively passive once he has volunteered his complaints. The popular expectation of therapist participation clashes particularly sharply with the theory, training and practices of contemporary psychotherapy, which deliberately leaves the burden of verbalization largely to the patient. . . . In summary, the lack of adequate research findings may indicate that not research but conventional practice is in the wrong and that therapy innovations are required."

There have been a very great number of published investigations of psychotherapy during the past thirty-five years; with adults and with children, of process and of outcome. One might reasonably suppose that we would have by this time some solid facts about psychotherapy. Surely we ought to be able to make a reasonable assessment of its effectiveness. Yet, there is no consensus on this score. The debate rages on, as if experimental scrutiny were still a thing of the future.

Surveys of evaluation studies (Eysenck, 1952; Levitt, 1957c) suggest that between 60% and 80% of patients subjected to a formal course of psychotherapy or merely evaluated and not treated, show "improvement." These findings may mean something, but they cannot be, and seldom are, accepted at strict face value. The methodological problems of evaluating the effects of therapy, and the status of untreated cases contraindicate definite, meaningful inferences. These problems have been delineated many times. The only generally accepted inference seems to be that the problems have not yet been satisfactorily resolved. Beyond this disheartening conclusion, the findings of decades of research

[1]Based on a paper presented in the symposium, "Current Status of Treatment and Management Techniques with Children," at the APA Convention, 1965.

Reprinted from *Psychotherapy: Theory, Research and Practice*, 1966, **3**, 163–166, by permission of the author and Dr. Eugene T. Gendlin, Editor.

have been correctly characterized by Colby (1964) as "disorder, confusion and impasse."

The interested parties appear now to have divided into three distinguishable camps. Each advances a hypothesis based on an analysis of the nature of the current impasse.

Hypothesis 1: The psychotherapy process is a very specialized instance of intimate, interpersonal interaction which defies, in principle, scientific examination and evaluation. A kind of Law of Indeterminancy prevails; the very energy employed in examining the therapeutic phenomenon alters its shape so that it can never be perceived veridically from without. Psychological treatment is an idiographic art which is not a suitable subject for true experimental investigation.

This hypothesis appears to have been adopted by a majority of practicing psychotherapists. This may explain why the sizable mass of psychotherapy research has evidently had very little impact on the practice of psychotherapy, as Strupp (1960) pointed out a few years ago.

Hypothesis 2: Measurement techniques used to evaluate the outcome of psychotherapy are insufficiently sensitive and reliable to be able to reflect the changes in patients which have actually occurred. Furthermore they are probably not even appropriate. It may well be that we have been using the wrong kind of measures, that we have been looking in the wrong place all these years.

This second hypothesis is espoused by those who maintain that the outcome studies which have so far been reported have little to contribute to knowledge. We must turn our attention to the process study, the examination of actual psychotherapy practices, of variables of the patient and therapist. Therein we shall eventually find the factors and measurements which are appropriate to use in evaluating therapy and we can then proceed to structure truly definitive outcome studies.

Hypothesis 3: The theoretical groundwork and practical implementation of conventional psychotherapy is faulty, and our approaches are in need of drastic alteration.

Those who endorse Hypothesis 3 point, for example, to investigations which show that the large majority of all psychotherapeutic courses are of 10 hours duration or less (Bahn and Norman, 1959). This is hardly sufficient time for an unwinding of the complex process which is thought to take place in intensive psychotherapy. In other words, it appears that the therapy which is actually being evaluated by researchers is considerably different from the therapy which is theoretically presumed to "cure" emotional illness.

Well, then, where to now, Psychotherapy?

I am going to ally myself, for the moment, with the third group. I will begin with an assumption excellently stated recently by Cartwright (1963):

In the last few years there have been number of studies showing that the major portion of the variance associated with the outcome of therapy can be accounted for by initial patient variables. In other words, how far the patient can go in using the opportunity of psychotherapy for making positive personality changes is largely predetermined by the kind of structure he brings to the experience. . . ."

I wish now to advance a particular hypothesis which is consistent with Cartwright's assumption. It employs a concept which is relatively new in psychotherapy research, though certainly not entirely unknown. It has been employed frequently in general research and theory in psychology. It may be called *"expectation-reality discrepancy" (ERD)*. My hypothesis is that there is a negative correlation between the effectiveness of any psychotherapeutic intervention and the discrepancy between the patient's expectation of the nature of the therapy process and the reality of the encounter. The more the patient finds that the therapeutic situation fails to conform to his preconception of it, the less it is likely to affect him favorably. I refer not to his faith or lack of faith in the effectiveness of the process, but rather to his perception of specific characteristics of the process itself.

Data bearing directly on the relationship between ERD and therapy outcome are scanty. However, there is considerable evidence that ERD is a widespread phenomenon. Every public opinion survey which has ever been carried out under any sort of circumstances indicates that the public is misinformed about the psychotherapy process.[2] The most recent comprehen-

sive study is that of Nunnally (1961). The findings which I will cite are based on one of Nunnally's samples whose mean education level was 13.8 years—clearly a highly educated group. Nunnally's subjects were asked to agree or disagree with a number of statements concerning performance of the psychiatrist in the therapeutic situation. Consider some of the findings:

The main job of the psychiatrist is to recommend hobbies and other ways for the mental patient to occupy his mind. Only 44% disagreed.

The main job of the psychiatrist is to explain to the patient the origin of his troubles. 72% agreed.

Hypnosis is often used by psychiatrists. Only 29% disagreed.

A person in treatment by a psychiatrist needs to make several visits each week. Only 44% agreed.

These beliefs are evidently unrealistic. The reality of a number of other statements was not nearly so clear. For instance,

Psychiatrists teach the patient to live for the future instead of the present. 53% agreed, 47% disagreed.

Psychiatrists try to teach their mental patients to hold in their strong emotions. 35% agreed and 65% disagreed.

What the psychiatrist does, may or may not be realistically construed in these fashions. The important point is that whatever reality may be, many people are not atuned to it.

And finally, it is worth noting that only 26% disagreed with "Psychiatrists are successful in treating most of their mental patients."

---

[2] It is of interest that Beisser (1964) comes to precisely the opposite conclusion although he cites in support a paper by Tannenbaum (1963) which in turn is based largely on Nunnally's book. Nunnally himself agrees with Beisser. It is hard to see how their conclusion is derived insofar as it includes the therapy process.

A recent study by Garfield and Wolpin (1963) with a sample of out patients descriptively similar to that of Nunnally, disclosed that 73% anticipated some improvement by the fifth psychotherapy session, and 70% expected complete recovery within 10 sessions or less. 45% believed that as much as 50% of the therapist's time would be given over to advice and direction; 33% emphasized the critical importance of an expert, directive role on the part of the therapist. 78% regarded lack of will power as an important cause of emotional illness.

A survey by Overall and Aronson (1963) dealt with outpatients of a lower socioeconomic strata than those of Nunnally and Garfield and Wolpin. This is one of the few studies in which an actual ERD was obtained. Perception of the process of an initial interview was assessed independently by patient and therapist with substantial correlation and degree of agreement between them. Expectation was obtained from the patient by means of a preliminary interview.

Sizable ERD's ranging between 40 and 57% were found for the following therapist behaviors:

Tell you what is wrong with you
Give you definite rules to follow
Tell you what is causing your trouble
Tell you ways to solve your problems
Tell you what is wrong with what you do

The prevalence of patient expectation of encountering these behaviors ranged from 60 to 75%. Reality—i.e., the percentage of patients who stated that they had, in fact, encountered them, ranged from 15 to 18%.

In the 10-year followup of psychotherapy at the Institute for Juvenile Research in Chicago (Levitt, 1957b), ex-patients were asked to indicate their affective reaction to the therapist assigned to them. Of 311 parents, 24% indicated that they had disliked the therapist or had felt neutral about him. Of 193 children who were able to recall an impression, 25% either had disliked the therapist or were neutral. These feelings were reflected in global estimates of the Clinic as a whole. Twenty-five percent of the treated parents were either poorly impressed by the Clinic, or were neutral. The comparable figure for children was 19%.

No serious attempt was made to determine patient expectations in the IJR followup, but a small number of interviewers recorded spontaneous criticisms volunteered by various of the ex-patient parents. By far the largest category—49% of all complaints—concerned the absence of directiveness and feedback from the therapist. It included such statements as "given no understanding of the child's problem" and "given no advice on handling of child or problem." A second major category, which encompassed 16% of the complaints, was resentment on the part of the parent at being made a focus of treatment. It seems plain that both of these categories reflect expectation-reality discrepancy.

In a retrospective study of former group therapy patients, Dickoff and Lakin (1963) reported that 50% had not had a positive affective reaction toward the therapist, and 54% had wished that he had taken a more active, directive role in the therapy process.

I do not think that there is very

much question but that expectations concerning the psychotherapy process are often misconceived. The psychotherapy outpatient seems to preconceive of the process as something resembling his dealings with the general medical practitioner. He expects that the course will take from 5 to 10 hours, and that he will experience a considerable amount of symptomatic relief in a few hours. He expects that the psychotherapist is going to be generally directive, that he will actively probe and find out in relatively short order what is wrong with the patient and will then proceed to tell him what the problem is and to offer one or more remedies. The patient sees himself as relatively passive once he has volunteered his complaints.

The popular expectation of therapist participation clashes particularly sharply with the theory, training and practices of contemporary psychotherapy, which deliberately leaves the burden of verbalization largely to the patient. When the patient is not substantially verbal, there may be extensive periods of uncomfortable silence. The few patients who find the burden tolerable without requiring participation by the therapist are almost always in the upper intellectual and educational brackets. The findings of White, Fichtenbaum and Dollard (1964) indicate that there are fewer silences in initial interviews among upper social class patients. Drop-outs from therapy had more than three times as much silence in initial interviews as continuers, but the extent of silence discriminated drop-outs in the lower classes only, and not in the middle class. Middle class patients with high ERD do not drop out and could con-

ceivably form a core of those for whom therapy will be relatively ineffective.

In one of the few investigations which bears directly on the relationship between ERD and the therapy outcome (Hoehn-Saric, *et al.*, 1964) a small group of patients was given a special educational pre-therapy session designed to provide accurate information about therapy. A comparable control group was admitted to treatment without benefit of this influence. The so-called Role Induction Interview (RII) covered four components:

1) a general exposition of psychotherapy;

2) a description and explanation of the expected behavior of a patient and of a therapist;

3) a preparation for certain typical phenomena in the course of therapy (e.g. resistance); and

4) the induction of a realistic expectation for improvement within four months of treatment. The patient was told that the therapist would not give the type of advice that he might expect from other physicians, that the therapist would talk very little but would listen carefully and try to understand and clarify his problems and feelings. It would be up to the patient, however, to find his own way to handle problems and to make decisions. . . . The patient was urged to talk freely to the therapist and cautioned that at first this would be difficult. . . . The importance of keeping appointments was stressed, especially when the patient was tempted not to come. (Hoehn-Saric, et al., 1964, pp. 270–271)

At the end of a 4-month period, the experimental ratings by therapist, patient, and independent interviewer revealed statistically significant improvement in the experimental group compared to the control group.

These results are far from convincing; the investigators themselves propose many qualifications. But as they say: "The results none the less strongly suggest that a systematic attempt to prepare the patient for his role in treatment has a catalytic effect on subsequent therapy" (p. 280). And it certainly cannot be denied that one of the most promising hypotheses of the basis of this effect is a reduction in ERD resulting from the RII.

In summary, the lack of adequate research findings may indicate that not research but conventional practice is in the wrong and that therapy innovations are required. In support of this view, the hypothesis has been raised that expectation-reality discrepancy (ERD) is negatively related to favorable therapy outcome. There is a great deal of testimony to support the conclusion that ERD is a widespread phenomenon.

Let me conclude by urging most strongly that those who have the facilities and the inclination to carry out psychotherapy research systematically investigate the ERD-outcome hypothesis.

Group Approaches

17

59 *Individual and Group Therapy of a Latency Age Child*

JOHN C. COOLIDGE, M.D.

MARGARET GALDSTON GRUNEBAUM

This presentation of a girl seen over a period of eight years suggests the need to increase the range of treatment techniques to include group and combined (group and individual) psychotherapy along with individual psychotherapy. The effectiveness of activity group treatment is illustrated.

During the past generation the traditional treatment in child guidance clinics for children of latency age has been individual, usually once a week, psychotherapy. We know that the child of this age group normally invests much of his energy in peer relationships, finding therein an opportunity to strengthen and broaden his own identity, both through group identification and by comparing the similarities between himself and others of his own age. This maturational process necessarily involves a partial exclusion of the adult world.

Certain children utilize psychotherapy to focus on selected areas of their difficulties which are manifestly represented in their peer relatedness. But often they insist that such difficulties do not exist. The limited effectiveness of psychotherapy with such children

Reprinted from the *International Journal of Group Psychotherapy*, 1964, **14**, 84–96, by permission of the senior author and Dr. Harris B. Peck, M.D., Editor.

is related to their need not only to deny the specific doubts, fears, and tensions which arise when with other children but also to prove to themselves that they have achieved the norms of peer trust as a bastion against infantile dependence upon the adult world. To admit frailty in this area is mistakenly perceived as surrendering to their original infantile status.

Activity group therapy is often able to prove effective with such children because its setting and techniques are compatible with the developmental phase of the latency child. Within the group, penetrating observations made by his peers are often more meaningful to the child than those offered as "interpretations" in individual psychotherapy. The immediate reward for giving up outmoded ways of adaptation is a closer bonding to the group. In the laboratory of the group there is no punishment for regression and there is mutual tolerance for trial and error attempts to master new social skills.

In clinics which offer three types of treatment—individual psychotherapy, group psychotherapy, and combined (group and individual) psychotherapy —there is an increasing need to clarify the specific therapeutic contributions which each type of treatment can best make. It is evident that with such knowledge therapists are in a better position to plan in advance for the treatment of each latency child and to be more flexible as treatment proceeds in adjusting therapeutic techniques to the specific characteristics of the patient.

The following case illustrates the considered use of all three modes of therapy.

INDIVIDUAL PSYCHOTHERAPY

Ellen C. was brought to the clinic at age five and a half, with the classical school phobia symptoms of morning agitation, nausea, vomiting, and tearful clinging to her mother. The problem about school was so acute that there was little parental concern about Ellen's almost complete inability to establish and maintain meaningful friendships with other children. Ellen and her mother were accepted for individual treatment. Our study of the situation revealed that there had been many disturbances in the family. Both parents had emigrated from Europe following war experiences. Neither was a content or secure person. Both had had unhappy relationships with their own parents. While pregnant with Ellen, Mrs. C. had developed severe toxemia, and a hemorrhage at seven months had necessitated an emergency caesarean section. This had been a highly traumatic event for Mrs. C., and there were many references in her contacts with her caseworker which indicated that she felt a deep resentment toward Ellen for somehow damaging her. Ellen weighed three pounds at birth and remained at the hospital for seven weeks. She suffered from a profound anemia during the first six months of her life which required several hospitalizations for study and treatment. Feeding difficulties emerged immediately. There were hour-long feedings during which she laboriously consumed only one or two ounces of milk. Eating has continued to be a source of concern and mutual tension between mother and daughter, as have sleep disturbances manifested by Ellen crying and demanding to sleep with her parents. In general, Ellen was a dissatisfied baby whose physical care took an enormous amount of time.

Nursery school was considered when Ellen was three, but the idea was abandoned. Mrs. C.'s need to isolate Ellen was augmented by pressure from the grandparents to keep Ellen away from crowds because of their fear of germs. By the age of four, Ellen had not been permitted or stimulated to play with other children.

Ellen's only sibling, Jonathan, was born when she was four. She reacted to this event with considerable regression, glued herself to her mother wherever she went and simply would not leave her side. An effort to enter Ellen in kindergarten a month later ended in total failure. At five, a second attempt at kindergarten was made possible by the presence of a very motherly school principal to whom Ellen transferred all her clinging impulses. However, the adjustment was most precarious. She constantly hovered close to an adult and refused to mingle or play with the other children. It was at this juncture that treatment started.

Ellen's mother was seen in casework treatment during all the five years that Ellen came to the clinic. Mrs. C. was always immaculately dressed, with literally never one hair out of place, and she stressed being "unemotional and reasonable." She was, at first intensely ambivalent about coming to the clinic, but only later revealed that she had developed symptoms of nausea, stomach-ache, and vomiting during the first month of casework, the very same symptoms Ellen manifested on school mornings. Her unresolved

hostile dependency toward her own mother soon came to light and she recalled her old feelings of being constantly disapproved of and ridiculed. She began to see that behind her confusion and anxiety about dealing with Ellen and her fear of "frustrating" her lay the same resentments her mother had felt toward her. As she recalled her own fearfulness and rebelliousness as a child, she reacted with increasing anger to Ellen's provocation and demandingness. Growingly she could see the intensity of the mutual anger between Ellen and herself, and finally was able to admit that she felt she hated Ellen when she did poorly; at such times her attempts to help Ellen with her homework became horrible wrangles. She became aware of Ellen's retaliatory wishes, understanding why she often looked dead to Ellen when the latter awoke early in the morning and observed her mother sleeping.

Mrs. C. also revealed her own childhood deficit in social areas. As a young girl in Europe she was highly restricted in her activities by the rigid, disapproving, and dictatorial policies of both her parents. She was expected to behave like a proper lady at all times and all spontaneous behavior, including her tomboyishness, was severely frowned upon. On the other hand, she was never really given a helping hand in developing social graces or in finding a feminine role. She was frequently told to protect herself, but neither parent would explain against what or why, consequently leaving the question shrouded in mystery and fear. It was no wonder then that Mrs. C. was quite unaware of both the depth of her own need to hold Ellen close to herself and of the severity of Ellen's real inability to relate with peers. One of the most important aspects of work with the mother was helping her to relinquish this hold and to allow her daughter social freedom. As a consequence of this increasing permission to move out of the home, Ellen became progressively often confronted with her peer problems.

Ellen's father, a dozen years her mother's senior, appeared to be disinterested in the children. He was a rigid, inflexible man who was easily perturbed by even the ordinary noise and activity of children. He withdrew from their care as much as he could. He was undemonstrative, took his wife's love for granted, and wanted to be waited upon. He was so intensely bound to his own mother that Mrs. C. once wistfully stated she had "married a mother-in-law rather than a husband." Her own fear of abandonment compelled her to repress her frustration and to cater to his idiosyncrasies rather than to protest. He resisted the clinic's attempts to involve him in the treatment program, but brought Ellen to the clinic several times when Mrs. C. was not able to. He revealed his concern for Ellen's unhappiness and raised the question of the possible use of tranquilizers, stating that he himself took Equinal at times of stress. He saw himself as an introvert who suffered silently along with Ellen. He explained his fear of emotional pain and told of his avoidance of serious theatre, stating that life was serious enough. He finally told Mrs. C. that he thought Ellen got her trouble from him, that he too had a "heaviness of heart" when he had to leave the house for work. Mrs. C. was amazed to learn that he could feel so intensely.

The first year of treatment revealed with clarity the nature of Ellen's human transactions. Her pinched pale face with dark shadows under the eyes displayed the effects of her ravaging anxiety. Her mannerisms and motions showed a mixture of intense restriction alternating with abrupt impulsive movements which gave to her demeanor an erupting, bursting quality. She was dressed immaculately, like a doll, and in many ways in her behavior seemed to alternate between being a doll to please her mother and showing violently that she was not a doll but a viable child.

In the first interviews, Ellen would not budge from her mother's side except to make short sorties to experiment with paints, crayons, or toys. Her mother whispered that she had never before used a brush. Anxiety and irritability arose quickly on each of these ventures, and after a span of several minutes she quickly retreated to her mother.

In the third interview, Ellen selected finger paints which at first she used most gingerly with one finger. Her control over her intense wish to mess broke down quickly and within several minutes both hands, the table top, and her own clothing were covered. She gesticulated with black dripping hands toward her mother. Then, out of anxiety, she asked her mother to wash her. Her mother angrily complied, scrubbing her arms forcefully in cold water in spite of Ellen's whimpering complaints. The next interview was cancelled, as were alternate interviews for the first three months. The ambivalence toward treatment was equally acute in both mother and child.

Gradually, Ellen's enormous preoccupation with her two-and-a-half-year-old brother, Jonathan, came into view. Behind this lay her confusion about sexual identity and a prodigious envy of Jonathan's masculinity. Total preoccupation with such problems completely consumed the therapy hours. In this respect, Ellen resembled a child of two and a half to four.

The controlled permissiveness of the therapeutic relationship provided Ellen with a badly needed opportunity to explore through direct action some degree of emotional expression. As already described, at first there was only precarious control over the original unmodified forces. Ellen, however, gradually found strength through the mechanism of identification with the aggressor, which she used increasingly as her chief mode of both expression and defense. For months she re-enacted the role of the fuming, exasperated teacher who bullied the student (therapist) for "unspeakable," yet unlabeled crimes. Her vindictive orders were issued from an angry distorted face while pounding on the table. Occasionally she erupted into a physical attack on the therapist, indicating the intensity of her bottled-up feelings. Her behavior revealed, with poignancy, the deep fear of annihilation in this little girl who had almost lost her life after birth. Attempts to clarify verbally the mechanisms or content only paralyzed her with fear and aggravated her behavior.

The first indication of concern about peer difficulties took place in the fourteenth month of treatment and heralded her first real recognition of the peer world around her. Until this time Ellen simply had not been developmentally ready to have friends. She initiated a game about school busses, and during this her therapist suggested she might have some concerns about fellow schoolmates. She replied quickly that the boys were fresh, said "ain't" and "shut-up" and other "unspeakable" terms, and half admitted that the actions of these boys caused her concern. She added that she herself never used such words but gave evidence that she might like to sometimes. She then promptly changed the subject. The rest of the hour was spent in tidying up the office as if to emphasize control. Her reaction to these boys, in effect, was an extension of her sibling difficulties. This became apparent in the next several sessions in which her envy of her brother reached new heights. She smashed an ashtray, threw things around, reported that she had told her brother he could not expect to have her mother all to himself and gave other indications of tormenting him. No more references to peer difficulties were made nor could they be solicited during the remainder of that year.

Ellen's school attendance improved considerably and treatment was discontinued with both mother and child at the end of the second year.

One year later, Ellen's mother returned asking for a consultation because of her daughter's increasing worry about her schoolwork. Ellen and her mother were reinstated in treatment. Ellen, now eight, looked and behaved as she had previously. She was listless and bored and complained about her schoolwork and teachers. She was asked if she had any friends and immediately she said she had none. In this consultation, her tenseness, irritability, and inhibition suggested that her extreme ambivalence was still holding her immobile.

However, that summer, the first of a series of more relaxed family vacations at the shore, seemed to help. The following fall Ellen showed for the first time a pleasant and friendly streak which heralded at long last some separation from her pre-genital past. In treatment there were indications that Ellen had an increasing desire for friends. Once she admitted she thought she was too bossy, and once she stated she wished she could have more friends, but in general Ellen could not deal therapeutically with the underlying difficulties.

There was still so little distance from oedipal and earlier developmental tasks that the intrusion of pre-genital impulses into her peer relationships was difficult for her to control. To prevent such regression and to keep her limited capacity for peer relatedness intact, Ellen held herself aloof when troubled by such events as the rambunctiousness of the boys in the bus. She was also reluctant to become too peer-oriented because of the threat this imposed to the mutual but neurotic closeness needed by both her and her mother. Perhaps most important of all was Ellen's wish to avoid the unbearable self-image of a lonely little girl who was deeply frightened of other children. Ellen was only too willing to let this sleeping dog slumber. Her reluctance to work on these problems was motivated by the unconscious fear of the regression which would necessarily have taken place in treatment if the conflicts underlying her peer difficulties were exposed. Thus, Ellen's defenses converged to block off communication, both in dramatic play and verbalization; the very tools through which individual psychotherapy is effective.

COMBINED THERAPY

When Ellen was ten, it was decided to recommend activity group therapy in addition to individual psychotherapy. The expectation was that group interaction would mobilize conflictual material which Ellen could bring back to her individual psychotherapy. It was further expected that the group process itself would hasten a realignment of internal forces and defenses and consequently lead to more appropriate adaptation.

True to the nature of Ellen's defenses she could not bring to her psychiatrist thoughts and feelings about the group. However, she quickly began to change. She developed more of an ordinary girl's demeanor and became more casual. She began to mention names of neighborhood friends and within several months received invitations to other girls' homes. Her mother reported strides in her social progress as indicated by a marked increase in the number of phone calls.

It was realized after a year of combined treatment that anxieties mobilized in the group would not be brought to her psychiatrist and that Ellen continued to view individual treatment only as an opportunity for companionship. On the other hand, strides being made in the activity group indicated that, given Ellen's patterns of defenses, this was currently the treatment of choice and could better provide for Ellen the tools for latency living. Consequently, individual psychotherapy was discontinued.

During Ellen's five years of individual treatment, some gains had been made. Her need for perfection, her exaggerated fear of attempting anything creative, and her marked fear of disapproval had been touched upon. The sibling rivalry continued to be a central focus and finally some of her seductive feelings toward her family members emerged. The earlier crude control over impulses and later identification with the aggressor were now largely replaced by a constrictive social conformity and reaction formation, which at least gave her a formula for behavior although at too great a cost. It was recognized that Ellen still was anxious, restricted and impoverished in her personality, and it was hoped that in the future she might be more accessible to individual psychotherapy and eventually be able to work through verbally her basic anxieties.

GROUP THERAPY

The pre-school child acquires a first identity from his parents, and with this as a foundation he is ready to begin the quest for an independent existence. He moves out from his family to join the society of children, and the peer group becomes the proving ground where the child learns to live with people outside the family.

Ellen was not able to take this important step forward because of fears that she would have to relinquish all claims on earlier satisfactions. Her problems were hard to reach, at this point, in individual therapy. This was in part due to her need to keep a tight lid on her conflicts and in part related to her developmental stage. The latency child is apt to shut adults out of much of his world.

When Ellen arrived at her first "club" meeting at the Judge Baker Guidance Center, she appeared as an attractive, well built, ten-year old. She greeted the new situation with a pinched, tight expression, which was to tell of her tension in group situations for many months to come. She entered the large meeting room and was greeted by her group leader who introduced herself to Ellen. In turn, Ellen learned the names of the five other girls who had also just been invited. It was many weeks before Ellen could tell some of these children apart, and indeed it was months before she got all their names straight. To her, at first, these five girls of her own age were an indistinguishable and frightening mass. She did not realize that they had been selected to attend this group with as much careful thought as was involved in the decision for her membership. While the six girls shared the same hunger for closeness to the adult and for friends, their strengths and problems were reviewed and weighed so that no personality problems would interfere unduly with the group's potential for promoting healthy functioning. What might be a problem in one child was selected to counterbalance a problem in another child. Thus, Ellen's overly rigid defense patterns were chosen to set off the impulsivity of another girl. The ease that another child had in expression of conflicts was chosen to stimulate the more reticent.

As is the procedure with each new child, Ellen was invited to look around her "club room." The walls were lined with cabinets which contained arts and crafts material: woodworking tools, clay, paint, leather and jewelry kits, etc. There were work tables, a toilet connected to the club room, and a kitchen area with shelves for food and cooking utensils, a stove, and a dining table. At this point, this rather casual setting filled Ellen with anxiety. She undoubtedly wondered if she would be accepted by the girls and if, in turn, she would like them. Further, she probably questioned who the adult was and what her expectations would be. Finally, she was concerned with the materials and whether she had the ability to use them well.

For the first time in her life Ellen entered a social situation which at least guaranteed the physical proximity of five other girls, although the guarantee obviously could go no further than the fact that most of these girls would be present week by week; companionship and emotional proximity would have to be achieved by Ellen herself. Still, this was an immediate improvement in her life situation, for at this time her behavior toward peers could not have attracted five constant playmates who would not walk away from her in response to her provocations. Secondly, although it would take Ellen and the others quite some time to discover this, she had close at hand an adult who was ready to protect, help, and feed. Unlike the adults known to these children at home, in school, or in neighborhood clubs, there would be no demands for behavior above the level of their emotional abilities and no retaliation for regressive expression. Finally, the total atmosphere was one in which Ellen could approach the children and the adult in her own fashion and at her own pace.

Ellen entered the group bringing with her the defensive and relationship patterns observed in her individual treatment and in her life at home.

In the first session, she responded to her own anxiety by turning to the adult to structure the situation, asking what she should do. She received the reply that she could do anything she liked. True to form, Ellen responded by removing herself from the children and the adult to work with paper and crayons. Her drawing, clearly a self-portrait, was of a flower, petals tightly held at the side of the stem, placed precisely in the center of the page and carefully bound with a heavy border. Although her back was turned and her head bent, she was ever watchful of the other children and of the adult.

About forty-five minutes before the end of this first meeting, Ellen sat down to the first of many group meals. The combination of her family's request that she maintain the dietary laws of her religion plus her own neurotic food habits increased her tension greatly. She carefully attended the leader's response to the active testing of a less inhibited girl who declared her dislike of one of the food items. The leader answered, "You don't have to eat anything you don't want," but, it was weeks before either she or the other children truly believed that the adult meant this.

In many ways Ellen's behavior during this first session typified her first weeks of reaction to the group experience. She remained on the sidelines with her back turned and yet was watchful. She discovered that the materials contained elements of safety, permitting her essentially to be present and busy and yet not have to interact directly. Even the range of materials available permitted her safety since she did not have to use the messiest, i.e., the clay and paint, or those which involved force and activity. She was free to maintain her rigid defenses against her impulses. Her drawing of the framed flower was repeated with little variation for quite some time.

Despite what appeared to be a picture of relative inactivity, a great deal was going on within the group and Ellen. While Ellen was watching, the other girls, according to their own problems, were more actively making their feelings and wants known. Ellen's eyes and ears were always focused on the hammer-banging activities, the arguments which erupted in jump-rope tournaments, and the smearing of paints and clay which were part of the more active testing and more open expression of conflict of the other children. At mealtime she viewed lapses in table manners with an increase in her own anxiety, and she scanned the leader's face for some trace of the responses she expected from an adult. One might say that while the other children were actively testing the leader, Ellen's quest went on vicariously through the actions of others.

But five girls will not let a sixth sit out for very long, and soon Ellen slipped into group interaction, letting herself be drawn by the others. While she was not yet able to take responsibility for her own actions and wishes, she would let herself be drawn into things by the other children. We might ask why it was that five girls would not allow another child to remain isolated from the group. There were undoubtedly many factors involved. Perhaps the children sensed Ellen's anxiety about them, anxieties which they shared but handled differently. Perhaps they saw her as too good and controlled, and their own increased regression could not tolerate her sharply contrasting behavior. Perhaps they feared that she would receive more from the adult in her side-line position and thus pulled her into their activities. Whatever the reason, we count on this characteristic in placing children like Ellen in groups.

By the middle of her first year in activity group therapy, Ellen was participating in tag, jump rope, conversation at the dinner table, and joint work with the materials, although she tended to seek out the more retiring girls like herself for partners. While her interactions increased, she was quick to retreat whenever any situation threatened to stimulate the expression of her own anger. Thus, she would return to solitary work with materials if any game disintegrated into an argument or if competition was part of the interactions. During this time Ellen turned more to the leader for protection and giving. She had learned that the adult could be approached for help at any time no matter how unrelated the requests were to the child's own actual abilities. In this vein Ellen came to the leader constantly to have directions read that she was able to read, to help her start on one project or another, to ask the leader's opinion of what colors to use.

As time went on, Ellen became freer to express her own true feelings. Her sense of safety was due to the direct feeding of the adult's support and her observation that the leader did not punish the other children when they exposed their conflicts in behavioral terms. With the release of her feelings, her group interactions lasted for a longer time. She no longer retreated from arguments but angrily stamped her feet and insisted that the girls conform to the rules and regulations. If retreating was necessary because of the potency of her feelings, her face wore the expression of her mood. Her activity of retreating was no longer drawing the flower but hammering out metal ashtrays. She was at least somewhat aware of the hostile expression that the activity involved for once she was heard to call out while pounding, "Does anyone have a headache?"

During this time, no matter what activity she engaged in, she brought with her, her battery of rules, exhibiting no flexibility. This rigid defense acted upon and was at the same time affected by those children whose concept of right and wrong was less intense than hers. Toward the end of her first year in group therapy one could hear Ellen declaring loudly that another child was a "cheat," which the latter admitted while at the same time accusing Ellen of being a "goody-goody." Ellen's expressions of hostility and her regressive swings were never as full as those of the other children, nor did they seem to tap fully the well of feelings within her; yet at the same time the tightness in this child's exchanges began to diminish.

As Ellen's exchanges with the children became freer the height of her conflict could be observed in her use of and approach to the leader. In every way short of the physical clinging of a toddler she clung to the leader. Her fear of loss of the adult was expressed in her attempts to capture the leader's attention and being for herself even as she involved herself in interactions with the other children. A barrage of anxious questions about her work were fired at the leader constantly: "Peggy,

do you think that I'll get this done today?" "Peggy, do you think my mother would like this kind of earring?"

In the second year of activity group therapy, Ellen was displaying her dilemma dramatically. In the language of behavior she was asking: will I lose my mother if I venture to grow? a question fraught with fear, longing, hostility, and healthy striving. The leader responded to each and every request but never lost sight of reality. Even if her questions had to be answered with an, "I don't know, Ellen," they were answered. And often the reply was given to Ellen that as soon as the leader did such and such for Ginny, she would work on Ellen's request. That Ellen became aware of some of the nature of her demands became obvious when, after a period of time, the requests came with a self-conscious smile and the anxiety in her voice decreased. Before she cut down on the requests, she went through a period in which the questions and demands had little or no force behind them; they were an empty ritual, once loaded with meaning but soon to be abandoned.

The most dramatic shifts in Ellen's behavior were seen at the dinner table. This was partially due to the fact that many of her greatest fears of regression and exposure of her oral-sadistic and dependent needs were stimulated around food. In addition the mealtime was intentionally structured both to feed and stimulate the working of sibling rivalry. A basic portion of food was served to all the children and then the extras were placed in the center of the table. Neither Ellen nor the other children realized that, by plan, there were never enough seconds to go around. In the first meetings of this group, the extras went unnoticed. Finally, a child freer in expressing her wants turned to the leader to request another helping and received the reply she was to hear for many sessions to come, "The extras belong to all the girls and it's up to you all as to what to do with them." This reply at first left the group silent and Ellen watchful. Some weeks later, a stronger though no more hungry child initiated the question to each girl in turn: "Is it okay with you if I have another?" To her distress and Ellen's, who quickly declined, she found that two girls wanted more food, though there were only two pieces. As is common in early stages of these groups, the children move into a kind of law of the jungle when they realize that the adult is not going to impose order. Battles rage, with primitive solutions like: "first come, first served" or "whoever gets their fork in first." True to form, Ellen remained apart from these wrangles, except that the fighting of the others made her sufficiently anxious so that she was prompted to offer sensible advice. Her ideas were usually rebuffed and it was pointed out that she had no say in the matter since she had said she did not want any more. It should be noted that Ellen's dietary customs were taken into account by the leader; whenever meat was served, there were items that she could eat that also became extras, so that she would not be excluded from this area by the food itself. Perhaps it was the provocation of the girls who pointed out to her that she had no say unless she claimed an extra, perhaps it was her greater freedom to assert herself that led Ellen soon to be counted in on desiring an extra.

In the middle of the second year,

Ellen and the girls reached a peak of conflict over two extra pieces of French toast. If they divided them in half, all would have their extras, pointed out Ellen, rightfully. But one child insisted on having a whole piece and this was too much for the rest. Ellen grabbed her half, screeching her reasonable idea over and over again and said, "You are all pigs and I can't stand the way you yell and argue." Ginny replied, "We are pigs, we're hungry and arguing never killed anyone." Ellen seemed stunned by this remark. Its impact could be observed in the weeks that followed as she permitted herself to assert and argue. In time, the girls worked out reasonable ways of managing the food.

The group was terminated after three years. By this time many changes could be observed in Ellen. Essentially, she was (and undoubtedly always will be) a person who relies on rules and regulations to structure her life, but she had attained a degree of flexibility and humor about herself so that she was no longer excluded from groups; indeed, she was able to make an important contribution in both her therapy group and elsewhere. In her over-all functioning there was a freer use of the energy and ability which had previously been so tightly bound.

Her mother's social worker observed that Mrs. C. watched intently the changes taking place in Ellen as she interacted with the group and vicariously received permission to act similarly. She consequently found greater rewards in her own increased social activities. It seemed as if the mother, at long last, had a chance to learn some of the basic ingredients of peer relatedness which she had never been allowed to acquire in her own youth.

CONCLUSIONS

The presentation of the work with Ellen reviews our attempt, following recognition of the relative failure of individual treatment, to find a therapeutic regimen which could circumvent Ellen's known defensive framework and offer more effective help. To some degree, this was achieved. Ellen belongs to that host of children who have been severely traumatized before the development of verbal communication. Such children suffer lifelong amorphous anxiety underlying the later more specific symptomatology, and they learn only with great difficulty to communicate such affect through the use of speech. Many such children showing similar signs of severe anxiety, irritability, hostility, and guilt swell clinic treatment lists, are treated for a greater or lesser number of years, and finally terminate with minimal or no basic improvement. It is our belief that child guidance clinics need to increase their range of treatment techniques to suit the varying needs of these children. We view activity group treatment as an important tool in the clinical armentarium. Since its mode of operation is essentially noninterpretive, it can often help these latency children whose emotional defect is primarily preverbal in origin and who are so often inaccessible to individual psychotherapy.

60 *Parallel Group Psychotherapy with the Parents of Emotionally Disturbed Children*

JACK C. WESTMAN, M.D.

EUGENE W. KANSKY, M.D.

MARY E. ERIKSON

BETTIE ARTHUR

ANN L. VROOM

Parallel group psychotherapy focuses on opening conscious verbal channels of communication between parents for insight-producing psychotherapy. Using separate mothers' and fathers' groups, periodically merged in joint meetings, tends to keep the therapy on the marital relationship and defines the defenses of the members. Phases of the therapeutic course with five families over a two-year period and evidence of intrapersonal and interpersonal changes in one family are presented.

Reprinted from the *International Journal of Group Psychotherapy*, 1963, **13**, 52–60, by permission of the senior author and Dr. Harris B. Peck, M.D.

Reaching the parents of emotionally disturbed children is an important challenge for child psychiatry (Ackerman, 1961; G.A.P. [Group for the Advancement of Psychiatry], 1957; Langford and Olsen, 1951). A variety of methods is available for gaining leverage on pathogenic forces in the family through the treatment of parents (Bell, 1961; Belmont and Jasnow, 1961; Dawley, 1959; Durkin, 1954; Glaser, 1960; Hallowitz and Stephens, 1959; Jackson and Weakland, 1961; Johnson, 1953; Lowry, 1948; Marcus, 1956; Martin and Bird, 1953; Mittelmann, 1948; Ritchie, 1960; Szurek, et al., 1942). This paper describes a plan of treatment built around parallel psychotherapy groups for mothers and fathers and specifically designed to meet common problems in clinical work with families. Three of these important difficulties are: (1) parents' lack of motivation for psychotherapy for themselves, (2) faulty communication between family members, and (3) impaired co-ordination of the therapeutic team in the clinic.

Achieving maximum effectiveness in the therapy of a child depends upon attracting both the father and the mother to the treatment process, but motivation problems in parents are often intensified when attempts are made to involve the father actively in treatment. The reluctance of the mother and father to share an interest in therapy frequently reflects pervasive faulty communication patterns within the family (Ackerman, 1958; Beukenkamp, 1959; Eisenstein, 1956; Grotjahn, 1960; Haley, 1959; Pollak, 1960; Ruesch, 1957). As a gross example, one father did not appear at the clinic because his wife had not told him of his scheduled appointments.

If communication patterns are teased out of the complicated matrix of family relationships, one can distinguish conscious and unconscious communication. Both verbal and nonverbal messages are transmitted at each level. In our clinic families, potent unconscious communication occurs between family members, while contradictory, inconsistent, or inadequate messages are transmitted at the conscious level. For example, one set of parents was enmeshed in a "cold war" in which underlying hostilities rarely broke through superficial pleasantries. At the other extreme, another family was in continual surface conflict but was held together by strong unconscious bonds. Most often the marriages of our clinic families are quite stable. As an illustration, if a wife projects her hostility on her husband and he characteristically turns his hostility against himself, a mutually satisfying relationship exists. If both parents project their hostility to a child, the marriage is compatible, but the child develops symptoms. In each case the parents have blind spots for their dominant unconscious communications. The projecting wife with a masochistic husband has no opportunity to become aware of her projections since they are readily accepted and unchallenged. Parents dominated by unconscious neurotic bonds cannot rationally deal with each other at a conscious verbal level, and thus they are handicapped in psychotherapy, which depends upon rational analysis and understanding of their behavior in each other's presence.

A third common problem is difficulty in making clinic teamwork a smoothly operating reality (Brody and Hayden, 1957; LaBarre, 1960). Szurek

(1952) points out that failures in the treatment of families may result from faulty co-ordination in the clinic. At times a disturbed family induces a similar disturbance in the therapeutic team, staff rivalries and personality differences providing fertile soil for the family's manipulative tendencies The very contagiousness of family disorder brings into bold relief the necessity of effective co-ordination of the therapeutic team.

In order to meet these problems, our strategy called for a therapeutic design which would capture the interest of both mothers and fathers, stimulate conscious verbal communication between parents as a basis for psychotherapeutic insight, and facilitate co-ordination of the team in the clinic. The ultimate goal was to raise parental communication from a blind, unconscious level to a more rational, conscious plane on which the parents could look at themselves and at each other more objectively.

METHOD

Group psychotherapy was chosen as the core of the program because of its usefulness in rapidly achieving a high degree of motivation in patients. Closed parallel groups of mothers and fathers were formed, tapping the natural curiosity spouses feel when each is in a similar but separate activity (Figure 1). Periodic merging of the groups, it was decided, would stimulate intergroup interest and give the parents an opportunity to see each other in action.

The clinic team consists of a separate therapist for each group, with the same observer in both groups. Weekly stereoscopic meetings of the group

therapists, observer, and child therapists are scheduled for sharing information within the team and comparing material from the separate group sessions. The children are treated individually as their needs indicate.

The material for this presentation is drawn from five families followed for two years in the parallel group therapy program. The groups met weekly for ninety minutes, with merged joint meetings at three-month intervals. Families with parents between the ages of 25 and 40 and with some college background were selected from the waiting list of the Out-patient Service of Children's Psychiatric Hospital.

At the beginning of therapy the over-all plan illustrated in the diagram was introduced to the parents. The channels of communication in the clinic were described. Appropriate respect for confidentiality outside of the families involved was requested, but confidentiality within the clinic-group-home system was not expected. Although they were not encouraged to discuss the group meetings at home, the parents were told they need not avoid discussions outside of the meetings. We did not directly encourage discussions at home because of the possibility that such a suggestion might cause or prevent outside interaction in an effort to please or frustrate the therapists.

OBSERVATIONS

The observations here are limited to the unique features of this structured treatment plan. We omit reference to the psychoanalytically oriented group therapy process and the treatment of the children for the sake of clarity.

OPEN CHANNELS OF COMMUNICATION
IN PARALLEL GROUP PSYCHOTHERAPY

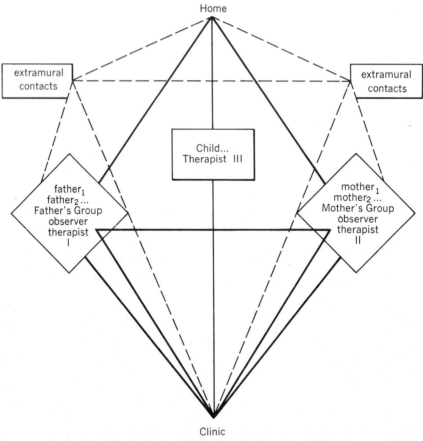

Fig. 1.

The Hale family was referred because their six-year-old daughter developed the school phobia syndrome after entering the first grade. At the time of initial evaluation, both parents were harmoniously preoccupied with their daughter's unhappiness and somatic symptoms. Because of the severity of her symptoms, Carol was enrolled in the hospital's day school. A part of the pathological interaction between parents and child was their mutual projection of their hostility onto the child. With Carol's improvement in the hospital school, open conflict appeared between the parents as they shifted their projections to each other. At this point, they entered the group therapy program. Carol was discharged from treatment several months later.

As the Hales became involved in their respective groups, "gossip sessions" after the group meetings began to replace their arguments at home. Mr. Hale told his wife of the faults and peculiarities of the other fathers. Mrs. Hale spoke bitterly of the other mothers. They began to displace their projections from each other onto members of the groups, permitting the return of relative harmony at home. In the fathers' group, Mr. Hale's projections were repeatedly interpreted. In the joint meetings the other fathers saw his wife's distortions and later demonstrated them to Mr. Hale. As he recognized his underlying hostility toward himself, he became clinically depressed. Mrs. Hale, at the same time, intensified her projections onto the other mothers as her husband was less inclined to return her hostility. Her accusations against the other mothers became so irrational that she was forced to face her own infantile conviction that she was unlovable. As Mr. Hale recovered from his depressive symptoms, Mrs. Hale began to show overt depression. She was continued in individual therapy for six months after the couple's two-year course in the parallel groups.

Although there were variations, the outline of the course with the Hales was repeated in other families. With the exception of one case, the children left treatment prior to the parents. All five families terminated with evident clinical improvement in their children and marriages.

The following tentative phases may be distilled from our experience with the five families:

Phase I: The Family Neurosis

On entering therapy each set of parents showed meshing of their neurotic personalities. Both of the Hales were basically infantile, passive-dependent persons who maintained a stable marriage by projecting their hostility onto their children. Their conscious communications centered around worry about their children. At an unconscious

level numerous messages revealed their hostility for the children and each other.

Phase II: Displacement to the Group

Projections were readily displayed from family members to the groups, resulting in improved relations at home. "After-group" discussions at home began with gossip about the other families and the transmission of messages between groups. For one couple the discussion of group meetings was the first interaction they had shared without leading to an argument in seven years of married life. The Hales' conscious verbal communication shifted from their children to criticisms of the other parents in the groups.

Phase III: Mirroring in the Groups

Married couples are handicapped in analyzing their relationship because of the blind spots created by the unconscious fit of their defenses. At home their pathological bonds are not recognized because they serve mutual neurotic needs, but in the group these bonds do not fit as well with other members and stand out as inappropriate. With the aid of the therapists and other group members, the parents begin to see themselves as others see them. Mr. Hale could not continue to remain unaware of his low self-esteem when a mirror was repeatedly held for him at group meetings.

Phase IV: Intrapersonal Change

With parallel groups the separation of spouses permits the gradual working through of insights at a rate consistent with the individual's tolerance of painful affects. The option of temporarily retreating to the old, but partially gratifying, neurotic interaction at home is always available. On the other hand, periodic confrontation with the spouse in the joint meetings keeps the focus on the husband-wife relationship. As the Hales were confronted with their own psychopathology, their conscious communications at home centered on themselves individually.

Phase V: Interpersonal Change

The ultimate goal of this program was to establish a new equilibrium in the family based less on unconscious neurotic bonds and more on mutual conscious tolerance and understanding. In the Hale family the first change was seen in the daughter who quickly improved when she was relieved of the pressure of the parents' projections. Mr. Hale's depression deprived his wife of his hostility which had given a core of reality to her projections onto him. With his later improvement and the appearance of her depression, Mr. Hale was able to partially fill his wife's dependency needs. In this family clinical symptoms shifted from the daughter to the father to the mother, ultimately exposing the mother's chronic depression which was the core of the family neurosis. After this was worked through, the family reached a new equilibrium, with visible evidence of less unconscious mutual hostility.

DISCUSSION

Both mothers and fathers showed a high degree of interest in the therapy groups. The mothers had initially expressed their desire for help through bringing their children to the clinic. The fathers were less involved in the clinic referral and less motivated for treatment for themselves. Meeting in separate groups offered the parents an opportunity to share feelings of guilt and failure with peers. The fathers saw their group as according them recognition equal to that given their wives. The parents supported each other in dealing with their spouses during and after the joint meetings. This was particularly true in the case of a passive father who used the other fathers' encouragement to stand up against his wife.

The curiosity stimulated by the separate groups heightened interest and opened channels of communication at home. For example, the mothers used each other as messengers to learn what their husbands were doing in the fathers' group. Husband and wife compared notes about the other families. As they did this, they found themselves talking less about dissatisfaction with their own children. Information transmitted between the groups underwent distortions that labeled the defenses of the bearer. As an illustration, Mrs. Hale repeatedly complained to her husband about another "rude, inconsiderate" mother. Mr. Hale gradually learned from the other fathers that his wife was in fact the "rude, inconsiderate" member of the mothers' group.

Although they came to the clinic because of their children, the parents rarely mentioned their youngsters as they became involved in the groups. Merging the fathers' and mothers' groups tended to focus the content of the parallel meetings and conversations at home on the marital relationship. The periodic joint meetings followed by separate sessions directly contrasted images developed of opposite partners with first-hand observations. For example, one father portrayed himself as the dominant force in his home. Witnessing his "puppy dog" behavior with his wife in a joint session led the other fathers to challenge his pseudomasculinity at the next fathers' group meeting. Several joint exposures and the working through of this confrontation during separate meetings were necessary before he could accept this unconsciously mediated pattern. In his wife's presence, he was unaware of his obvious submissiveness. The parents' unconscious interaction was modified first by conscious attention to the marriages of the other parents, second to themselves individually, and last to their own marriages.

The weekly team meetings in the clinic were leavened by the observer's reactions from her vantage point as a member of both groups. The stereoscopic view of life at home as reported separately by the husbands and wives provided the therapists with useful information for the clarification and interpretation of character operations. How much the open channels of communication in the clinic induced similar channels at home by example can

only be inferred. One parent remarked that the presence of the observer in both groups kept her "honest." The clinic team found that this design promoted a harmonious, constructive climate for teamwork.

The usefulness of this program for training group therapists warrants mention. Supervision of two groups can be provided at the stereoscopic conferences. The observer gains experience in group therapy in addition to filling a key position in the design.

SUMMARY

Parallel group psychotherapy is described as a method of inducing change in the families of emotionally disturbed children. The strategy of this program focuses on opening conscious verbal channels of communication between parents as a basis for insight-producing psychotherapy. The structure of the design with separate mothers' and fathers' groups periodically merged in joint meetings tends to keep the focus of therapy on the marital relationship and sharply outlines the defenses of the members. Phases of the therapeutic course with five families over a two-year period are noted. Evidence of intrapersonal and interpersonal change in one illustrative family is presented.

61 *Relationship between Psychotherapy with Institutionalized Boys and Subsequent Community Adjustment*[1]

ROY W. PERSONS

A one-year follow-up study evaluates the community adjustment of two groups of delinquent boys: one receiving group and individual therapy while incarcerated; the other serving as a matched control. The therapy group has a low rate of recidivism compared with the control group, commits fewer offenses, breaks parole less, and has a greater percentage of boys employed for a longer period of time. While still incarcerated, 30 of the 41 therapy boys are judged to be successfully treated, and these boys subsequently make a significantly better community adjustment in all spheres than any other group.

The results of a number of psychotherapy studies with social deviants have suggested that therapy may be a fruitful rehabilitative enterprise (Persons, 1965a, 1965b; Shore, Massimo, and Mack, 1965; Shore, Massimo, and Ricks, 1965). There is, however, a lack of controlled follow-up studies, using well-matched subjects, which investigate delinquents who received psycho-

therapy while incarcerated. The recent studies that have yielded positive findings have been concerned with non-institutionalized delinquents' improving their overt community behavior and incarcerated subjects' improving overt behavior within the institution and becoming better adjusted as measured by psychological tests. Illustrative of this type of study, Persons (1966) made an institutional evaluation of 82 incarcerated delinquent boys, 41 of whom received 20 weeks of therapy and 41 of whom received no therapy. The results indicated that the therapy group showed a superior adjustment as measured by psychological tests and a number of measures of overt behavior.

[1]The author wishes to express appreciation to the Ohio Youth Commission, I. Warrick, and Donald Mosher for assistance in this project. Portions of this paper were presented at the annual convention of the American Psychological Association held in New York City, September, 1966.

Reprinted from the *Journal of Consulting Psychology*, 1967, **31**, 137–141, by permission of the author and the American Psychological Association.

The present study is a community follow-up report on the 82 boys 1 year after the termination of therapy.

In the initial study (Persons, 1966), 41 pairs of incarcerated delinquents were prematched on a number of background variables; the selection process was designed with the objective of matching the therapy and control groups, subject for subject, on as many variables as possible. Each pair was selected so as to match as nearly as possible on the following variables: age, intelligence, race, socioeconomic background, type of offense, number of previous offenses, total time incarcerated during life, and nature of institutional adjustment. One member from each pair was randomly assigned to a therapy group and the other to a control group. The boys' socioeconomic backgrounds were estimated to be predominantly upper-lower and lower-middle class. There were 8 Negroes and 33 whites in each group. The mean age and intelligence quotient of the treated boys were 16.4 and 99.2, respectively, while the mean age and IQ for the controls were 16.3 and 97.6. The mean number of officially registered offenses prior to the current institutionalization was approximately four for each group, and the mean total time incarcerated for each group was approximately 11 months. The two most typical offenses for which the boys had been committed were auto theft and breaking and entering, but there were several boys in each group who had committed more serious crimes. The boys in both groups were serving indeterminate sentences, and in each group their institutional adjustments preceding treatment ranged from very good to very poor.

Each of the 41 boys in the therapy group came twice weekly for group psychotherapy, which met for an hour and a half per session. In addition, each boy had an average of 1 hour a week of individual psychotherapy. Thus, considering both individual and group therapy, each boy had 80 hours and 60 sessions of therapy over a 20-week period. There were five psychotherapists conducting interviews with six different groups of boys. In every case a boy had the same group and individual therapist. Throughout the 20 weeks the control group boys participated in the regular institutional program, but received no therapy. Following treatment, 30 of the 41 therapy boys demonstrated less pathological test scores, while only 12 controls showed improvement. The therapy boys showed better institutional adjustment, better interpersonal relationships, better performance in the institutional school, had fewer disciplinary reports, and received their institutional passes sooner than did the boys in the control group. Twenty of the 30 successfully treated boys became more similar to their particular therapist as indicated by personality measures, vocational interests, scholastic orientation, verbal statements of desire to be similar, physical appearance, and language habits (Persons and Pepinsky, 1966).

The critical question, of course, is whether the successfully treated boys' superior institutional adjustment persisted after release to the community. To answer this question, 1 year after the termination of the therapy period the Juvenile Placement Bureau had each parole officer submit a standard detailed report describing each boy's

TABLE 1.—Community Adjustment of
Therapy and Control Groups

	Therapy (N = 41)	Control (N = 41)
Subjects staying in community	28	16
Subjects reinstitutionalized	13	25
$\bar{\chi}$ offenses by returnees	1.94	3.07
Number of parole violators	20	32
$\bar{\chi}$ parole violations	1.75	3.91
Successes employed	20	6
Returnees employed	4	5
Successes' $\bar{\chi}$ time employed	6.2 mo.	3.2 mo.
Returnees' $\bar{\chi}$ time employed	2.3 mo.	1.9 mo.

activities since release from the institution. Each boy had meetings with his parole officer twice a month, and the parole officer visited in the boy's home. The parole officers had detailed information on all official and unofficial contacts with all law enforcement agencies, as well as employment information.

RESULTS AND DISCUSSION

Obviously, all 82 of the boys were not released the same day. The amount of time from the mean release date to the day the data were collected was 9.5 months, and there were no significant differences between the control and therapy groups concerning the time they were released; that is, on the average, the boys in both groups were released to the community 2.5 months after the therapy period ended.

A comparison of the therapy and control groups' community adjustment is presented in Table 1. In Table 1, "success" refers to those boys who have

not been reinstitutionalized, while "returnee" refers to boys who have been reinstitutionalized in *any* penal institution. Comparing the number of successes and returnees for both groups indicates superior community adaptation on the part of the therapy group (chi-square = 7.06, $p < .01$). The modal offense for which the therapy boys were reinstitutionalized was auto theft, and for the control boys, burglary and auto theft were the most frequently committed offenses. There was a trend for the therapy returnees to commit fewer offenses ($t = 1.55$, $p < .10$) than the control returnees. Analyzing the number of parole violations (behavior misconduct that does not necessarily involve legal infractions, but that does constitute a violation of the parole restrictions) does show that the therapy boys committed significantly fewer parole violations ($t = 4.01$, $p < .001$). A smaller proportion of therapy than control boys committed parole violations ($z = 2.74$, $p < .007$).

An evaluation made following therapy but while the boys still were incarcerated indicated that 30 boys had shown significant improvement. One year later, 25 of these 30 judged successfully treated boys were still in the community, whereas only 3 of the 11 nonsuccessfully treated boys were still in the community. As can be seen from Table 2, a z test between two proportions indicates that this difference is highly significant. Also, the judged successfully treated boys were much superior to the control group in their ability to stay in the community. The therapy boys that were judged as successfully treated did not differ from the control group in ability to stay in the community. A greater proportion of the judged successfully treated group remained in the community as compared with all other groups. Of the 20 successfully treated boys who became more similar to their therapist, 18 were still in the community 1 year later. Although this finding raises interesting questions, generalizations about the benefit of converging to the therapist are not appropriate because 7 of the 10 nonconverging successfully treated boys were also in the community a year later.

TABLE 2.—Proportion of Judged Successfully Treated (S), Judged Nonsuccessfully Treated (N), and Control Subjects (C) Staying in the Community

GROUP	PROPORTION	Z^a
N	.273	
		3.29****
S	.833	
S	.833	
		4.13****
C	.390	
N	.273	
		.69
C	.390	
S	.833	
		2.71***
All subjects	.536	

^{a}Z test between two proportions.
***$p = .007$.
****$p = .001$.

Following Meehl and R o s e n ' s (1955) base-rate suggestion, two different procedures were used to arrive at the base rates of recidivism. In this context recidivism refers to boys who have been released from this particular institution and who have been reinstitutionalized in *any* penal institution. The first base-rate figure was obtained merely by having the institution's classification officer estimate the proportion of released boys who would be reincarcerated in *any* institution within 9.5 months. His estimate was 65%. The second procedure involved drawing a sample of 100 case folders from the central record file in Columbus, Ohio, and tabulating the number of boys who had become reincarcerated in any institution within 9.5 months after release from the institution. Sixty-two percent of these sampled boys had been reinstitutionalized within 9.5 months. Table 3 presents a comparison of the groups in this study with the institution's base rates, using the latter and more conservative estimate.

TABLE 3.—A Comparison of the Institution's Base Rates with the Therapy and Control Groups

GROUP	PROPORTION	Z
Therapy subjects staying in community	.683	
		3.29****
Base rate of staying in community	.38	
Judged successfully treated subjects staying in the community	.833	
		4.22****
Base rate of staying in community	.38	
Control subjects reinstitutionalized	.61	
Base rate for reinstitutionalization	.62	
Judged nonsuccessfully treated subjects reinstitutionalized	.73	
		.69
Base rate for reinstitutionalization	.62	

****$p < .001$.

The judged successfully treated group and the total therapy group both had a significantly greater proportion of boys staying in the community as compared to the base rates. For the control and judged nonsuccessfully treated groups, there was no significant difference from the base rate in proportion of recidivism. The different therapy groups compared with base rates yield similar results as the therapy-control group comparisons.

TABLE 4.—Length of Time Each Group Was Employed

GROUP	$\bar{x}$ DIFFER-ENCE	df	t
Therapy success			
	4.3 mo.	22	2.70*
Therapy failure			
Therapy success			
	3.0 mo.	24	2.56*
Control success			
Therapy success			
	3.9 mo.	23	3.23**
Control failure			

*$p < .02.$
**$p < .01.$

Employment history provides yet another measure of community adjustment for the group of boys. Of all of the boys released, significantly more of the therapy boys were employed than control boys ($p < .01$). In considering just the boys successfully remaining in the community, there were significantly more therapy boys employed than were control boys (chi-square = 4.85, $p < .05$). Of the 24 boys in the therapy group who were employed, only 4 were reincarcerated while 20 remained in the community

($z = 4.66$, $p < .01$). Twenty-eight therapy boys remained in the community; of these 28, 20 were employed. Table 4 presents a comparison of the length of time the boys in each group were employed. The successfully treated therapy boys were employed significantly longer than any other group. There were no significant differences as to length of time employed between the therapy failure, the control success, and control failure groups; however, there was a trend for the boys in the control success group to be employed longer than the boys in the other two groups.

Approximately 90% of the boys were released to their homes with no significant difference between control therapy, success, and returnee boys concerning type of community placement. In an effort to compare the environment to which the boys would be released, the author carefully read each boy's case folder and rated his community placement environment from 1 to 9, extremely poor to extremely good. These judgments were based upon such criteria as: broken home, relationship with parents or parent surrogates, delinquency rate of the home area, family and financial status, and job possibilities. Although it was possible for a boy's home placement to be marked 9, in actuality the rankings were uniformly low and the highest ranking received by any boy was 5.5. There were no significant differences between the home situations of the therapy boys who remained in the community, therapy boys who were reinstitutionalized, control boys who stayed in the community, and control boys who were reinstitutionalized. Mean ratings for the groups were, respectively: 2.94, 2.46, 3.16, and 2.79. Despite the crudeness of such a home-rating method, another institutional psychologist[2] not associated with the project was asked to make similar ratings. The two separate ratings were strikingly in agreement with a .52 mean difference in the two rankings, and exact concordance in 73% of the homes rated. Sixty-eight percent of all the boys came from broken homes with 61% of the therapy returnees, 74% of the control returnees, 67% of the therapy community remainers, 68% of the control community remainers coming from broken homes. The most powerful observation which seems to defy meaningful numerical expression, made from reviewing the records and listening to the recorded interviews, was that almost every boy had never experienced a satisfactory relationship with his father or father surrogate.

---

[2]R. L. Uhl generously assisted in reviewing cases and making ratings.

More often than not the relationship was extremely stormy or the father was not a member of the family constellation.

The results of this study seem to indicate that psychotherapy can be an important factor in rehabilitation of delinquent youths. It should be particularly noted that only 5 of the 30 boys who were judged to be successfully treated subsequently became re-institutionalized. However, from these results it should not be construed that psychotherapy is a rehabilitative panacea. For maximum results it seems that a boy needs to have a successful therapy experience, a reasonably adequate community replacement, and employment. There were also some notable therapy failures, such as one armed robbery and an armed robbery and murder. Nevertheless, the results indicate that psychotherapy helped most of the boys reverse their antisocial behavior and become more responsible individuals.

From Childhood to Adolescence

18

62 Infant Vocalizations and Their Relationship to Mature Intelligence[1]

JAMES CAMERON

NORMAN LIVSON

NANCY BAYLEY

Correlations between infant development tests and later intelligence have been found previously to be very low. Through cluster analysis, one of the six-item clusters extracted from Bayley's California First Year Mental Scale, composed principally of vocalizations, significantly correlates with girls' later intelligence, increasingly with age, and more highly with verbal than performance scores. "These results strongly suggest that developmental psychologists need to rethink their previous conclusion that infant developmental test scores are unrelated to later measures of intelligence."

It is generally believed that infant (0 to 2 years) developmental tests cannot predict the level of intelligence of the growing child or the mature adult. Virtually all developmental research reports have reported insignificant correlations between the infant

[1]Supported, in part, by grant MHO-8135 from the National Institute of Mental Health. Marjorie P. Honzik contributed to earlier phases of work on this study.

developmental test scores, which are based on extensive and somewhat similar samples of the infants' relatively limited behavioral repertoire, and later indices of intelligence.[2] The presumption has grown that, until the effects of experience or the maturation of specific cognitive processes (hypothsis building, attention, extended memory) during the preschool years have occurred, testing infant intelligence for the purpose of estimating childhood or adult intelligence (as opposed to testing to detect infant developmental deviations) is a futile enterprise.[3]

In arriving at this conclusion, total scores (that is, the total number of items passed) at a particular age level have customarily been used. Whether a partial score, based on an empirically derived factor or subset of items selected from these infant tests, might predict later intelligence or some factor of intelligence remained an open question. In pursuing this line of investigation, we extracted six relatively independent item clusters from the data on the 115-item California First Year Mental Scale for the total sample

of children (males = 35, females = 39) in the Berkeley Growth Study.[4] The frequent testing of these children (generally at 1-month intervals) permitted use of the age at which each child *first* passed each test item as the basic data for this analysis. This treatment of the longitudinal data permitted any test item to correlate highly with any other item, regardless of the difference in the "average passing age" of the two items, so long as the children who were precocious in passing the earlier item were similarly ranked in precocity in passing the second item. This statistical advantage, not available in factoring simple pass-fail item data tests administered at a single age (where only a few test items are discriminating), permitted clusters to be composed of items drawn from the entire age range (0 to 1½ years) covered by the Bayley Scale.

One of the six factors which were extracted from the combined sample did appear to be related to girls' intelligence (but not boys'), as measured at years 6 through 26. Six of the seven items defining this factor involved the girls' early vocalization behavior. The items ranged in age placement on the Bayley Scale from 5.6 to 13.5 months, clearly well before the age when school-age intelligence is first predictable from total test scores. Predictabil-

---

[2]For example, the correlation between total development test scores at 8 months and I.Q. at 4 years is .02 (Bayley, 1949). A correlation of .32 between 6 months and 5 years is reported by Hindley (1965). However, one study on *preverbal vocalizations*, not overall intelligence, between 6 and 18 months reports r's of about .45 with I.Q. at 3 years (Catalano and McCarthy, 1954).

[3]Comparisons of the relations between children's I.Q.'s and abilities of true and of adoptive parents have been made by Honzik (1957) and by Bayley and Schaefer (1964). See also Whipple (1940).

[4]A full description of the longitudinal study can be found in Jones and Bayley (1941). The Tryon method cluster analysis is described in Tryon (1939, 1958). A full report of the cluster analysis of these infant developmental test data is in preparation as a monograph. A factor with slightly different item content, derived from scores for sexes combined, was reported by Bayley (1966).

ity of school-age intelligence increases markedly between 2 and 4 years. A useful prediction of adult intelligence cannot be made until after 4 years of age, when verbal and performance skills have matured to a considerable degree.[5]

The seven items and their age placements, in months, are: vocalizes eagerness (5.6), vocalizes displeasure (5.9), vocal interjections (8.1), says "da-da" or equivalent (8.5), pulls string adaptively (9.5), says two words (12.9), and uses expressive jargon (13.5). The seven items, with an average product-moment intercorrelation of .44, form a highly reliable scale (.84) as calculated by the Tryon cluster analysis computer program.[6]

Figure 1 plots the correlations between this factor and girls' I.Q.'s from 6 through 26 years. As the girls

[5]Correlations of .42 between 4 and 18 years, for 211 subjects, and .61 between 6 and 18 years, for 214 subjects, are reported by Honzik, Macfarlane, and Allen (1948). Bayley (1949), using an average of three consecutive tests to obtain more reliable scores, obtained r's of .62 between 4 and 18 years and .86 between 6 and 18 years for 40 subjects.

[6]Domain validity, as defined in the Tryon system, is equivalent to the correlation between subject's actual score in a particular domain of ability and a hypothetical score which measured *without error* his standing in that domain or area. See Tryon (1958) for computational formula.

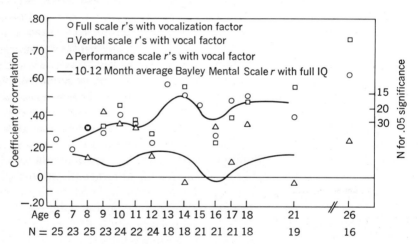

Fig. 1. Girls' vocalization-factor correlations with verbal, performance, and full-scale intelligence scores at ages 6 through 26 years. The bottom line represents a smoothed "base-line" curve of average 10- to 12-month total test scores' correlations with later full I.Q. The top smoothed curve indicates the increased prediction available from employing the vocalization-factor scores. Solid dots represent the actual vocalization factor—full-scale I.Q. correlations. Fluctuation in the two curves could be due to either fluctuating numbers of subjects or different I.Q. tests administered at different ages. Crosses and diamonds have been included to illustrate the better prediction by the vocalization factor of later verbal intelligence.

mature, the correlations between their intelligence scores and this early vocalization factor increase, reaching a range generally between .40 and .60 during the 13- to 26-years period. For the 6- through 26-years period, the correlations for the boys' early vocalization factor with intelligence are predominantly negative and never reach statistical significance.

At eleven ages during this 6- to 26-year age span, separate verbal and performance subscale scores were available, permitting us to detect whether this early vocalization factor correlated higher with verbal than with performance capabilities. Correlations with verbal intelligence were higher at 9 out of 11 ages.[7]

Despite the consistent trend of positive and increasing correlations across time and despite the confirming evidence of higher correlations with verbal as opposed to performance measures of intelligence, further assurance that these findings were not due to chance effects seemed in order. We therefore correlated the factor

_____
[7]At 6 and 7 years of age the Berkeley Growth Study subjects were given the 1916 Stanford-Binet, for which no methods are available for determining separate verbal and performance scores. At 13 and again at 15 years they received the Terman-McNemar test, which also has no separate verbal and performance scores. At ages 8 through 12 and again at 14 and 17 the revised Stanford-Binet intelligence tests (L and M) were administered, for which verbal and nonverbal factor score formulas are available (McNemar, 1942). At the remaining ages (16, 18, 21, and 26 years) the Wechsler-Bellevue test, which is divided into verbal and performance sections, was used.

coefficients (essentially the correlation of each item with the factor) on this early vocalization dimension for all 115 items from the Bayley Scale with each item's separate correlation with a composite intelligence score based on all available test scores from ages 13 through 18 years. In a sense, this procedure permitted evaluation of the predictive efficiency of the early vocalization dimension over all 115 items. In fact, the product-moment correlation coefficient describing this relation was .33. When the same set of 115 factor coefficients was correlated with separate verbal and performance composite intelligence scores (from data available at ages 14 through 18 years), as expected, the verbal intelligence correlation was higher (verbal $r = .24$, performance $r = .00$).

Figure 2 presents the scattergram corresponding to the first of these three correlations. Note that six of the seven definers fall in the outermost region of the top right quadrant, indicating that they contribute heavily to the correlation of .33. Of the four additional items which also occupy this area of the scattergram, one is an early vocalization item (vocalizes satisfaction, age placement = 6.5 months), while the other three are early assertive and adaptive acts (postural adjustment, 0.5 month: retains two cubes, 5 months; unwraps cube, 10.6 months).

These results strongly suggest that developmental psychologists need to rethink their previous conclusion that infant developmental test scores are unrelated to later measures of intelligence. Although these results should be replicated on data from other necessarily longitudinal studies, and

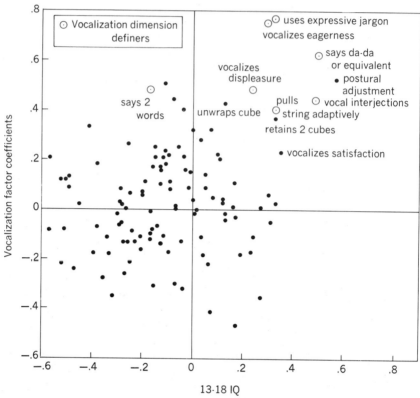

Fig. 2.   Scattergram of 115 Bayley First Year Mental Test items' factor coefficients on the vocalization factor plotted against each item's correlation with mean full-scale standardized intelligence scores from ages 13 to 18. Circled dots represent defining items of the vocalizing factor.

although even if replicated their power to predict mature intelligence will be modest indeed, these findings, if found valid, force us to reconsider our notions of the origins of intelligence (particularly with respect to sex differences), and to look more closely to the genetic structure of the child and the ecology provided by the parents for traces of these origins.

63 *Self-Image Disparity:*
A Developmental Approach[1]

PHYLLIS KATZ

EDWARD ZIGLER

The real-self, ideal-self, and social-self perceptions of fifth-, eighth-, and eleventh-grade children are studied. The major prediction is that real-ideal-self discrepancy is positively related to the individual's level of maturity. This hypothesis is based on two factors thought to relate to increase with maturity: capacity for guilt and cognitive differentiation. A subsidiary prediction is that measuring instruments most sensitive to the assessment of these factors should maximally reflect developmental changes in self-image disparity. Both the major and subsidiary predictions receive experimental support. Self-image disparity is found to be positively related to chronological age and intelligence. The larger disparity in older and brighter children is accounted for by both decreased self-evaluations and increased ideal-self images.

A frequently used measure in many empirical and theoretical contexts (cf. Wiley, 1961) has been the disparity between the individual's real-self image and ideal self. At least three different interpretations of this real-ideal-self disparity have been advanced. The most widely noted position is that of Rogers and his co-workers (Rogers and Dymond, 1954) who view such a disparity as a general indicator of maladjustment. Evidence of the popularity of this view can be seen in the practice of employing self-image disparity as an operational measure of mental illness (Scott, 1958).

A second position represents a qualification of the Rogerian thesis. A number of investigators have advanced evidence that while a large self-ideal disparity is invariably ominous, it

[1]This investigation was supported by grants M–6369 and MH–06809 from the National Institute of Mental Health, United States Public Health Service, and by a New York University Arts and Science research grant. The authors wish to thank Steven Gardner for his assistance in running the children and William Bacci, superintendent of the Carl Place, New York, school system for his aid in obtaining subjects.

Reprinted from the *Journal of Personality and Social Psychology*, 1967, **5**, 186–195, by permission of the senior author and the American Psychological Association.

would be found only among individuals employing particular psychological defenses, for example, sensitizers and psychoneurotics (e.g., Altrocchi, Parsons, and Dickoff, 1960; Hillson and Worchel, 1958). Within this position, maladjusted individuals employing other modes of defense, for example, denial, would be expected to show little self-ideal discrepancy.

A third position was recently advanced by Achenbach and Zigler (1963) who employed developmental theory to generate the prediction that real- ideal-self discrepancy was positively related to the individual's level of maturity. Using the social competence index devised by Phillips and Zigler (1961) as their measure of maturity, these investigators did find a greater disparity in more mature than in less mature individuals. Contrary to Rogerian theory, the magnitude of the disparity was unrelated to the level of the individual's psychological adjustment.

The developmental rationale underlying the predicted positive relationship between self-image disparity and maturity level was based upon two factors. The first of these was that the higher the maturity level, the greater the individual's capacity for incorporating social demands, mores, and values. The high developmental person, then, makes greater self-demands, is more often unable to fulfill them, and consequently experiences more guilt than the low developmental person (Phillips and Rabinovitch, 1958; Phillips and Zigler, 1961). The second factor is based upon the work of Werner and Piaget who have discovered a greater degree of cognitive differentiation at higher levels of development.

In any cognition, the more mature individual should employ more categories and make finer distinctions within each category than a less mature individual. This greater differentiating ability should result in a greater disparity when an individual first judges his real self and then his ideal self.

This view that self-ideal discrepancy is a product of both social guilt and cognitive differentiation was tested (Achenbach and Zigler, 1963) by employing a number of measures which differentially tapped these two factors. The disparity between real self and social self, that is, the self as one believes others see it (Brownfain, 1952), was assumed to be less influenced by social guilt and did indeed result in a smaller disparity than obtained with the real- ideal-self instruments. Furthermore, the assessment of these disparities by means of an adjective check list, which allows only a "yes" or "no," and is thus less sensitive to the effects of the cognitive differentiation factor, resulted in smaller disparity scores than obtained with a questionnaire format involving six alternatives to each item. Consistent with their developmental position, Achenbach and Zigler found that the differences between high and low maturity groups in self-image disparity were greatest on instruments involving both the guilt and differentiation factors (i.e., real- ideal-self questionnaire), smaller on instruments involving a single factor (real-ideal check list and real-social questionnaire), and nonexistent on a measure in which both factors were minimized (i.e., real-social check list).

Although the findings of the Achenbach and Zigler study were in keeping with developmental thinking, it should be noted that all of the subjects employed were adults whose developmental level was assessed by a social competence index consisting of the variables of education, intelligence, employment history, occupation, and marital status. Some exception could be taken to the assumption that such an index is a very sensitive indicator of developmental level. A more direct test of the developmental position suggests itself. This position clearly generates the view that there is an ontogenetic sequence in the development of self-disparity. A major purpose of the present study, then, was to test the specific prediction that younger children exhibit less disparity between perceived and ideal self than do older children.

Although chronological age is perhaps the most frequently used indicator of development, there is little question that chronological age is not the most sensitive reflector of the cognitive structures which are assumed to be changing with various developmental levels or stages (Piaget, 1932; Zigler, 1963). A better indicator of the child's cognitive structure, and thus his developmental level, in his mental age. In terms of the design of the present study, then, we would not only expect more self-image disparity with increasing age, but also more disparity in high- than in low-IQ children within each age level.

As in the earlier study, six measures were collected on every subject—three image measures (real self, ideal self, and social self), each in two formats (questionnaire and adjective check list). The general expectation here

was that the disparity would be highest where both guilt and cognitive differentiation were reflected, that is, real- ideal-self disparity on the questionnaire, and lowest where the effects of both these factors were minimized, that is, real- social-self disparity on the adjective check list. Furthermore, the developmental position would generate the prediction that the differences between developmental groups, defined by age and/or IQ, on self-image disparity should be greatest on measures sensitive to both factors, less on measures sensitive to a single factor, and least on measures relatively insensitive to both factors.

An ambiguity in the Achenbach and Zigler study was the failure to delineate the exact nature of the larger self-image disparity found in the more mature subjects. It would be interesting to discover whether a larger self-ideal discrepancy in more mature individuals was due to a lower self-evaluation, a higher self-expectation, or some particular combination of the two. The present study attempted to obtain data on this issue by assessing not only the amount of disparity, but these particular features of the disparity as well.

METHOD

Subjects

One-hundred-twenty children were randomly selected from all fifth-, eighth-, and eleventh-grade classes of the Carl Place, Long Island, public school system. The particular grades were chosen to include elementary school and junior and senior high school children. Since the questionnaires used were self-administering and dependent on the subject's ability to read, it was not deemed feasible to employ subjects younger than 10 years of age (fifth grade).

Within each grade level, subjects were dichotomized on the basis of Otis Quick-Scoring Mental Ability Test scores into high and low groups. The mean IQs of the low groups were 91, 93, and 94 for the fifth, eighth, and eleventh grades, respectively. The mean IQs of the high groups were 124, 127, and 125 for the fifth, eighth, and eleventh grades, respectively. An equal number of male and female subjects was employed within each age and intelligence classification. Thus, a three-way factorial design (Age × IQ × Sex) was employed which consisted of 12 groups of 10 subjects each.

Although a number of earlier studies (reviewed by Wiley, 1961) and a more recent one (McDonald and Gynther, 1965) have indicated no clear relationship between self-image disparity and socioeconomic status, use of the IQ variable sensitized the authors to the social class issue. For this reason a middle-class community was chosen that was very homogeneous in respect to socioeconomic status.

Self-Image-Disparity Measures[2]

Two self-image-disparity measures were employed. These were designed to be as similar as possible to those employed in the Achenbach-Zigler study and still be relevant for children. Some of the items used were taken from Coopersmith's (1959) scale of self-esteem. The first instrument was a questionnaire composed of 20 statements. The subject's task was to select one of six alternatives for each statement ranging from "very true" to "very untrue." Half of the statements

---

[2]Appended to the selection.

were negative, for example, "I often wish I were someone else," and half were positive, for example, "I'm popular with the other kids." The same 20 statements were used in different orders when assessing real self, ideal self, and social self. When measuring real self, response alternatives were phrased "This is very true of me," etc.; for ideal self, "I would like this to be very true of me"; finally, for social self, "People think this is very true of me." The most positive alternative was scored with 1 point ("very true" on positive items and "very untrue" on negative items), whereas the most negative received a score of 6. Thus, the possible range for each self-measure was from 20 (most positive) to 120 (most negative).

The second instrument consisted of a list of 20 adjectives, 10 positive, for example, "successful," and 10 negative, for example, "sneaky." For each adjective there were only two response alternatives, "yes" or "no." Analogous to the questionnaire, three different orders of the list were given to assess real self, ideal self, and social self. Positive responses were scored 0 ("no" to negative or "yes" to positive adjectives) and negative responses scored 1. The possible range on this instrument was from 0 (most positive) to 20 (most negative).

Considerable evidence has now been presented that the type of instruments used in this study are reliable in the chronological and mental age groups employed in this study (Engel, 1959; McAfee and Cleland, 1965; Perkins and Shannon, 1965).

Procedure

The instruments were group administered to entire classes in their schoolrooms. The subjects were told that the experimenter wanted to find out what chil-

TABLE 1.—Self-Image Scores for Each Group

GROUP	N	QUESTIONNAIRE					ADJECTIVE CHECK LIST				
		Absolute scores			Disparity		Absolute scores			Disparity	
		Real	Ideal	Social	Real–ideal	Real–social	Real	Ideal	Social	Real–ideal	Real–social
5th grade											
Low IQ	20	57.4	46.4	55.6	11.0	2.2	4.2	1.9	4.8	2.3	–.6
High IQ	20	51.2	40.0	49.0	11.2	2.2	3.2	.9	3.0	2.3	.2
8th grade											
Low IQ	20	61.6	46.2	54.2	15.4	7.4	5.5	1.0	4.3	4.5	1.2
High IQ	20	60.4	31.6	57.1	28.8	3.3	6.6	1.0	5.4	5.6	.8
11th grade											
Low IQ	20	57.4	38.4	51.4	19.0	6.0	4.6	.5	4.4	4.1	.2
High IQ	20	60.8	33.9	54.7	26.9	6.1	6.5	.6	5.4	5.9	1.1

dren thought about themselves. They were told that there were no right or wrong answers, that their responses would be kept in strict confidence, and that nobody at the school would be permitted to see the questionnaires. Specific instructions as to how to respond were printed at the top of each section, and a sample item was demonstrated by the experimenter on the blackboard. The questionnaires and adjective lists were always administered in the same order, namely, real self, ideal self, and social self with the three questionnaires first and the three adjective lists next.

RESULTS

The mean group absolute and disparity scores obtained on both the questionnaire and the adjective check list are contained in Table 1.

Disparity between Real and Ideal Self

A Lindquist (1953) repeated-measures analysis of variance (Measure × Age × IQ × Sex) was conducted on the real- and ideal-self questionnaire scores. The findings relevant to the hypotheses of this study are contained

in the within-subjects portion of this analysis. These findings revealed a significant measure effect ($F_{1,108} = 267.64$, $p < .001$), a significant Measure × Age interaction ($F_{2,108} = 11.60$, $p < .001$), and a significant Measure × IQ effect ($F_{1,108} = 11.12$, $p < .01$). As can be seen in Table 1, real-self scores are greater (more negative) than ideal-self scores. The two significant interactions indicate that the magnitude of this difference between real and ideal scores is influenced by both age and IQ. The Measure × Age interaction reflects the greater differences between real and ideal scores at Grades 11 and 8 than at Grade 5. The mean differences at these grades were 23.0, 22.1, and 11.1, respectively. The Measure × IQ interaction reflects the finding that the high-IQ subjects exhibit a greater discrepancy between real and ideal scores than do low-IQ subjects (22.3 versus 15.1).

In order to further assess these differential discrepancy scores, real-self and ideal-self questionnaire scores were analyzed separately in Age × IQ × Sex analyses of variance. The analysis of real-self scores revealed a significant difference associated with age

($F_{2,108} = 5.36$, $p < .01$). The real-self ratings were found to be more negative at Grades 11 and 8 than at 5 (59.1, 61.0 versus 54.3). A significant Age × IQ interaction ($F_{2,108} = 3.06$, $p < .05$) was also found. As can be seen in Table 1, this interaction reflected the different relative positions of high- and low-IQ children at the three grade levels. In the fifth grade, high-IQ subjects express more positive feelings about themselves than the low-IQ subjects; at the eighth grade, high- and low-IQ subjects are similar; and at the eleventh grade, high-IQ subjects express more negative real-self ratings than their less intelligent peers. On the ideal-self analysis, significant age ($F_{2,108} = 4.36$, $p < .05$) and IQ ($F_{1,108} = 18.77$, $p < .001$) main effects were found, indicating that the older or brighter the child, the more positive was his ideal self.

The repeated-measures analysis of variance of the real- and ideal-self scores on the adjective check list resulted in findings similar to those obtained on the questionnaire instrument. A significant measure effect ($F_{1,108} = 253.33$, $p < .001$) and a significant Measure × Age interaction ($F_{2,108} = 12.69$, $p < .001$) were found, reflecting greater negative scores on the real than on the ideal measure, and an increase in real-ideal disparity with age. A Measure × IQ interaction of borderline significance ($p < .10$) was also found. This trend was in the same direction as the significant findings on the questionnaire and reflects the tendency for greater real-ideal disparity in high- than in low-IQ subjects.

Analyses conducted separately on the real- and on the ideal-self adjective scores revealed only significant age effects on both the real ($F_{2,108} = 7.09$, $p < .01$) and ideal ($F_{2,108} = 4.22$, $p < .05$) scores. With increasing age, the real scores became more negative, and the ideal scores more positive.

Disparity between Real and Social Self

The repeated-measures analysis done on the real and ideal scores was also run on the real and social scores. On the real and social questionnaire scores this analysis resulted in a significant measure effect ($F_{1,108} = 45.30$, $p < .001$ and a significant Measure × Age interaction ($F_{2,108} = 3.93$, $p < .05$). As can be seen in Table 1, the social-self scores were smaller (more positive) than the real-self scores. The interaction indicates that the magnitude of difference between real- and social-self scores increases with age. Unlike the real-ideal discrepancy, however, the real-social discrepancy was not significantly influenced by IQ.

An Age × IQ × Sex analysis of variance conducted on the social questionnaire scores alone revealed no significant effects.

The repeated-measures analysis conducted on the real and social adjective check-list scores revealed a significant measure effect ($F_{1,108} = 10.59$, $p < .01$) and a significant Measure × Age interaction ($F_{2,108} = 6.80$, $p < .01$), similar to those found on the questionnaire instruments. Social-self scores were smaller (more positive) than real-self scores, and the difference between the two scores was greater at Grades 8 and 11 than at 5. In addition, a significant Measure × Age × Sex interaction ($F_{2,108} = 4.41$, $p < .05$) and a significant Measure × Age × Sex × IQ interaction ($F_{2,108} =$

TABLE 2.—Disparity Scores Defined by Number of Changes

GROUP	REAL–IDEAL–SELF DISPARITY		REAL–SOCIAL–SELF DISPARITY	
	Question-naire	Check List	Question-naire	Check List
5th grade				
Low IQ	11.00	5.10	10.80	5.60
High IQ	10.10	3.90	9.25	4.65
8th grade				
Low IQ	13.50	6.35	11.90	7.50
High IQ	15.20	6.90	10.55	6.70
11th grade				
Low IQ	12.55	4.80	11.30	6.80
High IQ	16.50	6.70	11.50	7.05
Total	78.85	33.45	64.80	38.30

3.24, $p < .05$) were found. These interactions primarily reflect the finding that fifth-grade male subjects perceived others evaluating them more negatively than they evaluated themselves. This trend was particularly pronounced in the low-IQ subjects at this age level. All other groups exhibited a real-social disparity in the opposite direction.

An Age × IQ × Sex analysis of variance conducted separately on the social adjective check-list scores revealed a significant Age × IQ interaction ($F_{2,108} = 3.18$, $p < .05$) and a significant Age × Sex interaction ($F_{2,108} = 5.59$, $p < .01$). The Age × IQ interaction reflects the fact that the social scores are greater for low- than for high-IQ subjects at Grade 5, whereas an opposite pattern is exhibited at Grades 8 and 11. The Age × Sex interaction can be described as follows: At the fifth grade the boys see themselves being evaluated more negatively than girls; at the eighth grade, girls see themselves being evaluated more

negatively than boys; finally, at the eleventh grade, boys and girls see themselves evaluated approximately the same.

Comparisons of Self-Image Disparity across the Different Measures

The findings reported to this point are generally in keeping with the major hypothesis that the magnitude of self-image disparity is related to developmental factors. A subsidiary hypothesis was that this positive relationship between development and self-image disparity is due specifically to two factors—an increase in guilt, and an ability to make finer cognitive judgments. A test of this hypothesis requires comparisons of self-image disparity on instruments differing in their susceptibility to the effects of these two factors. The expectation here was that the greatest disparity should be found on the instrument most sensitive to both factors (the real-ideal questionnaire), and the smallest disparity on the instrument least sensitive to both factors (the real-social adjective check list). Furthermore, it is the most sensitive instrument that should maximally reflect the developmental variables of age and IQ.

It is clearly inappropriate to test this hypothesis by comparing the discrepancy scores obtained on the questionnaires (a maximum possible score of 100) with those obtained on the check list (a maximum possible score of 20). In order to make all the discrepancy scores comparable, the following analyses were conducted on the total number of items changed between the two measures, ignoring magnitude of change. It should be noted that a discrepancy score defined by frequency of change was the same as that employed by Achenbach and Zigler (1963). Table 2 presents these discrepancy scores for each group.

These scores were subjected to a Measure (real-ideal versus real-social) × Instrument (questionnaire versus check list) × Age × IQ repeated-measures analysis of variance. With the expectation of the higher than expected scores obtained on the real-social check list, the findings of this analysis were consistent with the hypotheses advanced. The main effect of measure was significant ($F_{1,114} = 14.01, P < .001$), reflecting the finding that real-ideal disparity was greater than the real-social disparity across the two instruments. This would be predicted from the hypothesis since the real-ideal questionnaire is assumed to be sensitive to two factors, the real-ideal check list to one factor, and the real-social check list to no factors. Similarly, a significant instrument effect

($F_{1,114} = 401.41, p < .001$) was obtained reflecting the greater total discrepancy scores on the questionnaires (sensitive to two and one factor) than on the check lists (sensitive to one and no factors). A significant Measure × Instrument interaction ($F_{1,114} = 113.42, p < .001$) was found. This is a complex interaction that reflects a number of findings congruent with the predictions and one finding antithetical to the prediction. The discrepancy scores on the self-ideal questionnaire are significantly larger ($t = 5.21, p < .001$) than those made on the self-social questionnaire (predicted), whereas the discrepancy scores on the self-ideal check list tend to be smaller ($t = 1.85, p < .01$) than those on the self-social check list (opposite to prediction). The discrepancy scores on the self-ideal questionnaire were greater ($t = 17.16, p < .001$) than those on the self-ideal check list (predicted). Finally, the self-social questionnaire disparity is greater ($t = 11.11, p < .001$) than the self-social check-list disparity (predicted).

As predicted, a number of interactions between the particular disparity scores and the developmental variables were obtained. The effect of measure interacts significantly with both grade ($F_{2,114} = 4.24, p < .05$) and IQ ($F_{1,114} = 17.99, p < .001$), indicating that the difference between real-ideal and real-social scores is greater with increasing age and higher IQ. A significant Measure × Grade × IQ interaction ($F_{2,114} = 3.63, p < .05$) was found. Although a number of differences contribute to this interaction, a sizable portion of it would appear to be due to the finding that the greatest difference between high-and low-IQ groups was obtained with real-ideal disparities at the eleventh grade. A predicted Measure × Instrument × Grade interaction ($F_{2,114} = 11.37, p < .001$) was also found. This interaction primarily reflects the greater sensitivity of the self-ideal questionnaire disparity to grade differences. This is especially noticeable between the fifth and eighth grades, where the difference on this instrument is considerably greater than that found with the other three instruments.

The final significant finding revealed by this analysis was an Instrument × Measure × IQ interaction ($F_{1,114} = 7.65, p < .01$). As can be seen in Table 2, this interaction reflects the following: on the two real-ideal measures, high-IQ subjects have greater disparity scores than low-IQ subjects with the reverse being true for the two real-social measures, and the magnitude of this crossover effect is more pronounced on the questionnaire instruments than on the check-list instruments.

Further evidence that the instrument (real-ideal questionnaire) sensitive to both factors is most sensitive to the developmental variables of grade and IQ can be obtained directly from Table 2. It is with this measure of disparity that we obtain the greatest differences between grades and IQ levels. The only finding inTable 2 contrary to prediction is the larger discrepancy scores found in the real-social check list as compared to the real-ideal check list. However, the question of the comparability of these two scores must be raised. A phenomenon not encountered in the earlier study with adults (Achenbach and Zigler, 1963) must be noted. Whereas

the disparity on the real-ideal check list was typically in the expected direction, with the ideal being more socially desirable than the real, this was less true on the real-social check list. Unlike adults, the children were quite willing to report that they were seen by their peers as being less socially desirable on certain traits than they had reported themselves as being on the real-self check list. The failure to take into consideration the direction of the discrepancy in the scores reported in Table 2 may have led to an erroneous indicator of what we are primarily concerned with, namely, the disparity score predicated upon a change to a more positive social self. In order to investigate this possibility, new disparity scores were calculated for the real-ideal and real-social check-list data which included only the number of items in which the disparity indicated a change from negative to positive. These scores are presented in Table 3.

A comparison of these scores with those reported in Table 2 supports the

TABLE 3.—Frequency of Negative to Positive Changes in Adjective Check List

GROUP	DISPARITY	
	Real–ideal	Real–social
5th grade		
Low IQ	3.65	2.50
High IQ	3.10	2.35
8th grade		
Low IQ	5.35	4.35
High IQ	6.20	3.95
11th grade		
Low IQ	4.45	3.55
High IQ	6.15	4.20
Total	28.90	20.90

hypothesis that the larger disparity scores in the real-social check list reported in Table 2 were due to the large number of plus to minus instances. A Grade × IQ × Measure analysis of variance of the data reported in Table 3 revealed a significant measure effect ($F_{1,108} = 20.56$, $p < .001$) reflecting the predicted greater disparity on the real-ideal than on the real-social check-list scores. It thus appears that the one earlier finding that was in a direction opposite to that predicted by the two-factor developmental hypothesis was the result of ignoring directionality in the discrepancy scores. (In respect to the analysis of the data presented in Table 2, ignoring the directionality factor resulted in a more conservative test of the hypotheses under test, which nevertheless received substantial statistical support.)

Other Findings

The assumption that less mature subjects had a less differentiated response tendency than more mature subjects was tested further by running a repeated-measures analysis (Age × IQ × Sex × Measure) on the frequency with which each subject utilized the extreme response categories of "very true" and "very untrue" on each of the three questionnaires. These scores are presented in Table 4. The significant main and interaction effects found generally support the cognitive differentiation hypothesis. The children were found to make fewer extreme responses as they got older ($F_{2,108} = 3.75$, $p < .05$) with the brighter children giving fewer extreme responses than the less intelligent ones

($F_{1,108} = 6.40$, $p < .05$). As might be expected, ideal-self ratings evoked more extreme responses than either the real-self or social-self ratings ($F_{2,216} = 126.80$, $p < .001$). The significant Measure × Age ($F_{4,216} = 4.30$, $p < .01$) and Measure × IQ ($F_{2,216} = 9.10$, $p < .001$) interactions reflect the relative insensitivity of the ideal-self measure to the effects of age and IQ. It is on the real- and social-self measures that one finds a decrease in extreme responses with age and/or higher intelligence. A significant IQ × Sex × Measure interaction ($F_{2,216} = 3.65$, $p < .05$) was also found reflecting the one exception to the general findings. On the ideal-self ratings, and only on the ideal-self ratings, high-IQ boys were found to make more extreme responses than low-IQ boys. This may be accounted for by a higher level of aspiration on the part of brighter males, since extreme scores on ideal-self ratings may indicate perfectionistic strivings. It is interesting to note, however, that this exception did not occur in females.

TABLE 4.—Mean Number of Extreme Responses to Questionnaire

GROUP	MEASURE		
	Real self	Ideal self	Social self
5th grade			
Low IQ	8.8	13.3	11.6
High IQ	7.7	12.0	7.0
8th grade			
Low IQ	7.0	12.3	7.4
High IQ	5.4	11.9	5.0
11th grade			
Low IQ	6.6	11.8	7.7
High IQ	4.2	12.2	4.4

In order to assess the construct validity of the self-image-disparity concept, a correlation was computed between each subject's real-ideal disparity on the questionnaire and that obtained on the check list. The degree of relationship was highly significant ($r = .69, p < .001$).

DISCUSSION

The findings of the present study lend considerable credence to the view that self-image disparity increases with increasing maturity. Real-ideal-self disparity was found to be a positive function of both chronological age and IQ. This is a rather surprising finding in light of the conventionally dim view that has been taken of an increasing self-image disparity and the rather negative psychodynamics that are thought to accompany it (McCandless, 1961; Rogers and Dymond, 1954). The findings are in accordance with earlier results obtained with adults of varying maturity levels (Achenbach and Zigler, 1963) and suggest that self-image disparity might be better conceptualized as an index of development rather than a measure of maladjustment.

Although such a view is an unconventional one, further support can be found in certain underemphasized findings in the literature. Coopersmith (1959), in a study of fifth and sixth graders, did find that self-ideal discrepancy was positively related to anxiety. However, he also discovered that children having the largest self-ideal discrepancies received the highest ratings by others, had the highest need-achievement scores, and the highest actual achievement. This is reminiscent of Brownfain's (1952) finding that college students having unstable self-concepts made better grades and were rated more intelligent than students having more stable self-concepts. McAfee and Cleland (1965), employing retardates having mental ages similar to those of the youngest group in the present investigation, found that self-ideal disparity was unrelated to adjustment, but was positively related to IQ. Perkins and Shannon (1965), employing a sample of sixth graders, did not find a significant relationship between real-ideal disparity and IQ. However, as in the present study they did find a positive relationship between ideal scores and IQ. As noted by Achenbach and Zigler (1963), exponents of the stylistic approach to the understanding of self-image disparity, for example, Altrocchi, et al. (1960), Hillson and Worchel (1958), may well have obtained their findings (individuals with certain types of defenses have higher disparity scores than individuals employing other types of defenses) by inadvertently comparing individuals differing in maturity levels. As noted in the earlier paper (Achenbach and Zigler, 1963), the developmental position takes as its given the level of maturity attained by the individual and sees both the defenses employed and the amount of self-image disparity as an outgrowth of this level. Within this framework, the degree of self-image disparity would be expected to be low at low levels of maturity and high at high levels of maturity. However, since one finds both adjusted and maladjusted people at all levels of maturity, no simple relationship between degree of self-image disparity and adjustment would be expected.

While there have been studies with children indicating a positive relationship between self-image disparity and both paper-and-pencil tests of adjustment (Hanlon, Hofstaetter, and O'Connor, 1954) and judgments of being "less secure" (Bruce, 1958), the most consistent finding in research on children's self-image disparity is the positive relationship typically found between self-ideal disparity and anxiety (Bruce, 1958; Coopersmith, 1959; Lipsitt, 1958).

It is this consistently found self-image-disparity-anxiety relationship that has probably led workers, for example, McCandless (1961), to emphasize the ominous nature of an increasing self-image disparity. The implicit assumption that anxiety is an essentially negative agent in the individual's total psychic economy would appear to be open to considerable dispute. There are perhaps as many instances in which anxiety is beneficial as those in which it is detrimental to the individual (Ruebush, 1963). The key determinant would appear to be not the presence or absence of anxiety, but rather the individual's response to anxiety in particular situations. This basically positive view of anxiety is consistent with Hebb's (1958) argument that the capacity for anxiety increases as one ascends the phylogenetic scale due to the increasing cognitive capacity of the organism. Provided one can apply Hebb's position to ontogenetic development, the relationship between self-image disparity and anxiety becomes quite understandable within the developmental framework advanced

in this paper. Rather than being ominous in nature, increasing self-image disparity would invariably appear to accompany the attainment of higher levels of development, since the greater cognitive differentiation found at such levels must invariably lead to a greater capacity for self-derogation, guilt, and anxiety. As Achenbach and Zigler (1963) noted, the attainment of higher developmental levels does not constitute an unmitigated blessing. While such attainment guarantees the individual a greater ability to deal with whatever problems confront him, his greater cognitive differentiation also gives him the capacity to construct more problems for himself.

Support was found for the subsidiary hypothesis that self-ideal disparity, as usually measured, is a function of two underlying factors related to maturity level, namely, capacity for guilt and cognitive differentiation. On the basis of this hypothesis, it was predicted that various instruments differing in their sensitivity to these two factors should differentially assess the magnitude of the self-ideal disparity. Thus, the real-ideal questionnaire measure (assumed to be reflecting both social guilt and cognitive differentiation) was expected to be maximally sensitive to developmental trends, the real- social-self questionnaire (cognitive differentiation only) and real-ideal adjective (social guilt only) measures to be next most sensitive, and finally the real-social adjective measure (reflecting neither factor) to be least sensitive to age and intelligence effects. For the most part, the results supported these expectations.

An additional indication of the importance of the cognitive differentiation factor was revealed in the finding that the number of extreme responses is negatively related to maturity level, defined by both age and IQ. These findings were perfectly consistent with those reported by Light, Zax, and Gardener (1965). These investigators, employing exactly the same developmental rationale concerning cognitive differentiation as that utilized in this study, found that older and brighter children made fewer extreme responses in rating Rorschach inkblots on semantic differential scales.

Another finding of interest relates to the question of just what aspect of the self-image disparity changes with development. McCandless (1961) has posited that self-ideal-discrepancy scores could be easily replaced by single real-self measures. This argument is based upon the assumption that ideal-self ratings are not ordinarily subject to individual variation. The results of the present investigation contradict this assumption. The increase in real- ideal-self disparity with age was accounted for by both significantly lowered self-evaluations and more positively defined ideal-self ratings. Thus, both aspects of the disparity are related to development. In general, the magnitude of difference was greatest between the fifth- and eighth-grade children and least between the eighth- and eleventh-grade groups, thus suggesting that early adolescence may be a pivotal point in the development of self-image disparity.

The authors have presented their argument in such a way as to highlight the differences between this position and the Rogerian view that a large self-image disparity is ominous in nature. It should be noted, however, that this latter position is a logically appealing one, and considerable evidence has been presented indicating that a large self-image disparity is often accompanied in adults by a state of malaise and maladaptive behavior (Rogers and Dymond, 1954). Perhaps a judicious conclusion of the present study would be that future investigators should be cognizant of developmental factors when interpreting self-image-disparity findings a n d should expend some energy in determining exactly how the psychodynamic factors emphasized by many workers interact with the developmental phenomena investigated in this paper.

REAL SELF QUESTIONNAIRE

Introductory statement: Read each of the sentences carefully. Check the answer which tells how true of you the sentence is.
Response alternatives:
This is very true of me.
This is usually true of me.
This is slightly true of me.
This is slightly untrue of me.
This is usually untrue of me.
This is very untrue of me.

IDEAL SELF QUESTIONNAIRE

Introductory statement: For each sentence, think of how you would really like to be. Then check the answer that tells how true you would like the sentence to be.
Response alternatives:
I would like this to be very true of me.
I would like this to be usually true of me.
I would like this to be slightly true

of me.

I would like this to be slightly untrue of me.

I would like this to be usually untrue of me.

I would like this to be very untrue of me.

SOCIAL SELF QUESTIONNAIRE

Introductory statement: Read each sentence and try to imagine how people who know you judge you. For each sentence, check the answer which shows the way other people feel about you.

Response alternatives:

People think this is very true of me.

People think this is usually true of me.

People think this is slightly true of me.

People think this is slightly untrue of me.

People think this is usually untrue of me.

People think this is very untrue of me.

QUESTIONNAIRE STATEMENTS

(The same 20 statements are used in different orders when assessing real self, ideal self, and social self)
1. I like to help my friends.
2. I often get angry.
3. I'm popular with the other kids.
4. I prefer easy tasks to hard ones.
5. I am shy with people.
6. I get upset easily.
7. I'm pretty sure of myself.
8. I have trouble making up my mind.
9. I find it hard to get interested in things.
10. I often wish I were someone else.

11. I make friends easily.
12. I'm a lot of fun to be with.
13. I'm often sorry for the things I do.
14. I'm doing the best work that I can.
15. I'm pretty happy.
16. I don't like to be with other people.
17. I often feel ashamed of myself.
18. I usually don't let things bother me.
19. I am very easy to get along with.
20. I usually do what's expected of me.

REAL SELF ADJECTIVES

Introductory statement: For each of the following words, circle *yes* if it is true of you or circle *no* if it is not true of you.

IDEAL SELF ADJECTIVES

Introductory statement: For each of the following words think of how you would really like to be. Then circle *yes* if you would like the word to be true of you or circle *no* if you would not like the word to be true of you.

SOCIAL SELF ADJECTIVES

Introductory statement: Think of the way other people see you. Try to imagine just how people who know you think about you on each of the following words. For each word circle *yes* if other people think it is true of you, or circle *no* if other people think it is not true of you.

Adjectives: (The same 20 adjectives are used in different orders when assessing real self, ideal self, and social self)

| 1. easy-going | 11. good-natured |
| 2. selfish | 12. noisy |

3. moody	13. stubborn	7. shy	17. sneaky
4. lonely	14. popular	8. lazy	18. hot-tempered
5. smart	15. sad	9. friendly	19. successful
6. calm	16. honest	10. cheerful	20. fair

64 *Socio-Sexual Development in a Suburban Community*[1]

CARLFRED B. BRODERICK

Three hetorosexual attitudes and activities of children aged 10-11, 12–13, 14–15, 16–17 are explored in this cross-sectional study: social prejudice, attitudes toward romantic relations, and romantic experience (kissing, dating, girlfriend-boyfriend, going steady, love). In summary of the 10–11 year olds, it is found that they are "already leavened with heterosexual interest and activity. The foundations of future social and romantic relationships have already been laid in the general appreciation of adult romance, in the acceptance of marriage as a desirable eventuality, in the prevalence of special attachment to a member of the opposite sex, and in the crushes on relatively safe adults." The continuity between child and adolesecent development in sex attitudes and behavior is clearly depicted.

For many years the standard sequence of events leading up to full adult heterosexuality has been set forth as including the following: (1) a period of initial heterosexual orientation in which basic sex indentification and social and emotional skills are established through experiences within the family; (2) a period of sexual latency and segregation during which sex itself and particularly the opposite sex are of little or no importance; and (3) the period of adolescence when sex and the opposite sex

[1]This study was supported by a grant, MH–4974, from the National Institute of Mental Health and by the Pennsylvania State University. Acknowledgements are made to Stanley Fowler, Mary Harrison, Jay Richardson, and Robert Hobaugh for their extensive help in the design and execution of this study, and to Flora Ann Norris for her assistance in the preparation of this manuscript.

Reprinted from the *Journal of Sex Research*, 1966, **2**, 1–24, by permission of the author and Dr. Hugo E. Beigel, Editor.

begin to assume a position of focal importance.

Recent studies by Lewis (1958, pp. 30–31), by Broderick and Fowler (1961) and by Kanous, Dougherty, and Cohn (1962), however, have indicated that children who are theoretically in the "latency" period (ages 9–12) may have substantial heterosexual involvements. Further exploration of this phenomenon has led me to the belief that current theories of socio-sexual development do not sufficiently appreciate the essential continuity between the preadolescent and adolescent stages of development. As this paper will attempt to show, the heterosexual activities and attitudes typical of adolescents may also be well developed among younger children. The dramatic physiological, psychological and social changes which have everywhere been noted at puberty may be most accurately described as a simple quickening of tempo in a process that has continuous roots back into early childhood.

The present paper, however, is based on the findings of a preliminary cross-sectional study of children aged 10 to 17 in a suburban community in Pennsylvania. Its primary purpose is to provide documentation for the general point of view indicated above.

A secondary purpose is to provide more adequate descriptive material on socio-sexual development in this type of community than is presently available. Thirdly, it is hoped that this study will produce hypotheses for a subsequent longitudinal study. Where relevant, comparison will be made with the levels of heterosexual involvement found in a middle class, white Georgia community previously studied (Broderick and Fowler, 1961), and with data collected from Pennsylvania urban and rural communities in another phase of the project. Comparisons will also be made with the findings of other researchers.

The setting for the present report was an upper middle-class suburb of a medium-sized city. Sixty per cent of the fathers' occupations were professional or managerial. About 30% of the mothers worked, largely at professional or clerical jobs. Eighty per cent of the graduates of the high school went on to college. Only 7% of the parental marriages had been broken by death, divorce, or desertion.

The data were collected by means of questionnaires administered to the children by members of the research team. The study included virtually every child present in the 7th through 12th grades. Data were also collected

TABLE 1.—Total Number in Each Age–Sex Group

AGE	BOYS	GIRLS	TOTAL
10–11	98	90	188
12–13	106	115	221
14–15	172	159	331
16–17	96	110	206
Total	472	474	946

from the 5th and 6th grades in three of the four elementary schools in the district.

For the purposes of this paper the children were divided into sex and age-categories. The distribution of subjects is presented in Table 1. Differences between the sexes or between ages were tested by chi square. The .05 level of significance is used throughout.

For each level three basic questions were asked: 1) What was the level of social prejudice against the opposite sex? 2) What was the attitude toward romantic (as contrasted to merely social) relationships with the opposite sex in general? 3) What experience had there been with members of the opposite sex in a romantic context?

THE 10–11 YEAR OLDS

Social Prejudice

The work of Kanous, et al. (1962), and also our own earlier findings in Georgia, had both indicated that the almost total social segregation of the sexes reported in earlier studies was beginning to break down. The fact is, however, that despite considerable romantic involvement which will be noted later, the level of cross-sex social interaction was not very high among these 10–11 year olds.

The basic social unit at this age was the reciprocal friendship pair or triangle, and almost without exception these units were mono-sexual in their composition. Interconnecting these basic units was a web of less intimate, nonreciprocal relationships. It was among the latter—on the fringe, so to speak—that the large majority of heterosexual friendships were found. Among the five friends that the questionnaire permitted subjects to list, 30% of the boys and 38% of the girls listed at least one member of the opposite sex (Item 1, Table 2). It was indicative of the peripheral nature of these relationships that despite this sizeable percentage of cross-sex choices only about 3% of the whole sample were involved in reciprocal cross-sex friendships. Girls are more likely at this age, as at all ages, to choose a boy among their friends than boys are to choose a girl.

As in the case of racial prejudice, prejudice against the opposite sex is exhibited in different degrees depending on the situation. In order to check this, the subjects were asked to rank the desirability of having a companion of the opposite sex, a companion of the same sex or being alone in each of three different situations: eating in the school cafeteria, taking a walk, and going to the movies. Item 2, Table 2 shows the percentage of boys and of girls of this age who ranked as their first choice a companion of the opposite sex in each setting. Prejudice against the opposite sex was greatest in the cafeteria situation where only 8% of the boys and 17% of the girls preferred a cross-sex companion and least in the movie situation where 27% of the boys and 37% of the girls prefer to go with a member of the opposite sex.

It is probable that there are at least two features that discriminate these two settings. First, the level of visibility is different in the two cases. If there are negative sanctions against socializing with girls at this age, one

TABLE 2.—Heterosexual Attitudes and Activities of 10–11 Year-Olds

ITEM	BOY %	GIRL %
1. Chooses one or more cross-sex friends	30	38
2. Prefers cross-sex companion when		
Eating in school cafeteria	8	17
Taking a walk	8	31°
Going to the movies	27	37
3. Approves love scene in movie	30	57°
4. Would like to get married someday	61	79°
5. Has played kissing games		
Ever	33	46
This year	15	23
6. Has kissed, when it meant "something special"	15	14
7. Has begun to date	28	28
8. Has a girlfriend (boyfriend)	58	78°
9. Has gone steady	20	20
Is now going steady	8°	2
10. Has been in love	49	50

°The difference between the sexes is significant beyond the .05 level using Chi Square with 1 degree of freedom.

could scarcely find a setting more sure to evoke them than the school cafeteria. Secondly, it seems likely that the sanctions themselves would be more permissive in the case of the movie because of the vastly different symbolism of the two acts.

Eating together has always been a symbol of fraternal acceptance and social solidarity, and therefore social prejudices of every variety are always most evident in this type of situation. In this case the in-group whose solidarity is at stake is the monosexual clique and it is not surprising that few children wanted to break ranks in order to sit next to a member of the out-group, whatever his personal at-tractiveness might be. Heterosexual pairing in private is much less of a threat to group solidarity than defection in the public lunch room. Moreover, in our culture going to the movie is very often associated with dating and with the romantic status that goes with it.

This also applies to some extent to taking a walk, which, at all other ages, evoked less prejudice than the cafeteria setting, but more than the movie setting. Among these 10–11 year old boys walking with a girl was as firmly rejected as eating with one.

Girls were twice as ready as boys to cross the sex barrier in the school lunch room and four times as ready to walk with a boy as boys were to walk with a girl.

Attitudes toward Romantic Heterosexual Relationships

The data reviewed this far clearly establish the existence of social prejudice against the opposite sex at ages 10–11, but they also suggest that these prejudices may exist side by side with some romantic interest. The latter point was emphasized by the responses to two further items on the questionnaire. The first item showed a picture of children watching a love scene in a movie. The subjects were asked how the children of their own sex felt about what they were seeing. Assuming that the subjects own feelings corresponded to those imputed to the children in the picture, this item provided some index of the attitudes which these 10–11 year olds had toward adult romantic behavior. These data appear in Item 3, Table 2 and indicate that a majority of girls and nearly a third of the boys responded positively to a movie love scene even at this age.

A second item asked directly whether they would like to get married some day. In Item 4, Table 2 the percentage reporting *Yes* are shown. It is apparent that marriage was considered desirable by the large majority of 10–11 year-old children of both sexes, but especially by girls.

Romantic Experience

A wide range of items might be classified under the heading of romantic experience.

KISSING   One of the things which became clear in the pretesting stage of this study was that there are two basically different social settings for kissing which have quite different meanings for children. Kissing in kissing games is essentially exploratory without interpersonal implications. For this reason our data were divided into information on kissing games and information on kissing when "it means something special." Forty-six per cent of the girls had at some time played kissing games, but only half that many had done so within the last year. It would seem that some of the boys involved in these games must have come from an older age-group, since only one-third of the 10–11 year-old boys had ever played, and only 15% within the last year. This interpretation was supported by the figures for the 12–13 year-olds which showed an excess of boys who played kissing games during these years.

All of the kissing in the present sample was not done in games, however. Fifteen per cent of the boys and fourteen per cent of the girls report having "seriously kissed" a member of the opposite sex.

DATING   A few years ago a discussion of dating at ages 10 and 11 would have seemed inappropriate. Previous studies which have included these ages at all have reported only about 5% of this age group as dating (Michigan Univ. Survey, 1957; Smith, 1952). However, the earlier Georgia study found that approximately 40% of this age group claimed to have had at least one date, which indicated the presence, in some communities at least, of new norms. The children in the present sample were not so precocious as this, but in answer to the question "have you ever had a date?", 28% of the boys and an equal proportion of girls did claim to have began dating.

This was a considerably larger percentage of 10–11 year-olds than in any of the other Pennsylvania communities we studied. These differences were consistent with Lowrie's (1961) finding that more dating occurs among children whose parents are middle and upper class than among children whose parents were in the blue-collar class.

In order to find out more about dating at each age, those who had begun to date were asked a series of probe questions: How old had they been on their first date? How often did they go out? How many different people had they actually dated? Did they prefer single-, or double-, or group-dating? What time did they think children their age should have to be in after a date? The answers to these questions begin to provide some idea of what dating at ages 10–11 is like.

As we might have guessed, dating was a recent development for nearly all of these children. In fact, only 15% of the daters (4% of the whole sample of 10–11 year olds) had dated before the age of 10. Most of them (about two-thirds) went out only occasionally, once a month or less often. A few, however, did claim fairly high frequencies. Two boys (2% of all 10–11 year-old boys and 8% of those who dated) claimed to go out at least once every week; and five girls (6% of all 10–11 year-old girls and 20% of those who dated) claimed a similar frequency.

Among those who had begun to date, most (about three-fourths) had had only one or two dating partners. With regard to type of date, most boys (60%) preferred the single-date over any other arrangement at this age, as at most subsequent ages. Next in preference was the double-date (28%) and finally the group-date (12%). Girls were much less certain than boys about single-dating although it received more votes than any other type (44%). They were more comfortable than boys with the group-date which was their second choice (36%). Only 20% preferred double-dating at this age, but at every subsequent age it was the first choice among girls.

Boys felt that they should be home after a date by 9:00 or 10:00 and girls thought 9:00 or 9:30 were the most appropriate times.

When non-daters were asked when they would like to begin dating, one-third of the boys and one-half of the girls wanted to begin within the next two years. The desire to begin dating at early ages was far more common in this school than in either the industrial or rural settings we studied.

GIRLFRIEND-BOYFRIEND   One of the surprising findings of the Georgia study was that 86% of the boys and 96% of the girls of this age claimed to have a girlfriend or boyfriend. The present data supported these earlier findings to the extent that a majority did report a "sweetheart," but the majority was much reduced from the level of the Georgia sample. Fifty-eight per cent of the boys and 78% of the girls reported having a sweetheart. The sex difference was statistically significant and was consistent with the higher level of girls' romantic interest reported in several parts of the study.

The questionnaire, furthermore, included several probes phrased here as they appeared on the boys' schedules: "Does she know you like her? Do your friends know how you feel about her? Do your parents know how you feel about her?" About 40% of these relationships appear to have been wholly secret in that not even the other party knew about it. Girls were more likely than boys to confide their feelings to friends and parents. Both boys and girls were more likely to confide in friends than in parents. Both tendencies were statistically significant.

About 40% of these children felt certain that the other person reciprocated their feelings. The majority were unsure. Actually, even the 40% were over-sanguine in many cases. Of those for whom actual reciprocation could be checked (namely, for those who chose sweethearts from within the sample) only about 21% had their choices reciprocated.

It has been noted earlier in this paper that some 10–11 year old girls are interested in older boys. This is supported by our analysis of the ages of the chosen sweethearts. Of those 10–11 year olds who had sweethearts, only about 16% of either sex had sweethearts younger than themselves; but 25% of the boys and 42% of the girls claimed sweethearts older than themselves.

GOING STEADY Going steady is an institution most typical among high school students, but it was imitated by some of the elementary school children in the 10–11 age bracket. Twenty per cent claimed to have gone steady, although several of these children had never had a date. Informal interviews indicated that going steady at these ages might involve the exchange of tokens (inexpensive rings and pins) and a sort of proprietary relationship which was acknowledged by the couple and their classmates. It might involve little or no contact outside of school. At the time of the study only 8% of the boys and 2% of the girls in this age group described their relationship to their sweethearts as "going steady." The discrepancy between 8% and 2% suggests some degree of nonconsensus between boys and girls as to whether or not a relationship could be called "going steady."

LOVE As kissing games provide an emotionally safe training ground for developing competence, there seems to be a kind of practice emotion in the area of love—the "crush." Crushes on movie, TV, and recording "personalities" are surely the safest form of love. One can wish, yearn, dream, without the slightest risk of being rejected. Familiar adults such as school teachers or attractive married neighbors can also provide objects of affection almost as safe and somewhat more rewarding. Ages 10–11 seem to be the last ages that any great number of boys permit themselves the luxury of such emotions. At this age about one-fourth of the boys reported having had a crush on a famous person and an equal proportion, on a familiar adult. At subsequent ages, all but a few boys deny ever having had such a feeling. Girls, on the other hand, indulged in this romantic fantasy in larger numbers and for a longer period. At 10–11, 57% reported a crush on a famous personality and 33% on a familiar adult.

Children themselves made a distinction between these crushes and "love." As can be seen in Item 10, Table 2, approximately half of the 10–11 year olds felt that they had been in love at least once. A comparison of these percentages with those reported at later ages (See Item 10 in Tables 3, 4, and 5) reveals a curious thing: unlike the behavioral measures in this study (such as kissing or dating), the cumulative number who had been in love did not increase systematically from age to age but fluctuated uncertainly. Moreover, if one checks the data (not included in these tables) on when the individual reported he was first in love, one discovers that at virtually every age the large majority had first found love within the last year. From these two facts one may deduce that at each age there was a redefinition of what love is. It seems that old loves were systematically explained away as something less than love and only the more recent attachments were admitted. How much of this process was due to the discovery at each age of new facets of relationships which made earlier attachments seem shallower, and how much was simple rationalization, cannot be determined. Whatever the explanation, there seemed to be at each age and for each sex a large and relatively stable proportion of young people who claimed to have fallen in love for the first time within the last year. This phenomenon was already apparent at ages 10 and 11.

Summary of 10–11 Year-Olds

In summary it can be said that the 10 and 11 year-old children in this community live in a world dominated by mono-sexual associations, but already leavened with heterosexual interest and activity. The foundations of future social and romantic relationships have already been laid in the general appreciation of adult romance, in the acceptance of marriage as a de-

sirable eventuality, in the prevalence of special attachment to a member of the opposite sex, and in the crushes on relatively safe adults. At these ages kissing games become a fairly common pastime at parties. Over one quarter of these boys and girls have had their first date, and more wish they had.

Now let us see what changes occur in the next two years, which include the onset of puberty for most of the girls and for many of the boys.

THE 12–13 YEAR OLDS

Social Prejudice

In our discussion of the 10–11 year-olds we noted that the social separation of the sexes was substantial but that elements of budding romantic interest and involvement were also evident. Paradoxically, both the social segregation and the romantic interest increased in the 12–13 year-old group. Twelve years of age has traditionally been held as the age of greatest sociometric cleavage between the sexes, and this was fully substantiated by our data. If each age is examined separately, age 12 was characterized by the fewest cross-sex friendship choices among both boys and girls. It is true that comparisons with similar data from earlier generations show that the degree of sexual segregation is not as great as formerly—at least in this type of community—but there can be no doubt about the continuance of the traditional withdrawal pattern.

The paradoxical entrenchment of social segregation at the same time that romantic heterosexual contacts were increasing is well illustrated by the items showing the frequency of preference for a cross-sex companion in three different situations (Item 2, Table 3). The data showed that in the essentially fraternal act of eating together, mixed company was still very unpopular, while in the potentially more romantic situations of taking a walk and going to the movies, the preference for cross-sex companions was well up from the 10–11 year-old level. In fact, preferences for a cross-sex companion in these activities were expressed by over 40% of the children in each case. With one exception (girls in the movie situation), these levels were significantly different from 10–11 levels and also they were significantly different in each case from the eating situation.

There were no significant differences between boys and girls in their response to these items at this age.

Attitudes toward Romantic Heterosexual Relationships

A further reinforcement of our observation that romantic interest increases at this age despite sociometric withdrawal, came from the data on attitude toward the romantic scene in the movie. Comparison with the same Item in Table 2 shows a dramatic shift in the attitudes of boys. At 10–11, only 30% enjoyed the scene. At 12–13 the percentage who enjoyed it was up to 44%. The girls, a majority of whom had

TABLE 3.—Heterosexual Attitudes and Activities of 12–13 Year-Olds

ITEM	BOY %	GIRL %
1. Chooses one or more cross-sex friends	25	24†
2. Prefers cross-sex companion when		
Eating in school cafeteria	13	10
Taking a walk	41†	45
Going to the movies	50†	47
3. Approves love scene in movie	44†	63*
4. Would like to get married someday	66	94*
5. Has played kissing games		
Ever	58†	54
This year	33†	20
6. Has kissed, when it meant "something special"	23	29†
7. Has begun to date	60†	64†
8. Has a girlfriend (boyfriend)	55	79*
9. Has gone steady	24	19
Is now going steady	7	5
10. Has been in love	53	45

*The difference between the sexes is significant beyond the .05 level using Chi Square with 1 degree of freedom.

†The difference from the previous age is significant beyond the .05 level using Chi Square with 1 degree of freedom.

approved and enjoyed the scene at 10–11, shifted even further in the direction of approval. The difference between boys and girls remained substantial and was statistically significant.

Attitudes toward marriage provide one more evidence of a shift toward a more positive view of the opposite sex in the romantic context. An examination of Item 4 in Table 2 and in Table 3 permits a comparison between this age and the previous one. There has been a slight increase in the proportion of boys who wanted to get married (from 61% to 66%). For girls, however, the shift was dramatic. At 12–13 girls jumped from the 79% of 10–11 to 94% —a level similar to that of girls at each subsequent age. This corresponds exactly with the findings of a national study of young girls, which also found that 94% of the girls in this age group wanted unreservedly to get married someday (Michigan Univ. Surv., 1957).

Romantic Experience

KISSING   Kissing games rose to new heights of popularity at 12–13. One out of three boys and one out of five girls had played kissing games during the year. This was the peak year for this activity for boys, just as 10–11 was for girls. A gradually decreasing number of children played kissing games at each subsequent age. By the end of the 12–13 period over half of the children had been involved in this activity at some time in their lives.

In answer to the question "Have you ever seriously kissed a girl (boy)?" 23% of the boys and 29% of the girls answered "Yes," a considerable increase over the 15% and 14% levels of the previous period.

DATING   At twelve 48% of the boys and 57% of the girls were dating. At thirteen the figures were 69% for both. These levels were almost twice as high as those found in the rural and urban districts of Pennsylvania which we sampled. They were two or three times higher than the levels reported by Smith (1952) and in the Girl Scout study.

Typically boys and girls dated only a few times a year. Sixty per cent of the daters (about one-third of the entire age group) went out once per month or less. Only 15% of the dating boys and 10% of the girls went out as often as once per week. Thus it can be seen that although the percentage of children who dated was much higher at this age than at 10–11, the frequency of activity for children who dated had scarcely changed at all.

In the typical case a child in the dating column had been out with only 2 or 3 different persons in his whole dating career, but this was up from the previous period.

Preference for single-dating reached its low point at this age. Boys retreated from the strong preference for the single-date which they showed at other ages to the extent that only 44% preferred it at 12–13. Among girls this age only 24% prefer this more adventurous dating pattern. As interest in single-dating waned, interest in double-dating rose to its highest point (45% of the boys and 57% of the girls). The even greater safety of group-dating was preferred by 11% of the boys and 19% of the girls, but for the boys at least, this was the last age at which this alternative appealed to any appreciable number.

The majority of both sexes felt that a reasonable hour to return home from a date was 10 p.m. or possibly 11:00.

Boys were more inclined toward the later hour.

As at the earlier age, those who did not date hoped to begin within the next year or two.

GIRLFRIEND-BOYFRIEND   One of the interesting features about girlfriend boyfriend choices is that the percentage making these choices remained relatively constant at each age. But if the proportion of sweethearts chosen did not change, there was some evidence that the nature of the relationship did. Expected reciprocation had moved up to 48% and the actual reciprocation to 35%. It would seem that this reflects an important step toward real romantic relationships with the opposite sex and away from the largely imaginary character of earlier relationships.

Children of this age were somewhat more willing to reveal their romantic attachments than at earlier ages. The biggest increase was in the girls' communication with their friends. At this age and at subsequent ages girls were more likely to let their friends know how they felt (71%) than they were to let the boyfriend himself know (66%). Girls seemed to have acquired more confidence in their parents also, since the percentage who knew about their daughter's boyfriend jumped from 46% to 64%. Despite this increase, parents still trailed friends considerably.

Boys increased their confidences to friends and parents too, but not so dramatically as girls. For 62% of the boys their sweetheart knew, for 53% their friends knew, and for 40% their parents knew. It is clear that for boys particularly, a great deal of secretiveness was still a part of the sweetheart picture.

The tendency for girls to choose boyfriends older than themselves and for boys to choose girlfriends younger than themselves was accentuated at this age. Forty-seven per cent of the girls as compared to only 17% of the boys reported sweethearts one or more years older than themselves while 23% of the boys and only 14% of the girls reported sweethearts younger than themselves.

GOING STEADY   There was no important increase in the percentage of children who claimed they had ever gone steady. Nineteen per cent of the girls and 24% of the boys reported having gone steady at least once. Approximately 5% of both sexes were currently going steady at the time of the survey. It appears that steady-dating at this age remained something of an anomaly. While with respect to early casual-dating this suburban community was far in advance of the rural and urban communities sampled, early steady-dating was far more popular in the urban than suburban setting. Even the generally more conservative rural groups were not much behind the suburban sample where going steady was concerned.

LOVE   The age of crushes on teachers and other familiar adults and also on famous entertainers had passed for boys by 12–13. From this age and onward we found that fewer than 15% of the boys admitted ever having had such feelings. This probably does not mean that these boys had fewer crushes than the 10–11 year-olds in our sample, but that having had crushes was seen as being a little ridiculous and juvenile and was therefore denied by older boys.

Unlike the boys, a large proportion of girls (about half) continued to report having such crushes. Unfortunately our data did not permit us to be certain that these crushes were current, but our own feeling is that denial of this activity is probably a fairly reliable indication of the social stigma surrounding it for any age group. That this denial did not occur among 12–13 year-old girls, seems to indicate the acceptability in this group of crushes on adults.

As for "love" itself, as has been noted the pattern did not vary much from age to age. At 12–13 most of the loves which were claimed by 10–11 year-olds had been repudiated as something less than love. Approximately half reported having been in love at sometime, but in most cases it was within the last two years. Typically, students reported having had only one, or at most two, such loves in their whole experience.

Summary of 12–13 Year-Olds

This age group continues to show little inclination to form close social attachments to members of the opposite sex whether it be on a friendship or on a steady-dating basis. In contrast to this social rejection, interest in the opposite sex as an object of romantic attraction increases significantly.

The stage is set for the major shift toward heterosexual social involvement which comes with fully established adolescence.

THE 14–15 YEAR OLDS

Social Prejudice

The withdrawal of the two sexes into separate groups which was such a notable part of the social world of 12–

13 year-olds was beginning to diminish at 14–15. The percentage of boys who chose at least one girl among their friends rose from 25% to 39% (Item 1, Table 4). For girls, who are usually the more precocious in such matters, the percentage rose from 24% to 50%. An increasing proportion of girls reported not one, but two, members of the opposite sex among their friends, thus foreshadowing a basic change in the nature of the sociometric network at the next age. All of these data on cross-sex friendship contrasted with the findings of Gordon (1957) that in his entire tenth-grade sample not one person made a cross-sex friendship choice.

Preference for a companion of the opposite sex in various situations also increased. Both boys and girls continued to be rather conservative when choosing a companion in the school cafeteria situation. Out of every five boys and girls only one felt that he would actually prefer a member of the opposite sex.

For girls this age marked a big increase in their preference for a male companion in walking and movie situations. The percentage preferring boys was up from about 45% at 12–13 to a solid 75% at 14–15. For boys the level of cross-sex preference in the walking situation remained at 41%. In the movie situation the percentage preferring girls was up from 50 to 65.

Attitude toward Romantic Heterosexual Relationships

The impression that attitudes toward romance had taken a decisive upturn was reinforced by the responses of these young people to the romantic movie scene. Three out of four 14–15 year-old boys and girls enjoyed and approved such scenes.

Boys' attitude toward marriage improved still further at this age. Seventy-three per cent were sure they wanted to marry. The comparable figure for the girls was 91%.

Romantic Experience

KISSING   An analysis of Item 5 in Tables 2, 3, 4, and 5 indicates that at each age from 10 through 15 a new wave of young people discovered kissing games, played them at their parties off and on for a year or two, and then passed on to other activities. It appears also that the 14–15 group was the last among whom kissing games had a place for any significant number. Even at this age, although the large majority had at some time played kissing games, most of them had not participated within the last year. But if most 14–15 year-olds had passed on from kissing games to other pursuits, it is clear from Item 6 in Table 4 that one of these pursuits was kissing on a private enterprise basis. Actually in this instance the grouping of 14 and 15 year-olds together obscures an important development. At age fourteen 36% of the boys and girls had "seriously" kissed someone outside of kissing games. By 15 the percentages were 60 for boys and 69 for girls. If 12–13 was the big age for kissing games, it is clear that 15 was the age at which private kissing became a major phenomenon in this suburban community.

Consistent with this big increase in "serious" kissing we found an increase in the total number of kissing partners reported. Thus the majority of 14 year-olds who had kissed any one at all

had only kissed one to three persons, but for 15 year-olds two to six partners was a more typical range.

DATING   As previously stated, most children in this community had begun to date by the age of 13; however, an additional 15% joined the ranks of daters in the present age-period to bring the totals to 84% for both boys and girls.

Among those who dated there was some increase in frequency. For boys the per cent who claimed they went out at least once per week increased from 15% at ages 12–13 to 24% at 14–15. For girls the increase was from 10% to 34%. It remained true, however, that the majority of boys (53%) and a substantial number of girls (42%) who had begun to date went out only once per month or less.

The typical dater had been out with four or more different persons. Girls were more likely than boys to have dated this broadly. (Seventy per cent of the girls versus 56% of the boys). The difference was statistically significant.

Double-dating remained the most popular type of date for girls. 51% preferred it to 39% who preferred single-dating. Boys swung back to a preference for the single-date with 52% preferring this arrangement against 42% for the double-date. Group-dating retained very few advocates at this age: only 7% of the boys and 10% of the girls.

In the opinion of these young people 11:00 or 12:00 was the appropriate hour to come home after a date. Girls favored the earlier hour, and boys were about evenly divided.

GIRLFRIEND-BOYFRIEND   At 14–15 the definition of a "girlfriend" is sharply

TABLE 4.—Heterosexual Attitudes and Activities of 14–15 Year-Olds

ITEM	BOY %	GIRL %
1. Chooses one or more cross-sex friends	39†	50†
2. Prefers cross-sex companion when		
Eating in school cafeteria	21	22†
Taking a walk	41	75*†
Going to the movies	65†	74†
3. Enjoys love scene in movie	72†	77†
4. Like to get married someday	73	91*
5. Has played kissing games		
Ever	70	78†
This year	21†	18†
6. Has kissed, when it meant "something special"	49†	54†
7. Has begun to date	84†	84†
8. Has a girlfriend (boyfriend)	45	68*†
9. Has gone steady	41†	45†
Is now going steady	9	16†
10. Has been in love	64*	42

*The difference between the sexes is significant beyond the .05 level using Chi Square with 1 degree of freedom.

†The difference from the previous age is significant beyond the .05 level using Chi Square with 1 degree of freedom.

revised. At 14–15, only 45% did. At earlier ages 78% to 79% of the girls claimed to have a boyfriend. At 14–15, only 68% did. Some insight can be gained into the meaning of this downward turn in the extension of sweetheart choices by noting that at this age two out of three children expected reciprocation (compared to about half at 12–13). Actual reciprocation also rose sharply from the 35% levels of the previous age to about 55%. It appears that girlfriend-boyfriend relationships were becoming far more real.

This impression is reinforced by an examination of the relationship between friendship choices and sweet-heart choices. Near the beginning of the questionnaire, before the cross-sex focus of the study was apparent, each subject was asked to list his best friend and then four other persons he liked almost as well. Near the end of the questionnaire he was asked the name of his special girlfriend if he had one. By comparing names it was possible to determine whether a boy's girlfriend was listed as his best friend or, failing that, as one of his other four close friends. This comparison showed that the 14–15 year-old boy was significantly more likely than younger boys to list his sweetheart as a friend. Girls showed a similar pattern but the difference between this age and earlier ones was not statistically significant. For both, the big amalgamation of sweetheart and friend came at 16–17, but the movement in this direction at 14–15 was a further indication of the increasing social reality of the sweetheart relationship.

This point was further documented by the increased openness in communication about the relationship. At this age 85% of the boys and 74% of the girls were sure that the other person knew how they felt. Eighty-one per cent of the boys' friends and 77% of the girls' friends knew about it, and 67% of the boys' parents compared to 61% of the girls' parents. Parents lagged about 15 percentage points behind friends as confidantes.

The spread between the ages of sweethearts continued to increase at this age as more boys chose younger girls and more girls chose older boys. Fourteen to 15 year-old girls were more likely to choose up the age scale than their masculine contemporaries were to choose downward. For the first time a clear majority of girls (63%) reported boyfriends one or more years older than themselves.

GOING STEADY   Young people of 14 and 15, particularly the girls, began to show some indications of a greater interest in this social arrangement. At the time of the study 9% of the boys and 16% of the girls were currently going steady. The proportion who claimed that they had at some time gone steady at least once was about double the proportion reported at the earlier age, with 41% of the boys and 45% of the girls putting themselves in the experienced column. The big boom in steady dating lay ahead in the 16–17

age group, but the beginnings of this movement were already apparent. About one in ten of the total sample of 14–15 year old boys and a similar percentage of the girls claimed to have gone steady three or more times.

LOVE   This age period was distinguished by having the largest percentage of boys who felt that they had ever been in love (64%) and the smallest percentage of girls (42%). The sex difference was statistically significant. Some further light is cast on this difference by noting a related difference between the sexes at this age. As at all ages, the majority of subjects reported that they first experienced love within the last year. However, the percentage for boys was only 56% compared to 71% for the girls. Although not significant, this difference probably helped to account for the higher percentage of boys who reported ever being in love. It seems that these girls were more systematic than the boys in their repudiation of past loves and thus fewer appeared to have ever been in love. Boys, by contrast, were more prone to accept earlier attachments as being love and thus reported more loves. This interpretation is supported further by the fact that many more boys than girls claimed to have been in love two or more times.

Summary of the 14–15 Year-Olds

This is indeed an age of transition. The monosexual cliques of earlier ages have begun to open up to the opposite sex. In some situations, such as taking a walk and especially going to the movies, the preference for an opposite sex companion is general. Girls seem to be more advanced than boys of their own age, and the majority of them seek older boys as boyfriends while the boys are left to seek younger girls. The "secret love" is largely replaced by the publicly acknowledged girlfriend, and steady-dating begins to be more popular—especially among girls. Social interaction with the opposite sex has pushed forward on every front. Yet, as the next section shows, all of this is but prologue to the thoroughgoing heterosexuality of the social world of the 16–17 year-olds.

THE 16–17 YEAR-OLDS

Social Prejudice

In this community, 16–17 marks the passing of any substantial social sex prejudice. In fact the data suggest a basic restructuring of clique composition. Of those who chose five friends, 54% of the boys and 76% of the girls chose one or more members of the opposite sex among them (Item 1, Table 5). Among the girls, more chose two than chose only one cross-sex friend. This second cross-sex friend tended to be a close friend's sweetheart. It is our impression that among an important segment of the 16–17 year-olds in this community, the basic unit of the clique had become not the individual but the boy-girl pair.

By this age there was a great degree of consensus about the desirability of a cross-sex companion when going to

TABLE 5.—Heterosexual Attitudes and Activities of 16–17 Year-Olds

	ITEM	BOY %	GIRL %
1.	Chooses one or more cross-sex friends	54†	76*†
2.	Prefers cross-sex companion when		
	Eating in school cafeteria	34†	27
	Taking a walk	55†	74*
	Going to the movies	79†	93*†
3.	Enjoys love scene in movie	69	79
4.	Like to get married someday	75	94*
5.	Played kissing games		
	Ever	69	81*
	This year	13*	5†
6.	Kissed, when it meant "something special"	73†	82†
7.	Has begun to date	96†	97†
8.	Has a girlfriend (boyfriend)	59†	72*
9.	Has gone steady	65†	73†
	Is now going steady	29†	35†
10.	Has been in love	59	60†

*Sex difference significant beyond the .05 level using Chi Square with 1 degree of freedom.

†The difference from the previous age is significant beyond the .05 level using Chi Square with 1 degree of freedom.

the movies, with 79% of the boys and 93% of the girls favoring this arrangement. As at other ages, walking was the situation in which a cross-sex companion was next most desirable. These young people were still quite conservative in their choice of table mates. It appears that even at this age cafeteria social life involved segregation by sexes although there was some relaxing of this principle as compared with earlier ages. The differences between movies and walking and between walking and eating were significant for both boys and girls.

Attitudes toward Romantic Heterosexual Relationships

The high level of appreciation for romantic movies continued virtually unchanged into the present period. Attitudes toward marriage also continued unchanged from the previous age.

Romantic Experience

KISSING For the 16–17 year-olds kissing games were outmoded. As Item 5, Table 5 shows, only 13% of the boys and 5% of the girls played kissing games within the last year. Serious kissing, on the other hand, rose to new heights. At 16, 60% of the boys had kissed and at 17 it had jumped to 87%. Thus by 17 the boys had caught up with the girls, 82% of whom had kissed at 16 and 83% at 17. Most of these had kissed between four and ten different persons.

DATING By this age nearly everyone had begun to date. Only 4% of the boys and 3% of the girls had never dated. This unanimity was not observed in other communities. In the rural schools, for example, about 25% of the

boys and about 15% of the girls were still not dating at this age.

Four out of five of the daters had gone out with at least four different persons. The frequency of dating was also up. Fifty-eight per cent of the girls now went out regularly, at least once per week, compared to only 34% at 14–15. The boys were only a little behind, with 44% dating weekly.

Single-dating increased in popularity with both boys (62%) and girls (44%), but more girls (49%) still preferred double-dating. Only 5% of the boys and 6% of the girls preferred group-dating at this age. Both boys and girls believed that midnight was the most reasonable hour for returning home after a date, with some boys pushing for 1 a.m.

Despite all of this increase dating was reserved for weekends.

GIRLFRIEND-BOYFRIEND The tendency toward a more open and consequential sweetheart choice developed much more fully at this age. About the same proportion of children made sweetheart choices as at 10–11 or 12–13; namely, 59% for boys and 72% for girls. Only one in ten had any doubts about reciprocation, which is a big change from the one in three who were unsure at 14–15. Moreover, the actual reciprocation rate calculated for sweethearts who were in the sample rose to about 85%. In other words, the gap between expected and received reciprocation nearly disappeared at this age. Girls were more communicative about their boyfriends than previously. There remained, it is true, a small handful who were uncertain of the boy's feelings, uncertain as to whether he knew of their interest, and uncommunicative about their own feelings, but the very large majority were involved in an open, reciprocal relationship. It was known to their friends and parents and, we might add, approved of by their parents in most (92%) of the cases.

The boys differed from the girls in that they were a good deal less communicative about the relationship to friends and to parents.

Increasingly boys and girls of this age listed their sweethearts among their close friends. Nearly one-third of the boys named their sweethearts as their best friend compared to 8% at 14–15. When those who listed the sweetheart among their "other" friends were added to these, the total overlap between sweetheart and friend was about 50%. Only 21% of the girls listed their sweethearts as their best friend, but so many listed him among their "other" friends that sweetheart and friend overlapped in about two-thirds of the cases. This observation adds materially to the impression that by 16–17 the once secretive sweetheart choice had become a social relationship of some substance.

Among girls the preference for older boyfriends leveled off somewhat, however, the majority of girls continued to date older boys. Since these girls were juniors and seniors, many of them found their boyfriends outside the high school (56%).

STEADY DATING This was the first age at which the majority of young people reported having gone steady at some time, with 65% of the boys and 73% of the girls reporting this activity. This age also showed by far the highest rate of current steady-dating. Twenty-nine per cent of the boys and 35% of the girls reported going steady at the time of the study. These levels were two or three times as high as among 14–15 year olds.

In connection with our observations of the newly-developing pattern of mixed cliques, it seems likely that steady pairs formed the nuclei of these social groupings. A further evidence of the social meaning of going steady at this age is revealed by the answers of each age group to the question "Do you have to be in love to go steady?" Whereas at earlier ages the idea of romantic love as a prerequisite to going steady was held by 40% to 50% of the subjects, at 16–17 only 20% subscribed to this view. The other 80% apparently held that going steady was a desirable social arrrangement that need not involve any deep emotional attachment. Certainly this view is consistent with the social realities of the world of 16–17 year-olds. By 17 years of age 36% of the boys and 40% of the girls had gone steady at least twice. These figures included about one in ten who had gone steady four or more different times.

LOVE It has been seen that love was not generally held to be a prerequisite for going steady. Nevertheless about 60% of the subjects reported having been in love. As at every other age most of these had experienced love for the "first time" within the last year.

Summary of 16–17 Year-Olds

In many ways the growing tendency toward heterosexual interaction which we have noted at earlier ages comes to fruition at 16–17. The data suggest a social network in which mixed pairs play a key role. Young people increasingly go steady for pragmatic social reasons.

The processes of socio-sexual development in this community seem to be functioning smoothly, leading on toward the future stages of courtship, marriage and parenthood.

CONCLUSIONS

Although the longitudinal data necessary for a definitive test are not yet available, these cross-sectional data suggest a real continuity between prepubertal attitudes and experience and those of adolescence. For an important segment of the population studied, the years from 10 through 13 represented a period of preparation for later heterosexual involvement. It was a period marked by relative social isolation from the opposite sex but with all kinds of mechanisms for rehearsing the skills and feelings appropriate to the later relationships. Gradually, in a process of continual redefinition which appears to extend throughout the period of adolescence, these relationships became progressively more real, more open, more reciprocal, more consequential. Inevitably they also became less idealized and more practical.

Much work remains to be done in tracing the patterns of socio-sexual development in our culture, but even these preliminary findings suggest that we may need to modify our traditional points of view.

References

The date of each publication corresponds with the date given in a selection after an author's name.

ABERLE, D. F., and K. D. NAEGELE. 1952. Middle class fathers' occupational role and attitudes toward children. *American J. Orthopsychiatry*, 22, 366–378.

ACHENBACH, T., and E. ZIGLER. 1963. Social competence and self-image disparity in psychiatric and nonpsychiatric patients. *J. Abnormal Social Psychology*, 67, 197–205.

ACKERMAN, N. W. 1958. *The Psychodynamics of Family Life*. Basic Books.

———. (Ed.). 1961. Exploring the base for family therapy. *Family Service Association of America*.

ADAMS, E. B., and I. G. SARASON. 1963. Relation between anxiety in children and their parents. *Child Development*, 34, 237–246.

ADORNO, T. W., et al. 1950. *The Authoritarian Personality*. Harper & Row.

ALDOUS, J., and L. KELL. 1961. A partial test of some theories of identification. *Marriage Family Living*, 23, 15–19.

ALDRICH, C. A., and M. A. NORVAL. 1946. A developmental graph for the first year of life. *J. Pediatrics*, 29, 304–308.

ALLEN, K., et al. 1964. Effects of social reinforcement on isolate behavior of a nursery school child. *Child Development*, 35, 511–518.

ALLEN, W. F. 1937. Olfactory and trigeminal conditioned reflexes in dogs. *American J. Physiology*, 118, 532–540.

ALLINSMITH, W. 1954. The learning of moral standards. Unpublished doctoral dissertation, University of Michigan.

———. 1960. The learning of moral standards. In D. R. Miller and G. E. Swanson (Eds.), *Inner Conflict and Defense*. Holt, Rinehart and Winston, pp. 141–176.

———, and T. C. GREENING. 1955. Guilt over anger as predicted from parental discipline: A study of superego development. *American Psychologist*, 10, 320 (Abstract).

ALLPORT, G. W. 1954. *The Nature of Prejudice*. Addison-Wesley.

———, and B. M. KRAMER. 1946. Some roots of prejudice. *J. Psychology*, 22, 9–39.

ALTROCCHI, J., O. A. PARSONS, and H. DICKOFF. 1960. Changes in self-ideal discrepancy in repressors and sensitizers. *J. Abnormal Social Psychology*, 61, 67–72.

AMMONS, R. B. 1950. Reactions in a projective doll-play interview of white males two to six years of age to differences in skin color and facial features. *J. Genetic Psychology*, 76, 323–341.

AMSEL, A. 1958. The role of frustrative nonreward in noncontinuous reward situations. *Psychological Bulletin*, 55, 102–119.

ANASTASI, A., and C. DE JESUS. 1953. Language development and non-verbal IQ of Puerto-Rican preschool children in New York City. *J. Abnormal Social Psychology*, 48, 357–366.

ANDERSON, J. E. 1960. The prediction of adjustment over time. In I. Iscoe and H. W. Stevenson (Eds.), *Personality Development in Children*. University of Texas Press, pp. 28–72.

ANDERSON, R. C. 1964. *Shaping Logical Behavior in Six- and Seven-Year-Olds*. University of Illinois Press.

——, J. BOONE, and J. DANIEL. 1965. Common elements program for the card array task. *University of Illinois Training Research Laboratory Monographs*, 1, 1–200.

ANISFELD, M., S. R. MUNOZ, and W. E. LAMBERT. 1963. The structure and dynamics of the ethnic attitudes of Jewish adolescents. *J. Abnormal Social Psychology*, 66, 31–36.

ANTHONY, J. 1957. Symposium on the contribution of current theories to an understanding of child development: IV. The system makers: Piaget and Freud. *British J. Medical Psychology*, 30, 255–269.

ARMSTRONG, R. D. 1958. Reading success and personal growth. *Reading Teacher*, 12, 19–23.

ARONFREED, J. 1960. Moral behavior and sex identity. In D. R. Miller and G. E. Swanson (Eds.), *Inner Conflict and Defense*. Holt, Rinehart and Winston, pp. 177–193.

——. 1961. The nature, variety, and social patterning of moral responses to transgression. *J. Abnormal Social Psychology*, 63, 223–240.

ARONSON, E. and J. M. CARLSMITH. 1963. Effect of severity of threat on the devaluation of forbidden behavior. *J. Abnormal Social Psychology*, 66, 584–588.

ASHBY, W. R. 1956. *An Introduction to Cybernetics*. John Wiley.

ASHER, E. J. 1935. The inadequacy of current intelligence tests for testing Kentucky mountain children. *J. Genetic Psychology*, 46, 480–486.

ATKINSON, J. W. 1957. Motivational determinants of risk-taking behavior. *Psychological Review*, 64, 359–372.

AUBLE, D. 1953. Extended tables for the Mann-Whitney statistics. Bulletin, Institute Educational Research, 1: 2.

AUSUBEL, D. P. 1961. *Maori Youth*. Price, Milburn.

——, and H. M. SCHIFF. 1954. The effect of incidental and experimentally induced experience in the learning of relevant and irrelevant causal relationships by children. *J. Genetic Psychology*, 84, 109–123.

AYRES, L. P. 1909. *Laggards in Our Schools*. Russell Sage Foundation.

BAHN, A. K., and V. B. NORMAN. 1959. First national report on patients of mental health clinics. *Public Health Reports*, 74, 943.

BAKER, B. O., and J. BLOCK. 1957. Accuracy of interpersonal prediction as a function of judge and object characteristics. *J. Abnormal Social Psychology*, 54, 37–43.

BALDWIN, J. M. 1906. *Social and Ethical Interpretations in Mental Development*. Macmillan.

BANDURA, A. 1963. The role of imitation in personality development. *J. Nursery Education*, 18, 207–215.

——, and R. H. WALTERS. 1963. *Social Learning and Personality Development*. Holt, Rinehart and Winston.

BARKER, R. G., and H. F. WRIGHT. 1955. *Midwest and Its Children: The Psychological Ecology of an American Town*. Row, Peterson.

BARNDT, R. J., and D. M. JOHNSON. 1955. Time orientation in delinquents. *J. Abnormal Social Psychology*, 51, 343–345.

BARRON, F. 1958. The psychology of imagination. *Scientific American*, 199, 150–166.

BARROW, L. C., and B. H. WESTLEY. 1959. Intelligence and the effectiveness of radio and television. *Audio-Visual Communications Review*, 7, 193–208.

BARRY, H., M. K. BACON, and I. L. CHILD. 1957. A cross-cultural survey of some sex differences in socialization. *J. Abnormal Social Psychology*, 55, 327–332.

——, I. L. CHILD, and M. K. BACON. 1959. Relation of child training to subsistence economy. *American Anthropologist*, 61, 51–63.

BARTLETT, M. S. 1937. Some examples of statistical methods of research in agriculture and applied biology. *J. Royal Statistical Society Supplement*, 4, 137–170.

BARTOSHUK, A. K. 1962. Response decrement with repeated elicitation of human neonatal cardiac acceleration to sound. *J. Comparative Physiological Psychology*, 55, 9–13.

BATESON, G., et al. 1956. Toward a theory of schizophrenia. *Behavioral Science*, 1, 251–264.

BAYLEY, N. 1949. Consistency and variability in the growth of intelligence from birth to eighteen years. *J. Genetic Psychology*, 75, 165–196.

——. 1966. Learning in adulthood: The role of intelligence. In H. J. Klausmeier and C. W. HARRIS (Eds.), *Analysis of Concept Learning*. Academic Press, pp. 117–138.

——, and H. E. JONES. 1937. Environmental correlates of mental and motor development: A cumulative study from infancy to six years. *Child Development*, 4, 329–341.

——, and E. S. SCHAEFER. 1964. Correlations of maternal and child behavior with the development of mental abilities. *Society Research Child Development Monographs*, 29 (Whole Number 97).

BECK, R. C. 1961. On secondary reinforcement and shock termination. *Psychological Bulletin*, 58, 28–45.

BECKER, S. W., and J. CARROLL. 1962. Ordinal position and conformity. *J. Abnormal Social Psychology*, 65, 129–131.

BECKER, W. 1964. Consequences of different kinds of parent discipline. In M. L. Hoffman and L. W. Hoffman (Eds.), *Review of Child Development Research*, Volume 1. Russell Sage Foundation, pp. 169–208.

Beebe, G. W., and J. W. Appel. 1958. Variation in psychological tolerance to ground combat in World War II. Final Report, Department of the Army, Office Surgeon General.

Beisser, A. R. 1964. The paradox of public belief and psychotherapy. *Psychotherapy*, 2, 92–94.

Beittel, K. R., and R. C. Burkhart. 1963. Strategies of spontaneous, divergent, and academic art students. *Studies Art Education*, 5, 20–41.

Bell, H. M. 1939. The comparative legibility of typewriting, manuscript, and cursive script. *J. Psychology*, 8, 311–320.

Bell, J. E. 1961. Family group therapy. *Public Health Monograph*, Number 64.

Bell, R. R. 1965. Lower class Negro mothers' aspirations for their children. *Social Forces*, 43, 493–500.

Bell, W. 1957. Anomie, social isolation, and the class structure. *Sociometry*, 20, 105–116.

Bellack, A., and J. R. Davitz. 1963. The language of the classroom. USOE Cooperative Research Project Number 1497. Teachers College, Columbia University.

Belmont, L. P., and A. Jasnow. 1961. The utilization of cotherapists and of group therapy techniques in a family-oriented approach to a disturbed child. *International J. Group Psychotherapy*, 11, 319–338.

Berko, J., and R. Brown. 1960. Psycholinguistic research methods. In P. H. Mussen (Ed.), *Handbook of Research Methods in Child Psychology*. John Wiley, pp. 517–557.

Berkowitz, L. 1962. *Aggression: A Social Psychological Analysis*. McGraw-Hill.

Berlyne, D. E. 1957. Recent developments in Piaget's work. *British J. Educational Psychology*, 27, 1–12.

———. 1960. *Conflict, Arousal, and Curiosity*. McGraw-Hill.

Bernstein, B. 1958. Some sociological determinants of perception: An enquiry into subcultural differences. *British J. Sociology*, 9, 159–174.

———. 1960. Language and social class. *British J. Sociology*, 11, 271–276.

———. 1962. Linguistic codes, hesitation phenomena and intelligence. *Language Speech*, 5, 31–46.

Bertrand, A. L. 1962. School attendance and attainment: Function and dysfunction of school and family social systems. *Social Forces*, 40, 228–233.

Beukenkamp, C. 1959. The noncommunication between husbands and wives as revealed in group psychotherapy. *International J. Group Psychotherapy*, 9, 308–313.

Bieri, J. 1953. Changes in interpersonal perceptions following social interaction. *J. Abnormal Social Psychology*, 48, 61–66.

Bills, R. E. 1950. Nondirective play therapy with retarded readers. *J. Consulting Psychology*, 14, 140–149.

Blatt, S. J., and M. I. Stein. 1957. Some personality, value, and cognitive characteristics of the creative person. Paper presented at the annual meeting of the American Psychological Association.

BLUM, G. S. 1953. *Psychoanalytic Theories of Personality.* McGraw-Hill.

BOCK, W. E., et al. 1957. Social class, maternal health, and child care. New York State Department of Health.

BOVARD, E. W. 1951. The experimental production of interpersonal affect. *J. Abnormal Social Psychology,* 46, 521–528.

BRADLEY, M. A. 1957. The construction and evaluation of exercises for providing meaningful practice in second grade reading. Unpublished doctoral dissertation, Boston University.

BRECKENRIDGE, M. E., and E. L. VINCENT. 1965. *Child Development.* Saunders.

BREHM, J. W. 1961. Psychological reactions to choice reduction. Unpublished manuscript, Duke University.

BRENNAN, W. M., E. W. AMES, and R. W. MOORE. 1966. Age difference in infants' attention to patterns of different complexities. *Science,* 151, 354–356.

BRIDGER, W. H. 1961. Sensory habituation and discrimination in the human neonate. *American J. Psychiatry,* 117, 991–996.

BRODBECK, A. J. 1955. The mass media as a socializing agency. Paper presented at the annual meeting of the American Psychological Association.

———, and O. C. IRWIN. 1946. The speech behavior of infants without families. *Child Development,* 17, 145–156.

BRODERICK, C. B., and S. E. FOWLER. 1961. New patterns of relationship between the sexes among preadolescents. *Marriage Family Living,* 23, 27–30.

BRODIE, T. A. 1964. Attitude toward school and academic achievement. *Personnel Guidance J.,* 43, 375–378.

BRODY, N. 1963. N achievement, test anxiety, and subjective probability of success in risk taking behavior. *J. Abnormal Social Psychology,* 66, 413–418.

BRODY, S. 1951. *Patterns of Mothering.* International Universities Press.

BRODY, W., and M. HAYDEN. 1957. Intrateam reactions: Their relation to conflicts in family treatment. *American J. Orthopsychiatry,* 27, 349.

BRONFENBRENNER, U. 1958. Socialization and social class through time and space. In E. E. Maccoby, T. M. Newcomb, and E. L. Hartley (Eds.), *Readings in Social Psychology.* Holt, Rinehart and Winston, pp. 400–425.

———. 1960. Freudian theories of identification and their derivatives. *Child Development,* 31, 15–40.

BRONSHTEIN, A. I., et al. 1958. On the development of the functions of analyzers in infants and some animals at the early stage of ontogenesis. In Problemy evolyutaii fisiologicheskikh funktsii. (Problems of evolution of physiological functions.) Office of Technical Services Report Number 60–61011, pp. 106–116. Translation obtainable from the U. S. Department of Commerce, Office of Technical Services. Moscow-Leningrad: Akademiya Nauk SSSR.

BROOKS, N. 1960. *Language and Language Learning: Theory and Practice.* Harcourt, Brace & World.

BROWN, R. 1958. *Words and Things.* Free Press.

BROWNFAIN, J. J. 1952. Stability of the self-concept as a dimension of personality. *J. Abnormal and Social Psychology,* 47, 597–606.

BRUCE, P. 1958. Relationship of self-acceptance to other variables with sixth-grade children oriented in self-understanding. *J. Educational Psychology*, 49, 229–238.

BRUNER, J. S. 1961. The act of discovery. *Harvard Educational Review*, 31, 21–32.

——, J. GOODNOW, and G. A. AUSTIN. 1956. *A Study of Thinking*. John Wiley.

BUCK, J. 1949. The H. T. P. Technique. *J. Clinical Psychology*, 5, 37–74.

BURCHINAL, L. G., and J. E. ROSSMAN. 1961. Relations among maternal employment indices and developmental characteristics of children. *Marriage Family Living*, 23, 334–340.

BURKS, B., D. W. JENSEN, and L. M. TERMAN. 1930. *Genetic Studies of Genius: III. The Promise of Youth*. Stanford University Press.

BURTON, R. V., E. E. MACCOBY, and W. ALLINSMITH. 1961. Antecedents of resistance to temptation in four-year-old children. *Child Development*, 32, 689–710.

BUSS, A. 1961. *The Psychology of Aggression*. John Wiley.

CAMERON, W. J., and W. F. KENKEL. 1960. High school dating: A study in variation. *Marriage Family Living*, 22, 74–76.

CANTOR, G. 1963. Responses of infants and children to complex and novel stimulation. In L. P. Lipsitt and C. C. Spiker (Eds.), *Advances in Child Development and Behavior*. Academic Press, pp. 1–30.

CARLSMITH, J. M. 1962. Strength of expectancy: Its determinants and effects. Unpublished doctoral dissertation, Harvard University.

CARMICHAEL, L. 1954. The onset of early development of behavior. In L. Carmichael (Ed.), *Manual of Child Psychology*. John Wiley, pp. 60–185.

CARTWRIGHT, D., and A. F. ZANDER (Eds.). 1953. *Group Dynamics: Research and Theory*. Row, Peterson.

CARTWRIGHT, R. D. 1963. Two conceptual schemes applied to four psychotherapy cases. Paper read at the annual meeting of the American Psychological Association.

CASLER, L. 1961. Maternal deprivation: A critical review of the literature. *Society Research Child Development Monographs*, 26, 1–64.

CASTANEDA, A., B. R. McCANDLESS, and D. S. PALERMO. 1956. The children's form of the manifest anxiety scale. *Child Development*, 27, 317–326.

CATALANO, F. L., and D. McCARTHY. 1954. Infant speech as a possible predictor of later intelligence. *J. Psychology*, 38, 203–209.

CATTELL, J. McK. 1886. The time it takes to see the name objects. *Mind*, 11, 63–65.

CATTELL, R. B. 1950. *Personality: A Systematic, Theoretical, and Factual Study*. McGraw-Hill.

CENTERS, R. 1949. *The Psychology of Social Class*. Princeton University Press.

CHAPANIS, A., and W. C. WILLIAMS. 1945. Results of a mental survey with the Kuhlmann-Anderson intelligence tests in Williamson County, Tennessee. *J. Genetic Psychology*, 67, 27–55.

CHESS, S., and M. E. HERTZIG. 1960. Implications of a longitudinal study of child development for child psychiatry. *American J. Psychiatry,* 117, 434–441.

——, A. THOMAS, and H. G. BIRCH. 1959. Characteristics of the individual child's behavioral responses to the environment. *American J. Orthopsychiatry,* 29, 791–802.

CHILD, I. L., J. VEROFF, and T. STORM. 1958. Achievement themes in folk tales related to socialization practice. In J. W. Atkinson (Ed.), *Motives in Fantasy, Action, and Society.* Van Nostrand, pp. 470–492.

CHRONISTER, G. M. 1964. Personality and reading achievement. *Elementary School J.,* 64, 253–260.

CHURCH, R. M. 1957. Transmission of learned behavior between rats. *J. Abnormal Social Psychology,* 54, 163–165.

CLARK, A. W., and P. VAN SOMMERS. 1961. Contradictory demands in family relations and adjustment to school and home. *Human Relations,* 14, 97–111.

CLARK, K. B. 1963. Educational stimulation of racially disadvantaged children. In A. H. Passow (Ed.), *Education in Depressed Areas.* Teachers College, Columbia University, pp. 142–162.

——, and M. K. CLARK. 1939a. The development of consciousness of self in the emergence of racial identification in Negro preschool children. *J. Social Psychology,* 10, 591–599.

——, and ——. 1939b. Segregation as a factor in the racial identification of Negro preschool children: A preliminary report. *J. Experimental Education,* 8, 161–164.

——, and ——. 1940. Skin color as a factor in racial identification of Negro preschool children. *J. Social Psychology,* 11, 159–169.

——, and ——. 1950. Emotional factors in racial identification and preference in Negro children. *J. Negro Education,* 19, 341–350.

CLARK, W. W. November 1959. Boys and girls—are there significant ability and achievement differences? *Phi Delta Kappan,* 41, 73–76.

COFER, C. N. 1957. Reasoning as an associative process: III. The role of verbal responses in problem-solving. *J. Genetic Psychology,* 57, 55–68.

——, and H. M. HODGES. 1963. Characteristics of the lower-blue-collar class. *Social Problems,* 10, 303–334.

COHEN, J. A. 1960. A coefficient of agreement for nominal scales. *Educational Psychological Measurement,* 20, 37–46.

COLBY, K. M. 1964. Psychotherapeutic processes. *Annual Review Psychology,* 15, 347–370.

COLEMAN, J. 1961. *The Adolescent Society: The Social Life of the Teenager and Its Impact on Education.* Free Press.

COLEMAN, W., and A. H. WARD. 1955. A comparison of Davis-Eells and Kuhlmann-Finch scores of children from high and low socio-economic status. *J. Educational Psychology,* 46, 465–469.

COOPERSMITH, S. 1959. A method for determining types of self-esteem. *J. Educational Psychology,* 59, 87–94.

Cox, F. N. 1953. Sociometric status and individual adjustment before and after play therapy. *J. Abnormal Social Psychology,* 48, 354–356.

Craig, G. J., and J. L. Meyers. 1963. Developmental study of sequential two-choice decision making. *Child Development,* 34, 483–493.

Crandall, V. J., A. Preston, and A. Rabson. 1960. Maternal reactions and the development of independence and achievement behavior in young children. *Child Development,* 31, 243–251.

Curry, R. L. 1962. The effect of socioeconomic status on the scholastic achievement of sixth-grade children. *British J. Educational Psychology,* 32, 46–49.

Darby, C. L., and A. J. Riopelle. 1959. Observational learning in the rhesus monkey. *J. Comparative Physiological Psychology,* 52, 94–98.

Das, J. P. 1962. Supplementary report: Semantic generalization in probability learning. *J. Experimental Psychology,* 64, 423–424.

Davids, A., and A. N. Parenti. 1958. Time orientation and interpersonal relations of emotionally disturbed and normal children. *J. Abnormal Social Psychology,* 57, 299–305.

Davidson, H. H., J. W. Greenberg, and J. M. Gerver. 1962. Characteristics of successful school achievers from a severely deprived environment. Mimeograph.

——, and G. Lang. 1960. Children's perceptions of their teachers' feelings toward them related to self-perception, school achievement and behavior. *J. Experimental Education,* 29, 107–118.

Davidson, H. P. 1931. An experimental study of bright, average and dull children at the four-year level. *Genetic Psychology Monographs,* 9, 119–225.

Davidson, K. S., et al. 1958. Differences between mothers' and fathers' ratings on low anxious and high anxious children. *Child Development,* 29, 155–160.

Davis, A., and J. Dollard. 1941. *Children of Bondage.* American Council on Education.

——, and R. J. Havighurst. 1946. Social class and color differences in child rearing. *American Sociological Review,* 11, 698–710.

Dawley, A. 1959. Interrelated movements of parents and child in therapy with children. *American J. Orthopsychiatry,* 29, 748–754.

Dean, D. G. 1961. Alienation: Its meaning and measurement. *American Sociological Review,* 26, 753–758.

Dechant, E. V. 1964. *Improving the Teaching of Reading.* Prentice-Hall.

DeFries, J. C. 1964. Prenatal maternal stress in mice: Differential effects on behavior. *J. Heredity,* 55, 289–295.

——, J. P. Hegmann, and M. W. Weir. 1966. Open-field behavior in mice. *Science,* 154, 1577–1579.

DeMonchaux, C. 1957. Symposium on the contribution of current theories to an understanding of child development: III. The contributions of psychoanalysis to the understanding of child development. *British J. Medical Psychology,* 30, 250–254.

DENENBERG, V. H., and G. G. KARAS. 1959. Effects of differential infantile handling upon weight gain and mortality in the rat and mouse. *Science,* 130, 629–630.

DENNIS, W. 1935. The effect of restricted practice upon the reaching, sitting, and standing of two infants. *J. Genetic Psychology,* 47, 17–32.

——, and M. G. DENNIS. 1940. The effect of cradling practices upon the onset of walking in Hopi children. *J. Genetic Psychology,* 56, 77–86.

——, and P. NAJARIAN. 1957. Infant development under environmental handicap. *Psychological Monographs,* 71 (Whole Number 436).

DEUTSCH, M. 1960. Minority group and class status as related to social and personality factors in scholastic achievement. *Society Applied Anthropology,* Monograph Number 2.

——. 1962. The disadvantaged child and the learning process: Some social psychological and developmental considerations. Paper presented to Work Conference on Curriculum and Teaching in Depressed Urban Areas. Teachers College, Columbia University.

——. 1963. The disadvantaged child and the learning process. In A. H. Passow (Ed.), *Education in Depressed Areas.* Teachers College, Columbia University.

——, and B. BROWN. 1964. Social influences in Negro-white intelligence differences. *J. Social Issues,* 20, 24–35.

DEVINE, T. G. 1961. The development and evaluation of a series of recordings for teaching certain critical listening abilities. Unpublished doctoral dissertation, Boston University.

DEWEY, J. 1910. *How We Think.* Heath.

DICKOFF, H., and M. LAKIN. 1963. Patients' views of group therapy: Retrospections and interpretations. *International J. Group Psychotherapy,* 13, 61–78.

DIEDRICH, R. 1966. Teacher perceptions as related to teacher-student similarity and student satisfaction with school. Unpublished doctoral dissertation, University of Chicago.

DISHER, D. R. 1934. The reactions of newborn infants to chemical stimuli administered nasally. In F. C. Dockeray (Ed.), *Studies of Infant Behavior.* Ohio State University Press, pp. 1–52.

DOLLARD, J., and N. E. MILLER. 1950. *Personality and Psychotherapy.* McGraw-Hill.

DOOB, L. W. 1947. The behavior of attitudes. *Psychological Review,* 54, 135–156.

DORFMAN, E. 1951. Play therapy. In C. R. Rogers, *Client-Centered Therapy.* Houghton Mifflin, pp. 235–277.

——. 1958. Personality outcomes of client-centered child therapy. *Psychological Monographs,* 72:3 (Whole Number 456).

DOTSON, F. 1951. Patterns of voluntary association among urban working class families. *American Sociological Review,* 16, 687–693.

DOUVAN, E. 1956. Social status and success striving. *J. Abnormal Social Psychology,* 52, 219–233.

DROPPLEMAN, L. F., and E. S. SCHAEFFER. 1963. Boys' and girls' reports of maternal and paternal behavior. *J. Abnormal Social Psychology,* 67, 648–654.

DUNCAN, C. P. 1959. Recent research on human problem solving. *Psychological Bulletin,* 56, 397–429.

DURKHEIM, E. 1951. *Suicide.* Free Press.

DURKIN, H. E. 1954. *Group Therapy for Mothers of Disturbed Children.* Thomas Publishing.

DURRELL, D. W. 1956. *Improving Reading Instruction.* Harcourt, Brace & World.

——. 1961. Pupil-team learning: Objectives, principles, techniques. In J. A. Figurel, *Changing Concepts of Reading Instruction.* University of Delaware, pp. 75–78.

DYSINGER, W. S., and C. A. RUCKMICK. 1933. *The Emotional Responses of Children to the Motion Picture Situation.* Macmillan.

EASTON, J. 1959. Some personality traits of underachieving and achieving high school students of superior ability. *Bulletin Maritime Psychological Association,* 8, 34–39.

EDWARDS, A. 1960. *Experimental Design in Psychological Research.* Holt, Rinehart and Winston.

EDWARDS, A. M. 1927. Alphabetical index of occupations by industries and socio-economic groups. U.S. Government Printing Office.

EDWARDS, W. 1954. The theory of decision making. *Psychological Bulletin,* 51, 380–417.

EELLS, K., et al. 1951. *Intelligence and Cultural Experiences.* University of Chicago Press.

EISENSTEIN, V. W. (Ed.). 1956. *Neurotic Interaction in Marriage.* Basic Books.

ELLIS, L. M., et al. 1955. Time orientation and social class: An experimental supplement. *J. Abnormal Social Psychology,* 51, 146–147.

EMMERICH, W. 1962. Variations in the parent role as a function of the parent's sex and the child's sex and age. *Merrill-Palmer Quarterly,* 8, 3–11.

EMPEY, L. J. 1956. Social class and occupational aspirations: A comparison of absolute and relative measurement. *American Sociological Review,* 21, 703–709.

ENGEL, M. 1959. The stability of the self-concept in adolescence. *J. Abnormal Social Psychology,* 58, 211–215.

ENGLISH, H. B., and A. C. ENGLISH. 1958. *A Comprehensive Dictionary of Psy*olfactory stimuli in the human neonate. *J. Comparative Physiological Psychology,* 59, 312–316.

ENGLISH, H. B., and A. C. ENGLISH. 1958. *A Comprehensive Dictionary of Psychological and Psychoanalytical Terms.* Longmans, Green.

EPSTEIN, R., and S. S. KOMORITA. 1965a. The development of a scale of parental punitiveness towards aggression. *Child Development,* 36, 129–142.

——, and ——. 1965b. Parental discipline, stimulus characteristics of outgroups, and social distance in children. *J. Personality Social Psychology,* 2, 416–420.

ERIKSON, E. H. 1963. *Childhood and Society.* Norton.

ERVIN, S. M. 1960. Training and a logical operation by children. *Child Development,* 31, 555–563.

ESCALONA, S. 1958. The impact of psychoanalysis upon child psychology. *J. Nervous Mental Diseases,* 126, 429–440.

ESTVAN, F. J., and E. W. ESTVAN. 1959. *The Child's World: His Social Perception.* Putnam.

EYSENCK, H J. 1952. The effects of psychotherapy: An evaluation. *J. Consulting Psychology,* 16, 319–324.

——. 1953. *The Structure of Human Personality.* John Wiley.

FALCONER, D. S. 1960. *Introduction to Quantitative Genetics.* Oliver & Boyd.

FANTZ, R. L. 1961. The origin of form perception. *Scientific American,* 204, 66–72.

——. 1963. Pattern vision in newborn infants. *Science,* 140, 296–297.

——, M. ORDY, and M. S. UDELF. 1962. Maturation of pattern vision in infants during the first six months. *J. Comparative Physiology Psychology,* 55, 907–917.

FEATHER, N. T. 1959a. Subjective probability and decision under uncertainty. *Psychological Review,* 66, 150–164.

——. 1959b. Success probability and choice behavior. *J. Experimental Psychology,* 58, 257–266.

FENICHEL, O. 1945. *The Psychoanalytic Theory of Neurosis.* Norton.

FERGUSON, G. A. 1951. A note on the Kuder-Richardson formula. *Educational Psychological Measurement,* 11, 612–615.

FERSTER, C. B. 1958. Control of behavior in chimpanzees and pigeons by time out from positive reinforcement. *Psychological Monographs,* 72: 8 (Whole Number 461).

FESTINGER, L. 1957. *A Theory of Cognitive Dissonance.* Row, Peterson.

FEUER, G., and P. L. BROADHURST. 1962. Thyroid function in rats selectively bred for emotional elimination. *J. Endocrinology,* 24, 127–136, 253–262.

FIELDER, H. E. 1954. Assumed similarity measures as predictors of team effectiveness. *J. Abnormal Social Psychology,* 49, 381–388.

FLANDERS, N. A. 1965. Teacher influence, pupil attitudes, and achievement. Cooperative Research Monograph, Number 12. U.S. Government Printing Office.

FLAVELL, J. 1963. *The Developmental Psychology of Jean Piaget.* Van Nostrand.

FLUGEL, J. C. 1954. Humor and laughter. In G. Lindzey (Ed.), *Handbook of Social Psychology.* Addison-Wesley, pp. 709–734.

FORD, L. H. 1963. Reaction to failure as a function of expectancy for success. *J. Abnormal Social Psychology,* 67, 340–348.

FORGUS, R. H. 1954. The effect of early perceptual learning on the behavioral organization of adult rats. *J. Comparative Physiology Psychology,* 47, 331–336.

FREEDMAN, D. G., J. A. KING, and O. ELLIOTT. 1961. Critical period in the social development of dogs. *Science,* 133, 1016–1017.

FREEDMAN, M. B., et al. 1951. The interpersonal dimension of personality. *J. Personality*, 20, 143–161.

FREEMAN, F. N., K. J. HOLZINGER, and C. B. MITCHELL. 1928. The influence of environment on the intelligence, school achievement, and conduct of foster children. Twenty-seventh yearbook, National Society Study Education, Part I. University of Chicago Press, pp. 103–217.

FREUD, A. 1946. *The Ego and the Mechanisms of Defense.* International Universities Press.

———, and D. BURLINGHAM. 1944. *Infants without Families.* International Universities Press.

———, et al. 1945. *The Psychoanalytic Study of the Child.* International Universities Press.

FREUD, S. 1933a. *New Introductory Lectures on Psychoanalysis.* Norton.

———. 1933b. The passing of the oedipus-complex. In S. Freud, *Collective Papers*, Volume 2. Hogarth, pp. 269–282.

———. 1936. *The Problem of Anxiety.* Norton.

———. 1949. *An Outline of Psychoanalysis.* Norton.

———. 1951. Symposium on genetic psychology: II. The contribution of psychoanalysis to genetic psychology. *American J. Orthopsychiatry*, 21, 476–497.

———. 1960. *Jokes and Their Relation to the Unconscious.* Standard edition, Volume 8. Hogarth.

FULLER, J. L., and W. R. THOMPSON. 1960. *Behavior Genetics.* John Wiley.

GALLER, E. H. 1951. Influence of social class on children's choices of occupations. *Elementary School J.*, 51, 439–445.

GALLWEY, M. 1964. Personal communication.

GARFIELD, S. L., and M. WOLPIN. 1963. Expectations regarding psychotherapy. *J. Nervous Mental Diseases*, 137, 353–362.

GARRETT, H. E., A. I. BRYAN, and R. E. PERL. 1935. The age factor in mental organization. *Archives Psychology* (Whole Number 175).

GATES, A. I. 1961. Sex differences in reading ability. *Elementary School J.*, 61, 431–434.

———, and E. BOEKKER. 1923. A study of initial stages in reading by preschool children. *Teachers College Record*, 24, 469–488.

———, and G. A. TAYLOR. 1925. An experimental study of the nature of improvement resulting from practice in a mental function. *J. Educational Psychology*, 16, 583–593.

GESELL, A. 1946. *The Child from Five to Ten.* Harper & Row.

———. 1954. The ontogenesis of infant behavior. In L. Carmichael (Ed.), *Manual of Child Psychology.* John Wiley, pp. 335–373.

———, and F. L. ILG. 1942. *Infant and Child in the Culture of Today.* Harper & Row.

———, and ———. 1946. *The Child from Five to Ten.* Harper & Row.

——, and H. Thompson. 1929. Learning and growth in identical twin infants. *Genetic Psychology Monographs*, 6, 1–124.

——, and ——. 1941. Twins T and C from infancy to adolescence: A biogenetic study of individual differences by the method of co-twin control. *Genetic Psychology Monographs*, 24, 3–122.

Gewirtz, J. L., and D. M. Baer. 1958a. Deprivation and satiation of social reinforcers as drive conditions. *J. Abnormal Social Psychology*, 57, 165–172.

——, and ——. 1958b. The effect of brief social deprivation on behaviors for a social reinforcer. *J. Abnormal Social Psychology*, 50, 49–56.

——, ——, and C. H. Roth. 1958. A note on the similar effects of low social availability of an adult and brief social deprivation on young children's behavior. *Child Development*, 29 149–152.

Gibson, E. J. 1962. A developmental comparison of the perception of words, pronounceable trigrams and unpronounceable trigrams. Unpublished research memorandum, Cornell University.

——, and R. D. Walk. 1956. The effect of prolonged exposure to visually presented pattern on learning to discriminate between them. *J. Comparative Physiology Psychology*, 49, 239–242.

——, et al. 1962. The role of grapheme-phoneme correspondence in word perception. *American J. Psychology*, 75, 554–570.

Gildea, M. C. L., J. C. Glidewell, and M. B. Kantor. 1961. Maternal attitudes and general adjustment in school children. In J. C. Glidewell (Ed.), *Parental Attitudes and Child Behavior*. Thomas Publishing, pp. 42–89.

Glaser, K. 1960. Group discussions with mothers of hospitalized children. *Pediatrics*, 26, 132–140.

Glueck, S., and E. Glueck. 1950. *Unraveling Juvenile Delinquency*. Commonwealth Fund.

Goldbeck, R. A., and V. N. Campbell. 1962. The effects of response mode and response difficulty on programed learning. *J. Educational Psychology*, 53, 110–118.

Goldfarb, W. 1945. Psychological privation in infancy and subsequent adjustment. *American J. Orthopsychiatry*, 15, 247–255.

Goldstein, K. 1939. *The Organism*. American.

——. 1940. *Human Nature in the Light of Psychopathology*. Harvard University Press.

Gollin, E. S. 1958. Organizational characteristics of social judgment: A developmental investigation. *J. Personality*, 26, 139–154.

Gomme, A. B. 1964. *The Traditional Games of England, Scotland, and Ireland*. Dover.

Goodenough, E. W. 1957. Interest in persons as an aspect of sex differences in the early years. *Genetic Psychology Monographs*, 55, 287–323.

Goodenough, F. L. 1926. *Measurement of Intelligence by Drawings*. Harcourt, Brace & World.

——. 1940. New evidence on environmental influence on intelligence. Thirty-ninth yearbook, National Society Study Education, Part I. University of Chicago Press, pp. 307–365.

——, and A. M. LEAHY. 1927. The effect of certain family relationships upon the development of personality. *J. Genetic Psychology,* 34, 45–72.

GOODFIELD, B. A. 1965. A preliminary paper on the development of the time intensity compensation hypothesis in masculine identification. Paper read at meeting of San Francisco State Psychological Association.

GOODMAN, M. E. 1952. *Race Awareness in Young Children.* Addison-Wesley.

GORDON, H. 1923. Mental and scholastic tests among retarded children: An enquiry into the effects of schooling on the various tests. *Educational Pamphlets,* Number 44. Board of Education, London.

GORDON, J. E., and F. COHN. 1963. Effect of fantasy arousal of affiliation drive on doll play aggression. *J. Abnormal Social Psychology,* 66, 301–307.

GORDON, W. C. 1957. *The Social System of the High School.* Free Press.

GOULD, R. 1941. Some sociological determinants of goal strivings. *J. Social Psychology,* 13, 461–473.

GRATCH, G. 1959. Development of expectation of the nonindependence of random events in children. *Child Development,* 30, 217–227.

GRAY, S. W., and R. KLAUS. 1956. The assessment of parental identification. *Genetic Psychology Monographs,* 54, 87–114.

GREENACRE, P. 1945. Conscience in the psychopath. *American J. Orthopsychiatry,* 15, 495–509.

GREENE, J. E., and A. H. ROBERTS. 1961. Time orientation and social class: A correlation. *J. Abnormal Social Psychology,* 62, 141.

GRINDER, R. E. 1960. Behavior in a temptation situation and its relation to certain aspects of socialization. Unpublished doctoral dissertation, Harvard University.

GRONLUND, N. 1959. *Sociometry in the Classroom.* Harper & Row.

GROOT, DE, A. D. 1948. The effects of war upon the intelligence of youth. *J. Abnormal Social Psychology,* 43, 311–317.

——. 1951. War and the intelligence of youth. *J. Abnormal Social Psychology,* 46, 596–597.

GROTJAHN, M. 1960. *Psychoanalysis and the Family Neurosis.* Norton.

GROUP FOR THE ADVANCEMENT OF PSYCHIATRY. 1957. The diagnostic process in child psychiatry. Report Number 38.

GRUEN, G. E., and M. W. WEIR. 1964. Effects of concurrent delays of material rewards and punishments on problem-solving in children. *Child Development,* 35, 265-273.

GRUNZKE, M. E. 1961. A liquid dispenser for primates. *J. Experimental Analysis Behavior,* 4, 326.

GUILFORD, J. P. 1954. *Psychometric Methods.* McGraw-Hill.

——. 1956. Les dimensions de l'intellect. In H. Laugier (Ed.), *L'analyse Factorielle et Ses Applications.* Paris: Centre Nationale de la Recherche Scientifique, pp. 53–74.

——. 1959a. *Personality.* McGraw-Hill.

———. 1956b. Three faces of intellect. *American Psychologist,* 14, 469–479.

———. 1961. Factorial angles to psychology. *Psychological Review,* 68, 1–20.

———. 1967. *The Nature of Human Intelligence.* McGraw-Hill.

———, R. HOEPFNER, and H. PETERSEN. 1965. Predicting achievement in ninth-grade mathematics from measures of intellectual-aptitude factors. *Education Psychological Measurement,* 25, 659–682.

———, R. C. WILSON, and P. R. CHRISTENSEN. 1952. A factor-analytic study of creative thinking: II. Administration of tests and analysis of results. *Reports from Psychological Laboratory,* Number 8. University of Southern California.

GUMP, P. V., P. H. SCHOGGEN, and F. REDL. 1963. The behavior of the same child in different milieus. In R. G. Barker (Ed.), *The Stream of Behavior.* Appleton-Century-Crofts.

———, et al. 1955. *Wally O'Neill at Camp.* Wayne State University Press.

HAFNER, A. J., and A. M. KAPLAN. 1959. Children's manifest anxiety and intelligence. *Child Development,* 30, 269–271.

HAGGARD, E. A. 1954. Social status and intelligence: An experimental study of certain cultural determinants of measured intelligence. *Genetic Psychology Monographs,* 49, 141–186.

———, A. BREKSTAD, and A. SKARD. 1960. On the reliability of the anamnestic interview. *J. Abnormal Social Psychology,* 61, 311–318.

HALEY, J. 1959. The family of the schizophrenic: A model system. *J. Nervous Mental Diseases,* 129, 357–374.

HALL, C. S. 1954. *A Primer of Freudian Psychology.* New American Library.

HALLOWITZ, E., and V. STEVENS. 1959. Group therapy with fathers. *Social Casework,* 40, 183–192.

HANER, C. F., and P. A. BROWN. 1955. Clarification of the instigation to action concept in the frustration-aggression hypothesis. *J. Abnormal Social Psychology,* 51, 204–206.

HANLEY, C. 1951. Physique and reputation of junior high school boys. *Child Development,* 22, 247–260.

HANLON, T. E., P. R. HOFSTAETTER, and J. P. O'CONNOR. 1954. Congruence of self and ideal self in relation to personality adjustment. *J. Consulting Psychology,* 18, 215–218.

HARE, P., and R. T. HARE. 1956. Draw a group test. *J. Genetic Psychology,* 89, 51–59.

HARLOW, H. F. 1958. The nature of love. *American Psychologist,* 13, 673–685.

———, and R. R. ZIMMERMAN. 1959. Affectional responses in the infant monkey. *Science,* 130, 421–432.

HARRIS, D. B. (Ed.). 1957. *The Concept of Development: An Issue in the Study of Human Behavior.* University of Minnesota Press.

HARRIS, F. R., et al. 1964. Effects of positive social reinforcement on regressed crawling of a nursery school child. *J. Educational Psychology,* 55, 35–41.

HARRIS, I. D. 1959. *Normal Children and Mothers.* Free Press.

————. 1964. *The Promised Seed: A Comparative Study of Eminent First and Later Sons.* Free Press.

HARRIS, L. 1965. The effects of relative novelty on children's choice behavior. *J. Experimental Child Psychology,* 2, 297–305.

HART, B. M., et al. 1964. Effects of social reinforcement on operant crying. *J. Experimental Child Psychology,* 1, 145–153.

HARTLEY, R. E. 1959. Sex-role pressures and the socialization of the male child. *Psychological Reports,* 5, 458.

HARTSHORNE, H., and M. A. MAY. 1928. *Studies in the Nature of Character,* Volume I. Macmillan.

HARTUP, W. W. 1958. Nurturance and nurturance-withdrawal in relation to the dependency behavior of preschool children. *Child Development,* 29, 191–201.

HARVEY, O. J. 1953. An experimental approach to the study of status relations in informal groups. *American Sociological Review,* 18, 357–367.

HASTORF, A. H., S. A. RICHARDSON, and S. M. DORNBUSCH. 1958. The problem of relevance in the study of person perception. In R. Tagiuri and L. Petrullo (Eds.), *Person Perception and Interpersonal Behavior.* Stanford University Press, pp. 54–62.

HAVIGHURST, R. J., and L. L. JANKE. 1944. Relations between ability and social status in a midwestern community: I. Ten-year-old children. *J. Educational Psychology,* 35, 357–368.

HAWKES, G. R., L. G. BURCHINAL, and B. GARDNER. 1957. Pre-adolescents' views of some of their relations with their parents. *Child Development,* 28, 393–399.

HAYNES, H., R. WHITE, and R. HELD. 1965. Visual accommodation in human infants. *Science,* 148, 528–530.

HEALEY, W., and A. F. BRONNER. 1936. *New Light on Delinquency and Its Treatment.* Yale University Press.

HEATHERS, G. 1955. Emotional dependence and independence in nursery school play. *J. Genetic Psychology,* 87, 37–57.

HEBB, D. 1958. The mammal and his environment. In C. Ree, J. Alexander, and S. Tomkins (Eds.), *Psychopathology: A Source Book.* Harvard University Press, pp. 127–135.

HEBB, D. O. 1949. *The Organization of Behavior.* John Wiley.

————. 1958. *A Textbook of Psychology.* Saunders.

HEIDER, F. 1958. *Psychology of Interpersonal Relations.* John Wiley.

HEINECKE, C. M. 1953. Some antecedents and correlates of guilt and fear in young boys. Unpublished doctoral dissertation, Harvard University.

HEINSTEIN, M. I. 1963. Behavioral correlates of breast-bottle regimes under parent-infant relationships. *Society Research Child Development Monographs,* Number 88, 28, Number 4.

HEISS, J. S. 1960. Variations in courtship progress among high school students. *Marriage Family Living,* 22, 165–170.

HELD, R. 1961. Exposure-history as a factor in maintaining stability of perception and coordination. *J. Nervous Mental Diseases,* 132, 26–32.

————, and J. BOSSOM. 1961. Neonatal deprivation and adult rearrangement:

Complementary techniques for analyzing plastic sensory-motor coordinations. *J. Comparative Physiology Psychology,* 54, 33–37.

——, and S. Freedman. 1963. Plasticity in human sensorimotor control. *Science,* 142, 455–462.

——, and A. Hein. 1963. Movement-produced stimulation in the development of visually-guided behavior. *J. Comparative Physiology Psychology,* 56, 872–876.

Helgerson, E. 1943. The relative significance of race, sex, and facial expression in choice of playmates by the preschool child. *J. Negro Education,* 12, 612–622.

Hess, E. H. 1957. Effects of meprobamate on imprinting in water-fowl. *Annals New York Academy Science,* 67, 724–732.

——. 1959. Imprinting. *Science,* 130, 133–141.

Hewitt, L. E., and R. L. Jenkins. 1946. Fundamental patterns of adjustment. State of Illinois.

Hilgard, E. R. 1962. *Introduction to Psychology.* Harcourt, Brace & World.

Hilgard, J. R. 1932. Learning and maturation in preschool children. *J. Genetic Psychology,* 41, 36–56.

——. 1933. The effect of early and delayed practice on memory and motor performances studied by the method of co-twin control. *Genetic Psychology Monographs,* 14, 493–567.

Hill, W. F. 1960. Learning theory and the acquisition of values. *Psychological Review,* 67, 317–333.

Hillson, J. S., and P. Worchel. 1958. Self-concept and defensive behavior in the maladjusted. *J. Consulting Psychology,* 22, 45–50.

Himmelweit, H., A., N. Oppenheim, and P. Vince. 1958. *Television and the Child.* Oxford University Press.

Hindley, C. B. 1965. Stability and change in abilities up to five years: Group trends. *J. Child Psychology Psychiatry,* 6, 85–99.

Hirsch, J. (Ed.). 1967. *Behavior-Genetic Analysis.* McGraw-Hill.

Hoehn-Saric, R., et al. 1964. Systematic preparation of patients for psychotherapy: I. Effects on therapy behavior and outcomes. *J. Psychiatric Research,* 2, 267–281.

Hoepfner, R., J. P. Guilford, and P. R. Merrifield. 1964. A factor analysis of the symbolic-evaluation abilities. Report Number 33. Psychological Laboratory, University of Southern California.

Hoffman, L. W. 1964. Research findings on the effects of maternal employment on the child: Summary and discussion. In L. W. Hoffman and F. I. Nye (Eds.), *The Employed Mother in America.* Rand McNally.

Hoffman, M. L. 1960. Power assertion by the parent and its impact on the child. *Child Development,* 31, 129–143.

——. 1963a. Childrearing practices and moral development: Generalizations from empirical research. *Child Development,* 34, 295–318.

——. 1963b. Parent discipline and the child's consideration for others. *Child Development,* 34, 573–588.

——. 1963c. Personality, family structure, and social class as antecedent of parental power assertion. *Child Development,* 34, 869–884.

——. In press. Socialization practices and the development of moral character. In M. L. Hoffman (Ed.), *Character Development in the Child.* Aldine.

——, and H. D. SALTZSTEIN. 1960. Parent practices and the development of children's moral orientations. In W. E. Martin (Chm.), *Parent Behavior and Children's Personality Development: Current Project Research.* Annual meeting, American Psychological Association.

HONZIK, M. P. 1957. Developmental studies of parent-child resemblance in intelligence. *Child Development,* 28, 215–228.

——, J. W. McFARLANE, and L. ALLEN. 1948. Stability of mental test performance between two and eighteen years. *J. Experimental Education,* 17, 309–324.

HOROWITZ, F. D. 1963. Social reinforcement effects on child behavior. *J. Nursery Education,* 18, 276–284.

HOROWITZ, R. E. 1939. Racial aspects of self-identification in nursery school children. *J. Psychology,* 8, 91–99.

HUIZINGA, J. 1949. *Homo Ludens: A Study of the Play-Element in Culture.* Routledge.

HULL, C. L. 1943. *Principles of Behavior.* Appleton-Century-Crofts.

——. 1951. *Essentials of Behavior.* Yale University Press.

——. 1952. *A Behavior System.* Yale University Press.

HUNT, J. McV. 1961. *Intelligence and Experience.* Ronald.

——, and R. L. SOLOMON. 1942. The stability and some correlates of group status in a summer camp group of young boys. *American J. Psychology,* 55, 33–45.

HUSEK, T. R., and M. C. WITTROCK. 1962. The dimensions of attitudes toward teachers as measured by the semantic differential. *J. Educational Psychology,* 53, 209–213.

INGLE, R. B., and W. J. GEPHART. 1966. A critique of a research report: Programed instruction versus usual classroom procedures in teaching boys to read. *American Educational Research J.,* 3, 49–53.

INHELDER, B., and J. PIAGET. 1958. *The Growth of Logical Thinking from Childhood to Adolescence.* Basic Books.

——, and ——. 1964. *The Early Growth of Logic in the Child.* Harper & Row.

JACKSON, D. D., and J. H. WEAKLAND. 1961. Conjoint family therapy. *Psychiatry,* 24, 30–45.

JACKSON, P. W., and J. W. GETZELS. 1959. Psychological health and classroom functioning: A study of dissatisfaction with school among adolescents. *J. Educational Psychology,* 50, 295–300.

JACOB, F., and J. MONOD. 1961. On the regulation of gene activity. Cold Spring Harbor Symposium on Quantitative Biology, 26, 193–209.

JAKUBCZAK, F., and R. H. WALTERS. 1959. Suggestibility as dependency behavior. *J. Abnormal Social Psychology*, 59, 102–107.

JANKE, L. L., and R. J. HAVIGHURST. 1945. Relations between ability and social status in a mid-western community. II. Sixteen-year-old boys and girls. *J. Educational Psychology*, 36, 499–509.

JENKINS, R. L. 1964. Diagnoses, dynamics and treatment in child psychiatry. *Psychiatric Research Reports*, American Psychiatric Association, 18, 91–120.

——. 1966. Psychiatric syndromes in children in their relation to family background. *American J. Orthopsychiatry*, 36, 450–457.

——, and L. E. HEWITT. 1944. Types of personality structure encountered in child guidance clinics. *American J. Orthopsychiatry*, 14, 84–94.

——, E. NUREDDIN, and I. SHAPIRO. 1966. Children's behavior syndromes and parental responses. *Genetic Psychology Monographs*, 76, 261–329.

JENNINGS, H. H. 1947. *Leadership and Isolation*. Longmans, Green.

JENNINGS, H. S. 1930. *The Biological Basis of Human Behavior*. Norton.

JENSEN, A. 1963a. Learning ability in retarded, average, and gifted children. *Merrill-Palmer Quarterly*, 9, 124–140.

——. 1963b. Learning in the pre-school years. *J. Nursery Education*, 18, 133–139.

JOHN, V. P. 1963. The intellectual development of slum children: Some preliminary findings. *American J. Orthopsychiatry*, 33, 813–822.

JOHNSON, A. 1953. Collaborative psychotherapy: Team setting. In N. Heiman (Ed.), *Psychoanalysis and social work*. International Universities Press.

JOHNSTON, M. K., et al. 1966. An application of reinforcement principles to development of motor skills of a young child. *Child Development*, 37, 379–387.

——. n.d. Effects of positive social reinforcement on isolate behavior of a nursery school child. Unpublished manuscript.

JONES, H. E. 1943. *Development in Adolescence*. Appleton-Century-Crofts.

——, and N. BAYLEY. 1941. The Berkeley growth study. *Child Development*, 12, 167–173.

JONES, M. C. 1924. A laboratory study of fear: The case of Peter. *Pedagogical Seminary*, 31, 308-315.

JONES, M. H., and S. LIVERANT. 1960. Effects of age differences on choice behavior. *Child Development*, 31, 673–680.

KAGAN, J. 1956. The child's perception of the parent. *J. Abnormal Social Psychology*, 53, 257–258.

——. 1958. The concept of identification. *Psychological Review*, 65, 296–305.

——. 1965a. Impulsive and reflective children. In J. D. Krumboltz (Ed.), *Learning and the Educational Process*. Rand McNally, pp. 133–161.

——. 1965b. Reflection-impulsivity and reading ability in primary grade children. *Child Development*, 36, 609–628.

——, B. HOSKEN, and S. WATSON. 1961. Child's symbolic conceptualization of parents. *Child Development*, 32, 625–636.

———, and J. Lemkin. 1960. The child's differential perception of parental attributes. *J. Abnormal Social Psychology*, 61, 440–447.

———, and H. A. Moss. 1960. The stability of passive and dependent behavior from childhood through adulthood. *Child Development*, 31, 577–591.

———, et al. 1964. Information processing in the child: Significance of analytic and reflective attitudes. *Psychological Monographs*, 78 (Whole Number 578).

Kahl, J. A. 1959. *The American Class Structure*. Holt, Rinehart and Winston.

Kakihana, R., and G. E. McClearn. 1963. Development of alcohol preferences in BALB/c mice. *Nature*, 199, 511–512.

———, et al. 1966. Brain sensitivity to alcohol in inbred mouse strains. *Science*, 154, 1574–1575.

Kallman, F. J. (Ed.). 1962. *Expanding Goals of Genetics in Psychiatry*. Grune & Stratton.

Kanner, J. H., and R. L. Sulzer. 1961. Overt and covert rehearsal of fifty per cent vs. one-hundred per cent of the material in film learning. In A. A. Lumsdaine (Ed.), *Student Responses in Programmed Instruction*. National Academy of Sciences, National Research Council, pp. 427–441.

Kanous, L. E., R. A. Dougherty, and T. S. Cohn. 1962. Relation between heterosexual friendship choices and socio-economic level. *Child Development*, 33, 251–255.

Kantrow, R. W. 1937. An investigation of conditioned feeding responses and concomitant adaptive behavior in young infants. *University Iowa Studies Child Welfare*, 13: 3.

Katz, D., and K. W. Braly. 1958. Verbal stereotypes and racial prejudice. In E. E. Maccoby, T. M. Newcomb, and E. L. Hartley (Eds.), *Readings in Social Psychology*. Holt, Rinehart and Winston, pp. 40–46.

Keislar, E. R. 1961. Abilities of first grade pupils to learn mathematics in terms of algebraic structures. USOE Project Number 1090. University of California, Los Angeles.

———, and L. L. Mace. 1965. Sequence of listening and speaking in beginning French. In J. Krumboltz (Ed.), *Learning and the Educational Process*. Rand McNally, pp. 163–191.

———, and J. D. McNeil. 1962. A comparison of two response modes in an autoinstructional program with children in the primary grades. *J. Educational Psychology*, 53, 127–131.

Kelly, C. M. 1963. Mental ability and personality factors in listening. *Quarterly J. Speech*, 49, 152–156.

Kendler, H., and T. Kendler. 1956. Inferential behavior in preschool children. *J. Experimental Psychology*, 51, 311–314.

———, and ———. 1962. Vertical and horizontal processes in problem solving. *Psychological Review*, 69, 1–16.

Kendler, T. 1963. Development of mediating responses in children. *Society Research Child Development Monographs*, 28, 33–53.

Kessen, W. 1963. Research in the psychological development of children. *Merrill-Palmer Quarterly*, 9, 83–94.

KIMBLE, G. A. 1956. *Principles of General Psychology*. Ronald.

KIRK, S A. 1958. *Early Education of the Retarded Child. An Experimental Study*. University of Illinois Press.

KITAY, P. M. 1940. A comparison of the sexes in their attitudes and beliefs about women: A study of prestige groups. *Sociometry*, 3, 399–407.

KLINEBERG, O. 1935. *Negro Intelligence and Selective Migration*. Columbia University Press.

KOESTLER, A. 1964. *Act of Creation*. Macmillan.

KOFFKA, K. 1925. *The Growth of the Mind*. Harcourt, Brace & World.

KOHLBERG, L. 1963a. The development of children's orientations toward a moral order. *Vita Humana*, 6, 11–33.

———. 1963b. Moral development and identification. Sixty-second yearbook, National Society for the Study of Education, Part I. University of Chicago Press, pp. 277–332.

KOHN, A. R., and F. E. FIEDLER. 1961. Age and sex differences in the perception of persons. *Sociometry*, 24, 157–164.

KOOS, E. L. 1954. *The Health of Regionville*. Columbia University Press.

KOWITZ, G. T., and L. G. MAHONEY. 1964. Sex-linked factors in reading and arithmetic achievement. Paper presented at meeting American Educational Research Association.

KRECHEVSKY, I. 1933. Hereditary nature of "hypotheses." *J. Comparative Psychology*, 16, 99–116.

KROUT, M. H. 1939. Typical behavior patterns in 26 ordinal positions. *J. Genetic Psychology*, 54, 3–29.

KUMATA, H. 1960. Ten years of instructional television research. In W. Schramm (Ed.), *The Impact of Educational Television*. University of Illinois Press.

LABARRE, M. 1960. Dynamic factors in psychiatric team collaboration. *British J. Medical Sciences*, 33, 53.

L'ABATE, L. 1960. Personality correlates of manifest anxiety in children. *J. Consulting Psychology*, 24, 342–348.

LAMBERT, P., D. M. MILLER, and D. W. WILEY. 1962. Experimental folklore and experimentation: The study of programmed learning in Wauwatosa Public Schools. *J. Educational Research*, 55, 485–494.

LANDAUER, T. K., and J. W. M. WHITING. 1964. Infantile stimulation and adult stature of human males. *American Anthropologist*, 66, 1007–1028.

LANDIS, P. H. 1960. Research on teen-age dating. *Marriage Family Living*, 22, 266–267.

LANDRETH, C. 1942. *Education of the Young Child*. John Wiley.

———, and B. C. JOHNSON. 1953. Young children's responses to a picture inset test designed to reveal reactions to persons of different skin color. *Child Development*, 24, 63–80.

LANE, H. 1965. Programed learning of a second language. In R. Glaser (Ed.), *Teaching Machines and Programed Learning II: Data and Directions*. National Education Association, pp. 584–643.

LANGFORD, W. W., and E. OLSON. 1951. Clinical work with parents of child patients. *Quarterly J. Child Behavior*, 3, 240–249.

LAURITZEN, E. S. 1963. Semantic divergent thinking factors among elementary school children. Unpublished doctoral dissertation, University of California, Los Angeles.

LAZARUS, A. A. 1960. The elimination of children's phobias by deconditioning. In H. J. Eysenck (Ed.), *Behavior Therapy and the Neuroses*. Pergamon, pp. 114–122.

LAZOWICK, L. M. 1955. On the nature of identification. *J. Abnormal Social Psychology*, 51, 175–183.

LEBO, D. 1953. The present status of research in nondirective play therapy. *J. Consulting Psychology*, 17, 177–183.

LEHMANN, H. C., and P. A. WITTY. 1927. *The Psychology of Play Activities*. Barnes & Noble.

LEIGHTON, D., et al. 1963. *The Character of Danger*. Basic Books.

LESHAN, L. L. 1952. Time orientation and social class. *J. Abnormal Social Psychology*, 47, 589–592.

LEVIN, H., and E. WARDELL. 1962. The research uses of doll play. *Psychological Bulletin*, 59, 27–56.

——, and J. WATSON. 1963. The learning of variable grapheme-to-phoneme correspondences. U.S. Office of Education, Basic Research Program on Reading.

——, ——, and M. FELDMAN. 1964. Writing as pretraining for association learning. *J. Educational Psychology*, 55, 181–184.

LEVINE, J. In press. *An International Encyclopedia of the Social Sciences*. Macmillan.

LEVINE, S. 1957. Infantile experience and resistance to physiological stress. *Science*, 126, 405.

LEVINE, S. J. 1962. Psychophysiological effects of infantile stimulation. In E. L. Bliss (Ed.), *Roots of Behavior*. Hoeber, pp. 240–253.

LEVITT, E. E. 1953. Studies in intolerance of ambiguity: 1. The decision-location test with grade school children. *Child Development*, 24, 264–268.

——. 1957a. Ecological differences in performance on the children's manifest anxiety scale. *Psychological Reports*, 3, 281–286.

——. 1957b. A follow-up study of cases treated at the Illinois Institute for Juvenile Research. State of Illinois, Department of Public Welfare, Mental Health Project Number 5503.

——. 1957c. The results of psychotherapy with children. *J. Consulting Psychology*, 21, 189–196.

——. 1963. Psychotherapy with children. *Behavior Research Therapy*, 1, 45–51.

LEVY, D. M. 1928. Finger sucking and accessory movements in early infancy: An etiological study. *American J. Orthopsychiatry*, 7, 881–918.

——. March 1937. Finger sucking from the psychiatric angle. *Child Development*.

——. 1943. *Maternal Overprotection*. Columbia University Press.

LEWIN, K. 1935. *A Dynamic Theory of Personality*. McGraw-Hill.

——. 1936. *Principles of Topological Psychology*. McGraw-Hill.

——. 1938. The conceptual representation and measurement of psychological forces. *Contributions to Psychological Theory*, 1: 4.

——. 1948. *Resolving Social Conflicts: Selected Papers on Group Dynamics*. Harper & Row.

—— 1951, *Field Theory in Social Science: Selected Theoretical Papers*. Harper & Row.

——. 1954. Behavior and development as a function of the total situation. In L. Carmichael (Ed.), *Manual of Child Psychology*. John Wiley, pp. 918–970.

——, et al. 1944. Level of aspiration. In J. McV. Hunt (Ed.), *Personality and the Behavior Disorders*, Volume 1. Ronald, pp. 333–378.

LEWIS, D., and C. J. BURKE. 1949. The use and misuse of the chi-square test. *Psychological Bulletin*, 46, 433–489.

LEWIS, G. M. 1958. Educating children in grades, four, five, and six. U.S. Office of Education.

LEWIS, H. 1963. Culture, class, and the behavior of low-income families. Paper read at Conference on Lower Class Culture, New York City.

LI, J. C. R. 1957. *Introduction to Statistical Inference*. Edwards.

LIGHT, C. S., M. ZAX, and D. H. GARDENER. 1965. Relationship of age, sex, and intelligence level to extreme response style. *J. Personality Social Psychology*, 2, 907–909.

LINDQUIST, E. F. 1953. *Design and Analysis of Experiments*. Houghton Mifflin.

LINDZEY, G., H. D. WINSTON, and M. MANOSEVITZ. 1963. Early experience, genotype, and temperament in mus musculus. *J. Comparative Physiology Psychology*, 56, 622–629.

LIPSET, S. M. 1960. *Political Man*. Doubleday.

LIPSITT, L. P. 1958. A self-concept scale for children and its relationship to the children's form of the Manifest Anxiety Scale. *Child Development*, 29, 463–472.

——, and C. A. DeLUCIA. 1960. An apparatus for the measurement of specific response and general activity of the human neonate. *American J. Psychology*, 73, 630–632.

LORGE, I. 1945. Schooling makes a difference. *Teachers College Record*, 46, 483–492.

LOTT, B. E. 1961. Group cohesiveness: A learning phenomenon. *J. Social Psychology*, 275–286.

LOUGHLIN, L. J., et al. 1965. An investigation of sex differences by intelligence, subject-matter area, grade, and achievement level on three anxiety scales. *J. Genetic Psychology*, 106, 207–215.

LOURENSO, S. V., J. W. GREENBERG, and H. H. DAVIDSON. 1965. Personality characteristics revealed in drawings of deprived children who differ in school achievement. *J. Educational Research*, 59, 63–67.

LOWENFELD, V. 1939. *The Nature of Creative Activity*. Harcourt, Brace & World.

——. 1957. *Creative and Mental Growth.* Macmillan.

LOWRIE, S. H. 1956. Factors involved in the frequency of dating. *Marriage Family Living,* 18, 46–51.

——. 1961. Early and late dating: Some conditions associated with them. *Marriage Family Living,* 23, 284–291.

LOWRY, L. W. 1948. *Orthopsychiatry, 1923–1948: Retrospect and Prospect.* American Orthopsychiatric Association.

LUNDSTEEN, S. 1963. Teaching abilities in critical listening in the fifth and sixth grades. Unpublished doctoral dissertation, University of California, Berkeley.

——. 1964. Teaching and testing critical listening in the fifth and sixth grades. *Elementary English,* 41, 743–747.

LURIA, A. R., and S. Y. YUDOVITCH. 1961. *Speech and the Development of Mental Processes in Children.* Staples.

LYNN, D. B. 1959. A note on sex differences in the development of masculine and feminine identification. *Psychological Review,* 66, 126–135.

——. 1961. Sex differences in identification development. *Sociometry,* 24, 372–383.

——. 1962. Sex-role and parental identification. *Child Development,* 33, 555–564.

——. 1964. Divergent feedback and sex-role identification in boys and men. *Merrill-Palmer Quarterly,* 10, 17–23.

McAFEE, R. O., and C. C. CLELAND. 1965. The discrepancy between self-concept and ideal-self as a measure of psychological adjustment in educable mentally retarded males. *American J. Mental Deficiency,* 70, 63–68.

McCANDLESS, B. R. 1960. Rate of development, body build, and personality. *Psychiatric Research Reports,* 13, 42–57.

——. 1961. *Children and Adolescents.* Holt, Rinehart and Winston.

——, C. BALSBAUGH, and H. L. BENNETT. 1958. Preschool-age socialization and maternal control techniques. *American Psychologist,* 13, 320.

——, and H. R. MARSHALL. 1957. A picture sociometric technique for preschool children and its relation to teacher judgments of friendship. *Child Development,* 28, 139–147.

——, and C. C. SPIKER. 1956. Experimental research in child psychology. *Child Development,* 27, 75–80.

McCARTHY, D. 1961. Affective aspects of language learning. Presidential address, Division of Developmental Psychology, American Psychological Association. Mimeograph.

McCARTIN, R. A. 1963. An exploration at first grade of six hypotheses in the semantic domain. Unpublished doctoral dissertation, University of Southern California.

McCLEARN, G. E. 1962a. The inheritance of behavior. In L. J. Postman (Ed.), *Psychology in the Making.* Knopf.

——. 1962b. Genetic differences in the effect of alcohol upon behavior of mice.

In J. D. J. Havard (Ed.), *Proceedings of the Third International Conference on Alcohol and Road Traffic*. British Medical Association.

McCLELLAND, D., et al. 1958. The effect of the need for achievement on thematic apperception. In J. W. Atkinson (Ed.), *Motives in Fantasy, Action, and Society*. Van Nostrand, pp. 64–82.

MACCOBY, E. E. 1959a. The generality of moral behavior. *American Psychologist*, 14, 358.

——. 1959b. Role-taking in childhood and its consequences for social learning. *Child Development*, 30, 239–252.

——, and W. C. WILSON. 1957. Identification and observational learning from films. *J. Abnormal Social Psychology*, 55, 76–87.

McCORD, J., and W. McCORD. 1958. The effect of parental role model on criminality. *J. Social Issues*, 14, 66–75.

McCULLERS, J. C. and H. W. STEVENSON. 1960. Effects of verbal reinforcement in a probability learning situation. *Psychological Reports*, 7, 439–445.

McDONALD, R. L., and M. D. GYNTHER. 1965. Relationship of self and ideal-self descriptions with sex, race, and class in southern adolescents. *J. Personality and Social Psychology*, 1, 85–88.

MACE, L. L. 1966. Sequence of vocal response-differentiation training and auditory stimulus-discrimination training in beginning French. *J. Educational Psychology*, 57, 102–108.

——, and E. R. KEISLAR. 1965. Sequence of discrimination and differentiation training in the early primary grades. U.S. Office of Education Project Number 3–12–022.

MacFARLANE, J. W. 1938. Studies in child guidance: I. Methodology of data collection and organization. Society Research Child Development Monographs, 3: 6.

McGRATH, G. E. 1962. The influence of positive interpersonal relations on adjustment and effectiveness in rifle teams. *J. Abnormal Social Psychology*, 65, 365–375.

McGRAW, M. B. 1940. Neural maturation as exemplified in achievement of bladder control. *J. Pediatrics*, 16, 580–590.

——. 1943. *The Neuromuscular Maturation of the Human Infant*. Columbia University Press.

——, and L. B. MOLLOY. 1941. The pediatric anamnesis: Inaccuracies in eliciting developmental data. *Child Development*, 12, 255–265.

MACHOVER, K. 1949. *Personality Projection in the Drawing of the Human Figure*. Thomas Publishing.

McHUGH, W. J. 1961. Pupil-team learning in reading in the intermediate grades. In J. A. Figurel (Ed.), *Changing Concepts of Reading Instruction*. University of Delaware, pp. 78–81.

MacKINNON, D. W. 1938. Violation of prohibitions. In H. A. Murray (Ed.), *Explorations in Personality: A Clinical and Experimental Study of Fifty Men of College Age*. Oxford University Press, pp. 491–501.

MacLeod, R. B. 1945. The phenomenological approach to social psychology. *Psychological Review*, 54, 193–210.

McNeil, J. D. 1964. Programed instruction versus usual classroom procedures in teaching boys to read. *American Educational Research J.*, 1, 113–119.

———, and E. R. Keislar. 1963. Value of the oral response in beginning reading: An experimental study using programmed instruction. *British J. Educational Psychology*, 33, 162–168.

McNemar, Q. 1942. *The revision of the Stanford-Binet Scale: An Analysis of the Standardization Data*. Houghton Mifflin.

———. 1949. *Psychological Statistics*. John Wiley.

———. 1964. Lost: Our intelligence? Why? *American Psychologist*, 19, 871–882.

MacRae, D. 1954. A test of Piaget's theories of moral development. *J. Abnormal Social Psychology*, 49, 14–18.

Maddi, S. R. 1961. Exploratory behavior and variation-seeking in man. In D. W. Fiske, and S. R. Maddi (Eds.), *Functions of Varied Experience*. Dorsey, pp. 253–277.

Malpass, L. F. 1953. Some relationships between students' perceptions of school and their achievement. *J. Educational Psychology*, 44, 475–482.

———, and F. B. Tyler. 1961. Validation of the incomplete sentences test of school adjustment. Unpublished manuscript.

Maltzman, I. 1955. Thinking: From a behavioristic point of view. *Psychological Review*, 62, 275–286.

———. 1960. On the training of originality. *Psychological Review*, 67, 229–242.

Marcus, I. M. 1956. Psychoanalytic group therapy with fathers of emotionally disturbed preschool children. *International J. Group Psychotherapy*, 6, 61–76.

Marquis, D. P. 1931. Can conditioned responses be established in the newborn infant? *J. Genetic Psychology*, 39, 479–492.

Marshall, H. R. 1960. Personal communication.

———, and B. R. McCandless. 1957. Relationship between dependence on adults and social acceptance by peers. *Child Development*, 28, 421–425.

Martin, P. A., and H. W. Bird. 1953. An approach to the psychotherapy of marriage partners. *Psychiatry*, 16, 123–127.

Masling, J. M. 1954. How neurotic is the authoritarian? *J. Abnormal Social Psychology*, 49, 316–318.

Maslow, A. H. 1954. The instinctoid nature of basic needs. *J. Personality*, 22, 326–347.

———. 1954a. *Motivation and Personality*. Harper & Row.

Mazurkiewicz, A. J. 1960. Social-cultural influences and reading. *J. Developmental Reading*, 1, 235–240.

Mead, G. H. 1934. *Mind, Self, and Society*. University of Chicago Press.

Medley, D. M., and H. E. Mitzel. 1963. Measuring classroom behavior by systematic observation. In N. L. Gage (Ed.), *Handbook of Research on Teaching*. Rand-McNally, pp. 247–328.

Meehl, P., and A. Rosen. 1955. Antecedent probability and the efficiency of psychometric signs, patterns, or cutting scores. *Psychological Bulletin,* 52, 194–216.

MEIER, G. W. 1961. Infantile handling and development in Siamese kittens. *J. Comparative Physiology Psychology,* 54, 284–286.

MELZACK, R., and T. H. SCOTT. 1957. The effects of early experience on the response to pain. *J. Comparative Physiology Psychology,* 50, 155–161.

MERTON, R. K. 1949. *Social Theory and Social Structure.* Free Press.

MESSICK, S. J., and C. M. SOLLY. 1963. Probability learning in children: Some exploratory studies. *J. Genetic Psychology,* 90, 23–24.

MEYER, H. F. 1958. Breast feeding in the United States: Extent and possible trend. *Pediatrics,* 22, 116–121.

MEYER, W. J., and G. C. THOMPSON. 1956. Sex differences in the distribution of teacher approval and disapproval among sixth grade children. *J. Educational Psychology,* 47, 385–396.

MEYERS, C. E., et al. 1964. Four ability-factor hypotheses at three preliterate levels in normal and retarded children. *Society Research Child Development Monographs,* 29: 5.

MICHAEL, D. N., and N. MACCOBY. 1953. Factors influencing verbal learning from films under conditions of audience participation. *J. Experimental Psychology,* 46, 411–418.

MICHIGAN UNIVERSITY SURVEY. 1957. *Adolescent Girls.* Michigan University Survey Research Center.

MIKAELIAN, H., and R. HELD. 1964. Two types of adaptation to an optically-rotated visual field. *American J. Psychology,* 77, 257–263.

MILLER, D. R., and G. E. SWANSON. 1958. *The Changing American Parent.* John Wiley.

——, and ——. 1960. *Inner Conflict and Defense.* Holt, Rinehart and Winston.

MILLER, N. E. 1948. Theory and experiment relating psychoanalytic displacement to stimulus response generalization. *J. Abnormal Social Psychology,* 43, 155–178.

——, and R. BUGELSKI. 1948. Minor studies in aggression: The influence of frustration imposed by the in-group on attitudes expressed toward out-groups. *J. Psychology,* 25, 437–442.

——, and J. DOLLARD. 1941. *Social Learning and Imitation.* Yale University Press.

MILLER, S. M., and F. RIESSMAN. 1961. The working class subculture: A new view. *Social Problems,* 9, 86–97.

MILLER, W. 1958. Lower class culture as a generating milieu of gang delinquency. *J. Social Issues,* 14, 5–19.

MILNER, E. 1951. A study of the relationship between reading readiness in grade one school children and patterns of parent-child interaction. *Child Development,* 22, 95–112.

MINTZ, A. 1951. Non-adaptive group behavior. *J. Abnormal Social Psychology,* 46, 150–159.

MISCHEL, W. 1966. A social-learning view of sex differences in behavior. In E. E. Maccoby (Ed.), *The Development of Sex Differences*. Stanford University Press, pp. 56–81.

——, and C. GILLIGAN. 1964. Delay of gratification, motivation for the prohibited gratification, and responses to temptation. *J. Abnormal Social Psychology*, 69, 411–417.

MITTELMANN, B. 1948. The concurrent analysis of married couples. *Psychoanalytic Quarterly*, 17, 182–197.

MONEY, J. 1966. Cognitive defects in Turner's syndrome. Second invitational conference on human behavior genetics.

MORGAN, J., et al. 1962. *Income and Welfare in the United States*. McGraw-Hill.

MORGAN, J. J. B., and S. S. MORGAN. 1944. Infant learning as a developmental index. *J. Genetic Psychology*, 65, 281–289.

MORROW, W. R., and R. R. WILSON. 1961. Family relations of bright high-achieving and under-achieving high school boys. *Child Development*, 32, 501–510.

MORSE, N. C., and R. S. WEISS. 1955. The function and meaning of work and the job. *American Sociological Review*, 20, 191–198.

MOSHER, D. L., and A. SCODEL. 1960. A study of the relationship between ethnocentrism in children and the ethnocentrism and authoritarian rearing practices of their mother. *Child Development*, 31, 369–376.

MOWRER, O. H. 1950. *Learning Theory and Personality Dynamics*. Ronald.

——. 1960a. *Learning Theory and Behavior*. John Wiley.

——. 1960b. *Learning Theory and the Symbolic Processes*. John Wiley.

MULLAHY, P. 1952. *Oedipus Myth and Complex: A Review of Psychoanalytic Theory*. Hermitage House.

MUNN, N. L. 1955. *The Evolution and Growth of Human Behavior*. Houghton Mifflin.

MUNZINGER, H., and W. KESSEN. 1964. Uncertainty, structure and preference. *Psychological Monographs*, 78:9 (Whole Number 586).

MURDOCK, G. P. 1957. World ethnographic sample. *American Anthropologist*, 59, 664–687.

MURPHY, L. B. 1937. *Social Behavior and Child Personality*. Columbia University Press.

MURRAY, H. A., et al. 1938. *Explorations in Personality*. Oxford University Press.

MUUSS, R. E. 1960. A comparison of "high causality" and "low causality" oriented sixth grade children in respect to a perceptual "intolerance of ambiguity test." *Child Development*, 31, 521–536.

MYERS, G. C. 1928. The price of speed pressure. *Educational Research Bulletin*, 7, 265–268.

MYERS, J., and B. ROBERTS. 1959. *Family and Class Dynamics in Mental Illness*. John Wiley.

NEWMAN, H. H., F. N. FREEMAN, and K. J. HOLZINGER. 1937. *Twins: A Study of Heredity and Environment.* University of Chicago Press.

NEWTON, E. S., et al. 1959. Empirical differences between adequate and retarded readers. *Reading Teacher,* 13, 40–44.

NEWTON, N. R., and M. NEWTON. 1950. Relationship of ability to breast feed and maternal attitudes toward breast feeding. *J. Pediatrics,* 35, 860–875.

NICHOLSON, A. K. 1957. Background abilities related to reading success in first grade. Unpublished doctoral dissertation, Boston University.

NICKELL, M. 1962. Effects of different reinforcement stimuli: A comparison across age levels. Unpublished master's thesis, University of Utah.

NIHIRA, K., et al. 1964. A factor analysis of the semantic-evaluation abilities. Report Number 32, University of Southern California.

NISSEN, H. W., K. L. CHOW, and J. SEMMES. 1951. Effects of restricted opportunity for tactual, kinaesthetic, and manipulative experience on the behavior of a chimpanzee. *American J. Psychology,* 64, 485–507.

NUNNALLY, J. C. 1961. *Popular Conceptions of Mental Health.* Holt, Rinehart and Winston.

OETZEL, R. M. 1966. Selected bibliography on sex differences. In E. E. Maccoby (Ed.), *The Development of Sex Differences.* Stanford University Press, pp. 223–321.

OJEMANN, R. H. 1936. The modifiability of attitude and its significance for research in child development. Proceedings, Society for Research Child Development.

———. 1958. Basic approaches to mental health in the school. *Personnel Guidance J.,* 37, 198–206.

———, and K. PRITCHETT. 1963. Piaget and the role of guided experiences in human development. *Perceptual Motor Skills,* 17, 927–939.

———, et al. 1955. The effects of a "causal" teacher training program and certain curriculum changes on grade school children. *J. Experimental Education,* 24, 95–114.

OLSON, W. C., and B. O. HUGHES. 1940. Subsequent growth of children with and without nursery school experience. Thirty-ninth yearbook, National Society Study Education, Part I. University of Chicago Press, pp. 237–244.

OSGOOD, C. E. 1953. *Method and Theory in Experimental Psychology.* Oxford University Press.

———, G. J. SUCI, and P. H. TANNENBAUM. 1957. *The Measurment of Meaning.* University of Illinois Press.

O'SULLIVAN, M., J. P. GUILFORD, and R. DEMILLE, 1965. Measurement of social intelligence. Report Number 34, University of Southern California.

OVERALL, B., and H. ARONSON. 1963. Expectations of psychotherapy in patients of lower socioeconomic class. *American J. Orthopsychiatry,* 33, 421–430.

PAGE, E. B. 1958. Teacher comments and student performance: A seventy-four classroom experiment in school motivation. *J. Educational Psychology,* 49, 173–181.

PAPOUSEK, H. 1961. Conditioned head rotation reflexes in infants in the first months of life. *Acta Pediatrics,* 50, 565–576.

PARSLEY, K. M., et al. 1963. Are there really sex differences in achievement? *J. Educational Research,* 57, 210–212.

PARSONS, T. 1954. *Essays in Sociological Theory.* Free Press.

PASSOW, A. H. 1963. *Education in Depressed Areas.* Teachers College, Columbia University.

PAYNE, D. A., and W. W. FARQUHAR. 1962. The dimensions of an objective measure of academic self-concept. *J. Educational Psychology,* 53, 187–192.

PEEL, E. A. 1959. Experimental examination of some of Piaget's schemata concerning children's perception and thinking, and a discussion of their educational significance. *British J. Educational Psychology,* 29, 89–103.

PERKINS, C. W., and D. T. SHANNON. 1965. Three techniques for obtaining self-perceptions in preadolescent boys. *J. Personality Social Psychology,* 2, 443–446.

PERSONS, R. W. 1965a. Degree of effect expression in psychotherapy and degree of psychopathy. *Psychological Reports,* 16, 1157–1162.

———. 1965b. Psychotherapy with sociopathic offenders: An empirical evaluation. *J. Clinical Psychology,* 21, 204–207.

———. 1966. Psychological and behavioral change in delinquents following psychotherapy. *J. Clinical Psychology,* 22, 337–340.

———, and H. B. PEPINSKY. 1966. Convergence in psychotherapy with delinquent boys. *J. Counseling Psychology,* 13, 329–334.

PETERSON, G. H., and F. SPANO. 1941. Breast feeding, maternal rejection and child personality. *Character Personality,* 10, 62–66.

PETRIE, C. R. 1961. An experimental evaluation of two methods for improving listening comprehension abilities. Unpublished doctoral dissertation, Purdue University.

PHILLIPS, L., and M. S. RABINOVITCH. 1958. Social role and patterns of symptomatic behavior. *J. Abnormal Social Psychology,* 57, 181–186.

PHILLIPS, L., and E. ZIGLER. 1961. Social competence: The action-thought parameter and vicariousness in normal and pathological behavior. *J. Abnormal Social Psychology,* 63, 137–146.

PIAGET, J. 1929. *The Child's Conception of the World.* Harcourt, Brace & World.

———. 1930. *The Child's Conception of Physical Causality.* Harcourt, Brace & World.

———. 1932. *The Moral Judgment of the Child.* Routledge.

———. 1948. *The Moral Judgment of the Child.* Free Press.

———. 1952. *The Child's Conception of Number.* Routledge.

———. 1952a. *The Origins of Intelligence in Children.* International Universities Press.

———. 1953a. *Logic and Psychology.* Manchester University Press.

———. 1953b. *The Origins of Intelligence in the Child.* Routledge.

———. 1962. *Play, Dreams, and Limitations in Childhood.* Norton.

———, B. INHELDER, and A. SZEMINSKA, 1960. *The Child's Conception of Geometry.* Basic Books.

POLANI, P. E., et al. 1960. A Mongoloid girl with 46 chromosomes. *Lancet,* 1, 721–724.

POLLAK, O. 1960. A family diagnosis model. *Social Service Review,* 34, 19–31.

POLYA, G. 1954. *Patterns of Plausible Inference.* Princeton University Press.

POWERS, F. 1962. Pupil acceptance of teacher authority. *School Society,* 90, 249–250.

PRATT, K. C. 1954. The neonate. In L. Carmichael (Ed.), *Manual of Child Psychology.* John Wiley, pp . 215–291.

PRESTON, R. C. 1962. Reading achievement of German and American children. *School Society,* 90, 350–354.

PRICE, W. H., and P. B. WHATMORE. 1967. Criminal behavior and the XYY male. *Nature,* 213, 815.

PYLES, M. K., H. R. STOLZ, and J. MACFARLANE. 1935. The accuracy of mothers' reports on birth and development data. *Child Development,* 6, 165–176.

QUINE, M. V. O. 1960. *Word and Object.* Massachusetts Institute of Technology Press.

RABINOWITZ, W., and R. M. W. TRAVERS. 1955. A drawing technique for studying certain outcomes of teacher education. *J. Educational Psychology,* 45, 257–273.

RACHMAN, S., and C. G. COSTELLO. 1961. The aetiology and treatment of children's phobias: A review. *American J. Psychiatry,* 118, 97–105.

RADKE-YARROW, M. J. 1946. *The Relation of Parental Authority to Children's Behavior and Attitudes.* University of Minnesota Press.

RAINWATER, L. 1960. *And the Poor Get Children.* Quadrangle Books.

RAMBUSCH, N. M. 1962. *Learning How to Learn: An American Approach to Montessori.* Helicon.

RAMSAY, O. A., and E. H. HESS. 1954. A laboratory approach to the study of imprinting. *Wilson Bulletin,* 66, 196–206.

READ, H. E. 1945. *Education Through Art.* Pantheon.

READ, K. H. 1955. *The Nursery School.* Saunders.

REDL, F., and D. WINEMAN. 1951. *Children Who Hate.* Free Press.

REYMERT, M., and R. HINTON. 1940. The effect of change to a relatively superior environment upon the IQ's of one hundred children. Thirty-ninth yearbook, National Society Study Education, Part II. University of Chicago Press, pp. 255–268.

RHEINGOLD, H., and N. BAYLEY. 1950. The later effects of an experimental modification of mothering. *Child Development,* 30, 363–372.

——, and ——. 1959. The later effects of an experimental modification of mothering. *Child Development,* 30, 363–372.

RIESEN, A. H. 1947. The development of visual perception in man and chimpanzee. *Science,* 106, 107–108.

——. 1950. Arrested vision. *Scientific American,* 183, 16–19.

——. 1958. Plasticity of behavior: Psychological series. In H. Harlow and C. Woolsey (Eds.), *Biological and Biochemical Bases of Behavior.* University of Wisconsin Press, pp. 425–450.

RIESSMAN, F. 1962. *The Culturally Deprived Child.* Harper & Row.

RIGBY, M. K., et al. 1957. The application of sociometric technique to women recruits: I. Prediction of individual success or failure in recruit training. Technical Report Number 8, U.S. Office of Naval Research.

RITCHIE, A. 1960. Multiple impact therapy: An experiment. *Social Work,* 5, 16–21.

ROBBINS, L. C. 1961. Parental recall of aspects of child development and child rearing practices. Unpublished doctoral dissertation, New York University.

ROBERTS, J. M., and B. SUTTON-SMITH. 1962. Child training and game involvement. *Ethnology,* 1, 166–185.

ROBERTS, R. C. 1967. Some evolutionary implications of behavior. *Canadian J. Genetics Cytology,* 9, 419–435.

ROBERTSON, W. O. July 1961. Breast feeding practices: Some implications of regional variation. *American J. Public Health.*

ROBINS, L. N., and P. O'NEAL. 1958. Mortality, mobility and crime: Problem children thirty years later. *American Sociological Review,* 23, 162–171.

ROBISON, S. M. 1960. *Juvenile Delinquency: Its Nature and Control.* Holt, Rinehart and Winston.

RODMAN, H. 1963. The lower-class value stretch. *Social Forces,* 42, 205–215.

ROFF, M. 1956. Preservice personality problems and subsequent adjustments to military service: Gross outcome in relation to acceptance-rejection at induction and military service. USAF School Aviation Medical Reports, Numbers 55–138.

——. 1957. Preservice personality problems and subsequent adjustments to military service: The prediction of psychoneurotic reactions. USAF School Aviation Medical Reports, Numbers 57–136.

——. 1960. Relations between certain preservice factors and psychoneurosis during military duty. *Armed Forces Medical J.,* 11, 152–160.

ROGERS, C. R. 1951. *Client-Centered Therapy.* Houghton Mifflin.

——, and R. DYMOND. 1954. *Psychotherapy and Personality Change.* University of Chicago Press.

ROHRER, J. H., and M. S. EDMONSON (Eds.). 1960. *Eighth Generation: Cultures and Personalities of New Orleans Negroes.* Harper & Row.

ROKEACH, M. 1960. *The Open and Closed Mind.* Basic Books.

ROSEN, B. C. 1959. Race, ethnicity and the achievement syndrome. *American Sociological Review,* 24, 47–60.

ROSENBERG, B. G., and B. SUTTON-SMITH. 1964a. The measurement of masculinity and femininity in children: An extension and revalidation. *J. Genetic Psychology,* 104, 259–264.

——, and ——. 1964b. Ordinal position and sex-role identification. *Genetic Psychology Monographs,* 70, 297–328.

ROSENBLITH, J. F. 1959. Learning by imitation in kindergarten children. *Child Development,* 30, 69–80.

——. 1961. Imitative color choices in kindergarten children. *Child Development,* 32, 211–223.

ROSENHAN, D. 1965. Cultural deprivation and learning: An examination of method and theory. Research Memorandum 65–4. Educational Testing Service.

——. 1966. Double alternation in children's binary-choice responses: A dilemma for theories of learning and arousal. *Psychonomic Science,* 4, 431–432.

——, and J. A. GREENWALD. 1965. The effects of age, sex, and socioeconomic class on responsiveness to two classes of verbal reinforcement. *J. Personality,* 33, 108–121.

ROSENZWEIG, M. R. 1964. Effect of heredity and environment on brain chemistry, brain anatomy, and learning ability in the rat. *Kansas Studies Education* 14(3), 3–34.

——, et al. 1960. A search for relations between brain chemistry and behavior. *Psychological Bulletin,* 57, 476–492.

ROSS, R. 1964. A look at listeners. *Elementary School J.,* 64, 369–372.

ROTTER, J. B. 1954. *Social Learning and Clinical Psychology.* Prentice-Hall.

RUEBUSH, B. 1963. Anxiety. In H. W. Stevenson (Ed.), *Child Psychology: Sixty-second yearbook of the National Society for the Study of Education,* Part I. University of Chicago Press, 460–516.

RUESCH, J. 1957. *Disturbed Communication.* Norton.

SAAYMAN, G., E. W. AMES, and A. MOFFETT. 1964. Response to novelty as an indicator of visual discrimination in the human infant. *J. Experimental Child Psychology,* 1, 189–198.

ST. JOHN, C. W. 1932. The maladjustment of boys in certain elementary grades. *Educational Administration Supervision,* 18, 649–672.

SAKODA, J. M., B. H. COHEN, and G. BEALL. 1954. Test of significance for a series of statistical tests. *Psychological Bulletin,* 51, 172–175.

SAMPSON, E. E. 1962. Birth order, need achievement, and conformity. *J. Abnormal Social Psychology,* 64, 155–159.

SANFORD, N. 1955. The dynamics of identification. *Psychological Review,* 62, 106–118.

SARASON, S. B., et al. 1958. A test anxiety scale for children. *Child Development,* 29, 105–114.

——, et al. 1960. *Anxiety in Elementary School Children.* John Wiley.

SARNOFF, I., et al. 1958. A cross-cultural study of anxiety among American and English school children. *J. Educational Psychology,* 49, 129–136.

SAX, G., and J. P. OTINA. 1958. The arithmetic reasoning of pupils differing in school experience. *California J. Educational Research,* 9, 15–19.

SCHAEFER, E. S., and R. Q. BELL. 1958. Development of a parental attitude research instrument. *Child Development,* 29, 339–361.

SCHAEFER-SIMMERN, H. 1948. *The Unfolding of Artistic Activity.* University of California Press.

SCHLESINGER, K., R. C. ELSTON, and W. BOGGAN. 1966. The genetics of sound induced seizure in inbred mice. *Genetics,* 54, 95–103.

SCHMUCK, R., M. B. LUSZKI, and D. EPPERSON. 1963. Interpersonal relations and mental health in the classroom. *Mental Hygiene,* 47, 289–299.

SCHNEPP, G. P. 1960. Survey of going steady and other dating practices. *American Catholic Sociological Review,* 20, 238–250.

SCHRAMM, W., J. LYLE, and E. B. PARKER. 1961. *Television in the Lives of Our Children.* Stanford University Press.

SCHULZ, R. W. 1960. Problem-solving behavior and transfer. *Harvard Educational Review,* 30, 61–77.

SCOTT, J. P. 1963. The process of primary socialization in canine and human infants. *Society Research Child Development Monographs,* 28: 1.

——, E. FREDERICSON, and J. I. FULLER. 1951. Experimental exploration of the critical period hypothesis. *J. Personality,* 1, 162–183.

——, and M. MARSTON. 1950. Critical periods affecting the development of normal and maladjustive social behavior of puppies. *J. Genetic Psychology,* 77, 25–60.

SCOTT, W. 1958. Research definitions of mental health and mental illness. *Psychological Bulletin,* 55, 1–45.

SEARLES, L. V. 1949. The organization of hereditary maze-brightness and maze-dullness. *Genetic Psychology Monographs,* 39, 279–325.

SEARS, R. R., E. E. MACCOBY, and H. LEVIN. 1957. *Patterns of Child Rearing.* Row, Peterson.

SEEMAN, J., and B. EDWARDS. 1954. A therapeutic approach to reading difficulties. *J. Consulting Psychology,* 18, 451–453.

SEEMAN, M. 1959. On the meaning of alienation. *American Sociological Review,* 24, 783–791.

SEROT, N. M., and R. C. TEEVAN. 1961. Perception of parent-child relationship and its relation to child adjustment. *Child Development,* 32, 373–378.

SHERMAN, M., and C. B. KEY. 1932. The intelligence of isolated mountain children. *Child Development,* 3, 279–290.

SHERRIFFS, A. C., and R. F. JARRETT. 1953. Sex differences in attitudes about sex differences. *J. Psychology,* 35, 161–168.

SHOLTY, M. 1912. A study of the reading vocabulary of children. *Elementary School Teacher,* 12, 272–297.

SHORE, M., J. MASSIMO, and R. MACK. 1965. Changes in the perception of interpersonal relationships in successfully treated adolescent delinquent boys. *J. Consulting Psychology*, 29, 213–217.

——, ——, and D. Ricks. 1965. A factor analytic study of psychotherapeutic change in delinquent boys. *J. Clinical Psychology*, 21, 208–212.

Siegel, A. E., and J. M. Andrews. 1962. Magnitude of reinforcement and choice behavior in children. *J. Experimental Psychology*, 63, 337–341.

Siller, J. 1957. Socio-economic status and conceptual thinking. *J. Abnormal Social Psychology*, 55, 365–371.

Silverman, B. E., and M. Alter. 1961. Response mode, pacing, and motivational experiments in teaching machines. United States Naval Training Device Center.

Silverman, W., F. Shapiro, and W. T. Heron. 1940. Brain weight and maze learning in rats. *J. Comparative Psychology*, 30, 279–282.

Simpson, M. 1935. Parent preferences of young children. Contributions to Education, Number 652. Teachers College, Columbia University.

Simpson, R. L., and M. Miller. 1961. Social status and social alienation. Paper read at meeting of Southern Sociological Society.

——, and ——. 1963. Social status and anomia. *Social Problems*, 10, 256–264.

Sinks, N. B., and M. Powell. 1965. Sex and intelligence as factors in achievement in reading in grades four through eight. *J. Genetic Psychology*, 106, 67–79.

Skeels, H. M., and H. Dye. 1939. A study of the effects of differential stimulation in mentally retarded children. Proceedings, American Association Mental Deficiency, 44, 114–136.

——, and E. A. Fillmore. 1937. Mental development of children from underprivileged homes. *J. Genetic Psychology*, 50, 427–439.

——, et al. 1938. A study of environmental stimulation: An orphanage preschool project. *University Iowa Studies Child Development*, Number 4.

Skinner, B. F. 1938. *The Behavior of Organisms: An Experimental Analysis*. Appleton-Century-Crofts.

——. 1950. Are theories of learning necessary? *Psychological Review*, 57, 193–216.

——. 1953. *Science and Human Behavior*. Macmillan.

Skodak, M. 1939. Children in foster homes: A study of mental development. *University Iowa Studies Child Welfare*, 16: 1.

——, and H. M. Skeels. 1949. A final follow-up of one hundred adopted children. *J. Genetic Psychology*, 75, 85–125.

Smedslund, J. 1961. The acquisition of conservation of substance and weight in children. *J. Scandinavian Psychology*, 2, 11–20, 71–87, 153–160, 203–210.

Smith, N. B. 1928. Matching as a factor in first grade reading. *J. Educational Psychology*, 19, 560–571.

Smith, S. 1939. Age and sex differences in children's opinion concerning sex differences. *J. Genetic Psychology*, 54, 17–25.

——. 1942. Language and non-verbal test performance of racial groups in

Honolulu before and after a fourteen-year interval. *J. Genetic Psychology,* 26, 51–93.

SMITH, W. A. 1952. Rating and dating: A restudy. *Marriage Family Living,* 14, 312–317.

SOLOMON, R. L., and L. C. WYNNE. 1954. Traumatic avoidance of learning: The principle of anxiety conservation and partial irreversibility. *Psychological Review,* 61, 353–385.

SPEARMAN, C. 1927. *Abilities of Man.* Macmillan.

SPEER, G. S. 1940. The mental development of children of feeble-minded and normal mothers. Thirty-ninth yearbook, National Society Study Education, Part II. University of Chicago Press, pp. 309–314.

SPITZ, R. A. 1945. Hospitalism: An inquiry into the genesis of psychiatric conditions in early childhood. *Psychoanalytic Studies Child,* 1, 53–74.

———. 1949. The role of ecological factors in emotional development in infancy. *Child Development,* 20, 145–155.

SPOCK, B. 1957. *Baby and Child Care.* Pocket Books.

STAGNER, R., and C. S. CONGDON. 1955. Another failure to demonstrate displacement of aggression. *J. Abnormal Social Psychology,* 51, 695–696.

STANDING, E. M. 1959. *Maria Montessori: Her Life and Work.* American Library Guild.

STEPHENS, J. M. 1951. *Educational Psychology.* Holt, Rinehart and Winston.

STEVENSON, H. W. 1961. Social reinforcement with children as a function of CA, sex of E, and sex of S. *J. Abnormal Social Psychology,* 63, 147–154.

———, and D. B. CRUSE. 1961. Effectiveness of social reinforcement with normal and feebleminded children. *J. Personality,* 29, 124–135.

———, and R. D. ODOM. 1962. The effectiveness of social reinforcement following two conditions of social deprivation. *J. Abnormal Social Psychology,* 65, 429–431.

———, and M. W. WEIR. 1959. Variables affecting children's performance in a probability learning task. *J. Experimental Psychology,* 57, 403–412.

———, and E. F. ZIGLER. 1958. Probability learning in children. *J. Experimental Psychology,* 56, 185–192.

———, et al. 1960. Social interaction in an interracial nursery school. *Genetic Psychology Monographs,* 61, 41–75.

STOLUROW, L. M. 1961. Teaching by machine. Cooperative Research Project Monograph, U.S. Government Printing Office.

———, and C. C. WALKER. 1962. A comparison of overt and covert response in programmed learning. *J. Educational Research,* 55, 421–432.

STOLZ, L. M. 1960. Effects of maternal employment on children: Evidence from research. *Child Development,* 31, 749–782.

STOTT, L. H., and R. S. BALL. 1963. Evaluation of infant and preschool mental tests. *Merrill-Palmer Quarterly.*

STRONG, E. K. 1931. *Change of Interest with Age.* Stanford University Press.

STROUD, J. B., and E. F. LINDQUIST. 1942. Sex differences in achievement in the elementary and secondary schools. *J. Educational Psychology,* 33, 657–667.

STRUPP, H. H. 1960. *Psychotherapists in Action.* Grune & Stratton.

SUCHMAN, J. R. 1961. Inquiry training: Building skills for autonomous discovery. *Merrill-Palmer Quarterly,* 7, 147–169.

SUSSMAN, M. B. 1961. Needed research on the employed mother. *Marriage Family Living,* 23, 368–374.

SUTTON-SMITH, B. 1965. Play preference and play behavior: A validity study. *Psychological Reports,* 16, 65–66.

——. 1966. Piaget on play: A critique. *Psychological Review,* 73, 111–112.

——, and P. GUMP. 1955. Games and status experience. *Recreation,* 48, 172–174.

——, and B. G. ROSENBERG. 1959. *Play and Game List.* Bowling Green State University.

——, and ——. 1965. Sibling perceptions of power styles within the family. Paper read at meeting of American Psychological Association.

——, ——, and F. F. MORGAN. 1963. Development of sex differences as in play choices during preadolescence. *Child Development,* 34, 119–126.

SZUREK, S. A. 1952. Some lessons from efforts at psychotherapy with parents. *American J. Psychiatry,* 109, 296–301.

——, A. JOHNSON, and E. FALSTEIN. 1942. Collaborative psychiatric therapy of parent-child problems. *American J. Orthopsychiatry,* 12, 511–516.

TAGIURI, R., N. KOGAN, and J. S. BRUNER. 1955. The transparency of interpersonal choice. *Sociometry,* 18, 624–635.

TANNENBAUM, P. H. 1963. Communication of science information. *Science,* 140, 579–583.

TANNER, J. M., and B. INHELDER (Eds.). 1957. *Discussions on Child Development,* 2 Volumes. International Universities Press.

——, and ——. 1958. *Discussions on Child Development,* Volume 3. International Universities Press.

TASCH, R. G. 1952. The role of the father in the family. *J. Experimental Education,* 20, 319–361.

TAYLOR, K. W. 1954. *Parent Cooperative Nursery Schools.* Teachers College, Columbia University.

TEAHAN, J. E. 1958. Future time perspective, optimism, and academic achievement. *J. Abnormal Social Psychology,* 57, 379–380.

TEMPLIN, M. C. 1957. *Certain Language Skills in Children.* University of Minnesota Press.

——. 1944. Attitudes of elementary school children to school, teachers, and classmates. *J. Applied Psychology,* 28, 134–141.

TERMAN, L. M. 1925. *Genetic Studies of Genius: I. Mental and Physical Traits of a Thousand Gifted Children.* Stanford University Press.

——, and M. A. MERRILL. 1937. *Measuring Intelligence.* Houghton Mifflin.

——, and M. H. ODEN. 1947. *Genetic Studies of Genius: IV. The Gifted Child Grows Up.* Stanford University Press.

——, and ——. 1959. *Genetic Studies of Genius: V. The Gifted Group at Mid-Life.* Stanford University Press.

TERRELL, G. 1958. The need for simplicity in research in child psychology. *Child Development*, 29, 303–310.

THIBAUT, J. 1950. An experimental study of the cohesiveness of underprivileged groups. *Human Relations*, 3, 251–278.

THOMAS, A., and S. CHESS. 1957. An approach to the study of sources of individual differences in child behavior. *J. Clinical Experimental Psychopathology*, 18, 347–357.

——, et al. 1960. A longitudinal study of primary reaction patterns in children. *Comprehensive Psychiatry*, 1, 103–112.

——, et al., 1961. Individuality in responses of children to similar environmental situations. *American J. Psychiatry*, 117, 798–803.

THOMPSON, W. R., and W. HERON. 1954. The effects of restricting early experience on the problem-solving capacity of dogs. *Canadian J. Psychology*, 8, 17–31.

THORNDIKE, E. L. 1920. Intelligence and its uses. *Harpers*, 140, 227–235.

THORNDIKE, R. L. 1948. Growth of intelligence during adolescence. *J. Genetic Psychology*, 72, 11–15.

TINKER, M., and D. PETERSON. 1940. Eye movements in reading a modern face and old English. *American J. Psychology*, 54, 113–115.

TOLMAN, E. C. 1952. A psychological model. In T. Parsons and E. A. Shils (Eds.), *Toward a General Theory of Action*. Harvard University Press, pp. 279–361.

TRITES, D. K., and S. B. SELLS. 1957. Combat performance: Measurement and prediction. *J. Applied Psychology*, 41, 121–130.

TRYON, C. M. 1944. The adolescent peer culture. Forty-third yearbook, National Society Study Education. University of Chicago Press, pp. 217–239.

TRYON, R. C. 1939. *Cluster Analysis*. Edwards.

——. 1940. Genetic differences in maze-learning ability in rats. Thirty-ninth yearbook, National Society Study Education, Part I. University of Chicago Press, pp. 111–119.

——. 1958. Cumulative communality cluster analysis. *Educational Psychological Measurement*, 18, 3–35.

TSCHECHTELIN, M. A., M. J. F. HIPSKIND, and H. H. REMMERS. 1940. Measuring the attitudes of elementary school children toward their teachers. *J. Educational Psychology*, 31, 195–203.

TUCKER, D. 1961. Physiology of olfaction. *American Perfumer*, 76, 48–53.

TUDDENHAM, R. D. 1951. Studies in reputation: III. *J. Educational Psychology*, 42, 257–276.

——. 1952. Studies in reputation. *Psychological Monographs*, 66, 1 (Whole Number 333).

TUNE, G. S. 1964. Response preferences: A review of some recent literature. *Psychological Bulletin*, 61, 286–302.

TURNER, E. A., and J. C. WRIGHT. 1965. Effects of severity of threat and perceived availability on the attractiveness of objects. *J. Personality Social Psychology*, 2, 128–132.

U.S. Department Health, Education, and Welfare. 1955. Infant Care. Children's Bureau Publication Number 8. U.S. Government Printing Office.

URSPRUNG, H. 1965. Genes and development. In R. L. De Haan and H. Ursprung (Eds.), *Organogenesis*. Holt, Rinehart and Winston.

VALENTINE, C. W. 1948. A study of the beginnings and significance of play in infancy. *British J. Educational Psychology*, 8, 188–200.

VANDENBERG, S. G. 1965. Multivariate analysis of twin differences. In S. G. Vandenberg (Ed.), *Methods and Goals in Human Behavior Genetics*. Academic Press.

VAN WAGENEN, R. K., and R. M. W. TRAVERS. 1963. Learning under conditions of direct and vicarious reinforcement. *J. Educational Psychology*, 54, 356–362.

VERNON, P. E. 1948. Changes in abilities from 14 to 20 years. *Advancement Science*, 5, 138.

VEROFF, J., et al. 1960. The use of thematic apperception to assess motivation in a nationwide interview study. *Psychological Monographs*, 74: 12.

VYGOTSKY, L. 1962. *Thought and Language*. John Wiley.

WADDINGTON, C. H. 1957. *The Strategy of the Genes*. Macmillan.

WAELDER, R. 1933. The psychoanalytic theory of play. *Psychoanalytic Quarterly*, 2, 208–224.

WALKER, H., and J. LEV. 1953. *Statistical Inference*. Holt, Rinehart and Winston.

WALKER, R. N. 1962. Body build and behavior in young children: I. Body build and nursery school teachers' ratings. *Social Research Child Development Monograph*, 27: 84.

———. 1963. Body build and behavior in young children: II. Body build and parents' ratings. *Child Development*, 34, 1–23.

WALLACE, M. 1956. Future time perspective in schizophrenia. *J. Abnormal Social Psychology*, 52, 240–245.

———, and A. I. RABIN. 1960. Temporal experience. *Psychological Bulletin*, 57, 213–236.

WALSH, A. M. 1956. *Self-Concepts of Bright Boys with Learning Difficulties*. Teachers College, Columbia University.

WALTERS, R. H., and E. RAY. 1960. Anxiety, social isolation, and reinforcer effectiveness. *J. Personality*, 28, 358–367.

WARNER, W. L., M. MEEKER, and K. EELLS. 1949. *Social Class in America*. Science Research Associates.

WEIR, M. W. 1964. Developmental changes in problem-solving strategies. *Psychological Review*, 71, 473–490.

———, and J. C. DEFRIES. 1964. Prenatal maternal influence on behavior in mice: Evidence of a genetic basis. *J. Comparative Physiology Psychology*, 58, 412–417.

WELLMAN, B. L. 1945. IQ changes of preschool and nonpreschool groups during the preschool years: A summary of the literature. *J. Psychology*, 20, 347–368.

WHEELER, L. R. 1942. A comparative study of the intelligence of East Tennessee mountain children. *J. Educational Psychology*, 33, 321–334.

WHERRY, R. J., and D. H. FRYER. 1949. Buddy ratings: Popularity contest or leadership criteria? *Personnel Psychology*, 2, 147–159.

WHIPPLE, G. M. (Ed.). 1940. Intelligence: Its nature and nurture. Thirty-ninth yearbook National Society Study Education. University of Chicago Press.

WHITE, A. M., L. FICHTENBAUM, and J. DOLLARD. 1964. Evaluation of silence in initial interviews with psychiatric clinic patients. *J. Nervous Mental Diseases*, 139, 550–557.

WHITE, B. 1965. Rearing conditions and the development of visual attentiveness in human infants. Paper read at Eastern Psychological Association.

——, and P. CASTLE. 1964. Visual exploratory behavior following postnatal handling of human infants. *Perceptual Motor Skills*, 18, 497–502.

——, ——, and R. HELD. 1964. Observations on the development of visually-directed reaching. *Child Development*, 35, 349–364.

WHITE, M. S. 1957. Social class, child rearing practices, and child behavior. *American Sociological Review*, 22, 704–712.

WHITE, R. W. 1959. Motivation reconsidered: The concept of competence. *Psychological Review*, 66, 297–333.

WHITING, J. W. M. 1954a. The cross-cultural method. In G. Lindzey (Ed.), *Handbook of Social Psychology*, Volume 1. Addison-Wesley, pp. 523–531.

——. 1954b. Fourth presentation. In J. M. Tanner and B. Inhelder (Eds.), *Discussions on Child Development*, Volume 2. Tavistock, pp. 185–212.

——. 1959. Sorcery, sin, and the superego: A cross-cultural study of some mechanisms of social control. In M. R. Jones (Ed.), *Nebraska Symposium on Motivation*. University of Nebraska Press, pp. 174–195.

——. 1960. Resource mediation and learning by identification. In I. Iscoe and H. W. Stevenson (Eds.), *Personality Development in Children*. University of Texas Press, pp. 112–126.

——, and I. L. CHILD. 1953. *Child Training and Personality: A Cross-Cultural Study*. Yale University Press.

——, R. KLUCKHOHN, and A. ANTHONY. 1958. The function of male initiation ceremonies at puberty. In E. E. Maccoby, T. Newcomb, and E. L. Hartley (Eds.), *Readings in Social Psychology*. Holt, Rinehart and Winston, pp. 359–370.

WHYTE, W. F. 1933. *Street Corner Society*. University of Chicago Press.

WICKENS, D. D., and C. WICKENS. 1940. A study of conditioning in the neonate. *J. Experimental Psychology*, 26, 94–102.

WILEY, R. 1961. *The Self-Concept*. University of Nebraska Press.

WILEY, W. E. 1928. Difficult words and the beginner. *J. Educational Research*, 17, 278–289.

WILKINS, W. L. 1954. Selection of Marine Corps platoon leaders. *Armed Forces Medical J.*, 5, 1184–1191.

WILLIAMS, R. M. 1947. *The Reduction of Intergroup Tension.* Social Science Research Council.

WILLIAMS, S. B., and H. J. LEAVITT. 1947. Group opinion as a predictor of military leadership. *J. Consulting Psychology,* 11, 283–291.

WILSON, F. I., and C. W. FLEMING. 1938. Spelling substitutions in children. *J. Genetic Psychology,* 53, 3–11.

WINSTON, H. D., and G. LINDZEY. 1964. Albinism and water escape performance in the mouse.

WINTER, W. 1961. Values and achievement in a freshman psychology course. *J. Educational Research,* 54, 183–186.

WIRT, R. D., and W. E. BROEN. 1956. The relation of the Children's Manifest Anxiety to the concept of anxiety as used in the clinic. *J. Consulting Psychology,* 20, 482.

WITTROCK, M. C., E. R. KEISLAR, and C. STERN. 1964. Verbal cues in concept identification. *J. Educational Psychology,* 55, 195–200.

WOHLWILL, J. F., and R. C. LOWE. 1962. An experimental analysis of the development of the conservation of number. *Child Development,* 33, 153–167.

WOLF, M., T. RISLEY, and H. MEES. 1964. Application of operant conditioning procedures to the behavior problems of an autistic child. *Behavior Research Therapy,* 1, 305–312.

WOLFENSTEIN, M. 1953. Trends in infant care. *American J. Orthopsychiatry,* 23, 120–130.

WOLPE, J. 1958. *Psychotherapy by Reciprocal Inhibition.* Stanford University Press.

——. 1961. The systematic desensitization treatment of neuroses. *J. Nervous Mental Diseases,* 132, 189–203.

WOOD, B. D., and F. N. FREEMAN. 1932. *An Experimental Study of the Educational Influences of the Typewriter in the Elementary School Classroom.* Macmillan.

WOODWARD, E. K. 1962. Perception of artificial words by beginning readers. Unpublished master's thesis, Cornell University.

WOODWORTH, R. S. 1958. *Dynamic Psychology.* Holt, Rinehart and Winston.

——, and H. SCHLOSBERG. 1954. *Experimental Psychology.* Holt, Rinehart and Winston.

WRIGHT, C. R., and H. H. HYMAN. 1958. Voluntary association memberships of American adults: Evidence from national sample surveys. *American Sociological Review,* 23, 284–294.

YARROW, L. 1961. Maternal deprivation: Toward an empirical and conceptual re-evaluation. *Psychological Bulletin,* 58, 459–490.

YARROW, M. R. (Ed.). 1958. Interpersonal dynamics in a desegregation process. *J. Social Issues,* 14: 1.

YOST, P. A., and A. E. SIEGEL. 1962. Nonverbal probability judgments by young children. *Child Development,* 33, 769–780.

ZAWADZKI, B. 1948. Limitations of the scapegoat theory of prejudice. *J. Abnormal Social Psychology*, 43, 127–141.

ZIGLER, E. 1961. Social deprivation and rigidity in the performance of feeble-minded children. *J. Abnormal Social Psychology*, 62, 413–421.

——. 1963. Metatheoretical issues in developmental psychology. In M. Marx (Ed.), *Psychological Theory* (2d ed.). Macmillan, pp. 341–369.

——, and P. KANZER. 1962. The effectiveness of two classes of verbal reinforcers on the performance of middle- and lower-class children. *J. Personality*, 30, 157–163.

——, J. LEVINE, and L. GOULD. 1966a. Cognitive processes in the development of children's appreciation of humor. *Child Development*, 37, 507–518.

——, ——, ——. 1966b. The humor response of normal, institutionalized retarded, and noninstitutionalized retarded children. *American J. Mental Deficiency*, 71, 472–480.

——, and J. WILLIAMS. 1963. Institutionalization and the effectiveness of social reinforcement: A three-year follow-up study. *J. Abnormal Social Psychology*, 66, 197–205.

Name Index

Subject Index